Learn Android App Development

Wallace Jackson

Apress

Learn Android App Development

ISBN-13 (pbk): 978-1-4302-5746-2

ISBN-13 (electronic): 978-1-4302-5747-9

Distributed to the book trade worldwide by Springer Science+Business Media New York, 233 Spring Street, 6th Floor, New York, NY 10013. Phone 1-800-SPRINGER, fax (201) 348-4505, e-mail `orders-ny@springer-sbm.com`, or visit `www.springeronline.com`. Apress Media, LLC is a California LLC and the sole member (owner) is Springer Science + Business Media Finance Inc (SSBM Finance Inc). SSBM Finance Inc is a Delaware corporation.

For information on translations, please e-mail `rights@apress.com`, or visit `www.apress.com`.

Apress and friends of ED books may be purchased in bulk for academic, corporate, or promotional use. eBook versions and licenses are also available for most titles. For more information, reference our Special Bulk Sales–eBook Licensing web page at `www.apress.com/bulk-sales`.

Any source code or other supplementary materials referenced by the author in this text is available to readers at `www.apress.com/9781430257462`. For detailed information about how to locate your book's source code, go to `www.apress.com/source-code/`.

This book is dedicated to everyone in the open source community who is working diligently to make professional level software and new media development tools available for everybody to use to achieve their dreams and goals. Last, but certainly not least, to my family, friends, and neighbors for their help, assistance, and those great late night BBQs.

Contents at a Glance

About the Author xxi

About the Technical Reviewer xxiii

Acknowledgments xxv

Introduction xxvii

■ Chapter 1: Building an Android IDE for Version 4.2: Acquiring, Installing, and Configuring an Android Development Environment 1

■ Chapter 2: Exploring Android App Development: The Lingo of Android and Building Your First Hello World App! 31

■ Chapter 3: Java for Android Primer: Enhancing Our Hello World Application 55

■ Chapter 4: Layouts and Activities: Using ViewGroup Classes 77

■ Chapter 5: Android Intents and Events: Adding Interactivity 111

■ Chapter 6: Android UI Design: Using Views and Widgets via XML 137

■ Chapter 7: Android Graphics Design: Concepts and Techniques 165

■ Chapter 8: Compositing in Android: Advanced Graphical User Interface Design 191

■ Chapter 9: Android Image Animation: Frame-Based Animation Using XML Constructs 217

■ Chapter 10: Android Vector Animation: Procedural Animation via XML Constructs 239

■ Chapter 11: An Introduction to Video: Concepts and Optimization 273

■ Chapter 12: Digital Video in Android: Using the VideoView Class 301

■ Chapter 13: An Introduction to Audio: Concepts and Optimization 321

■ Chapter 14: Playing Audio in Android: The MediaPlayer Class 345

■ Chapter 15: Audio Sequencing: Android SoundPool Class 363

■ Chapter 16: Android Intents: Inter-Application Programming 383

■ Chapter 17: Android Services: Using Background Processing 411

■ Chapter 18: Broadcast Receivers: Android Inter-Application Communication 433

■ Chapter 19: Android Content Providers: Access to Datastores 451

■ Appendix A: Building an Android IDE for Version 4.12 and Earlier: Acquiring, Installing, and Configuring an Android Development Environment 487

Index 509

Contents

About the Author xxi

About the Technical Reviewer xxiii

Acknowledgments xxv

Introduction xxvii

Chapter 1: Building an Android IDE for Version 4.2: Acquiring, Installing, and Configuring an Android Development Environment 1

Our Plan of Attack 2

Foundation of Android Programming: Java 6 3

Installing the JDK 3

The Android Developer Tools (ADT) Bundle 6

Downloading the Android ADT IDE 6

Configuring Android Virtual Devices (AVDs) 18

Creating Your Nexus 7 Tablet Emulator 19

Creating Your Nexus S Smartphone Emulator 20

Creating Your Android iTV Emulator for GoogleTV Support 21

New Media Tools Used in Android Development 26

Digital Imaging Software: GIMP 2.8.4 26

Digital Audio Software: Audacity 2.0.3 27

Digital Video Software: EditShare Lightworks 11 ... 28
3D Modeling and Animation Software: Blender 3D ... 29
Summary ... 30
Chapter 2: Exploring Android App Development: The Lingo of Android and Building Your First Hello World App! ... 31
Android Application Development Lingo ... 32
The Foundation of Android: The Linux 2.6 Kernel ... 32
Android Optimization: The Dalvik Virtual Machine (DVM) ... 32
Android Activities: The Presentation Layer ... 33
Android Services: The Processing Layer ... 33
Android Broadcast Receivers: The Communications Layer ... 34
Android Content Providers: The Data Storage Layer ... 35
Android Intents: Inter-Application Communications ... 35
Android Manifest: Application Permissions Definition ... 35
Creating Your First Android Application ... 36
Anatomy of an Android Application Project ... 41
Android Application Project: XML Mark-Up ... 44
Creating User Interface Screen Layouts in Android Using XML ... 44
Creating Option Menus in Android Using XML ... 46
Setting Constant Values for Your Android Application Using XML ... 47
Android Application Project: Java Coding ... 49
Defining the Android Classes via Import Statements ... 49
Creating Our Application Infrastructure Using the onCreate() Method ... 50
Running Your Hello World App in the Android 4.2 Emulator ... 51
Setting Up Logcat after Your First Android 4.2 Emulation ... 52
Summary ... 53
Chapter 3: Java for Android Primer: Enhancing Our Hello World Application ... 55
Java's Highest Level: The Application Programming Interface ... 55
Organizing the Java API: The Package ... 56

The Foundation of Java: The Object 57
Blueprint for a Java Object: The Class 59
Defining a Java Object's Functions: The Method 61
Coding a Java Class in Eclipse: Creating the WorldGen Class 64
Creating Our New WorldGen Java Class 64
Creating WorldGen Objects Using the WorldGen Class 68
Comments, Warnings and Errors Inside of ADT Eclipse 72
Creating a Java Interface for the Public: The IntWorldGen Interface 72
What a Java Interface Does for Our WorldGen Class 72
Creating a Java Interface for Our WorldGen Class 73
Summary 75
Chapter 4: Layouts and Activities: Using ViewGroup Classes 77
Android Screen Layout Containers: The ViewGroup Class 78
Android ViewGroup Subclasses: Layout Container Types 78
Relative Layout Positioning: The Android RelativeLayout Class 79
Creating a Start-Up Screen: Defining Our RelativeLayout via XML 80
Adding a Menu to Our Activity: The Menu Inflater and Menu XML 91
Defining the Add a New Planet Screen: Creating Android Activities 96
Defining the Configure Planet Activity: The LinearLayout Container 102
Defining a Travel to Planet Activity: The FrameLayout Container 104
Defining the Attack on Planet Activity: Our Second Linear Layout 105
Adding our Application Activities to our XML: AndroidManifest.xml 107
Summary 108
Chapter 5: Android Intents and Events: Adding Interactivity 111
Android High-Level Communication: The Android Intent Object 112
The Component Name 112
The Action 113
The Data Reference 113
The Type Reference 113
Android Category Constants 114
Flags and Extras 114

Implicit Intents: Intent Filters that Define Implicit Intent Handling....114
Using Explicit Intents: Making Our Hello_World Menu Functional....116
Inflating Our Menu....117
Adding the New Planet Intent....118
Adding the Rest of the Intents....119
Enabling Our New Planet Activity's User Interface: Event Handling....120
Enabling Our ConfigPlanet Activity User Interface: Event Handling....124
Enabling Our TravelPlanet Activity User Interface: Event Handling....125
Enabling Our AttackPlanet Activity User Interface: Event Handling....127
Event Handling for Keypads or Keyboards: OnKey Event Handlers....130
Other Event Handler Methods: OnFocusChange and OnLongClick....133
Summary....134
Chapter 6: Android UI Design: Using Views and Widgets via XML....137
Android User Interface Elements: Android View and Subclasses....137
Optimizing Our NewPlanet Activity UI: The ImageView UI Widget....138
Putting Our Image Assets in Drawable DPI Folders....138
Referencing and Aligning Our Planet Image Source Files....139
Adding Screen Caption Text and Done Button....141
Adding the Java Code to Incorporate Our New User Interface Elements....144
Introducing (and Utilizing) the Android Toast Class....145
Optimizing Our ConfigPlanet Activity UI: Button and Text UI Widgets....146
Creating Complex User Interface Designs Using Nested Layout Containers....147
Introducing the Android EditText User Interface Element for Editable Text Fields....148
Adding the Java Code to Incorporate Our Configure a Planet Screen's New User Interface Elements....149
Optimizing Our TravelPlanet Activity: Android's VideoView Widget....153
Configuring Our VideoView User Interface Element....153
Adding the Java Code to Incorporate Our Travel to a Planet Screen's New User Interface Elements....154
Optimizing Our AttackPlanet Activity UI: ImageButton UI Widgets....155
Putting the Image Assets in Place....155
Referencing, Aligning, and Compositing Our Attack Icon Image Source Files....156
Adding a Screen Caption TextView to Our XML Mark-up....158

Creating a More Complex User Interface Design Using Nested LinearLayout Containers 158
Fine-Tuning Our UI Design and Adding Text Labels to Our Attack Icons 160
Adding Java Code to Incorporate Our Attack a Planet Screen User Interface Elements 161
Summary 162
Chapter 7: Android Graphics Design: Concepts and Techniques 165
Android Graphics Design Highest Level: The Drawable Class 166
Direct Subclasses of the Android Drawable Class 166
Indirect Subclasses of the Android Drawable Class 167
Digital Imaging's Lowest Level Picture Element: The Pixel 167
Shaping an Image Using Pixels: Resolution and Aspect Ratio 168
Fashioning the Color of a Pixel: The Concept of Color Depth 169
Defining Transparency in an Image: The Concept of Alpha Channel 171
Image Format Support in Android: PNG8, PNG24, WEBP, JPG, GIF 172
Portable Network Graphics (PNG) Format 172
Joint Photographic Experts Group (JPEG) Format 172
Graphics Information (GIF) Format 172
Web Photo (WEBP) Format 172
Reducing the Image Data Footprint: Image Compression Concepts 173
Upgrading Our NewPlanet Activity: Applying the Imaging Concepts 174
Adding a Stars Image Background to Our HelloWorld App 174
Editing Our Screen Layout XML to Reference the Stars Background Image 174
Adjusting Our XML Tag Parameters to Accommodate the New Stars Background Image 175
Adjusting Our TextView Tag's textColor Parameter to Increase the Contrast 176
Upgrading Our TravelPlanet UI: Creating an Alpha Channel for Our AttackVirus 178
Adding Transparency: Creating an Alpha Channel Mask 178
Inverting the Alpha Channel to Select the Virus 180
Saving Our Work So Far in the GIMP XCF Native Format 183
Using the Canvas Size Tool to Re-Center Our Newly Masked Image 183
Using GIMP's File Export (Save As) Dialog to Save Our New Image in a PNG32 File Format 184
Creating Our Other Resolution Density Image Versions Using the Image Resize Tool 186
Summary 188

Chapter 8: Compositing in Android: Advanced Graphical User Interface Design 191

Multi-State UI Elements: The Normal, Pressed, and Focused States 192

Creating Our ImageButton Multi-State Image Source Files 192

Importing Our Gold Hoop Image for Compositing 195

Centering Our Soldier's Face in the Gold Hoop by Moving Its Layer Position 196

Erasing the Unwanted Pixels Outside the Gold Hoop 196

Exporting Our attackinvadepress Button Icon State 197

Creating Our attackinvadefocus Image Button State 198

Creating Our Other Resolution Density Multi-State ImageButton Icons 198

Implementing Multi-State Buttons in XML: Android's Selector Tag 199

Creating a New Android XML File of Resource Type: Drawable 199

Adding Android <item> Tags to our attack_invade.xml Multi-State XML Definition 200

Referencing Our New Multi-State ImageButton XML Definitions from Our Activity Screen Layout XML 200

Compositing Our UI Elements: Alpha, Color, Gravity, and TextStyle 202

Modifying Our activity_config XML Parameters to Composite Space Background Image with Our UI Elements 203

Improving the Contrast of Our EditText Fields Using Background Color and Alpha Transparency 204

Formatting the Text Characteristics Inside Our EditText UI Elements 205

Upgrading Our App Home Screen: Adding an ImageView Tag and textColor Parameters 207

Custom Activity Screen Title and App Icon: Details Make a Difference 211

Creating Our Activity Screen Title Constants in the strings.xml File 212

Configuring Activity Screen Labels in Our Hello_World AndroidManifest XML File 212

Summary 215

Chapter 9: Android Image Animation: Frame-Based Animation Using XML Constructs 217

Frame-Based Animation: Concepts and Data Optimization 217

Implementing Frame Animation in XML: The Animation-List Tag 218

Creating a New Android XML File of Resource Type: Drawable for Frame Animation 219

Adding Our Frame Animation <item> Tags Specifying the Animation Frames 220

Referencing Our Frame Animation Definition XML File from Our attack_virus.xml File 221

Leveraging the Android state_enabled Parameter to Make Our Virus Animate on Activity Screen Launch....... 222

Advanced Frame Animation in XML: Using Animated Backgrounds 222

Adding Our Animation Frame <item> Tags in Our anim_forcefield.xml File 223

Compositing Within a Single UI Element: Using Both the Source Image and Background Image Together 224

Coding Our AnimationDrawable Object in Java to Implement Our Forcefield Animation 226

Full-Screen XML Frame Animation: Background Image Transitions 230

Setting Up the <item> Tags for an Image Transition XML Definition 231

Upgrading Our App API Level Support in the AndroidManifest XML for Hello_World 232

Adding a TransitionDrawable Object in Our Java Code to Implement the Image Transition 233

Summary 237

Chapter 10: Android Vector Animation: Procedural Animation via XML Constructs 239

Procedural Animation Concepts: Rotation, Scale, and Translation 240

Implementing Rotational Animation: The Attack Bomb UI Icon 241

Completing the Rotate Tag 242

Adding Java Code for the Rotation 244

Implementing Scalar Animation: The Pulsing Attack Virus UI Icon 245

Completing the Scale Tag 246

Adding Java Code for the Scaling 247

Implementing Alpha Channel Animation: Beam Me Over to a Planet 248

Completing the Alpha Tag 248

Adding Java Code for the Alpha Animation 250

Combining Bitmap and Procedural Animation 251

Configuring the Animation in XML 252

Implementing a Background Behind a Fade 254

Adding Java Code for the Animation 256

Implementing Complex Animation: XML <set> Parameter Grouping 257

Configuring the Set Tag 260

Adding Image Scaling 261

Adding an Alpha Procedural Animation 263

Adding Java Code for the Animation 266

Implementing Motion Animation: The XML <translate> Parameter 268

Configuring the Translate Tag 269

Adding Java Code for the Translation 270

Summary 271

■ Chapter 11: An Introduction to Video: Concepts and Optimization 273

The Foundation of Digital Video: Pixels, Frames, FPS, and Codecs 274

Important Digital Video Attributes: SD, HD, Streaming, and Bit-Rates 274

Storing Video: Resolution 275

Accessing Digital Video Data: Captive and Streaming 275

Digital Video Formats: Support for Digital Video Codecs in Android 276

Digital Video Optimization: Playback Across Devices and Resolution 277

Digital Video Creation: Creating our Mars Planet Surface Fly-Over 278

Generating Uncompressed Frames 279

Configuring the Render Engine 281

Rendering the Animation 282

Creating the Resolution Files 283

Digital Video Compression: Key Concepts and Techniques 285

Importing the Video 286

Compressing the Video 290

Using Digital Video Assets in Android: The Resource's Raw Folder 296

Playing Digital Video in the UI Design: Android's VideoView Class 299

Summary 299

■ Chapter 12: Digital Video in Android: Using the VideoView Class 301

Using Android MediaController Class to Play Video 301

Creating a Java videoUri Object in the TravelPlanet Activity 302

Creating a MediaController Object to Play Our Digital Video 303

Controlling Video Playback in Our travelVideo VideoView 304

Testing Video Playback in Eclipse ADT's Nexus S Emulator 305

Scaling a VideoView to Fit a Screen Using a RelativeLayout 306

Modifying Our UI to Support the MediaController Transport 308

Adding a Button UI Element to Return Us to Home Screen 310

Troubleshooting Our VideoView User Interface Design 312
Adding the Return to Home Planet Button to the Java Code 314
Fine-Tuning Our Travel to Planet User Experience Design 316
Summary 318
Chapter 13: An Introduction to Audio: Concepts and Optimization 321
The Foundation of Analog Audio: Sound Waves and Air 321
The Foundation of Digital Audio: Sampling, Sample Resolution, and Sampling Frequency 322
Key Digital Audio Attributes: CD Audio, HD Audio, Audio Streaming, and Audio Bit-Rates 324
Digital Audio Formats: Support for Popular Digital Audio Codecs in Android 325
Digital Audio Optimization: Playback Across Devices 327
Setting Up Audacity 2 with Plug-Ins and Codec Libraries 328
Digital Audio Creation: Finding Hello World Sound Effects 329
Digital Audio Compression: Key Concepts and Formats 330
Setting Sample Rate and Sample Resolution in Audacity 331
Export an Uncompressed PCM Baseline .WAV Format File 332
Export a Lossless .FLAC Open Source Audio Format File 334
Export Lossy Ogg Vorbis Open Source .OGG Format Files 335
Exporting to a Lossy MPEG-3 Format .MP3 Audio File 335
Exporting to a Lossy MPEG-4 Format .M4A Audio File 336
Exporting a Narrow Band MPEG-4 Format .AMR Audio File 337
Using Digital Audio Assets in Android: The Project Resource Raw Folder 339
Playing Digital Audio: The Android MediaPlayer Class 342
Summary 342
Chapter 14: Playing Audio in Android: The MediaPlayer Class 345
The Android Media Player: Methods and the State Engine 346
Setting Up a MediaPlayer Object and Loading It with Digital Audio Data 349
Writing Our Custom setAudioPlayers() Java Method 349
Using Our Media Player Object: Starting Audio Playback Using the .start() Method 351
Coding the Other Special Effect Audio MediaPlayer Objects 352
Looping Background Ambient Audio for Our MainActivity 354

Creating Voice Synthesis for Our NewPlanet.java Add a Planet Activity 356
Optimizing Our Alien Voiceover Audio Sample Using Audacity 2.0 357
Creating Button Click Audio FX for Our Configure a Planet Activity 360
Summary 361
Chapter 15: Audio Sequencing: Android SoundPool Class 363
MIDI and Audio Sequencing: Concepts and Principles 364
Digital Audio Synthesis: Basic Concepts and Principles 364
An Introduction to SoundPool: Class Rules and Methods 366
Android Digital Audio Synthesis and Sequencing Caveats 368
Using SoundPool for Our Attack a Planet Activity 368
Setting Up SoundPool: The SoundPool Object 369
Loading the SoundPool Data: The Android HashMap Class 371
Configuring the SoundPool: Using Android AudioManager 372
Configuring Your HashMap: Using the .put() Method 373
Coding a playSample() Method: Using SoundPool .play() 375
Android SparseIntArrays: Using the SparseIntArray Class 376
Calling Our SoundPool Objects: Using Our playSample() Method 380
Summary 381
Chapter 16: Android Intents: Inter-Application Programming 383
Android Intent Messaging: First, the Global Overview 384
Android Intent Implementation: Three Different Types of Intent Usage 384
Activities 385
Android Services 385
Broadcast Receivers 386
Android Intent Structure: Anatomy of an Android Intent 386
Intent Object Components: Specify a Component Name Parameter 387
Intent Object Actions: Specifying an Action Parameter 388
Intent Object Data: Sending Data for the Action to Act Upon 389
Intent Object Category: Using a Category Constant Parameter 389
Intent Object Data Types: Setting a MIME Data Type Parameter 390

Intent Object Extras: Using Extras in Your Intent Object 391
Intent Object Flags: Using Flags with Your Intent Object 392
Explicit Versus Implicit Intents: Which Intent Type to Use 392
Explicit Intents 393
Implicit Intents 393
Implicit Intent Resolution: Introducing Intent Filters 393
Creating Intent Filters: Using the <intent-filter> XML Tag 394
Using an Intent Object to Launch an Activity in Hello World 395
Creating the LinearLayout XML for Our TimePlanet.java Activity 398
Configuring the AndroidManifest.xml for Our TimePlanet Activity 402
Adding an Atomic Clock Button Tag to Our activity_config.xml File 404
Coding an Intent Object in Java for Our ConfigPlanet.java Activity 405
Coding an Intent Object in Java for Our TimePlanet.java Activity 407
Summary 409
Chapter 17: Android Services: Using Background Processing 411
Android Service Basics: The Rules and Characteristics 412
Processes or Threads: Valuable Foundational Information 413
How to Specify a Process: Using android:process XML Parameters 414
The Android Process Lifespan: How to Keep Your Processes Alive 415
Some Caveats Regarding Threads: Don't Interfere with a UI Thread 417
Should My Android Application Use Services or Threads? 418
Implementing a Music Service in Our TimePlanet Activity 419
Configuring Our AndroidManifest file to Add a <service> Component 422
Writing Java Code in Our TimePlanet Activity to Launch the Service 423
Creating a New Service Subclass for Our MusicService.java Class 424
Coding Our MusicService Class Service Lifecycle Methods in Java 427
Refining Our TimePlanet Class Context Reference Using TimePlanet.this 428
Testing the MusicService Component 430
Summary 431

■Chapter 18: Broadcast Receivers: Android Inter-Application Communication................. 433

Android BroadcastReceivers: Basic Concepts and Types 434

Broadcasting Your Intent: Activity versus Broadcast Receiver Intents 435

Secure Broadcasts: BroadcastReceiver Security Considerations... 436

The BroadcastReceiver Lifecycle: Rules and Regulations 437

Processing Broadcasts: How a Broadcast Affects an Android Process 438

Broadcasting Inside Your Application: The LocalBroadcastManager 438

Registering a Broadcast Receiver: Dynamic versus Static Registration..................................... 439

Implementing a Broadcast Receiver in Our Application 439

Designing Our Alarm Broadcast Receiver User Interface Using XML 440

Adding Our AlarmReceiver BroadcastReceiver Android Manifest XML.. 442

Coding Our startTimerButton and startTimer( ) Method Using Java.. 443

Coding Our startTimer() Java Method 445

Creating Our AlarmReceiver BroadcastReceiver Subclass.. 446

Coding Our AlarmReceiver BroadcastReceiver Sublass 448

Summary...450

■Chapter 19: Android Content Providers: Access to Datastores 451

Database Fundamentals: Concepts and Terminology..452

MySQL and SQLite: An Open Source Database Engine..453

Android Content Providers and Content Resolvers: An Introduction.................................454

Addressing the Content Provider: Using a Content URI 455

Android OS Content Providers: Databases That Are Part of the OS 456

The Android MediaStore Databases 457

The Android CalendarContract Databases.. 457

The Android ContactsContract Databases 458

Deprecated Content Providers: Deprecated Database Structures....................................459

Content Provider Access: Adding Permissions in Manifest 460

Content Provider Activity: Creating an AlienContact Class 464

Content Provider Activity: Prepare the AlienContact Class 465

Content Provider User Interface: Creating activity_contact.xml... 466

Coding User Interface Elements in the AlienContact Class... 470

Using a ContentResolver: Coding Our listAliens() Method 471
Adding Alien Contacts to the ContactsContract Database 474
Adding the AlienContact Activity to the Home Screen Menu 477
Testing the listAliens() Method in the AlienContact Activity 480
Android ContentValues: Code an addToAlliance() Method 482
Summary 485

Appendix A: Building an Android IDE for Version 4.12 and Earlier: Acquiring, Installing, and Configuring an Android Development Environment 487

Our Plan of Attack 488
Foundation of Android Programming: Java 6 489
Installing the JDK 489
Installing an Integrated Development Environment: Eclipse 492
Android SDK and Android Developer Tools 497
Eclipse's Android Development Tools Plug-in 504
Configuring the Android Development Environment 506
Configuring Your Android Virtual Devices 506

Index 509

About the Author

Wallace Jackson has been writing for leading multimedia publications about his work in new media content development since the advent of *Multimedia Producer Magazine* more than two decades ago, when he wrote about computer processor architectures for the magazine centerfold (a removable "mini-issue" insert) distributed at SIGGRAPH. Since then, Wallace has written for several other publications about his work in interactive 3D and new media advertising campaign design, including *3D Artist, Desktop Publishers Journal, CrossMedia, AVvideo* and *Kiosk Magazine* and has written several popular application programming books on Android development for Apress (Springer) over the past several years.

Wallace is also the CEO of Mind Taffy Design, a new media content production and digital campaign design and development agency in Northern Santa Barbara County. Mind Taffy Design has created open source technology (HTML, Java, and Android) digital new media content deliverables over the past two decades for many of the top-branded manufacturers in the world, including Sony, Samsung, IBM, Epson, Nokia, TEAC, and Mitsubishi.

Wallace received his undergraduate degree in Business Economics from the University of California at Los Angeles (UCLA) and his graduate degree in MIS Design and Implementation from the University of Southern California (USC). His post-graduate degree in Marketing Strategy is also from USC, where he also completed the Graduate Entrepreneurship Program.

About the Technical Reviewer

Michael Thomas has worked in software development for over 20 years as an individual contributor, team lead, program manager, and Vice President of Engineering. Michael has over 10 years' experience working with mobile devices. His current focus is in the medical sector using mobile devices to accelerate information transfer between patients and health care providers.

Acknowledgments

I would like to acknowledge all the fantastic editors and their support staff at Apress who worked so long and hard on this book, making it the ultimate all-around Android application production book.

James Markham, for his work as the lead editor on the book, and for his experience and guidance during the process of making this book great.

Mark Powers, for his work as the coordinating editor on the book, and for his diligence in making sure I either hit my deadlines or surpassed them.

Linda Seifert, for her work as the copy editor on the book, and for her attention to detail and conforming the text to Apress writing standards.

Michael Thomas, for his work as the technical reviewer on the book, and for making sure I don't make any mistakes, because code with mistakes does not run properly, if at all, unless they are very lucky mistakes, which is quite rare in computer programming.

Frank Serafine, my close friend and the world's finest and most respected sound designer and a popular musician for contributing the audio samples used in this book's apps from his stellar (no pun intended) work on some of the world's most popular science fiction movies and television shows.

Finally I'd like to acknowledge **Oracle** for acquiring Sun Microsystems and continuing to enhance Java so it remains the premiere open source programming language, and also **Google** for making Android the premiere open source operating system and for acquiring ON2's VP8 video codec and making it available to all of us multimedia producers.

Introduction

The Android OS is currently the most popular OS in the world today, running on everything from watches to HD smartphones to touchscreen tablets to eBook readers to interactive television sets.

Since there are billions of Android consumer electronics devices owned by people all over the world, it stands to reason that developing applications for these people might just be an extremely lucrative undertaking, given that you have the right concept and design. This book will go a long way toward helping you to learn how to go about creating an attractive Android application which spans multiple types of Android device types and supports multiple Android OS versions.

I wrote *Learn Android App Development* as the next level up from my *Android Apps for Absolute Beginners* title, targeting those readers who are more technically proficient, and who are familiar with computer programming concepts and techniques. That being said, this would be a good follow-on title to the *Android Apps for Absolute Beginners* title, and both cover the latest Android 4.2.2 Jelly Bean Plus Android operating system version.

I designed this book to be a far more comprehensive overview of the Android application development work process than most Android app development books. For this reason, this book covers the use of a wide variety of other open source software packages, such as GIMP and Audacity, for instance, and how their usage fits into the overall Android application development work process. This approach serves to set this book distinctly apart from the other Android application development titles currently on the market.

The book starts out with installing the latest Java and Android SDKs and the Eclipse IDE with the Android ADT Bundle, and then progresses through creating a basic Android application and then adding to that application with each chapter. We continue this process until all the major concepts are covered and implemented in one comprehensive Android application. This approach more closely parallels real world application development, where an application is continuously added to over time, making it more and more robust and feature filled as time goes on, while making sure each new feature does not cause the application to crash.

We look at Java objects and constructors, user interface design using XML mark-up, digital imaging and graphics design, digital video and animation, audio sampling and audio sequencing, and other advanced new media concepts and multimedia application features, as that is what is popular in Android application development today. We look at core Android OS areas, including Content Providers (SQLite Databases), Broadcast Receivers, Services, and using Events, Intents, and Activities, all in great detail.

We cover the foundational knowledge that you will need to be able to work in the more advanced areas that the Android OS encompasses. Some of these include digital image compositing, digital video optimization, procedural animation, database design, multi-screen resolution support, 3D rendering, and similar advanced topics regarding which an Android developer needs to know at least the basics in order to work intelligently within their application design and development work process.

If you want a comprehensive overview of Android, Eclipse, Java, XML, and the Android Developer Tools environment, as well as knowledge about how to optimally use these technologies with leading open source new media content design and development tools, then this book will be of great interest to you.

Chapter 1

Building an Android IDE for Version 4.2: Acquiring, Installing, and Configuring an Android Development Environment

The first thing that we need to do before we can learn Android Application Development is to put together a working Android Application Development Environment on our development workstation. Hopefully you have an entry-level quad-core AMD or Intel computer with 4GB or more of DDR memory and Windows 7 or Windows 8; the computer that I will be using for this book is a $398 ACER 64-bit quad-core AMD, running at 3.1GHz with 4GB of DDR3 memory and 1TB hard disk drive and Windows 7 that I picked up at Walmart.

Fortunately for us Android App developers, very powerful 64-bit computers are readily available for a few hundred dollars! If you have a 32-bit computer, that will also work just as well for Android Application Development, because the Android 4.2 Development Environment comes in both 32-bit and 64-bit flavors. Additionally, all the software that we will be using for app development in this book is free for commercial use, also known as open source, so the cost of starting up your own Android Application Software Development business is quite low these days indeed.

If for some reason, you want to use a development environment that predates Android 4.2.2 (which I would strongly recommend against), there is an Appendix at the end of this book that covers the much more involved work process for installing the Android 4.1.2 development environment.

Our Plan of Attack

In this chapter, we will make sure that our system has the very latest versions of the Oracle Java 6 Software Development Kit (Java SDK, also known as the JDK, or Java Development Kit) programming environment, as well as the Android Software Development Environment, which consists of the Google Android Software Development Kit (SDK), Android Development Tools (ADT) Plug-ins for Eclipse, and the Eclipse 4.2 Integrated Development Environment (IDE).

All these installed together at once are cumulatively known as the **Android ADT Bundle**, which, as of Android 4.2, you can now download all at once, in under 400MB, at the **Android Developer** website at `http://developer.android.com`.

Before Android 4.2 Jelly Bean+ (Android API Level 17), developers had to download and install each of these components individually, which was quite tedious. If you want to do it this way, or see what it would be like to have to do it this way (and gain a greater understanding of what is going on between Eclipse and Android SDK and Android ADT) you can see the long-version of the install in Appendix A of this book.

Once our JDK is downloaded and installed, we will then download and install an Android Integrated Development Environment (IDE) called the **Android ADT Bundle**, the foundation of which is the Eclipse 4.2 Juno for Java EE IDE. Eclipse makes developing Android Apps easier by providing us with a slick Graphical User Interface (GUI) with which we can write, run, test, and debug our Android application code.

Eclipse runs "on top of" the Java Runtime Environment (JRE), because Eclipse is written in Java, and thus it uses the Java Platform to run its own codebase, which makes up the Eclipse IDE user interface and feature set, which you will see (as you progress throughout this book) is quite extensive indeed.

This is the primary reason that we downloaded and installed the Java 6 JDK first, so that the Java SDK and JRE are in place on our workstation. In this way, once we get into installing the ADT Bundle, which is based on Eclipse, Eclipse can easily find the Java Runtime Environment (so that Eclipse can launch and run). Once Eclipse is able to find Java it can use the Java SDK to build the Java programming code foundation for our Android Development Environment, because Android APIs (SDK) are based on the Java 6 APIs (SDK).

Once we have the ADT Bundle downloaded and installed and working smoothly on top of Java 6, we essentially have installed, all in one bundle, the Google Android Software Development Kit (SDK), the Eclipse 4.2.2 IDE, and all the ADT plug-ins needed to develop for Android 4.2.2 API Level 17.

For a bird's—eye view, if this process were formulated into an equation, it would look something like this:

JDK (Java 6 SDK) + ADT Bundle (Eclipse + Android SDK + ADT Eclipse Plug-Ins) = Custom Android IDE

As part of the Android Bundle installation and configuration for development usage work process (the second major part), we will install some **Android Virtual Device** (AVD) Emulators, which will live inside Eclipse 4.2, and which will allow us to test our applications on various Android Virtual Devices, such as a Virtual Nexus 7 Tablet, or a Virtual Nexus S Smartphone, or even a Virtual GoogleTV Set. So let's get started with this process now, so we can get it over with, and start developing apps in the next chapter!

Foundation of Android Programming: Java 6

The foundation of Android Application Development, both from a programming as well as an Integrated Development Environment (IDE) standpoint, is Java 6. Android Applications are written using the Java 6 programming language (and using XML as well, which we'll get into in more detail in Chapter 2), and Android Apps are developed inside the Eclipse 4.2.2 IDE, which is also written in the Java 6 programming language, and which runs on top of the Java 6 Runtime Environment, also known as the JRE. To put it mildly, the exact order in which you set up the various software components that make up your Android Development Environment is very important, and is the reason for this first chapter.

So that we have both the Java programming language, which we gain access to via the JDK or Java Developer Kit, as well as the Java Runtime Environment (JRE), which is part of the JDK, go to the Oracle TechNetwork and download the latest JDK 6 installation software and install it on your machine. We do this first because Eclipse needs Java to run, that is, Eclipse can be said to run "on top of" the Java platform and language. Android also requires Java, as well as Eclipse, for its Android Developer Tools (ADT) plug-ins, so we install the Java Platform and Java Environment first, then the Android ADT Bundle.

Let's get started.

Installing the JDK

The first thing we must do is get to the Java SDK download page, and there are two ways to do this; one is generic, one is precise. The generic way, which will always work, even if Oracle changes the location of its Java SDK download page (which it probably won't), is to use Google Search with the keyword phrase **"Java SDK Download",** which should bring up the Oracle TechNetwork Java download URL. The second way is to type the URL for the page directly into the browser. Here is the URL:

```
http://www.oracle.com/technetwork/java/javase/downloads/index.html
```

What this points to is the Internet (HTTP) and the Oracle website in their TechNetwork area (folder) in the Java area (sub-folder) for the Java SE or Standard Edition area (sub-sub-folder) in the Downloads area (sub-sub-sub-folder). There are three primary versions of Java: SE or Standard Edition for individual users, EE or Enterprise Edition for large collections of users, and ME or Micro Edition for older mobile flip-phones. Most modern smartphones use Android and Java SE, rather than Java ME. One of the really cool things about Android is that it uses the full Standard Edition of Java (known as Java SE) just like a PC does. This is because Android runs "on top of" a full version of the Linux OS Kernel, so an Android consumer electronics device is essentially a full-blown Linux computer, for all practical purposes.

Once you type in this URL, you arrive at the Java 6 JDK download page, and you need to find the Java 6 JDK download portion of the page, which looks like the (partial) page section shown in Figure 1-1.

***Figure 1-1.** The Java SE 6 JDK download section of the Oracle TechNetwork Java SE webpage*

Scroll about halfway down the page and click the blue **DOWNLOAD** button under the JDK (remember, the JDK contains *both* the JDK and the JRE, so don't download the JRE at all), as shown in Figure 1-1.

This takes you to the Java 6 JDK download page shown in Figure 1-2, where you first accept the software licensing agreement, and then download either the Windows 32-bit version or the Windows 64-bit version of Java 6.

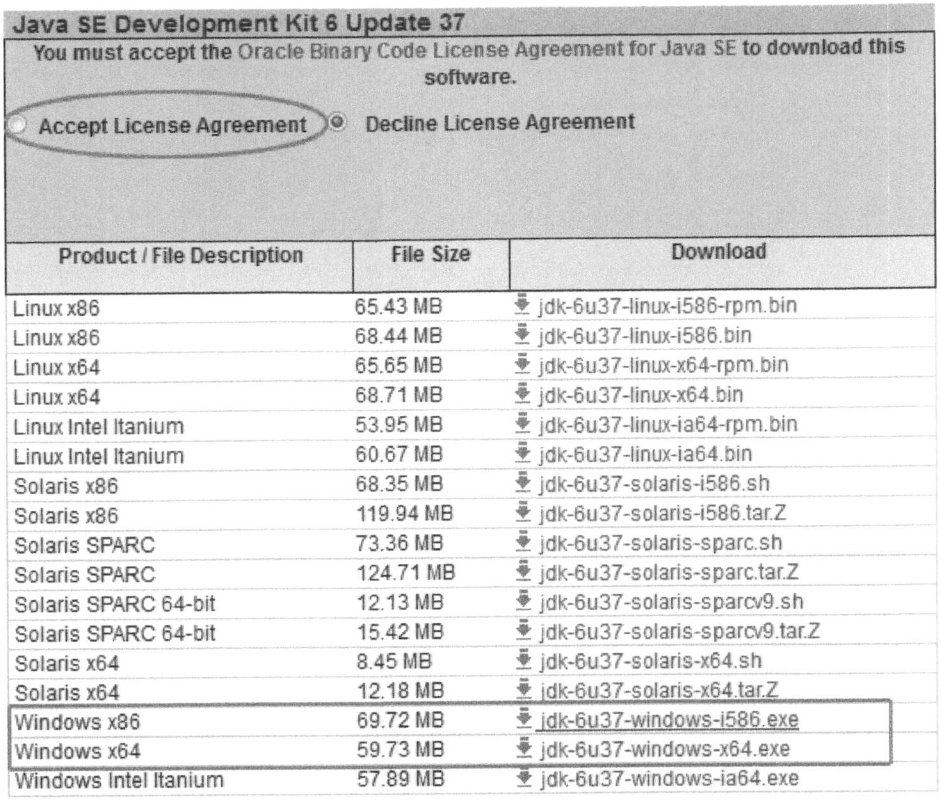

Java SE Development Kit 6 Update 37

You must accept the Oracle Binary Code License Agreement for Java SE to download this software.

Accept License Agreement   Decline License Agreement

Product / File Description	File Size	Download
Linux x86	65.43 MB	jdk-6u37-linux-i586-rpm.bin
Linux x86	68.44 MB	jdk-6u37-linux-i586.bin
Linux x64	65.65 MB	jdk-6u37-linux-x64-rpm.bin
Linux x64	68.71 MB	jdk-6u37-linux-x64.bin
Linux Intel Itanium	53.95 MB	jdk-6u37-linux-ia64-rpm.bin
Linux Intel Itanium	60.67 MB	jdk-6u37-linux-ia64.bin
Solaris x86	68.35 MB	jdk-6u37-solaris-i586.sh
Solaris x86	119.94 MB	jdk-6u37-solaris-i586.tar.Z
Solaris SPARC	73.36 MB	jdk-6u37-solaris-sparc.sh
Solaris SPARC	124.71 MB	jdk-6u37-solaris-sparc.tar.Z
Solaris SPARC 64-bit	12.13 MB	jdk-6u37-solaris-sparcv9.sh
Solaris SPARC 64-bit	15.42 MB	jdk-6u37-solaris-sparcv9.tar.Z
Solaris x64	8.45 MB	jdk-6u37-solaris-x64.sh
Solaris x64	12.18 MB	jdk-6u37-solaris-x64.tar.Z
Windows x86	69.72 MB	jdk-6u37-windows-i586.exe
Windows x64	59.73 MB	jdk-6u37-windows-x64.exe
Windows Intel Itanium	57.89 MB	jdk-6u37-windows-ia64.exe

Figure 1-2. Accept the Java 6 License Agreement and download Windows x86 32-bit – or Windows x64 64-bit .exe file

If you are using Linux OS or Solaris OS, you can find 32-bit and 64-bit versions for these operating systems here as well. Note that before you can download the Windows x86 32-bit .exe file or the Windows x64 64-bit .exe file, you must click the radio button selector next to the "Accept License Agreement" option at the top of the webpage section, as shown in Figure 1-2. Once you do this, the download links on the right become bold, and you can click them to download the installation file.

Click the **jdk-6u43-windows-i586.exe** link (or whatever that latest update revision happens to be) if you have a 32-bit Windows OS such as Windows XP, or the **jdk-6u43-windows-x64.exe** link (or whatever that latest update revision happens to be) if you have a 64-bit Windows OS such as Windows 7 or Windows 8, and then download the JDK 6 installer file to your Downloads folder on your workstation. Note that you do *not* need to download both files.

Removing Any Outdated JDKs

Before you install the current Java 6 JDK, you should check your system to make sure that no preexisting (older) versions of Java are already installed on your workstation. This is done in Windows via the Control Panel, which is accessed via the Windows Start Menu. Launch the Control Panel now, and find the icon labeled "Programs and Features" and launch the Programs and Features dialog shown in Figure 1-3.

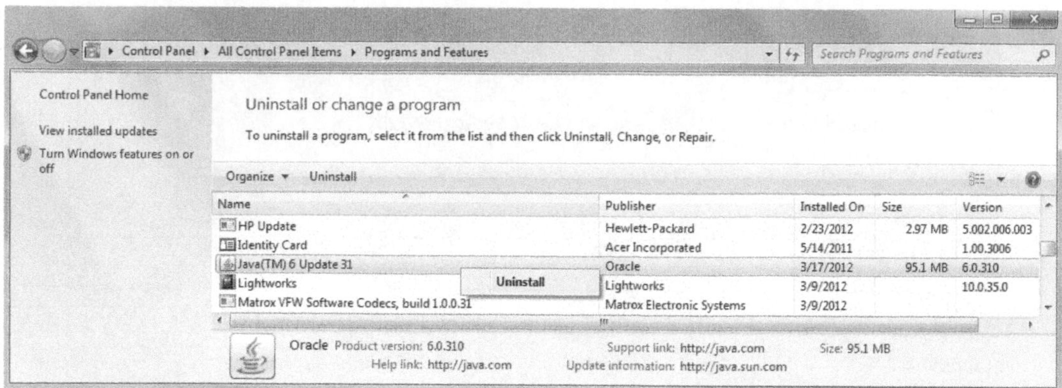

Figure 1-3. Right-click the existing Java installation, and select Uninstall to remove it from your system

Notice on my workstation that I already have 32-bit Java 6 Update 31 installed. Because I want to install the most recent 64-bit development software possible during this installation process, I am going to uninstall the previous Java 6 Update 31 installation, as well as any older versions of Eclipse and Android (if they exist, which they didn't on this particular workstation) using the exact same work process.

To do this, you need to select the older version of Java, and then right-click it, and select the **Uninstall** option, as shown in Figure 1-3. Windows then proceeds to remove the older version(s) of Java (and Eclipse and Android, if needed) from your system.

Next, go into your **Downloads** folder (or your desktop, or wherever you saved your file download), and double-click the **jdk-6u43-windows-i586.exe** or the **jdk-6u43-windows-x64.exe** file to start the Java 6 installation. Accept the default settings for the installation, which should proceed fairly quickly if you have a modern day workstation with a fast hard disk drive and at least 3GB of memory.

Once the Java 6 JDK installation is finished, you will be ready to download and install the Android ADT Bundle. Let's do that next, so that we have an Android IDE set-up to use for our future Android application development in the rest of the book.

The Android Developer Tools (ADT) Bundle

As of Android 4.2 Jelly Bean, the Android Software Development Kit, or Android SDK, is bundled with the Eclipse IDE and Android Development Tools (ADT) in one large 400MB download called the ADT Bundle.

Downloading the Android ADT IDE

The first thing we must do is get to the Android Developer webpage, and there are again two ways to do this; one generic, the other precise. The generic way, which will always work, even if Google changes the location of its Android Developer webpage (which it probably won't), is to use Google Search with the keyword phrase "Android Developer Website", which should bring up the `Developer.Android.com` website URL. The second way is to type the URL (I suggest that you memorize this URL) for the Android Developer webpage directly into the browser: `http://developer.android.com/index.html`.

Once you type in the URL, you arrive at the Android Developer website home page, and you need to find the **Get the SDK** button at the bottom of the page, which looks like the menu shown in Figure 1-4.

About Android	Get the SDK	Open Source	Support	Legal

Figure 1-4. Selecting the Get the SDK button to go to the Android SDK download page on the `Developer.Android.com` *site*

Once you click the **Get the SDK** button you are taken to the **Get the Android SDK** page, where you see a large blue button that says: **Download the SDK - ADT Bundle for Windows** (or it may say for Linux or for Macintosh, if you are currently using those operating systems; the website auto-detects your OS and gives you the proper download link). Click this blue button, as shown in Figure 1-5, to go to the downloads page to get the Android SDK ADT Bundle installer .zip file, which is now available in 32-bit and 64-bit versions.

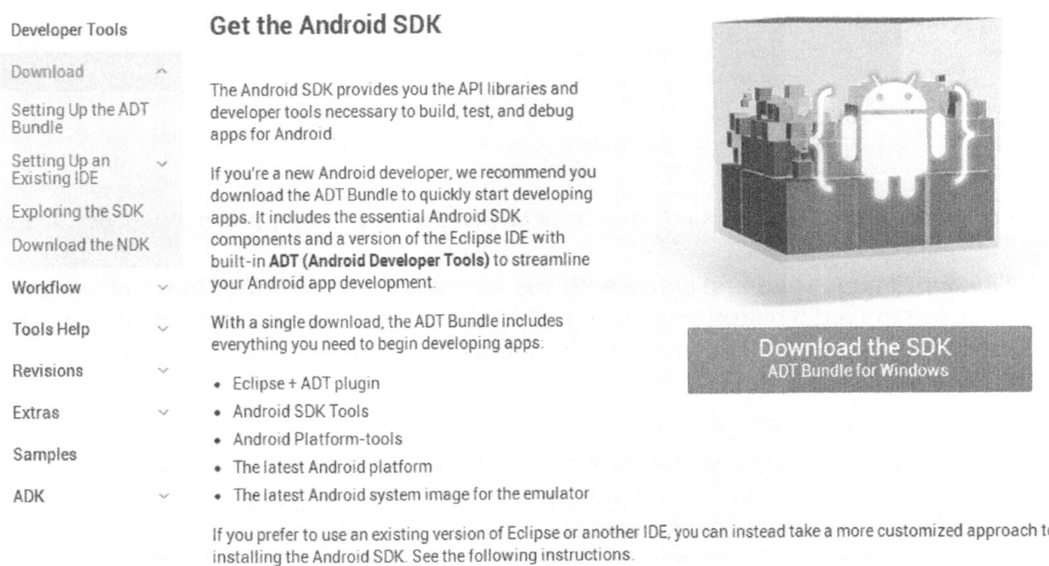

Developer Tools
Download
Setting Up the ADT Bundle
Setting Up an Existing IDE
Exploring the SDK
Download the NDK
Workflow
Tools Help
Revisions
Extras
Samples
ADK
Get the Android SDK
The Android SDK provides you the API libraries and developer tools necessary to build, test, and debug apps for Android.
If you're a new Android developer, we recommend you download the ADT Bundle to quickly start developing apps. It includes the essential Android SDK components and a version of the Eclipse IDE with built-in ADT (Android Developer Tools) to streamline your Android app development.
With a single download, the ADT Bundle includes everything you need to begin developing apps:
Eclipse + ADT plugin
Android SDK Tools
Android Platform-tools
The latest Android platform
The latest Android system image for the emulator
If you prefer to use an existing version of Eclipse or another IDE, you can instead take a more customized approach to installing the Android SDK. See the following instructions.
Download the SDK
ADT Bundle for Windows

Figure 1-5. The Download the SDK for Windows ADT Bundle button on the Get the Android SDK page on `Developer.Android.com`

Once you click the **Download the SDK ADT Bundle** button, you are taken to the page shown in Figure 1-6 where you can read the licensing agreements for the software packages (Android 4.2.2 SDK, Eclipse 4.2.2, Android Developer Tools, etc.) that you are downloading in the bundled installation.

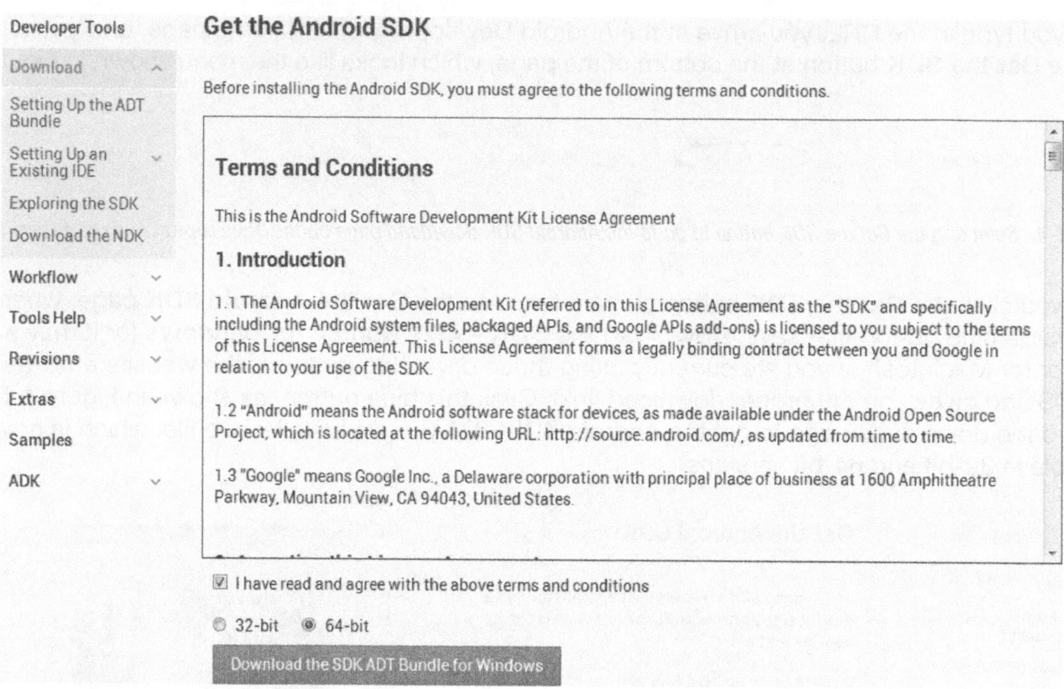

Developer Tools
Download
Setting Up the ADT Bundle
Setting Up an Existing IDE
Exploring the SDK
Download the NDK
Workflow
Tools Help
Revisions
Extras
Samples
ADK
Get the Android SDK
Before installing the Android SDK, you must agree to the following terms and conditions.
Terms and Conditions
This is the Android Software Development Kit License Agreement
1. Introduction
1.1 The Android Software Development Kit (referred to in this License Agreement as the "SDK" and specifically including the Android system files, packaged APIs, and Google APIs add-ons) is licensed to you subject to the terms of this License Agreement. This License Agreement forms a legally binding contract between you and Google in relation to your use of the SDK.
1.2 "Android" means the Android software stack for devices, as made available under the Android Open Source Project, which is located at the following URL: http://source.android.com/, as updated from time to time.
1.3 "Google" means Google Inc., a Delaware corporation with principal place of business at 1600 Amphitheatre Parkway, Mountain View, CA 94043, United States.
I have read and agree with the above terms and conditions
32-bit
64-bit
Download the SDK ADT Bundle for Windows

***Figure 1-6.** The Agree to Terms and Conditions and Download the SDK ADT Bundle for Windows page on `Developer.Android.com`*

After you click the **"I have read and agree with the above terms and conditions"** checkbox, and have then selected the radio button for the type of OS (32-bit or 64-bit) that you are running, you can click the **Download the SDK ADT Bundle for Windows** button and download the appropriate zip file for your OS type.

Because I have a Windows 7 64-bit Quad-Core AMD system, I selected the 64-bit SDK version, which was only recently available as of Android 4.2 API Level 17, also known as Jelly Bean Plus. Before Android 4.2 came out in late November 2012 (over the Thanksgiving holiday believe it or not), Android application developers had no choice but to use a 32-bit development software environment, even if they developed on a 64-bit workstation. So if you like to keep everything 64-bit clean on your 64-bit workstation, you're in luck! Let's start the download and get that 400MB file downloading and onto our workstation's hard disk drive now.

Installing the Android ADT IDE

Once the 400MB download has finished, open your Windows Explorer File Navigation and File Management Utility, and find the .zip file in your system's Downloads folder. If you can't find it, put the a partial name of the zip file using wildcard characters in the Search box at the upper right, and select your Computer or C:\ drive on the left, and Windows Explorer will find the file for you.

Here's the search string I use: `adt-bundle*.zip` (an asterisk wildcard expands to fit anything else in filename).

Once you find the **adt-bundle-windows** zip archive file, right-click it to get a context-sensitive menu of everything that can be done to or with that file, and choose the **Extract All...** option to extract all the files and folders inside of the zip archive onto your hard disk drive. This is shown in Figure 1-7 (circled in red).

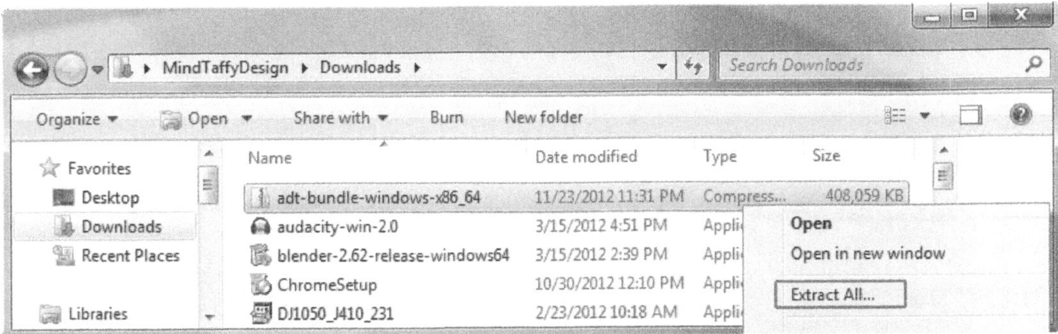

Figure 1-7. Right-clicking the adt-bundle zip file in your Downloads folder and selecting the Extract All... option

Next you will see an **Extract Compressed (Zipped) Folders** dialog, asking you to select your destination directory in which to extract the ADT Bundle files and folder hierarchy. As shown in the top dialog in Figure 1-8, the archive extraction utility places the current location of the file into your system Downloads folder as its destination path, which is not surprising, as it really doesn't know where you want to put these files, so it makes an assumption and puts itself right where the zip file is "standing" currently, so to speak. Let's change that location, and put the files in a more logical location on our workstation.

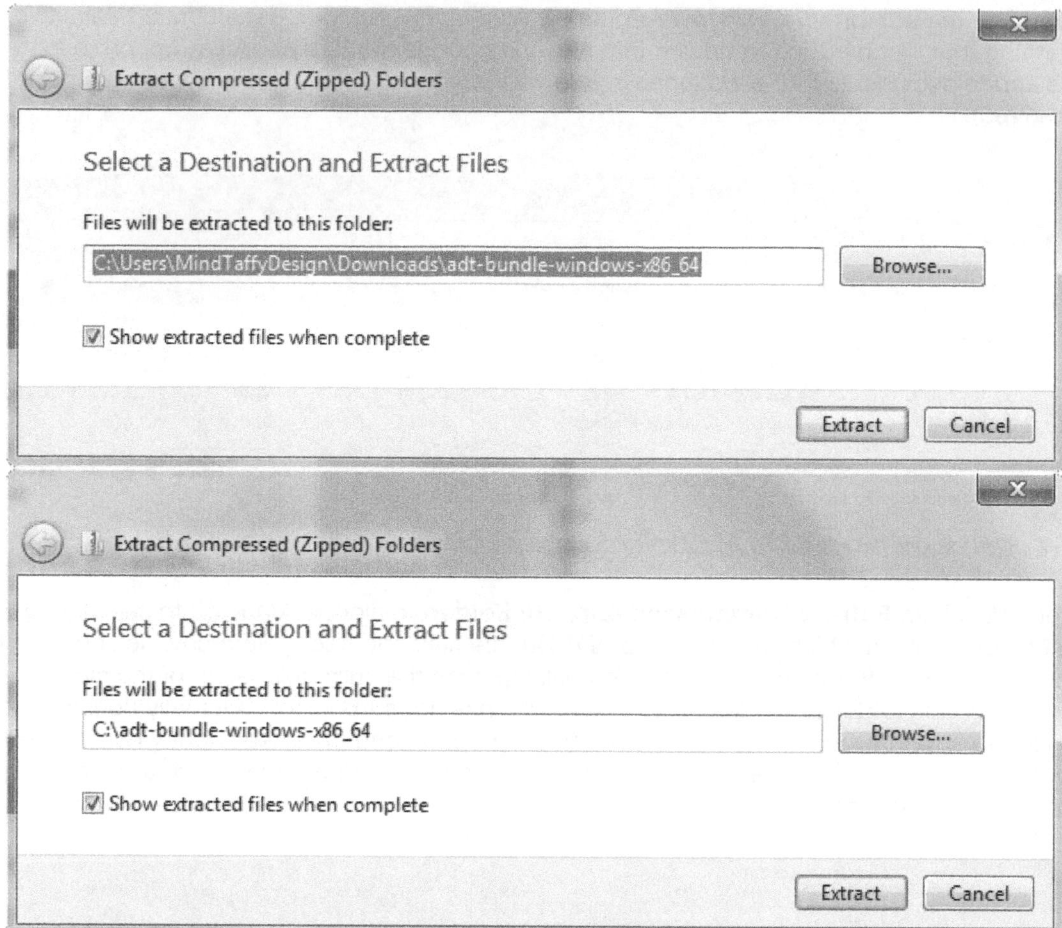

***Figure 1-8.** Changing the extract files destination folder from C:\Users\Username\Downloads to C:\adt-bundle-windows*

Because we don't really want our ADT Bundle installed into our Downloads folder (which we use primarily to hold our file downloads), the easiest work process is to move it up to the top or "root" of our C:\ primary hard disk drive, so let's click the cursor right in front of the adt-bundle in the filename, and then backspace over the Downloads, (*Your User Name Here*), and Users sections of the auto-generated pathname.

In this way, you end up with the C:\ hard drive specifier right in front of the `adt-bundle-windows-x86 .zip` filename that you just downloaded as your folder name. This installs the ADT Bundle in the Root (top) of your C:\ drive, on your primary hard disk partition, where you can easily see it and find it anytime that you need to. The resulting path is shown in the lower part of the screen shot in Figure 1-8.

Note that if you wanted to, you could also remove the `windows` and `x86` parts of the folder name and name the folder `C:\ADT` or `C:\ADT-Bundle` if you wanted to, or `C:\Android_Development_Environment` or something similar. Because you are going to find and set-up the Quick Launch Icon for this Application Executable, it doesn't matter what you call this top-level folder, as long as you can easily locate it.

Once you click the **Extract** button, you get a small progress dialog, shown in Figure 1-9, which shows you all the 8,740 items (584 megabytes) that are being inflated and copied onto your hard disk drive. After this process is complete, open your Windows Explorer file viewing utility, and find the **eclipse.exe,** which is the Eclipse 4.2.2 application's executable file.

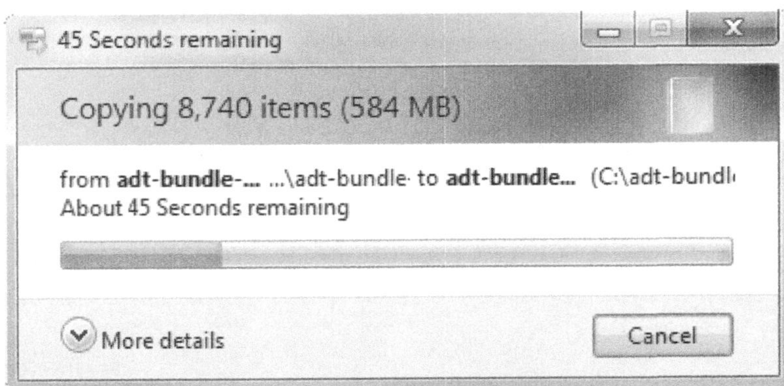

***Figure 1-9.** Extracting the 8,740 files totaling 584MB from the 400MB ADT Bundle zip file*

To do this, open the C: drive on the left navigation panel in the Windows Explorer utility, and then look for the **adt-bundle-windows-x86** filename that you downloaded, installed, and named, and under that you will find the eclipse folder and its sub-folders, as shown in Figure 1-10. If you used your own custom name, such as `ADT_Bundle`, then look for whatever name you decided to use for your ADT Bundle folder.

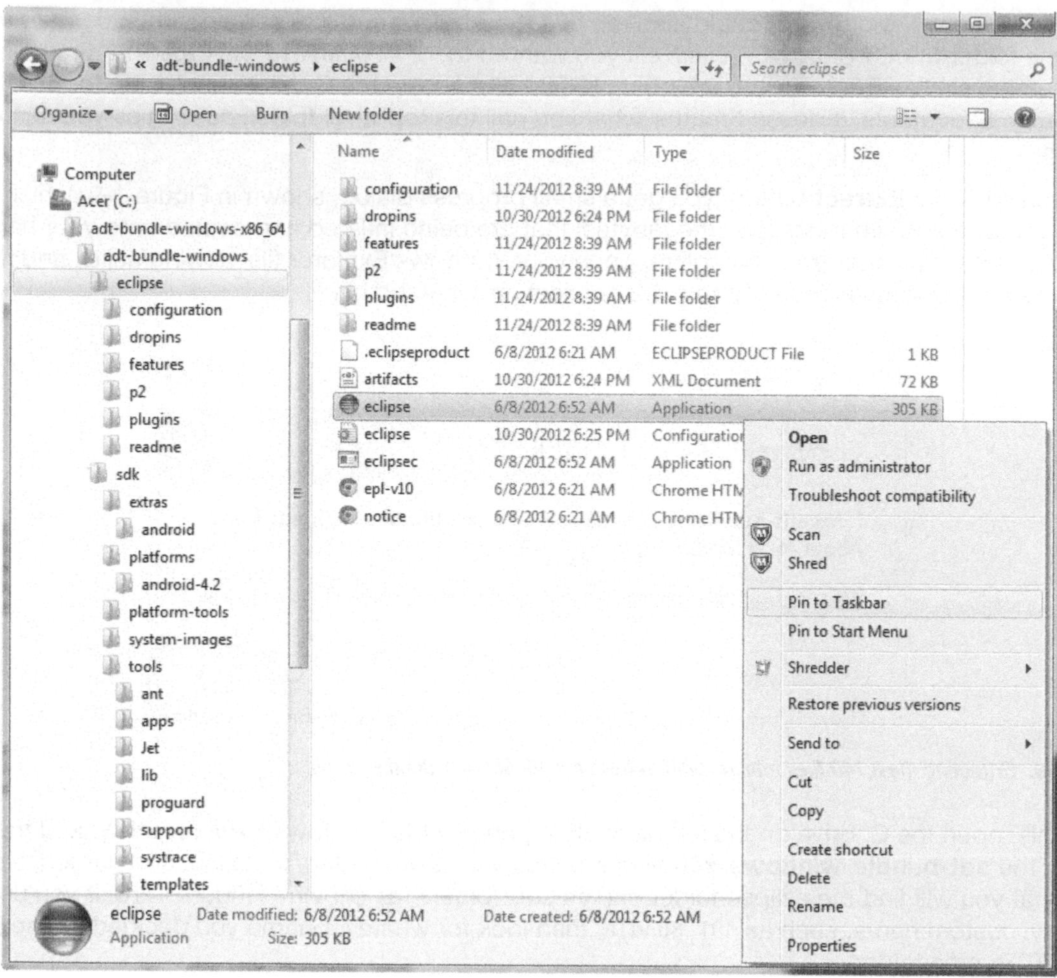

Figure 1-10. Finding the Eclipse Application file in Windows Explorer and right-clicking to invoke the Pin to Taskbar feature

Setting Up a Quick Launch Icon on Your Taskbar

Look for a purple sphere next to the word **eclipse** with a file type of "application" and that is your Eclipse IDE software executable file. Next, right-click this **Eclipse application file** to get another context-sensitive menu of commands, and then choose the **Pin to Taskbar** command in the third section of this menu. This installs Eclipse as a Quick Launch Icon in your Taskbar Program launch area. This work process is also shown in Figure 1-10.

Once you select the **Pin to Taskbar** command from the right-click menu, the Eclipse 4.2 ADT Bundle purple sphere launch icon appears on your Windows Taskbar. This is usually located at the bottom of the OS screen, but can be docked (via dragging) onto the top, or even the left or the right of the screen. Figure 1-11 shows the Eclipse 4.2 ADT Bundle Launch Icon installed on my Win7 Taskbar along with other professional open source software packages (GIMP, Blender 3D, Audacity, Lightworks, OpenOffice, and Chrome, shown in that order), many of which we'll be installing later on in this chapter.

Figure 1-11. The Eclipse 4.2 ADT Bundle Launch Icon is shown on the far left side of the Windows Taskbar

Click the Eclipse Quick Launch Icon and make sure Eclipse for ADT fires up; if it does, it means that you have installed Java 6 correctly, and that Eclipse ADT Bundle has successfully found Java, and is using it to run its integrated development environment. The start-up screen is shown in Figure 1-12.

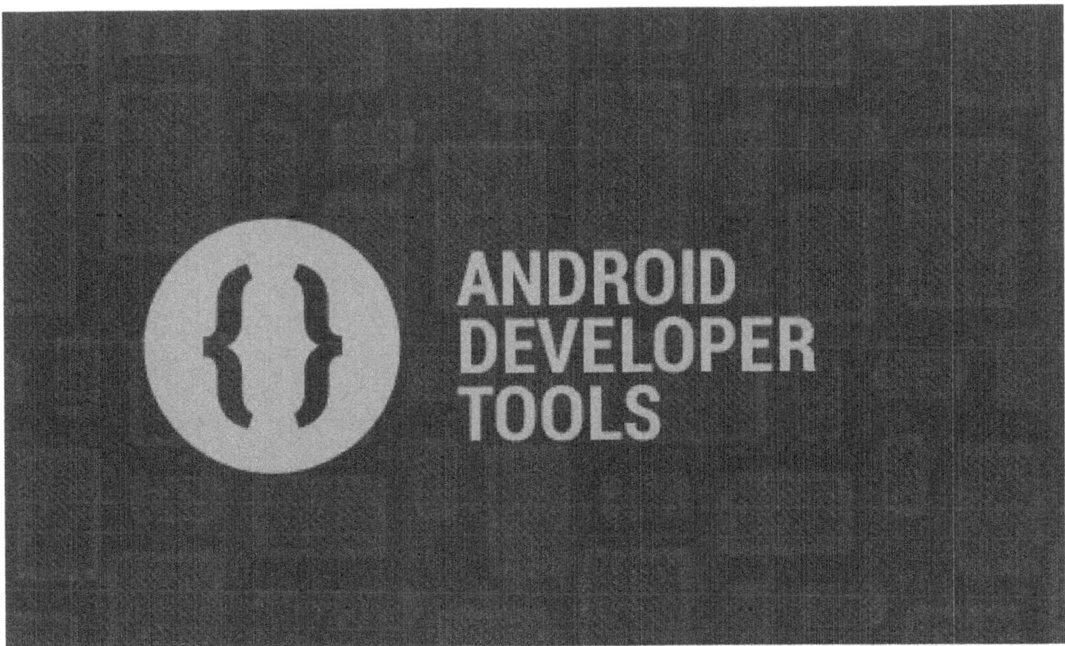

Figure 1-12. Launching the Android Developer Tools version of Eclipse 4.2.2 via your newly installed Quick Launch Icon

It is important to note that as of Android 4.2 Jelly Bean+, that the Eclipse Juno 4.2 start-up screen is now gone, and the new ADT Bundle start-up screen shows that Eclipse is now an integrated part of the 64-bit **Android Developer Tools** software bundle that we have just installed.

Launching and Configuring the Android Developer Tools IDE

After you launch the Eclipse 4.2 for Android Developer Tools software, the first screen that you see pop up is the **Contribute Usage Statistics** dialog. You only see this screen the first time you launch the Eclipse ADT Bundle, so select the option that you want for usage statistic sharing now. You can always change your mind (the option chosen) later on, if you like, via the Android ➤ Usage Stats menu sequence.

I selected the **Send Usage Statistics to Google** (Yes) option, so that Google can see how I use Eclipse and ADT, and so they can make improvements to the product. You can also select the No option with zero negative repercussions. This dialog is shown in Figure 1-13.

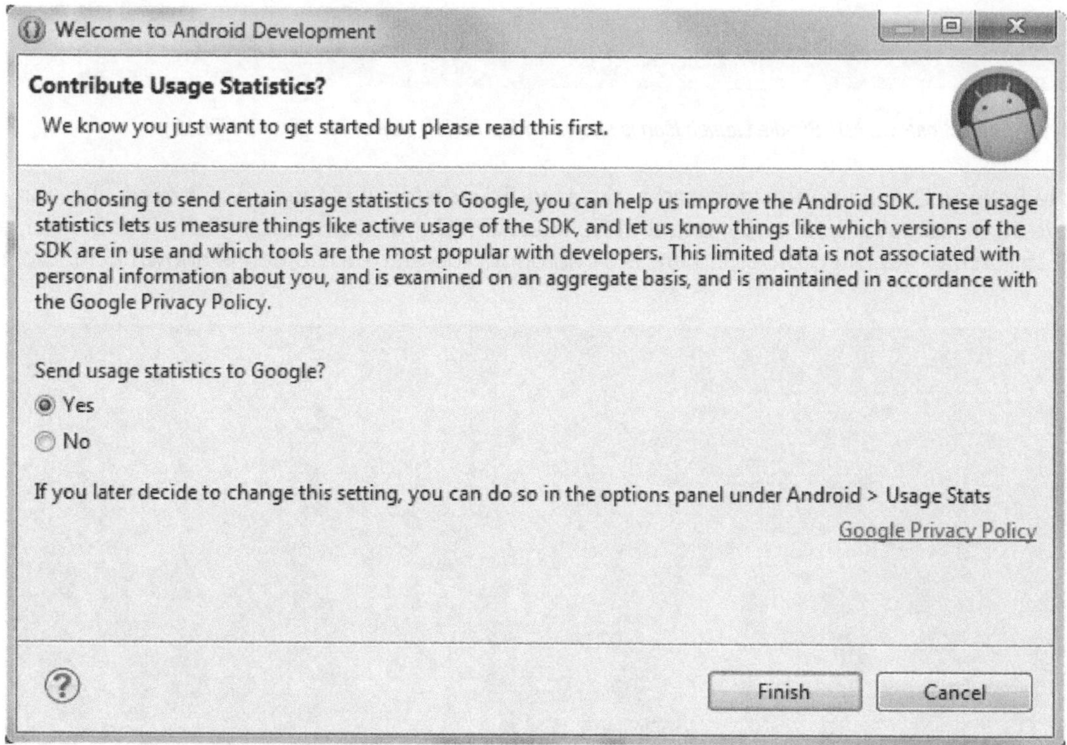

Figure 1-13. Contribute Usage Statistics dialog encountered on initial launch of Eclipse ADT software

Once you make your selection, click the **Finish** button, and the Eclipse ADT Bundle continues to launch the Android Integrated Development Environment (IDE).

When you launch the Android Developer Tools version of Eclipse 4.2 for the first time, you will see an **Android IDE Welcome** screen. Everything on that screen we will be covering in the first few chapters of this book, so read it all if you want, and then close it using the **X** in the right side of the **Android IDE Tab** at the top. Once you do this, an empty version of the Eclipse IDE then appears, as shown in Figure 1-14.

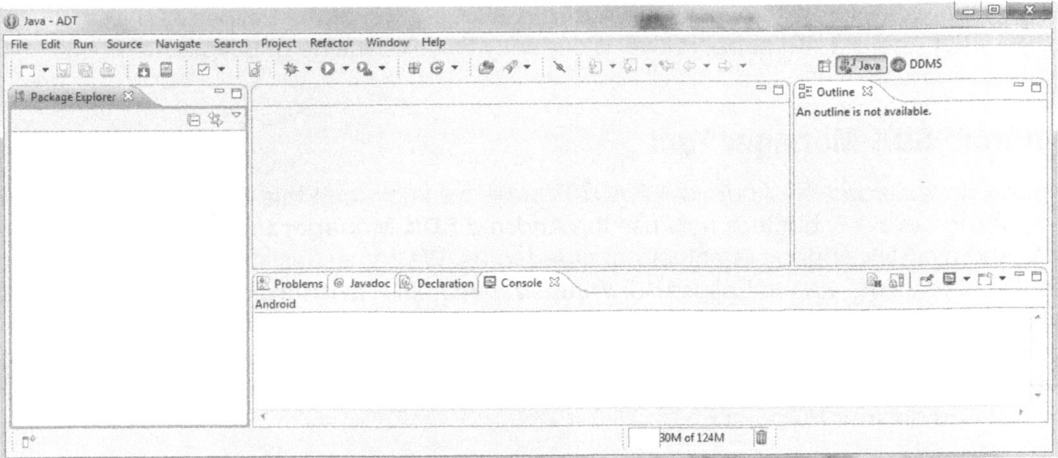

***Figure 1-14.** Eclipse 4.2 for ADT on first launch showing empty Package Explorer, Editing, Console, and Outline panes*

The first thing that we want to do is to make sure the ADT Bundle that we just installed is completely up to date. We do this via the **Help** menu, and its **Check for Updates** command, located near the bottom. Once you have selected this option, you see the dialog shown in Figure 1-15. If there are updated versions of any of the 8,740 files that were installed during your ADT Bundle installation, you will see the **Checking for Updates...** function "fetching" them, and updating the older versions that are on your system currently.

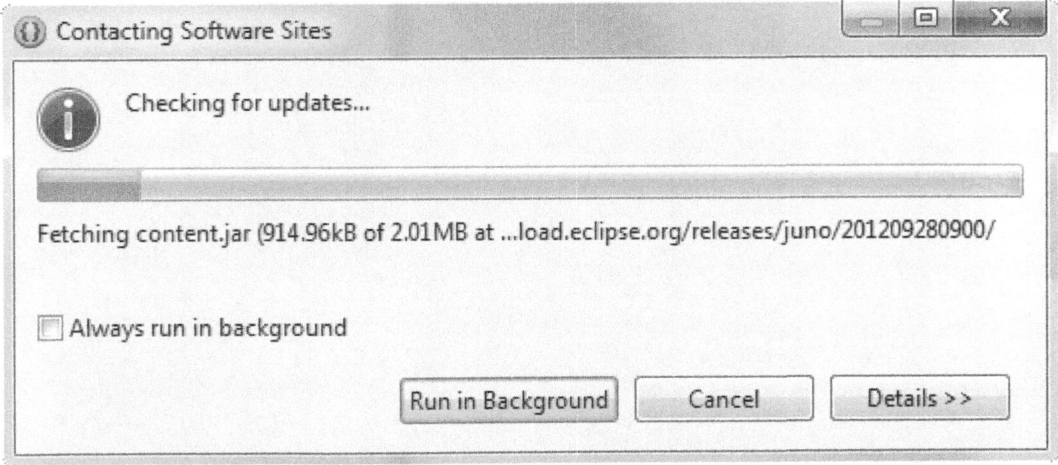

***Figure 1-15.** Checking for Android software updates online, using the software repositories at Eclipse and Google*

Now let's take a look at how to access the **Android SDK** portion of the Eclipse ADT Bundle at any time to see what Android API support level is currently installed inside of Eclipse.

The Android SDK Manager Tool

Because we downloaded the Android 4.2 ADT Bundle, we know that this is going to be at least Android 4.2 API Level 17, but let's now use the **Android SDK Manager** tool to dive deeper in, and to see what Android SDK support is actually afforded to us. We can access the Android SDK part of the Android IDE at any time via the Eclipse 4.2 **Window** menu, and its **Android SDK Manager** option, located in the bottom section of that menu. Clicking this option opens up an Android SDK Manager window, which shows which API Levels (Android OS Versions) we have currently installed (on our system) in our Android IDE. Let's do that now so that you can see what the ADT Bundle installation actually installed on your PC.

As you can see in Figure 1-16, this includes the Android SDK Tools, the Android SDK Platform Tools, the Android SDK 4.2 Platform, the ARM Processor system image (for testing in the Emulator we'll be setting up soon), and the Android Support Library. The **Android Support Library** allows previous versions of Android to be supported, so that we do not necessarily need to download all the other API Levels to support all the hardware devices out there. This is important to note, and is the primary reason why we are only going be to using Android API Level 17 installed during this process in the examples in this book and not download any of the other Android APIs shown in Android SDK Manager at this time.

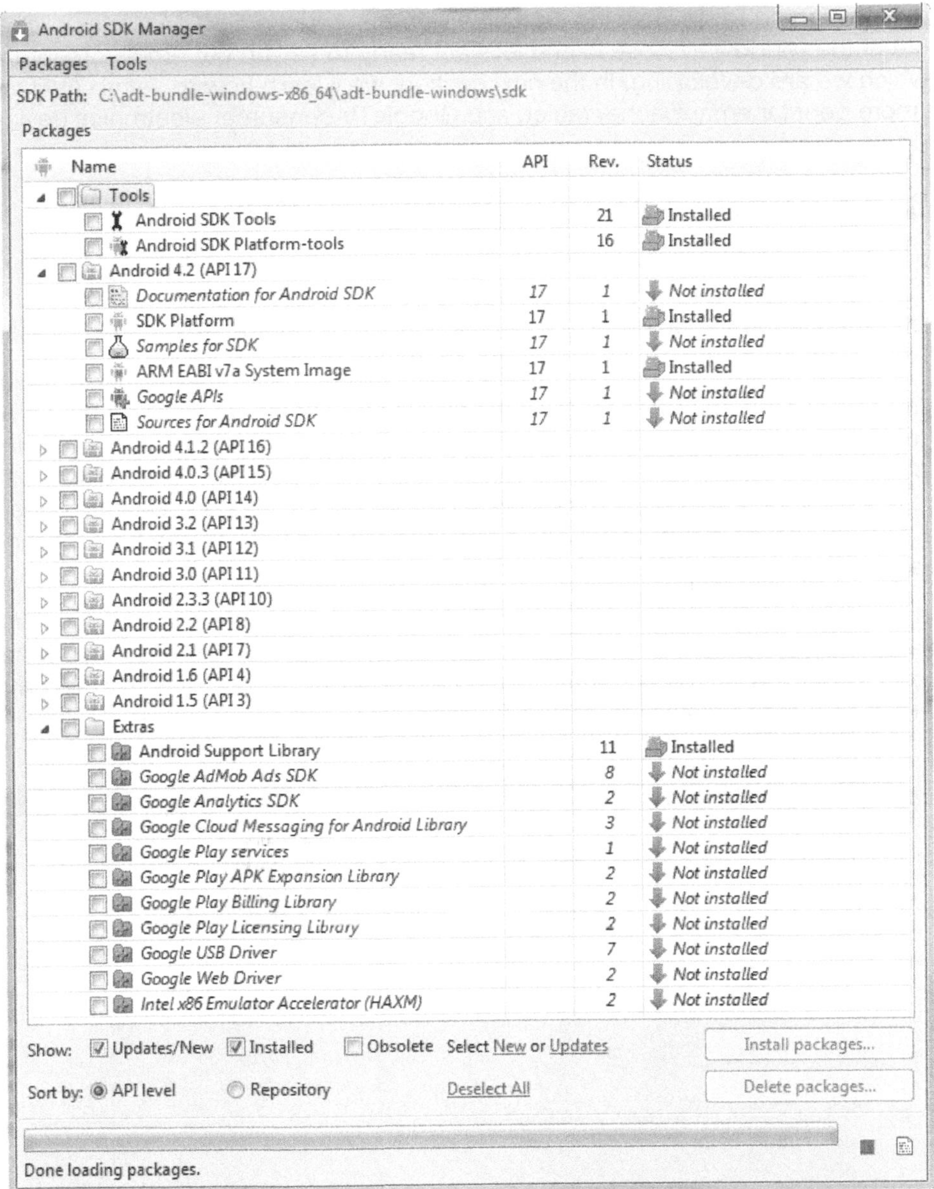

Figure 1-16. Android SDK Manager dialog, showing the libraries and packages installed in the ADT Bundle

In the future, if you absolutely need to develop for other versions of Android, such as 2.3.7 for Amazon Kindle Fire, or 4.0.4 for Amazon Kindle Fire HD, for instance, simply select those Android versions, and click on the **Install packages...** button at the bottom right of the window. I strongly suggest that you do this one API Level at a time, and only for those Android API Levels that you are absolutely sure that you need to develop for, as each involves downloading hundreds of megabytes of files and documentation.

Because we are not going to do anything right now with the Android SDK Manager, click the red X at the top right of the window to close it, and let's get ready to set-up our emulators for the Android devices for which we are developing. In the next section, we'll learn how to set up AVD emulators for some of the more popular smartphone, tablet, and GoogleTV consumer electronics devices.

Configuring Android Virtual Devices (AVDs)

The last step in the process to get your Android Development Environment ready for the rest of this book is to set up your **Android Virtual Devices** (AVDs). An **AVD** is an **emulator** that mimics an Android smartphone, tablet, e-reader, iTV Set (GoogleTV) or set-top box consumer electronics product and allows you to test your Android Apps on your workstation.

Having an emulator is desirable because the work process of constantly uploading your application onto an actual physical Android device (hardware) is much more tedious than right-clicking your project and selecting Run As Android Application. That's not to say that you shouldn't test your app out once in a while on a real Android hardware device, but the AVD allows you to test as you develop, and with much greater speed and frequency. In this section, we'll create three such devices: a Nexus 7 tablet, a Nexus S smartphone, and an Android iTV Set.

Because you are already in Eclipse, go into the **Window** menu, and select the **Android Virtual Device Manager** option near the bottom. This opens up the **Android Virtual Device Manager** dialog, which lists your AVDs. You currently have no AVDs set-up, and it says: **No AVD available** within the central area of the dialog, as shown in Figure 1-17.

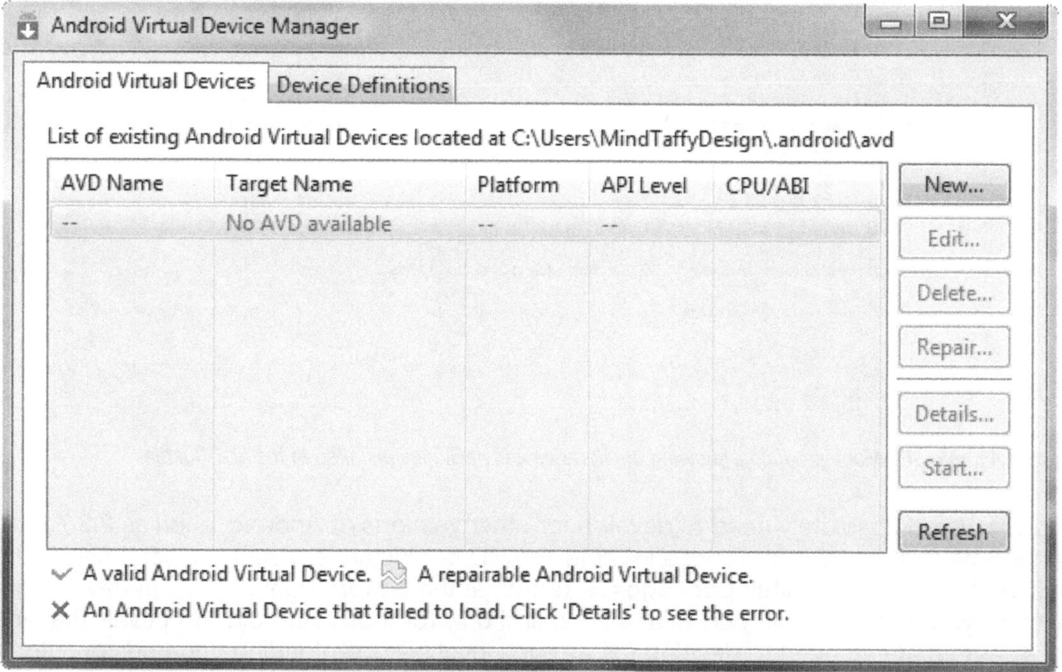

Figure 1-17. Android Virtual Device Manager dialog–click the New... button to add an AVD

To add a new AVD to your Eclipse environment, click the **New...** button at the top right of the dialog, and open the **Create a New Android Virtual Device (AVD)** dialog.

Creating Your Nexus 7 Tablet Emulator

The first thing that we want to do is to name our emulator, so enter: **Android_4.2_Emulator_Nexus_7** in the **Name:** field, as shown in Figure 1-18. In the **Device:** field, use the drop-down menu (via the down arrow) to select the **Nexus 7** Tablet option. Then select the **Target:** for the emulator, which is the API Level for the emulator, which is Android 4.2, or API Level 17, which is the current latest revision of the Android OS.

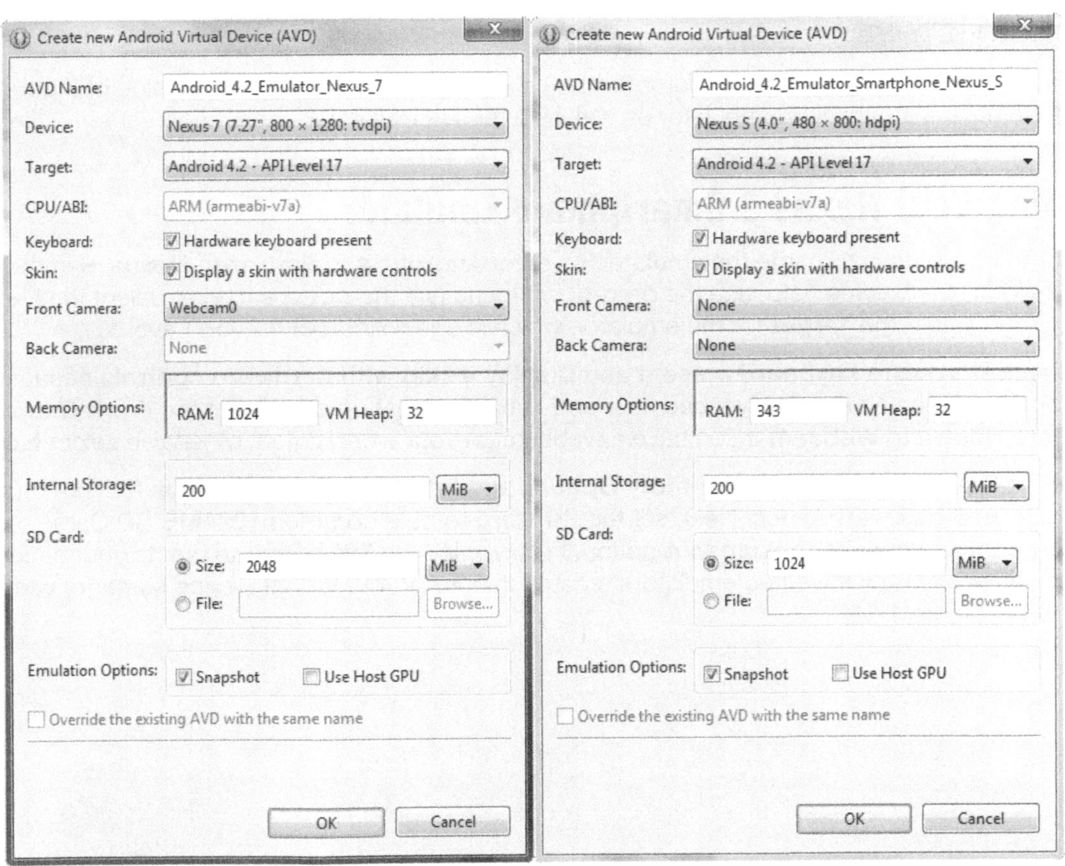

***Figure 1-18.** Creating a New Android Device (AVD) for a Nexus 7 tablet and a Nexus S smartphone using the AVD Manager*

Because the Nexus 7 uses an ARM (armeabi-v7a) processor, this field is automatically set for you, and cannot be changed. Next, check **Hardware keyboard present** and **Display a skin with hardware controls** because those options fit the Nexus 7 for users who own the wireless keyboard, which most serious users do.

Set the **Front Camera** option drop-down to: **Webcam** if you have a webcam installed on your workstation, otherwise select **None**. This is a new Android AVD Emulator feature starting with Android 4.2. Note that before Android API Level 17, the Android Emulator (AVD) did not support camera testing of any kind.

The Nexus 7 AVD Profile sets the **Memory Options** and **Internal Storage** settings for you, based on the Nexus 7 manufacturer's hardware specifications. Next, set the **SD Card** to be a common **2048MB** SD card configuration, and check the **Snapshot** option.

Finally, click the **OK** button to create the first of three Android 4.2 AVD Emulators, this one for the Nexus 7 Tablet. If you are going to develop for some of the other popular API level tablets, utilize exactly the same work process and add other emulators named **Kindle Fire** (use Android 2.3.7 API Level 10 and HDPI) or **Kindle Fire HD** (use Android 4.0.4 API Level 15 and XXHDPI), for instance, if you need to test your applications for delivery on those other specific hardware platforms.

Next, let's create a Smartphone Emulator for the Nexus S, as shown on the right-side of Figure 1-18, so that we have a smartphone emulator as well as a tablet emulator.

Creating Your Nexus S Smartphone Emulator

The first thing we do is to name the emulator, so enter **Android_4.2_Emulator_Nexus_S** in the **Name** field. In the **Device** field, use the drop-down menu (via the down arrow) to select the **Nexus S** option. Then select the **Target** for the emulator, which is again Android 4.2 API Level 17.

Next check **Hardware keyboard present** and **Display a skin with hardware controls** because those options fit the Nexus S advanced user and make app testing easier. Set the **Front Camera** option drop-down to **Webcam** if you have a webcam on your workstation, otherwise select **None**.

The Nexus S AVD Profile sets the **Memory Options** and **Internal Storage** settings for you, based on the Nexus S hardware specs. Next, set the **SD Card** to be a common **1024MB** SD Card configuration, and check the **Snapshot** option. Finally, click the **OK** button to create your second AVD Emulator. We now have two emulators created in our Android Virtual Device Manager window, as shown in Figure 1-19.

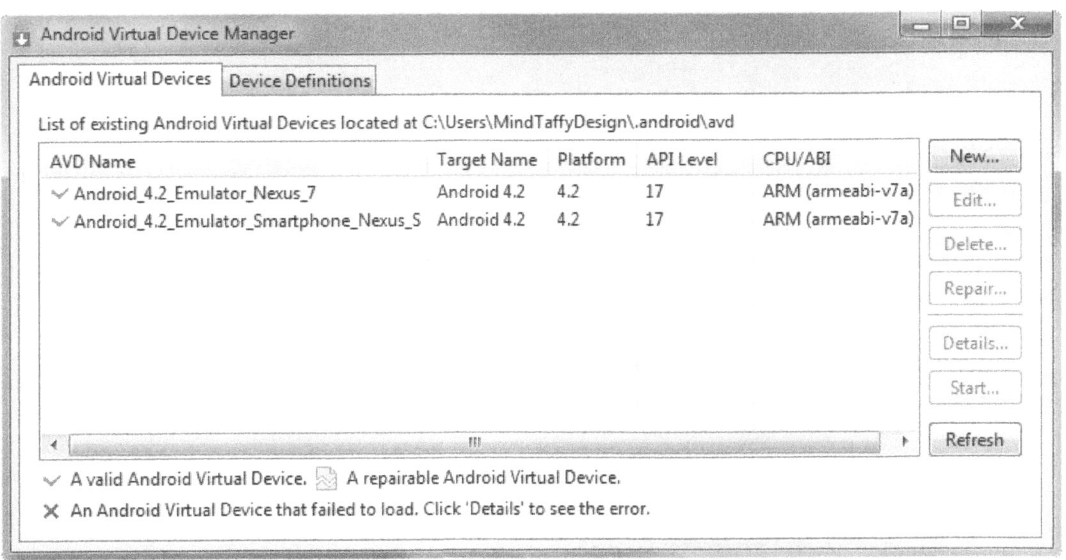

Figure 1-19. Android Virtual Device Manager showing two new emulators for the Nexus 7 Tablet and Nexus S Smartphone

The only other type of Android virtual device that we should really create to test our content on in this book is the newest genre of Android device to hit the market—the iTV, or Interactive Television Set.

Creating Your Android iTV Emulator for GoogleTV Support

Android iTV sets run a branded version of the Android OS called GoogleTV and are available as iTV Sets or Set-Top Boxes (STBs) or Home Media Centers (HMCs) or even as USB sticks such as the Philips product.

Fortunately, I just got the new Philips GoogleTV USB stick product to use for an Android application development project for one of my clients. Thus I have the specifications for the product I'll need to create my own custom AVD device definition specification to use to create an AVD to use for testing.

The first thing I need to do is see whether it is on the list of preconfigured AVDs on the right-side tab labeled Device Definitions, as seen in Figure 1-20. However, the Philips GoogleTV USB stick is not one of them, so we need to go into yet another series of dialogs to add the Philips GoogleTV product to the list of products currently in the AVD Manager Device Definitions dialog. One of the reasons I am adding an iTV emulator to our tablet and smartphone emulators is specifically to show you this work process, as it is hidden even deeper in the AVD Manager than the AVD creation process is.

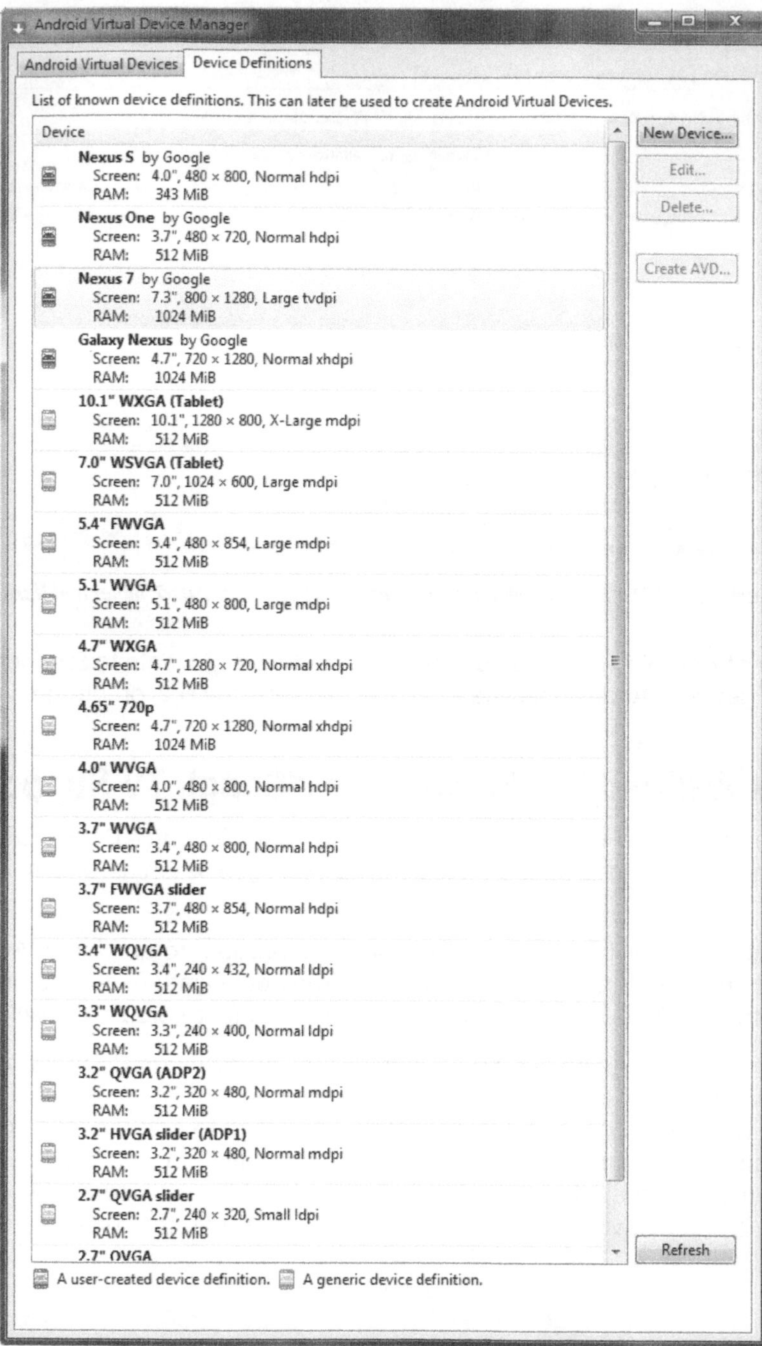

Figure 1-20. The AVD Manager Device Definitions tab, where you can select from predefined AVD devices or create your own

The key to unlocking this New Device Definition work process is, you guessed it, the **New Device...** button, located on the top right of the Android Virtual Device Manager's **Device Definitions** tab panel. Click the **New Device...** button, and you get the **Create New Device** dialog, shown in Figure 1-21.

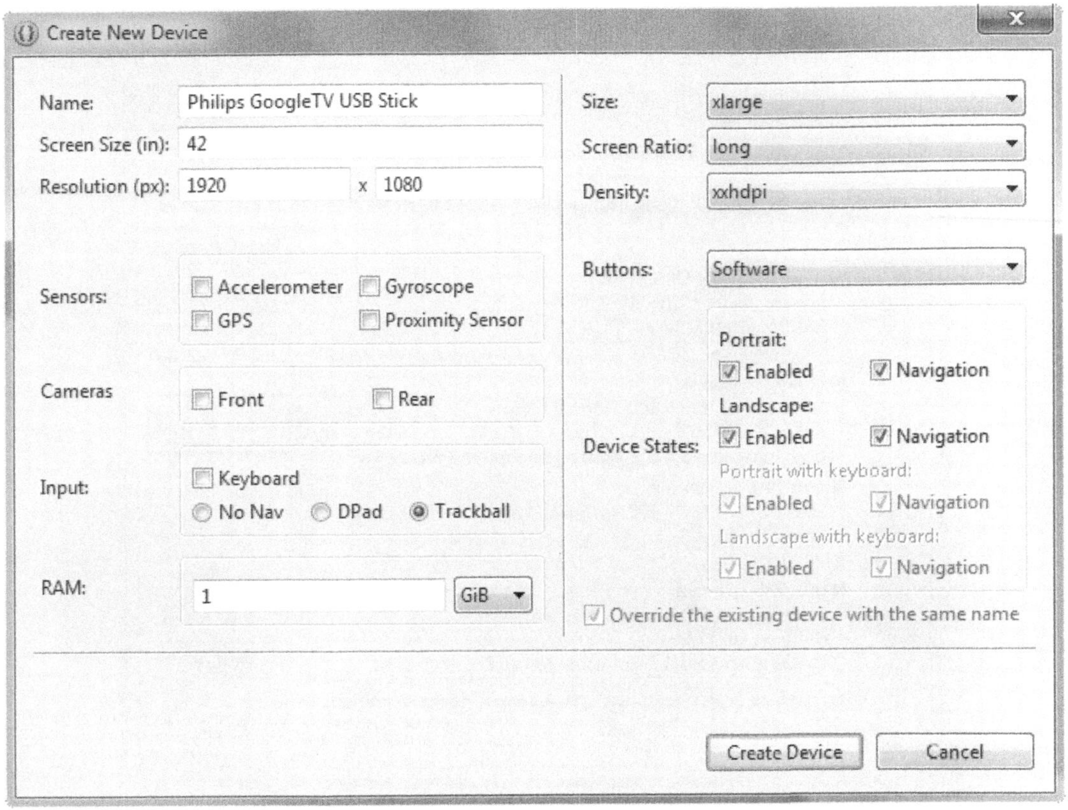

Figure 1-21. The Create New Device dialog in the Device Definitions tab of the AVD Manager window

The Create New Device dialog lets us create a custom product device definition for the Device Definitions tab in the Android Virtual Device Manager window. Let's create one for the Philips GoogleTV USB stick now. In the **Name:** field, place the product name of Philips' GoogleTV USB stick, and also enter the most common **Screen Size:** of **42** inches, and its physical pixel resolution of HDTV **1920 x 1080** pixels. Because HDTVs don't have **sensors**, leave these four options unchecked, and because the GoogleTV USB stick doesn't have any **cameras**, leave these two options unchecked as well. The Philips GoogleTV USB stick product uses a mouse, so select the **Input:** section option of **Trackball**.

The product features 1GB of RAM, so enter a **1** in the **RAM:** field, and select the **GiB** drop-down menu selection. The product has an extra-large size, so select the **xlarge** value for the **Size:** option, and **long** for the **Screen Ratio:** option, because HDTVs are widescreen devices. The Pixel Density is 1920 by 1080 pixels regardless of screen size, so select **XXHDPI** for the **Density:** setting. Because this product is a USB stick, select **Software** for the **Buttons:** option and then enable the **Portrait** and **Landscape** mode checkboxes, as shown in Figure 1-21, because the product works well in both of these modes.

After all these new product specifications are entered correctly, you can click the **Create Device** button at the bottom of the dialog to add the new product definition to the Device Definitions tab of the AVD Manager window, as shown in Figure 1-22.

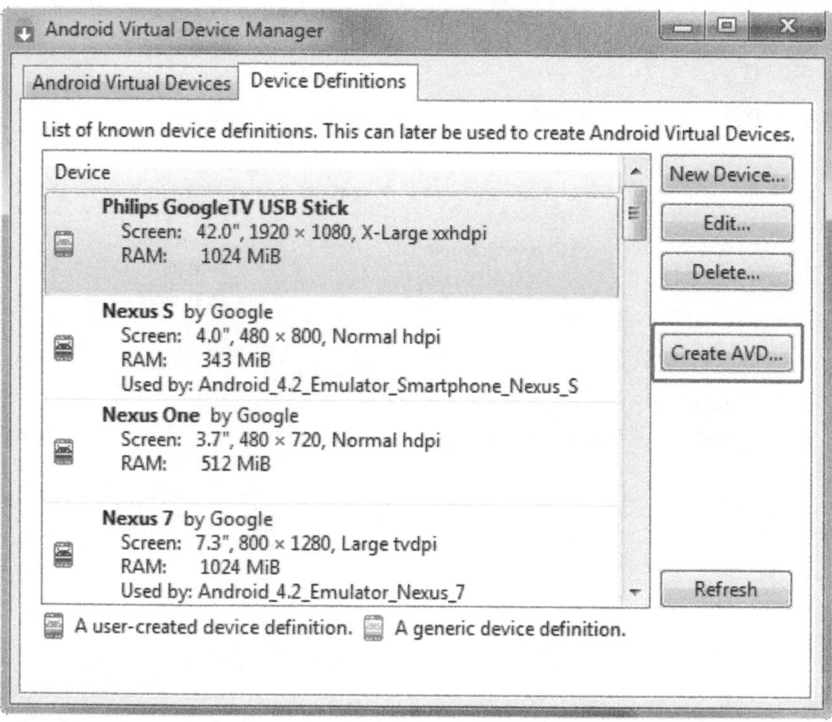

***Figure 1-22.** Philips GoogleTV USB Stick added to the AVD Manager Device Definitions list*

Now that we have the Philips GoogleTV USB stick product in the Device Definitions tab, we can select it as shown in Figure 1-22 and create a New Android Virtual Device Emulator using this product definition by clicking on the Create AVD... button in the middle of the dialog.

This opens up the **Create new Android Virtual Device (AVD)** dialog, shown in Figure 1-23, with the proper device settings in the relevant areas of the dialog, much like we observed when we created our AVD Emulators for the Google Nexus products shown in Figure 1-18.

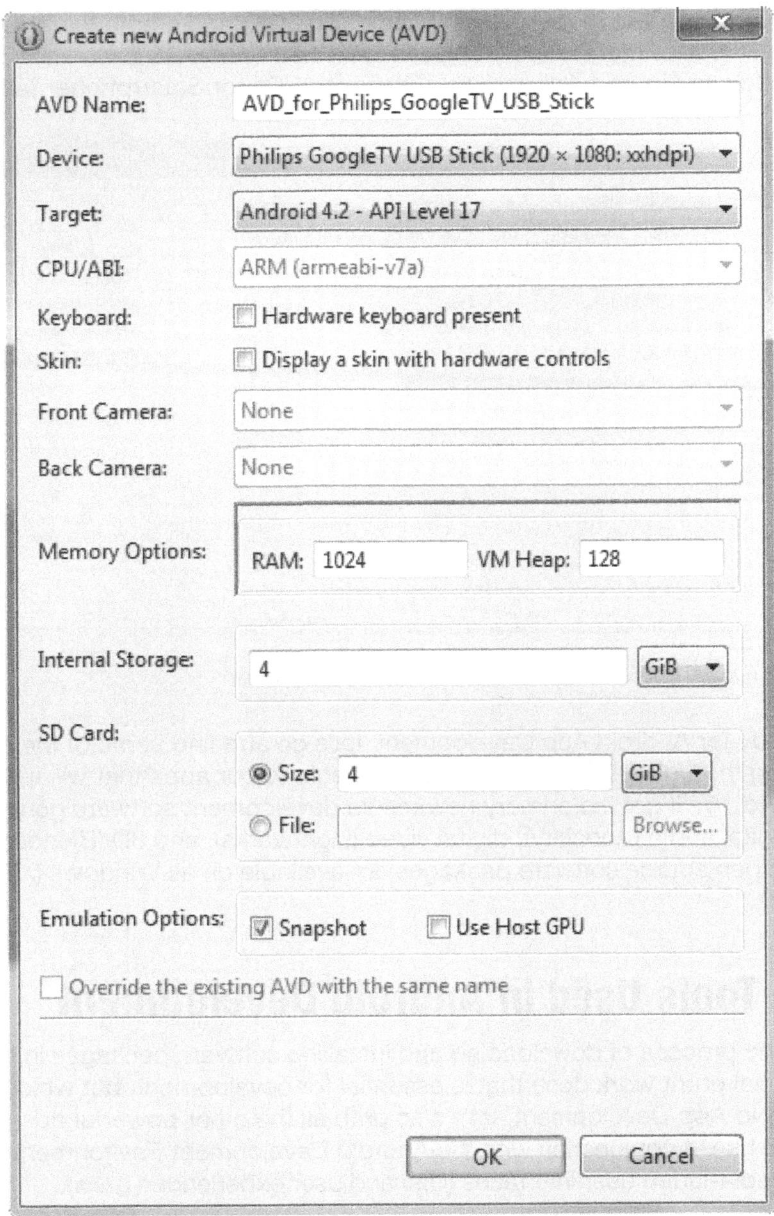

Figure 1-23. Creating a new Android Virtual Device for the Philips GoogleTV USB stick

Notice that ADT names the device for us as **AVD_for_Philips_GoogleTV_USB_Stick** and that it selects this product for us in the second **Device:** drop-down menu as well. The **Target:** default **Android 4.2 API Level 17** is also set for us automatically so all we have to do is fill out the **Internal Storage** and **SD Card** values, which are both **4GB**.

Select the Snapshot option and make sure the **Keyboard** and **Skin** options are unchecked, because the product has no keyboard or hardware control features. Notice that our Memory (RAM) setting is correct at **1024** megabytes (1GB), just as we set it earlier in the **Create New Device** dialog.

Once you are finished filling out all the relevant fields, click **OK**, and create the AVD for the Philips GoogleTV USB stick. Notice that Philips GoogleTV USB Stick AVD has been added to the AVD Manager main window in Figure 1-24, and we now have AVDs for Smartphone, Tablet, and iTV.

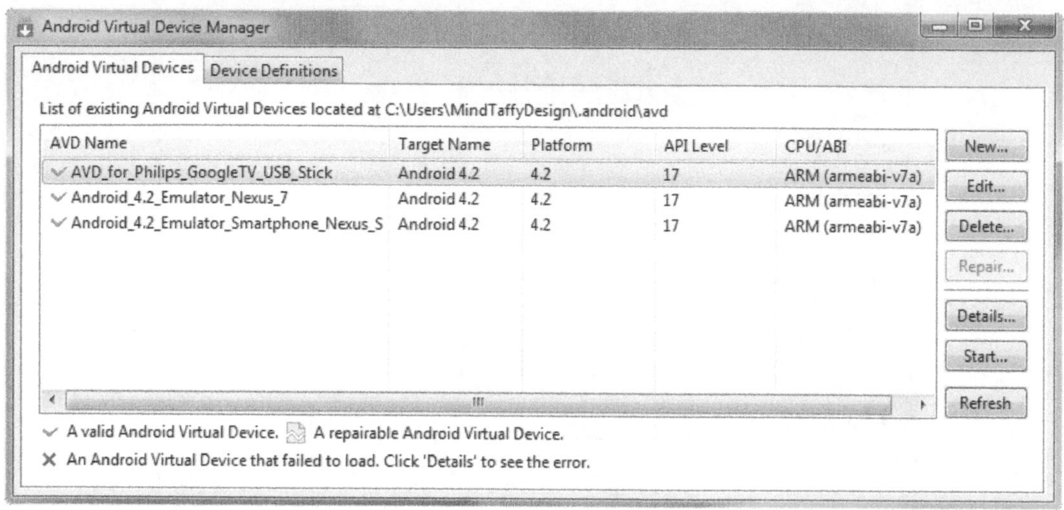

***Figure 1-24.** The Philips GoogleTV USB Stick is added as an Android Virtual Device*

Now that we're ready for Android App Development, let's go and find some of the new media tools that we will be using throughout this book to add elements to our apps that will make them stand apart from the crowd. We'll get the primary new media development software genres of digital imaging (GIMP), digital audio (Audacity), digital video (Lightworks), and 3D (Blender). All these professional-level open source software packages are available on all Windows (XP, Vista, 7 and 8) and Linux platforms.

New Media Tools Used in Android Development

Because we're in the process of downloading and installing software packages in this first chapter to get all the essential grunt work done that is essential for development, but which is not teaching us any actual Android App Development, let's also grab all the other powerful open source software that we will need to use in conjunction with the Android Development Environment to create truly memorable, rich media-laden user interfaces (UIs) and user experiences (UXs).

We'll get all this software download and installation stuff out of the way here in the first chapter and build ourselves a content development workstation that will serve us well for all types of new media content development.

Digital Imaging Software: GIMP 2.8.4

First, let's install the leading open source digital imaging software package GIMP 2.8.4 for Windows. If you have Photoshop CS6 that's great, but to make sure all the readers have a professional imaging app, you will need to download and install GIMP because it's free!

You can find GIMP **GIMP.org**. At the top right of the page, you will see a **Download** button as well as a **Downloads** link (see Figure 1-25), which when clicked takes you to the GIMP 2.8 Downloads page. Next click the download link for the GIMP program version that matches the OS that your system is currently running. For my Windows 7 workstation, I downloaded the .EXE installer for the Windows XP, Vista, Windows 7 and Windows 8 version of GIMP 2.8.4.

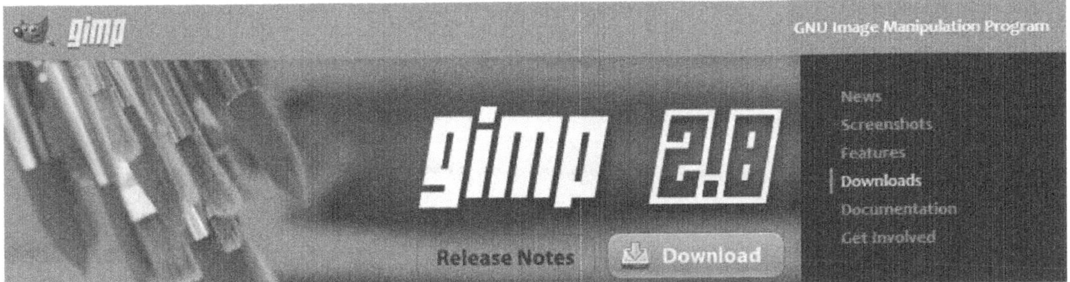

***Figure 1-25.** The GIMP 2.8 Download button and Downloads link located at the* `www.gimp.org` *website*

Find the .EXE installer file in your Downloads folder, and double-click it to install the software using the suggested defaults. Then, find the file in your Program Files folder, and right-click the Application EXE file, and **Pin to Taskbar** so it lives in the Launch Icons area of your Taskbar as shown previously in Figure 1-10. You are now one more step closer to creating an extremely powerful new media Android Application Development workstation. Let's get a leading digital audio editing software package next.

Digital Audio Software: Audacity 2.0.3

Next, let's install the leading open source digital audio software package, Audacity 2.0.3 for Windows. If you have Reason, SoundForge, or ProTools, that's great, but to make sure we all have a professional audio engineering app, you will need to download and install Audacity 2.0.3, because it's also free! You can find Audacity at the **SourceForge.net** open source website.

Type **Audacity** in the Search bar on the homepage, and you will find the **Audacity.SourceForge.Net** software download page, shown in Figure 1-26. On the top left of the page, you will see a **Download** button that takes you to the download for the software, in my case, the Windows OS version.

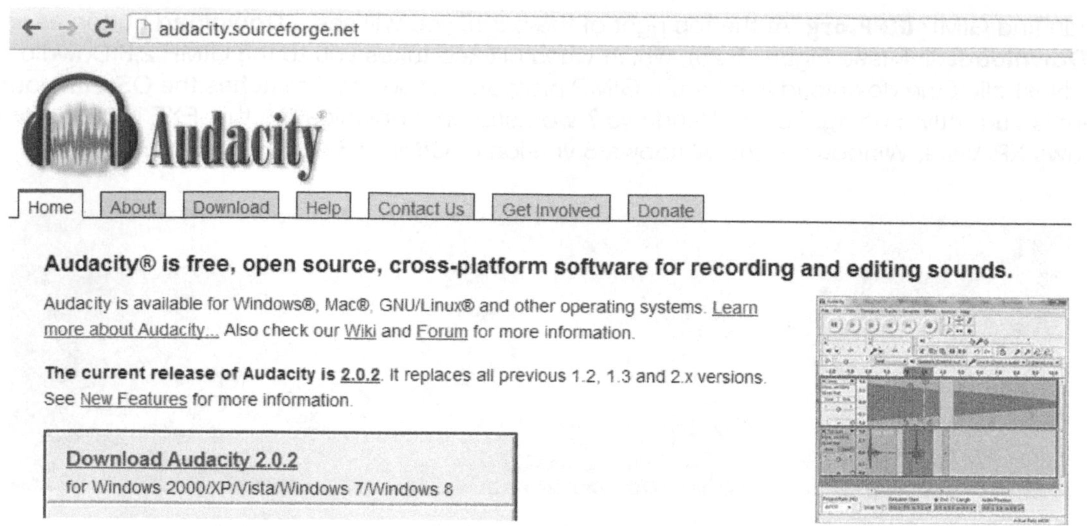

Figure 1-26. The Audacity 2.0.3 Project at SourceForge.Net–Click the Download link for Windows 2000/XP/Vista/Windows7/ Windows8

Next, click the download link for the program version that matches the OS of your system, in my case, I downloaded the .EXE installer for the Windows version. Find the .EXE installer file in your system's Downloads folder, and double-click it and install the software with its defaults.

Next, find the file in its **Program Files** folder, and right-click the Application EXE file and **Pin to Taskbar** so that it lives on your Launch Icons area of your Taskbar, as shown previously in Figure 1-10. You are now yet another step closer to creating that uber-powerful new media Android application development workstation right there on your desk.

Digital Video Software: EditShare Lightworks 11

Next, let's install the leading open source digital video editing software package, **EditShare Lightworks 11** for Windows. If you have FinalCut or AfterEffects CS6 that's great, but to make sure all of us have a professional video editing app, you should download and install Lightworks, because it's free! You will find Lightworks 11 at **www.LWKS.com**, and on the top right of the page, you will see a **Download** button that takes you to the Downloads page as shown in Figure 1-27.

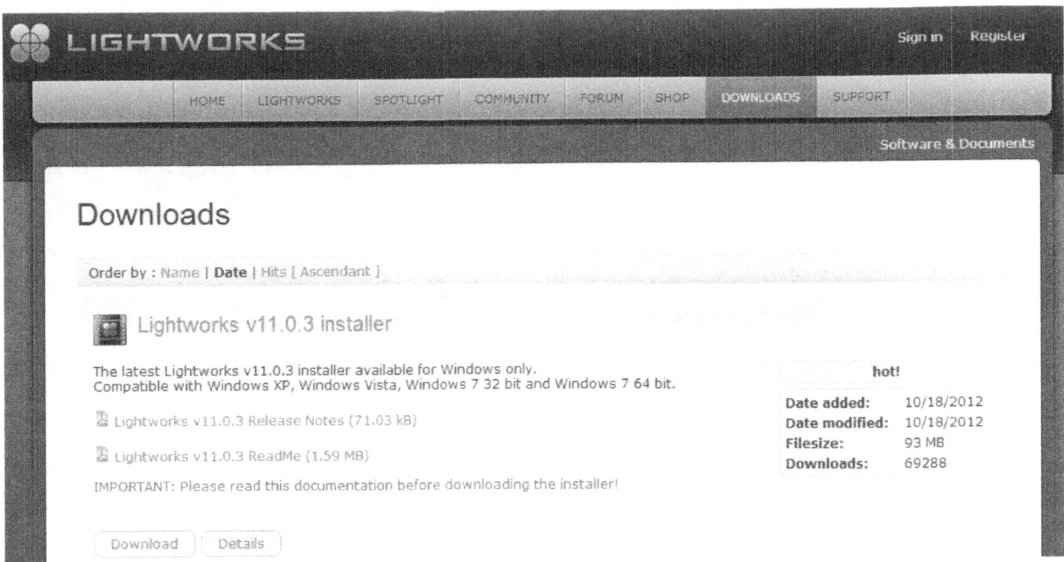

***Figure 1-27.** The EditShare Lightworks 11 Downloads page for Windows installer*

To download this free software you must sign-in or register and then you can click the Download link for the Lightworks program version that matches the OS and Bit-Level of your system.

In my case, I downloaded the .EXE installer for the Windows 7 64-bit version, which is around 100MB.Be sure to download the Release Notes and ReadMe files as well, and read them thoroughly as this is a high-end software package that used to cost thousands of dollars.

Once the download is complete, find the .EXE installer file in your system's Downloads folder, and then double-click it, and install the software using its default settings. If you are only installing one Lightworks "seat" (one copy, on one machine), set it as number 1 (enter 1 or 001 in the first dialog that appears during install). Note you may need to backspace over the default number in this first dialog and actually type a **1** to get the next step button to come alive (to become not dimmed out and click-able).

Then, find the file in its Program Files folder, and right-click the Application EXE file and **Pin to Taskbar** so it lives on your Launch Icons area of your Taskbar, as shown previously in Figure 1-10. You are now one more step closer to creating that powerful new media Android application development workstation that you always dreamt about.

3D Modeling and Animation Software: Blender 3D

Finally, let's install the leading open source 3D modeling, rendering, and animation software package, Blender 3D 2.66 for Windows. If you have Lightwave or Maya, that's great, but to make sure all of us have a professional 3D application you should download and install Blender 3D because you guessed it again—It's free!

You can find Blender 3D at **`www.Blender.org`**, and on the top left of the Blender home page, you will see a **Download** menu or, if you prefer, at the top right a **Download Blender** link that will take you to the Downloads page (see Figure 1-28).

***Figure 1-28.** The Blender 3D website located at `Blender.Org` showing the Download menu (top) and Download Blender link (right)*

First, click the Download Blender link and on the Downloads page look for the program version that matches the OS and Bit-Level of your system. In my case, I downloaded the .EXE installer for the Windows 64-bit version. Once the installer file has downloaded, find the Blender .EXE installer file in your Downloads folder, double-click it, and install the software with its defaults.

Next, proceed with the usual work process of finding the file in its Program Files folder and right-click the Application EXE file and **Pin to Taskbar** so it lives on your Launch Icons area of your Taskbar, as was shown previously in Figure 1-10.

You are now finished creating a comprehensive new media Android Application Development workstation to use throughout this book as well as for your future software development projects. This new media development workstation will allow you to develop highly professional Android applications that feature advanced 3D imagery, digital audio, digital video, and digital imagery. Congratulations! You have just installed open source software that, if you paid for it, would have cost you well over one hundred times what you just paid for this book. Not a bad return on investment!

Summary

In this first chapter, we got all our ducks in a row (or better yet, we got all our Jelly Beans in a row) to prepare for the Android App Development that we are going to do in the remaining chapters in this book.

We acquired and downloaded a gaggle of extremely valuable content production software, for everything from Java to Eclipse to Android, as well as all the leading new media applications for the primary four new media genres: 3D modeling, digital video editing, digital audio editing and digital image editing.

We learned how Eclipse runs on top of Java, and how the Android SDK is integrated into the Eclipse IDE via the ADT Tools plug-ins to create a seamless Android Development Environment. We saw that as of Android 4.2, the ADT Bundle installation is now far easier than it was in the past, and Appendix A confirms this and shows at a deeper level how Eclipse 4.2, Android 4.1 SDK, and all the ADT Plug-ins integrate together seamlessly.

In Chapter 2 we will get right down to business and create our first Hello World App, to see how Android sets up everything using Java and XML along with our new media resources. We'll learn about the terminology Android uses to describe the different areas and capabilities of an Android Application and even use one of these in the Hello World App that we build later on in the chapter.

Chapter 2

Exploring Android App Development: The Lingo of Android and Building Your First Hello World App!

Because this book is geared toward readers already familiar with computer programming principles and work processes, everyone is familiar with the universal concept of the **Hello World** programming example, which is used to show us all the basics regarding how any given programming language and platform gets its basic code structure up and functioning.

Because I want to fast-track our readers to an intermediate level as rapidly as possible within this book, I am going to get the Hello World app up and running here in the second part of the chapter. First, I will discuss the terminology used in Android application development. We'll then use the Hello World app example to show you how Android structures its programming environment and expose you to the basic Android Application Development work process.

We will take a look at how to create a new Android application project inside Eclipse, how that project is structured and organized in the Eclipse Package Explorer, how Android uses XML mark-up to define data structures, project parameters, OS permissions and user interfaces quickly and easily, so that we don't have to do this in Java, how our new media assets are named and stored in predefined logical resource folder hierarchies, and of course, how the Java programming language bootstraps and pulls it all together via Android Packages, Classes, Methods and Constants. Android Development is definitely unique.

First, however, we will need to spend a little time up-front learning about the various components of an Android Application. We will learn what the various Android components are termed inside of the

Android environment. Android uses some very unique terminology or lingo to describe the various Android application components, and we will learn this lingo as well as how these components all work seamlessly together.

Then, in the next part of this chapter, we can get down to work and build our very first Android application, using some of this new terminology and some XML mark-up and the Java programming language.

Android Application Development Lingo

Android uses very unique terminology to describe the various components or areas of its application development. In this section, I define what these areas are, and what they most closely equate to in other common programming languages such as C++ or Java. Plus, I'll give you a little more insight as to what open source technologies besides Java and XML drive Android under the hood, as well as how Android optimizes its Java into binaries for use on Embedded (Portable Consumer Electronics) Devices.

The Foundation of Android: The Linux 2.6 Kernel

The foundation of the Android OS is the **Linux 2.6 Kernel**; just like the Eclipse IDE runs on top of Java, Android runs on top of a full version of the latest Linux operating system. So yes, any and all Android devices are essentially fully functional Linux computers, which is why you see Android devices these days with dual-core, quad-core, and octa-core processors, just like "real" computers feature. The same thing goes for memory—most Android devices have at least one full gigabyte (1GB) of RAM (random access memory), and many feature 2GB, and soon you will see Android devices that have 3GB or 4GB of RAM.

The Android OS uses the core libraries of the Linux OS to do all the low-level things with files, memory, and processing that are done using any computer OS, and because Linux is so highly optimized, it can do this with less memory (more efficiently) than other OSes can. Why is the new Windows 8 OS so memory efficient all of a sudden? Because it has to compete with Linux (Android), that's why. It is rumored that Google has Android 4.2.2 running on top of the much more recent Linux 3.8 Kernel and that Android 5.0 will run on top of this more modern Linux Kernel later on in 2013.

Android Optimization: The Dalvik Virtual Machine (DVM)

An Android application developer uses the Android SDK and its Java programming language to access lower-level OS functions, as well as other higher-level functions that Android provides for using various new media assets, SQLite databases, and hardware features of the Android devices, such as cameras, gyroscopes, GPS, and the like.

When you compile your Java code and other assets (XML, audio, images, etc.) Android uses a DVM, or Dalvik Virtual Machine, technology to optimize these into a highly optimized binary format, much like an executable file, only even more optimized to run on smaller, more portable devices. If you look inside your Android APK file, you will see a .DEX file for your application in the root of your project. This is stands a Dalvik executable file.

DVM is not something an Android developer needs to be concerned with during day-to-day development, I am just mentioning it here so that if you happen to come across it on an Android-related Google search someday, you'll have the context to know what it is and what the DVM is doing in the overall development process. Next let's get into the lingo of Android and learn about each of the four major components of an Android application and what they are and how they work together to form a single cohesive Android app.

Android Activities: The Presentation Layer

Android uses the term **Activity** to describe the "front-end" screens of your application that your users view.

An Activity is a collection of design elements that, working together, compose each screen view of your application. These would include such things as user interface elements, text, background graphics, 3D, foreground content, digital video, pop-up menus, animated elements, and other visual design components that serve to provide an interface between what your application does (its Activities), and the end-user who is utilizing your application. We learn about Activities in detail in the first two parts of this book.

In Android terms, Activities generally consist of a **Layout Container**, which organizes and arranges a series of user interface elements called **Widgets**, along with your application's content, into predefined screen areas. If you want to include graphical elements, to make your designs more compelling, then you would use **Drawables**, which is Android's terminology for graphic elements such as images or animation.

Animation in Android uses both Widgets and Drawables; Drawables are used for frame-based animation (raster animation), and Widgets are used in procedural or tween-based animation (vector animation), as drawables can be as well. Amazingly, Android calls animation exactly what it is: animation. There is one other term in Android that is the same as it is in other programming languages: **Events**. Events allow the many elements that comprise our Activities to be processed using **Event Handling** code, just like in many other programming languages. Because readers of this book are familiar with programming, and because Event Handling is needed to make user interface designs in the first half of this book functional, I am going to cover Events early on in this book, so that we can create more robust applications sooner.

We will learn more about the Android **Activity** Class, and designing screen layouts via Android **Layouts**, which leverage the Android **ViewGroup** Class, in Chapter 4. We'll learn more about User Interface Design via Android Widgets, which leverage the Android **View** Class, in Chapter 5. Finally, we will learn more about **Events** in Chapter 6, and **Drawables** in Chapters 7 through 10, when we cover advanced User Interface Design and Graphics Design using Digital Images, Digital Video and Animation within Android.

Android Services: The Processing Layer

Whereas Activities represent the front-end or foreground of your Android application, Android **Services** represent the back-end, or background processing, the heavy lifting if you will.

The Android **Service** Class is used to create Java classes that do repetitive processing tasks, usually via programming constructs called loops or via data-fetching processes, such as streaming, in the background, while your user is simultaneously uses your application via its the front-end user interface activities. A good example of this would be a user playing an MP3 audio file while using your app.

There are many uses for Service classes in Android, obvious and common uses would be playing audio MP3 and digital video MP4 files for entertainment, streaming new media files from a remote server, converting text to speech (speech synthesis), calculating game logic while playing the game, processing Android Live Wallpapers or Android Daydreams, using Bluetooth or NFC to transfer large new media files between end-users in real-time, running a spelling checking process, any overly complex mathematical calculations, 3D rendering, and anything else that requires so much processor overhead (power) that it makes the Activity user interface or content become stilted and unprofessional.

Fortunately for Android Developers, most modern-day Android devices, such as smartphones, tablets, e-readers, and iTV sets, come with a minimum hardware configuration of a dual-core (two central processing units, or CPUs) processor, and many more are now becoming available with quad-core (four CPU) processors, and now octa-core (eight CPU) processor Android devices are appearing on the market. This means that there is plenty of processing power for your Android Service classes to leverage!

One of the more powerful options in the Android Service class is to have your background processing Service placed into its own **thread** (I like to call it spawning, but it is known in programming terminology as a **process**), which, with so many CPUs present in an Android device, could actually translate into your Service classes being allocated their own CPU cores.

Android also features a number of specialized Service classes that are already sub-classed (we will learn about this Java terminology in Chapter 3) from the primary Android Service class. For example, there are SpellCheckerService, WallpaperService, TextToSpeechService, DreamService, IntentService, AccessibilityService, VpnService, and AbstractInputMethodService classes also available for use by Android Developers. We will be learning all about Services in Chapter 17 of this book.

Android Broadcast Receivers: The Communications Layer

Android communicates inside its application infrastructure via **Broadcast Receivers**.

These are usually used for inter-application communication, as well as to provide alerts for your users, many times from the Android OS or Android device itself. For instance, if the phone is ringing, or if the tablet is about to run out of battery power, the Android OS sends out a Broadcast Receiver that your application programming logic can respond to with some sort of custom action. Other common messages relate to the camera being used to take a picture, a time-zone change, a data download completion, a language preference change, a video cache is complete and ready for playback, and so forth.

Similar to Android Services, Broadcast Receivers run in the background, and you can configure your app code to “trap” any type of Broadcast Receiver that you feel is necessary for your application and its end-users to be concerned with. Once your code detects a Broadcast Receiver that it needs to respond to, it can invoke the appropriate user interface element in the appropriate Activity, and alert the end-user to the change in the OS or device status. We will be taking a close look at Broadcast Receivers in Chapter 18.

Android Content Providers: The Data Storage Layer

Android has a unique term for a common concept: Data Storage. Whether it is stored in memory, in files on an SD Card, or in a SQLite database, stored data in Android is accessed via a **Content Provider**.

The primary (and best) way to store and share data across Android applications to use the open source **SQL** technology, which is a part of the Android OS. This is the **SQLite** database management tool package. Android has an entire package dedicated to the SQLite database management paradigm, called **android.database.sqlite,** which contains everything you will need to create and access SQLite databases.

Android Content Provider SQLite databases are used for Android device user-defined data storage by the Android OS across the board. We will be learning more about some of the more important databases to an Android device user, such as the **Contacts** databases and the **Calendar** databases, later on in this book. There are also new media related databases that keep track of a user's images, audio files, and video assets and playlists.

We'll learn more about Android Content Providers and learn about creating, populating, modifying, and deleting Android SQLite databases, in Chapter 19.

Android Intents: Inter-Application Communications

An Android application communicates between its primary components via an **Intent**.

For example, you can use Intents to communicate between your Activities and Services, and you can do everything from launching new tasks or activities, to sending out new task instructions to existing ones.

The Intent object holds information regarding which application component needs to perform the required task. This includes what actions need to be taken to complete that task, a definition of the data that the task uses to perform that action, and, optionally, that data's MIME type and any flags (settings) and other optional data or information that may be needed to completely convey what exactly needs to be accomplished via the Intent object that is being sent from one Android app module to another. Yes, Intents are one of the more complicated areas of the Android OS, as far as their implementation goes.

Each type of of Android component, Activities, Services, or Broadcast Receivers, has its own type of Intent object. This assures that Intents do not get mixed up and keeps everything well organized. So to start up a Service via an Intent, you pass over a Context.startService(); Java method call with your Intent. For an Activity, use a Context.startActivity(); Java method call, and for a Broadcast Receiver use a Context.sendBroadcast(); Java method call. We will learn all about this in Chapter 3 (Java) and Chapter 16 (Intents).

Android Manifest: Application Permissions Definition

Finally, Android utilizes the term **Manifest** to describe the XML file that "bootstraps," or defines and launches, any given Android application. Android uses XML to define many things, and like the index.html file used to launch websites, Android apps launch via their project APK's AndroidManifest.xml file.

In the root level of any Android application **.APK** (Android PacKage) file, you will find a file named: **AndroidManifest.xml** that contains XML mark-up tags that define everything that the Android OS needs to know about your application. This includes, but is not limited to, what Android OS versions the app supports, what Activities, Broadcast Receivers, and Services the app contains, what permissions the app needs to access secure databases and Internet resources, and Intent Filters that need to be established.

We'll discuss Android Manifest in the chapters where we need to define special Activities, Services, Broadcast Receivers, or assign permissions to application components. This will turn out to be quite a few, by the time we hit the end of this book.

Creating Your First Android Application

Let's not waste any more time, as we have a lot to cover in this chapter, so let's get right down to it and fire up Eclipse via the Quick Launch Icon that you set up in Chapter 1. We will create a Hello World application framework in this section that we will use to build a world generation toolkit that you can use as a jumping off point for creating your own interplanetary games.

Accept the default path to the workspace folder that Eclipse set up for you in your Users folder, and launch the IDE onto your screen. Go into the **File** menu, and find the **New** sub-menu at the top, and then select the **Android Application Project** sub-menu.

Alternatively, you can also use the **File ➤ New ➤ Project...** menu sequence, which is how it used to be accessed prior to Android 4.2. This opens a **New Project** dialog, which lists the different types of projects that you can create inside of Eclipse. Find the **Android** project type, and click the triangle UI element to the left to open up the sub-menu of Android application types, and then select the **Android Application Project** and finally click on the **Next ➤** button at the bottom of the dialog.

Either of these work processes will open the **New Android Application** dialog, where we can set all the top-level attributes of our Hello World Android application, as shown in Figure 2-1.

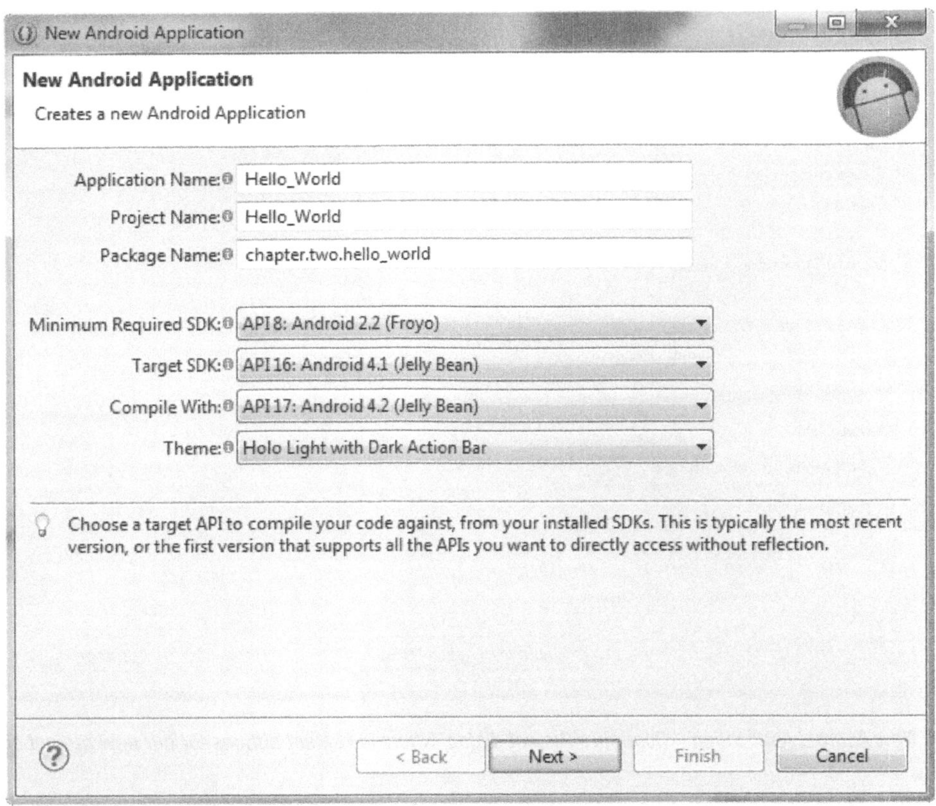

Figure 2-1. Naming our Application, Project, and Package in the New Android Application dialog in Eclipse

First enter the **Application Name**, Hello_World, into the first field in the dialog. Notice that as you type in Hello_World that the second field, **Project Name**, is also being filled out via a dual-typing feature. This means that Android wants our App Name and Project Name to be the same, and because of this, I am going to use an underscore instead of a space in our Hello World app name, as this is a fairly common programming practice, and because I don't like to use spaces in my file names or folder names.

The third field allows us to create our package name for our new Android application project, and to use a consistent package naming convention for this book, let's use: **chapter.two.hello_world** as our package name, which should use all lowercase letters and underscores. Next, we need to select our **Minimum Required API** Level of support for our Android application, which we will set to nine versions of backward compatibility via the **Android 2.2 API Level 8** setting, because there are still lots of Android 2.2 and 2.3.7 devices on the market that we need to provide support for. We also need to set our **Target SDK** Level, which is the target Android API Level for which we are developing, in this case it's the **Android 4.1 API Level 16,** as that is the emulator that we installed back in Chapter 1. We'll compile with the current Android 4.2 API Level 17 that we just installed in Chapter 1 because that's the latest (and most bug-free) software that we have, and you always want to compile with the latest development software code. Now click the **Next ➤** button and proceed to the next dialog as shown in Figure 2-2.

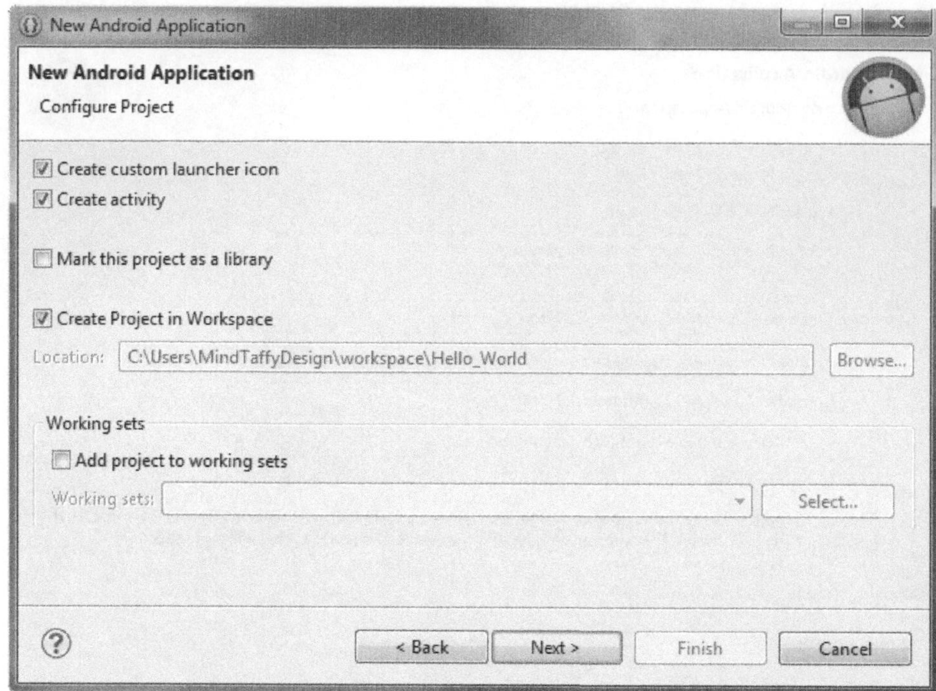

***Figure 2-2.** The New Android Application – Configure Project dialog, where we select options for our new project creation*

In the **Configure Project** dialog, check the **Create custom launcher icon** checkbox and the **Create Activity** checkbox at the top of the dialog, as well as the **Create project in Workspace** checkbox in the bottom of the dialog, and then click **Next ➤** to proceed to the **Configure Launcher Icon** dialog, as shown in Figure 2-3.

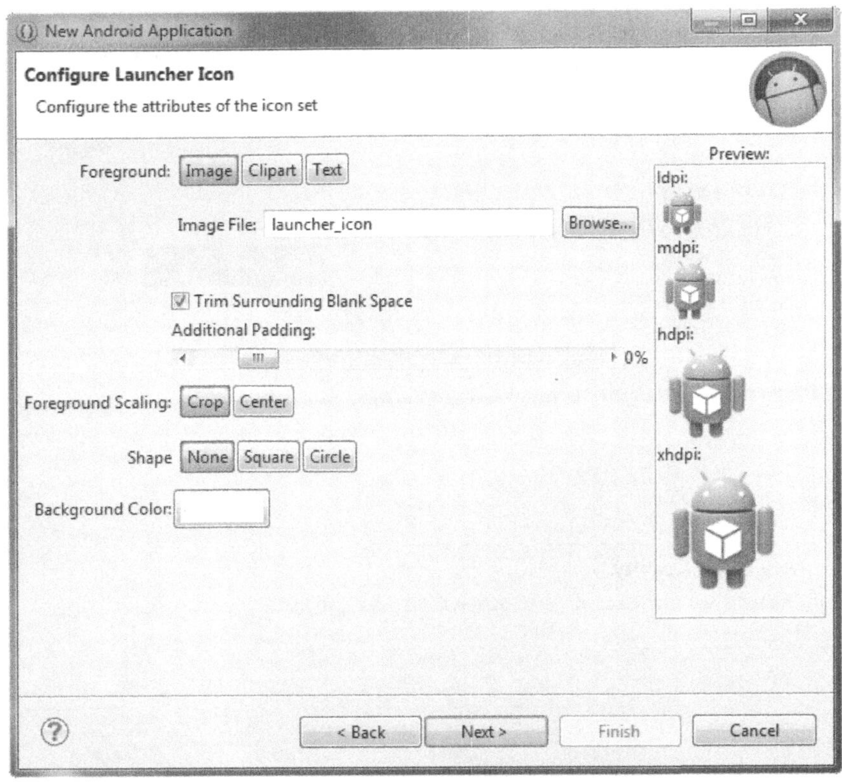

Figure 2-3. The Configure Launcher Icon dialog where we can select a predefined Android Application Launch Icon

This dialog allows you to select a predefined Android App launch icon from an image, clipart, or text asset, many of which have already been provided for you. Let's select the default for now (as we are doing in all these dialogs) just to see what the default New Android Application Project creation process does so we have a minimum baseline understanding to build from. After you have chosen your application Launcher Icon (which Android names ic_launcher.png, as we'll see later on in this chapter), click **Next ➤** to proceed to the **Create Activity** dialog, where we will create a **BlankActivity** for our application. We are selecting a **BlankActivity** so that we can see the minimum code that Android will generate via the New Android Application Project series of dialogs. The dialog is shown in Figure 2-4.

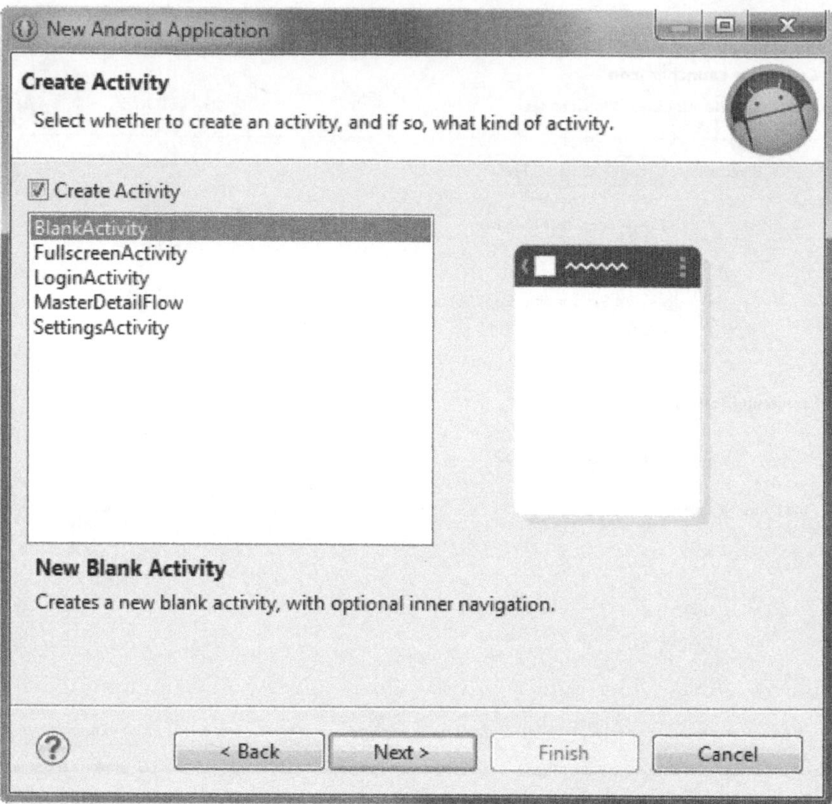

Figure 2-4. The Create Activity dialog in the New Android Application Project series of dialogs

You are probably wondering what an Activity is in Android, and what exactly its function is. An **Activity** is a screen area that holds content and user interface (UI) designs that provide a front-end (display area) for your application to interface visually with your end-users. As you will see in this chapter, the main activity is defined via XML mark-up and then inflated via Java code in your application onCreate() method in your Main Activity class. The Activity contains Layout Containers that are specified by the Android **ViewGroup** Class (logical as Layouts are groups of Views) that contain Android **View** Class Widgets that are UI elements and content containers.

Click the **Next ➤** button and proceed to the **New Blank Activity** dialog shown in Figure 2-5 where we will set the parameters for our Android application's Activity, much like we did in the first New Android Application dialog. Let's accept the default (suggested) names, just to become familiar with what Android would like us to call the various main components of our application, and name our Activity **MainActivity** and name our Layout XML file **activity_main** with a navigation type of **None**—again, this is so we can see the minimum bootstrap code that will be provided for us by the New Android Application Project series of dialogs. Now click **Finish** and let ADT proceed with the new project creation process.

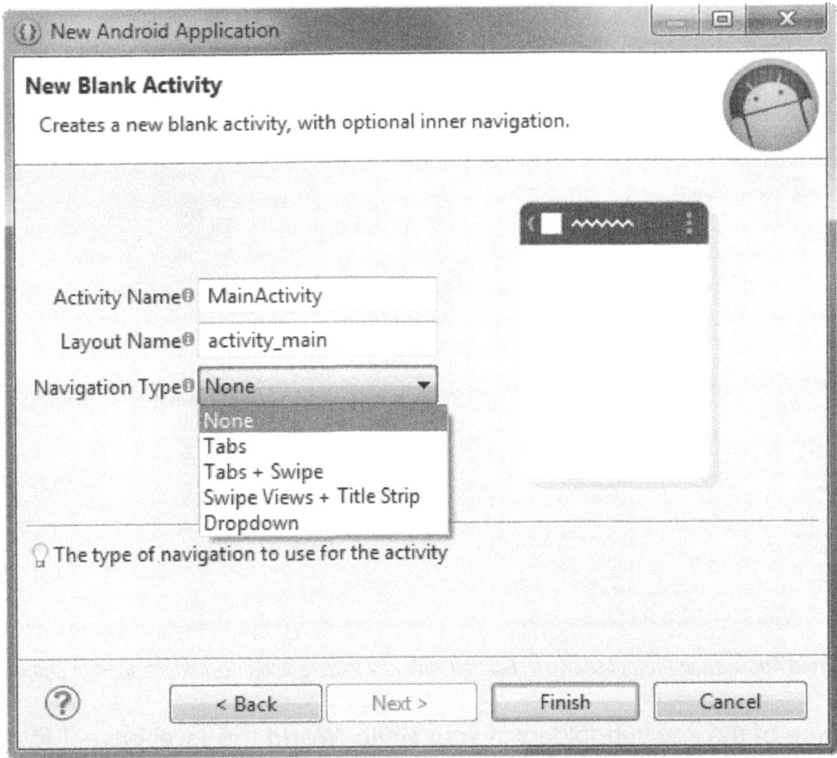

Figure 2-5. The New Blank Activity dialog, where we name our Activity and select its Navigation Type

Once you click the final Next button in the last dialog, Android Development Tools (ADT) will check your current installation (SDK and Plug-Ins set-up) to make sure that you have everything that you need to create the Android Application Project that you just specified. For instance, if you specified Android 2.2 through 4.1 support, but only installed API Level 10 (2.3.7) through API Level 16 (4.1.2), then an **Install Dependencies** dialog will appear asking you to install API Level 8 (2.2). Once you click the Install/Upgrade button these additional APIs will be pulled over from the Google repositories and installed on your system to be used in your Eclipse Android Development configuration. Now we're ready to develop our new Hello World application inside of the Eclipse IDE, which will appear, populated with the new Android application project, once the Install Dependencies download is complete (if needed) and its install process has been completed. Next let's take a look at the virgin Android Project that ADT has so kindly created for us!

Anatomy of an Android Application Project

Let's take a look at what the ADT New Android Application Project helper has created for us in our Eclipse IDE, starting with the Package Explorer project navigation pane on the left side of the IDE. The Package Explorer Utility allows us to navigate through the project assets hierarchy for our Android application at any time during its development, much like the Windows Explorer Utility allows us to navigate our hard disk drive and OS. Figure 2-6 shows what Eclipse will look like after the new project pops up on the screen in the IDE.

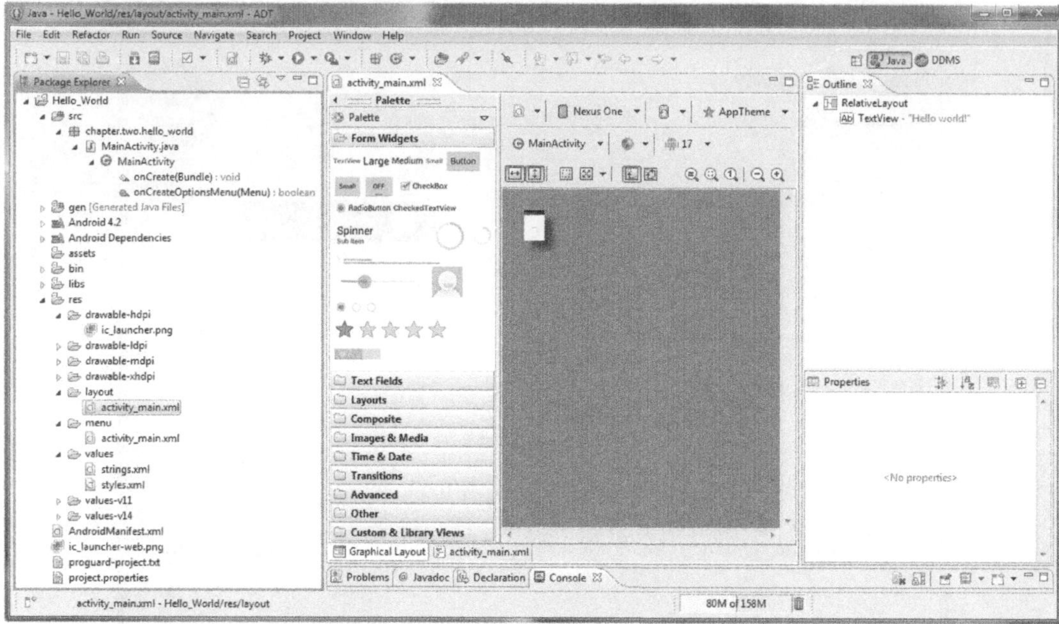

Figure 2-6. New Android Application Project shown in Eclipse with key folders and sub-folders open to show project assets

Let's open up some of the key sub-folders in your **Hello_World** top-level project folder by clicking on the little triangle UI elements next to each folder that point to the right. For now, let's focus on the folders named **src** (source code) and **res** (resources), as those are the most important folders in any Android Project. Open up the **src** folder, which contains one sub-folder named **chapter.two.hello_world** that you might remember we specified in the New Android Application dialog as our package name.

Dig a little bit deeper and look under the **chapter.two.hello_world** folder, where you will find our **MainActivity.java** file, which contains the Java code that the New Android Application creation process has written for us, and which "bootstraps" or launches our Activity (main screen) user interface layout and menu code, which happens to be defined via XML files in the **layout** and **menu** folders. We'll open this Java file in a later section of this chapter and take a look at that Java code and what it does exactly. All your Java code files will be kept in this package-name folder for any Android application that you develop.

Also notice in Figure 2-6 that I clicked the right-facing arrow triangle next to the **MainActivity.java** file, and that the Package Explorer also shows the Java Methods that are within this Java code, so it seems that the Eclipse Package Explorer not only navigates files, but also code structures as well. This is a pretty vanguard feature for an IDE.

The other primary application assets folder that we need to take a closer look at is the resources or **res** folder, which, as you may have guessed, is where all the XML and new media resources that Android applications will inevitably draw on to create its User Experience (UX) are kept in immaculate order. Click the triangle UI icon next to the **res** folder, as shown in Figure 2-6, and open it up, so you can see its many sub-folders that were created for us by the New Android Application Project helper.

The first four folders you see at the top all start with the word **drawable** which, as you might surmise correctly, is an Android application asset that can be drawn to the screen via the Activity that we learned about earlier. A drawable can be an image, a shape, a frame animation, an image transition, an icon, or any similar graphics-related content or user interface elements needed for your application. Also notice that there are four drawable folders—one for each level of screen density: low, medium, high, extra high. It is important to note that as of Android 4.2.2 there is also an Extra, Extra High (XXHDPI) classification.

Click the triangle UI element next to any one (or all four, if you like) of the drawable folders, and you will see the **ic_launcher.png** Launcher Icon, which we created in the third **Configure Launcher Icon** dialog of the New Android Application Project series of dialogs. Note that just having your application icon named correctly (ic_launcher.png) and placed in the correct drawable folder is all that you have to do to have an icon appear for your application. That's right: zero coding. We'll get into how to optimize icons and graphics for these different drawable folders later on in Part 2 of this book.

These four drawable folders allow Android Developers (such as yourself) to provide custom pixel-perfect graphic elements across all genres of Android devices, from smartphones to tablets to e-readers to iTV sets. Low Density Pixel Imagery (LDPI) is optimized for the smallest of Android screens, such as 120 DPI (which also stands for **Dots Per Inch**) flip-phones or MP3 players, which usually have small 320 by 240 pixel screens. Medium Density Pixel Imagery (MDPI) is for entry-level smartphones (480 by 320 and 640 by 480 resolution) that use a 160 DPI pixel screen density.

High Density Pixel Imagery (HDPI) fits mainstream smartphones and the 5" to 7" mini-tablets (800 by 480, 854 by 480, and 960 by 540 resolution) that use 240 DPI pixel density screens. eXtra High Density Pixel Imagery (XHDPI) uses 320 DPI pixel density screens, and fits HD smartphones and larger 8" to 11" tablets (1024 by 600, 1280 by 720, and 1280 by 800 resolutions). Interactive Television Density Pixel Imagery (TVDPI) also uses 320 DPI (at 1920 by 1080 and 1920 by 1200 resolutions) and fits the new GoogleTV iTV sets. We'll cover this topic in far more detail in Part 2 of this book, which covers graphics design and animation for Activity User Interface and Content Development.

The next folder down is the **layout** folder; click the triangle UI element to open it, and you will see that it currently contains the Layout XML file for our Activity, named **activity_main.xml** as we previously specified in the fifth dialog in our New Android Application Project series of dialogs. This file contains all the XML mark-up tags that define our Activity Screen Layout and its User Interface elements. We'll open this in the Eclipse IDE in the next section of this chapter and eventually customize the XML tags to create an even cooler Hello World user experience.

Each of the Activities (user interface screens) that you define for your application will have its own XML file in this **layout** folder, each containing unique tags that define what each application screen will look like. So, if your app has a Log-In screen, for instance, there would also be an activity_login.xml file in this folder, which would contain completely different XML mark-up (tags) than the activity_main.xml file does.

The next folder down is the **menu** folder, which holds XML files that define your Android application menu structure for each Activity user interface screen. Click the triangle UI element next to the **menu** folder to open it, and you will see that it currently contains the Menu XML file for our Activity, which Android has named **activity_main.xml** as previously specified in the fifth dialog in our New Android Application Project series of dialogs.

The reason that the Layout and Menu XML files have the same name is because normally you will have both UI elements and menus for each of your application (activity) screens, so the most logical way to group them is by their file names. Because these files are in different folders, they are kept separate, and therefore can have the same file name, which Android will look for by using the first part of the file name, as well as by the folder it is in. We'll open up both these files in the Eclipse IDE a little later on in the chapter, and later we will even customize their XML tags to create a more advanced Hello World Layout and Menu system, so that you can better experience how exactly Activities work inside of Android.

The last three sub-folders in the resource folder are the **values** folders, which hold our constants or "hard-coded" values for our application, such as strings, themes, dimensions, colors, and the like, so that they can all be later accessed (and changed with the greatest of ease) in one centralized location within your project hierarchy. Android wants all values externalized into these folders, as we will see with the strings.xml file in the next section. As you will see throughout the book, if you do not use values properly Eclipse flags your code with triangular yellow warning icons in the IDE. Android OS is kind of strict!

Next let's take a closer look at how Android leverages XML mark-up to allow team members, primarily non-programmers in design roles, to contribute to the application development process. XML is used for many things in Android development, such as User Interface Design, Application Configuration in the AndroidManifest.xml file, and much more.

Android Application Project: XML Mark-Up

Your application's Java code in **MainActivity.java** references the activity_main.xml files that we have seen in both the layout and menu folders, and in fact when Eclipse opens up after the New Android Application Project creation process, it automatically opens up the Activity Layout XML file **activity_main.xml** from the **layout** folder in its central main editing area. This can be seen in Figure 2-6, which shows what Eclipse looks like when it first opens up your new application project. Notice in the central area that the activity_main.xml is open (note name in top tab) in the **Graphical Layout** editor (note name in bottom tab).

Creating User Interface Screen Layouts in Android Using XML

Let's click the **activity_main.xml** tab at the **bottom** of the Eclipse central editing pane, as shown in Figure 2-7, and see exactly how this XML mark-up works inside your Android Application. Here's the XML mark-up to define a Relative Layout Container and place some Hello world! text inside it:

```
<RelativeLayout xmlns:android="http://schemas.android.com/apk/res/android"
    xmlns:tools="http://schemas.android.com/tools"
    android:layout_width="match_parent"
    android:layout_height="match_parent"
    tools:context=".MainActivity" >

    <TextView
        android:layout_width="wrap_content"
        android:layout_height="wrap_content"
        android:layout_centerHorizontal="true"
        android:layout_centerVertical="true"
        android:text="@string/hello_world" />

</RelativeLayout>
```

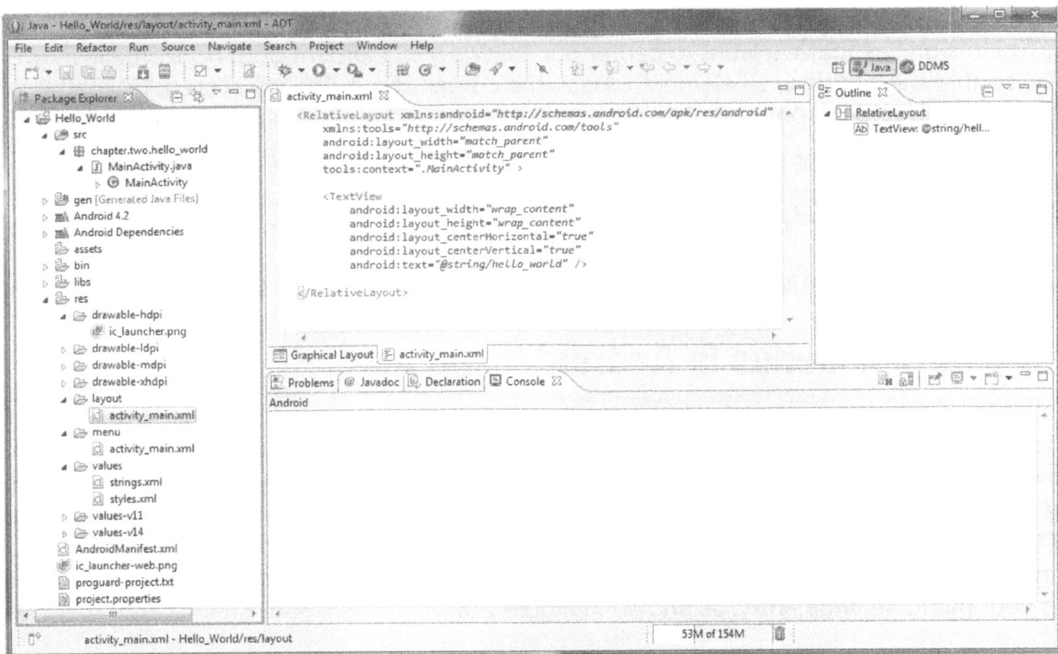

***Figure 2-7.** Using the XML Editing tab at the bottom right of the main editing area to view the activity_main Layout XML*

The first XML **tag** shown in the **<RelativeLayout>** tag, which provides a Layout Container that will hold our user interface elements, in this case text, and eventually, imagery and buttons, for example. Inside of the RelativeLayout tag you will find several parameters, each of which follow the following format:

```
platform:feature="setting value"
```

For instance, the first parameter is **xmlns:android** and referenced the XML platform (XMLNS means eXtended Mark-up Language Naming Schema) and defines a location on the Internet where the XML tags for use with Android that are used in this XML document are publicly defined and referenced in one central location. The second parameter **xmlns:tools** is also from the XML platform, and defines where on the Internet the XML tools used in this XML document are defined publicly. The **tools:context** tag tells where these tools will be utilized, in this case in our MainActivity Java class, referenced via **.MainActivity** setting value held in quotes within that parameter.

The other parameters in the Layout XML file are all from the Android platform and define parameters that pertain to the Android OS, for instance, android:layout_width and android:layout_height are both set to the **match_parent** value, which tells the Relative Layout container to expand to fill the entire display screen.

Now let's look at the parameters in the **<TextView>** tag that sets our Text within our Relative Layout container. We again see the **android:layout_width** and **android:layout_height** parameters, but this time they reference the **wrap_content** setting, which essentially does the exact opposite of what the match_parent setting does. Instead of expanding the tag to fill its container, **wrap_content** "shrink-wraps" the container, or in this case user interface element, around its content! Let's look at the layout centering parameters and the string.xml file values that the android:text parameter references next.

The **android:layout_centerHorizontal** and **android:layout_centerVertical** parameters are both set to **true,** which signifies that we want to center our TextView UI element both horizontally as well as vertically, so that the TextView UI element lives in the center of our Activity screen, no matter what the screen density, orientation, or resolution is that the user's device might be using at the time.

The final and most important parameter for the TextView UI element is the actual text content that that UI element is to contain, and this is accessed via the **android:text** parameter. The setting value contained in quotes is set to **@string/hello_world** which is Android OS specific symbolic notation for:

```
C:\Users\Username\workspace\Hello_World\res\values\strings.xml <string> tag named: hello_world
```

Creating Option Menus in Android Using XML

We'll be looking at the **strings.xml** file in our **values** folder later on in this chapter to see how this text value is set as well. First, let's take a look at the other **activity_main.xml** file that is contained in the **menu** folder, and analyze the Menu XML code that ADT has written for us. Right-click the **activity_main.xml** file inside the **menu** folder in your Package Explorer (shown in Figure 2-6), and select **Open** or simply select the file and use the **F3** key on your keyboard to open it. A second tab opens in the central editing area of Eclipse labeled **activity_main.xml** and you will see XML mark-up defining your menu settings entry, as shown in Figure 2-8.

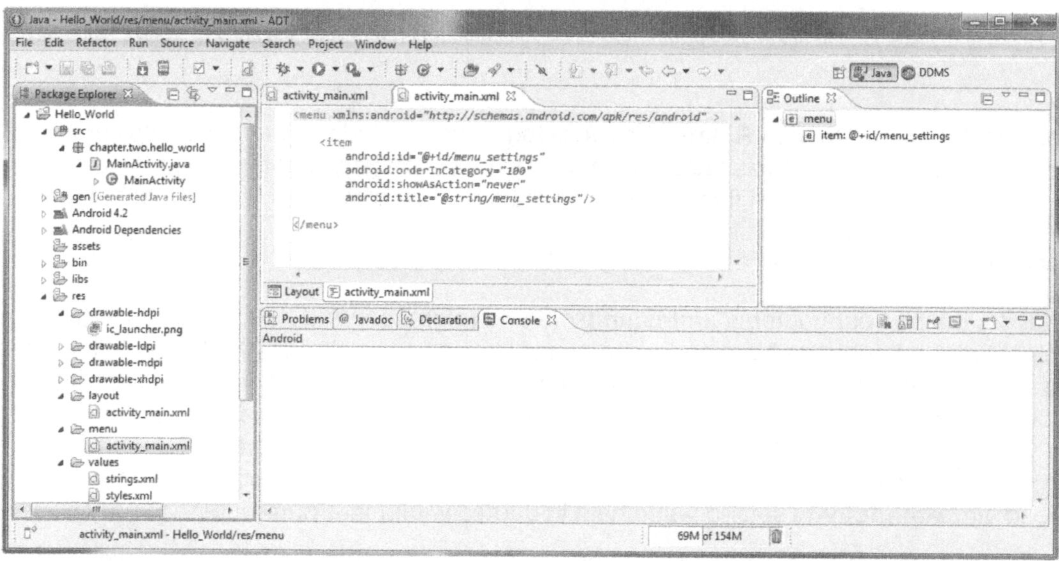

Figure 2-8. The Menu XML file shown in the second (menu) activity_main.xml tab in the Eclipse central code editing area

Menu XML files in Android also use mark-up structures called **Tags** to define menu items via the **<menu>** tag container and inside of it the **<item>** tags for each menu item. In this case there is only one menu item called **Settings** however, later on we'll add some more menu items and make them active, so that you have a complete understanding of how to implement menu items in your apps.

It is important to note that when you run your app the menu pops up when you use the Menu key (button) in your Android Emulator, even though the menu item when clicked does not do anything yet. This allows you to define your Activity menu user interface and test it before you write the code to implement what it actually does. So let's look at the Menu XML code that Android created for us now line by line:

```
<menu xmlns:android="http://schemas.android.com/apk/res/android" >

    <item
        android:id="@+id/menu_settings"
        android:orderInCategory="100"
        android:showAsAction="never"
        android:title="@string/menu_settings"/>

</menu>
```

As you can see, the opening tag in any XML file, in this case the "parent" **<menu>** tag, contains a HTTP reference to the Android XML Naming Schema, just like the **<RelativeLayout>** tag did in the **layout** folder version of the **activity_main.xml** file that we looked at earlier. Inside the <menu> tag we "nest" <item> tags that define each menu item, and each <item> tag in turn has its own parameters that define what each menu item is named, what it says on the menu, what order it appears in, and whether it shows as an Action Icon in Android 3.x, 4.x, or 5.x operating systems. Let's go over each parameter.

The first **android:id** parameter names this menu item **menu_settings** so that we can reference it in our Java code. The second **android:orderInCategory** parameter sets the order that the menu item will be in a menu that has more than one menu item, as most menus do. As we add menu items later on, we will set this parameter to 200 (and so on) to determine the importance of each menu item function that we add.

The third **android:showAsAction** parameter determines whether your menu shows on the Action Icon Bar on Android OS version 3.x and 4.x (and soon 5.x) devices. In this case, we are using the **none** setting, because we want backward-compatibility to Android 1.6 and 2.x devices such as the Amazon Kindle Fire (2.3.7). A **none** setting pops-up the menu at the bottom of the screen as you will see when you run the Hello_World app in the 4.2 Emulator later. If you are developing apps solely for Android 3.x and later, you can use the **ifRoom** parameter as a setting instead, and your menu items will appear in the Android Action Bar, if there is room for them, that is.

The final **android:title** parameter is the title, or label, for the menu item within the pop-up menu itself. Because this menu title is a string constant, it is set in the **values** folder in the **strings.xml** file. In fact let's look at that now by right-clicking the **strings.xml** file in the **values** folder and selecting the **Open** command!

Setting Constant Values for Your Android Application Using XML

The **strings.xml file** opens in its own editing tab in the central area of Eclipse as shown in Figure 2-9, if you want to see the strings edited visually, click the bottom **Resources** tab on the left or use the XML view tab on the right, labeled with the **strings.xml** filename.

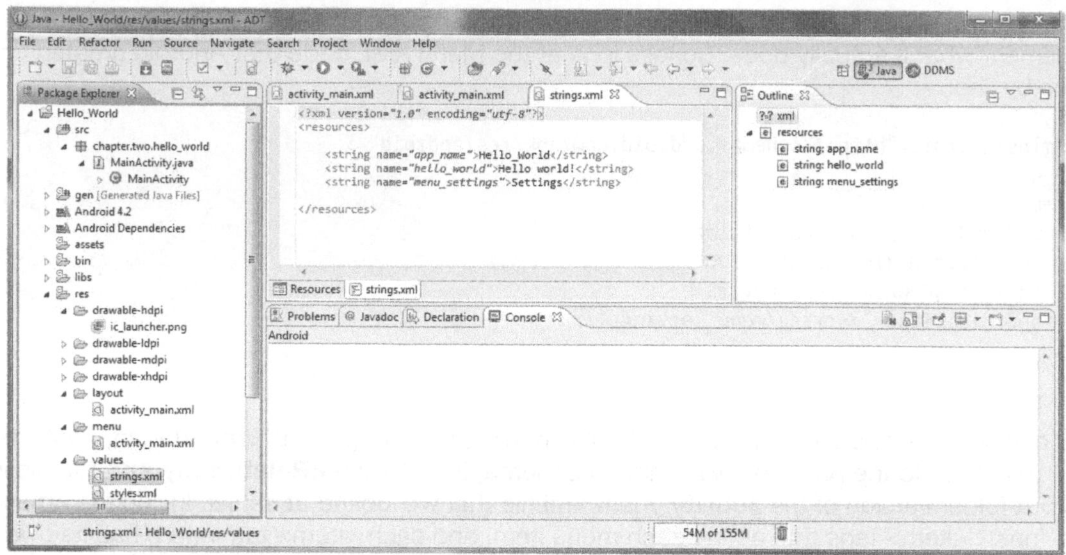

***Figure 2-9.** The strings.xml file (located in the values folder) shown in the Eclipse central editing pane in XML coding mode*

Because we're learning XML code in this section of the chapter, I chose to show the XML mark-up view pane in the Eclipse ADT Editor shown in Figure 2-9.

Let's look at that XML mark-up code now, to see how we define constants:

```
<?xml version="1.0" encoding="utf-8"?>
<resources>
    <string name="app_name">Hello_World</string>
    <string name="hello_world">Hello world!</string>
    <string name="menu_settings">Settings</string>
</resources>
```

The first XML tag declares we are using XML version 1.0 and that we are using text (font) encoding paradigm UTF-8, which accommodates a fairly large character set that spans many common languages. The second "parent" tag is the <resources> tag that holds our <string> resources that are nested inside the Resources container. The first **<string>** tag is named **app_name** and its value holds the name for the application **Hello_World** that appears at the top of the application in the emulator when we run it. The second **<string>** tag is named **hello_world** and its value holds the text that is used in the TextView UI element that displays: **Hello world!** that appears in the middle of the application Activity screen in the emulator when we run it. The third **<string>** tag is named **menu_settings** and its value holds the name for the first menu option title: **Settings** that appears at the bottom of the application in the emulator when we run it and click the Menu button or icon on the right side of the emulator screen.

Now that we've covered the plethora of options and values that can be set via the XML mark-up in our Android application, let's take a look at how Java calls, starts up, and inflates all these XML assets via various onCreate() methods.

Android Application Project: Java Coding

Now let's take a look at the Android application Java code assets themselves that live in the Project Explorer hierarchy we examined in detail earlier in the chapter. We'll again start at the very top of the Project Folder hierarchy, and look in the **src** folder and under our package folder we'll find the MainActivity.java Java source code file that contains our MainActivity class and onCreate() methods.

Assuming your **src** and package-name folders are open and you can see the MainActivity.java file, click the **MainActivity.java** file to select it, and hit the F3 key on your keyboard, or alternatively you can right-click the file name, and select the **Open** menu item from the context-sensitive menu that will appear. A fourth tab opens at the top of the Eclipse central editing pane and you should see something like what is shown in Figure 2-10.

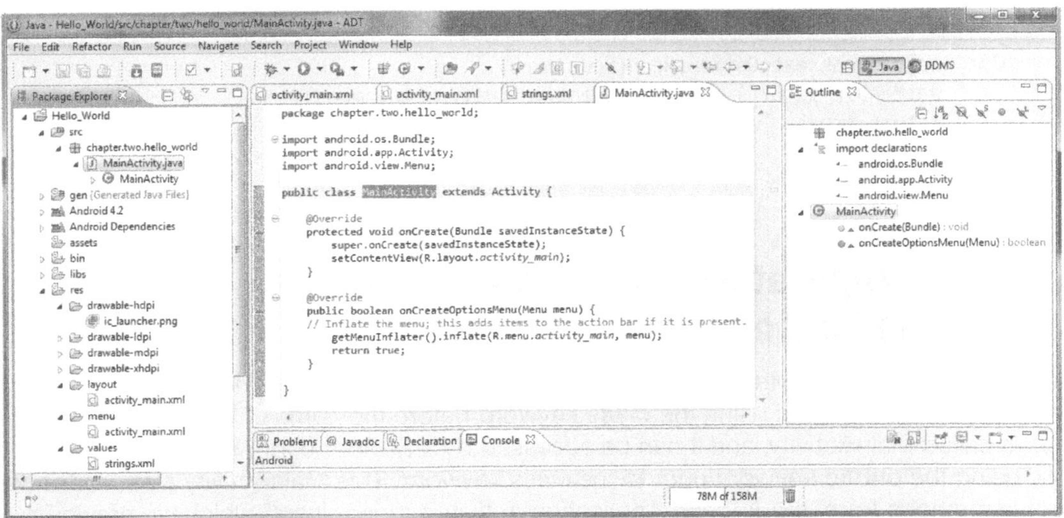

Figure 2-10. The MainActivity.java file shown in the Eclipse central editing pane ready for further editing

Notice that a tab opens in the central part of Eclipse that says **MainActivity.java** at the top and contains the Java code that is in that file. This central part of Eclipse is the code editing pane and can have more than one tab open at a time, as we have seen when we opened our Layout and Menu XML files for review and editing. So, let's take a look at our Java code now.

Defining the Android Classes via Import Statements

There are three **import** statements at the top that reference other Java code that we will use in the Java class and its methods below it. Note we will get into all this Java terminology in greater detail in the next chapter. To see all the **import** statements, click the + UI symbol next to the first **import** statement, and you can see all three import statements.

The first **onCreate()** method uses the first **Bundle** class, the second **Activity** class extends our MainActivity class, and the third **Menu** class creates a menu via the **onCreateOptionsMenu()**

method. All these Android classes are discussed in greater detail in the first two parts of this book. Here is the Java code that creates our Activity (User Interface) and Menu for our Hello_World application as it was created for us in the ADT New Android Application Project helper:

```
package chapter.two.hello_world;

import android.os.Bundle;
import android.app.Activity;
import android.view.Menu;

public class MainActivity extends Activity {
        @Override
        public void onCreate(Bundle savedInstanceState) {
                super.onCreate(savedInstanceState);
                setContentView(R.layout.activity_main);
        }
        @Override
        public boolean onCreateOptionsMenu(Menu menu) {
                getMenuInflater().inflate(R.menu.activity_main, menu);
                return true;
        }
}
```

Creating Our Application Infrastructure Using the onCreate() Method

Next, let's take a look at the **MainActivity** Java class and the **onCreate()** method that lives inside of it. In Java, you declare a class using the **class** keyword before the name of the class. In this case, our class is called MainActivity, and it can be accessed by any other code, so it is also declared as public using the **public** keyword prior to the class keyword. This MainActivity class **extends** (or borrows methods from) the Android Application Activity "super class," which we previously imported at the top of this code using the **import android.app.Activity;** line of code. Our complete MainActivity class declaration reads as follows:

```
public class MainActivity extends Activity { ... }
```

The first method in our class is also **public** and also is declared as **void,** which means that it does not return any value to the calling function (in this case the Android OS), it just does something, which in this case is to create our initial Activity or User Interface Screen via the **onCreate()** method. The onCreate() method is passed a **Bundle** object by the Android OS that is called **saveInstanceState** and contains the states (settings) of the user interface elements in our Activity in the form of a Bundle of values and settings.

Inside the onCreate() method are two method calls. The first method call uses the **super** keyword to pass the **saveInstanceState** Bundle object up to the **android.app.Activity** superclass and its onCreate() method. The second method call sets the Content View (Activity Screen) for the application via the **setContentView()** method, along with a reference to our **activity_main.xml** file in the **layout** folder that we looked at earlier in the chapter. That looks like this: **setContentView(R.layout.activity_main);** where the **R** equates to the Hello_World Project path down to the **layout** folder, or C:\Users\Username\workspace\

Hello_World\res\ so as you can extrapolate from this information, **R.layout.activity_main** actually translates into (means to Android):

```
C:\Users\Username\workspace\Hello_World\res\layout\activity_main.xml
```

This serves to load your XML **layout** definition through the Java **setContentView()** method in the **Activity** subclass (remember the extends Activity part of our class declaration). Next, let's look at the second method **onCreateOptionsMenu()** that similarly serves to create your Activity's Options Menu from the activity_main.xml Menu XML file using the **getMenuInflater()** method accessed via the **android.view.Menu** class **import** statement we looked at earlier.

The getMenuInflater() method calls an **.inflate()** method that has two parameters, a **Menu** object named **menu** passed into the method via onCreateOptionsMenu(Menu menu) and the path to our activity_main.xml file in the menu folder via the now familiar **R.menu.activity_main** which equates to:

```
C:\Users\Username\workspace\Hello_World\res\menu\activity_main.xml
```

So, basically, the .inflate() method takes the **Menu** object named **menu** and inflates it with the XML Menu definition referenced in **R.menu.activity_main**. Note that Android uses the first part of the filename (not the .xml part, it does not use the file extension) to reference both XML and graphics (drawable) files. Once the Menu object menu is inflated and ready for use it returns a **true** value to the OS.

Running Your Hello World App in the Android 4.2 Emulator

Now let's compile and run all this XML and Java code and see what it does in the Android 4.2 Emulator that we created in Chapter 1 for the Nexus S smartphone. To launch the emulator, simply right-click the **Hello_World** Project top-level folder in the Eclipse Package Explorer, and select the **Run As ➤ Android Application** menu item. When the Android 4.2 Emulator for the Nexus S smartphone appears you will see the Hello_World app and its Hello world! exclamation on the emulator screen as shown in Figure 2-11.

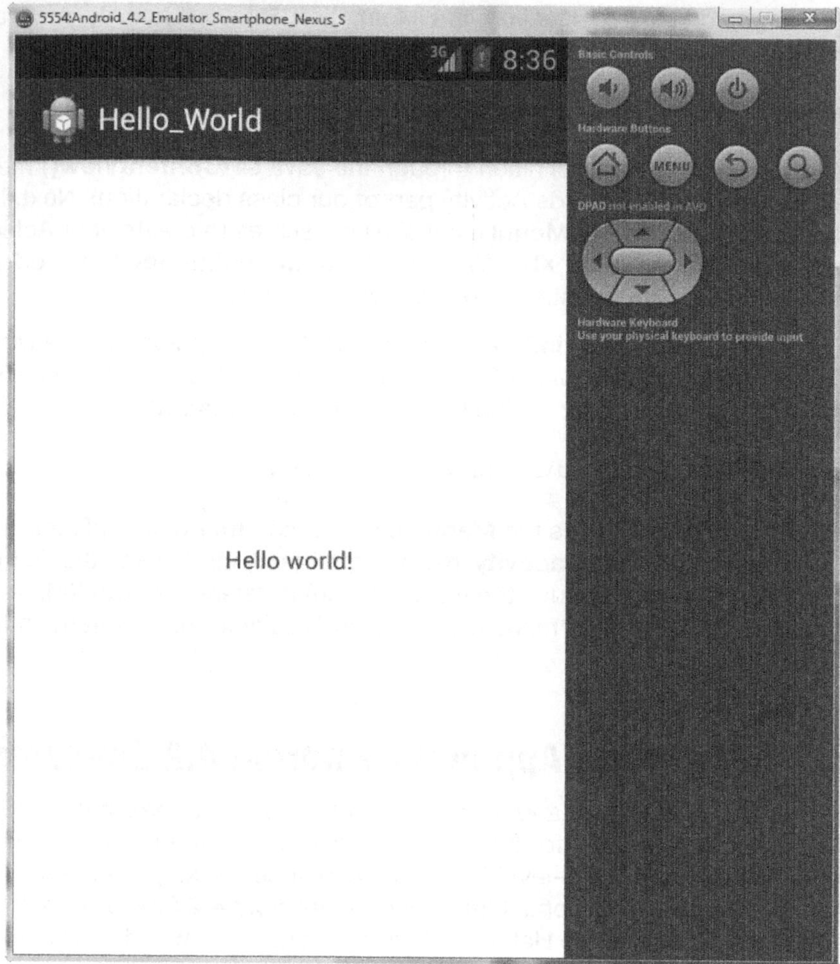

Figure 2-11. Running our Hello_World Android Application in the Android 4.2 Nexus S Smartphone Emulator

We can see the Application Name we specified in the New Android Application Project series of dialogs, as well as the Launch Icon we chose and the text message we set in the strings.xml file. Our XML Layout tags centered the text perfectly, and now we are ready to click the X at the top right and exit the emulator.

Setting Up Logcat after Your First Android 4.2 Emulation

Once you exit your Android 4.2 Nexus S Smartphone Emulator for the first time, you will notice that you get an error dialog that informs you that Logcat is not set up for your Eclipse Android Development environment and offers to set it up for you. This **Auto Monitor Logcat** dialog is shown in Figure 2-12.

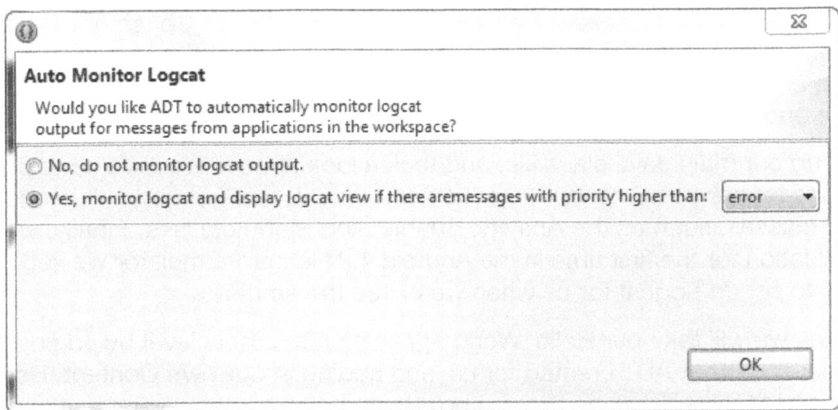

Figure 2-12. Auto Monitor Logcat dialog that appears after the first launch of any emulator in ADT

Android's Logcat stands for Log Catalog and is an automatic logging system that provides you with a convenient method for collecting and viewing all Android system debugger output. Detailed logs from various applications and parts of the operating system are collected within a series of circular buffers, which then can subsequently be viewed and even filtered by the Logcat pane inside of the Eclipse IDE.

You can also use the Logcat from an ADB shell to view the log messages once you become a more advanced Android Developer. More information can be found at the following URL:

http://developer.android.com/tools/help/logcat.html

You will find that the Logcat utility is helpful in researching errors that may pop up during your application development process. If you cut and paste the error message right out of the Eclipse Logcat pane into the Google search bar and press Return or click Search you can quickly find other developers who are getting the same error message in their applications and see how they solved it.

Summary

In this chapter you created your first Android Hello World application, with the help of the Android Developer Tools (ADT) New Android Application Project "helper" series of dialogs. In the next chapters, we will modify this basic code to build a more impressive Hello World application, so that you can take your knowledge of Eclipse, XML mark-up, and Java coding in Android to the next level.

The first thing we looked at was the work process for creating a New Android Application Project via a handful of dialogs that allow developers to set a myriad of options to create a "bootstrap" application shell that they can then modify and morph into the application they want to develop. This involves naming the application, Java class and XML files, determining Android OS version support, selecting application launch icons, naming and selecting Activity types, and selecting navigation modes.

Next we looked at the Eclipse IDE and its very useful Package Explorer pane and used that utility to examine the anatomy of the Android Hello_World application structure that the New Android Application Project helper created for us. We looked at the Source Code and Resource Folder hierarchies and where files are kept for graphic assets, XML definitions, and Java code.

Next we opened the key XML files used for Layout, Menu, and String Constant definitions for our Hello_World Application Project and examined what makes them tick: Tags and Parameters. We learned about the Eclipse center code editing pane and the top and bottom tab areas that allow us to select what file and what editing mode we are working in.

Next we opened up our main Java class file, and took a look at how the Java code pulls together our XML definitions for our user interface, menus and content, and learned a little about some of the core Android classes, such as the Activity, Bundle, and Menu classes. Finally, we ran our Hello_World application for the first time in the Android 4.2 Nexus S Emulator we set up in Chapter 1, and allowed ADT to set up Logcat for us when we exited the emulator.

In the next chapter, we will take our Hello_World application to a new level by adding to and changing the initial code that ADT created for us, and adding in our own Content, User Interface elements, Icons, and Menu selections to learn how to take the bootstrap application that ADT creates for us and morph it into something customized to achieve our own Prime Directive. At the same time we'll learn more about Java, XML, icons, and other Android secrets that we didn't uncover in the first two chapters.

Chapter 3

Java for Android Primer: Enhancing Our Hello World Application

In this chapter, we will take the Hello World application that we created in the previous chapter using the New Android Application Project helper, and add in our own Java code to make it much more interesting. At the same time, we are also going to use this chapter to give those readers who are not Java programmers a high-level overview of the various code structures that we will be using in this book via the Java programming language and its objects, variables, methods, classes, packages, modifiers, and so on.

I am going to try and seamlessly meld these two objectives, enhancing our Hello World app and summarizing Java concepts at a high level, into one cohesive chapter that defines the approach and capabilities of Java within the context of our Hello World application. Using Java code, we will add the capability to our Hello World application so it generates new worlds, as well as to colonize and protect them.

Java's Highest Level: The Application Programming Interface

As with any programming language, the highest level of that language is called the **API**, or **Application Programming Interface**, which is the sum-total of the entire programming language itself, in its latest revision, all in one collection or place. As you all know, if you want to develop in any given programming language, you must go and get (and eventually learn) the API for that programming language in order to develop an application under that programming language using its development paradigm.

In this respect, Java is no different than any other programming language. In the rest of this chapter, we'll discuss the lingo of Java, as well as its various programming constructs, as we did in the previous chapter for the lingo that various modules in Android use. In this way, you will know conceptually what we're talking about during the remainder of this book.

Organizing the Java API: The Package

Java provides a method of organizing the code in your programming projects into logical modules, or collections of code, called **Packages**. In the Java programming language, a **Package** is a collection of Java **Classes**, which we will learn about in greater detail in the next section of this chapter.

We have already created a **package** for our Hello_World project in Eclipse, during the New Android Application Project series of helper dialogs that we utilized in Chapter 2. These five dialogs were used to help create our app's basic Java and XML code foundation for our Hello World application.

Because we created our Hello_World application in Chapter 2 of this book, we logically named our Java package: **chapter.two.hello_world** and we then declared it at the top of our **MainActivity.java** file Java code like this:

```
package chapter.two.hello_world;
```

Packages are **declared** at the top of each Java code module that utilizes their **classes** and **methods** (more about these soon) contained within those packages. Packages are always declared using Java's **package** keyword.

Project package names usually use lowercase characters, and tell the user what the code in the package does. For this reason, we need to use logical package naming conventions that tell other users of our package what it is that the package is, and if possible, what it is that it does.

Note that packages containing functional classes, especially in Android, will sometimes use an uppercase letter on the last name in the package. You will see this often in the Android OS, as classes are named with uppercase letters, such as **String, View, Activity, Object, Bundle,** and so on.

Our **chapter.two.hello_world** package that we created earlier in Chapter 2 currently contains one class named **MainActivity** whose Java source code is located within a file called **MainActivity.java** located under our project's source code folder (named src). In this chapter, we will create another all new class from scratch, named **WorldGen**, which will allow us to create new Worlds (planets) for our Hello World application, while also teaching you the basic Java concepts, just in case you're not a Java programmer.

As you use more and more of the Android OS features, you will find that package names in Android will always logically reflect what that package is, as well as what it does, and also where that package came from within the Java and the Android OS hierarchy.

Let's take a closer look at this, for instance, using the Android packages that we have already brought into our Chapter 2 Java code using the Java **import** statements. These import statements are located in our MainActivity Java code file, just underneath our **package** declaration statement:

```
import android.os.Bundle;
import android.app.Activity;
import android.view.Menu;
```

The **import** command in Java is used to–you guessed it–import other Java packages. Imported packages are collections of logically bundled-together functional classes that have already been written and tested for you and which are currently available for commercial use within your application.

In the case of Android OS application development, the import statement allows us to use pre-existing Java code (kept in packages) specifically written to support Android OS functionality, which is provided for use within our Android applications, and which we will learn about in much greater detail in this book, as we use more and more of these packages.

One of the most powerful things about Java is that we can import these entire libraries, or packages, of code that have already been written and tested, and then utilize them for our own benefit (even for profit), within our own Android applications, without having to pay nary a penny for that software's (code) development. It's a fairly amazing open source software development business proposition, if you think about it.

Let's take a closer look at those three import statements referencing core Android packages and their classes that were created for us in our MainActivity.java file during the Eclipse ADT New Android Application Project sequence of dialogs that we utilized in Chapter 2.

Reviewing the Java Import Statements

The first one, **android.os.Bundle** references the Android OS. The middle reference tells us the code is OS related and Bundle in the final part of the package name tells us that this package is a collection of Java classes and methods relating to the **Bundle** features in Android.

The second import statement, **android.app.Activity** is also Android related. The second part tell us that it relates to **app**lication functionality and the final part of the package name tells us that this package contains a collection of classes and methods that are used to provide the **Activity** features in Android. This package is an important one, and is used in all Android apps. The next few chapters will focus specifically on Activities.

The final import statement, **android.view.Menu** is an Android package that relates to the view (screen-related) Android functionality. It supports a large collection of **View** classes (and subclasses called **Widgets**, which we will be learning about in the next few chapters). The Android View classes relate to Android **View** (screen layouts and user interface widgets) features, many of which we'll be utilizing to enhance our Hello_World user interface design and user experience functionality. But first we need to learn a little bit more about the Java programming language and Java Objects. In this case we are importing the **Menu** classes and methods from the **android.view** package so we can implement our menu system.

The Foundation of Java: The Object

Java is an **Object Oriented Programming (OOP)** Language. Like C++, Java uses programming constructs called **objects** to model the data and functions used within its programming logic. Java objects are like descriptions of those real-life objects that you see around you in everyday life.

Just like real-life objects you encounter each day, such as automobiles, appliances, computers, buildings, ships, airplanes, and so on, a Java object also features unique attributes and utility (i.e., capabilities that can enhance your everyday life), very similar to those real-life objects that you use each day.

In Java, to "model" or create an object, you will create a Java **class** that holds that object's **states** and **behaviors**. We'll learn more about **classes** in the next section of this chapter, but to understand classes, we must first understand objects, so let's discuss objects in greater detail here.

The functionality of an object can be described via its **behavior**; that is, those things that the object can do or perform. Objects gain this functionality via programming constructs called **methods,** which we will soon learn more about and use in our Hello World app later in this chapter.

Each characteristic of an object can be defined via a **state**; that is, data that describes an object's attribute at any given moment in time. Objects gain these attributes via programming constructs called **instance variables,** which we will learn about and use in our app later in this chapter.

Let's use our Hello World app as an example, and define some Worlds or Planets, each of will be represented as an object, so that you can see these concepts in action.

First, let's define some of the attributes or states of our World objects:

- **Planet Name**–A **String** data type or text value, for instance, "Earth"
- **Planet Mass**–An **integer** value representing Yottagrams; Earth is 5,973 YG
- **Planet Gravity**–A real or **float** value for gravity; Earth=9.78 m/s squared
- **Planet Colonies**–An **integer** data value, representing a number of colonies
- **Planet Population**–A 64-bit **double** value, representing a number of people
- **Planet Bases**–An **integer** value, representing the number of military bases
- **Planet Military**–An **integer** value, representing the number of military personnel
- **Planet Protected**–A **Boolean** value, telling us whether planet forcefield is on

Next, let's define at least a dozen object behaviors or functions that can be attributed to these new World objects:

- **WorldGen**–Constructs new Worlds, that is, it generates a new World object
- **Set Planet Colonies**–Adds any number of new colonies to a planet surface
- **Get Planet Colonies**–Returns the number of colonies on the planet surface
- **Set Planet Military**–Adds any number of military bases to planet surface
- **Get Planet Military**–Returns a number of military bases on planet surface
- **Turn ForceField On**–Turns on forcefield protecting the planet atmosphere)
- **Turn ForceField Off**–Turns off forcefield protecting a planet atmosphere
- **Get ForceField State**–Returns the forcefield status on/true or off/false
- **Set Colony Immigration**–Adds people into each colony on a planet surface)
- **Get Colony Immigration**–Return the population currently on planet surface
- **Set Base Protection**–Adds military to protect Military Bases on a planet
- **Get Base Protection**–Returns the number of military personnel on a planet

As you can see, these are behaviors or things that each new World object can do, or can change, about its existence and states or characteristics.

As you will also see later on in this book, objects can also contain other objects, in an object hierarchy. This is similar to the folder hierarchy on your system's hard disk drive, for instance. This allows more complex objects to be built modularly in a more organized and logical fashion.

An example of this concept in our Hello World application example is that WorldGen objects (which we are defining and creating in this chapter) are used with, and add complexity to, the **java.lang.Object** top-level object, which we will learn more about in the next section of this chapter.

One of the central concepts in Object Oriented Programming (OOP) is the concept of **Data Encapsulation,** which is where an object's states or its **instance variables** can only be changed via its own functions or **methods**.

The reason for data encapsulation is so that objects are self-contained, and can be created and tested within a vacuum, without being affected by anything else within the overall software package that is being created.

This allows for a modular code development process to be implemented, and is often termed **code modularity**. Writing code in self-contained code **modules** allows for bugs and other problems to be isolated more easily, within logically organized functions each developed separately within the overall software development project.

This code modularity lends itself perfectly to maximizing code re-use, and thus allows software development teams to each focus on developing their own modules and functions within the overall software package development process. In this way, everyone's coding efforts are usable by every other team member, once the code modules are written, tested, debugged, and ultimately are then released for use by all the other team members.

Blueprint for a Java Object: The Class

The primary vehicle in Java for coding the blueprint for a Java object is called the **Class**, and once a Java Class, or a collection of Classes in the form of a Java Package is released for use, even more complex Classes or Packages can be created using that code via a process called **subclassing**.

In Java this is an example of the OOP concept called **inheritance**, where an existing Java class can later be used to create an even more detailed or complicated version of that original class. Other commonly used terms for a subclass are: a **child** class, a **derived** class, and an **extended** class.

The new class that is **derived** from (or a **derivative** of) the original class is called the **subclass**, and the original "parent" class is then termed the **superclass**. Superclasses can be referenced through their subclasses via the **super** keyword, which we will see in use throughout this book. Other commonly used terms for a superclass are: **parent** class or the **base** class.

This class **hierarchy** can be seen on the Android developer website at the top of any given Android class description webpage, where a hierarchy of where each Android class originated from is shown, starting with the top level **java.lang.Object** superclass, and proceeding down through a hierarchy of subclasses, each of which were created to add some additional features and functionality to the superclass above it.

```
java.lang.Object > Object Subclass > Subclass Subclass > etcetera
```

So, if you want to see where features have been added to each class level, start at the top at java.lang.Object (where object features originate) and progress down the tree to see what classes were subclassed at each level.

Let's look at an example of an Android class hierarchy for the Java **String** data type class. This class originates at the java.lang.Object class, and thus the Android **java.lang.String** class subclasses from the **Object** class to add String data type capability to Java and Android. We will use the String data type to define our planetName instance variable for our WorldGen object that we will be creating.

String objects allow an **array** (collection) of text to be created via the **char** (character) **primitive data type**. Thus, String data type objects are really a collection (via an array) of characters (via the **char** data type), whereas all the other common data types in Java are called **primitives** or primitive data types. Lowercase string in your code will not represent a String data type to Java, and will be considered an object or variable name, so this is something to be aware of if you are using lots of text.

To summarize, just remember that the top-level **java.lang.Object** or Java Language Object class is the mother of all Java classes, as it provides the foundation for all Objects in Java, however big or small they might be. Now, let's move on to learn how to code these Java classes, so that we can use them to spawn or create or **instantiate** some new Java objects!

Just as a blueprint defines how any given structure will be constructed, so too does a Java **class** define how an object will be constructed. A Java class is made up of **instance variables** that hold the object state values, a **constructor** that constructs each new object, as well as **methods** that operate on its variables so that the object can have some functionality. It is also important to note that variables defined inside of methods are called **local variables,** while any variables defined outside of methods but inside of a class structure are called instance variables.

How does one create an object using a class, you might wonder? After the class is coded, which defines the object's states (instance variables) and its functions (methods), we can utilize that class definition to create an **instance** of an object. An instance is a single occurrence of that object, and each **instantiation** or occurrence of that Java object can be a unique and different collection of that particular object's states or attributes.

Using our Hello World application example from the previous chapter, let's create a new class that generates new World objects for our existing Hello World application. To declare this class, which we will call **WorldGen**, we will utilize the following Java syntax:

```
public class WorldGen { instance variables and methods go between curly brackets }
```

Just like in any other programming language, the first things that we will want to declare at the top of our Java classes are the instance variables, which we are going to use to hold the attributes or states of our WorldGen objects. In Java, this is done by using the following generalized format:

```
<data type> then <variable name> then = then <set variable value> then ;
```

So, for object state instance variables that we described in the previous section, we would write the variable description lines of code as follows:

```
String planetName = "Earth"; (shown only to demonstrate how to set a default value)
int planetMass;
double planetGravity;
```

```
int planetColonies;
long planetPopulation;
int planetBases;
int planetMilitary;
boolean planetProtection;
```

We are using a default value above for the planetName String variable that would apply to planet **Earth** to show you how to include a default initial value within your class variable declarations. When you include a default value, as it is with any programming language, it is called **initializing** that variable. Normally, you would declare the variables and set them later via your **constructor** method, which we will be looking at in the next section.

If you are a programmer (which we are assuming you are), you are already familiar with **String** (text), **integer** (non-decimal whole numbers), **double** (up to 64-bit value real, or decimal, numbers), **long** (up to 64-bit value high-precision numbers), **char** and **boolean** (true/false values) **data types**.

Now that we have defined our object's states or instance variables, let's go ahead and define our object's behaviors next, using some Java **methods**.

Defining a Java Object's Functions: The Method

To define a function or **method** within your Java class, you would use the following format to name and **declare** that method in your Java code:

```
<Modifiers> <Return Data Types> <Method Name> (parameters) {Java code}
```

Methods generally go after the instance variable declarations in a class (although they don't absolutely have to, this is simply a convention for better code organization and readability, for other viewers of your code).

For our behaviors or functions that we described earlier, the one WorldGen constructor, and 11 methods, would be declared as follows (we'll code in their functionality next):

```
public WorldGen            (String name, int mass, double gravity) {...}
void setPlanetColonies     (int numColonies) {...}
int  getPlanetColonies     () {...}
void setPlanetMilitary     (int numBases) {...}
int  getPlanetMilitary     () {...}
void turnForceFieldOn      () {...}
void turnForceFieldOff     () {...}
boolean getForceFieldState () {...}
void setColonyImmigration  (int numColonists) {...}
long getColonyImmigration  () {...}
void setBaseProtection     (int numForces) {...}
int  getBaseProtection     () {...}
```

The keyword placed immediately before the method name is called a **modifier** in Java. Modifiers in Java can be used with classes, methods, or variables. There can be more than one modifier, if needed, to define a class, method, or variable's characteristics. There are two types of modifiers, **access control** modifiers, and modifiers which do not define any access control.

There are four levels of access control modification: **no modifier** (see all the preceding methods, except for the constructor method) where the method or variable is visible to the entire package that it is contained in; the **public** modifier, which means that any Java class, even classes outside of the package, can use that method or variable; the **private** modifier, which means that only the class that a method or variable is defined in can use that method or variable; and the **protected** modifier, which means that the method or variable is visible to the package, as well as to all subclasses which may be created from that class.

There are several other types of modifiers which do not affect access control, such as: **static**, **final**, **abstract,** and **synchronized** modifiers.

Besides the modifiers, there are also **return data types** that are declared before a Java method. The **void** data return type that we are using in so many of our methods signifies that all these methods return no data value back to the calling entity when the void method is called. The other return data types that we are using, **int**, **long,** and **boolean**, return data to the calling entity of that precise primitive data type, respectively.

Now let's look at adding some functionality to these methods via code that exists inside the curly braces that define the beginning and end of each method. The first **WorldGen()** method is a special type of method called a **constructor**, and this method code is written as follows:

```
public WorldGen (String name, int mass, double gravity) {
        planetName = name;
        planetMass = mass;
        planetGravity = gravity;
        planetColonies = 0;
        planetPopulation = 0;
        planetBases = 0;
        planetMilitary = 0;
        planetProtection = false;
}
```

A Java constructor differs from a method in a number of distinct ways. First of all, it does not use any of the data return types, such as **void** and **int**, because it is used to create an object, rather than to perform a function. Indeed, that's why it's called a constructor in the first place; because its function is solely to construct or create the new object.

Note that every class that creates Java objects will feature a constructor with the **same name as the class** itself, so a constructor is the one method type whose name can (and will, always) start with an uppercase letter.

Another difference between a constructor and a method is that constructors cannot have non-access-control modifiers, so be sure not to declare your constructor as: **static**, **final**, **abstract**, or **synchronized**.

Inside this WorldGen() constructor, we take three important **parameters** for our new planet's name, mass, and gravity, and set them inside of the constructor method. We will also be initializing the other object instance variables to zero, to create a clean, virgin, unprotected world.

Next, let's code our other six methods, which perform those functions that modify the state of our world. This provides a number of useful world building capabilities to the users of our Hello_World application.

The first **setPlanetColonies()** method is much simpler than our WorldGen() constructor method, and it allows us to add new Colonies to our world object. The Java code for this method is written as follows:

```
void setPlanetColonies (int numColonies) {
        planetColonies += numColonies;
}
```

The **void** data return type that is declared before our setPlanetColonies() method name declares what type of value will be returned by this method. In this case, this method does not return any data value at all, so we will declare it as void (or devoid of any data return type or data value).

Also note that our method name begins with a lowercase letter, and uses uppercase letters for words that are internal to the method name. In the computer programming industry, this naming convention is called **CamelCase**.

Inside our **setPlanetColonies()** method **body** we will utilize an **assignment operator** that adds the numColonies integer parameter to the planetColonies instance variable for this object. As programmers, we know that this is a shorthand (fast) way to add the number of colonies parameter passed into the method to the total number of Planet Colonies held in a planetColonies instance variable, which we declared at the head of our WorldGen class.

We'll do something very similar with the **setPlanetMilitary()** method, which will look like this, once we code it in Eclipse:

```
void setPlanetMilitary (int numBases) {
        planetBases += numBases;
}
```

Next, let's write the **turnForceFieldOn()** and **turnForceFieldOff()** methods, which set the boolean parameter, indicating whether a planet's protective forcefield is on or off. By default, as we can see from the body of our **WorldGen()** constructor method, we initialize the planetProtection variable to false for a planet when it is initially created (instantiated), so that planets are not initially protected by any forcefield.

```
void turnForceFieldOn () {
        planetProtection = true;
}
void turnForceFieldOff () {
        planetProtection = false;
}
```

Now let's code our **setColonyImmigration()** method, which lets us add Colonists to our World's Colonies. This method adds the number of Colonists parameter passed over to the method to the planetPopulation count instance variable using the addition assignment operator.

```
void setColonyImmigration (int numColonists) {
        planetPopulation += numColonists;
}
```

Finally, let's code our **setBaseProtection()** method, which lets us add Military Forces to our World's Military Bases. This method add**s** the number of forces parameter passed over to it to the planetMilitary count variable using the addition assignment operator.

```
void setBaseProtection (int numForces) {
        planetMilitary += numForces;
}
```

Now we are ready to open up our project in Eclipse ADT and create our new WorldGen Java class. We will write all this code that we previously developed into the Eclipse central text editor pane, so we can later use it in our app to create, populate, and protect new worlds.

Coding a Java Class in Eclipse: Creating the WorldGen Class

First we need to fire up Eclipse ADT by clicking the Quick Launch Icon that we set up in Chapter 1, and accept the default workspace folder location for our project, which should be C:/Users/YourName/workspace/ or similar, unless of course you have set it to a different location.

Once Eclipse ADT opens its main IDE window, you will see your Hello World project that we created in Chapter 2. The tabs should still be open for the Java and XML editing panes that we used in Chapter 2.

Because the MainActivity class that we created contains the Java code for starting the app's Main Activity window (and hence its name), we are going to leverage the modular nature of Java, and create our own separate WorldGen class to generate (spawn) world objects with.

Creating Our New WorldGen Java Class

One of the primary reasons that Java is modular is to allow us to organize code by its logical functionality, so that we can write classes to create our new world objects and have other classes that launch and define our user interfaces and our content Activity screens.

To create a new Java class inside the Eclipse ADT, use the **File ➤ New ➤ Class** menu sequence, which opens up the **New Java Class** dialog, as shown in Figure 3-1.

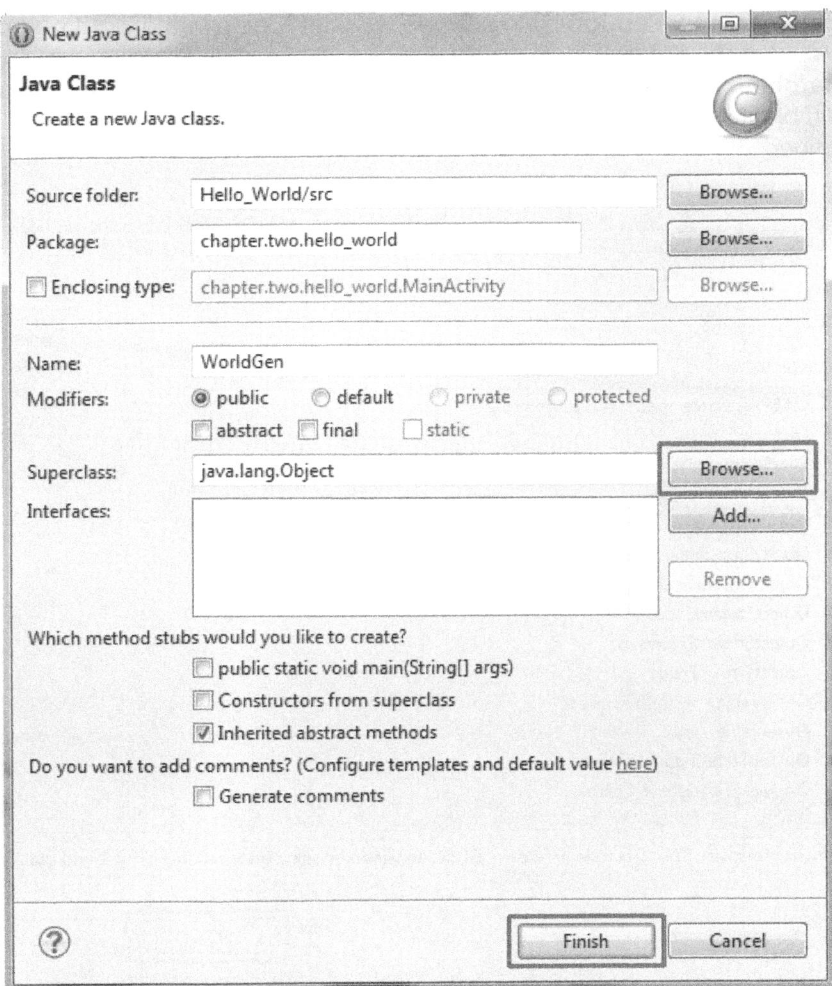

Figure 3-1. Creating our WorldGen class using the New Java Class dialog

This New Java Class dialog contains about a dozen fields, checkboxes, and radio buttons that allow us to configure our New Java Class in a similar fashion to what the New Android Application Project dialogs allowed us to do when we configured our new Android application project settings.

When the dialog opens up, you will see that it has populated several of the fields for you automatically; the first two are set correctly, with your package name and the Hello_World source code folder location. The **Superclass** field is set to your MainActivity class (the dialog will assume that an existing Java class is going to be used as the superclass), and so we will want to set that to the **java.lang.Object** class instead, because our WorldGen() class is going to generate world objects, and not Activities.

First, name your class **WorldGen** using the **Name:** field, and then click the **Browse . . .** button on the right side of the **Superclass** field, so that we can browse through all the available classes in Android to locate the Java **Object** class from which we want to subclass our WorldGen class.

This opens the **Superclass Selection** dialog, where we start typing in the word **object** in the **Choose a type:** field at the top of the dialog, as shown in Figure 3-2. After we type in the "o" character, the **Matching items:** section of the dialog in the center populates, and we can then select (click) the Object item, as shown. Finally, click **OK** at the bottom, and our java.lang.Object Superclass is defined.

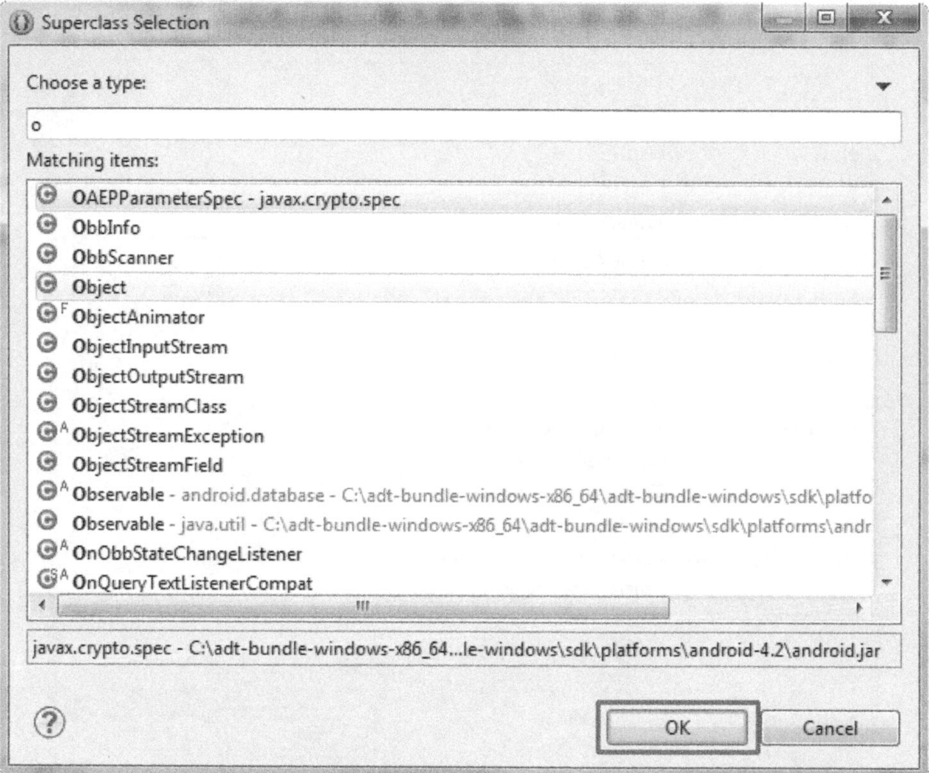

***Figure 3-2.** Using the Superclass Selection dialog to browse for the java.lang.Object class*

After you click **OK** you are returned to the **New Java Class** dialog, where you can click **Finish** to create your new WorldGen() Java Class. Eclipse adds the new Java class file, code, and information into all three of its primary panes: the Package Explorer pane on the left, the Code Editing pane in the center, and the Code Outline pane on the right, as shown in Figure 3-3.

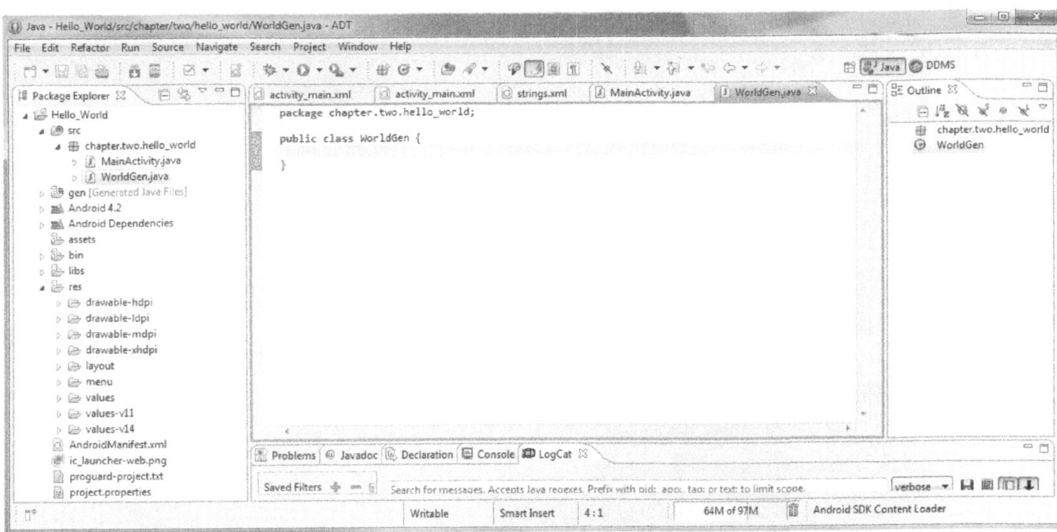

***Figure 3-3.** Eclipse ADT IDE with empty WorldGen class code structure created via the New Java Class dialog*

Notice at the top of the code editing pane that the New Java Class dialog also writes your **package** Java statement for you, as well as your WorldGen Public Class declaration, which means that we're ready to add in the Java code that we wrote in the previous section of this chapter.

Note that we made our WorldGen class **public**, so that any Java class, even Java classes which are not included in our package, could call or **invoke** our WorldGen object constructor, as well as our WorldGen methods, This allows other Java packages to create new worlds for their apps as well.

We could have also left the **public** modifier off this class declaration entirely, which would have signified to the Java compiler that only the classes in our chapter.two.hello_world package could generate new worlds. In this particular case, that would have worked just as well for our app, as the MainActivity class is also inside our package. In fact, that might be interesting for you to try as an experiment later on sometime (removing the public modifier) to get some more experience.

Now, let's type in all the Java code that we created in the previous two sections of this chapter in the Eclipse ADT editing pane in the center of the IDE. Alternatively, as a short-cut you can cut and paste it. Make sure that everything is inside those two curly brackets (also called braces) that define the boundaries of the WorldGen class.

The results are shown in Figure 3-4, and as you can see, Eclipse ADT finds zero errors in our code, and conveniently summarizes all our instance variables, our constructor, and methods in the outline pane on the right.

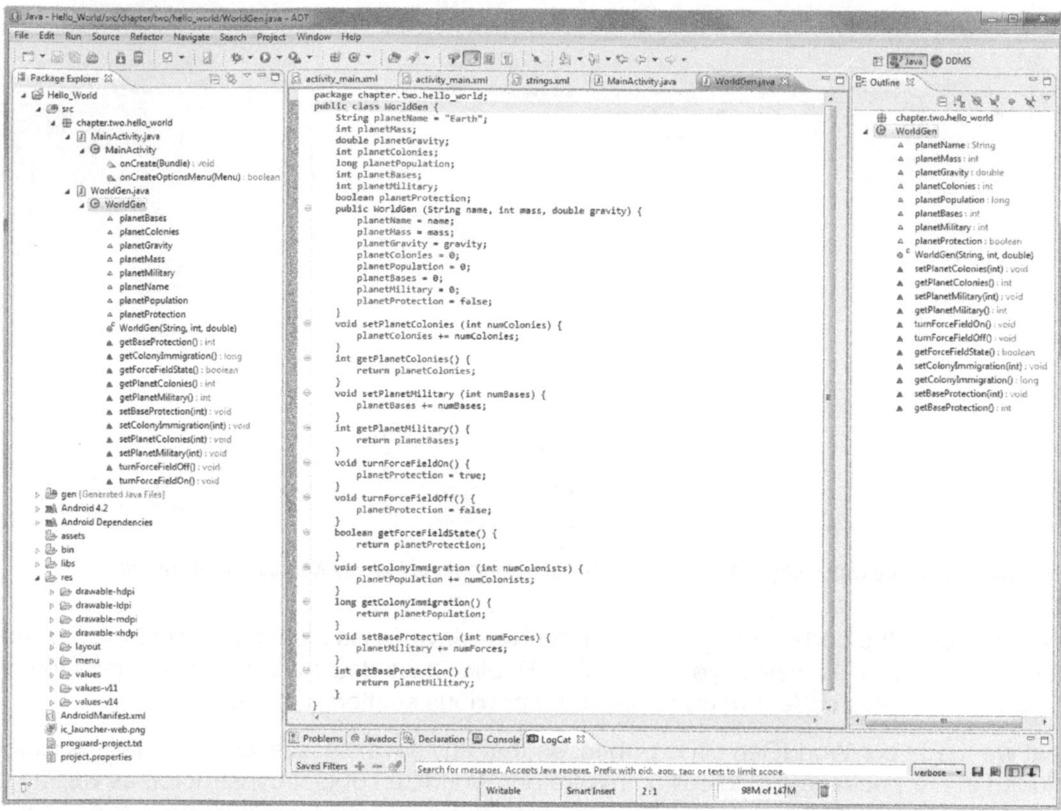

***Figure 3-4.** Java code for the WorldGen class entered into the Eclipse ADT Integrated Development Environment*

Now that we have written our WorldGen class, we can have code in our other classes utilize the class to create WorldGen (World) objects.

Creating WorldGen Objects Using the WorldGen Class

We'll do this (for now) inside our MainActivity class, just to show you how it's done, and then in later chapters, we'll have this code called via other Java methods and classes, and possibly from some of our new XML user interface elements, such as menus, buttons, text fields, and so on.

Click the MainActivity.java top tab in the Eclipse central editing pane, so that we can switch over to viewing the Java code for our main Activity. We will add in an object declaration using the Java **new()** method, which allows us to create new Java objects.

We will do this in our **onCreate()** method, right after the statements that create our main Activity via the **super.onCreate()** method call, and after the **setContentView()** method call, because we will need to have created our Activity, and have set its content view, before we can do anything else.

The format for creating Java objects using a constructor method call is

```
<Declare Constructor Method> <Object Name> = new <Constructor Method Call>
```

So, to create a WorldGen object, we declare it (WorldGen), and then name it (earth), and then finally call our constructor method via the **new** keyword, as shown in Figure 3-5, like this:

```
WorldGen earth = new WorldGen("Earth", 5973, 9.78);
```

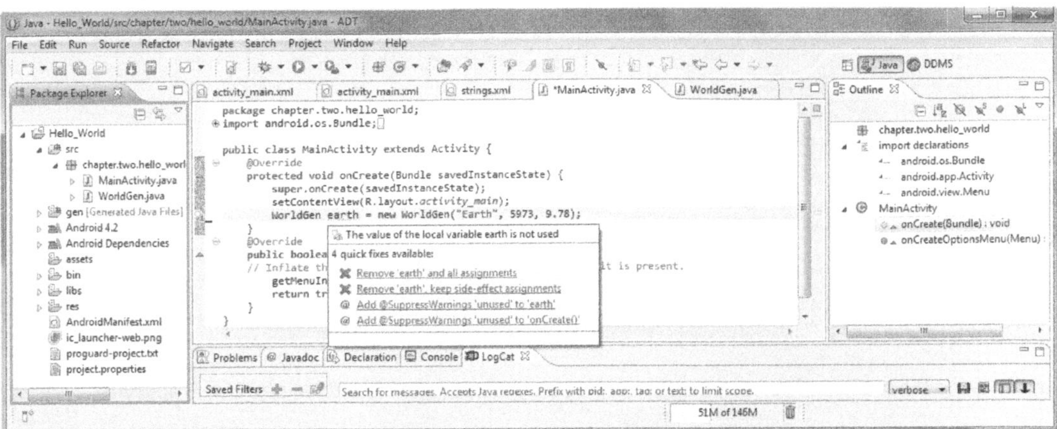

***Figure 3-5.** Adding Java code to our MainActivity class to generate a new World object via our WorldGen class*

Basically, this line of code should be read like this: I want to declare a **WorldGen** object named **earth** and it's going to be a **new** object and it needs to use the constructor method called **WorldGen** with these three parameters **("Earth", 5973, 9.78)** passed over to it, which are defined in its method.

Note in Figure 3-5 that after we type in our code to create the new **earth** WorldGen object, the word **earth** is underlined with a wavy yellow line. In Eclipse, this is a **warning** about that word in the code, and to have Eclipse tell you what it's warning you about, you can simply place the mouse over the underlined word, and up pops a yellow dialog that tells you what Eclipse thinks the problem is. This also works with the tiny yellow warning icon in the left margin of that line of code.

In this case, the warning reads: **The value of the local variable earth is not used** and this is because we have just declared it, and have not even had time to use our new earth object yet. So, in this case, we ignore the warning, and type in a second line of code that uses the earth object.

We will do this to show you how an object calls or **invokes** its methods, but also (just a little bit) we'll do this to get rid of that pesky little yellow warning icon and wavy underline in Eclipse. On the line right after we create our new earth WorldGen object, let's use this WorldGen object to invoke one of the WorldGen methods for adding Colonies to our world.

To invoke a method from or on an object, we utilize something called **dot notation**. In its simplest form, this notation takes the following format:

```
<Object Name>.<Method Name>(Method Parameter List)
```

In this case, we will add one new colony to the new WorldGen object earth, via a fairly simple line of Java code, which reads as follows:

```
earth.setPlanetColonies(1);
```

As you can see in Figure 3-6, this eliminates the Eclipse warning on the earth object declaration, because that object is now in use, creating new colonies via the setPlanetColonies() method. Whew! We now have clean code showing in our IDE. What a relief!

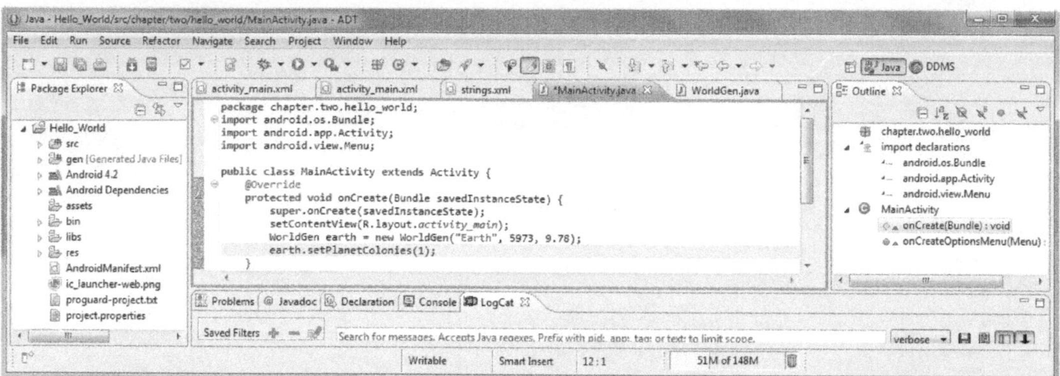

***Figure 3-6.** Invoking the setPlanetColonies() method on our newly created earth WorldGen object in Eclipse ADT*

Now let's utilize the other set attribute related methods to add in the other object configuration settings that will set up our new world with Colonies, Military Bases, Inhabitants, and Soldiers, as well as turning on the forcefield to protect the planet from external attack.

Add a line after the line that sets the planet colonies and type in the object name **earth** again. Notice that Eclipse underlines the line in red (because it is unused as yet), and that once you press the period character to add the dot notation attachment of a method call, Eclipse opens up a dialog containing all the methods, variables, and other calls that you can make from the earth object via dot notation.

This is shown in Figure 3-7, and is a pretty useful function, as Eclipse is now referencing your own code in its own user interface helper dialogs.

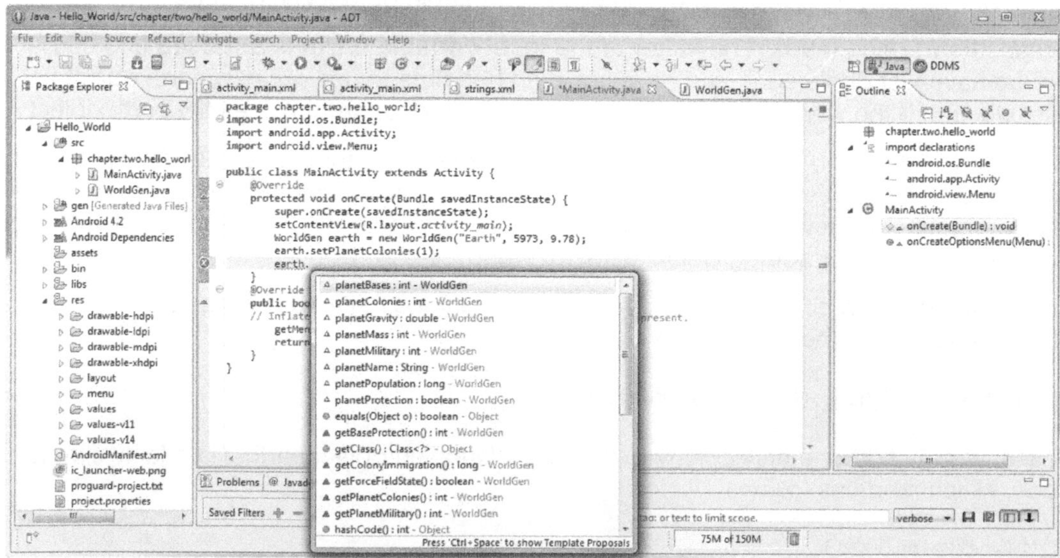

***Figure 3-7.** Using the Eclipse Object methods Helper Pop-Up to set our other new object characteristics*

Find the **setPlanetMilitary()** method in the list, and then double-click it to add it as the next object method call, and then enter a **1** inside of the parameter list parentheses to create (add) a new Military Base for the New World object.

Next, add another line after that one, and again type in the earth object name and a period character and then select the **setColonyImmigration()** method from the pop-up list that appears and set Immigration to **1000** immigrants.

Note that you can also simply type **earth.setColonyImmigration(1000);** and you can ignore the Eclipse supplied pop-up dialog entirely, as it disappears right after you start to type the method name that you want to reference via the object dot notation.

Next, let's bring in 100 Soldiers to staff the military base that we earlier added to our world object. On the next line down, type in: **earth.setBaseProtection(100);** or by type in **earth** and then a period and select the **setBaseProtection** method from the dialog.

Finally, add one more line after that, and turn on the planet's forcefield, using the **earth.setForceFieldOn();** object method call, so that our newly formed planet is now protected on the outside of its atmosphere.

Note that this last method call does not require any parameters to be passed over, so the parentheses are empty, and contain no value. That is because this method is a switch of sorts and simply by calling it, we are flipping the On switch for our planet's protective forcefield.

Figure 3-8 shows all our new Java code in the MainActivity class for creating our new WorldGen object, as well as for setting its methods in the Eclipse central editing pane (error free) once we've typed it all in.

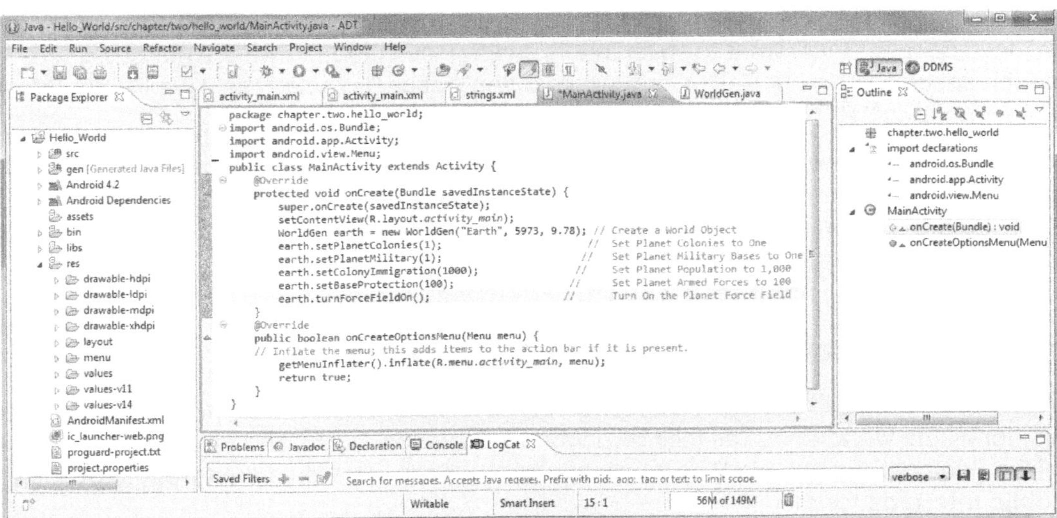

***Figure 3-8.** Java code in MainActivity.java to create a new WorldGen object named earth and call its set methods*

Comments, Warnings and Errors Inside of ADT Eclipse

Note in Figure 3-8 that we have also **commented** our Java code for creating our new WorldGen object using the **double forward slash** character sequence.

This is how we add single line comments after each line of code in Java, as you can see in the screen shot in Figure 3-8 of our final object instantiation code.

It is important to try and make your comment text as readable as possible, so try to line up your comments, and clearly separate them from your code. Make your comments as clean and concise as possible, in this way they will benefit other programmers who later try and read your code and decipher what it is that you are doing with it.

It is also important to notice that Eclipse colors your comments green to make them stand out to the viewer. Also notice that Eclipse colors other key Java code for readability as well, such as coloring Java keywords in purple, variable names in blue, and all other code in black.

Warnings are underlined using yellow and potential compiler errors are underlined in red. To see what Eclipse thinks may be wrong, mouse over the underlined text, or click the warning or error icons on either side of that line of code in the main Eclipse code editing central window pane.

Now that we've learned about Java objects, classes, methods, and variables, let's look at one final Java construct called an Interface that allows us to define our Java class for public use and define publicly its methods.

Creating a Java Interface for the Public: The IntWorldGen Interface

The final Java concept that I want to cover in this chapter, even though we are not going to implement it specifically in our Hello World Android application, is that of the Java **Public Interface**.

Java interfaces have lots of rules, and introduce some new concepts that we have not yet covered in this chapter, such as the **abstract** and **static** modifiers, so it's best to discuss interfaces last. Additionally, we will need to have all our methods coded before we develop public interfaces for any given class, and because we have now completed this, it works out well all the way around. What are interfaces used for, you might wonder.

What a Java Interface Does for Our WorldGen Class

If we were going to release our WorldGen Java class that we created within this chapter in its own package, for all the world to use as their own World Generation Toolkit and for creating their own customized personal Hello World Planet Creation applications, we would then want to define the Java **Public Interface** for them.

This Java **interface** would then define precisely how to interface with (what methods to use and how to utilize them) our WorldGen class. We will go ahead and actually do this in this part of the chapter, to show you how this is done, but we will not actually implement (add) these changes to our code that we wrote earlier in this chapter. This is because our WorldGen class was expressly written for our own Hello World Android application use and will not be released to the general public.

If you want to make these changes (make all the methods public, just like the constructor) to the code, and implement this interface, the code will still work, so you can do this as an additional exercise if you want to.

In Java, a **public interface** to a class is most often used to give users of your class a snapshot of all its methods as well as what types of data values these methods operate on (or with). This is done so that users know what your class methods do, and via what variable data types those things are done. The general format for coding a Java interface is as follows:

```
<Access Control Modifier List> interface <Interface Name> { ... }
```

All methods declared within an interface are **abstract** by definition, that is, they cannot be used directly, but must be subclassed to be used, which is what the **abstract** modifier signifies.

In a nutshell, **abstract** classes are classes which are written (meant) to be subclassed, but which cannot be used to create objects directly. To be able to create an object from an abstract class you subclass that abstract class, which makes it into a **concrete** class (as long as the subclass class is not declared with the abstract modifier before the word class within the subclass's class declaration). If we made WorldGen abstract like this:

```
public abstract class WorldGen { ... }
```

Then to create WorldGen objects we would have to subclass a concrete class from the now abstract WorldGen class, now designed as a WorldGen template:

```
public class WorldGenPlanets extends WorldGen { ... }
```

Notice the keyword **extends**, which is used to subclass WorldGenPlanets from WorldGen. Because there is no abstract modifier in WorldGenPlanets, it is a concrete class and as long as it implements all the WorldGen **superclass** methods, then it can be used to create WorldGenPlanet objects.

Because all **methods** declared within an interface are inherently abstract, they do not need to be declared as such using the Java abstract modifier. Similarly, because an interface is intended (again, inherently) to **expose** these methods to the public, the **public** access control modifier is also implicitly assumed, and thus also does not have to be explicitly declared.

Finally (no pun intended), all methods declared within a Java interface are inherently declared as **final**, so the Java **final** modifier also does not have to be explicitly included. The **final** modifier makes something, well, final, so that it cannot be modified later, kind of like a lock function.

A variable defined as **final** is essentially a **constant**, and is **initialized** one time only, and it is then fixed from that time onward. Any attempt to modify a final variable in your code triggers a compiler error (or an error notification inside of Eclipse before compile time). Final variables differ from constants in that a constant value is known at compile time, whereas a final variable's value might not be known at compile time.

Creating a Java Interface for Our WorldGen Class

A quick example of this would be as follows. Say that we had made our planetName, planetMass, and planetGravity instance variables for our WorldGen class set with the final modifier.

If we had set it up this way, then once these variables were set, via any given instance of our WorldGen() constructor method, those three instance variables would then be set as final; however, they would not be set as constant values at compile time, but instead they would be set at run-time by each creation of a unique WorldGen object via our public WorldGen() constructor method.

A class declared as final cannot be subclassed; examples of Java classes declared as final, so that they cannot be changed, are **java.lang.String** and **java.lang.System**. Thus, if we had declared our WorldGen class as:

```
public final class WorldGen { ... }
```

Then the code statement we made earlier on this page would not be allowed:

```
public class WorldGenPlanets extends WorldGen { ... } // This will generate an error!
```

A method declared as final cannot be **overridden** (that is, its code cannot be changed, replaced, or enhanced) in any subclass, essentially locking that method and its functionality, so that it cannot be changed later on.

The reason a method might be declared with a final modifier is because it probably contains some critical functionality that should not be changed for any number of reasons, including code stability, function preservation, or consistency maintenance. Needless to say, the final modifier is indeed a useful tool in the Java language for making sure that your code is used properly. In any event, just remember that all methods declared inside of a Java interface are inherently public, abstract, and final.

An interface for **WorldGen** as it exists currently would be coded like this:

```
public interface IntWorldGen {
        void setPlanetColonies(int numColonies);
        int  getPlanetColonies();
        void setPlanetMilitary(int numBases);
        int  getPlanetMilitary();
        void turnForceFieldOn();
        void turnForceFieldOff();
        boolean getForceFieldState();
        void setColonyImmigration(int numColonists);
        long getColonyImmigration();
        void setBaseProtection(int numForces);
        int  getBaseProtection();
}
```

Notice we don't need a constructor method in an interface definition, only methods are included. You **implement** a Java interface using this syntax:

```
public class WorldGen implements IntWorldGen { ... }
```

The **implements** keyword carries the constructor method for the class over to the new interface implementation with it, so, in this case, either class name or interface name can be used to create new objects, like this:

```
IntWorldGen earth = new IntWorldGen("Earth", 5793, 9.78);
```

Is the same thing as doing this:

```
WorldGen earth = new WorldGen("Earth", 5793, 9.78);
```

In other words, once WorldGen implements the IntWorldGen interface, both of these object instantiations will call the WorldGen constructor method.

Summary

In this chapter, we took a closer look at some of the more important Object Oriented Programming (OOP) concepts within the Java programming language. At the same time, to practice implementing these concepts within our Hello_World application code, we applied these concepts to create the **WorldGen** World Generation Class.

We can use this Java class to take our Hello_World Android application created in Chapter 2 to the next level, once we write some XML mark-up to add in some cool screen layouts, menus, text, buttons, user interface designs, graphic imagery, and animation over the next few chapters.

We first looked at the highest level Java construct, the **API** or the **Application Programming Interface**, and then we took a look at the Java **Package** and how it organizes our project code. We then looked at how packages in Android contain useful Android classes that we may want to **import** and leverage within our own Hello_World Android application, as well as other applications as we progress through this book.

Next we looked at the concept of the Java **object**, the foundation of OOP, and a central coding construct within the Java programming language. We learned that Java objects model real-world objects, complete with both attributes (instance variables) and functionality (methods).

The next logical step was for us to look at how we create Java objects using Java **classes**, which are code constructs that allow us to define instance variables and methods containing local variables.

Drilling down one more level into the class structure we looked at Java **methods**, and how these methods are created. We wrote a dozen methods, so that we now have a World Generation Toolkit for our Hello_World Android application. I hope you didn't assume that we were just going to do the run-of-the-mill print "Hello World!" on the screen Hello World app in this book, because we are actually going to do just the opposite and create the most awesome Hello World sample application implementation ever created!

After we learned a bit of Java OOP theory and lingo it was time to fire up Eclipse ADT and actually code our WorldGen class for real. We learned about how Eclipse flags warnings and errors for us in its IDE and how to mouse-over and mouse-click these to find out what Eclipse thinks is wrong with our code. We also learned how to have Eclipse collect our methods and variables for us when we type our object name and then press the period key, as well as how to comment our code for enhanced readability.

Finally, we took a look at Java public interfaces and how they define what methods should we use should we decide to implement an interface for any of our classes, which we will be doing with some of the Android classes later on in this book.

In the next chapter we will start building our screen layouts, menu, and user interface for our Hello_World Android application, but this time we'll be using XML mark-up code (for the most part) to define these elements.

Chapter 4

Layouts and Activities: Using ViewGroup Classes

Now that we have created the Java code in Chapter 3, which generates robust new worlds (WorldGen) for our Hello_World application, we need to start building the **front-end** for our Android application, what I like to call the **user interface design**.

The user interface (UI) design, as well as the user experience (UX), and the application content for that matter, is all delivered via the primary screen of the Android consumer electronics device that your target end-user or customer is using to view your Android application. User Experience (UX) is the sum total of the User Interface Design, its usability, and the perceived impact of the content.

In this chapter, we are going to take a closer look at the lowest level, indeed the **foundation**, for any screen design in Android. This is called the Android **Layout Container**, and it is implemented in Android using the **ViewGroup** class. The Android **ViewGroup** class is a subclass of the Android **View** class, which is itself a subclass of the Java **Object** class we learned about in Chapter 3. Luckily, we already understand Java class hierarchies.

I am again going to try to seamlessly meld two objectives in this chapter; enhancing our Hello World app again by adding layout containers and menus, and teaching you how to code menus and screen layouts using **XML** and all about Android **View** and **ViewGroup** class concepts at the same time.

We'll define a few different types of screen layout containers within our Hello_World app, and give each of them basic user interface elements for now, which later on, we will replace (upgrade) with more advanced user interface elements, graphics, video, and animation in Part 2 of the book. We'll also learn how to create Android **Activities**, which we'll use to hold our layout containers and to define logical areas in our Hello_World app.

Android Screen Layout Containers: The ViewGroup Class

In Android, screen layouts are created, defined, and organized via the Android **ViewGroup** class, which is subclassed from the more generalized **View** class. The View class must be imported into every Android application via the familiar **import android.view.View;** statement.

Because the Android **View** class manages our screen interface in every way, it ends up having a significant number of subclasses, and most of those **View** subclasses themselves have even more specialized subclasses, as you will be seeing in this chapter, as well as in the next chapter covering user interface design, and, in general, throughout the rest of this book.

Needless to say, Views are important in Android, as they provide an interface between your app and its end-users. The Android View package is used in the bootstrap (basic) Android application that is created in the New Android Application Project dialogs, because to use the screen for your app, you must have imported the View class to be able to do this.

The Android View class has a large number of specialized subclasses, many of which we discuss in greater detail in Chapter 5. This chapter is dedicated to one very special View subclass called **ViewGroup**, which allows View subclasses in the form of **Widget** subclasses (user interface elements) to be organized seamlessly.

ViewGroup is a subclass of `View` because the Android `View` class provides those top-level screen management characteristics (size, dimensions, orientation, and similar screen properties) as well as functionality (event processing, focus, etc.) that we will be covering in detail in Chapter 5.

The `ViewGroup` subclass adds in global screen layout attributes and methods that allow developers to define and fine-tune screen layout organization characteristics and top-level functionality.

Just like the Android View class provides higher-level attributes and functions to its `ViewGroup` subclass, the `ViewGroup` **base** class provides higher-level screen layout parameter attributes and screen layout creation functions for its own subclasses.

The reason that I mention this here is because the `ViewGroup` class is not used directly to implement any specific layout container in Android; it can thus be defined or classified as a **base** class to its many subclasses.

So, just remember that all the different types of screen layout container classes currently available to Android developers to create user interface designs under (with) are actually subclasses of the Android `ViewGroup` base class.

Android ViewGroup Subclasses: Layout Container Types

Android provides several mainstream layout container types as subclasses of the ViewGroup class. These classes are the ones that you will use in most of your projects, and are the ones which we will cover in this book.

These ViewGroup subclasses are named: **RelativeLayout** (default layout type, created in the New Android Application Project dialogs), **FrameLayout** (used for single item layouts), and **LinearLayout** (for user interface elements that need to conform to a row or column format, such as in-line button strips and top-down lists).

There are some other layout container types that are **deprecated**, and those we will not cover, because they have been discontinued. Deprecated means discontinued, but still supported (however not recommended) for use, so that older code that uses this deprecated code still functions. Deprecated layout containers in Android and the API Levels at the time that they were deprecated include **AbsoluteLayout** (Level 3) and **SlidingDrawer** (Level 17).

There are also some layout container types that are essentially the exact opposite of deprecated, that is, they are so new (API Level 13 and later) that they are not yet finished in their code implementation by Google, and by using them, you risk having to change your code later, when all the features are finally in place. Additionally, these only work in API Levels 13 through 17, and do not support API Levels 3 through 12, which legacy consumer electronics products still support. What we want to focus on in this book are layout containers that work across all Android devices.

API Level 13 (Honeycomb) and later layout containers include **Grid Layout**, **ViewPager,** and **PagerTitleStrip**, and we will not cover these.

Note that we also don't discuss the **FragmentBreadCrumbs** layout container, as its complexity is outside the scope of an introductory book on learning Android application development.

The first layout container that we look at is one of the most commonly used, and the Android OS default : the **RelativeLayout**. Because the `RelativeLayout` is already set up in your bootstrap Hello_World activity_main.xml file we'll go ahead and show you how to use it properly.

Relative Layout Positioning: The Android RelativeLayout Class

We will start with the **RelativeLayout** class, because that is the default layout container that the Eclipse ADT has set up for us in our New Android Application Project series of dialogs. We will use that and learn about RelativeLayouts first, as they are the most commonly used.

The `RelativeLayout` container is aptly named, as it arranges user interface elements (UI widgets, which are subclassed using the Android `View` class, which we will learn about in the next chapter) using **relative positioning**.

You will see how Relative Layouts are created, populated with parameters and then fine-tuned as we start coding our Hello_World app start-up screen user interface elements by using the Android XML mark-up language in the next section of this chapter.

We'll use our current **MainActivity** screen Activity as our start-up screen. Because we already have a "default" or initial Earth world defined, we'll use this on our application home screen to show our end-users where they are currently located–Earth. That way, we don't have to rewrite any code!

We'll also show you how to define a menu, so that you can call the other screen (Activity) definitions. We use different types of screen layout containers in those activities, so that you can learn how each is implemented. We cover menus in this chapter because the menu code was already written in Chapter 2, so it is logical to go ahead and implement our menus as early on as possible, so that you learn how to implement menus for your Activity screens. Besides, menus are a part of UI design, right?

Creating a Start-Up Screen: Defining Our RelativeLayout via XML

The first screen (Activity) layout container that we define is our Hello World application start-up screen, which was defined in Chapter 2. The Java code is located in the **MainActivity.java** and the XML mark-up is in the **activity_main.xml**, and as it currently exists, it is a RelativeLayout container with a Hello World! text message inside it.

We want to transmute this current start-up screen into an info chart of sorts showing our app end-user current attributes for the World on which the end-user is currently located. We use some Java code and XML mark-up changes (fairly minor ones). When the app first launches this is the Earth object we defined in Chapter 3. We are going to let our users travel between worlds, so we have to make this screen access **variable** content (rather than fixed text values) right from the get go, making it a bit more difficult. Let's design our screen output as follows:

```
Planet Name:           Earth          <planetName instance variable>
Planet Mass:           5,973 YG       <planetMass instance variable>
Planet Gravity:        9.78 m/s       <planetGravity instance variable>
Planet Colonies:       1              <planetColonies instance variable>
Planet Population:     1,000          <planetPopulation instance variable>
Planet Military:       100            <planetMilitary instance variable>
Planet Bases:          1              <planetBases instance variable>
Planet Forcefield:     On             <getForceFieldState() method call>
```

What this translates into inside our Relative Layout container is eight text fields (on the left) containing eight string **constants** and eight text fields on the right that access our WorldGen object methods and variables and that can be set via Java code when our user travels to another world.

Even though we cover user interface elements in detail in the next chapter, we will have to cover at least one View subclass (TextView) here to create this Current World Information start-up screen. So let's click our Eclipse Quick Launch Icon and get started!

Eclipse opens our Hello_World application exactly as we had it configured in Chapters 2 and 3. There should be edit tabs at the top already open for activity_main.xml (res/layout folder), activity_main.xml (res/menu folder), strings.xml (res/values folder), MainActivity.java (src/chapter.two.hello_world folder), and WorldGen.java (src/chapter.two.hello_world folder). Let's get started by clicking on the strings.xml edit tab.

Creating the String Constants for Our Start-Up Screen

Let's add our start-up screen info text label constants first, because our TextView widgets in our RelativeLayout container is going to access them. As you can see there are already string constants defined in this XML file for our App name (Hello_World) and Hello_World greeting message, as well as for one menu label (Settings) that we are going to change a bit later on.

Click the editing tab for **strings.xml** and add in **<string>** XML tags for the eight world info field labels that we defined earlier in this section. The XML tags should look like this and are also shown in Figure 4-1:

```
<string name="planet_name_label">Planet Name: </string>
<string name="planet_mass_label">Planet Mass: </string>
<string name="planet_gravity_label">Planet Gravity: </string>
```

```
<string name="planet_colonies_label">Planet Colonies: </string>
<string name="planet_population_label">Planet Population: </string>
<string name="planet_military_label">Planet Military: </string>
<string name="planet_bases_label">Planet Bases: </string>
<string name="planet_forcefield_label">Planet Forcefield: </string>
```

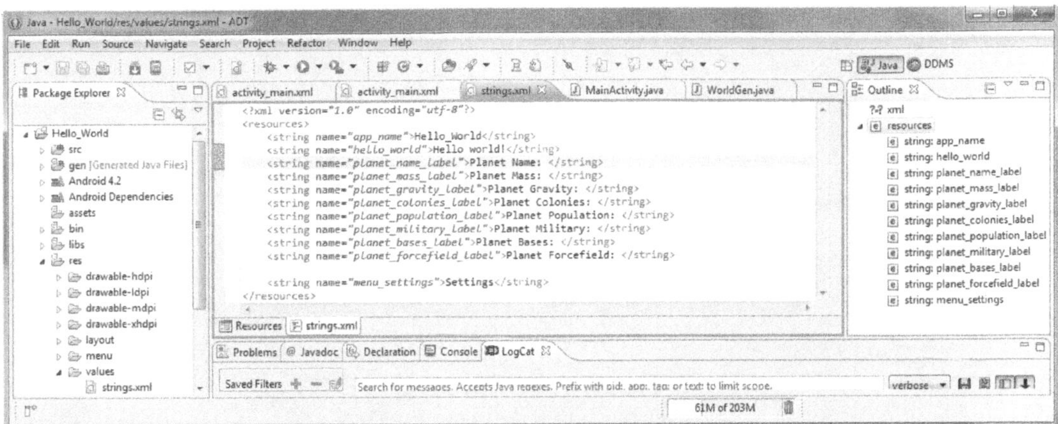

***Figure 4-1.** Adding our eight start-up screen text constants in the strings.xml file in Eclipse*

Note that we have added a space after each semicolon so that our variable data that we will add later on does not touch our label text constant. As programmers we must always be thinking ahead about UX issues such as this.

Adding Text to Our Start-Up Screen UI via <TextView>

Now click the **activity_main.xml** tab that holds the `RelativeLayout` XML container, the far left edit tab in Figure 4-1. We don't need (or want) to center any of these new TextView elements vertically or horizontally, so the first thing we will want to do is to remove those two XML parameters.

Next, let's add an **android:id** parameter to the first TextView UI element, right after the opening **<TextView>** tag. This way once we copy and paste in all of the TextView tags we can identify each of the TextView tags in our RelativeLayout by name, based on how we configure this first one.

This ID is also used so that we can reference each of the UI elements both from Java, as well as in our XML mark-up, and is done using the now familiar **android:id** XML parameter. The parameter is written like this:

```
android:id="@+id/textView1"
```

Finally, change the last parameter in the TextView, **android:text** to point to **@string/planet_name_label** that we created previously in our strings.xml file. The completed TextView UI element XML mark-up is shown in Figure 4-2.

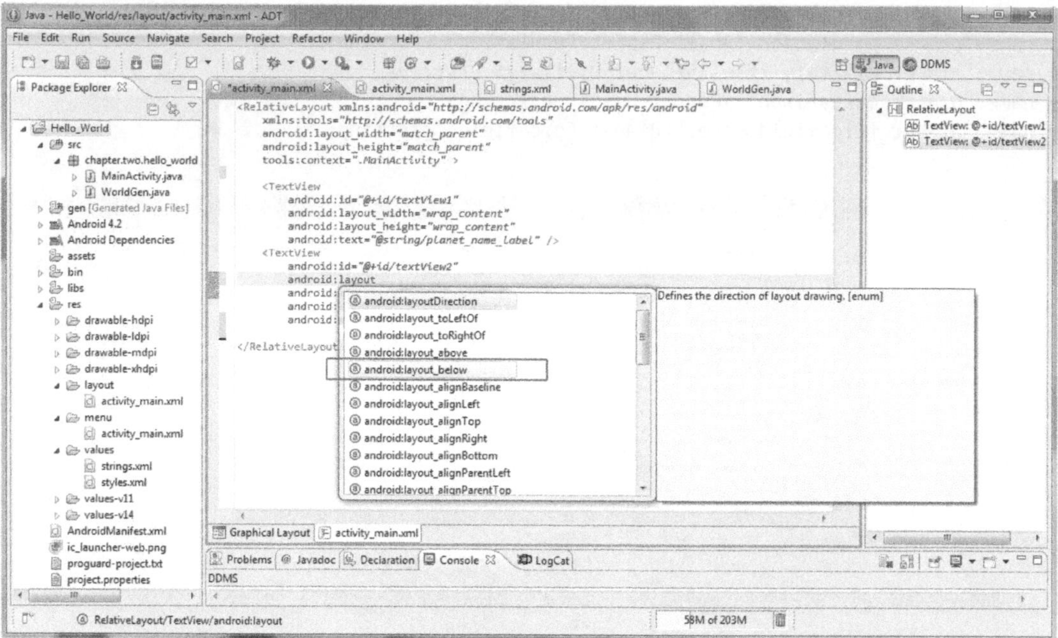

***Figure 4-2.** Adding TextView XML tag in Eclipse and configuring the Relative Layout Parameter via pop-up dialog*

Because there is only one UI element on our Activity screen, there is still no Relative Layout Positioning going on here, so let's copy and paste this first TextView UI element right underneath itself, so that we have two, and can then explore positioning them relative to each other.

Name the second one **textView2** by editing the **android:id** parameter, as shown in Figure 4-2, and then remember to change the tag's **android:text** parameter as well, to point to the **planet_mass_label** string constant that we defined in the strings.xml file in the values folder earlier.

Next, let's add our relative positioning parameter by adding a line under the android:id parameter and typing in the word **android**. Notice that right after you press the **colon** character that comes after the **android** part of the parameter name, and before the **layout** part of the parameter name, you trigger an Eclipse parameter helper dialog, as shown in Figure 4-2.

The XML parameter selector helper dialog always pops up with parameter suggestions, just like we observed in Chapter 2 after we pressed the period key when defining our Java objects.

After you press the colon key, continue typing the word **layout** and notice that as you type, Eclipse refines the contents of the pop-up helper, based on what it thinks that you are looking for, again shown in Figure 4-2.

After you have finished typing *android:layout* you then have listed all the possible relative layout parameters that can be used with the RelativeLayout container.

As you can see in Figure 4-2, there are about three dozen of them (there are one dozen showing and because the scroll bar is one-third the length of the height span I am estimating that times three) and you will need to select the fifth one down on this list.

Double-click the **android:layout_below** parameter to select it for usage (because we want our TextView UI elements to layout below each other). Once this relative layout parameter has been added to the Eclipse

XML editing pane, type inside the two quotation characters that are provided to you by the helper utility the **@+id/textView1** reference, which is a reference to the first TextView UI element located directly above it.

Note that if you were inside a **LinearLayout** container, for instance, this parameter pop-up helper dialog would contain parameters that were compatible with the **LinearLayout** type of Android Layout Container.

Next, we'll copy and paste six times this second TextView XML construct that we have created using the first TextView XML tag, so that we don't have to type all the TextView tags and their parameters six more times.

For each of the six copied TextView tags, let's edit the **@string** variable in each of the copied TextView tags' **android:text** parameter so that they match up with the final (last) six <string> tag constant names that we have defined previously inside our strings.xml file in the values folder.

Finally, let's edit the **android:layout_below** parameters for each of the six copied TextView tags, so each points to, or **references**, the **android:id** parameter of the TextView UI element that is directly above each of them.

The eight XML tags for our text label constants for our Hello_World app Start-Up screen are now defined inside our **activity_main** RelativeLayout XML container, and should look like the screen shown in Figure 4-3.

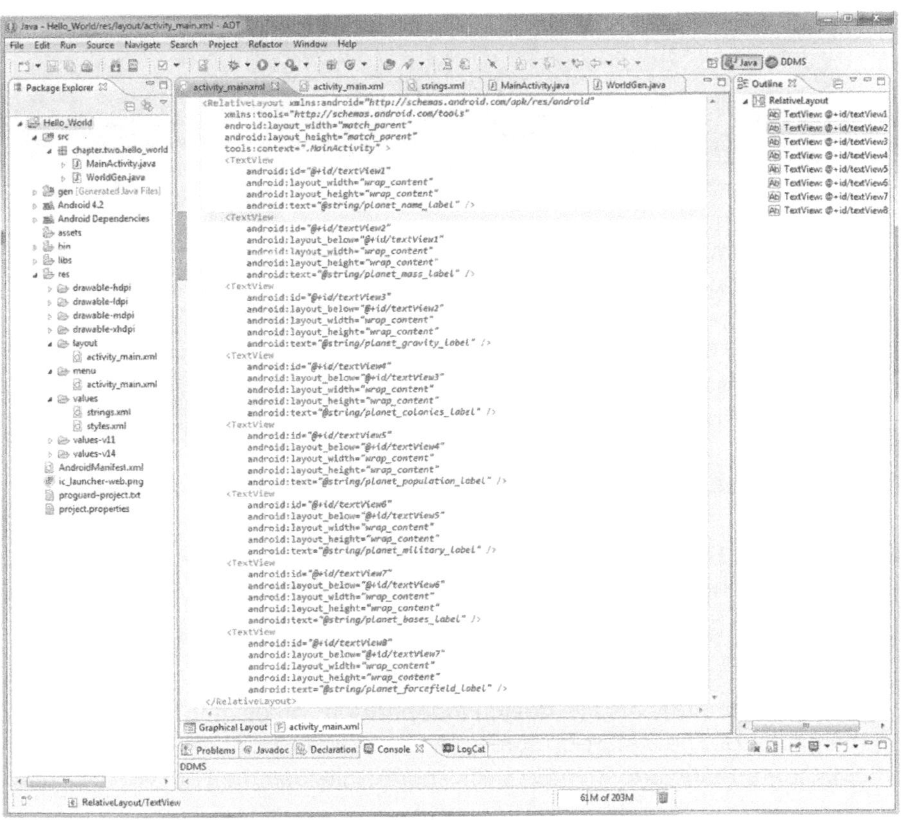

***Figure 4-3.** Our eight basic TextView XML tags with Relative Layout (layout_below) parameters configured*

Note that there are two different ways to close an XML tag. One way is to close each TextView tag with a **/>** symbol after the tag parameters. This is the way to close a tag that does not have any other tags **nested** inside of it.

The other way to close an XML tag in the case where there are other tags nested inside of the XML tag, is by closing the opening tag using just a **>** symbol, and then having the tag name ending with the /> symbol after any nested items inside of that tag. This is the case with our **<RelativeLayout>** tag here.

We can see these two different tag closing methodologies in action here, in Figure 4-3, with our current Relative Layout tag and the TextView tags that are now nested inside of it.

Now let's compile and run our Hello_World Android application, to see how our start-up screen looks thus far. Make sure that all the code you wrote is saved (you can use **CTRL-S** in any tab to **Save** at any time), and then you can right-click the project folder in the Package Explorer pane on the left, and then select the **Run As Android Application** menu option.

As you can see in Figure 4-4, the text labels for our start-up screen line up perfectly relative to each other, so our Relative Layout parameters are working well. The only thing we need to do to perfect our User Experience is to move our eight text labels a little bit to the right, so that they are not touching the left edge of the user's screen.

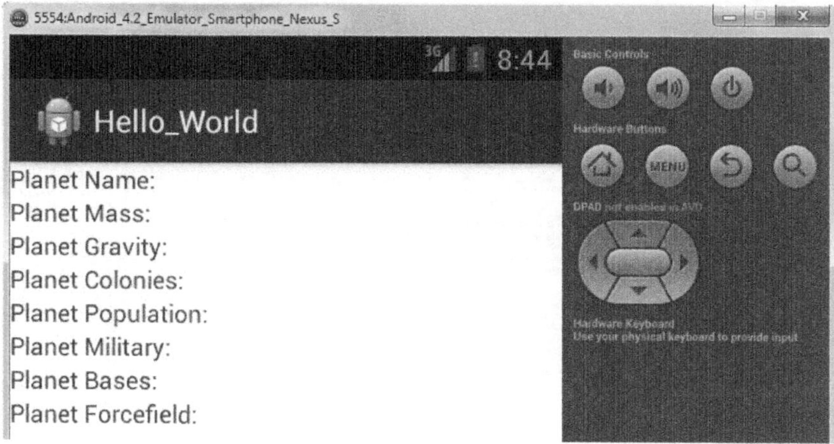

***Figure 4-4.** Running our RelativeLayout in the Nexus S Emulator, to see how relative positioning works*

We'll do this by using the RelativeLayout container left margin parameter **android:layout_marginLeft**. This requires we add a single line of XML mark-up to each of our eight TextView tags as follows:

```
android:layout_marginLeft="5dip"
```

This moves our text constant labels five **device independent pixels** (**DIP** or **DP**) to the right, creating a straight left margin for our new start-up screen. Add this line of XML mark-up to each TextView, right after the android:id parameter, and then to check your results use the **Run As Android App** command.

Adding Data to Our Start-Up Screen UI via <TextView>

Now we are ready to add the TextView UI elements that will hold the actual data values for our WorldGen object. We will use some new relative layout parameters that are similar to the ones we just used to complete the left half of this screen's user interface design.

Again let's take another shortcut and copy the first TextView tag, rename its ID from textView1 to **dataView1** and make some other changes to create our object data variable TextView user interface element tag, as follows:

```
<TextView
        android:id="@+id/dataView1"
        android:layout_toRightOf="@+id/textView1"
        android:layout_marginLeft="36dip"
        android:layout_width="wrap_content"
        android:layout_height="wrap_content"
        android:text="@string/planet_name_label" />
```

The first thing we've added is an **android:layout_toRightOf** parameter that tells us that this first TextView UI element that is going to hold our Planet Name variable data value is laid out **toRightOf** (to the right of) our first Planet Name label constant in our relative layout container.

The second thing that we need to modify is the **android:layout_marginLeft** parameter, which serves to push the variable data out, away from the label constant. For now, I left the **android:text** parameter in (we'll remove it later on in the work process), so that we can line up our variable data in a straight line in the middle of the screen so that it looks professional.

Let's push out the variable data text (using the Planet name "dummy" text for now) by setting the `marginLeft` to **36dip**, so that it is spaced out a little farther than the longest label constant (Planet Population) on the left side of the screen. This gives us a baseline for lining up the other variable data text UI elements. The XML code is shown in Figure 4-5.

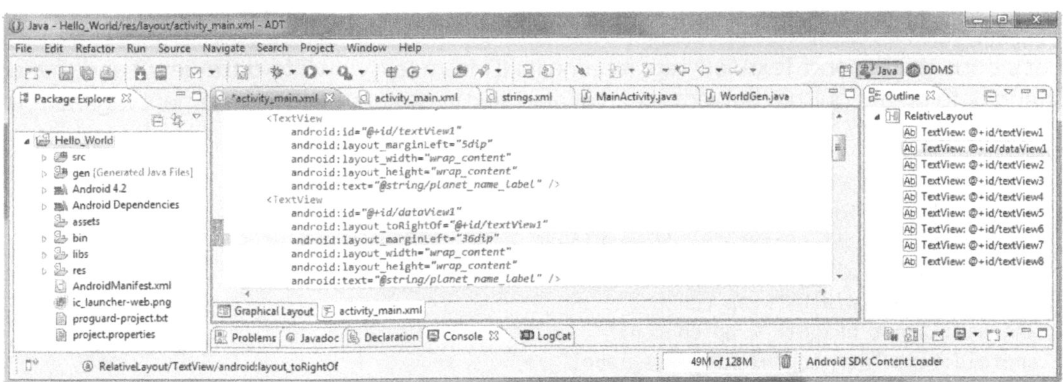

***Figure 4-5.** Adding our variable data TextView using the android:layout_toRightOf parameter*

Now I will show you exactly how I got to this 36 DIP setting value without using the **Run As Android App** (emulator) a bunch of consecutive times as I refined that parameter, as that work process can be very time consuming!

There is a new feature in the Eclipse XML mark-up editing pane called the **Graphical Layout Editor** (I often call it the **GLE**, for short) which can be accessed at the bottom left of the XML editing pane via a small tab, as shown circled in red in Figure 4-6.

Figure 4-6. Using the Eclipse Graphical Layout Editor to preview our Relative Layout parameter settings

Clicking on this GLE tab "renders" the XML code that you have written in a simulation of what the emulator is going to show you when you run that UI Design via your MainActivity Java code. Note that this GLE can also be used to write your XML code for you, using drag-and-drop features that you can see around its perimeter. Because we're all coders here, I'm going to approach this book strictly from a code writing standpoint, and use this GLE feature primarily as a short-cut for rendering design previews, to save on timely emulator launching cycles during our UI design process.

Again, let's copy the second TextView tag, rename its ID from textView2 to **dataView2** and make some other changes to create our next object data variable TextView user interface element tag, as follows:

```
<TextView
        android:id="@+id/dataView2"
        android:layout_toRightOf="@+id/textView2"
        android:layout_alignStart="@+id/dataView1"
        android:layout_alignBelow="@+id/dataView1"
        android:layout_width="wrap_content"
        android:layout_height="wrap_content"
        android:text="@string/planet_mass_label" />
```

We rename the **ID** to dataView2, make sure that it is **toRightOf** textView2, set the **alignBelow** parameter to be below dataView1, and also replace the **marginLeft** parameter with an **android:layout_alignStart** parameter.

This new relative layout parameter that we are using aligns the starting (pixel) location of a UI element, and we set it to reference the dataView1 that we just created, so that dataView1 and dataView2 line up perfectly.

For now, we leave the android:text reference set to the same planet mass string that we used in the textView2 tag, although later on we can remove it, as eventually our Java code will set this value, and we will not need it to check alignment (which is why we are leaving it in here for now).

Once we make these changes, shown in Figure 4-7, we can use dataView2 as a template and copy and change it slightly, to create dataViews 3 through 8.

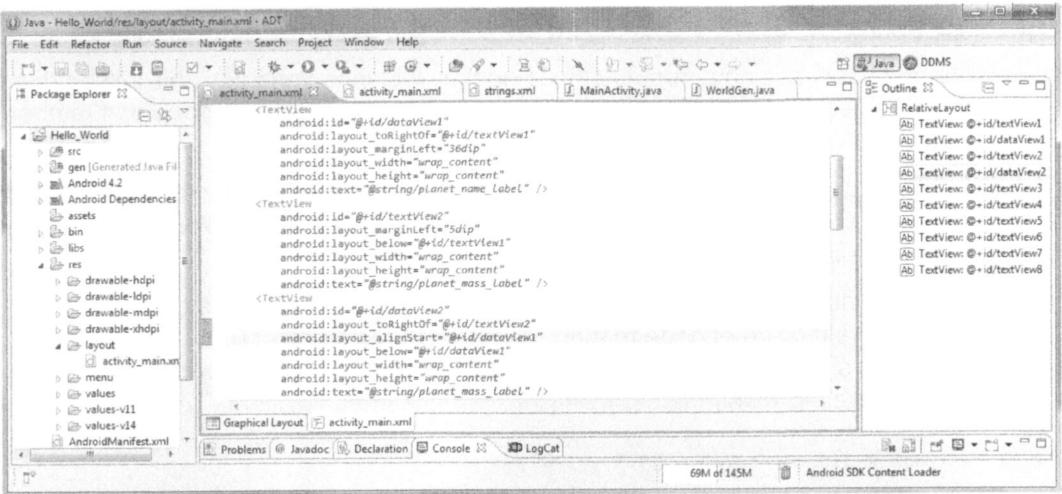

Figure 4-7. Using the android:layout_alignStart parameter to line dataView2 with the left side of dataView1

After we have copied and pasted in TextView tags for dataView3 through dataView8, we can click the Graphical Layout editor tab at the bottom of the screen and see our dummy text variables perfectly aligned, as shown in Figure 4-8.

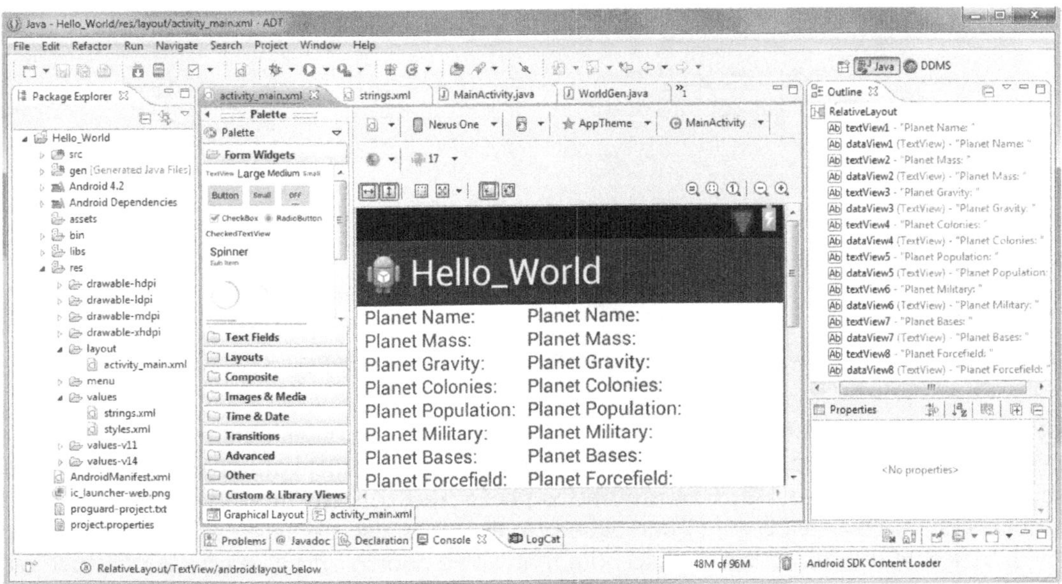

Figure 4-8. Dummy data text variables lined-up in Graphical Layout view using layout_alignStart parameter

Note that the only relative layout parameter we have any flexibility in changing its value for when we copy it is the **android:layout_alignStart** parameter. It can be set to reference dataView1 or the data view above it. I used the dataView above it, as it was just easier to add one to each number for each copy of the dataView tag from the previous one that I had copied. That was my work process for copying these dataView tags.

Writing Data into Our Start-Up Screen UI Using Java

Now we need to have our Java code replace these dummy instance variables (this will be done at runtime) with actual object variable data values. This requires that we write a couple of methods in our `MainActivity` class.

The first method we write will serve to consolidate our `onCreate()` method, by taking all that object creation code we put in there, back in Chapter 2, and creating a **setStartUpWorldValues()** method to set the values for our initial (default) world object and location in an orderly fashion.

Because we are also writing a **setStartUpScreenText()** method that accesses our `earth WorldGen` object, we need to move the line of code that creates our `WorldGen` object up to the top of our `MainActivity` class, as shown in Figure 4-9, so that all methods inside that class can access it. The line of Java code reads as follows:

```
WorldGen earth = new WorldGen("Earth", 5973, 9.78);
```

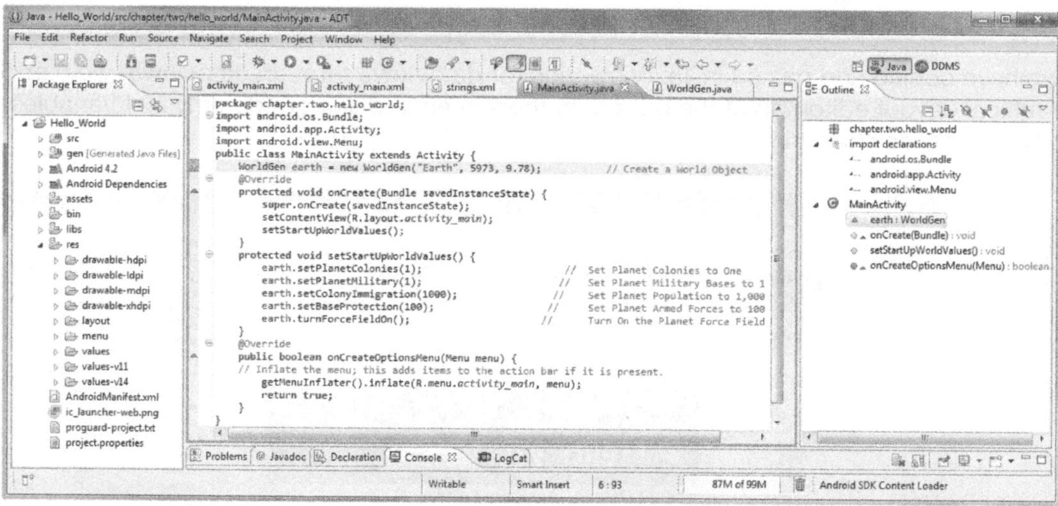

***Figure 4-9.** Rewriting the WorldGen object creation and configuration code as setStartUpWorldValues() method*

The rest of the `WorldGen` method calls that populate our `earth WorldGen` object with its instance variable data settings now go inside the curly braces for our **protected void setStartUpWorldValues()** method, as shown in Figure 4-9. This method is **protected** so that other methods in this class (and subclasses), such as `onCreate()` can access (call) it. It is also declared as **void** because it performs a task that returns no value. Also note that we've copied and aligned our comments along with the code.

Now it's time to write our second **setStartUpScreenText()** method, which will populate the dataView TextView UI elements with the data from our `WorldGen` object named **earth**. This requires two lines of Java code for each dataView TextView object; one to create, name and reference the TextView UI element and a second to set its **android:text** parameter value to the value of each earth WorldGen object instance variable data field.

To declare and name our first TextView object, we use this line of code:

```
TextView planetNameValue = (TextView)findViewById(R.id.dataView1);
```

This declares the object to be of type TextView, names it, and references it to the dataView1 tag that we designed in our activity_main.xml file.

Notice in Figure 4-10 that when we type in the TextView object type, that Eclipse uses a wavy red underline, and when we mouse-over the underlined object type to see why, Eclipse informs us that **TextView cannot be resolved to a type** and gives us some potential solutions, the most obvious of which is the first **Import TextView**, because we know from Chapter 2 that we have to import an object class before we utilize it inside of our own code.

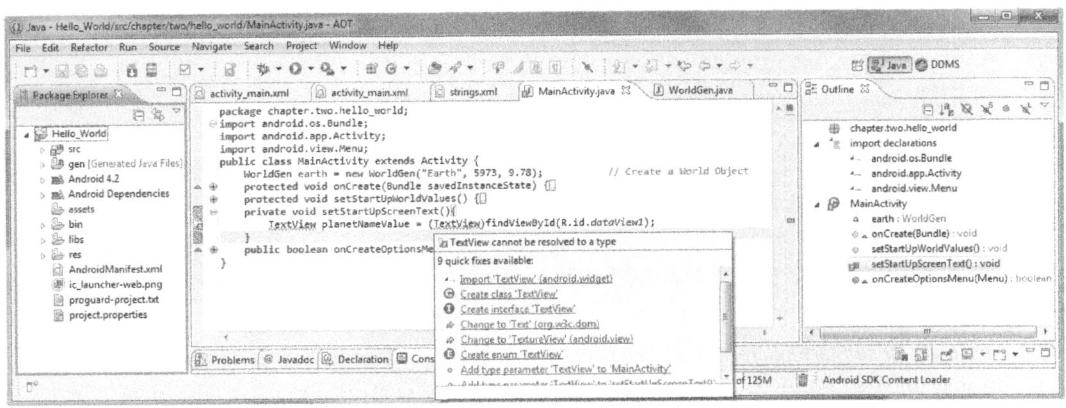

Figure 4-10. Coding a setStartUpScreenText() method and adding a dataView TextView and its import statement

So click the **Import TextView (android.widget package)** option, and let Eclipse write our import statement for you, and as you will see in Figure 4-11, it's now in place and ready for use.

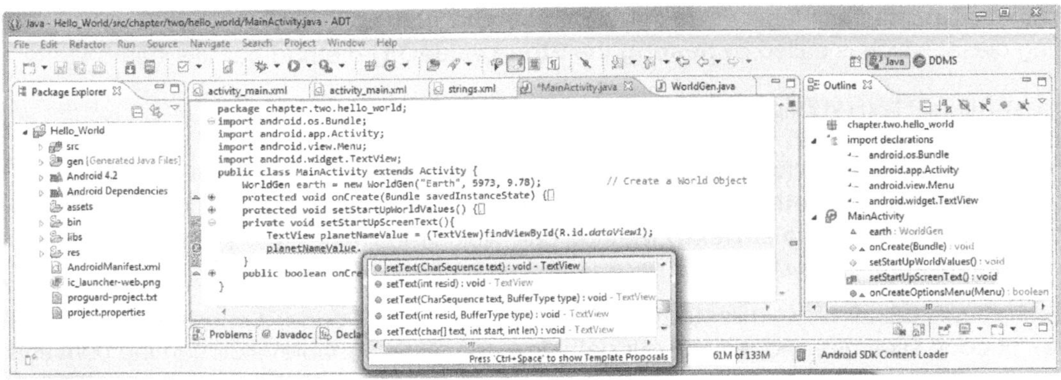

Figure 4-11. Using the Java .setText() method call to set our planetNameValue TextView object for dataView1

The second line of code we need to write takes the TextView object we just declared named **planetNameValue** and uses it to call one of the methods of the TextView class used to set text values. No surprises here, this method is called the **setText()** method. You will notice that after you type in the **planetNameValue** object name, and type the period character, that Eclipse will bring up its object method selection helper dialog shown in Figure 4-11. Scroll down to the **setText(CharSequence text)** method listed, and double-click it to add this dot call to this method to your object.

Enter a reference to the **earth.planetName** object and instance variable data value inside the parentheses for the method call as shown in Figure 4-12. Now let's code our second two lines of code for the planetMass data.

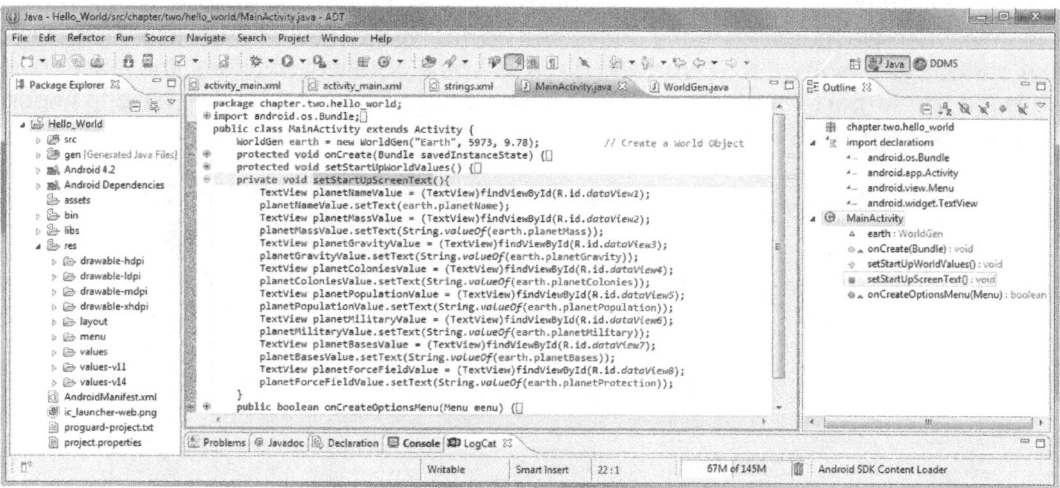

Figure 4-12. *Java code for setStartUpScreenText() that populates dataView UI elements with Earth object data*

Copy the TextView planetNameValue line of code, and change planetNameValue to **planetMassValue** and then reference **dataView2** instead of dataView1 in the **findViewById()** method call. Then copy the planetNameValue.setText() line of code and change the planetNameValue object name to match the planetMassValue object name created in the previous line of Java code.

Because planetMass is an integer data value, we will have to **nest** a method inside of our **.setText()** method that converts the integer value into a String value. This is done via the **.valueOf()** method of the String class, which is called by **nesting** the **String.valueOf()** method call like this:

```
planetMassValue.setText(String.valueOf(earth.planetMass));
```

This line of Java code nests two method calls, which passes the return value of the **String.valueOf(earth.planetMass)** method call, which converts the integer value to a String value, over to the **planetMassValue.setText()** method call, which requires a String value as input, all in one very compact (nested) code statement.

The next six lines are all very similar to these two, so let's take the coder's shortcut and copy the last two lines of code six times and replace our dataView and planetVariableValue naming conventions accordingly. The result of all this arduous Java coding work is shown in Figure 4-12.

Now let's run our Hello_World Android application in the Nexus S Emulator and see this start-up screen bear the fruits of our labor. Right-click on the Project folder, and select **Run As Android Application** and you will see that our XML and Java coding work has produced an impeccable app UI screen that creates a data information screen for the earth WorldGen object that we created earlier and that will serve as the initial Home World for our Hello_World application. This is shown in Figure 4-13.

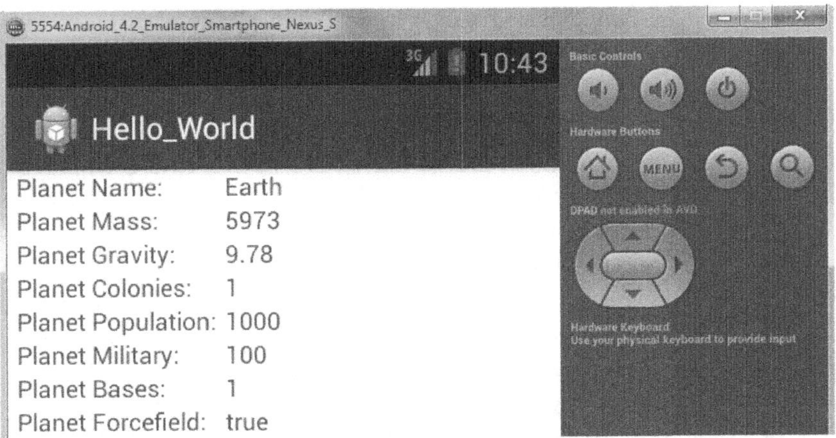

***Figure 4-13.** Running the Hello_World app with the dataView TextView UI elements populated with object data*

Next, let's add a menu system to the bottom of our Home (Start-Up) Screen!

Adding a Menu to Our Activity: The Menu Inflater and Menu XML

The first thing that we need to do is to define our start-up screen menu. Menus in Android usually have five or fewer entries, so let's pick five primary functions that we need to define layout screens (Activities) for later in this chapter. After all, this is the layout design chapter.

Our Hello_World planet generator will need to have screens that allow its users to select a new world, set its attributes, visit that planet (in times of peace), attack that planet (in times of war), and return to the Home (Start-Up) Screen that we'll call **Show Home Planet**, in case the user leaves planet Earth, and travels to one of the other planets they create.

Thus, the logical Start-Up (Home) Screen menu selections, along with what Java Activity, XML mark-up filename, and layout container type they would invoke (or call) when the menu item was selected, would be as follows:

```
Add a New Planet      Call NewActivity.java, activity_new.xml          RelativeLayout
Configure Planet      Call ConfigActivity.java, activity_config.xml    LinearLayout
Travel to Planet      Call TravelActivity.java, activity_travel.xml    FrameLayout
Attack on Planet      Call AttackActivity.java, activity_attack.xml    LinearLayout
Show Home Planet      Stay in MainActivity.java, activity_main.xml     RelativeLayout
```

Note that we have designed our menu **labels** to be evenly spaced (the text lines up nicely). This is so that our menu looks as attractive to our end-users as possible, enhancing our application's **user experience** or UX.

To add menu items to our MainActivity screen, we will use XML mark-up to define our menu items in a file named **activity_main.xml** that is located in the **menu** folder within our res (resources) folder. But, we already have an activity_main.xml file in the **layout** folder, you are thinking to yourself intelligently. That is correct; however, that file is in the **layout** folder and thus is a **different file** than the activity_main.xml file that is also in the **menu** folder, even though it has the exact same filename.

Each layout container XML definition and menu XML definition for each of your Activity screens should have the same filename, which is really very logical if you think about it for a bit, as each screen (Activity) in your application (if it is an advanced app) will have complex user interface or content elements (layout XML) defined, as well as menu selections (menu XML) defined, for each Activity (functional application area and screen).

Notice that I'm interchanging these screen/Activity terms, at least for a little while, so that you will get used to the lingo of Android. Before we show you how to code separate Activity classes for these screens our menu is going to call, let's modify the current activity_main.xml file that the New Android Application Project series of dialogs created for us, so that it contains our five menu labels, instead of just the one Settings label.

You should still have the menu folder version of activity_main.xml open in your Eclipse IDE from our work in Chapter 2, if it's not open in the IDE, simply open the menu folder and right-click the activity_main.xml file and select the **Open** option from the context-sensitive menu. Then click on that XML edit tab, and copy the <item> tag four more times, to create our five item menu. Before we copy the existing <item> tag, let's first edit it so it matches up with our first menu item that we designed previously.

Change the **android:id** from menu_settings to **menu_add** and the **android:title** to **menu_add_planet** and then copy the <item> tag four times underneath the first tag. Change the android:id parameters for menu_add to: menu_config, menu_travel, menu_attack, and menu_home, respectively.

Then change the **android:orderInCategory** values to: 200, 300, 400 and 500, and **android:title** parameters to: menu_config_planet, menu_travel_planet, menu_attack_planet, and menu_home_planet, respectively.

Each <item> tag should thus have the same basic format, as follows:

```
<item android:id="@+id/menu_function"
        android:orderInCategory="Number Value for Order in Menu"
        android:showAsAction="never"
        android:title="@string/menu_string_constant" />
```

The result of this work process is shown in the final XML menu mark-up in Figure 4-14.

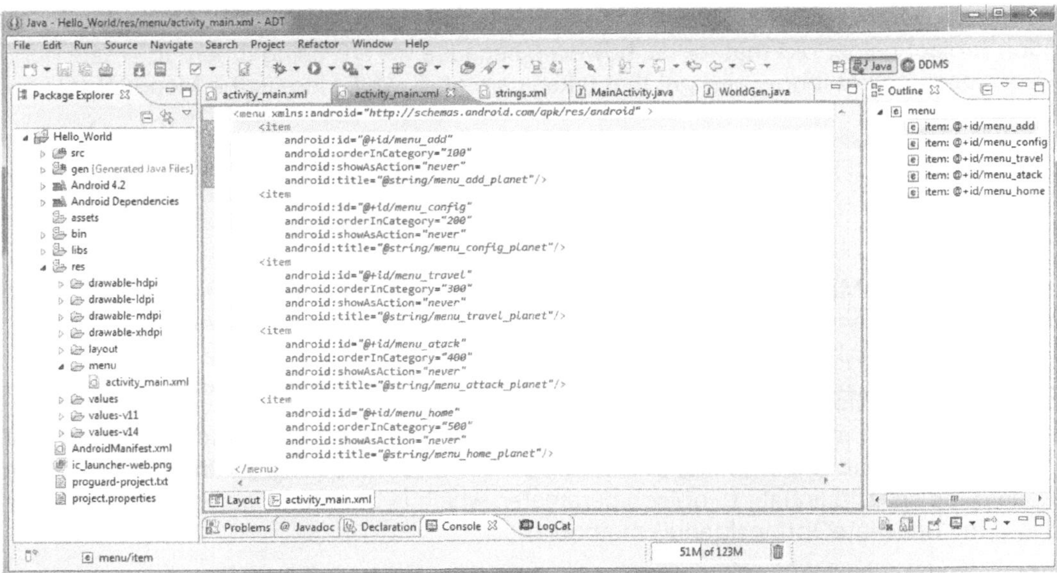

***Figure 4-14.** Adding our five menu items to the existing activity_main.xml menu definition file in the menu folder*

Now we need to add the menu label text constants to our strings.xml file, so click the strings.xml tab at the top of Eclipse next, and edit the tag that is there already for the <string> named menu_settings to turn it into a **menu_add_planet** <string> tag with the label value: **Add a New Planet.**

Once you have done that, copy that <string> tag four times, and edit the <string> tags to create four new menu_config_planet, menu_travel_planet, menu_attack_planet and menu_home_planet string constants, as shown in Figure 4-15. Each <string> tag should follow this same basic format:

```
<string name="menu_add_planet">Add a New Planet</string>
```

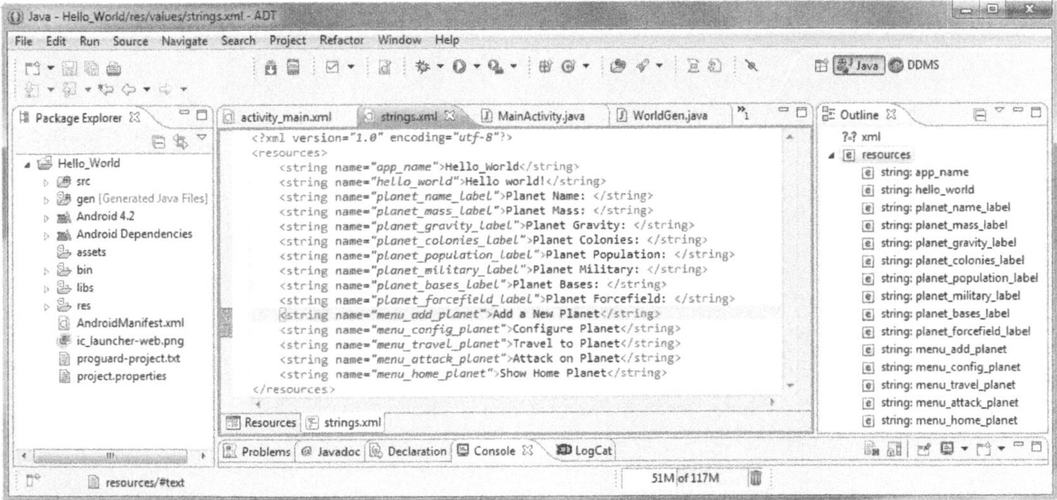

***Figure 4-15.** Adding our five menu label string constants to the strings.xml file in the values folder*

We don't need to write the Menu Inflater code to create the menu, because the New Android Application Project helper did that for us, however, because we are using it here to create our menu, let's take a closer look at it now and get that taken care of as well. Here is the Menu Inflater code:

```
public boolean onCreateOptionsMenu(Menu menu) {
        getMenuInflater().inflate(R.menu.activity_main, menu);
        return true;
}
```

The **onCreateOptionsMenu()** method is part of the Android Activity class, and it is used to create the **options menu** for any given Activity. In this particular case, it is our **MainActivity** subclass of **android.app.Activity**, which is imported at the top of our MainActivity.java file.

This method passes a Menu object named menu into the method, where it is populated with your menu XML parameters via an **inflate()** method, which references your **\resource\menu\activity_main.xml** file via the first (inflate from) parameter in the method of **R.menu.activity_main** and then inflates that data into the second (inflate to object) parameter, which is the **menu** object declared and passed into the onCreateOptionsMenu() method.

The **getMenuInflater()** method calls the inflate() method and uses it to populate the MenuInflater object for the Activity. The **MenuInflater** class is a member of the android.view package (**android.view.MenuInflater**) and it takes your menu XML definition and **instantiates** the inflated **menu** object using those **<menu>** and **<item>** tags and their parameters.

Once the **getMenuInflater().inflate()** process has been completed without any failures, the **onCreateOptionsMenu()** method exits, and returns a **true** value, which signifies that a menu resource has been properly implemented.

We can now right-click our project folder and select the **Run As Android Application** command to compile and run our Java and XML code. Let's take a look at how our menu looks in action in the emulator shown in Figure 4-16.

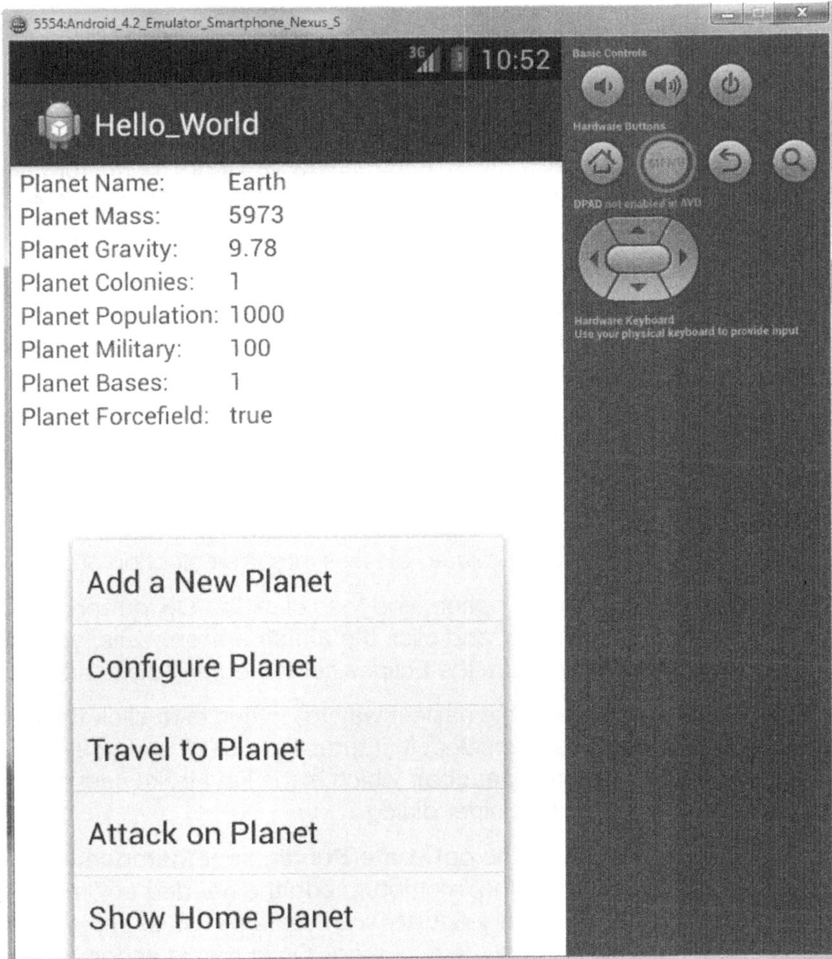

Figure 4-16. Main Activity start-up screen with a functioning menu

Before we can actually implement these menu options in our Java code, we need to create the layout containers (via XML mark-up) and activities (via Java code) for each of them. This is because selecting each of these menu items switches the application into each of these activities.

So let's create four new Activity Java classes, each with their own custom Layout Container XML definitions, for the first four menu options shown in Figure 4-16 that encompass the major functional areas of our Hello_World Android application.

These new Activities and their layout containers give us plenty of application function screens to work with over the next few chapters in the book, where we will be learning about events, intents, UI widgets, graphics design, and animation in Android.

Defining the Add a New Planet Screen: Creating Android Activities

The first thing we need to do is create a **NewPlanet** class for our Add a New Planet menu item, so right-click your Hello_World project folder and select the **New ➤ Class** menu item. We will use the same work process as we did when we created our WorldGen class in Chapter 2, except this time, we will be subclassing the **android.app.Activity** class, because we are creating an Activity, and not a World Object Generator.

The primary difference in these two types of classes is that an Activity class does not have a constructor method, whereas a class that generates objects would. This is because Activities are not generated at runtime, and need to be defined in the AndroidManifest.xml file.

In the **New Java Class** dialog click the **Browse . . .** button located next to the **Package** field. Select the **chapter.two.hello_world** package, and then enter **NewPlanet** into the **Name:** field to name our new Activity class. This Activity class is named after what it will allow our end-user to add in a new planet.

Next click the **Browse . . .** button next to the **Superclass** field and type **Activity** (typing just **Act** gets the same results) to bring up all the Activity-related classes into the selection area.

Select the **Activity - android.app** package option, and then click the **OK** button. Leave the other default settings as they are set in the dialog, and click the **Finish** button. Voila, your **NewPlanet.java** class is created and opened for editing inside the Eclipse central editing pane area.

Next, we add an **onCreate()** method, and the easiest way to do this is to click the blank line in the new class (between the two curly braces) to select it (it turns light blue) and hold down the **Control** (Ctrl) key and at the same time press the **Spacebar,** which is the keystroke sequence needed to bring up the Eclipse ADT method selector helper dialog.

Scroll down halfway in the dialog and find the **onCreate(Bundle saveInstanceState) : void** method, as shown in Figure 4-17, and double-click that method to add the needed onCreate() method into our NewPlanet (class) Activity subclass. Every Activity you create needs to implement an onCreate() method so that it can create the Activity in system memory. Once that is accomplished, you can then define an area with which to view your application content, which we will do next.

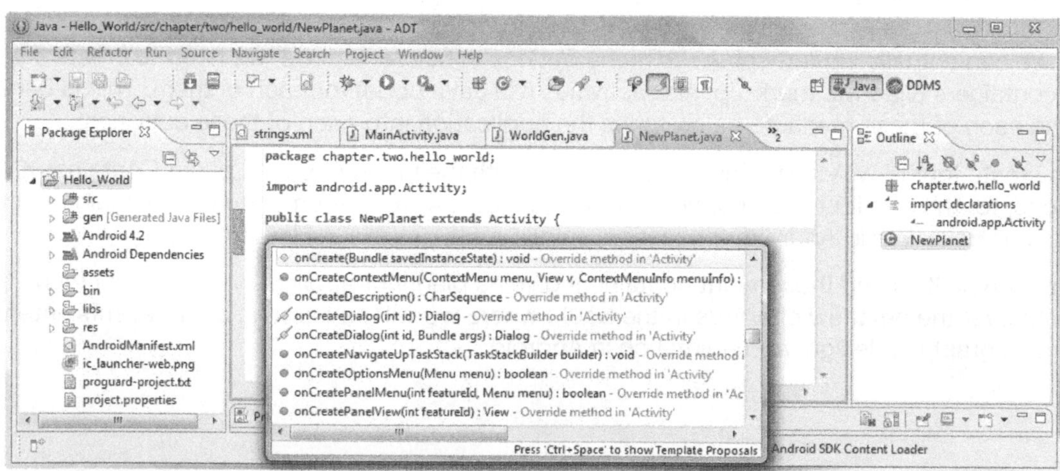

Figure 4-17. The Control-Spacebar keystroke sequence invokes the method selector helper dialog

After the **super.onCreate()** method call, we need to add a line that calls the **setContentView()** method, similar to what is in our MainActivity.java file. In fact, you can take the programmer's shortcut and cut and paste that line of code, and then modify it to reference the **activity_add.xml** file that we are going to create next. The code should read as follows:

```
setContentView(R.layout.activity_add);
```

Notice that when you do this that Eclipse uses a wavy red underline to flag the **activity_add** reference, as shown in Figure 4-18, and we already know that this is because the referenced file does not exist yet, so we ignore the error for now, because we are about to create that layout XML file as the next step in this Activity creation work process.

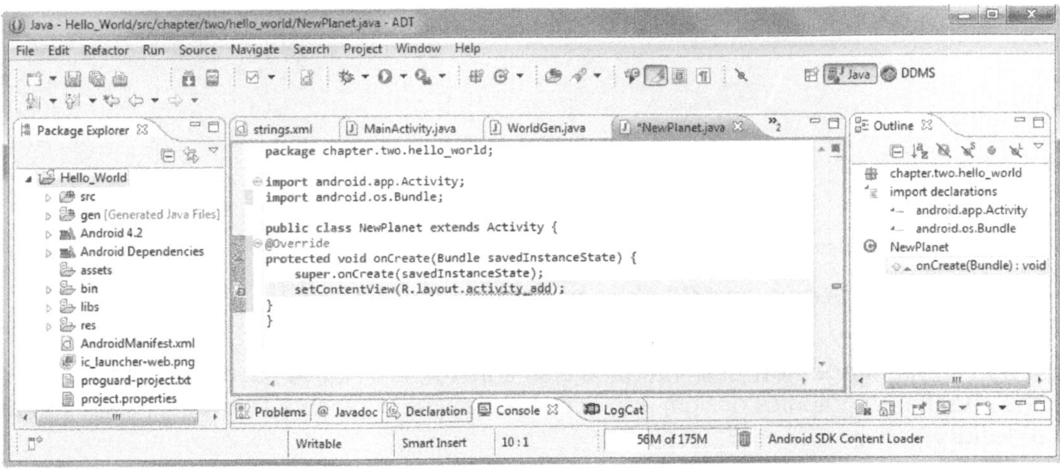

***Figure 4-18.** Adding the setContentView() method call and reference to a not yet created activity_add.xml file*

Right-click the Hello_World project folder a second time in the Package Explorer, and then select the **New ➤ Android XML File** menu option. Select the Layout XML type from the drop-down (if it's not set that way already) and specify the **Hello_World** Project. Next add the **activity_add** file name (first part only, the dialog adds the .xml extension for you) that we are going to use, and select the **RelativeLayout** layout type from the selection area in the center of the dialog, as shown in Figure 4-19. Then click the **Finish** button and to create the XML file in the layout folder and opened for you in the central editing pane of Eclipse.

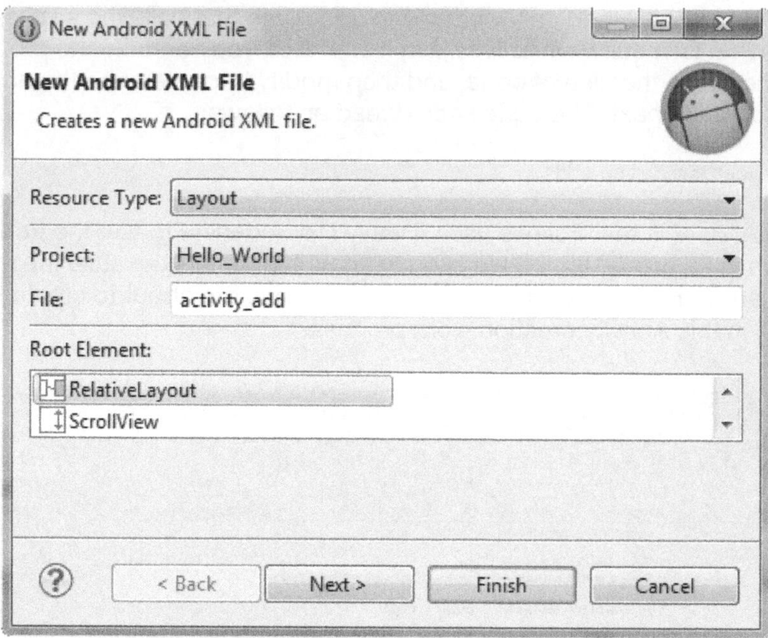

***Figure 4-19.** Creating a RelativeLayout layout XML file via the New Android XML File dialog*

Now let's add some **ImageView** user interface elements to the Relative Layout container, so we can later (in the chapter on graphics design) add in some pictures of planets as a visual selection user interface design.

This time we are going to use the Graphical Layout Editor (GLE) to add the first **<ImageView>** tag, just so that you can see how its drag and drop functions work. Because this is a book for programmers, we are not going to leverage the GLE as much as we would in a book from the Apress Absolute Beginners' series on how to create Android apps, but you should see how it works, just in case you want to use it in your own work process sometime (other than as an XML code previewing tool or shortcut).

Click the tab to the lower left of the central edit pane and select the Graphical Layout Editor mode. Find and click the **Images & Media** drawer on the left, so that we can access the **ImageView** user interface elements, or **widgets**, which we will be learning about in greater detail in future UI Design Chapter 6. Grab the ImageView, as shown in Figure 4-20, and drag it onto the simulated application screen and drop it near the center.

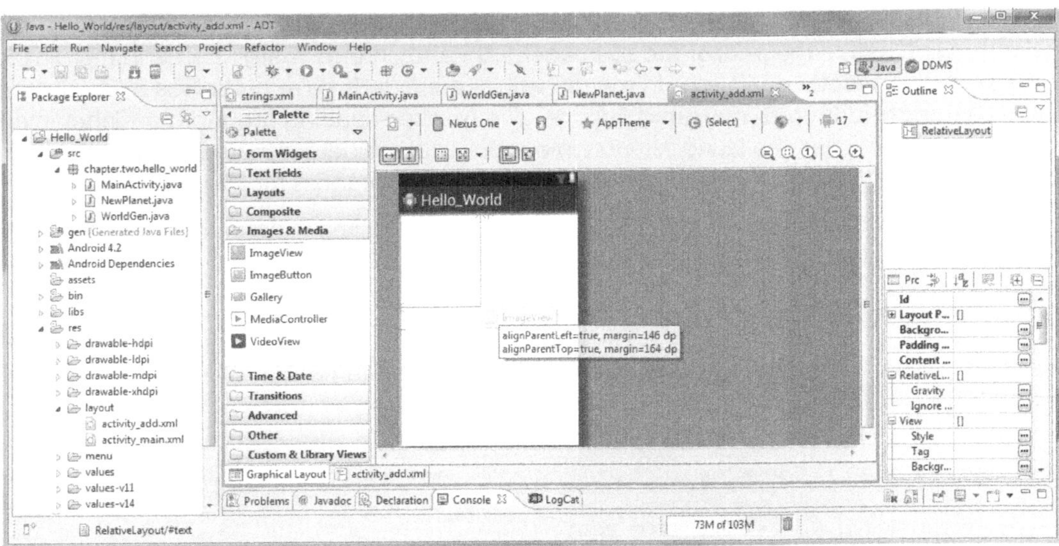

Figure 4-20. Using the Graphical Layout editor pane to create the initial ImageView tag and parameters

Notice that during the drag-and-drop operation that a tool-tip gives you parameter and positioning information in real-time, as you drag your UI element around the screen. Be sure to play around and experiment with this feature, as it is an excellent learning tool to see what parameters are available. After you drop the ImageView UI element, click the XML editing tab (labeled activity_add.xml) at the bottom of the screen and see the XML code that was generated for you. It should look something like this:

```
<?xml version="1.0" encoding="utf-8"?>
<RelativeLayout xmlns:android="http://schemas.android.com/apk/res/android"
  android:layout_width="match_parent" android:layout_height="match_parent" >
    <ImageView
        android:id="@+id/imageView1"
        android:layout_width="wrap_content"
        android:layout_height="wrap_content"
        android:layout_alignParentLeft="true"
        android:layout_alignParentTop="true"
        android:layout_marginLeft="146dp"
        android:layout_marginTop="164dp"
        android:src="@drawable/ic_launcher" />
</RelativeLayout>
```

Notice that the ImageView tag is underlined with a wavy yellow line, and if you mouse-over it, it will tell you that you are missing a content description tag, which Android wants to see included to help the disabled. Add a new line and type in android and then a colon and find the **android:contentDescription** parameter in the dialog that pops up. The XML mark-up should look something like this with a string variable referenced:

```
android:contentDescription="@string/content_desc_earth"
```

Next, let's make a few minor changes to this ImageView tag, before we copy it to create our six world selector UI. Change the **android:id** to imageEarth, and change marginLeft and marginTop to a 5dp (or 5dip) value. In fact, because both margin values are 5, let's save ourselves a line of mark-up and simply use **android:layout_margin="5dp"** to give us even spacing around our planet images. Notice, for now, that we use the launcher icon in our drawable folder as a **placeholder graphic** until we create our different world images in the graphic design Chapter 6 a bit later on.

Because we reference content description strings for the sight-impaired in our ImageView tags, let's add our six planet content description strings next, and get that over with. The format for each <string> tag is

```
<string name="content_desc_planet">Planet Name</string>
```

Let's use the six most common planet names for our string constants: Earth, Mars, Venus, Jupiter, Saturn, and Neptune. See Figure 4-21.

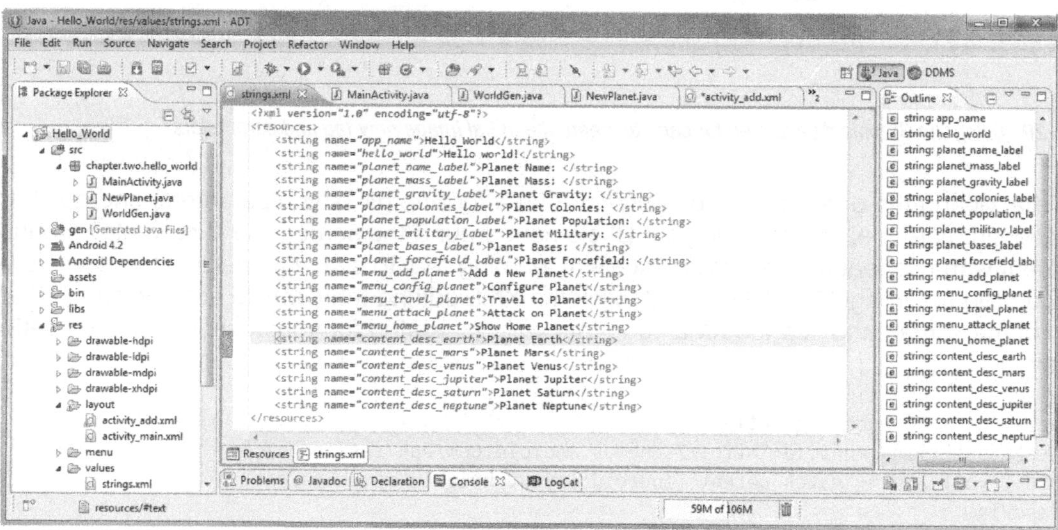

Figure 4-21. Adding the six planet content description string tags to our strings.xml file in the values folder

Now copy the first ImageView tag and paste it underneath, and change the ID to **imageMars.** Let's also remove the alignParentLeft and alignParentTop, as these are only needed for the top-left ImageView, to make sure that the alignment for this RelativeLayout starts in the top-left corner of the layout (the Parent container). Next, let's add an **android:align_toRightOf** parameter that references the imageEarth ID, because we want the second ImageView aligned right next to (to the right of) the first one. Also change the contentDescription to reference the **@string/content_desc_mars.**

Copy the second ImageView tag and paste it underneath again. Next change the ID to **imageVenus** and change the layout_toRightOf parameter to **layout_below** and reference the imageEarth ID, because we want the third ImageView to be aligned below (underneath) the first ImageView. Also, remember to change the contentDescription tag to reference **@string/content_desc_venus.**

Copy the third ImageView tag and paste it underneath again. Change the ID to **imageJupiter** and the layout_below parameter to reference imageMars and add an **android:layout_toRightOf** parameter referencing **imageVenus**, so that imageJupiter is below imageMars and to the right of imageVenus. Edit the contentDescription to point to **@string/content_desc_jupiter** as well.

The first <ImageView> tag aligns itself relative to the parent container and its XML mark-up code would look like the following:

```
<ImageView android:id="@+id/imageEarth"
        android:layout_width="wrap_content"
        android:layout_height="wrap_content"
        android:layout_alignParentLeft="true"
        android:layout_alignParentTop="true"
        android:layout_margin="5dp"
        android:contentDescription="@string/content_desc_earth"
        android:src="@drawable/ic_launcher" />
```

Note that once you copy this XML mark-up to create the other needed five <ImageView> tags, that you will have to change certain **android:layout** parameters to align each ImageView UI element properly, relative to the other UI elements that are around it. This is shown in Figure 4-22.

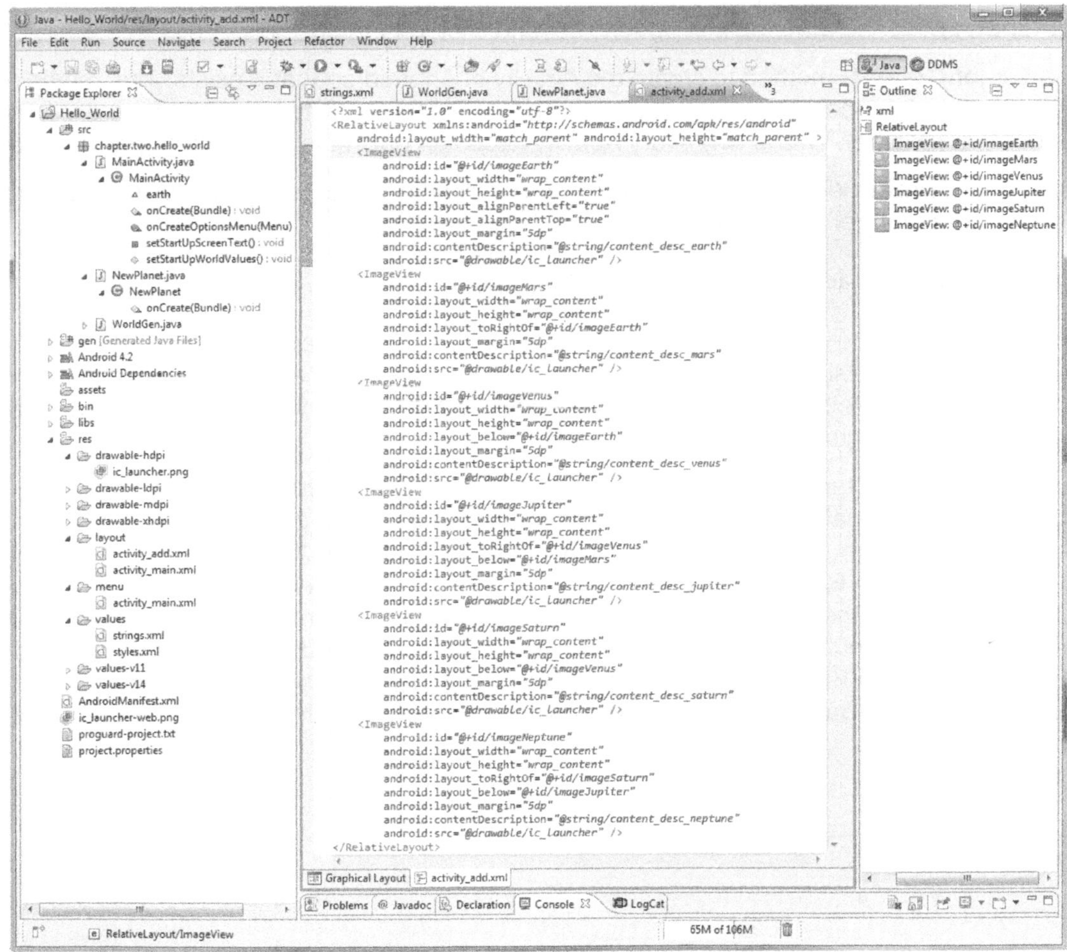

***Figure 4-22.** RelativeLayout XML mark-up to define Add a New Planet screen user interface with placeholder graphic*

Finally, copy the last two ImageView tags for imageVenus and imageJupiter, and paste them underneath imageJupiter and change their IDs to imageSaturn and imageNeptune respectively. Change their contentDescription references to **content_desc_saturn** and **content_desc_neptune**, and their layout_below parameters to reference imageVenus and imageJupiter, respectively. Make sure that the imageNeptune ImageView also has an **android:layout_toRightOf** parameter, which forces it to align to the right of imageSaturn. The six completed ImageView tags are shown in Figure 4-22.

Defining the Configure Planet Activity: The LinearLayout Container

Next, we are going to create our Configure Planet UI screen, which involves creating another Activity subclass called **ConfigActivity.java** with a LinearLayout container defined in an **activity_config.xml** file. Because you have already done this once before I will forego the screenshots and figures as you can reference the previous section for those if needed.

First, right-click the Hello_World project folder and select **New ➤ Class** and create a Java class for the chapter.two.hello_world package that subclasses android.app.Activity and is named **ConfigPlanet**. Leave the other default options set and click on **Finish**.

Next, add an **onCreate()** method to create the Activity in Android so that it exists. This method is called when you reference (access) the Activity, and creates the Activity in system memory (allocates memory for it at runtime). This is why every Activity needs an onCreate() method **implemented**.

Next, add a **setContentView()** method that references **activity_config.xml** that we create next to hold our LinearLayout definition, like this:

```
setContentView(R.layout.activity_config);
```

Next, right-click the Hello_World project folder again and select the New ➤ Android XML file and create a LinearLayout XML file to define the LinearLayout user interface design. Select resource type: **Layout**, project: **Hello_World**, filename: **activity_config**, and root element: **LinearLayout** in this dialog (reference Figure 4-19) and click **Finish**.

Next, add some Button tags inside of our LinearLayout container, so you can see what a LinearLayout does. In a later chapter 5, we'll wire these up so that they perform the tasks they are supposed to, but for now, we are just going to be concerned with the XML layout file definition. Click on the Graphical Layout Editor tab at the bottom of the XML editing pane (the **activity_config.xml** tab should be active at the top of the pane), and drag a **Button** UI element out of the **Form Widgets** drawer and onto the simulated app screen. Then switch to the XML editing pane and change the **android:id** value for the Button tag to **coloniesButton** and then the **android:text** parameter to reference the **@strings/button_name_colonies** value which we will create next. This can be seen in Figure 4-23.

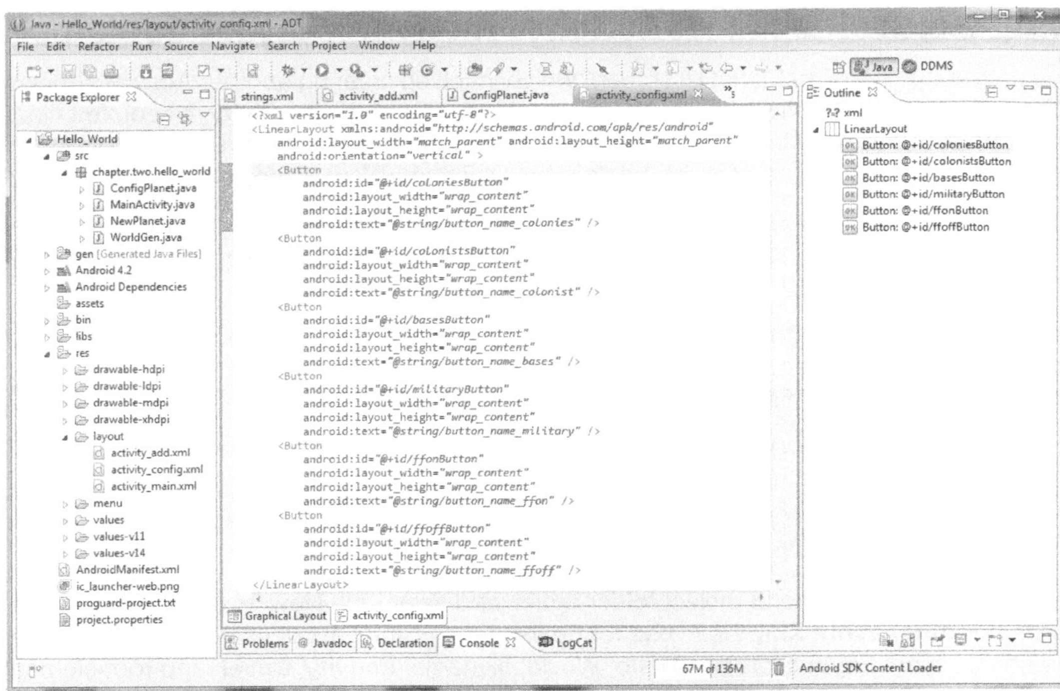

***Figure 4-23.** Filling the LinearLayout with Button UI elements for use with the World Configuration UI screen*

Each <Button> tag should have the following parameter mark-up structure:

```
<Button android:id="@+id/coloniesButton"
        android:layout_width="wrap_content"
        android:layout_height="wrap_content"
        android:text="@string/button_name_colonies" />
```

Next, copy the Button tag five more times underneath the first tag and edit the ID and Text parameter values to match what each of the button UI elements are going to do. Thus, we change colonies to colonists, bases, military, ffon (forcefield on), and ffoff (forcefield off), respectively.

Next, add six string tags that define the text labels for each button, and which are referenced via the **android:text** Button tag parameter, like this:

```
<string name="button_name_colonies">Add Colonies</string>
<string name="button_name_colonists">Add Colonists</string>
<string name="button_name_bases">Add Bases</string>
<string name="button_name_military">Add Military</string>
<string name="button_name_ffon">Forcefield On</string>
<string name="button_name_ffoff">Forcefield Off</string>
```

I'll forego the extra screenshot here, but these <string> tags can be seen later in Figure 4-25 (along with the string tags we need to add the attack methods for our AttackPlanet class and Activity subclass).

Next, let's go ahead and create our TravelPlanet class Activity subclass, as well as a FrameLayout container, so that later we can add digital video of intergalactic travel to the other planets in our application.

Defining a Travel to Planet Activity: The FrameLayout Container

Next, we create our Travel to Planet UI screen, which involves creating another Activity subclass called **TravelActivity.java** with a FrameLayout container defined in an **activity_travel.xml** file. Because you have done this before, I'll skip most of the figures, as you can reference the NewPlanet.java section for those, if you need to, it's back in the Defining a New Planet Activity Screen section.

First, right-click the Hello_World project folder and select **New ➤ Class** and create a Java class for the chapter.two.hello_world package that subclasses android.app.Activity and is named **TravelPlanet**. Leave the other default options set, and then click **Finish**.

Next, add an **onCreate()** method to create the Activity in Android so that it exists. This method is called when you reference (access) the Activity, and creates the Activity in system memory (allocates memory for it at run-time). This is why every Activity needs an onCreate() method **implemented**.

Next, add a **setContentView()** method that references **activity_travel.xml,** which we create next to hold our LinearLayout definition, like this:

```
setContentView(R.layout.activity_travel);
```

Next, right-click the Hello_World project folder again, and select the **New ➤ Android XML File** and create a **FrameLayout** XML file to use for defining the FrameLayout user interface design. Select resource type: **Layout**, project: **Hello_World**, filename: **activity_travel**, and root element: **FrameLayout** in this dialog (reference Figure 4-19) and click on **Finish**.

Next, add a **VideoView** tag inside the FrameLayout container. A FrameLayout is the perfect layout to use with full-screen digital video, as a FrameLayout contains only one single UI element. In a later chapter, we add the digital video assets, but for now, we're just going to be concerned with our XML layout file definition.

The basic **<VideoView>** tag XML mark-up is implemented as follows:

```
<VideoView android:id="@+id/travelVideoView"
            android:layout_width="match_parent"
            android:layout_height="match_parent" />
```

This <VideoView> XML mark-up is nested inside the <FrameLayout> tag, as shown in Figure 4-24.

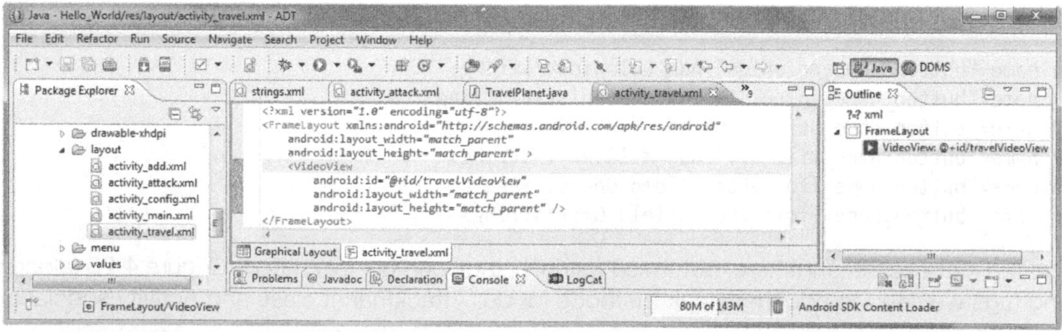

***Figure 4-24.** Adding a FrameLayout container and VideoView UI element to our activity_travel.xml file in Eclipse*

Click the Graphical Layout Editor tab at the bottom of the XML editing pane (the **activity_travel.xml** tab should now be active at the top of the editing pane), and drag a **VideoView** UI element out of the **Images & Media** drawer and onto the simulated app screen.

Next, switch over to the XML editing pane, and change the **android:id** value for the VideoView tag to **travelVideoView**. This can be seen in Figure 4.24.

Finally, we add the AttackPlanet.java class Activity subclass, and yet another LinearLayout, which holds ImageButton tags. Now we have a five screen framework set up for our Hello_World application for use during the rest of this book.

Defining the Attack on Planet Activity: Our Second Linear Layout

Next, we create our Attack on Planet UI screen, which involves creating another Activity subclass called **AttackActivity.java** with a LinearLayout container defined in an **activity_attack.xml** file. Because you have already gone through this before, I will forego the screenshots and figures, as you can reference the Defining the Add a New Planet Screen section for those, if needed.

First, right-click the Hello_World project folder and select **New ➤ Class** and create a Java class for the chapter.two.hello_world package that subclasses android.app.Activity and is named **AttackPlanet**. Leave the other default options set as they are, and click on **Finish**.

Next, add an **onCreate()** method to create the Activity in Android so that it exists. This method is called when you reference (access) the Activity, and creates the Activity in system memory (allocates memory for it at runtime). This is why every Activity needs an onCreate() method **implemented**.

Next, add a **setContentView()** method that references: **activity_attack.xml,** which we create to hold our LinearLayout definition, like this:

```
setContentView(R.layout.activity_attack);
```

Next, right-click the Hello_World project folder again and select the **New ➤ Android XML File** and create a LinearLayout XML file to use for defining the LinearLayout user interface design. Select the resource type: **Layout**, project: **Hello_World**, filename: **activity_attack**, and root element: **LinearLayout** in this dialog (reference Figure 4-19), and click **Finish**.

Next, add in some **ImageButton** tags inside the LinearLayout container, so we can add some attack icons and features to our Hello_World (or maybe we should we have named it Goodbye_World) Android application.

Note that in a later chapter, we'll wire these up so that they perform the tasks they are supposed to, but for now, we are just going to be concerned with our XML layout file definition.

Before we add the ImageButton tags, let's first define the four <string> labels that they will reference. These are shown in Figure 4-25 at the very bottom of the screenshot. They are the last four <string> tags listed in the <resources> parent tag container whose name parameters start with: content_desc.

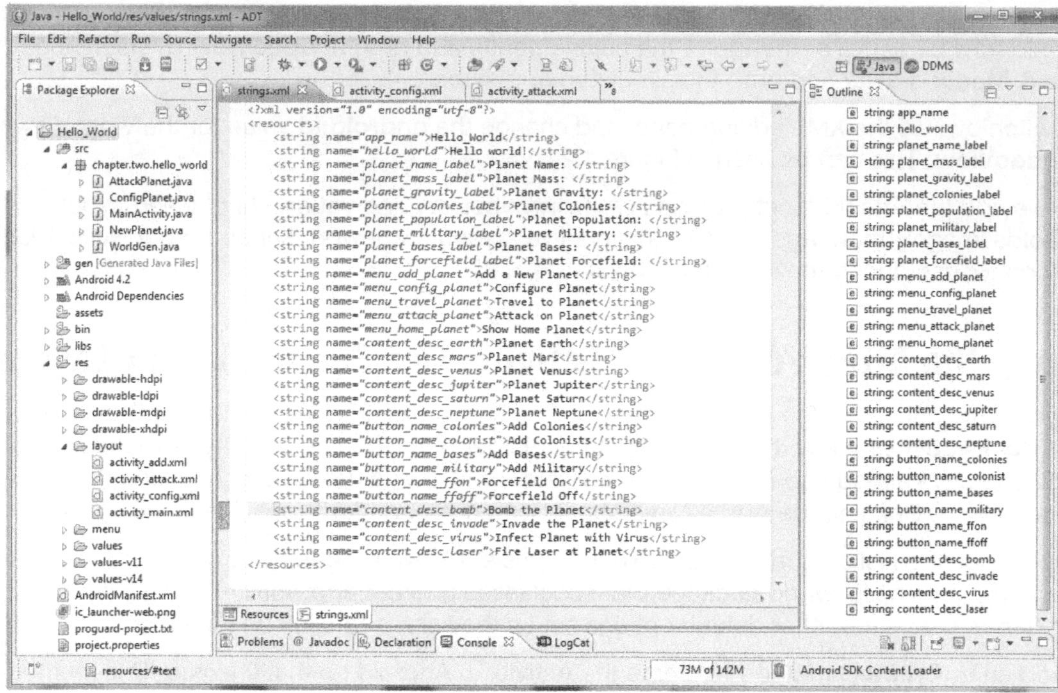

Figure 4-25. Adding the string tags for our activity_config.xml and activity_attack.xml layout string references

There are four graphical (image or icon) buttons that allow us to initiate four different types of attacks on a planet: Bomb, Invade, Infect, and Laser.

Because graphics in Android (ImageView and ImageButton UI elements) require a Content Description tag to help the visually impaired, let's add four string constants that reflect these modes of attack in our strings.xml file (values folder) referenced via android:contentDescription, like this:

```
<string name="content_desc_bomb">Bomb the Planet</string>
<string name="content_desc_invade">Invade the Planet</string>
<string name="content_desc_virus">Infect Planet with Virus</string>
<string name="content_desc_laser">Fire Laser at Planet</string>
```

Next, click the **activity_attack.xml** tab at the top and **Graphical Layout** tab at the bottom, and drag-out an **ImageButton** UI element (see Images & Media) and select the app launcher icon as a placeholder graphic to use for now. Then go into XML editing mode and change its ID to **bombButton** and add the string reference **@string/content_desc_bomb** to point to the string tag just you added. The <ImagButton> mark-up for the tag should look like this:

```
<ImageButton android:id="@+id/bombButton
             android:layout_width="wrap_content"
             android:layout_height="wrap_content"
             android:contentDescription="@string/content_desc_bomb"
             android:src="@drawable/ic_launcher" />
```

Copy and paste this three more times below the tag and change the bomb ID reference to invade, infect, and laser as shown in Figure 4-26, and change the contentDescription reference to invade, virus, and laser, respectively.

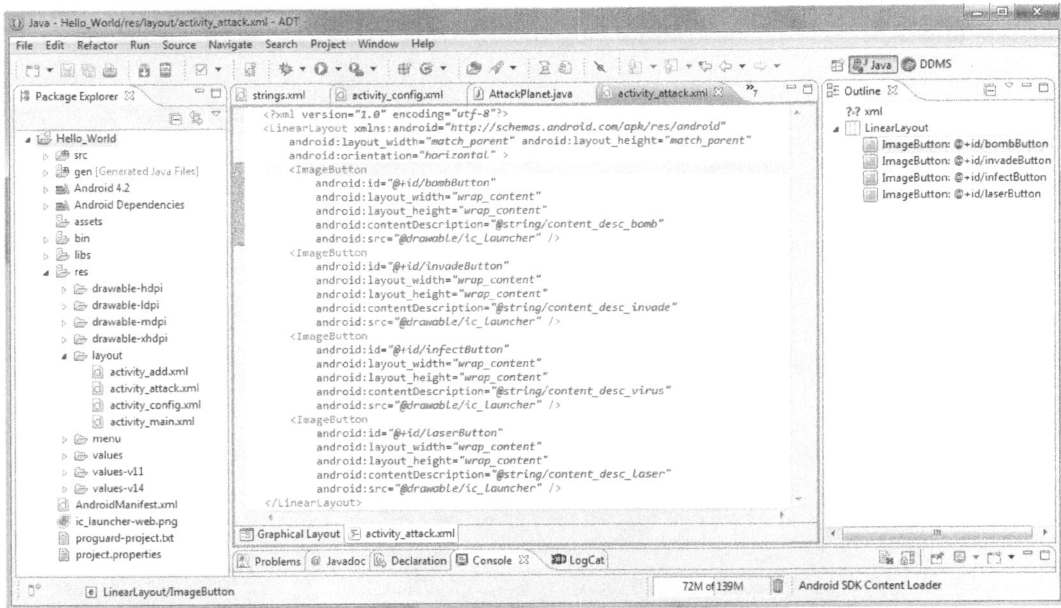

Figure 4-26. LinearLayout XML definition for the activity_attack.xml file for our AttackPlanet.java Activity class

Now that all our Activities and their Layout Containers are defined, the last thing we have to do is to declare these four new Activity screens to the Android OS using <activity> tags in our AndroidManifest.xml file.

Adding our Application Activities to our XML: AndroidManifest.xml

The last thing we need to do to be 100 percent sure that everything that we have done in this chapter compiles and runs cleanly is to add in declarations of our usage of these Activities into the **AndroidManifest.xml** file. This is done by adding **<activity>** tags, each of which defines the use of one Activity, as well as provides the Android OS with the name of the Activity via a specific naming convention.

The format for the <activity> tag and required Activity subclass name is

```
<activity android:name="chapter.two.hello_world.NewPlanet" />
<activity android:name="chapter.two.hello_world.ConfigPlanet" />
<activity android:name="chapter.two.hello_world.TravelPlanet" />
<activity android:name="chapter.two.hello_world.AttackPlanet" />
```

Here are all four <activity> tags, so you can see what needs to be added to the AndroidManifest.xml file, after the MainActivity class <activity> tag created back in Chapter 2. You can see that the full reference to the class name includes the package and class name.

As you can see in Figure 4-27 our new <activity> tags "throw" no errors or warnings in Eclipse. There was one warning on my **android:targetSDKVersion** that said it was not the latest version so I changed the value from the **16** API Level Android 4.1.2 JellyBean version that the New Android Application Project helper placed into this **<uses-sdk>** tag, over to the current **17** API Level Android 4.2.2 **Jelly Bean +** version. As I mentioned previously, Eclipse ADT can, and will, make some mistakes, which you may need to fix later on!

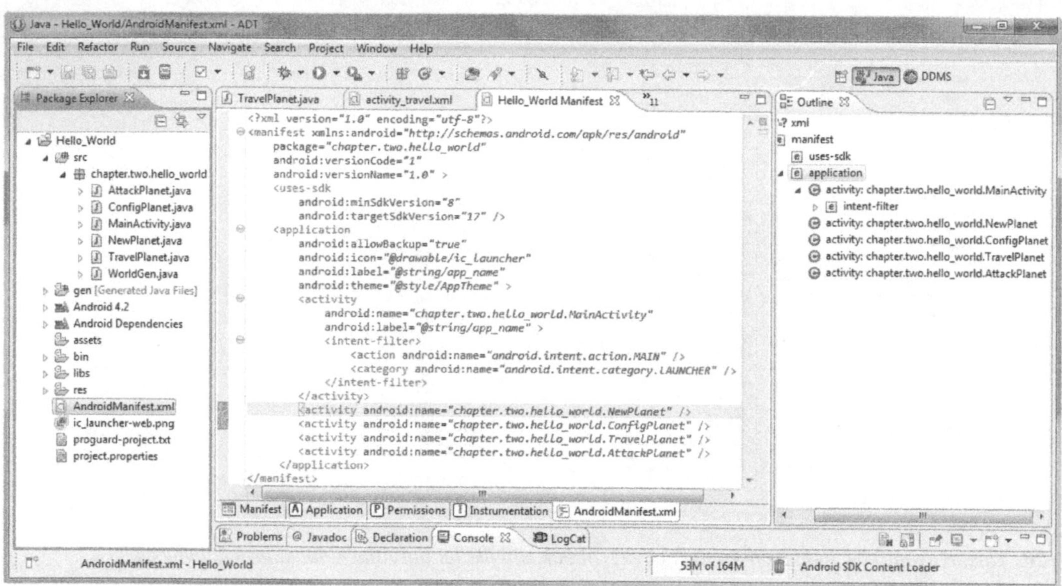

***Figure 4-27.** Adding four <activity> tags to Hello_World AndroidManifest.xml file to define each Activity subclass*

To be sure that everything we have created in this chapter is in perfect working order (we added lots of impressive Java code and XML mark-up), I'm now going to right-click the Hello_World project folder in the Eclipse Package Explorer, and select the **Run As Android Application** menu sequence to launch our trusty Nexus S emulator and see whether our application will run.

After a few minutes of loading the emulator and its user interface, and then replacing the previous application screen, this app runs perfectly, and I see the same exact screen that we saw earlier in Figure 4-4.

Sometimes, if the new app version does not appear, you can click the **run previous arrow** (a left-pointing, swoop-around arrow) in the emulator (on the top-right bank of buttons, in the second row, third button from the left), and it will relaunch the Hello_World app for you (or will at least hurry things up a little bit). Whew! We really got a *ton* of critical application infrastructure (Activity screens, Functional classes, Layout XML) in place during this chapter. Pat yourself on the back!

Summary

In this chapter, we learned all about Android Layout Containers, including those layout types that are **deprecated** (no longer in use) and those that have been recently added for API 14 to 17 (Android 4.x) development usage.

We then utilized the three most frequently used Screen Layout Containers that are currently available and recommended for use across all Android API Level (API 3 through 17) Application Development: the **RelativeLayout** container, the **LinearLayout** container, and the **FrameLayout** container.

To practice implementing these mainstream Android screen layout containers using XML mark-up within our ever-evolving Hello_World Android application, we then designed and created four new **Activity** screens for our application. We then implemented the three different types of Layout Containers inside these four new Android Activity subclasses.

To create all these new application Activity classes, we again used our trusty **New ➤ Class** menu sequence, to create four Java classes, which we used to support our Layout Containers via Android Activities, which are functional screen areas for an Android application.

We named these new Java classes, which subclass the **android.app.Activity** class, as follows: NewPlanet.java, ConfigPlanet.java, TravelPlanet.java, and AttackPlanet.java. We have now created a handful (five) of our own custom Java classes from scratch, and we're only in Chapter 4!

We learned how to create an Android Activity subclass and how to **implement** the necessary **onCreate()** and **setContentView()** methods, which are needed to define the memory and screen areas for each of our Hello_World Activities.

While we were doing all this Java coding and XML mark-up, we were also learning about the Eclipse IDE and how it flags our errors, warns us about conventions that it wants to see implemented, and offers us helper dialogs that make our class, method, and variable selections much easier.

We learned how to use the **Graphical Layout Editor (GLE)** and how the tabs at the bottom of a the Eclipse central editing pane give us different views of the data, whereas the editing pane tabs at the top of the editing pane allow us to select what code or mark-up we are working with.

Finally, we added several **<activity>** tags to our **AndroidManifest.xml** file, so that our four new Activities would be declared for use (and be visible) to the Android operating system. We ran our new app code, and it worked!

In the next chapter, we will start "wiring up" our new Screen Layouts, UI elements, and Activities that we learned about and created in this chapter to our WorldGen class and objects that we created back in Chapter 3. We will use Android **Intents** and **Events**, both of which allow Android's Activities and user interface elements to talk with each other.

Chapter 5

Android Intents and Events: Adding Interactivity

In this chapter, we will take our Hello World Android application that we have created thus far during the previous three chapters, and add in some more Java code to start the process of making it interactive and usable.

Now that we have created the Android application project (in Chapter 2), defined our `WorldGen` object structure (in Chapter 3), created our five user interface layout containers, four Activity screens, and an application menu structure (Chapter 4), it is time to wire all these together so that the user can use the main menu to navigate through the application's functional screens to experience actual results when they click some of the (placeholder) user interface elements.

At the same time, we are also going to use this chapter to teach two very important concepts in Android programming: **Intents** and **Events**. These even rhyme in a strange way! Both Intents and Events allow communication inside your application, which is why they allow interactivity to be implemented.

Intents allow communication at a more global level within the Android app, allowing the components of an Android application, such as the functional Activity subclasses that we created in the previous chapter, to be called and accessed (via Java code) whenever they are needed by the end-user.

Events allow communication at a much more localized level within an Android application, as they enable the lowest level component parts of an app, which are usually the user interface elements, or **widgets**, to talk, or more accurately to **call back**, to your Java and XML programming logic.

Because you are already a programmer, you are probably familiar with the concept of **event handling**. In the second half of this chapter, we will cover exactly how this is done in Java and Android, as well as what events are supported in Android, and how they are processed. Let's get started!

Android High-Level Communication: The Android Intent Object

An Android Intent is actually an object, so the Android Intent class in the package **android.content**, is a subclass of the **java.lang.Object** class. It is in the Android Content Provider **android.content** package because Intents can be used to quickly access database records, which we will learn about later on in this book. An Intent object can be (and usually is) very simple, however, it can also be complex, as an Intent object can have up to seven different parts or components to it. We cover Intents in far greater detail at the end of this book (in Chapter 16), but need to use them in our app at this stage, so we are going to cover them at a precursory level in this chapter.

The Intent is aptly named, as it is actually an object that describes something that needs to be accomplished, and is sent from one component of an application to another component. This is similar to the way a personal intent to perform or to accomplish something is communicated in real life.

The primary areas of Android applications that can process Intent objects include Activities, which we have created already; Services, which are used for background processing, and which we cover later on; and Broadcast Receivers, which are used for sending messages to the Android end-user.

Each of these three different functional areas of Android has its very own Intent object that is optimized for dealing with the unique attributes of each of these areas. After all, Activities are optimized to display screen interfaces, Services for doing heavy background processing, and Broadcast Receivers for broadcasting communication messages, and thus each of these application components must have different Intent object handling structures to work optimally and seamlessly with each other.

So what types of information does one of these Intent objects pass between application components? Functional areas of an Intent object include:

- The **component name** of the component (class) which needs to process the intent
- The **action** that needs to be performed
- The **data** that the action needs to operate on
- The **type** of data (a MIME type) that is being processed
- The **category** that this processing falls under
- Any **flags** and **extras** that are needed to further define this processing that needs to be performed

The Component Name

The most important field in the Intent object is the **component name**, and the instance variable for each Intent object contains a **reference** to the full **path** to the class that the Intent object is **targeting**. An Intent that contains a component name is termed an **explicit** Intent, whereas an Intent that does *not* specify a component name is termed an **implicit** Intent.

The full path to a class name includes the **package name** and also the **class name**, if the class were in another package. So if you were going to launch our NewPlanet Activity class from another package, you would use **chapter.two.hello_world.NewPlanet.class** as the complete path name to the class. If you were inside the chapter.two.hello_world package (such as we will be, in the Intent examples later in this chapter) you would use **NewPlanet.class** as a **run-time reference** to our `NewPlanet.java` class code.

The Action

The next most important variable in the Intent object is the **action**, and there are many **predefined action constants** within the Android OS that can be accessed via Intent objects. If you want to review them all, go to **http://developer.android.com/reference/android/content/Intent.html**.

Some examples of commonly used actions used with **Activity** classes for the Android OS include:

- `ACTION_DIAL` (Display a phone number to dial)
- `ACTION_CALL` (Make a phone call)
- `ACTION_MAIN` (Start the main activity for the app)
- `ACTION_EDIT` (Edit a database)

Some commonly used actions with **Broadcast Receivers** include:

- `ACTION_TIMEZONE_CHANGED` (User has moved into a new time zone)
- `ACTION_POWER_CONNECTED` (User has plugged in the device)
- `ACTION_SHUTDOWN` (User has shut down the Android device)

The Data Reference

The next most important reference in the Intent is the **data** reference, which points to the data that the action is to act upon. Every action needs something to act upon (some data value to use or change) and every data value needs some action to be specified (what to do to or with the data). Thus, Intent actions and data go hand in hand, and data is usually specified using something called a **URI** or **Universal Resource Identifier**.

The Type Reference

The next most important reference within the Intent is the **type** reference, which refers to a **MIME Type**, which is a standard data classification used in Internet 1.0 (HTTP) and 2.0 (Mobile or Consumer Electronics) platforms.

MIME originally stood for **Multipurpose Internet Mail Extensions** and it was initially created to define e-mail (attachment) data types supported by e-mail servers, but MIME has since been adopted by many different types of data servers, and now, even on the client-side, by the Android OS itself.

It is important to note here that if any of the seven areas of the Intent object parameter classifications are left out that Android will **infer** what should go in that parameter slot. This is probably easiest for an omitted MIME Type, because it's easier to infer than the MIME Type for an MP3 audio data file should be: **Content-Type: audio/mp3** or that the proper MIME Type for an MP4 video data file should be: **Content-Type: video/mp4**.

Android Category Constants

The next most important reference in an Intent object is Android **category** constants, which are used to define a specific area of the Android OS to target the Intent toward. Some more popular **category constants** include:

- **CATEGORY_DEFAULT**
- **CATEGORY_BROWSABLE**
- **CATEGORY_TAB**
- **CATEGORY_LAUNCHER**
- **CATEGORY_INFO**
- **CATEGORY_HOME**
- **CATEGORY_PREFERENCE**
- **CATEGORY_CAR_DOCK**
- **CATEGORY_DESK_DOCK**
- **CATEGORY_CAR_MODE**
- **CATEGORY_APP_MARKET**

The category constants are all listed, and described (via links), at **`http://developer.android.com/reference/android/content/Intent.html`**.

An example of how a category would be used with an Intent action would be, for instance: to launch your user's Android device Home Screen, you would utilize an Intent object that was preloaded with the **ACTION_MAIN** action constant as well as the **CATEGORY_HOME** category constant.

Flags and Extras

The last two reference types that can be added to a more complicated and involved Intent object structure are **flags** and **extras**. Flags, as you know from your programming experience, are Boolean values that are like option switches that can be passed over with the Intent object. Extras are other types of data that are needed, such as text or other object structures.

Because we are not going to cover Intents at an advanced level in this book, we will not be using flags and extras in our Intent objects, but I wanted to let you know that they are included in the Intent object hierarchy and are available if your advanced Intent object design requires them.

Implicit Intents: Intent Filters that Define Implicit Intent Handling

As I mentioned earlier, **Implicit Intents** are `Intent` objects that do not specify any **component specifier** within the Intent object itself, that is, the Intent object does not specify (does not direct the Intent) where it needs to go to get **handled** or processed to its resolution.

In this situation, the Android OS has to **infer** by using the other `Intent` object parameters what area in the OS (or more precisely, what code that is currently executing in system memory) that it needs to pass the `Intent` object over to for the successful processing or **resolution** of that Intent.

Android performs this inference process based on a careful comparison of all the various actions, data, MIME types, and categories that are in fact defined inside the `Intent` object, using the code components that are currently available in system memory with which to process that intent.

You can also create your own inference engine using **intent filters**, which can be defined using **XML tags** in the application **AndroidManifest.xml** file. You can find much more detailed information regarding Intent Filters at **developer.android.com/reference/android/content/IntentFilter.html**.

Designing Android applications that process implicit intents and leverage intent filter XML is beyond the reach of an introductory book on learning Android application programming; however, we'll cover the concept here, to give you a general idea of what can be accomplished with them and in which situations you would want to use implicit intents and intent filters.

Intent filter structures are declared inside the `AndroidManifest.xml` file, by using the **<intent-filter>** tag. They filter implicit intents based on three of the seven attributes of an Intent object; the Intent **action**, its **data**, and possibly its **category**, if included and applicable.

Intent filter tags can be contained (nested) inside the **<activity>** and **<activity-alias>** XML tags, as well as inside the **<service>** and the **<receiver>** tags. This is because, as we learned earlier in the chapter, there are different types of Intent objects for each of these three unique Android areas: Activities, Services and Broadcast Receivers.

If you want to review more detailed information regarding implementing Intent Filter structure definitions by using the **<intent-filter>** tag, visit the **Intent Filter Element** Android developer page, located at **developer.android.com/guide/topics/manifest/intent-filter-element.html**.

Intent filter tag structures are used to define a description of `Intent` object configurations that need to be matched. They also allow a **priority** attribute that can be implemented, if more than one match is encountered.

Intent filters are tested for **action** matches first, then for **data** matches, and finally for **category** matches. If no action intent filters have been specified, then the action parameter of the intent will not be tested at all, moving the testing process on down to test the data parameter of the intent. Similarly, if no data intent filters have been specified, then only intents that contain no data will be matched.

For Intent filters that include data characteristics, a data parameter gets broken down into four categories, including the **data type** (MIME Type), the **data scheme** (such as http://), the **data authority** (server host and server port, specified as host:port), and finally the **data path**.

The **data path** to your strings.xml file, for instance, would be specified **C:/Users/UserName/workspace/Hello_World/res/values/strings.xml**.

For instance, in the following intent filter data parameter specification **content://com.apress.projects:500/project_files/android/file_number_2**, the data scheme is **content://** and the data authority (host is specified first) is **com.apress.projects:500** (port is specified second), and the data path is **/project_files/android/file_number_2**, respectively.

Here is a brief example of an intent-filter data definition that specifies (from the inside of an application AndroidManifest.xml file) that videos (MPEG4 H.264 format data) and audio (MPEG3 format data) will be remotely accessed from the internet, using the HTTP data scheme:

```
<intent-filter>
<data android:mimeType="video/mp4" android:scheme="http" />
<data android:mimeType="audio/mp3" android:scheme="http" />
</intent-filter>
```

Implicit intents and intent filters are most often used in more advanced application development scenarios, when an application is designed to be used by other developers or used with other applications where the methods of that usage are not known in advance by other developers. In this case, intent filter structures will need to be built to handle unforeseen access to the application feature set by external developers who have not been educated as to how to access the application data structures and features.

We will focus on **explicit intent** structures for our application development in this book as we know which application components we will be targeting.

Using Explicit Intents: Making Our Hello_World Menu Functional

Now it's time to use Explicit Intents to take our Hello_World Android Application to the next level, by making our application menu functional.

Over the past three chapters, we have coded custom Java program logic into six different classes, five of which we created 100% from scratch. So far, we have created Java code that allows our users to create new worlds, colonize those worlds, travel to each world, militarize a world, protect a world using a forcefield, and even mount an attack on another world.

We have written Java code to create WorldGen objects, and written XML tag mark-up to define screen layouts that hold user interface elements, menus, and buttons which access different features of our Android application. Our four new classes that we wrote in the previous chapter utilize Activities to hold all these UI elements within their own functional screens.

Without Explicit Intents, however, these are all just isolated components, which cannot be used together to do anything significant. Sure, each will do something in and of itself, like creating new planets (NewPlanet.java), configuring a given planet with colonies, colonists, bases, and army forces (ConfigPlanet.java), traveling to a planet (TravelPlanet.java), or attacking a planet (AttackPlanet.java). But to make the app a useful sum of its component parts, we need to access all these functional screen modules (Activities) via our Home Screen options menu system, which requires that we use Intent objects to call and to **start** these Activities.

So, the next thing we need to do is to leverage explicit Intent objects to enable our four primary menu items to call the Activity subclasses that we have created to hold these different functional areas of our application. Let's set up our menu functionality now so that we can use explicit intents to call these Activities we have created.

Inflating Our Menu

Menu creation involves the **onCreateOptionsMenu()** method, which contains our app options menu **inflation** routine, which we have already utilized to create our primary application menu, by **inflating** our menu XML definition.

To make this options menu functional requires that we add a second method to our `MainActivity.java` class. The **onOptionsItemSelected()** method is used with the `onCreateOptionsMenu()` method, and contains all the code that allows the various menu options to be selected and executed on a case by case basis. This is done via the Java **switch** code construct, which some of you programmer types may have also referred to as **case** statements.

Let's write this code now, so that we can see how it all works together. First, use the tiny minus sign on the left of each of the methods in our `MainActivity.java` class to close up the code views for all those Java methods to give us some more code editing room inside of the editing pane.

Next let's add a line of white space (by pressing the return key) after the `onCreateOptionsMenu()` method, and then press the **Ctrl-Spacebar** keystroke combination, which we learned in the previous chapter. This brings up the method selector helper dialog, at which point we can then locate the **onOptionsItemSelected()** method, and double-click it to implement it on the inside of the current `MainActivity.java` class (Activity subclass).

Notice that it has **public** access control, so all code can access the menu options, and a **boolean** return type, so that a processing status (true for processed, and false for failed to process) can be returned to the calling entity. The method takes a **MenuItem** object, named **item**, as its parameter.

Inside the `onOptionsItemSelected()` method we will use a **switch** statement to select between the five menu options, or cases, with code inside of each **case** branch in the `switch` statement, which will be executed when that case arises. The `switch` statement itself needs the **ID** for the **MenuItem** object as its parameter, and because the `MenuItem` object named **item** is passed into the `onOptionsItemSelected()` method as its parameter, we can also use the **.getItemId()** method on the MenuItem object named **item** inside of the switch statement parameter area, which we code all in one line of code like this:

```
switch(item.getItemId()) { the case statements will go inside of these brackets }
```

So, let's type this into our method, and then add our first case branch, using the **menu_add** ID parameter that we created in the previous chapter for our Add a Planet menu item, like this:

```
case R.id.menu_add:
```

This is all shown in Figure 5-1, along with the next step, where we add in our explicit Intent object, which calls our `NewPlanet` Activity class.

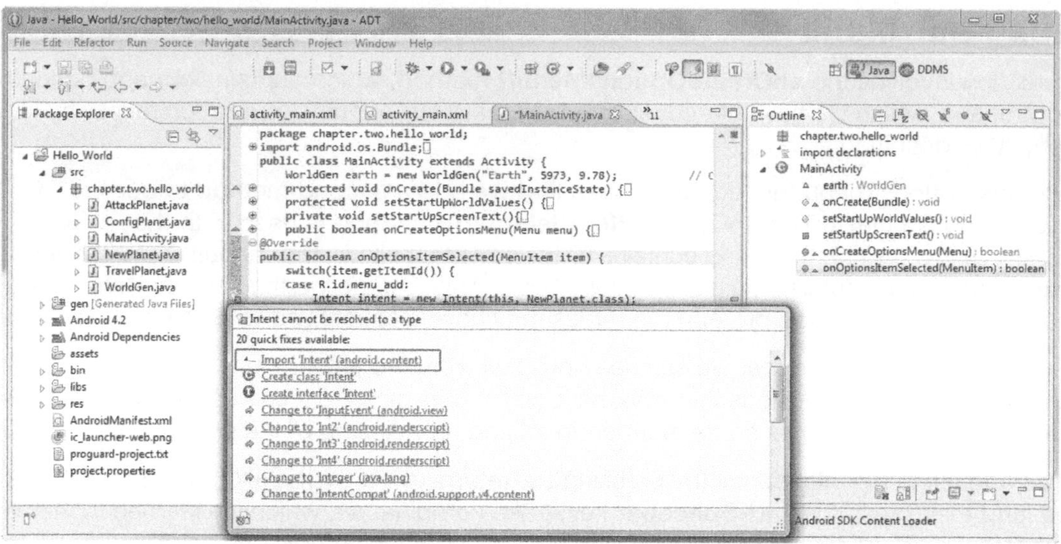

***Figure 5-1.** Adding an onOptionsItemSelected() method to process our menu options and importing Intent class*

Adding the New Planet Intent

On the next line of code, we create our first explicit Intent object, which we use to call the **NewPlanet** Activity subclass that we wrote in the previous chapter. This is done in a similar fashion to how we declared our WorldGen objects in Chapter 3, using the **new** keyword, like this:

```
Intent intent = new Intent(this, NewPlanet.class);
```

Notice in Figure 5-1 that Eclipse underlines our Intent object declaration with a wavy red error line, which we realize at this point is because the Intent class has not been properly declared for use in our code by using an **import** statement. Let's mouse-over that red-underlined Intent keyword, and when the helper dialog pops up, select the option to **Import Intent** from the **android.content** package in which the Intent class is contained.

As you are now familiar with this object declaration process, you realize that the line of code above declares an **Intent** object named **intent** and loads it with a **new** Intent object with the current context of **this** and then points it toward the `NewPlanet` Activity class via a **NewPlanet.class** run-time class reference. Since we will be adding more Intent objects to this `switch` structure later on, we will name this Intent object **intent_add** to more clearly reflect which Intent object it is.

```
Intent intent_add = new Intent(this, NewPlanet.class);
```

Next add in a line of code that calls the Intent object's **.startActivity()** method, which uses the Intent object we just created to start the Activity subclass NewPlanet.class that we just defined in the previous line of code and which is called from the current context object (this) using the code:

```
this.startActivity(intent_add);
```

Finally, we add a **break;** statement, so that we can exit this section of the `switch case` statement after the code we need executed has been processed.

This is shown in Figure 5-2, along with the rest of the `case` statements which we'll add in the next few paragraphs. Each individual **case** statement inside of the Java **switch** container needs to be structured just like this:

```
case R.id.menu_add:
        Intent intent_add = new Intent(this, NewPlanet.class);
        this.startActivity(intent_add);
        break;
```

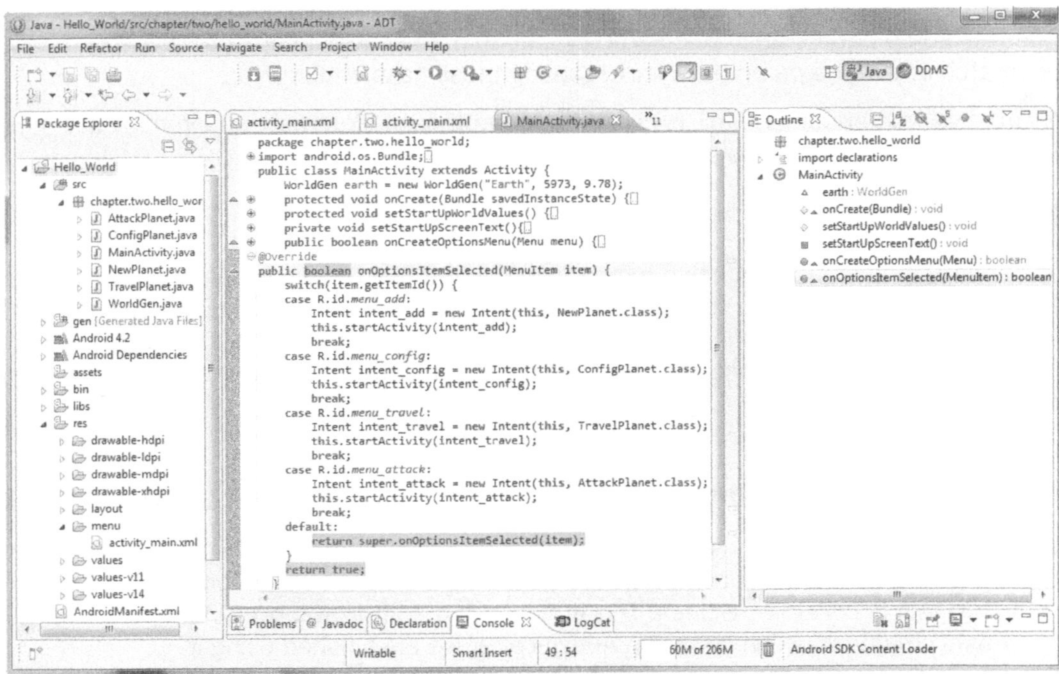

***Figure 5-2.** Adding five case statements that send Intent objects, calling our Hello_World functional Activity screens*

We will add in the rest of the case statements for our menu options inside of our Java switch container in the next section of this chapter.

Adding the Rest of the Intents

Next, let's take the programmer's short-cut, and copy and paste the first `case` statement right underneath itself and make the changes needed to make it call our `ConfigPlanet.java` Activity subclass. Change the `R.id` reference to **R.id.menu_config** and the name of the Intent object to **intent_config** and set the Activity class called to **ConfigPlanet.class** so that we open up the correct screen when the Configure Planet menu option is selected.

Half of our Activity subclasses are now called via Intent objects from our options menu; let's add the other two using the same copy and paste method we just used. Copy either the first or the second case statement in our switch code structure under the second case statement, to add a third case statement, and then change the R.id reference to **R.id.menu_travel** and the name of the third Intent object to **intent_travel** and a third Activity class call set to **TravelPlanet.class** so that we open up the Travel to a Planet screen when the Travel to Planet menu option is selected.

Let's call the fourth AttackPlanet Activity subclass within the next case statement, by pasting the case statement again, underneath the third case statement to create a fourth case statement, and then change the R.id reference to point to **R.id.menu_attack** and the name of the fourth and final Intent object to **intent_attack** along with the fourth Activity class call set to **AttackPlanet.class** so that we open up our apps Attack a Planet function screen when the Attack on Planet menu option is selected.

Finally, at the bottom of every `switch` or `case` statement, we can have a **contingency** statement that processes some code that is executed only if none of the case statements inside of the switch construct match any of the parameters for executing those case statements.

In the Android **switch** statement, this is called the **default** case statement and in this case, it returns control to the superclass via a line of code that reads:

```
default: return super.onOptionsItemSelected(item);
```

This is essentially the same as returning a false value for the entire `switch` statement, and passes control back up to the superclass's `onOptionsItemSelected()` method. Let's right-click our Project Folder and **Run As Android Application** and run our code to see if it works. The menu items now call each of the Activity classes and layout containers that we designed in the previous chapter (review Figure 4-16).

Enabling Our New Planet Activity's User Interface: Event Handling

Now that we can start our Activity subclasses from our `MainActivity` class options menu, we need to be able to use those Activity subclasses to perform their respective functions, and then return users to our `MainActivity` Home Screen. This is done via the **android.app.Activity** class (or our subclass) **finish()** method, which closes an Activity after we are finished using it.

Let's code part of our **NewPlanet.java** class (Activity subclass), to show you how the **finish()** method is implemented, as well as to show you how to use the **onClick()** event handling method to process a click on one of our New Planet images (or for now, on one of our placeholder images).

First, we'll add a line of code after our `onCreate()` and `setContentView()` methods that we created when we created the class, and create an **ImageView** object used to reference an **imageMars** UI element we defined earlier in our **activity_add.xml** file. This is done by declaring an ImageView object named **marsImage** and by referencing it to the XML UI element definition using the **findViewById()** method referencing the XML **android:id** parameter as follows:

```
ImageView marsImage = (ImageView)findViewById(R.id.imageMars);
```

Notice that when we enter this line of code into Eclipse, that it will red underline this ImageView class reference, because we have not yet imported it for use. Let's mouse-over this highlighted code element, and select the **Import ImageView (`android.widget` package)** initial option, and have Eclipse ADT write that import code statement for us, as shown in Figure 5-3.

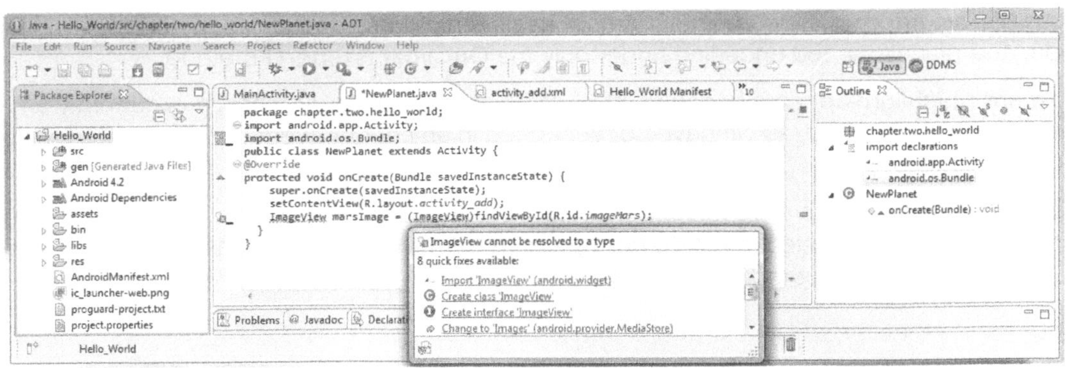

Figure 5-3. Create an ImageView object named marsImage in NewPlanet.java that references XML UI definition

Now that we have defined our marsImage UI object for use in Java, we want to attach a method to it by using dot notation that allows it to process a user's click (or touch, if a touchscreen device is being used). This is done using the **.setOnClickListener()** method from the `View` class.

Let's set up an `OnClickListener()` method for our `marsImage` ImageView UI object using the **new** keyword and `setOnClickListener()` method like this:

```
marsImage.setOnClickListener(new View.OnClickListener() { code goes in here } );
```

What this compact line of code does is to declare a new **OnClickListener()** method in the **View** class inside of a **setOnClickListener()** method attached to a **marsImage** ImageView object that we created one line of code earlier.

Notice that Eclipse again red underlines our Java code because we're using methods from a View class that is not yet imported into our `NewPlanet.java` code. So now let's mouse-over the View class reference in the code, to get the helper dialog shown in Figure 5-4 that will **Import View** (`android.view` package) for us, so that we don't have to write the import code ourselves.

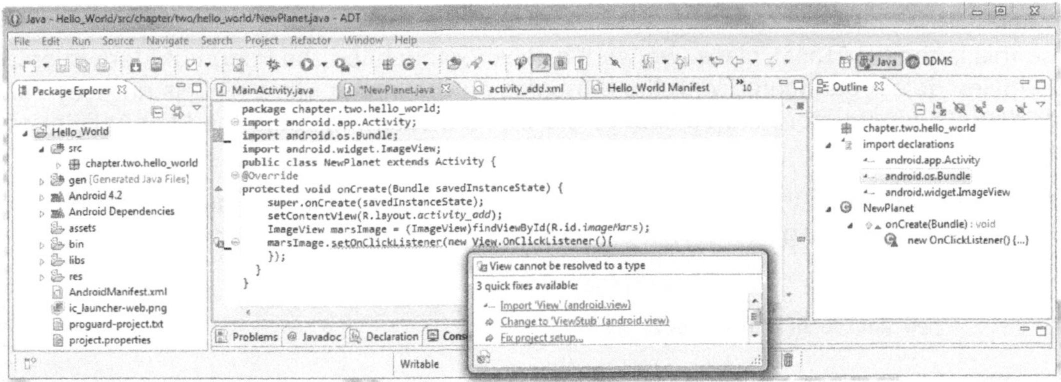

Figure 5-4. Add setOnClickListener method to marsImage ImageView Object and creating new OnClickListener()

Once our **import android.view.View;** statement has been put in place for us, Eclipse re-evaluates our code, and places the red underline under only the **OnClickListener()** method.

This new error highlight appears because, at least for now, this listener method is currently an empty or **unimplemented** method, as we have not yet added in any of our event handling code inside of the two curly braces.

Let's take the opportunity to have Eclipse write some more code for us and again mouse-over the red underlined code, and select the **Add unimplemented methods** option, as shown in Figure 5-5. Voila! Eclipse writes this method:

```
@Override
public void onClick(View v) {
  //Add Code To Process Here
}
```

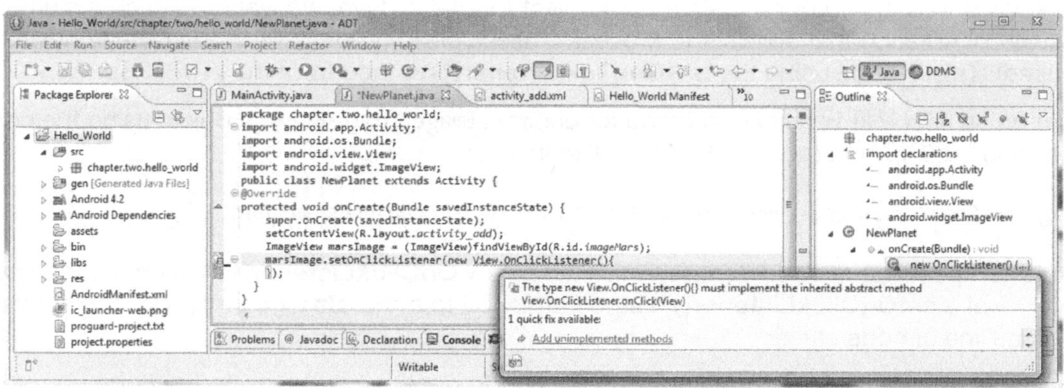

***Figure 5-5.** Implementing the inherited abstract method View.OnClickListener.onClick(View) via Eclipse helper*

Next, we add in the code to process what we want to happen (when a user clicks on a `marsImage` ImageView UI element) inside of this **onClick()** method, which is passed a View object (named v) that it needs to process.

Because this is the `NewPlanet` class, we want a click (or touch) on the image of Mars to create a new WorldGen object configured with the attributes for the planet Mars. This is done by calling our **WorldGen()** constructor method like we did with the **earth** object in the MainActivity.java class earlier.

Our first line of code inside the **onClick()** event handler creates a new `WorldGen` planet object named **mars** and then configures its name, mass, and gravity via parameters passed to the `WorldGen()` constructor:

```
WorldGen mars = new WorldGen("Mars", 642, 3.7);
```

Notice that once we type in this new object creation line of code, Eclipse yellow underlines the **mars** object, because it is not yet utilized. We could just ignore the warning, shown in Figure 5-6, but in the interest of a clean code editing view, we'll add a Colony to Mars, to satisfy Eclipse.

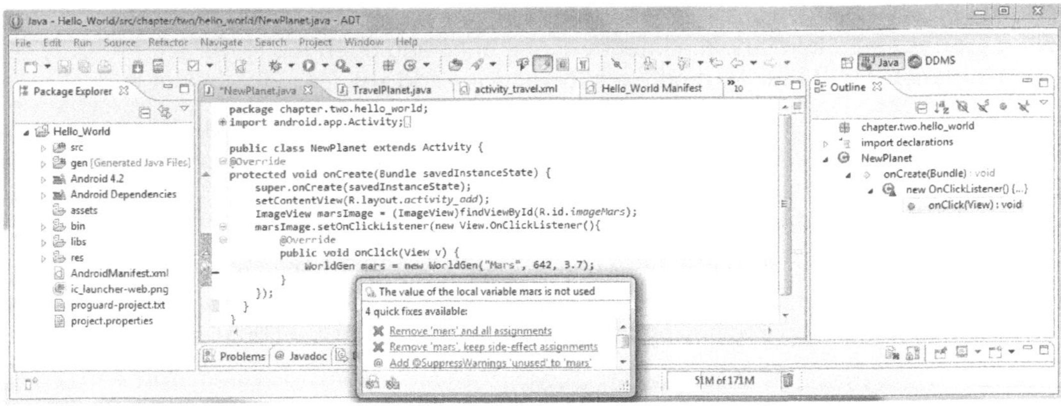

***Figure 5-6.** Add WorldGen() constructor method call to onClick(View) event handler method creating mars object*

To add a Colony to Mars we would call the `.setPlanetColonies(1)` method from the **mars** object we just **instantiated** using dot notation like this:

```
mars.setPlanetColonists(1);
```

Next, we need to tell the `NewPlanet` Activity that we are finished using it and wish to return to the MainActivity Home Screen for our application. This is done using the **finish()** method, which is our next line of code in the `onClick()` event handler method, as shown here and in Figure 5-7:

```
finish();
```

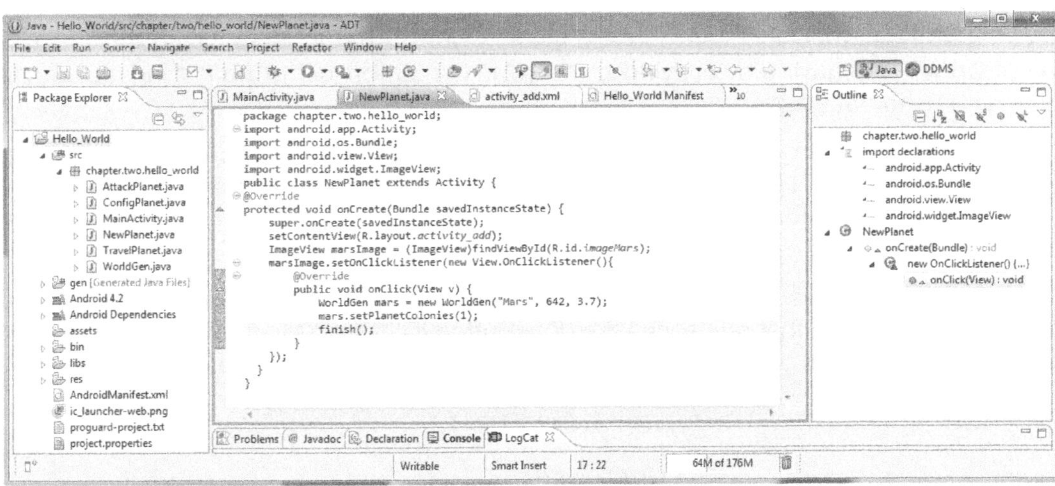

***Figure 5-7.** Call .setPlanetColonies() method on mars object to use local mars variable; call finish() Intent method*

Now let's right-click the `Hello_World` project folder, and select **Run As Android Application**, which saves all our code changes for us, if we haven't been saving them via CTRL-S, and launches the Nexus S emulator to run our `Hello_World` app with our new Intent and Event processing code.

The screen again looks like Figure 4-16 when you click the emulator Menu button. Next, click the **Add a New Planet** menu item and the Intent will reference and open the NewPlanet Activity screen and its Add a Planet layout that we created in the activity_add.xml file in the layout folder.

Now, let's see if our event handling code works properly. Click the top right (Mars) image placeholder icon, and the `onClick()` event handler creates the new Mars planet with one colony, and should then return you to the application's Home Screen, via the `finish()` method call at the end of our `onClick()` method code statements.

Next let's add event handling to our other app functional activity screens so that our app options menu structure can be used to navigate amongst the various areas of our app. That way, we have the basic structure of our app in place by the time we finish the first section (Part 1) of this book.

Enabling Our ConfigPlanet Activity User Interface: Event Handling

Next, let's prepare our **ConfigPlanet** Activity and UI Layouts to return our users to their Home Screen when they are done configuring the current planet. We do this by adding a **Done Configuring** button to our activity_config.xml and a matching **button_name_done** string constant to our strings.xml file. Then, we'll wire up this XML Done button using Java code to allow our users to return to the Hello_World Home Screen when the Done button is clicked. I will not use a lot of screen shots for this section as you've seen the work process before and so they are not needed.

On the top right of your Eclipse editing tabs in the central pane there is a number (in Figure 5-7 it is a 10); click this to drop-down a menu containing all your open editing tabs. Select the **activity_config.xml** editing tab, so that we can add the Done Configuring button XML mark-up.

Copy and paste the last button in this XML layout definition underneath itself, and change the **android:id** tag to **doneButton** and the **android:text** tag string constant reference to **button_name_done** and press Ctrl-S to save the XML file. Then click the "tabs not shown number" drop-down menu again, and select the **strings.xml** editing tab, and add the new **button_name_done** string tag along with the value of **Done Configuring** by copying and pasting the button_name_ffoff string tag, and then change its name and data value.

Now that our XML mark-up editing is complete, we can turn to our Java code editing in the **ConfigActivity.java** class. Here we need to add a **Button** object on which to attach our `onClick()` event handling for the Done button, just like we did for the ImageView UI element in the previous section.

Let's go through a similar work process as to what we did in our `NewPlanet` class, and add a Button object named **doneButton** that references the doneButton ID in the XML file that we just finished editing. We do this by using the **findViewById()** method, using a single line of code, as follows:

```
Button doneButton = (Button)findViewById(R.id.doneButton);
```

Next, we'll use this doneButton Button UI object that we have just created and attach an **OnClickListener()** method to this UI object, via the familiar **.setOnClickListener()** method that creates a new `OnClickListener` like this:

```
doneButton.setOnClickListener(new OnClickListener() { our code goes in here } );
```

The Java event handling code that we use for our Done Configuring button that returns the user to the Home Screen (`MainActivity`) involves again using the Activity class's **finish()** method, inside the **onClick()** event handler, as shown in our modified `ConfigPlanet` class in Figure 5-8.

```
@Override
public void onClick(View v) {
    finish();
}
```

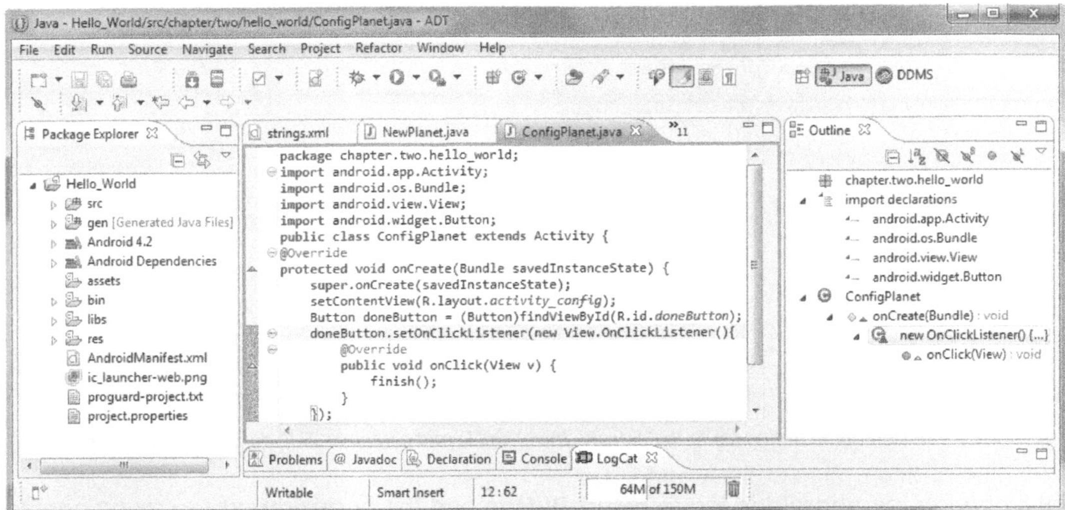

***Figure 5-8.** Adding an .OnClickListener() method to our doneButton Button object in the ConfigPlanet.java class*

Next, we will modify our `TravelPlanet.java` class, so that it can be called from the main options menu and later return users back to the Home Screen.

Enabling Our TravelPlanet Activity User Interface: Event Handling

As we did for our ConfigPlanet class, let's now prepare our **TravelPlanet** Activity and UI Layouts to return users to their Home Screen when they are done traveling around the currently active planet.

We do this by adding a **Return Home** button to our **activity_travel.xml** and a matching **button_name_return** string constant to our strings.xml file. Then, we'll wire up the XML Return Button UI element using some Java event handling code that allows our users to return to their Hello_World Home Screen whenever the Return button is clicked by the user.

On the top right of your Eclipse editing tabs in the central pane is a number (in Figure 5-8, it's an 11); click this again to drop-down the selection menu containing all your open code modules. Select the **activity_travel.xml** editing tab, so that we can add the Return Home button XML mark-up that our Java event handler code is going to reference.

Let's take a shortcut, and copy and paste the last button we used in your `activity_config.xml` layout definition, and use that under our **<VideoView>** UI element tag, so that we have a button to use in this layout container, as shown in Figure 5-9. The <Button> XML mark-up should look like this:

```
<Button android:id="@+id/returnButton"
        android:layout_width="wrap_content"
        android:layout_height="wrap_content"
        android:text="@string/button_name_return" />
```

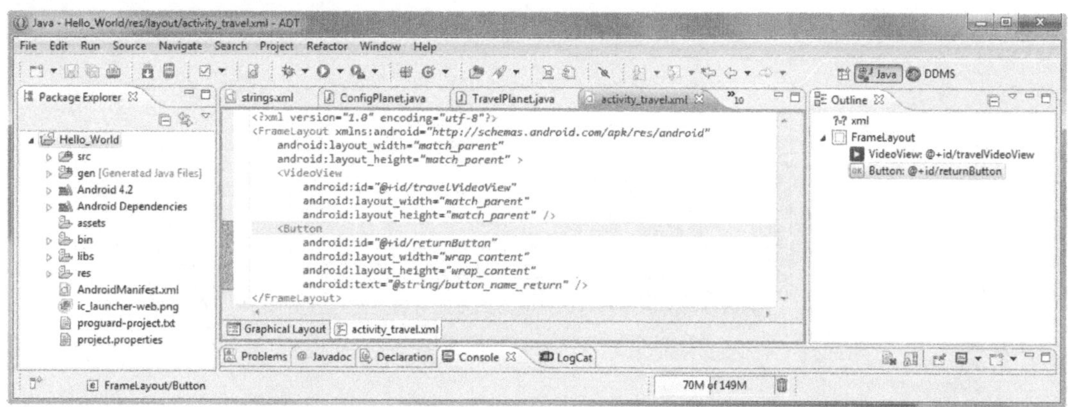

***Figure 5-9.** Adding a Return Home Button tag to the activity_travel.xml layout container XML definition in Eclipse*

Next, let's change the **android:id** tag to **returnButton** and the **android:text** tag string constant reference to **button_name_return** and then press Ctrl-S to save our modified XML layout container definition.

Again click the tabs-not-shown-number drop-down menu, and this time, select the **strings.xml** editing tab, so we can add the string constant our new Button UI object references. Add the new **button_name_return** string tag, along with the value of **Return Home** by again copying and pasting the `button_name_done` string tag immediately underneath itself and then change the values from done to return, and from Done Configuring to Return Home.

Now that our XML mark-up editing is completed we can turn to our Java code editing in the **TravelActivity.java** class, where we need to add in another **Button** object, to which to attach our next **onClick()** event handling method for the Return Home button, just like we did inside our `ConfigActivity.java` class in the previous section.

Let's go through a similar work process as in our ConfigPlanet class, and add a Button object named **returnButton** that will reference the returnButton ID in the XML file that we just finished editing. We do this by using a **findViewById()** method, using a single line of code, as follows:

```
Button returnButton = (Button)findViewById(R.id.returnButton);
```

Next use the returnButton Button UI object that we have just created and attach an **OnClickListener()** method to this UI object via the familiar **.setOnClickListener()** method that creates a **new** OnClickListener like this:

```
returnButton.setOnClickListener(new OnClickListener() { your code goes in here } );
```

The Java event handling code that we use for our Done Configuring button that returns the user to the Home Screen (MainActivity) involves again using the Activity class's **finish()** method, inside of the **onClick()** event handler, as shown in the following Java code:

```
@Override
public void onClick(View v) {
        finish();
}
```

This is shown in our modified `TravelPlanet` class in Figure 5-10.

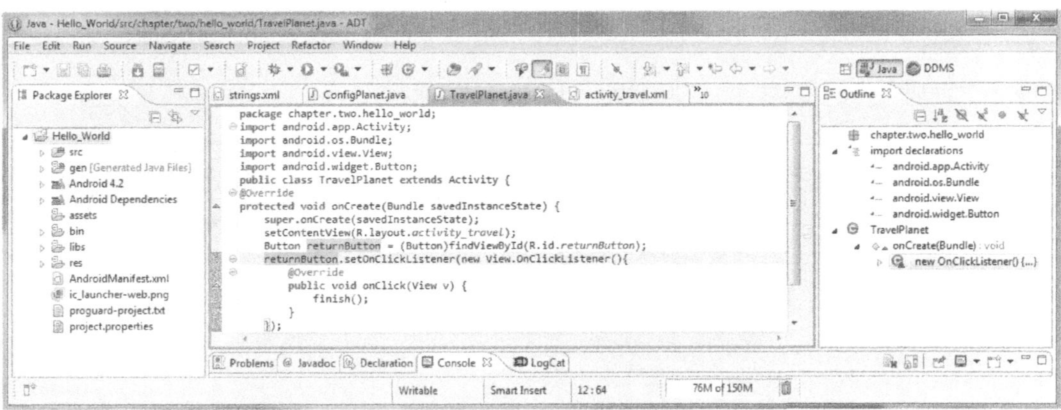

***Figure 5-10.** Adding the returnButton Button UI object and event handling code to our TravelPlanet.java class*

We are getting close! Once we modify our **AttackPlanet.java** class to return to our app's Home Screen, our entire Hello_World user interface navigation infrastructure will have its high-level navigation in place, allowing our end-users to travel (no pun intended) between our application's functional activity screens via our main options menu, and then to return from each of those app screens to the primary application home screen.

Enabling Our AttackPlanet Activity User Interface: Event Handling

Like we did for our TravelPlanet class, let's now prepare our **AttackPlanet** Activity and UI Layouts, so we can return our users to their app Home Screen when they are done having fun attacking the other planets.

We do this by adding an **Exit Attack Mode** ImageButton UI widget to our **activity_attack.xml** layout specification. Note that because we are using an ImageButton UI element, that we do *not* need to add a **button_name_exit** string constant to our `strings.xml` file. Later, we will wire up our Exit ImageButton element using event handler code which allows our users to return to the Hello_World Home Screen when an Exit ImageButton is clicked.

On the top right of your Eclipse editing tabs in the central pane there is a number (in Figure 5-10, it's a 10); click this again to drop-down the selection menu containing all your open code modules. Select the **activity_attack.xml** editing tab, so that we can add the Exit Attack Mode button XML mark-up that our Java event handler code is going to reference.

Let's take a shortcut and copy and paste the last `ImageButton` tag that we originally defined in our `activity_attack.xml` layout definition, and use that as our fifth `ImageButton` UI element, so we have another matching image button for use in this layout container, as shown in Figure 5-11. The fifth <ImageButton> tag and its parameters should look like the following XML mark-up:

```
<ImageButton
    android:id="@+id/exitButton"
    android:layout_width="wrap_content"
    android:layout_height="wrap_content"
    android:contentDescription="@string/content_desc_exit"
    android:src="@drawable/ic_launcher" />
```

`Make sure that you add a <string> tag to your strings.xml file for your Exit button content description parameter that says Exit to Home Planet using the following XML mark-up:`

```
<string name="content_desc_exit">Exit to Home Planet</string>
```

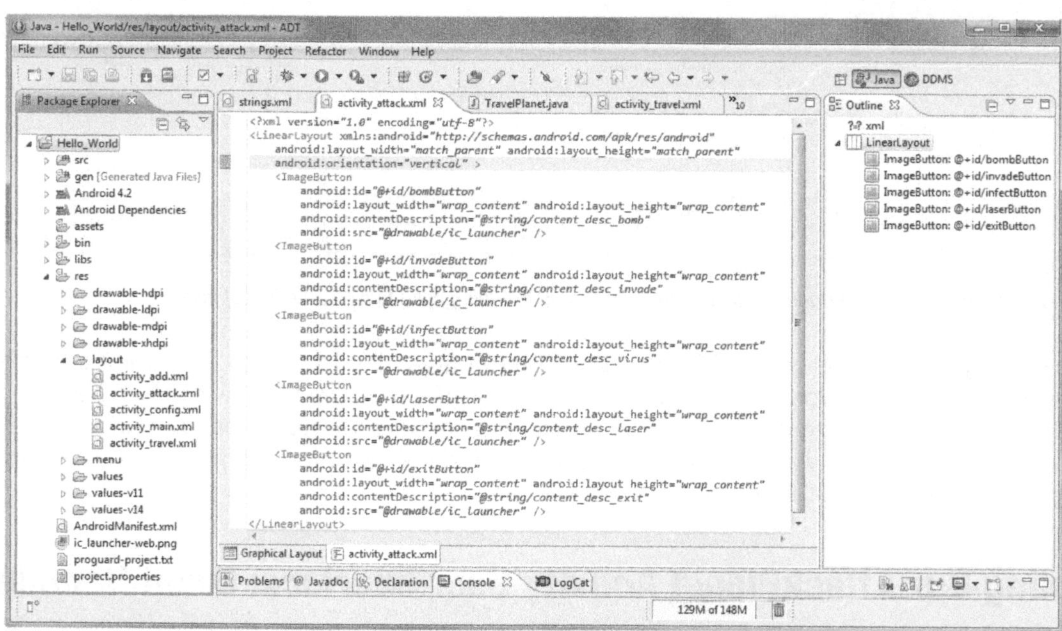

***Figure 5-11.** Adding a fifth Exit Attack Mode ImageButton UI element tag to our activity_attack.xml layout markup*

Also notice in Figure 5-11 that we changed the **android:orientation** parameter for our LinearLayout container tag from **horizontal** to **vertical**. This is so that our five image buttons (currently icon placeholder images, until we reach Chapter 7) will fit more easily up and down the screen rather than along the top now that there are five of them.

Now that our XML mark-up editing is completed, we can work on our Java code editing in the **AttackActivity.java** class. Here we need to add an **ImageButton** object on which to attach our next **onClick()** event handling method, to make our Exit Attack Mode button interactive, much like we did inside of our `TravelActivity.java` class in the previous section.

Let's undertake a similar work process to what we did in our `ConfigPlanet` class, and add an `ImageButton` object named **exitButton** that references the exitButton ID in the XML file that we just finished editing. We'll do this using a **findViewById()** method, via a single line of code, as follows:

```
ImageButton exitButton = (ImageButton)findViewById(R.id.exitButton);
```

Next we'll use the `exitButton ImageButton` object that we have just created and attach an **OnClickListener()** method to this UI object via the familiar **.setOnClickListener()** method that creates a **new** `OnClickListener` like this:

```
exitButton.setOnClickListener(new OnClickListener() { the code will go in here } );
```

The Java event handling code that we will use for our Exit Attack Mode button that returns the user to the Home Screen (MainActivity) involves again using the Activity class's **finish()** method, inside of the **onClick()** event handler, as shown in our modified `AttackPlanet` class in Figure 5-12.

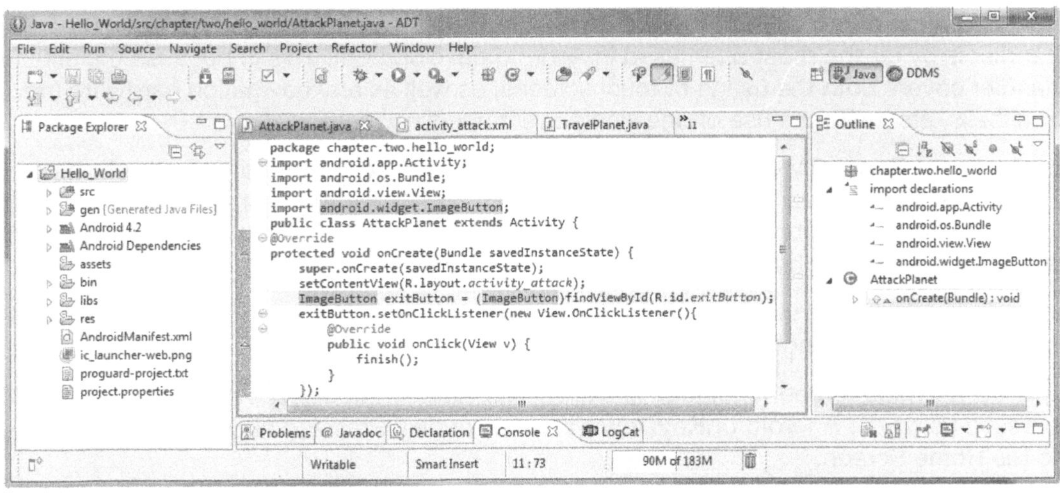

***Figure 5-12.** Add ImageButton UI object named exitButton to AttackPlanet.java class to handle events & finish()*

Now right-click the `Hello_World` project folder, and select **Run As Android Application**, which again launches our Nexus S emulator, so that we can test our app with its new Intent and Event processing code.

The screen again looks like Figure 4-16 when you click the emulator Menu button. Next, click the **Configure Planet** menu item and the Intent references and opens the ConfigPlanet Activity screen and its Configure Planet layout we created in the `activity_config.xml` file. Now let's see whether our event handler code is working. Click the **Done Configuring** button, and the `onClick()` event handler calls the `finish()` method and returns us to the Home Screen.

Next, click the **Travel to Planet** menu item, and see whether the Intent references and opens the TravelPlanet Activity screen and its Travel to Planet layout we created in the activity_travel.xml file. To see if our event handler code is working, click the **Return Home** button. That `onClick()` event handler should also call our `finish()` method and return us home.

Finally, click the **Attack on Planet** menu item, and the Intent references and opens the AttackPlanet Activity screen and its Attack Planet layout that we created in the `activity_attack.xml` file. Let's also test whether our event handler code for the ImageButton UI element is working properly. Click the **Exit Attack Mode** ImageButton, the icon at the bottom left, and see whether our `onClick()` event handler calls the `finish()` method.

Now that everything is working well for navigating around our Hello_World application's functional screens, let's cover one more important area in event handling–keys**.** Because a large percentage of Android devices these days have keys of some sort or another, we'll look at the **onKey()** method of event handling next, just so we cover all the "majors" in this chapter!

Event Handling for Keypads or Keyboards: OnKey Event Handlers

Up until now, we have used the `onClick()` event handler to capture the user touching our Activity screen UI elements, or navigating using a navigation arrow pad and center select button that is found on many Android devices.

We've focused most of our coverage so far on the `onClick()` handler method because the `onClick()` event handler is by far the most often used in Android development. This is because the `onClick()` event handler covers both the usage of touchscreens, as well as any navigation hardware (navigation keys, trackballs, etc.) with the use of one single event handling method.

With the advent of GoogleTV or Android iTVs, we also need to consider that more keyboards (or keypads) will become available for use by our end-users. There are also smartphone (and even tablet) models with slide-out or attachable mini-keyboards still available in the market, so I'm going to cover the **onKey()** event handling method here in this chapter as well.

Let's add a keyboard shortcut to our app that exits each of our Activity screen functional areas using the common **X** key, signifying the word **exit**.

To do this we will need to code methods in each of our Activity subclasses that listen for the **X** key being pressed using the Android **onKeyDown()** event handler. Pressing an **X** key will return our users to the Home Screen.

The `onKeyDown()` method takes in two parameters, one integer and one object and then evaluates them. The first parameter contains the **keyCode,** which is an **integer** value that represents the assigned numeric value (constant) for the key that is being depressed. The second parameter is a **KeyEvent** object named event that is the key event that is being handled.

The `onKeyDown()` method is **public** so everything can access it, and **boolean**, as it returns a **true** (handled) or a **false** (not handled) **return data value**.

The code to compare the **keyCode** passed into this event handler with the **KeyEvent** class constant for the letter X (**KEYCODE_X**) uses a basic **if-loop** inside of the **onKeyDown()** event handling method. The code looks like this:

```
public boolean onKeyDown(int keyCode, KeyEvent event) {
        if (keyCode == KeyEvent.KEYCODE_X) {
               finish();
               return true;
       }
       return false;
}
```

Let's type this code into our `ConfigActivity.java` class, right after the `onCreate()` method, because we want our Activity screen to "trap" the user pressing the **X** key to return to the Home Screen at any time.

Notice that as we type in this code, Eclipse sees we do not have the Android **KeyEvent** class declared for use via an **import** statement. Once you have finished typing in the method, mouse-over the KeyEvent keyword, and have Eclipse add our `import` statement for us, as shown in Figure 5-13.

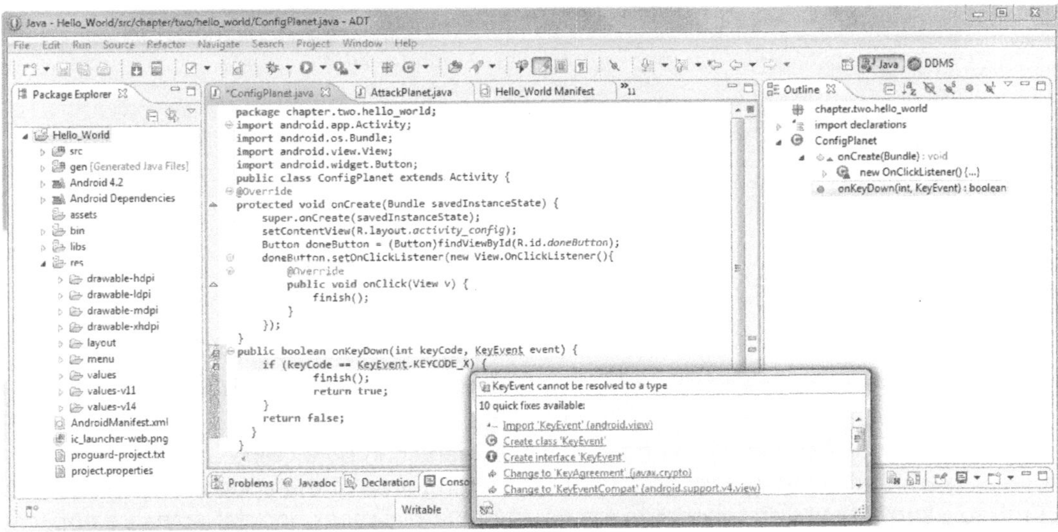

***Figure 5-13.** Adding an onKeyDown method and removing the error highlights by selecting: Import KeyEvent*

What the Java code does inside the `onKeyDown()` method is fairly basic, but I'll cover it here for those not as familiar with Java. We use a == numeric **comparison operator** inside of an if-loop, or in this case, it's utilized more as an if-statement, to compare a keycode integer representing the key that was pressed by the user to a `KEYCODE_X` constant that is part of the KeyEvent class to see whether X was pressed by the user.

If an X key was pressed (if the two values equate to being the same), then the statements inside of the if construct are executed, and the **finish();** code statement is executed, and a **true** value is returned from the called method, signifying that it has completed its event handling successfully.

If any other key is pressed (if the two values do not equate to being the same), then the statements inside of this if construct are *not* executed, and the method will return a **false** value signifying that the event was not acted upon. Note that any other event handlers we may create could still operate on that event; the event is said to **bubble** from one handler to the next, until it is handled (or never handled if we don't specify that key).

Figure 5-14 shows our completed **ConfigActivity.java** class event handling code, which we will now replicate (probably via cut and paste, if we're really smart) in our other three Hello_World Activity subclasses.

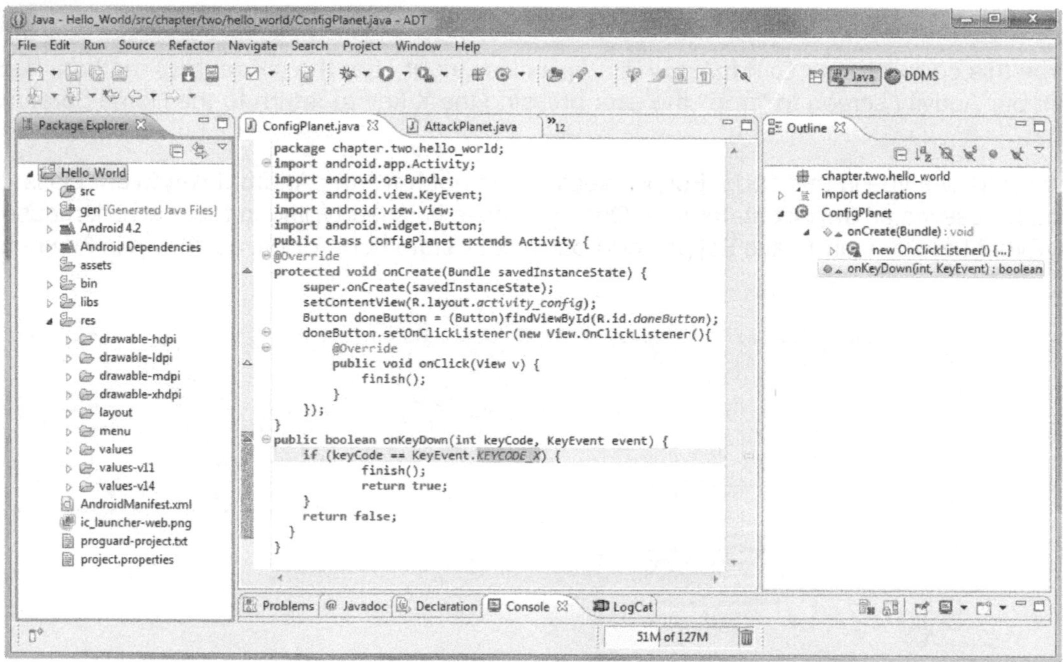

***Figure 5-14.** Final Java code for ConfigPlanet class to handle both click and key events for our app's navigation*

We do this so that each of our application functional screens can be exited easily by the user by simply pressing an **X** key, if they happen to go to the wrong area of the application by mistake. As you probably know, keyboard shortcuts are common across most popular software applications.

Let's do our code replication work process first, before we utilize the now familiar **Run As Android Application** function to test our application one final time, and before we move on to conquer the User Interface Design and User Experience Design sections of this book.

Select the `onKeyDown()` method in its entirety, and press the **Ctrl-C** key to copy it to your system clipboard, and then drop-down the **active tabs menu** by clicking the number (in Figure 5-14, it's a 12) on the right of the tabs area. Next, select your **TravelPlanet.java** file, and use the **Ctrl-V** keyboard sequence to paste the `onKeyDown()` method code block at the bottom of the TravelPlanet class, right before the final curly brace.

We need to also do this for our **NewPlanet.java** and **AttackPlanet.java** classes as well, so that all four of our application's Activity subclasses implement our new **X Key for Exit** key shortcut feature. Replicate this work process now, so that the `onKeyDown()` event handling is present in all four of our functional screen Activity subclasses.

Finally, we need to test our application navigation that we have added in this chapter in its entirety. Right-click our project folder select the **Run As Android Application** menu option, and launch the Nexus S emulator so that we can see whether everything we have implemented is working correctly.

To test the application once it is running, invoke the options menu, and click each of the four application areas, and then press the **X** key on your computer keyboard (the emulator uses your computer's keyboard to simulate a device keyboard), and be sure that your application returns the end-user to their Home Screen.

You will find that if you test the `onClick()` event handling at this point, that both types of events are handled perfectly alongside of each other. Our application is now ready for us to add actual features!

Other Event Handler Methods: OnFocusChange and OnLongClick

There are four other primary Android event handling methods that we are not going to cover in this chapter, but we will be implementing them later in the book, as we add in more complex user interface elements, graphic designs, animation, and new media assets and features to our application.

The first is the **OnLongClick()** event handling method, which is the Android equivalent of the right-click on a computer or other device using a mouse. A **LongClick** is invoked by touching and holding the screen, trackball, or the center selection button on any Android device.

An `onLongClick()` event handler is implemented in your Java code just like an onClick() event handler is.

The second type of event handler is an **OnCreateContextMenu()** event handler method, which creates **Context Menus** for use in Android. Context Menus are also similar to the menus found in a PC O/S that are accessed via right-clicking an object or area of the software to get a menu of **Context-Sensitive** options that are available specifically for that object.

The third type of event handler is the **OnFocusChange()** event handler method, which is used for handling **focus** events that are sent out by user interface elements when the user progresses from one element to the next.

When an end-user is using a given user interface element on an application screen, that UI element is said to have the **focus**, and when the user stops using that UI element, and starts using another UI element, then the focus is said to have **changed**.

When the focus changes from one of the UI elements to another, Android OS sends out a **FocusChanged** event that can be trapped by the `OnFocusChanged()` event handling method. This can be extremely useful for **fine-tuning** your application UI control, as well as for tracking precisely how the user is accessing your UI elements, and thus how a user is using your application.

Finally, there is also an **OnTouch()** event handler in Android, that handles only touchscreen events. I would suggest using the `onClick()` event handler for touchscreen devices (as well as non-touchscreen devices) to cover the widest array of Android devices with the least amount of coding.

However, if you are sure that all your users will have and use only touchscreen Android devices, you can then use the `onTouch()` event handling method as well as, or in place of, your `onClick()` methods.

The `OnTouch()` event handler is also used for Android OS features that can only use the touchscreen, the best example of this is an Android feature called **gestures**, the implementation of which is beyond the introductory scope of this book.

Summary

In this chapter, we learned about two of the most powerful and useful code constructs in the Android programming language: the **Intent** and the **Event**.

Intents and Events allow us to "wire up" our Android application, so to speak, so that when our end-users click on our user interface elements, such as our options menu items, ImageButtons, text Buttons or ImageViews, our application is able to process those clicks (or touches) and go where the application needs to go (Intents calling Activity screens), and to do what it needs to do (Events calling program logic to implement something).

First we learned about the anatomy of an **Intent object**, and the **seven** primary functional areas (component, action, data, type, category, flags, extras) that an Intent object can include. We learned why each of these areas are important, and why they are needed to process the Intent object, and what each of these areas do for (or in) the Intent processing request.

We learned about **implicit Intents** and the **<intent-filter>** tags inside the **AndroidManifest.xml** file, which implement these Intent Inference Engines that can be custom built by advanced developers. We learned that Intent Filters will process actions, then data, and then categories, to ascertain how developers want their Intents to be processed and executed.

We then learned about and implemented **explicit Intents** in our Hello_World application to implement the options menu structure we created in previous chapters, and have our menu call our four custom Activity subclasses that we created previously to hold our application functional screens.

Once we got our menu navigation working we needed to learn about event handling to use our user interface elements in each of our application functional screens to return us to our app's Home Screen.

We learned about the `onClick()` event handler and how to implement it in our Java code to trap click events on our various UI elements (widgets) so that our users could call the Activity finish() method and return to the main app Activity (Home Screen).

We then coded `onClick()` event handlers for a variety of popular Android user interface widgets, including **ImageView** objects, **Button** objects, and **ImageButton** objects. By doing this we enabled seamless navigation to and from each of the primary functional screens (Activities) within our app.

Next we learned about the onKey() event handlers and set up onKeyDown() handlers that allow us to trap our users hitting the **X** key, so that we could implement an **exit** keyboard shortcut for our application. After that we went over some of the other Android event handlers, which we will be implementing as we need them during the other three parts of this book.

We will be utilizing these **Intent** and **Event** capabilities often throughout the rest of this book; I just felt that we needed to get these basic Intent and Event concepts and principles taken care of very early on, here within the first part of the book. You're coders–you can handle it. No pun intended, of course.

I covered this topical material early on because these Intent and Event Java objects and methods are so very important to getting our application to work at a more advanced level, before we start to make it look really pristine, during the second part (User Interface Design) of this book.

In the second part of the book we will take the application infrastructure that we have created in the first part of the book, and start to focus on user interface design as well as graphics design for our Hello_World app, enhancing our User Experience (UX) and making Hello_World look more like a professional Android application.

In the next chapter, we will learn about Android UI Design widgets, and start fine-tuning our user interface designs for our five primary screen areas in our Hello_World Android application. However, in Chapter 6 we will mainly be using XML mark-up (for the most part) to refine and enhance our UI elements.

Also in Chapter 6 we will explore many of these primary UI element options (as XML parameters) for fine-tuning our User Interface "look and feel," as well as exploring the precise pixel placement of our UI elements on our Android application's screen real estate.

Chapter 6

Android UI Design: Using Views and Widgets via XML

In this chapter, we will take our Hello World application, which we created during the first part of the book, and work toward making the application user interface design for its various functional screens considerably more professional. In Android, this is done primarily via XML UI parameters for Android user interface **widgets**, which we already know are **View** subclasses.

At the same time, we are also going to utilize this chapter to give those of our readers who are not user interface designers a taste of the various design considerations that are encountered in striving to make a UI design appear professional, while also remaining easy to use for the end-users.

I'm going to again attempt to simultaneously accomplish these objectives; enhancing our Hello World application user interface considerably, while also covering key XML UI parameters at a low-level, in one unified chapter which will outline the techniques and capabilities of using XML to define user interface elements within the context of our Hello World application.

Android User Interface Elements: Android View and Subclasses

As I mentioned earlier in the book, all user interface elements, at least the visual ones that the user interfaces with to control the application, are **subclasses** of the Android **View** class, which means that a View is itself an object and a subclass of the **java.lang.Object** master Object class.

Some of the most common user interface widget objects and layout container objects, including ViewGroup, ImageView, and TextView, are **direct sublasses** of the View class. Others that we have already utilized, such as Button, VideoView, and ImageButton, are **indirect subclasses** of the View class.

Indirect subclasses are simply subclasses of subclasses; for instance, the Android **Button** class, which can be found (imported) via the **android.widget** package (you would import android.widget. Button in order to use a Button UI element object) is subclassed from the **android.widget.TextView**

class. This is because a Button object has all the features that a TextView object has, plus additional features (the button look and feel elements), so it is logical to subclass a TextView object to create a Button object.

Other View direct subclasses that we will be looking at later in this book include AnalogClock and ProgressBar; however, many of the user interface widgets that we will be using are farther down in the View class hierarchy (that is, they're more specialized user interface feature implementations) and are thus indirect subclasses of the Android View class.

In this chapter we're going to focus on **mainstream** View classes or widgets that are used across all Android application development projects. Our app UI widgets will include direct subclasses **TextView** and **ImageView**, because images and text are the most important and often used elements in any app, as well as **Button**, **ImageButton**, **EditText**, and **VideoView** UI element widgets.

Optimizing Our NewPlanet Activity UI: The ImageView UI Widget

Let's start with our first options menu item and Activity screen, defined in the **NewPlanet.java** class, which we wrote back in Chapter 3. This UI screen lets us click an image of a Planet to create that basic planet object inside of our Hello World Android application. If you forgot what it looks like, it's shown again in this chapter, with planet images, in Figure 6-2.

As it sits right now, we are using the default Android application launch icon that the New Android Application Project dialog series created for us in Chapter 2 as a placeholder image. In this section we'll finally replace those placeholder images with actual planet images, and later on we'll use XML parameters to format them to fit the screen with professional results.

I have created four different resolution versions of each planet; one that is 256 pixels square for iTVs, one that is 192 pixels square for tablets, one that is 128 pixels square for touchscreen smartphones, and one that is 96 pixels square for mobile phones with smaller 240 or 320 pixel screens.

Putting Our Image Assets in Drawable DPI Folders

Next copy each of these planet image files into their appropriate drawable folder under the resource (res) folder. Note that we will be getting into all the theory behind developing these different resolution graphics assets very soon, in Chapter 7. For now, I'll simply cover the basics of what we are doing here, so we can use drawables (bitmap imagery) in our user interface design work inside this chapter.

Let's start with planet **Earth**, as that is our first XML **ImageView** tag, in our **activity_add.xml** layout container that we developed in Chapter 3. Using the Windows Explorer file manager, copy the **earth256.png** file into your Hello_World project **resource** folder, in the **drawable-xhdpi** folder at:

```
C:/Users/YourNameHere/workspace/Hello_World/res/drawable-xhdpi/
```

XHDPI stands for **Extra High Density Pixel Imagery**, and this folder contains our highest resolution image assets, in this case, a 256 pixel square Earth image. Next copy the **earth192.png** file into the **drawable-hdpi** folder, used for **High Density Pixel Images**, and then copy the **earth128.png**

file into the **drawable-mdpi** folder, used for **Medium Density Pixel Images**, and finally, copy the **earth96.png** file into the **drawable-ldpi** folder used for **Low Density Pixel Images**.

Next, we are going to rename each of these four image files to **earth.png**. We do this because earth.png is the image asset name that we are going to reference in our XML mark-up and Java code, and Android automatically looks at what screen size is being used by the user, and go into the correct folder and get that resolution density image asset. We will be getting into this concept further in Chapter 7.

Next, we need to copy and rename the other five planet image assets, so that we have six .png files in each of the four drawable folders. Each of the four folders should have six .png files, each starting with just the name of the planet, and in all lowercase characters.

Next, we have to use the **Refresh** command in Eclipse to **update** our project folders to display these new assets that we have copied into these folders from "outside of" Eclipse (using the Windows Explorer file manager).

To do this, right-click your project folder and select **Refresh** from the menu, or alternatively you can left-click the folder and press the **F5** function key on your computer keyboard. What this does is to tell Eclipse to scan all your project folders and files, and to update the Package Explorer navigation pane, as well as its own tracking routines, so that these image files, when called inside our code, will not get flagged as missing (or not present) from our project assets hierarchy.

Referencing and Aligning Our Planet Image Source Files

Next, we need to go into our **activity_add.xml** RelativeLayout XML file and change our XML mark-up that we wrote back in Chapter 4 to point to the proper planet filenames, which are referenced in each **ImageView** tag using the **android:src** parameter. Change the placeholder image, currently **@drawable/ic_launcher**, with the name of each planet in lowercase letters. The parameter for the first ImageView tag **imageEarth** would be as follows:

```
android:src="@drawable/earth"
```

After you do this for all six ImageView tags, click the **Graphical Layout** tab at the bottom of the editing pane, and use its preview feature to see if all six planets are showing. If they are, then you've done the previous steps in this work process correctly. Notice that all six planets, as a group, need to be moved over to the right a little bit. To accomplish this we will add the now familiar **android:layout_marginLeft** parameter. Because we want the entire layout (the group of planets as a whole) to be moved over, we will put this marginLeft parameter inside the **parent** RelativeLayout tag, as shown in the shaded line of code in Figure 6-1.

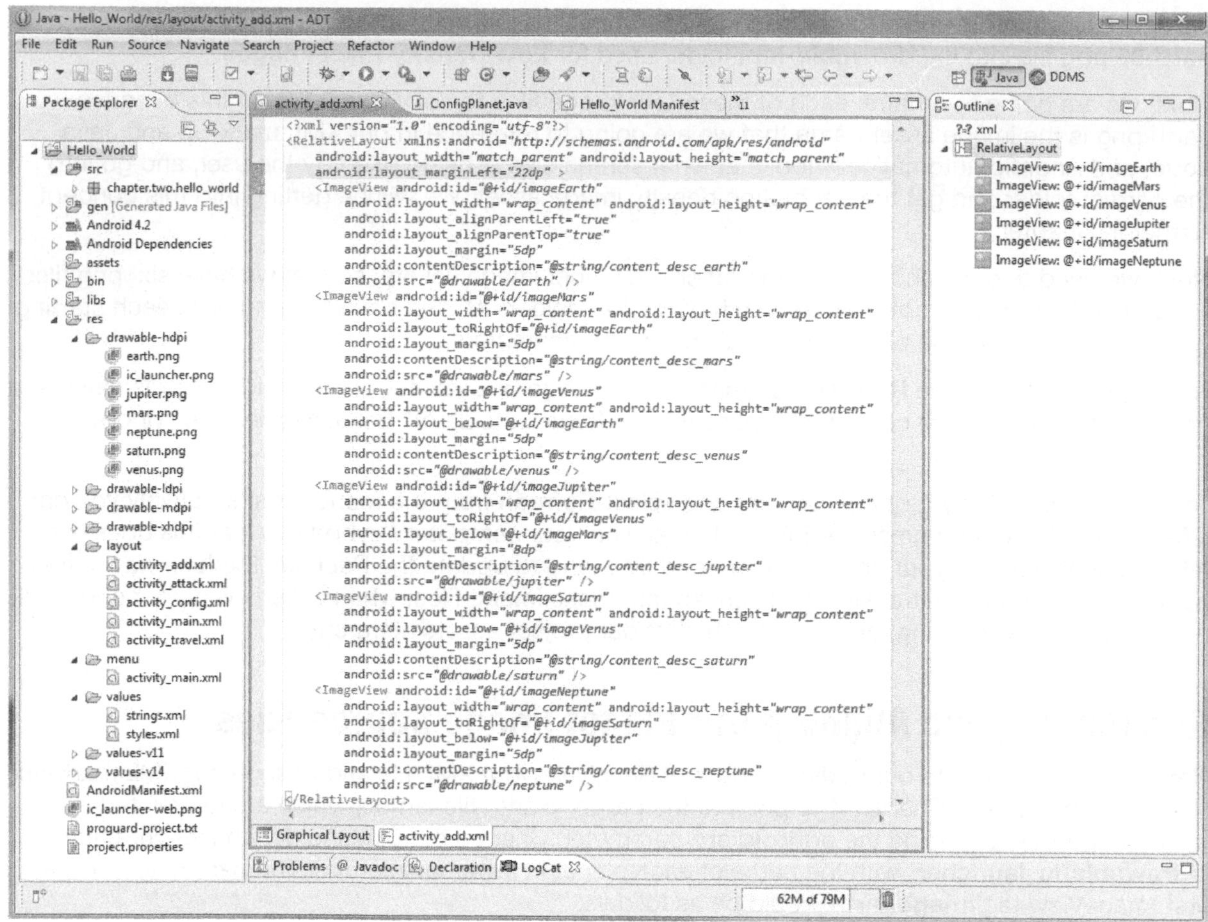

***Figure 6-1.** Add RelativeLayout parameter to center all planets and set the android:src parameter to new imagery*

Use a setting value of 22 **Density Independent Pixels** (DIP, or DP) to center our New Planet selection ImageView PNG graphics on our NewPlanet Activity class user interface screen via the following line of XML markup:

```
android:layout_marginLeft="22dp"
```

Now go back and click the bottom **Graphical Layout** tab to preview this new **android:marginLeft** parameter you have added, and see how this 22 DIP setting pushes the group of planets into the center of the display screen for a more professional UI screen appearance. This is shown in Figure 6-2, along with the Eclipse **Properties** pane on the right, which you can make larger in your Graphical Layout Editor tab screen by placing your mouse over the top border of the Properties pane, when your cursor turns into a double-arrow drag-to-resize-me indicator, at which time you can drag this border up, giving yourself a larger properties editing area to work with.

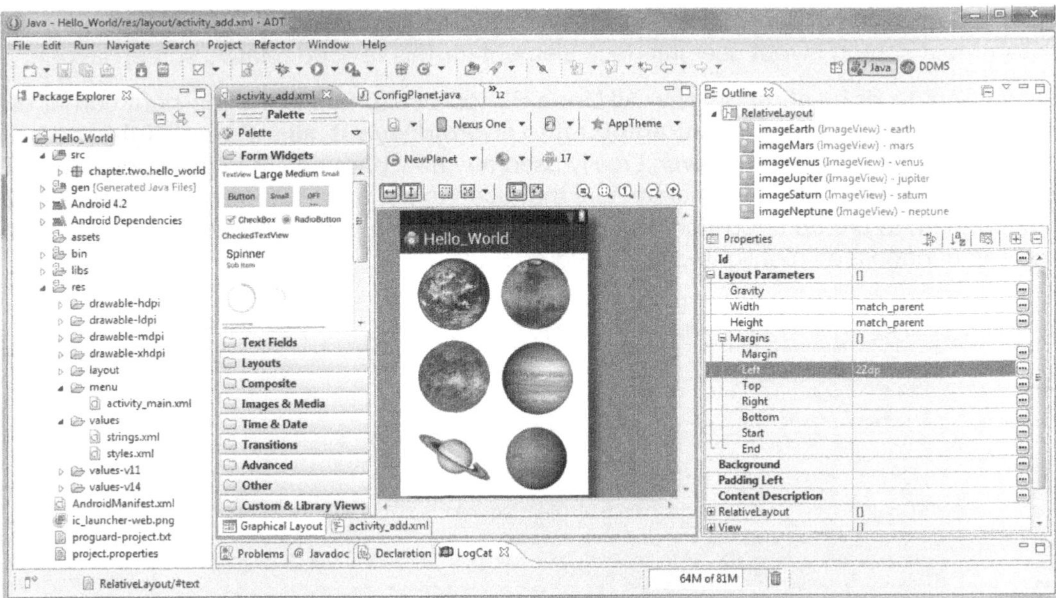

Figure 6-2. *Preview of activity_add XML code, with planet images and new margin settings in Properties panel*

Notice that the parameters that you coded in the XML mark-up view pane are also set in the Properties pane view, so you can add parameters in this way as well, if you want. Highlighted in blue is our Left Margin Layout Parameter 22dp setting that we just added. Also notice the simulated app user interface screen in the center, along with a much more professional view of our six planets. Things are shaping up nicely for this Activity.

Adding Screen Caption Text and Done Button

The next thing that makes this screen completely professional is adding a **TextView** UI widget (tag) at the top of the screen to tell users what the screen is for, as well as a **Button** they can click when they're finished adding planets. The **doneAddingButton** Button UI element (tag) calls our **finish()** Activity method, and clicking the planet ImageView UI elements generates those new objects. We'll write our Java code later on in the chapter; for now we are learning UI design via XML, so let's add our tags.

First, let's add in a **Button** user interface element tag, so that our users can exit this screen when they are done adding planets. The easiest way to accomplish this is to go into the **activity_config.xml** XML mark-up, and to copy the Done Configuring Button tag, and then paste that mark-up at the top of the **activity_add.xml** file, under the RelativeLayout container tag.

Change the **android:id** value to **@+id/doneAddingButton** and the **android:text** value to **@string/button_name_done_add**, and then go into your **strings.xml** file and copy and paste the **button_name_done** <string> tag, and create a **button_name_done_add** named string constant, with a value of: **"All Done!"**

The next thing that we want to do is to cut and paste (not copy) both the **android:layout_alignParentLeft** and **android:layout_alignParentTop** tags from the imageEarth

ImageView tag, and utilize them in the Button tag we are adding. This is because the Button tag is now the top-most screen layout user interface element for this revised relative screen layout.

Because we want to **right-align** the new **All Done** Button UI element in the top-right corner of the screen, change **android:layout_alignParentLeft** to **android:layout_alignParentRight** and leave the android:alignParentTop alone. We haven't really used any new parameters in our **doneAddingButton** UI element, we just "borrowed" the parameters that used to be in the top-left ImageView UI element, and changed them to create a top-right Button UI element. Next we will add a TextView UI element for our screen caption (see highlighted line in Figure 6-3).

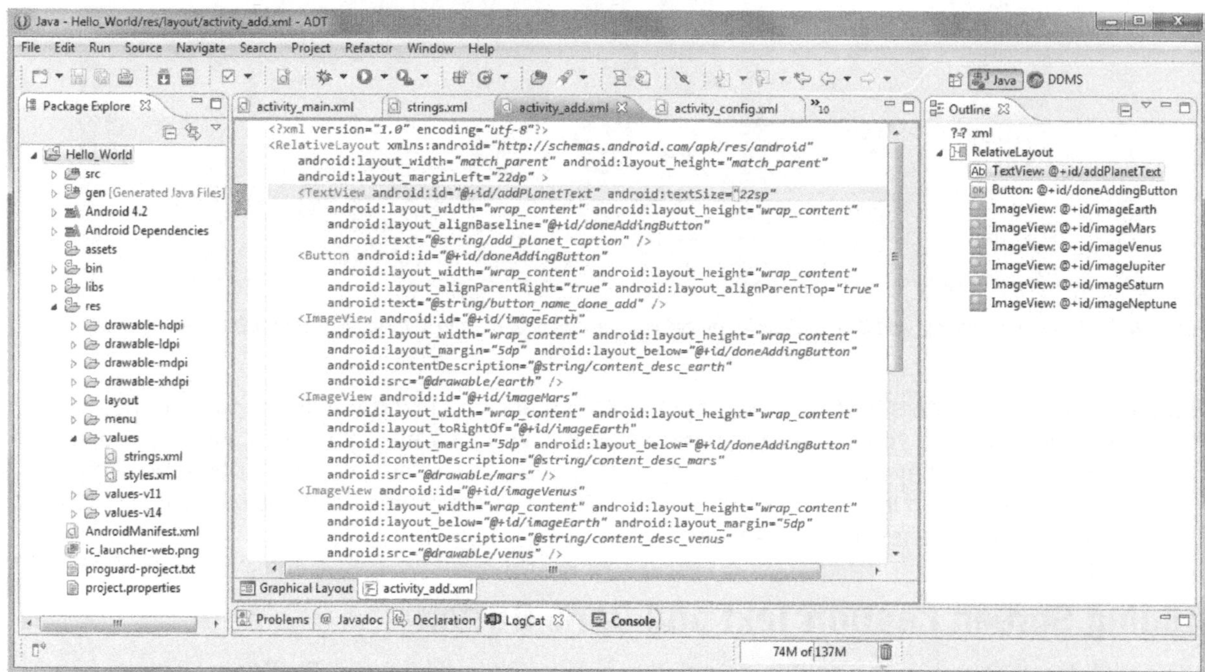

Figure 6-3. ***Adding a TextView tag to add a screen caption and a doneAddingButton Button tag to exit Activity***

Next let's copy the first TextView UI element (tag) from our **activity_main** XML layout container, and paste it above the Button tag we just created. Change the **android:id** to **@+id/addPlanetText** and the **android:text** parameter to point to **@string/add_planet_caption**, and then go into your strings. xml file and copy and paste the **hello_world** <string> tag and use it to create a **add_planet_caption** named string constant, with a value of: "**Click Planet to Add**" so that our users know what to do when they get to this screen.

Preview the UI design via the Graphical Layout Editor tab at the bottom of the edit pane, and you'll notice that the text is a bit small, so go back into XML edit mode and add an **android:textSize** parameter set to **22sp** right after the **android:id** parameter in the TextView tag as shown in Figure 6-3.

Text fonts use **standard pixels (sp)** rather than density independent pixels to define their values. If you try and use **dp** or **dip** with any font-related sizing, Eclipse will flag it and warn you to use **sp** values for sizing text.

The next thing we need to do is to align our screen caption text with the Button UI element, so that it looks professional and well-aligned, at the top of the screen layout. We can do this with one single parameter, called **android:layout_alignBaseline** which will align a UI element with a baseline alignment to another UI element, in this case, with our Button UI element.

Let's implement that now, by setting the alignBaseline parameter to point to the android:id value of our Button UI element using the parameter code:

```
android:layout_alignBaseline="@+id/doneAddingButton"
```

This line of code is also shown in Figure 6-3 and when we now click the Graphical Layout Editor tab at the bottom of the edit pane we see both our larger font size and our Baseline alignment implemented in the UI design.

Also notice in Figure 6-4 that Eclipse actually shows us the baseline that it is using to align the text in the Button tag UI element with the screen caption TextView UI element. If you look closely you will see a green line that proves that our TextView and Button object are now Baseline aligned.

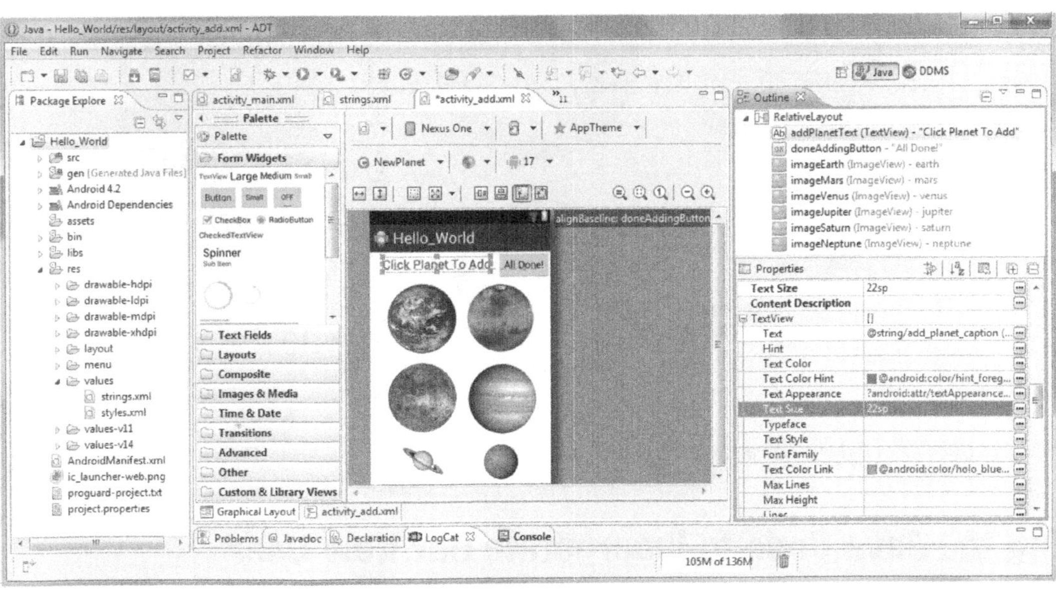

***Figure 6-4.** Viewing the TextView layout_alignBaseline parameter result relative to the doneAddingButton Button*

If you are not seeing a green baseline, go back into XML edit mode pane and click the line of code for the alignBaseline parameter to highlight it.

Once that line of code is highlighted (in light blue), it will be the one that is previewed (specifically) in the Graphical Layout Editor view, once you click that tab again. Also notice in Figure 6-4 that I highlighted our Text Size parameter in the Properties pane, showing that it could also be set there as well. Next, let's **Run As Android Application**, and see how our NewPlanet.java Activity screen user interface layout looks with all our new changes in place. The results can be seen in Figure 6-5.

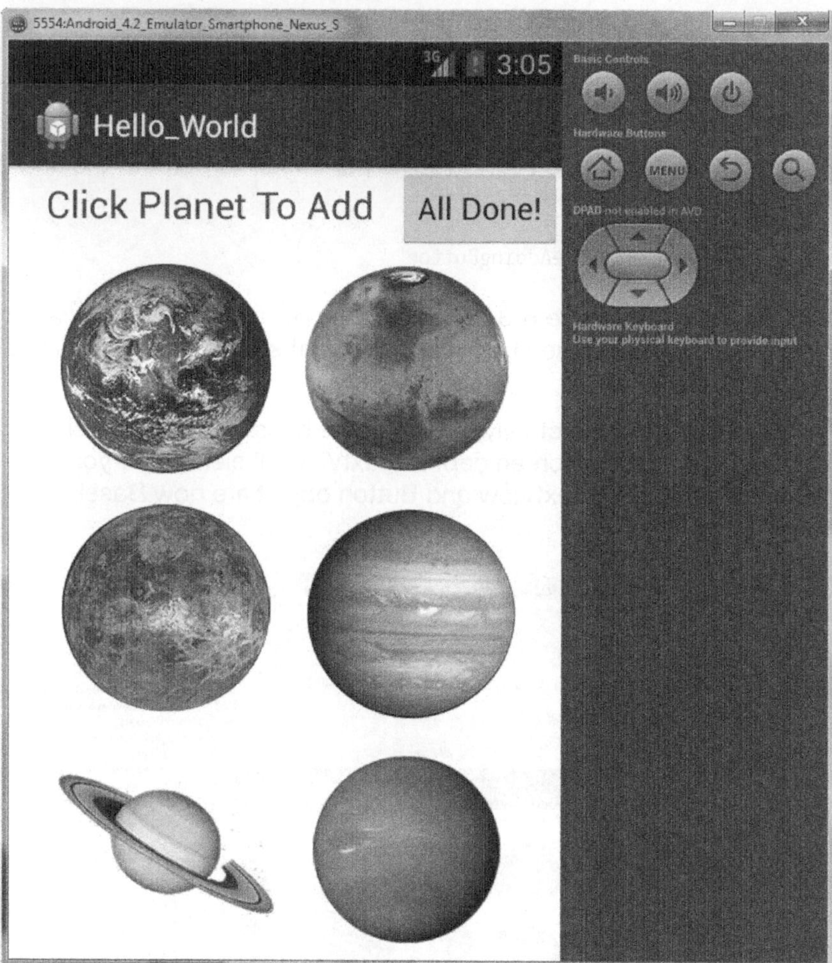

***Figure 6-5.** Our NewPlanet Activity screen in the Nexus S emulator*

Adding the Java Code to Incorporate Our New User Interface Elements

Finally, we need to make a couple of additions to our **NewPlanet.java** Java code to assimilate the changes we made in our XML UI designs into the Java code functions of this Add a New Planet Activity for our Hello_World Android application. The first thing we need to do is add a **Button** object.

Setting up our Button UI object in Java is similar to how we set up the ImageView object to handle a click on our Mars ImageView object. We declare our Button object using a line of Java code that declares a **Button** object, names that object **doneButton,** and wires it up to our XML definition via the **findViewById()** method referencing a **doneAddingButton** ID like this:

```
Button doneButton = (Button)findViewById(R.id.doneAddingButton);
```

Next, we utilize the familiar **.setOnClickListener()** method to set a **new View.OnClickListener()** for the doneButton Button object. This in turn contains an onClick() event handler that listens for a click and then executes a **finish()** method for our Activity, allowing the user to exit the Activity screen, and return to the Home Screen. The code looks like this:

```
doneButton.setOnClickListener(new View.OnClickListener() {
        @Override
        public void onClick(View v){
                finish();
        }
});
```

Next, we need to remove the finish() method call from the onClick() event handler method that is attached to our **marsImage** ImageView object, because we now have our **doneButton** UI Button to use to exit our Activity, and we no longer want the screen to go away when we click one of the planets.

In place of the finish() method, let's add a **Toast** object and method call, to let our users know that the Mars object was in fact created. This is a logical place to introduce Android **Toast** objects, because they are usually used for user interface and user experience optimization and enhancement.

Introducing (and Utilizing) the Android Toast Class

Android Toast objects are used to send messages onto your Activity screen that appear for a predefined period of time sending a message to the user. In our case they will send the message "Mars Created" when the user clicks on the marsImage ImageView UI element so that the user knows that the Mars object has been created by the user clicking the image of that planet.

Toast objects are from the **android.widget.Toast** package and class and are a subclass of java.lang. Object (and not a subclass of android.view.View, as it does not need any of the View class features) because they are simple by nature, although they are also very effective when used well.

Declaring a Toast object is done most simply by using the **.makeToast()** method off of a Toast object. The method requires the current context, the message to be Toasted, and the duration in the form of a constant. There are two duration constants, **LENGTH_LONG** and **LENGTH_SHORT**, and we will be using the LENGTH_SHORT constant for a quick visual confirmation that our Mars planet has been created. The Toast call is coded as follows:

```
Toast.makeText(NewPlanet.this, "Mars Created", Toast.LENGTH_SHORT).show();
```

Notice that we have appended the Toast **show()** method using dot notation to the end of the Toast. makeText() method call. This is a great example of Java method **chaining** and this technique allows us to make more dense code, where an entire block of code can be written within a single line of code. To write this single line of code "long-hand," using two separate lines of Java code, you would code the following:

```
Toast myToast = Toast.makeText(NewPlanet.this, "Mars Created", Toast.LENGTH_SHORT);
myToast.show();
```

As you can see here the first line of code we wrote was much more compact!

Now add this line of code we developed to Toast a message to the screen in place of the **finish()** method call we had before and our finished NewPlanet Java code will look like the code shown in Figure 6-6.

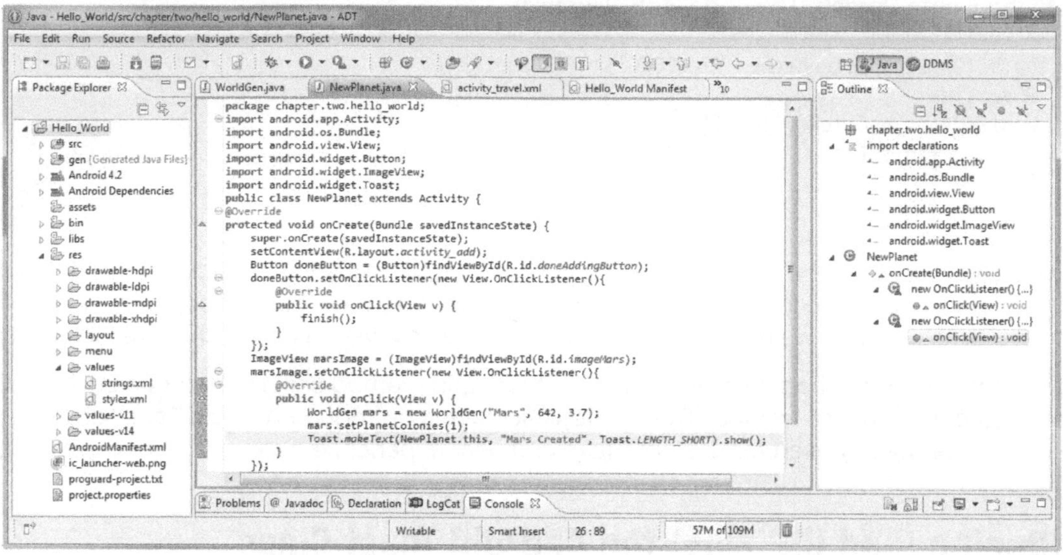

***Figure 6-6.** Adding a Button object and a Toast object and .makeText method call to our NewPlanet.java Activity*

Notice that when we **Run As Android Application** to test our code, that we now get a screen that has an All Done button, and it creates a Mars object when we click the Mars image, and Toasts us feedback that the Mars object has been created.

We'll finish the Java code for this area of our application a little bit later on, right now we are focusing on our user interface design, so let's continue, and fine-tune our UI for our **ConfigPlanet** Activity screen next.

Optimizing Our ConfigPlanet Activity UI: Button and Text UI Widgets

Let's refine our user interface design for our second options menu item, Configure Planet, by enhancing the XML mark-up in our **activity_config.xml** file. First, we'll condense some of our Button tag XML mark-up by putting two tag parameters on each line, so we can fit some new UI element tags on the screen. Notice that tag parameters need only be separated by a single space character; parameters do not need to be on their own line. This can be seen in Figure 6-7, inside the **LinearLayout**, where our Button tags now only take up around a dozen lines of markup. To enhance this UI design and make the screen more functional, we will need to place some **editable text fields** on the right side of our UI screen across from each of our buttons.

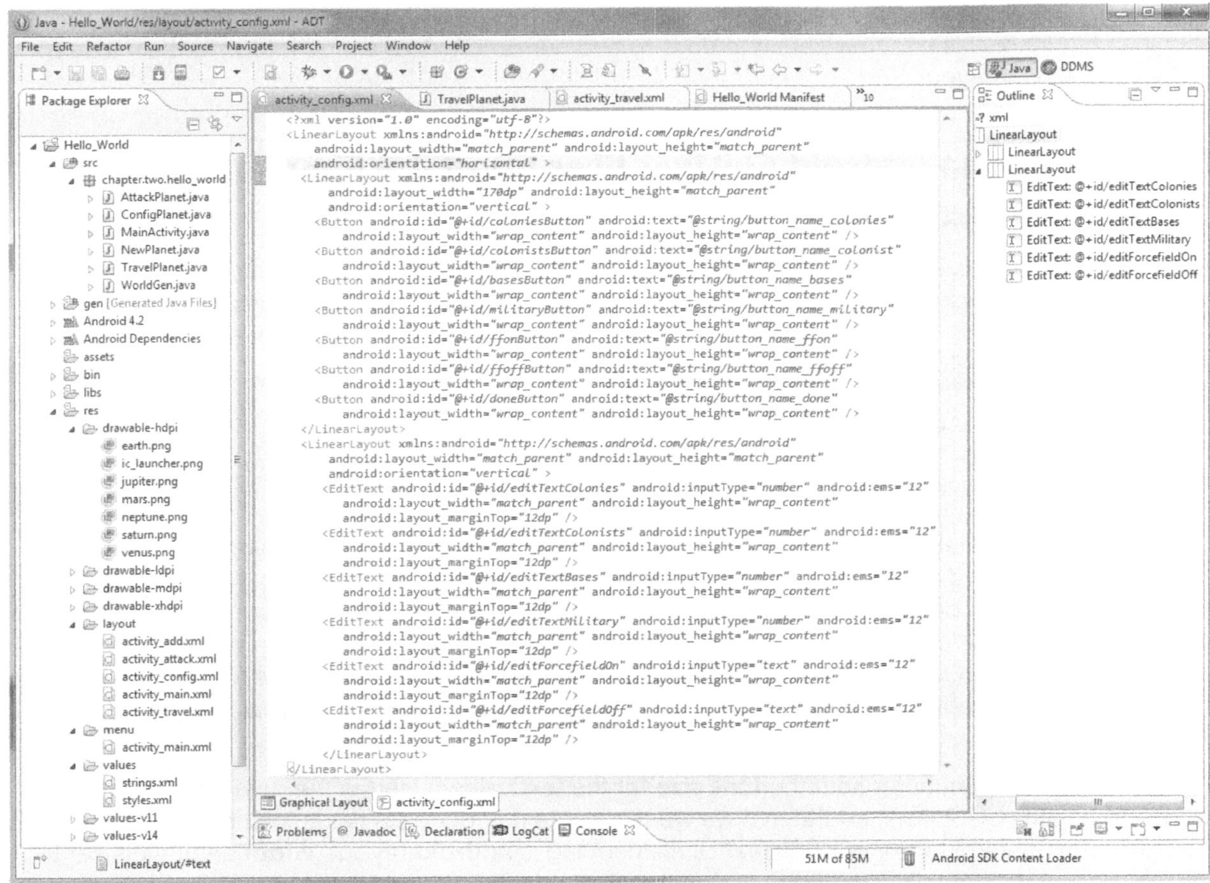

Figure 6-7. Adding EditText UI element tags and nesting two LinearLayouts to create a side-by-side UI layout

Creating Complex User Interface Designs Using Nested Layout Containers

To accomplish this, we need to nest two LinearLayout containers together, one for the left-side vertically aligned **Button** UI tags, and the other for the right-side vertically aligned **EditText** UI element tags. Let's copy the LinearLayout opening tag, and paste it underneath the LinearLayout closing tag to start a new container, as shown in Figure 6-7. Copy a LinearLayout closing tag underneath that, so that our closing tag is in place as well.

Then copy the LinearLayout opening tag and paste it **above** the LinearLayout opening tag, to create a new top-level LinearLayout container, and change its **android:orientation** parameter from **vertical** to **horizontal**, because the two nested LinearLayout containers are going to be beside each other. Then copy the LinearLayout closing tag again as well, and paste it at the very bottom of the layout container so that the first **horizontal** LinearLayout tag wraps the two internal (nested) **vertical** LinearLayout container tags.

To set a width ratio between the two nested LinearLayouts we need to add an **android:layout_width** parameter to the first (left) tag, to define how much of the screen (**170dp**) it will have. The right LinearLayout takes the rest.

If you like, you can change the indentation of the nested tags slightly to show what is nested, as shown in Figure 6-7. Next, all we have to do is to add our **EditText** UI element tags to the inside of the second LinearLayout.

Introducing the Android EditText User Interface Element for Editable Text Fields

To add an EditText User Interface element, we can either drag the EditText UI element onto the right side of the screen, using the Graphical Layout Editor, or hand-code the EditText tag and its parameters, by writing the mark-up for one element, and then copying it five times while changing the parameters to match the Button ID and Input Type:

```
<EditText android:id="@+id/editTextColonies" android:inputType="number"
          android:ems="12" android:layout_width="match_parent"
          android:layout_height="wrap_content" android:layout_marginTop="12dp" />
```

The first EditText UI field is opposite the Add Colonies Button and has an **android:id** of **editTextColonies** and an **android:inputType** of **number** (matches up with integer data). The inputType parameter defines the type of data the field uses and needs to match up with the data type used in the Java code that will access that field, as we will see a bit later on when we write our Java code to populate these data fields. We use number and text data types for our inputType parameters but if needed there are other types, such as **numberDecimal,** for real (decimal) numbers as well.

The **android:ems** parameter sets the **font size** for the text values used in the data field, and we will start with a value of 12 ems, and then if we want larger text in our data fields, refine it from there a bit later. The next parameter for our EditText UI element tag is **android:layout_width** and that is set to **match_parent**, which tells Android to match the width of the EditText UI element (field) to the parent container object (tag), which in this case is the second nested LinearLayout.

The **android:layout_height** parameter in our EditText tag has a **wrap_content** value, which is essentially the opposite of a **match_parent** value. The wrap content constant means to conform the edges of the UI element to the content contained therein, whereas the match parent constant means the opposite: expand the edges of a UI element to the container that it is contained in.

Finally, we will use an **android:layout_marginTop** parameter of **12dp** to line up each of our EditText fields with our Buttons, so that we have even spacing between the data fields, and so that each lines up with the bottom edge of the Button UI element that is immediately to the left of it.

Now that we have coded one representative EditText tag, let's copy it five more times underneath itself and change the **android:id** parameters to match the button ID names and change the **android:inputType** parameter to **text** for the two Forcefield indicator fields, which will contain text values.

The end result of upgrading our Configure Planet Activity screen XML to include EditText data editing fields in side-by-side Linearlayouts can be seen in Figure 6-7, which shows our final XML code and an overview of the UI elements that we are using in the Outline pane on the right-hand side of Eclipse. Check to make sure that the current UI settings look good on the emulator screen by using the **Run As Android Application** work process.

Adding the Java Code to Incorporate Our Configure a Planet Screen's New User Interface Elements

Next, let's modify our **ConfigPlanet.java** Activity class Java code to "wire it up" to these new UI elements, so it becomes functional within our app.

The first thing that we want to do is to replicate our Button code for our **doneButton** Button object so that all our Buttons on the Activity screen are functional. Notice in Figure 6-8 that I made the **onClick()** code block a bit more compact by placing the **finish();** statement inside of the curly braces on one line, because for now, there is only that one code statement.

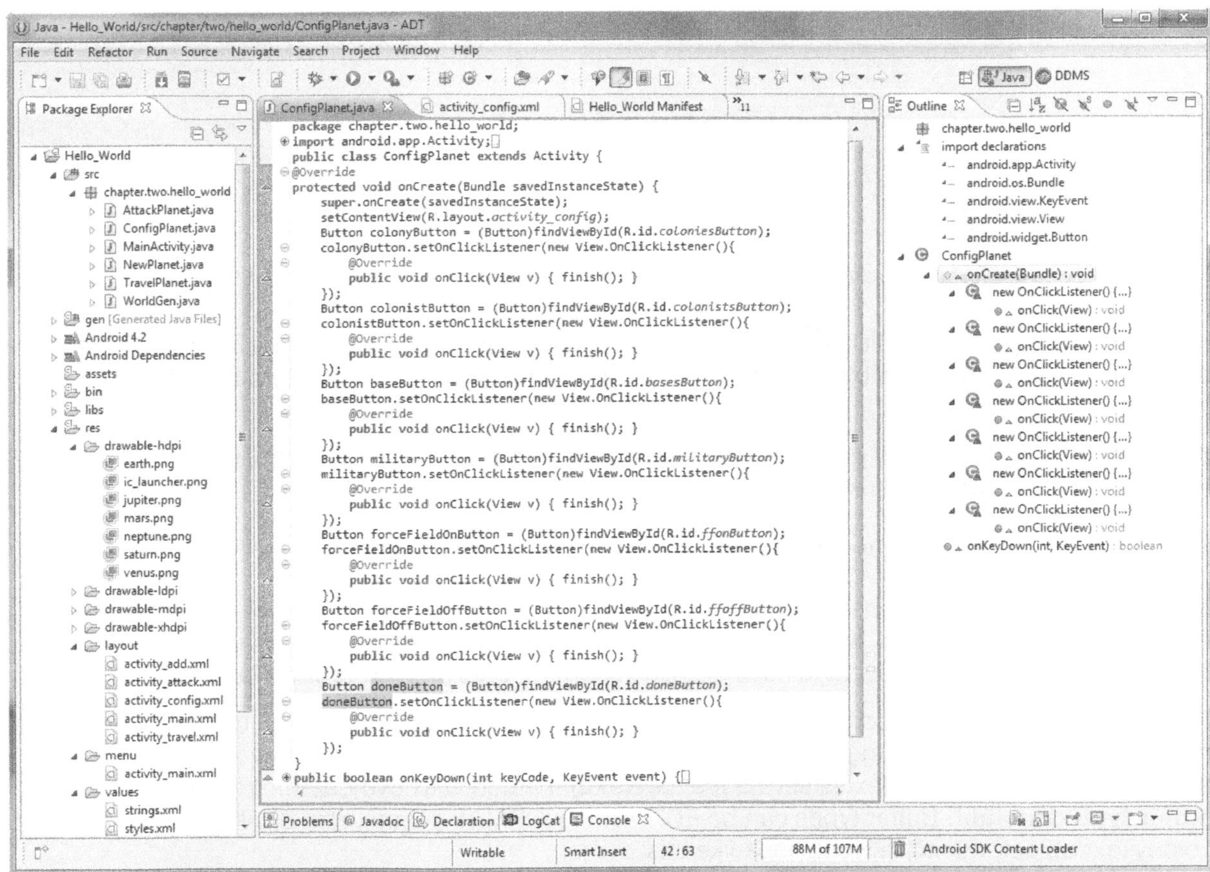

Figure 6-8. Adding Button objects and onClick() event handlers for each to our Java code in ConfigPlanet.java

Next, we need to copy all the doneButton related (5) lines of Java code **six times** underneath the doneButton code block as shown in Figure 6-8, so we create colonyButton, colonistButton, baseButton, militaryButton, forceFieldOnButton, and finally forceFieldOffButton blocks of code. Make sure to reference the correct XML ID names for each Button UI element in each code block, and make sure that the **.setOnClickListener()** method is connected to the correct Button object name that is defined in the line immediately above it. Finally, click the top minus sign icon in the left margin next to each block of code to collapse the code blocks as shown in Figure 6-9 so we have more editing room.

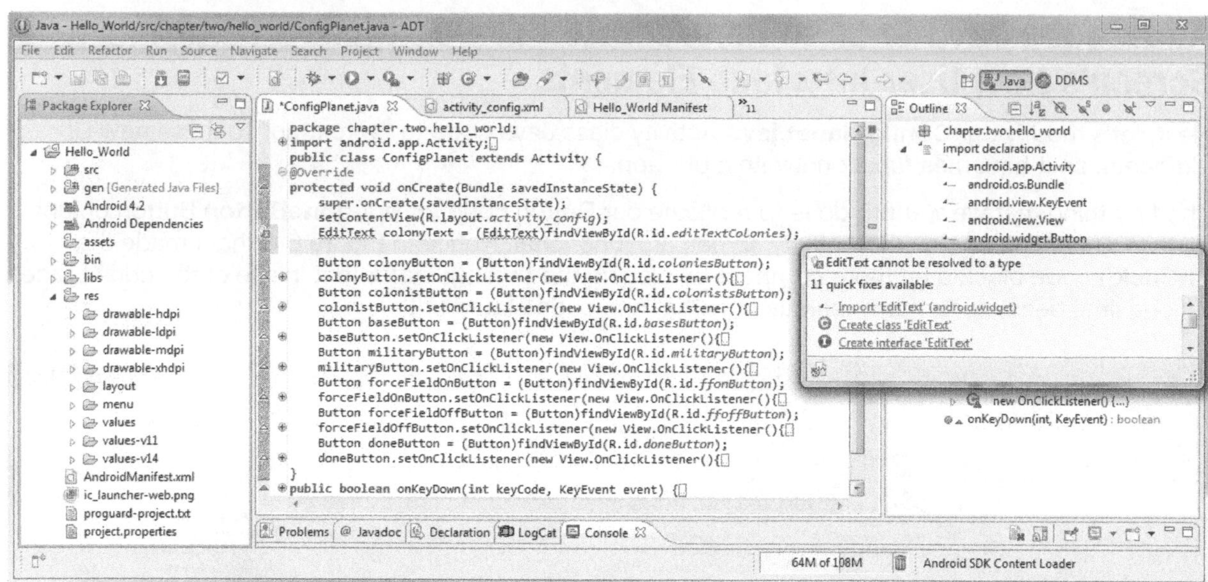

Figure 6-9. Add an EditText object named colonyText and Invoke Eclipse's auto-import feature via: Import EditText

Now it is time to add our EditText UI objects to our Java code, so that we can utilize the data values that are put into these fields by the user in our program logic as we continue to build this app throughout the book.

You should be getting pretty good at declaring UI elements inside the Java code, using their widget type, name, and **findViewById()** method, like this:

```
EditText colonyText = (EditText)findViewById(R.id.editTextColonies);
```

Notice in Figure 6-9 that Eclipse error flags our EditText object, because we are not allowed to use it in our code until we import it, so mouse-over the red-underlined object, and click the **Import EditText android.widget** package option, to have Eclipse import our **android.widget.EditText** class.

The next thing we need to do is to set a default value inside our EditText field that conforms to how many of that attribute we suggest that users add. In the case of Colonies, we are using a "1" value, to add a Colony at a time. Text is set via the **.setText()** method with two parameters, a **value**, and a **buffer type constant**. Buffer types can be EDITABLE, NORMAL (Fixed), and SPANNABLE. For our colonyText object, our code would look like this:

```
EditText colonyText = (EditText)findViewById(R.id.editTextColonies);
colonyText.setText("1", EditText.BufferType.EDITABLE);
```

Now all we have to do is copy those last two lines of Java code five times underneath the first two lines, and change the colony to colonists, bases, military, forcefieldOn, and forcefieldOff. Then, make sure the XML ID tag names for each EditText UI element match our XML in **activity_config.xml**, and then change the "1" value to "100" for **colonistsText** and to "10" for **militaryText** to set more reasonable default values for those data fields.

For our forcefieldOn and forcefieldOff **text** data fields, we will use a "Forcefield is Off" for the forcefieldOffText data default setting, and a null (empty quotes) setting for the forcefieldOnText data default setting.

The final Java code for all of the five copied two-line code blocks should look like the following:

```
EditText colonistText = (EditText)findViewById(R.id.editTextColonists);
colonistText.setText("100", EditText.BufferType.EDITABLE);
EditText basesText = (EditText)findViewById(R.id.editTextBases);
basesText.setText("1", EditText.BufferType.EDITABLE);
EditText militaryText = (EditText)findViewById(R.id.editTextMilitary);
militaryText.setText("1", EditText.BufferType.EDITABLE);
EditText forcefieldOnText = (EditText)findViewById(R.id.editTextForcefieldOn);
forcefieldOnText.setText("", EditText.BufferType.EDITABLE);
EditText forcefieldOffText = (EditText)findViewById(R.id.editTextForcefieldOff);
forcefieldOffText.setText("Forcefield is Off", EditText.BufferType.EDITABLE);
```

Now we have set up our EditText UI elements in only a dozen lines of Java code as shown in Figure 6-10. Later we will add Java code to the onClick() event handlers for our Button UI elements that will take the data values from these EditText fields that we have set up using the **.getText()** method and set our WorldGen object data variables with those values accordingly.

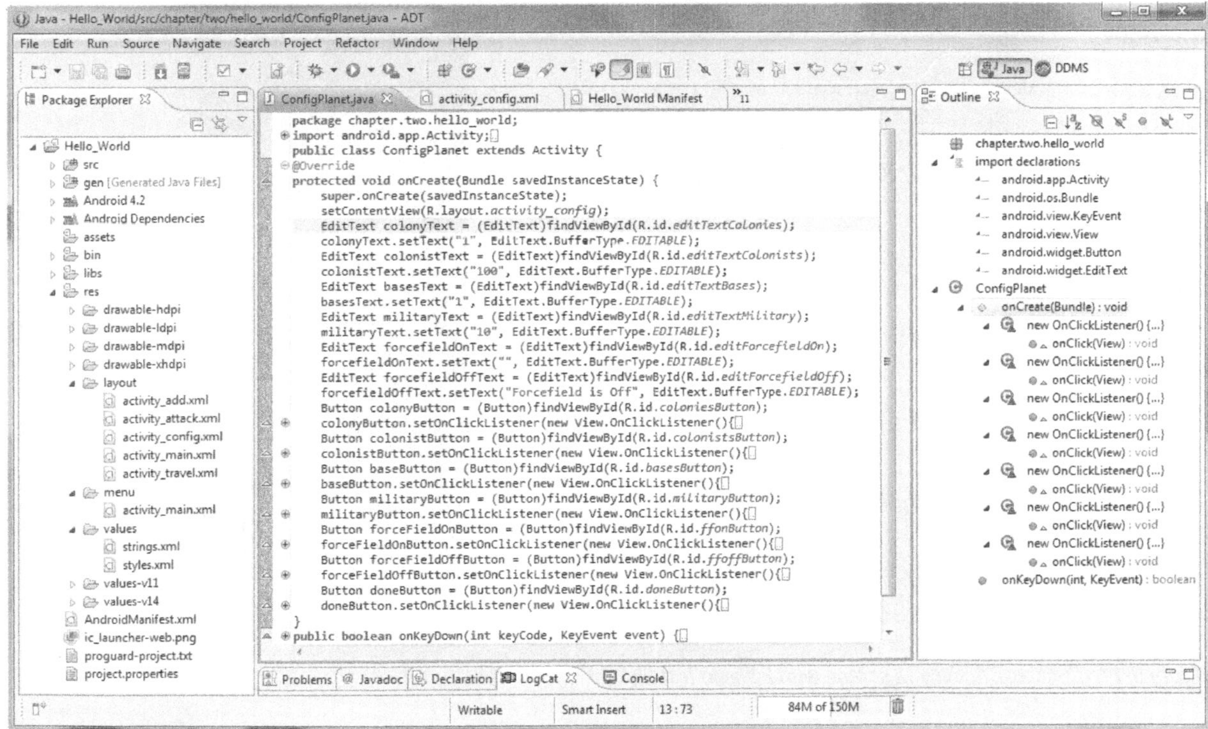

Figure 6-10. Copying the six EditText objects and .setText() methods to implement our EditText UI fields in Java

Next, we need to ascertain if our XML mark-up and Java code is giving us the more refined user interface design results that we have been trying to implement. Right-click the project folder and select the **Run As Android Application** menu item, and when the Nexus S emulator launches hit the menu button and the Configure Planet menu selection, and observe the UI screen.

Notice that we estimated the ems font size setting correctly, and that the data in the EditText fields is a nice size, so we will keep those tag parameter settings. However, the bottom of the EditText fields is not lining up perfectly with the bottom of the Button elements; it looks like the **android:layout_marginTop** values of **12dp** are too large, and that pushes each data field down too far from the data field above it. So let's reduce the marginTop value by 33% to a value of **8dp** and **Run As Android Application** again.

As you can see in Figure 6-11 our Configure Planet UI screen lines up well and the data values set in our Java code appear correctly in each UI data field, just like we designed it. In Chapter 7, we add translucent buttons and spice things up quite a bit more, but for now, this Activity screen's user interface design has been upgraded and implemented in our Java code, so let's move on, and dial in our Travel to Planet Activity screen next. We're making great progress on this app!

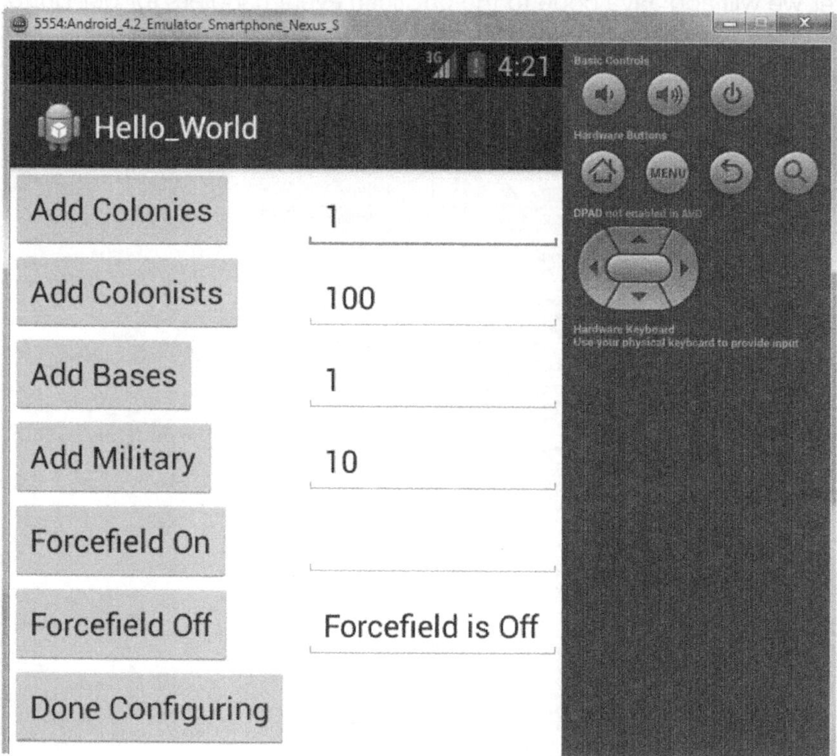

***Figure 6-11.** Configure Activity UI screen with Editable Text Fields implemented*

Optimizing Our TravelPlanet Activity: Android's VideoView Widget

Our TravelPlanet.java Activity class has the simplest XML mark-up code and will have the most complicated Java code (when we get into the chapters on Video, Chapters 11 and 12), as we will be working with an advanced type of new media: digital video. Our goal in this section is to make the Travel to Planet section of our application more professional in its appearance and user experience, and we are going to do that by getting rid of that Button that lies on top of our video viewscreen so that users can enjoy fullscreen video playback. To accomplish this we'll need to remove the Button UI element from our UI.

Configuring Our VideoView User Interface Element

Go into the **activity_travel.xml** editing tab, and delete the Button UI element tag in its entirety from the FrameLayout container, as shown in Figure 6-12. Because we no longer have the button to click to exit our Activity, we will need to make the VideoView itself clickable, so let's look for a parameter that will let us accomplish this. Type **android**, and then press the **colon** key to get the parameter options helper dialog from Eclipse, and then scroll down and look for any parameters that deal with clickability.

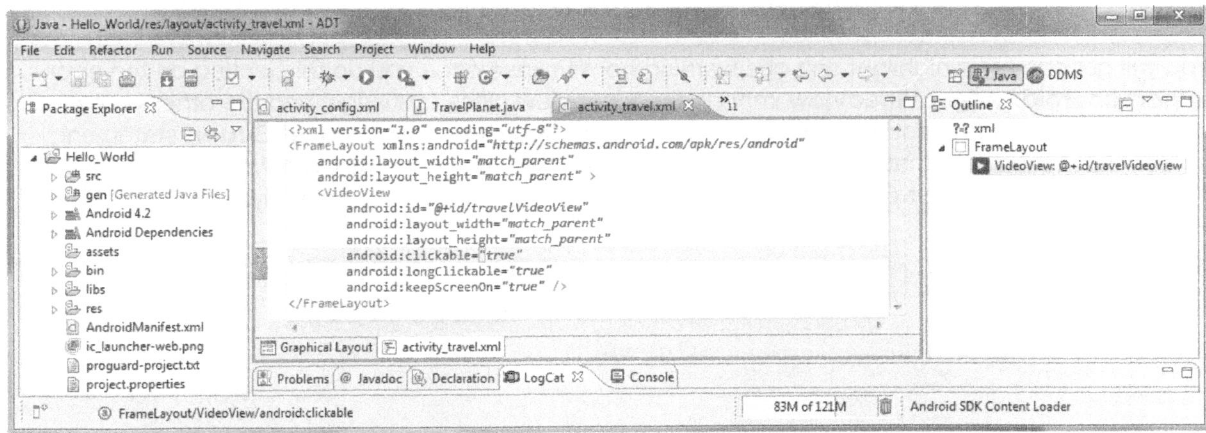

Figure 6-12. *Removing the Button UI element tag and making the VideoView UI element clickable instead*

Notice there are two parameters called android:clickable and android:longClickable on the list, double-click **android:clickable** to add it, and then using the same work process go back and double-click the **android:longClickable** parameter to add it as well, while we're here writing mark-up. We implement clicks as well as long-clicks on our video screen using Android **onTouch()** events (because video is playing on the touchscreen) in our Java code later on in this chapter, as well as in Chapters 11 and 12, where we will be covering Digital Video in much greater depth.

Next, we add another UI parameter that enhances our user experience during the digital video playback, when our users are taking a tour of (traveling over) a planet's surface. Many Android devices prioritize power savings over user experience, and because we don't want our Android device screen to dim (or even to go dark) during our user's travel experience, we're going to look for a parameter that addresses this issue.

Again type in the **android** keyword and the **colon** key **activator** and bring up the parameter options helper dialog from Eclipse, and look for a parameter that will keep our Android device screen on during the VideoView playback.

It is important to note here (if you haven't noted it already) that this Eclipse parameter options helper dialog will *only* populate its view with parameters that relate to (are usable with) the tag that you are typing the android keyword and colon activator within. Thus, this is a great way to find out exactly what parameters are available for each user interface element's tag. Double-click the **android:keepScreenOn** parameter and add it.

Once you are finished editing your XML for the activity_travel.xml file, it should look like Figure 6-12. Now we just need to change our Java code to access what we have done in our XML editing session, so that everything fits together like a glove.

Adding the Java Code to Incorporate Our Travel to a Planet Screen's New User Interface Elements

The first thing we need to do is to either remove the Java code that instantiates our Button object, or edit it, replacing our Button object with a **travelVideo** VideoView object as in this line of code:

```
VideoView travelVideo = (VideoView)findViewById(R.id.travelVideoView);
```

You will get one error highlight and one warning from Eclipse once you do this; acting on the error **import android.widget.VideoView** imports the VideoView class for usage, and the other yellow warning highlights the fact that you no longer need an **import android.widget.Button** statement, so you can now delete that import statement if you want to (you don't absolutely have to–it's a warning level and will not prevent the code from compiling and working correctly).

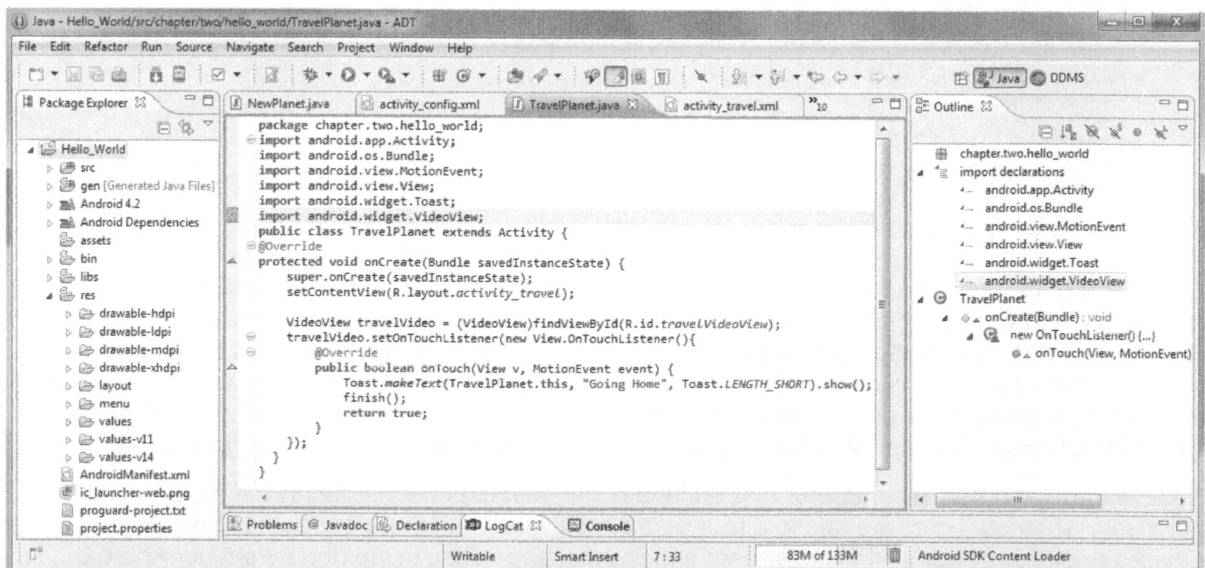

Figure 6-13. Replacing the Button and onClick() handler with a VideoView object and onTouch() handler in Java

Once we have created our travelVideo VideoView object, we can set an event listener on it. Because digital video is best used via a touchscreen device, let's take the opportunity to use the **onTouch()** event listener, instead of the onClick() event listener. To set the **OnTouchListener()**, use this code:

```
travelVideo.setOnTouchListener(new View.OnTouchListener() {
   @Override
   public boolean onTouch(View v, MotionEvent event) {
        Toast.makeText(TravelPlanet.this, "Going Home", Toast.LENGTH_SHORT).show();
        finish();
        return true;
   }
});
```

With this code, all our user has to do is to touch the screen (where the video will eventually be after we add it) and the **onTouch()** event handler broadcasts a **Toast** to the screen that says "Going Home" and then executes the Activity **finish()** method, taking the user back to the Home Page. So now, our VideoView UI element handles the event that the Button UI element used to, and the Button is not blocking our view of the Video viewscreen. This UI design has a more professional user experience.

In Chapter 7, if we need the touch event to control video playback or the video transport, then we might change the touch event into a longClick. For now, we are just putting the foundation in place, so that we can expand on it later on, but in a way such that it works well within the current application functionality. That is the best way to develop our code, by making sure that it works well at every level of its development.

So, let's **Run As Android Application**, and be sure that the code works as it should. Once the app starts, hit the menu button, and select the Travel to Planet menu option, and it will take you to a black screen (blank video viewscreen) where you can click (simulating a finger touch) in the middle of the screen. Once you do this, a Toast message comes up that says "Going Home" and the app returns to the Home Screen. Now that we have 75% of our application Activity screens working, we need to fine-tune our Attack a Planet screen, and then we'll be ready to get into some graphics design!

Optimizing Our AttackPlanet Activity UI: ImageButton UI Widgets

Before we modify the XML mark-up for our **ImageButton** tags in our **attack_activity.xml** LinearLayout container, we should put the image elements that our ImageButton tags will use for custom button icons into the correct resolution drawable resource folders. We did this earlier in the Configure Planet section of this chapter, regarding our six planet images that our ImageView tags used (only these icons are cooler). Let's do this first.

Putting the Image Assets in Place

Copy the 96 pixel versions of the five ImageButton graphic .png files into your **Hello_World/res/drawable-xhdpi/** folder. They are named attackbomb96px.png, attackinvade96px.png, attackvirus96px.png, attacklaser96px.png, and attackexit96px.png. A slick way to do this is to select the first one, and then hold down the **Ctrl** key on your keyboard, while selecting the other four. This allows non-contiguous file selection, whereas the **Shift** key will select a range of files (click the first file, hold down Shift, then click the last file in a desired range). Then right-click, select **Copy**, and then select the target folder, and right-click that and select **Paste**.

Once they are in the **/res/drawable-xhdpi** folder, remove the **96px** part of the filename, so that the files (eventually, once we are finished with all this copying) all have the same generic names: attackbomb.png, attackinvade.png, attackvirus.png, attacklaser.png, and attackexit.png.

Next, do the exact same work process for the **80px** versions of these five files, copying them into the **/res/drawable-hdpi** folder, and removing the 80px part of the filename so they are all generically named. Do the same work process again, with the **64px** versions of these five files that need to go into the **/res/drawable-mdpi** folder, and finally again with the **48px** versions of the five files, which go into the **/res/drawable-ldpi** folder.

Referencing, Aligning, and Compositing Our Attack Icon Image Source Files

Now we are ready to go into the Eclipse XML editing pane, and add the tag parameters that we need to enhance new user interface screen design. We will also need to change the image source filenames specified in the tag's **android:src** parameter, so that our impressive new custom ImageButton graphic icons are correctly referenced in each respective ImageButton tag.

Let's modify our ImageButton tags first (Figure 6-14), with our new filenames, as well as functional parameters, such as sound effects, background color values, and margins to put some space on our UI screen between the image graphics.

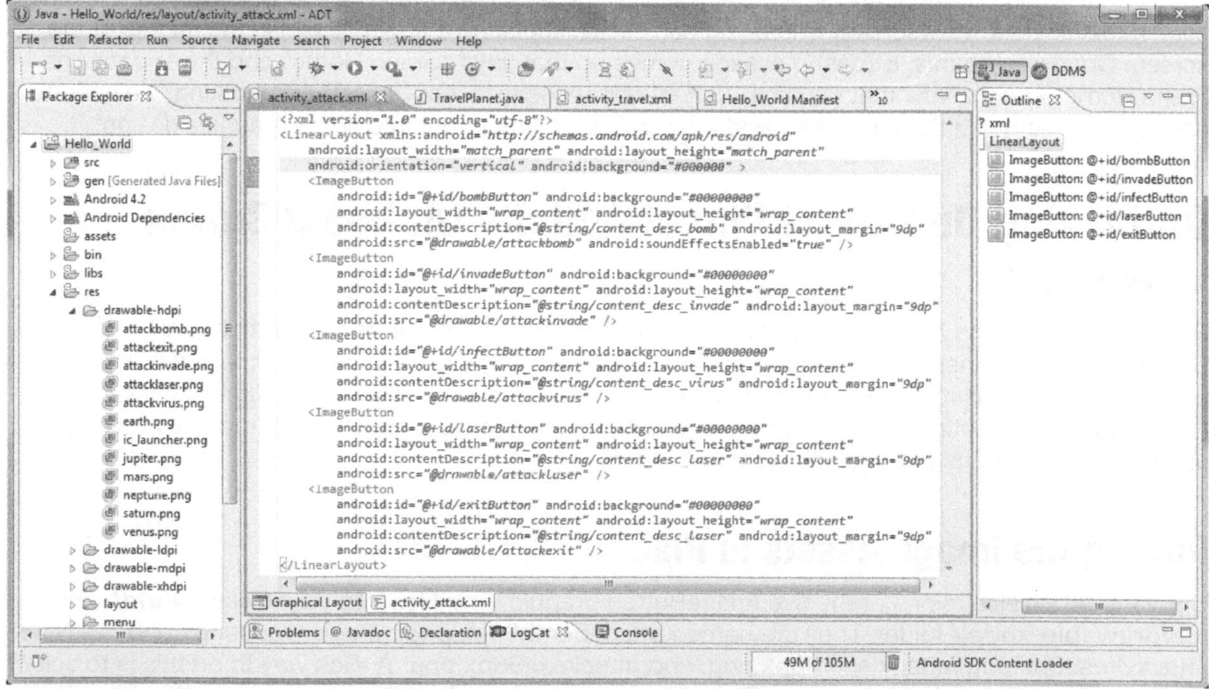

***Figure 6-14.** Upgrading ImageButton tag parameters to reference new images and add background transparency*

Because eventually (after Chapter 7) all our application screens will have dark or black backgrounds, featuring the starfields and plasmafields found in space, let's add a new parameter to our LinearLayout container that gives it a black background. We'll accomplish this via the **android:background** parameter, and as we will learn in the Chapter 7, the color **black** is represented in computers via a **#000000** value.

While we're adding **android:background** parameters, let's add the same tag parameter to each ImageButton, and use the value **#00000000**, which is the value for **transparent**, as the extra two zeros control transparency. Again we will be learning all about why this is in the next chapter on graphics.

Next, we will change the **launcher_ic** placeholder graphic (finally!), with our generic attack graphic names that are now located in each of our four resolution-specific drawable folders. If you don't see their names in the Package Explorer **/res/drawable** folders, as shown in Figure 6-14, then you may have forgotten to right-click the Hello_World folder and to **Refresh** the IDE's "view" of your project folder on your hard disk drive, after you copied the files into their proper folders earlier using Windows Explorer.

Once Eclipse can "see" the new files, change the launcher icon **android:src** parameter reference for each ImageButton to the first part of the new filename, as shown in Figure 6-14. To space out the ImageButton UI elements on a screen a bit more professionally, add an **android:layout_margin** parameter with an initial value of **9dp** to put some space (no pun intended, at least not yet) around each of the new graphics we are using for our ImageButton.

Finally, let's use the **parameter helper dialog** to find a sound effects tag parameter, by typing **android** and then pressing the **colon** key. Scroll down and search for a tag parameter relating to enabling sound effects for the ImageButton. Double-click to add the **android:soundEffectsEnabled** parameter and **once you locate it on the list** set its value to **true.**. Make sure that you make all four of these changes and additions for each of your five new ImageButton tags, as shown in Figures 6-14 and 6-15. Next we will add text.

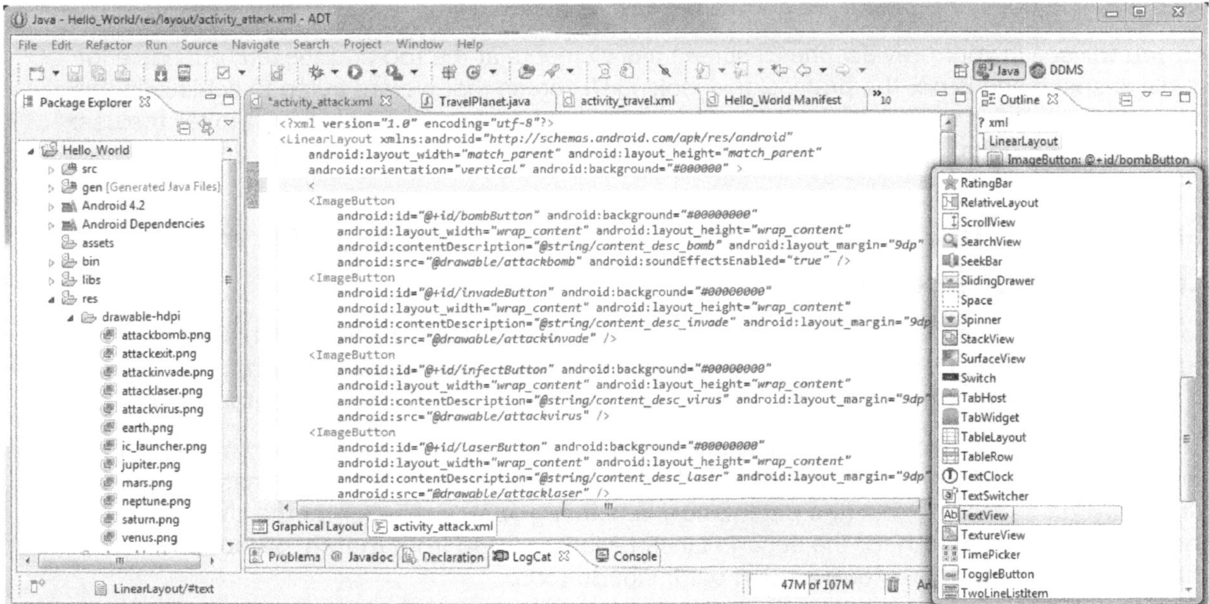

Figure 6-15. Pressing the left-facing chevron < character to invoke the add a tag helper dialog in Eclipse

Adding a Screen Caption TextView to Our XML Mark-up

To make sure the user knows what to do when they arrive at this Attack UI screen, let's add in a **caption** at the top of our UI screen which tells the user what action to take when they are on this screen. Add a line of space before the first ImageButton tag (press your return key), as shown in Figure 6-15, and then press the **left-facing chevron < key (Shift-Comma)** on your keyboard, and notice that an **add a tag helper dialog** pops up in Eclipse.

Find the **TextView** tag, and **double-click** it to add it to your XML mark-up. Notice that there are hundreds of tags, enough to fill several books, and that you can use this pop-up helper to explore some of the less often used tags available. In this book, we are going to cover the tags you will most frequently use to implement text, images, video, animated UI elements, and the like, but feel free to explore the more niche UI elements via this cool feature when you have time. Now let's configure our TextView caption.

Because our UI screen background is now black, let's make our caption text **white** by using the **android:textColor** parameter and a data value of **#FFFFFF,** which as we will soon learn is the **hexadecimal** value for white. Set your text size to **18** standard pixels (**sp**), using an **android:textSize** parameter, and make sure to add the standard **layout_width** and **layout_height** parameter settings of **wrap_content**; if you forget these, Eclipse will flag your XML.

Finally, add an attack_planet_caption <string> tag to your strings.xml file, which sets this value: **Select Attack Type Using Icon** and then reference it via an **android:text** parameter, via a **@strings/attack_planet_caption** value.

To preview what you have done so far, you can use the **Graphical Layout** tab at the bottom of the edit pane, or use the **Run As Android Application** work process to get an even more precisely rendered view of what your UI screen will look like on an Android smartphone. As this Attack UI screen becomes more complex and detailed, you'll see that the Graphical Layout preview is just an estimate, and does not provide as good a preview as the emulator.

As you will see in your preview, the UI screen has elements at the top and the left, but has a lot of black space and is not the professional looking UI screen that we are trying to achieve in this chapter, so we need to add some text to the right side of each ImageButton icon to tell the user what each icon does.

Creating a More Complex User Interface Design Using Nested LinearLayout Containers

To create a more complex UI, we will need to follow a work process similar to what we did to take our Configure Planet UI screen to the next level, and so let's add two nested **vertical** LinearLayouts (one for ImageButtons and the other for TextViews) inside of one parent **horizontal** LinearLayout.

Copy the top LinearLayout tag underneath itself and change the **orientation** parameter on the first (now parent) LinearLayout to **horizontal**. Delete the **android:background** parameter for the second LinearLayout, as the first one (the parent) now sets that global parameter for the UI screen. Change the **android:layout_width** for the second LinearLayout to **70dp** from **match_parent** as we now want the left LinearLayout to conform around our ImageButtons.

Remember to make sure that there are two nested LinearLayout closing tags at the bottom of your XML definition and then copy the second LinearLayout tag and paste it after the second to last LinearLayout closing tag, to create a third LinearLayout tag. Copy the TextView UI element into the second nested vertical LinearLayout container, as that container will be holding our TextView UI elements. Also, make sure that your second nested LinearLayout container also has a closing tag at the bottom of the XML UI definition, and indent the nested LinearLayouts as shown in Figure 6-16.

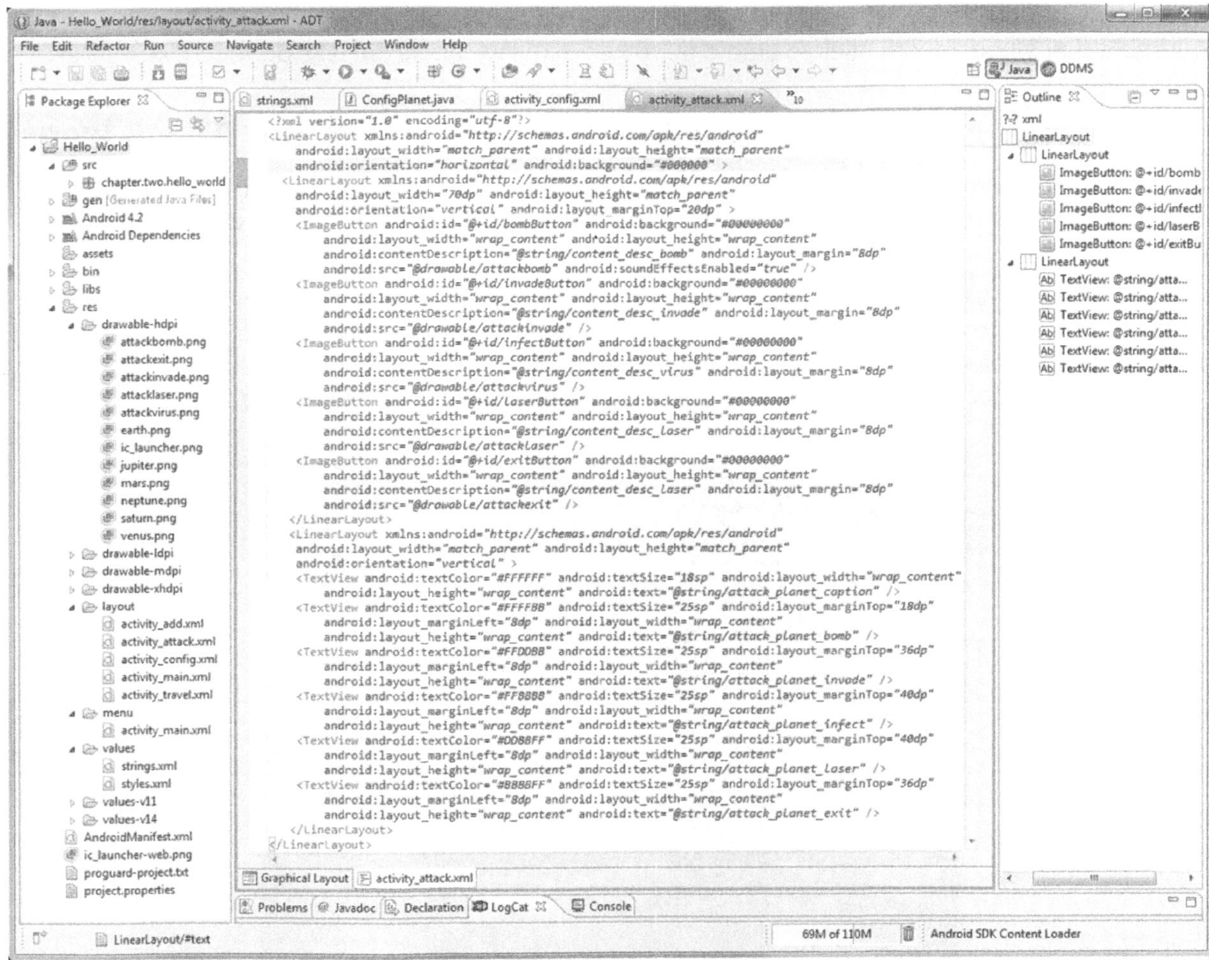

***Figure 6-16.** Nesting LinearLayout containers to add in TextView tags to label our Attack Planet Option icons*

Next, let's copy the **attack_planet_caption** TextView underneath itself to create an **attack_planet_bomb** TextView tag that we can configure for some larger and more colorful text to label what each Attack ImageButton icon does. Change the **android:textColor** value to **#FFFFBB** to make it **yellow** and change the **android:textSize** value to **25dp** to make it 40% larger than the caption text. Add an **android:layout_marginTop** tag with an **18dp** value, to push the text down from the screen caption, next to the first ImageButton.

Now, **render** the UI screen via your **Graphical Layout** and **Run As Android Application** work processes, and see how it looks. We still need a little fine-tuning before we copy this TextView tag four more times underneath itself to create our other TextView labels, so let's do that next.

Fine-Tuning Our UI Design and Adding Text Labels to Our Attack Icons

Add an **android:layout_marginLeft** parameter, with a device independent pixel (DIP, or DP) value of **8dp** to push our text a little bit away from our ImageView icon, and toward the center of the user interface screen.

Now we are ready to copy and paste this **attack_planet_bomb** TextView four more times underneath itself, to create our other attack_planet TextViews. Make sure to change the **android:text** parameters to reference <string> tag constants that you have created in your strings.xml file that create text labels for each of the TextViews according to what they do (see Figure 6-17).

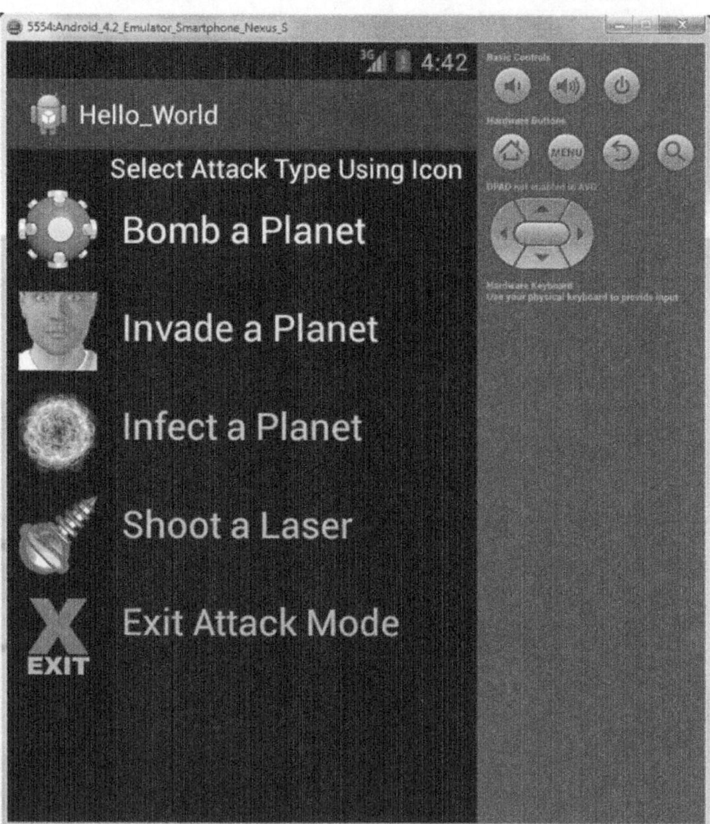

Figure 6-17. Attack Planet UI screen preview in Nexus S emulator

Adjust the **android:layout_marginTop** parameter for the copied TextView tags to between 36dp and 40dp to space the labels near the center of each icon graphic, as shown in Figure 6-17. This is an iterative process, where you tweak these values and go back and forth from the emulator, until you have values that put each label in the middle of each icon on the screen. Next, change the textColor values to set a color gradient from yellow to purple.

Next, we need to upgrade our Java code in our **AttackPlanet.java** Activity subclass, to implement the four ImageButton objects that we have not yet implemented. Remember that we've already coded our exitButton ImageButton object earlier and had it call our Activity finish() method, and that Java code we will leave as-is, and, in fact, we will copy it and then paste it four more times, to create our other four ImageButton objects next.

Adding Java Code to Incorporate Our Attack a Planet Screen User Interface Elements

Copy the code block that includes the ImageButton object creation, and the .setOnClickListener code block that implements the OnClickListener() and onClick() methods four times underneath the exitButton object set-up code.

Leave the exitButton code as the fifth and final block of code, and go up to the first code block, and change the **exitButton** to **bombButton** in all three locations (name, reference, and method call). Next, let's change the **finish()** method call to a **Toast.makeText()** method call, which tells our users what was done when they clicked the ImageButton icon graphic.

Our **.makeText()** Toast object method has an AttackPlanet class context, a Bombs Away! text message, and a short display length duration, like this:

```
Toast.makeText(AttackPlanet.this, "Bombs Away!", Toast.LENGTH_SHORT).show();
```

Next, perform this same work process to create **invadeButton**, **infectButton,** and **laserButton** ImageButton objects with onClick() event handlers that toast **Troops Sent**, **Virus Spread,** and **Laser Fired!** messages, respectively.

Figure 6-18 shows how the five code blocks should look once you are done!

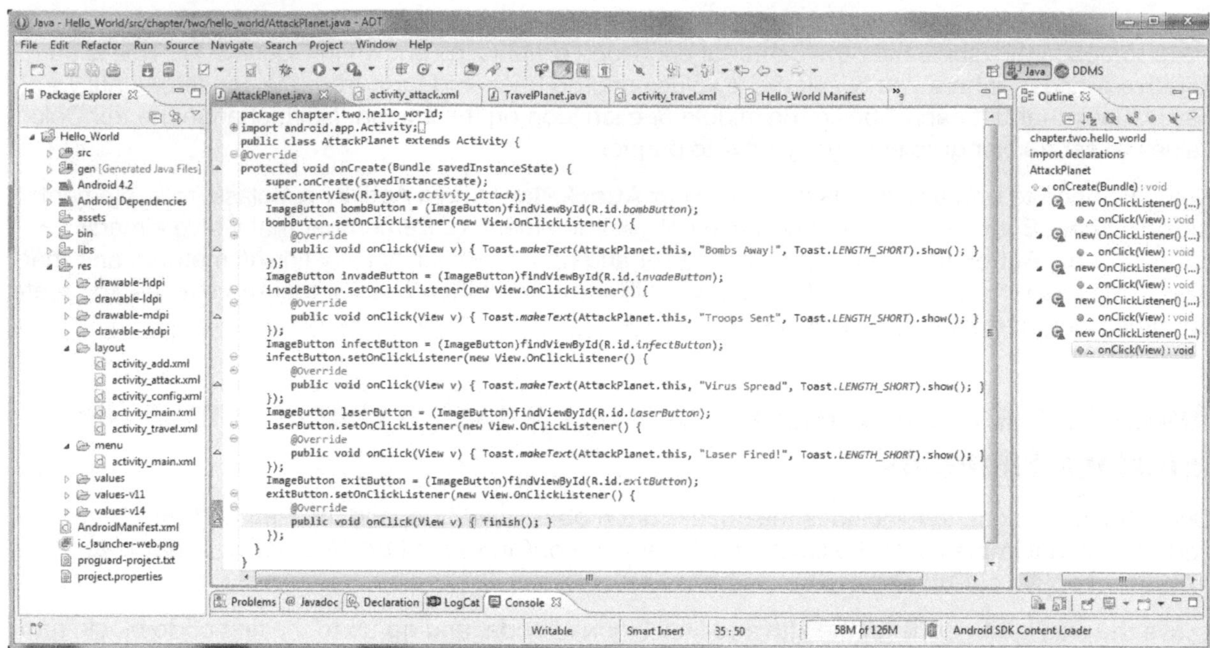

***Figure 6-18.** Adding our ImageButton objects and onClick() handlers in AttackPlanet.java for each attack method*

Now, we can test our AttackPlanet Activity User Interface in its entirety.

Right-click the project folder and Run As Android Application to launch the Nexus S emulator. After it loads, click the Menu button and select the Attack on Planet menu item, and after the Attack Planet UI screen appears, click each of the first four ImageButton icon graphics, and watch your Toast messages appear perfectly at the bottom of the UI screen. Then click the fifth Exit ImageButton, and watch the screen exit and return you Home!

We have now implemented the XML mark-up and Java code that makes our entire Hello World application 100% functional at the basic user interface design level, as well as at the navigational level. We are ready to implement some very cool rich media elements in the next couple sections of this book.

We will add these new media elements over the next several chapters, which cover graphics design, animation, digital video, and digital audio. This should be a lot of fun, as we now get to make this application really fun and game-like for all our end-users!

Summary

In this chapter, we took a much closer look at some of the most often used Android **android.widget package** user interface classes, and implemented them in our Java code as functional UI objects for our own Hello World application. We learned that UI element widgets are subclassed from the venerable Android **View** class, and we took a look at the most important and most universally used UI widget classes across Android application development projects.

During the chapter we learned more about Eclipse features, especially how we can bring up tag helper dialogs and parameter helper dialogs simply by typing **<** (the left-facing chevron character) on a blank line, and by typing in the **android** keyword, and then the **colon** key activator. This is a great way to explore the hundreds of tags and parameters that are available in the Android OS at any given time (on any given API Level installation).

For our New Planet Activity, we took a closer look at Android's **ImageView** class, as well as at the Android **TextView** and **Button** classes, and we then implemented each of these UI element types at a more advanced level using some of their custom parameters in XML. We then instantiated each of these UI element objects inside our Java code base, to create a highly visual user interface for a New Planet selection screen that we needed for our users to use to select and create new planets inside our application.

For our Configure Planet Activity, we leveraged the Android **Button** class, as well as text editing fields via the Android **EditText** class, and we then implemented each of these UI element types with their custom parameters in XML, and then instantiated them in Java, to create our data entry user interface for a planet configuration data entry screen that we needed for our users to be able to define planet attributes in our application.

For our Travel Planet Activity, we looked at the Android **VideoView** class, and we implemented some advanced parameters in XML, so that our VideoView could be Clicked and LongClicked (or Touched and LongClicked) to implement features. We also made sure that any Android device screen would remain on during our Video content playback using an **android:keepScreenOn** parameter. Finally, we instantiated our VideoView object in Java, and implemented an **OnTouchListener()** and **onTouch()** event handler, to create a sleek user interface for an Inter-Planetary Travel digital video playback screen needed for our users to travel to the surface of their planets in our app.

For our Attack Planet Activity we looked at the Android **ImageButton** class, which allows Android developers to implement buttons that are made out of graphical assets, such as images and animation. We will be looking at this widget in more detail in the next chapter on graphics design, as you might imagine, but wanted to cover the basics before we got to that part of the book. We added custom button icon graphics to our ImageButtons to replace the placeholder images we were using and added other parameters that set the stage for our making this screen support sound effects and compositing that we will learn in future chapters. We then wired up these ImageButtons in our Java code, and made this UI screen both functional and professional in its user interface design.

We learned during this chapter about the Android **Toast** class and object, and how to implement a Toast, to broadcast feedback messages to our users to give them visual updates as to what tasks our app is doing during their use of our user interface screen Activity subclasses.

In the next chapter we will learn about using graphics in Android apps and we will start customizing our screen layouts and user interfaces for our Hello World Android application, using both XML mark-up code (for the most part), as well as Java code to define and implement these wow-factor user experiences and user interface elements. The next few chapters are going to be really fun, because we will be making our app commercially viable!

Chapter 7

Android Graphics Design: Concepts and Techniques

In this chapter, we will learn about the foundational concepts of digital imaging and graphics design in Android, as well as how these concepts are implemented in the Android OS, as well as some digital imaging techniques.

We will learn about the **android.graphics.drawable** package, and the Android **Drawable** class, and the many types of Drawable objects that are supported in Android. We will also learn what **ARGB** means, what an **Alpha Channel** is, and all about digital imaging concepts such as **Pixels**, **Color Depth**, **Dithering**, **Resolution**, **Aspect Ratio**, **Layers**, **Blending**, **Image Compression,** and **Formats**.

We will then apply this new knowledge to take our Hello World application that we have created thus far to an all new level of professionalism, by adding some space-related background elements and making sure that they are implemented seamlessly, via a digital imaging technique that is called **compositing**, which we will also be learning more about within this chapter.

To implement all these new digital imaging features in our application, we will continue to learn about applying XML user interface parameters in new ways, as we have been doing since Chapter 2, and as we will continue to do throughout the rest of this book.

This chapter will be more about covering graphics design elements, digital imaging concepts, and imaging techniques than it will be about programming concepts, because these days, Android applications are more and more about visual design, 3D, graphics design, animation, digital imagery, and other new media elements than ever before, making this chapter a real necessity.

Let's get started by learning about the Android **graphics** package and the **drawable** classes, which make all this visual magic come alive for our end-users and allow us developers to implement what is in our mind's eye in Java code and XML mark-up in a logical and structured fashion.

Android Graphics Design Highest Level: The Drawable Class

Similar to what we saw with the Android **View** class in the previous chapter relative to UI elements or **widgets**, the Android **Drawable** class is also the highest level class for **graphics design** related objects, which are called **drawables** in Android, because they are drawn onto our display screen.

This is the reason that some of the sub-folders in your project's resource folder start with the word *drawable*, as they contain those graphics design elements for your application. So far we have used digital image drawables but before we are done, we will have used several other types of drawables as well, to implement things like animation or image cross-fading effects.

As with the View class, the Drawable class is not usually used directly, but it has a myriad of subclasses. Like with View subclasses, Drawable has both **direct subclasses** and **indirect subclasses**. These Drawable subclasses do all the heavy lifting in Android graphics, for this reason, throughout this book we will be importing and leveraging many of them within our application. Let's go over which Drawable subclasses are direct, which are indirect, and what these Drawable sublasses do for our application.

Direct Subclasses of the Android Drawable Class

The **direct subclasses** of the Drawable class essentially equate to which types of graphics design elements we can use in our Android applications.

By far the most often used direct subclass of the Drawable class is called the **BitmapDrawable** subclass, which is used for **digital images**, such as the PNG files we have used so far in our app as well as for WEBP, JPEG or GIF.

The **ColorDrawable** is the most basic level Drawable class, and it's used to define the **color** of a screen, like we did when we defined the **black** screen color for our Attack Planet Activity user interface screen in Chapter 6.

The **GradientDrawable** is used to create a gradient of colors from one color into another, and can be defined by any shape. Shapes supported in Android GradientDrawables include: line, rectangle, ellipse (oval), circular, ring (hoop or torus), and a gradient can be drawn **linear** (straight, any angle), **radial** (emanate from a point), or **sweep** (linear but rotate around a point).

The **ShapeDrawable** is used to create a **vector** shape in Android. A vector or shape is a 2D line or curve that defines the outside of a 2D volume, like a heart or a star. Those familiar with Adobe Illustrator will be familiar with vector shapes, as well as gradients and color graphics tools.

These last three Drawable subclasses that we've discussed (ColorDrawable, GradientDrawable, and ShapeDrawable) give Android OS many of the same basic features that a vector software package, such as Illustrator or InkScape, will feature, only we have them here in Android on a Java code level. This gives us the ability to create the same type of vector artwork that we can create in InkScape and then make the art interactive or animated via Java.

The **LayerDrawable** lets us handle multiple layers of imagery, much like one sees in Photoshop or GIMP digital imaging software, and their image layers features. This is a more advanced drawable, for use in advanced gaming and real-time compositing applications. We'll learn more about image **layers** and **compositing** later on in this chapter, as well as how they are used.

The **InsetDrawable** allows us to use an area or subset of the screen called an **inset** to display graphics (drawable) elements. This is used for things like widgets, which use only a part of the display screen as the required screen area for their application or purpose. A clock for the device home screen might be a good example of something that may use an InsetDrawable.

Indirect Subclasses of the Android Drawable Class

The **indirect subclasses** of Drawable are significantly more complicated or detailed graphics functions that leverage the direct subclasses to create even more complex graphics design effects and motion, such as animation.

For instance, the Android **TransitionDrawable**, which **cross-fades** two images to create an image **transition**, is a subclass of **LayerDrawable**. Because these LayerDrawable objects handle multiple images in layers, they are a logical class to subclass to create the TransitionDrawable class, which takes two images and animates their **alpha channel** values (yes, we'll cover this soon as well) to create impressive and useful image cross-fading effects.

Besides the TransitionDrawable class, we will also be making quite a bit of use of the **AnimationDrawable**, another key indirect subclass of Drawable that implements **Frame Animation** in Android. We will cover Frame Animation, as well as **Vector Animation**, in a later chapter specifically focusing on Animation. Since we are covering the major drawable indirect subclasses here, I will mention it now to put it into the correct context for you.

The **LevelListDrawable** is used for progress bars and similar applications where a graphic element needs to be replaced on the screen based on a level of activity of some kind. A similar **StateListDrawable** class is used to replace graphic elements based on a different state change that may be encountered during an application runtime. A StateListDrawable can access graphics elements in any particular order, that is, out of order, whereas a LevelListDrawable accesses graphics in order, from one level to another.

Both the LevelListDrawable and StateListDrawable are subclassed from the Android **DrawableContainer** direct subclass, which is not usually used or called directly, but which can be used to create your own custom drawable container, if the LevelList or StateList drawable containers do not fit your needs precisely enough.

Because most applications (and most websites, for that matter) use **bitmaps** for their graphics design purposes, the next few sections of this chapter address the concepts and characteristics of **bitmap images** in greater detail, as these are key to creating Android application user experiences that are both beautiful, as well as professional. We will start with the foundation of a bitmap image, the **pixel**, and build up from there, just like a digital image itself is built–one pixel at a time!

Digital Imaging's Lowest Level Picture Element: The Pixel

Digital images are made up of tiny dots of color; if you have ever used the **zoom** feature in a digital imaging software package, such as GIMP, you probably know that already. Each element of a picture is called a **pixel**, which is a conjugation of the word **pictures** (called pix in popular slang) and the word **element** (el). I opened up GIMP 2.8 and zoomed in on the 48 pixel version of our Attack Virus to 800% from normal (100%), so that you can see the individual picture elements (pixels) that make up the image in Figure 7-1. We'll be using GIMP 2.8 for our digital imaging work process in this book because it is open source and all our readers can download and install it for free (as we did in Chapter 1). Note the zoom setting at the bottom of the software in a drop-down widget for easy access to new settings. Also note in the top of the screen that there is information on the filename, color depth, layers, and resolution, all of which we will be getting into in greater detail in the next three sections of this chapter.

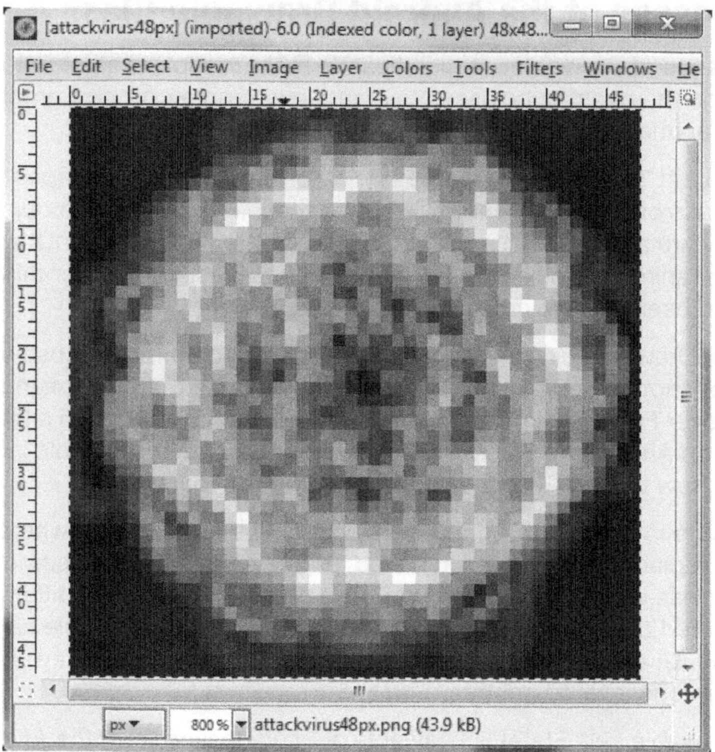

***Figure 7-1.** Our Attack Virus picture elements (pixels)*

Pixels are defined using **bits**, which as programmers we all know are binary values that represent data, in this case, color values. This is why images are called **bitmaps**, because they are actually maps of bit values, defining color values for each pixel using binary (**hexidecimal**) data formats. This is why we have **8-bit** images (8 bits of data are used to define each pixel) and 24-bit images, as well as 32-bit images, which we will be learning all about soon in the section regarding **color depth** later in the chapter.

Shaping an Image Using Pixels: Resolution and Aspect Ratio

In Figure 7-1 at the top-right of the GIMP window, you see a **48x48** notation. This is the **resolution** of the image in pixels, that is, 48 pixels wide and 48 pixels high. Image resolution is expressed in 2D, or two dimensions, as width by height. The image volume, or the number of pixels in an image, is calculated by multiplying width by height, so our 48x48 pixel image contains 2,304 pixels within its volume. Our Nexus S emulator screen is 800x480 resolution, and contains 384,000 pixels.

So the concept of resolution is fairly simple, assuming that you know how to use a calculator to multiply two numbers together! This new concept of **aspect ratio** is a little bit more complicated, as it involves the **ratio** of how many pixels wide to how many pixels in height a screen resolution is.

Aspect ratio is most important when it comes to **scaling** an image, which is resizing an image up or down. If you do not **maintain** the aspect ratio when you are scaling your image (or video), your imagery will become distorted. This is a common mistake in digital imaging and digital video; we have all seen those images of people who look like coneheads, or look a bit wide in the face. This is why digital image scaling (resizing) dialogs have a **keep aspect ratio locked** feature, which you should almost always have selected.

Calculating an aspect ratio is a lot like finding the least common denominator in fraction math, because the aspect ratio is a lot like a fraction. is the aspect ratio is expressed as W:H or Width:Height. So technically the aspect ratio for our Nexus S is 800:480, but in the industry this is usually reduced to the smallest two numbers that can show this ratio.

So, let's work backward (this is how I do this calculation in my head, without using a calculator) and drop the zero. 80:48 is also technically a correct aspect ratio for an 800x480 display. Because they are even numbers, let's divide them in half and get 40:24 and again to get 20:12. Now we are getting closer to a single-digit number pair! Since they are both still even, let's cut them in half again and get 10:6, now one of the sides has a single-digit number. They are both still even numbers so again divide them in half and we have 5:3, which is the correct aspect ratio for an 800x480 screen.

Other common aspect ratios include 16:9 (HDTV), since 1920 divided by 16 times 9 equals 1080, and 4:3 was the original computer monitor aspect ratio for all resolutions except for 1280x1024, which was a 5:4 aspect ratio. Another popular Android Smartphone resolution (and mini-tablet resolution) is 854x480, which is also 16:9. So an 800x480 screen is 5:3 and an 854x480 screen is 16:9, although they seem close in resolution, they are far apart when it comes to UI design, because they are vastly different aspect ratios. We deal with the disparity between these two particular close (resolution) but far apart (aspect ratio) resolutions later on in this book in Chapter 12.

Notice that the closer the numbers are to being equal, the more square the image is; our 48x48 pixel image in Figure 7-1 has 1:1 aspect ratio. A 2:1 aspect ratio image simply means that the image is twice as wide as it is tall, and a 3:1 or a 4:1 aspect ratio image could be called downright panoramic!

Fashioning the Color of a Pixel: The Concept of Color Depth

Now that we have covered pixels, resolution, and aspect ratios, we can get into the pixel coloration itself, and discuss color theory. There are two types of color display, **subtractive color** used in print, where ink colors subtract from each other, and **additive color**, which is used in lit display (display uses light) products, where color values are added to each other.

In subtractive color, red and green (ink) values yield purple colors, whereas in additive color, red and green (light) values yield yellow colors. Quite a bit of difference! Subtractive color, used in the printing industry, follows a **CMYK** color model, which stands for **Cyan Magenta Yellow Black** (I guess they took the K off the wrong end of the word black).

Additive color is used in the consumer electronics industry for products that feature display screens, and follows an RGB color model. **RGB** stands for **Red Green Blue**, and by using these three colors of light, any color in the visible light spectrum can be created. Different colors are created by varying the intensity (dark, or fully off, to light, or fully on) of each of the RGB color **components**.

In the digital world, each of these RGB colors can have 8-bits, or 256 levels, of color intensity. So for red, 0 would be all the way off, or black (no red value at all) and 256 would be all the way on, or 100% red.

Since we have **8-bits** of color value for each of the RGB color **channels** in an image, the image can be said to be a **24-bit color** image, also known as a **truecolor** image. Truecolor images can display **16,777,216** different color values, which can be calculated by multiplying 256 by 256 (65,536 colors, also known as **16-bit color**) and then multiplying that value by 256 again.

As we saw in the previous chapter, the 256 levels can be represented with only two characters using **hexidecimal**, or Base-16 numeric representation, where instead of counting from 0 to 9 (Base-10), we count from zero to F, giving us 16 values for that one character "slot." Because 16 times 16 is 256, two slots give us the ability to represent 256 different values.

To get the **orange** color value for our Invade Planet option in Figure 6-17 in the previous chapter, we used the hexidecimal color value **#FFDDBB**, which means full intensity (256) of Red, less intensity (196, or 14 times 14) of Green, and even less intensity (144, or 12 times 12) of Blue.

In addition to 24-bit truecolor images, there are also 8-bit **indexed** color images. Indexed color images use an 8-bit **index** of 256 colors in a **palette** to **approximate** all of the colors in an image. This works better for some images than others, for instance an image of puffy white clouds in a clear blue sky might work well as an indexed color image, because the 256 color values utilized can be spread out over the white and blue shades needed to simulate a truecolor image using only 256 colors, instead of 16,777,216.

Indexed color images are generally much smaller in data footprint (file size) than truecolor images (three times smaller before compression) and can do a pretty good job of representing the colors in an image. The icons that we used in the Attack Planet UI screen in Chapter 6 all use indexed color, as can be seen in Figure 7-1 at the top of the screenshot where it specifies Indexed color. Since our Virus Cell uses shades of pink, purple, and red, it is a very good candidate for using indexed color to simulate a truecolor image quality result, using far less data (2.86 kilobytes).

Even with more than a few different colors in the image, an indexed color image can yield an impressive result, as can be seen in our Attack Laser image shown in Figure 7-2 in the next section. In general, the more pixel resolution you have in an image, the better indexed color will work. I'll show you how to optimize the results of an indexed image compression in a section on compression techniques right after the next section on Alpha!

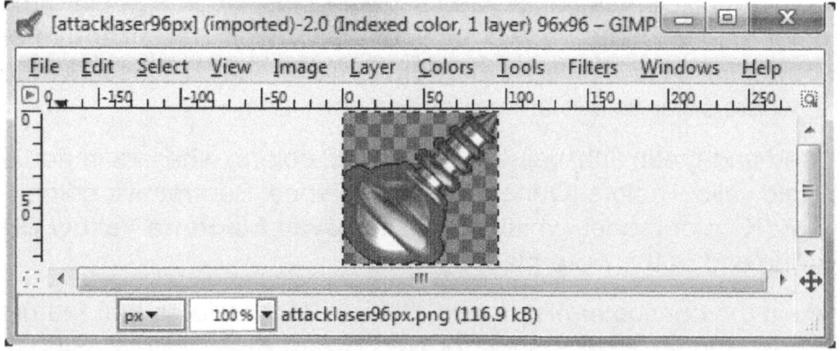

***Figure 7-2.** Attack Laser digital image with its alpha channel showing via a checkerboard pattern*

Defining Transparency in an Image: The Concept of Alpha Channel

Whereas a 24-bit image has three (RGB) color **channels**, a **32-bit image** has four (**ARGB**) color channels. The fourth channel in a 32-bit image is called the **alpha channel**. Like each of the image's RGB channels, an alpha channel can also have **256 levels**, but instead of defining color intensity, these 256 levels define the **transparency** level (or translucency) for that pixel.

The primary use for a fine-tuned, pixel-by-pixel control over transparency is **image compositing**, which is the process of composing a number of image **layers** together, to create one final image or special effect. The alpha channel in the attacklaser image, shown in Figure 7-2 would be black (0 or transparent) around the laser cannon and white (256 full **opacity**) where you see the laser cannon in the image. GIMP represents transparency via a **checkerboard** pattern, as you can also see in Figure 7-2.

If you want to see how effective an alpha channel can be in compositing an image over just about any other graphics, look in the upper-left corner of the screen shot in Figure 7-2, where GIMP has composited your laser cannon over its window titlebar. Looks like it was designed to be there, doesn't it? Almost all our images that we are using in our Hello World app–the planets, laser cannon, soldier and bomb–have an alpha channel in place so that when we put starfields and plasma clouds behind them, the backgrounds will show through every little detail in the image perfectly. That is, the imagery composites **seamlessly**.

We have already turned UI element parameters completely transparent, using an **ARGB** setting in XML of **#00000000**. The first two zeroes specify **opacity** to be 100% off, and thus transparency is 100% on. **Opaque** is the opposite of transparent and thus the level of opacity and the level of transparency are analogs of each other. If a pixel is 30% transparent it is 70% opaque.

Alpha channels are used frequently in application development because we often want to use content development **engines**, in this case Android, as an image compositing tool. In image compositing, each layer in the composite carries an alpha channel, or an alpha data component, to define what shows through that layer and what data on that layer will apply itself in some fashion to the final image composite result (the resulting visual image).

Besides using image layers and their alpha channels, compositing involves using a **blending algorithm** on each layer that sums (or differences) pixel data values, based on complex algorithms that can create image compositing special effects such as **Overlay**, **Screen**, **Darken**, **Lighten**, **XOR**, and so on.

Android supports these blending modes via the **PorterDuff** algorithm, in a package and class called **android.graphics.PorterDuff**, and thus not only is Android like InkScape on steroids; it's also like GIMP 2.8.4 on steroids! Coding blending algorithms is a bit beyond the scope of an introductory book on Android such as this, but it will be in my "Pro Android Graphics Design" book (Apress,11/2013) if you want to take Android Digital Imaging to the next level!

Image Format Support in Android: PNG8, PNG24, WEBP, JPG, GIF

Now that we have a handle on the different attributes in a digital image, we can discuss some different **file formats** supported in Android, because each of these image file formats have different combinations and levels of support for things like color depth and alpha channels.

Android OS has a preference for some of these formats over the others, and that will dictate the order in which I cover the formats in this section.

Portable Network Graphics (PNG) Format

The format Android prefers over all others is **Portable Network Graphics** or **PNG** (pronounced **Ping**) file format. PNG comes in two flavors, **PNG8** or indexed color PNG and **PNG24** or truecolor PNG. Because PNG24 can also "carry" an alpha channel, technically a 24-bit PNG with an alpha would be a **PNG32**.

Android likes PNG format images because PNG use **lossless** image compression that yields the highest quality result because PNG images do not lose any of the original image quality (or data) during the compression process.

Joint Photographic Experts Group (JPEG) Format

The next most desirable image format for use in Android is **JPEG**, which stands for **Joint Photographic Experts Group**. This image format uses **lossy** image compression, which "throws away" some of the original image data to achieve a better compression result, but at the expense of image quality. If you zoom into a JPEG image you will see areas that look dirty or discolored; these are compression **artifacts**, and are one of the reasons that JPEG format is not a preferred image format for Android development.

Another important aspect of JPEG image format is that it cannot carry an alpha channel, and thus it cannot be used in image compositing, unless it is the bottom layer in the image compositing layer stack, or unless the alpha information is attached to it later on, inside of an application.

Graphics Information (GIF) Format

The least desirable image format to use in Android is the Compuserve **GIF** format, which stands for **Graphics Information Format**. A GIF image only supports 8-bit indexed color, and has a larger data footprint (a weaker compression algorithm) than a PNG8 file will have. Try not to use GIF in your Android development unless you absolutely have to.

Web Photo (WEBP) Format

There is one additional image format that has been added to the Android OS since its 4.0 (API Level 14 Ice Cream Sandwich) version and later, called: **WEBP**. WEBP stands for **Web Photo** and it is similar to PNG32 but has about a 25% better (smaller) data footprint; that is, its compression algorithm is superior to PNG24 and PNG32.

However, if you want to deliver your Android apps to the millions of users that are using Android 1.5 through 3.2 (API Levels 3 through 13) devices, you will probably want to use the PNG24 and PNG32 formats, as well as PNG8 when it works well (as we are doing for the Hello World app in this book).

Reducing the Image Data Footprint: Image Compression Concepts

Once we have defined our image and alpha channel, and what file format we are going to use, the final step we go through after our image is created and composited and any alpha channels are defined and added is to **compress** the image to obtain the **smallest file size possible**.

> **Note** The reason that we do compress the image is because the total size of our Android app is the sum total of all our images plus our Java code and XML mark-up, and since we all know that text compresses better than pixels do, the majority of an app's data footprint reflects how well we optimize our new media assets.

I'll go over the key factors in this section that affect the compression **algorithm**, and thus the final **data footprint** of an image file size, after the compression process (the compression algorithm) is finally applied.

Resolution is the biggest factor to adjust to get better compression (file size) results of your image. As we learned earlier the sheer number of pixels to be compressed always comes down to pixel Width times Height.

Without compression, the raw data size for an image would be calculated as follows: Pixel Width times Pixel Height times 3 (for RGB) or 4 (for ARGB).

So, for our ARGB 96 pixel laser cannon, shown in Figure 7-2, the original uncompressed image data was **9,216** pixels (96x96) times **4** (ARGB), which is **36,864** total pixels to compress, or 9,216 pixels in each of the four image channels. 36,864 divided by 1,024 (the number of pixels in one kilobyte of data) gives us a **raw** file size of exactly **36 kilobytes**, or **36KB**.

Our final file size for our 96 pixel laser cannon image is **4.89KB,** which is **7.36** times smaller (36 divided by 4.89), or **13.6%** (4.89 divided by 36) of an original raw data footprint. 100% minus 13.6% yields 86.4% compression.

What did we do to compress this image almost 87%, and have it still look great? Well, since we didn't have the option of changing its resolution, we instead changed its color depth. Color depth is the next most important factor in image compression. This is because you have to factor the number of pixels by multiplying that against the number of color channels, and if you can reduce this multiplier, you also greatly reduce the resulting file size. So instead of using a 32-bit PNG we used an 8-bit PNG; by doing this we reduced the amount of pixels we were compressing from 36,864 to 9,216.

As you can see in top of the screenshot in Figure 7-2 the attacklaser.png is an 8-bit indexed color PNG image, yet it looks like it's an even higher quality truecolor image. This is because I used **dithering**, a key option available for 8-bit image compression.

Dithering involves simulating more than the 256 allowed colors in an 8-bit Indexed color palette. This is done by using subtle dot patterns that mix two colors together, to form a third color halfway between the two. This technique tricks the eye into thinking that there are more than 256 colors being used to create the image. Because of smaller pixel sizes (pixel size is termed dot pitch) found in the popular XXHDPI (super extra high density pixel image) Android screens these days, dithering is a valuable technique.

Dithering is especially useful for 8-bit images that exhibit a color depth conversion characteristic called **banding**, as it can mitigate or eliminate the banding by simulating 512 colors via this technique. Note that dither patterns in the image data can increase the file size a little bit, so be sure and toggle the dithering option on and off, to see if image quality is improved enough to merit that few extra bytes of data that it might add to the image's data footprint.

Upgrading Our NewPlanet Activity: Applying the Imaging Concepts

Now it's time to take a look at how some of these concepts apply to our Android application development. Let's add a starfield background to our NewPlanet Activity screen, so that our planets are out in space where they belong.

Adding a Stars Image Background to Our HelloWorld App

The first thing we need to do is copy these starfield image assets into their respective folders. Copy stars320x480.png to the drawable-ldpi folder, stars480x800.png into the drawable-mdpi folder, stars1024x600.png into the drawable-hdpi folder, and finally the stars1280x720.png file into the drawable-xhdpi folder. Be sure and rename each one to be simply **stars.png** after you copy each resolution version to its respective drawable folder.

First of all, notice that these are indexed PNG8 files, and range from 6KB to less than 24KB, even though the largest one is HD resolution. Stars are a perfect example of a great image type to use for an indexed file format, as there's lots of black area and not much image detail or color variation so the compression results for PNG8 in this type of scenario are amazing.

Editing Our Screen Layout XML to Reference the Stars Background Image

Next, open the **activity_add.xml** file and add an **android:background** parameter that references the stars.png file via the **@drawable/stars** path addressing mechanism as shown in Figure 7-3. Then select the Hello_World project folder, and hit your **F5** key to refresh the project view, or right-click the project folder, and select the **Refresh** menu option. Then click the **Graphical Layout** tab at the bottom of the editing pane to preview our image compositing result. As you can see in Figure 7-4, the planets look great against that starry background, but our caption text seems to have disappeared, and there is a 22 DIP white stripe going down the left side of our user interface screen.

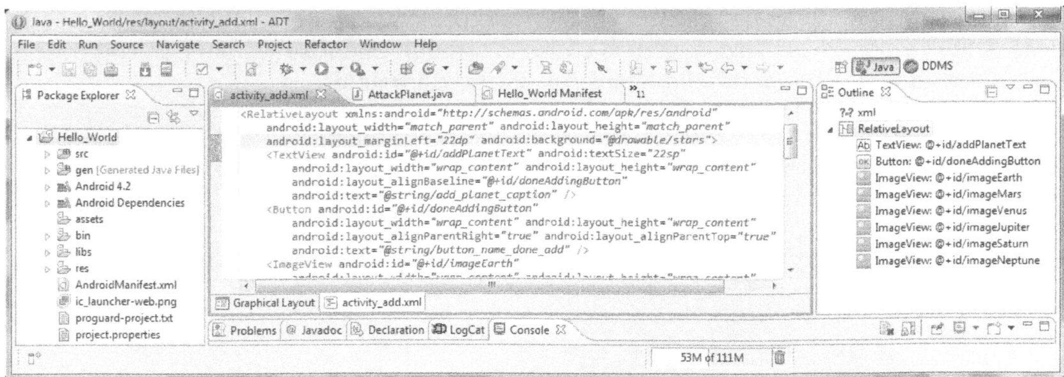

Figure 7-3. Adding a starfield background image to our activity_add.xml file to composite planets with some stars

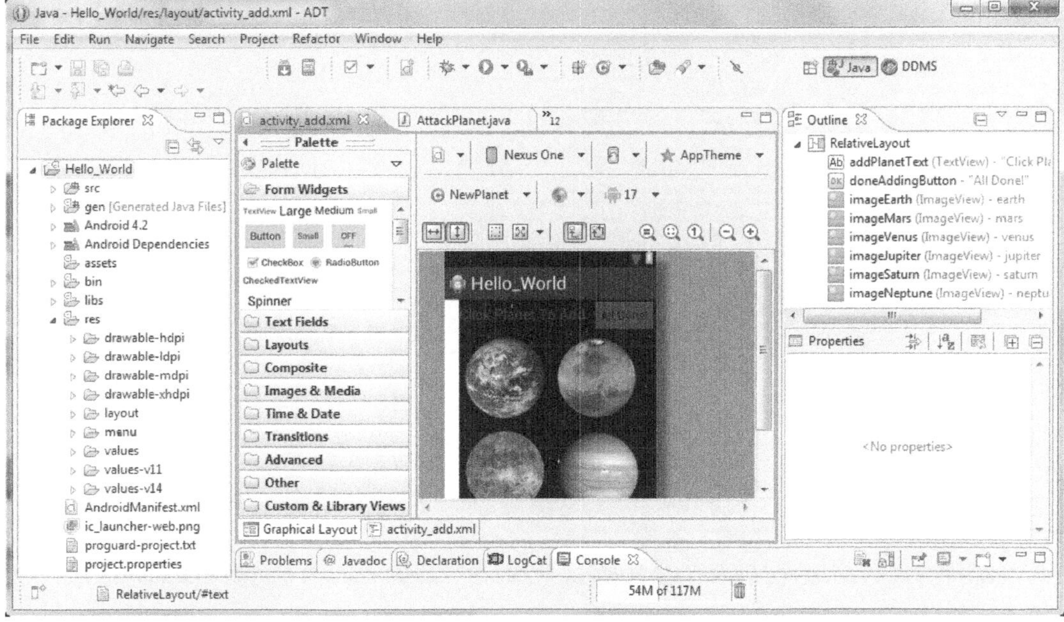

Figure 7-4. Previewing our android:background parameter using the Graphical Layout Editor tab in Eclipse

This isn't the professional UI result that we were expecting, so we need to change a few tag parameters in our tags, to make adjustments now that we have the dark starry background, instead of the white background color (see Figure 7-4).

Adjusting Our XML Tag Parameters to Accommodate the New Stars Background Image

What is happening here is that we have been using the **marginLeft** parameter in our RelativeLayout layout container to center the planets as a group; now that we have a background image set for that layout container, the marginLeft parameter is also pushing that background image over by 22 dip as well, causing the white stripe on the left.

Android OS uses a white default application background color, just like it does for all its layout containers default color value. This is what is showing through because we are pushing over the entire layout container via the android:marginLeft="22dp" parameter.

To correct this, we will remove the **marginLeft** parameter from the Relative Layout container tag, and instead we will put it in each of our ImageView tags to push them over by the same amount, as shown in Figure 7-5.

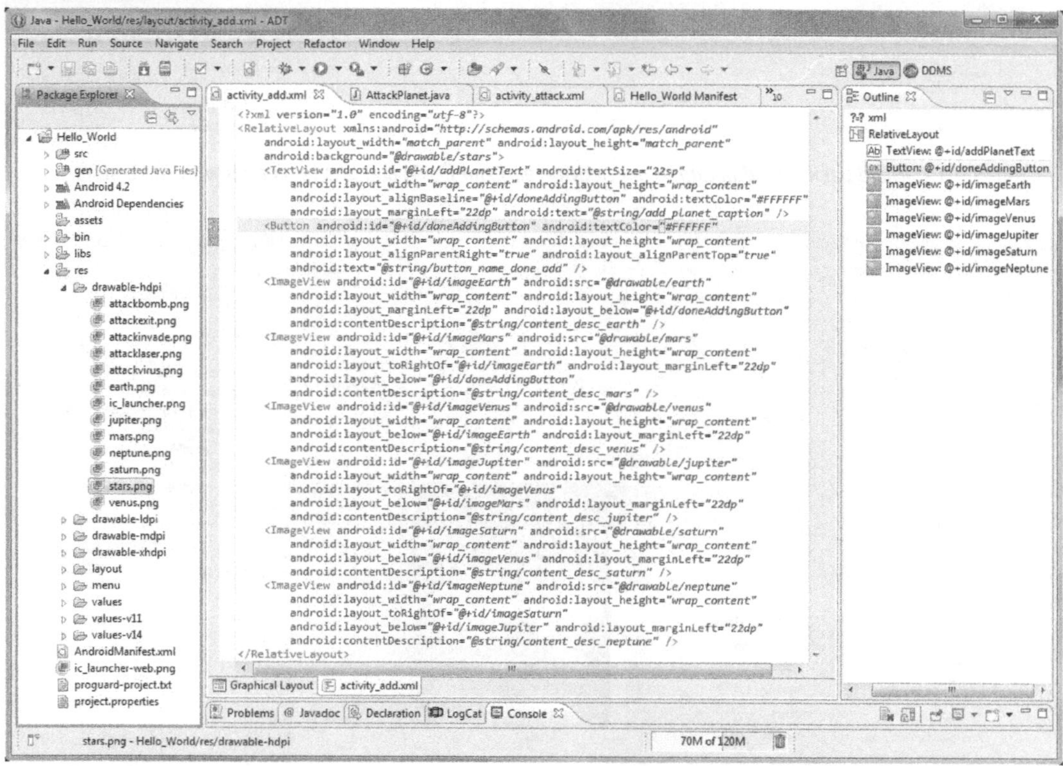

Figure 7-5. *Modifying our TextView and Button tags to add white text color parameter and MarginLeft parameters*

We will also need to put another copy of the marginLeft parameter into the TextView, to push it back over as well, so that it doesn't touch the left edge of the user interface screen.

Adjusting Our TextView Tag's textColor Parameter to Increase the Contrast

Next, we need to add an **android:textColor** parameter set to **#FFFFFF** (white) to the TextView and Button tags, so that we can see the caption and button labels against the stars.png background. Another important concept for us to learn about in digital imaging theory is that of **contrast**, and to have readable text, we need high contrast, that is, bright color text against a dark color background. This tag parameter addition is shown in Figure 7-5.

Now that we have made android:marginLeft and android:textColor parameter changes to the tags that required them, it is time to use **Run As Android Application** and invoke the Nexus S emulator, and to actually see what our newly upgraded Add a Planet user interface screen looks like.

As you can see in Figure 7-6 the text is now readable due to the **high contrast** between the white text and dark starfield background, and the button looks good as well. Did you notice that the button background is darker once we put the stars.png image behind it? That is because the button background is not only grey, it is also transparent as well, in fact, you can see a little star right at the top of the button that is showing through this transparency.

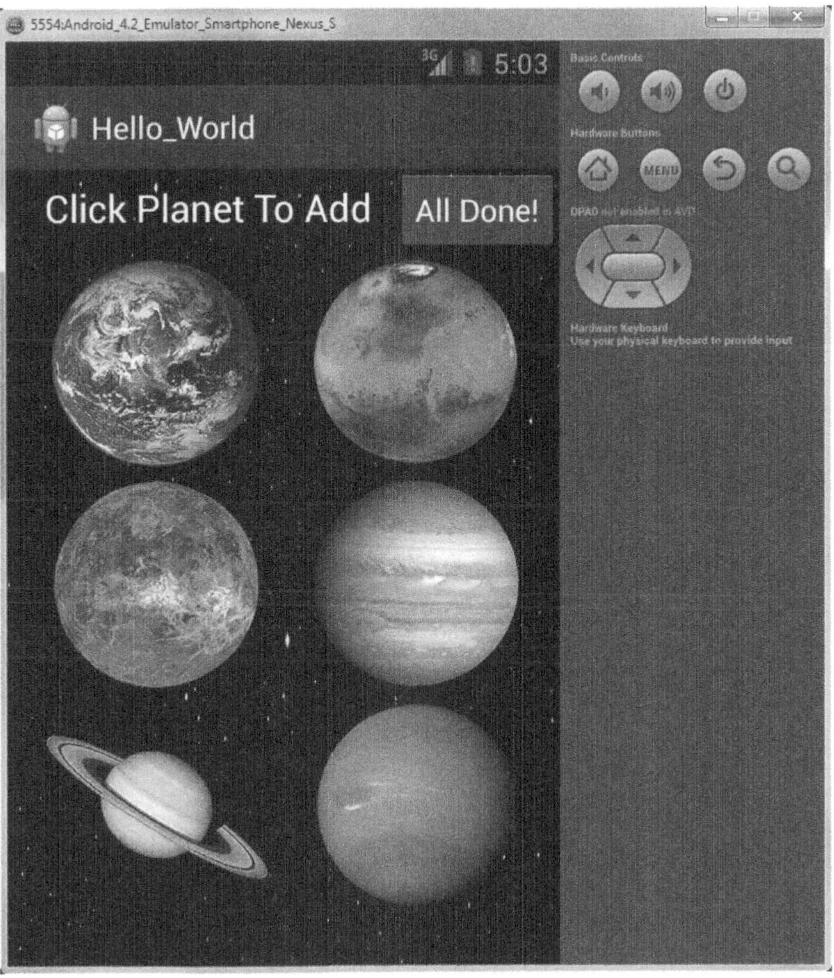

***Figure 7-6.** Previewing our image compositing result in the Nexus S emulator*

This is an example of **blending**, which I covered earlier, where the button background color is algorithmically added to each background pixel color. This allows you to put buttons over images with a more professional visual result. Note that this blending amount can also be changed in XML parameters or in Java code.

Because this looks so good, let's also go ahead and add the stars.png image to the AttackPlanet user interface screen background. Using an image **asset** more than once in an application is a great way to get more mileage out of your image assets, and that helps make your app's data footprint smaller.

Upgrading Our TravelPlanet UI: Creating an Alpha Channel for Our AttackVirus

Before we add the android:background parameter to our activity_attack.xml file like with did for our Add a Planet screen in the previous section, we need to create an alpha channel for one of the icon images for our UI. You may have noticed when copying the icons into your project subfolders, that one of these images, attackvirus.png, has a solid, black background around the virus, instead of featuring transparency as the other four icons have.

Let's go through the work process involved in rectifying this, using the GIMP open source image editing software, so you know how this is done, and so later on, we can put a virus over any background with seamless results.

Adding Transparency: Creating an Alpha Channel Mask

Launch GIMP 2.8.4, and then use the **File ➤ Open** menu sequence to open the **attackvirus.png** file (see Figure 7-7) located in the project resource **drawable-xhdpi** folder because that file has **96 pixels** of resolution. In digital imaging, we always start with the highest resolution and work down to avoid any **pixellation**.

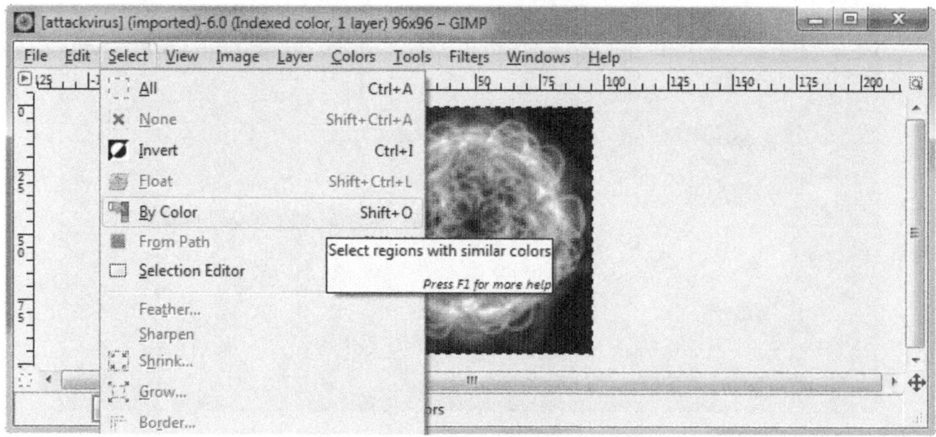

***Figure 7-7.** Open the attackvirus.png file in the drawable-xhdpi folder and then invoke the Select By Color tool*

Click the **Select** menu and the **By Color** image area selection tool, which will put you into a **contiguous color selection mode** that will select areas of color that contain collections of pixels with the same RGB color value.

Once you are in the tool mode set the **Threshold** (selection sensitivity) to a value of **40**, and click on the **black pixels** in one of the four corners of the image. Since there are several different color values within our virus cell itself, it is a more logical work process to select colors that are **not** in the virus cell, rather than trying to select the virus cell colors. Once your **selection marquee** (marching ants outline) looks like it does in Figure 7-8 use the **Delete** key on your keyboard to remove the black pixels.

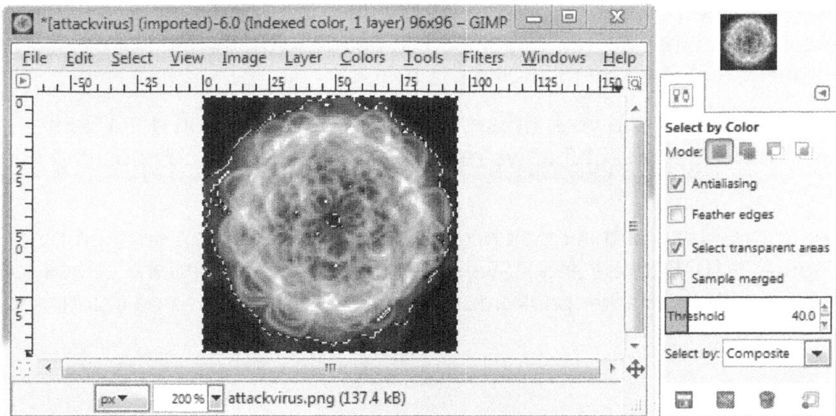

***Figure 7-8.** Select By Color selection marquee showing selection and options dialog with Threshold set at 40*

Once you press the Delete key, you will see the white background color used in GIMP (just like Android uses as its app background color), which will make further editing (clean-up) of our alpha channel image **mask** easier (Figure 7-9).

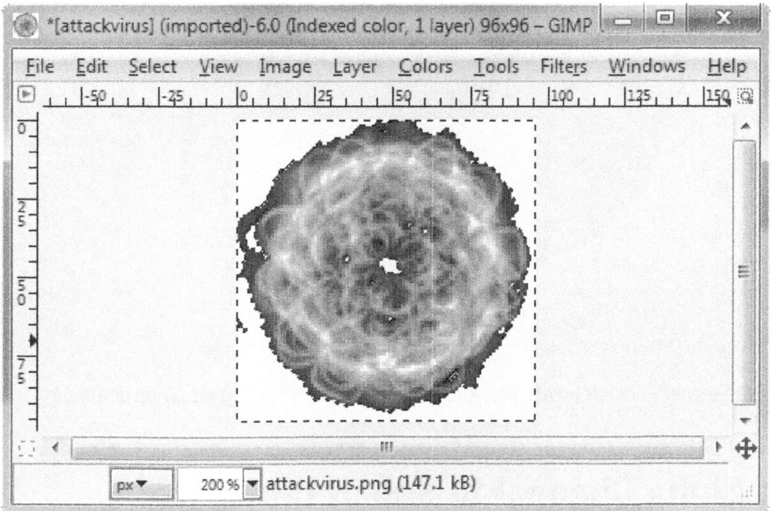

***Figure 7-9.** Delete the selected black color values showing GIMP default white background color*

A mask defines the part of an image that is going to show or be used in an image composite, thus, this process that we are undertaking here is called **masking** the attack virus cell from the image of the attack virus cell.

Next drop-down the **Select** menu again and pick the **None** option to make sure nothing is selected in the image before we edit it. Then select the **Eraser** tool (look for an old-school eraser in your tool palette) and set the tool settings to **1 Pixel**, **square Aspect Ratio** (0 value) and **Angle** set 0 (square to screen), and select **Pencil Generic** from the **Dynamics** drop-down menu. Using the Eraser tool, click the fringe black pixels that did not get selected, because they were not close enough to the black pixel value that you clicked on to invoke the tool.

This process is called **cleaning up your mask**, and is done so that you get a tighter selection area around the attack virus image object that we're going to use later for compositing effects in our Android application.

A before and after comparison of this black pixel clean-up process can be seen by comparing Figure 7-9 with Figure 7-10. Be sure and leave some dark pixels around the edges to effect a better blending effect with the darker backgrounds that we are going to be using in the Hello World application.

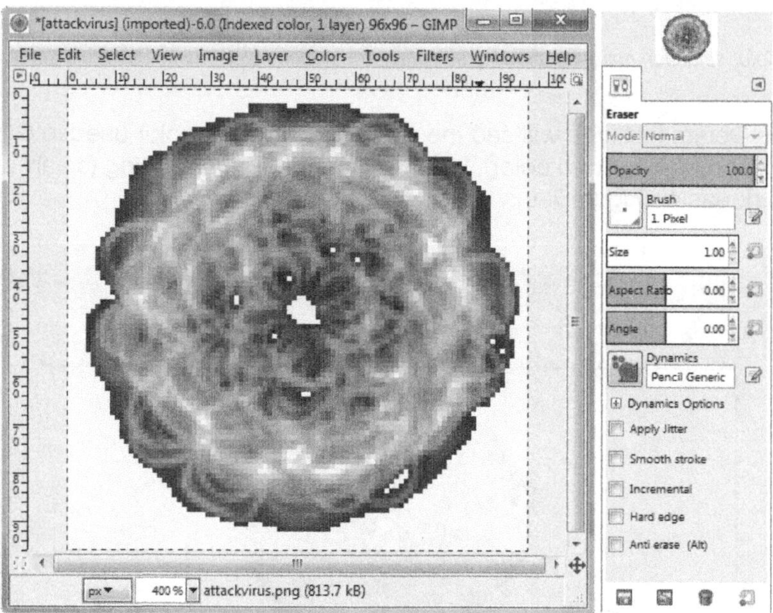

***Figure 7-10.** Using the Eraser tool to clean up our mask in preparation for creating an alpha channel*

Inverting the Alpha Channel to Select the Virus

Now we are going to re-select our new object via the mask we just cleaned up by again using the **Select By Color** tool, and clicking the now white areas in the corner of the current image. This more precisely selects the virus (or rather what is not the virus) as you can see in Figure 7-11. Next invoke the **Select ➤ Invert** menu operation to change our selection from what is not the virus to the virus itself.

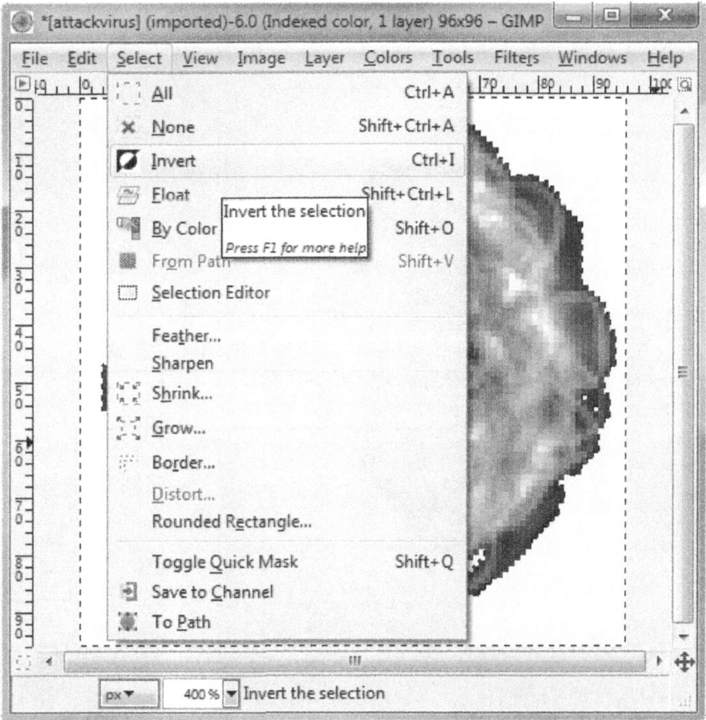

***Figure 7-11.** Inverting the selection using Select ➤ Invert*

Go ahead and **Invert** your selection mask to get a final attack virus object pixel collection properly selected. Now, we are going to use the **Edit ➤ Copy** to copy the attackvirus pixels to our system clipboard.

Now that we have just the pixels for our attackvirus image object selected and copied to the clipboard, we can paste them into a new file. When we do this, GIMP will put an alpha channel (transparency) in the pixel locations that do not have any pixels in them.

GIMP 2.8 also automatically sets the new image pixel resolution, based on the horizontal and vertical number of pixels used in the selection data in the system clipboard. In this case, this is 90 by 89, as can be seen in Figure 7-12, in the window header for the new attackvirus image with alpha channel in the bottom left of the screenshot. Look on the right of that screen shot, and you will also see the **ARGB channels** for the new image and the alpha channel that has been created for us via **Paste As ➤ New Image**.

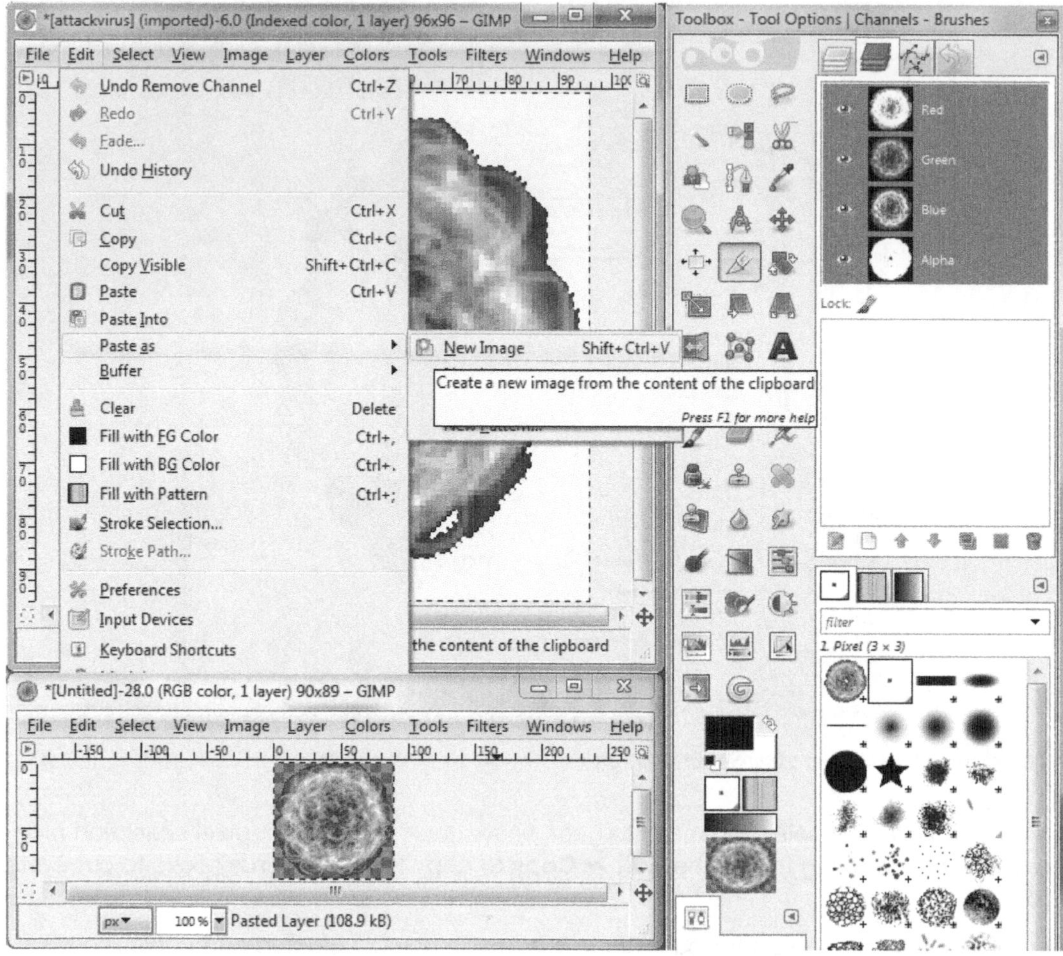

***Figure 7-12.** Using Paste As ➤ New Image to create new image (lower left) with alpha channel (upper right)*

It is also important to notice in Figure 7-11 and Figure 7-12 that if you hold your mouse over a menu item or a toolbox icon, that GIMP will pop-up a tool-tip telling you exactly what that tool will do if you select it for use. This is a key way to explore what GIMP can do and learn its features.

In Figure 7-12, which not only shows us the new untitled image that we will generate from the next operation but that operation menu selection as well (I created a 2-in-1 screenshot to save space), you will see that the **Edit** menu has a **Paste As** sub-menu, which itself has a sub-sub-menu containing a **New Image** paste function which will paste the copied attackvirus pixels in your clipboard into an all **New Image File** (named untitled). The tool-tip says: **Create a new image from the content of the clipboard**. What the tool-tip doesn't say is: GIMP automatically creates your alpha channel for you in pixel locations where there are no pixels present in the clipboard.

Notice in the alpha channel in the top right of Figure 7-12 that GIMP uses white pixels (on or visible) where the virus is, and black pixels (off or transparent) where we originally edited our selection mask. Also note that above the image channels the channels icon is represented as layers of RBG values in three dimensions; this is a great way to think about color channels, even though, ultimately, it is mathematics that sums these ARGB values to define each pixel's color and translucency levels.

Saving Our Work So Far in the GIMP XCF Native Format

Because our new image is **untitled** let's use the **File ➤ Save As** menu sequence to give our new image with alpha a name, and save it, so we don't lose all our work. I named the file: **attackvirusnew.xcf** (GIMP native format) and put it into **drawable-xhdpi** with attackvirus.PNG, as shown in Figure 7-13.

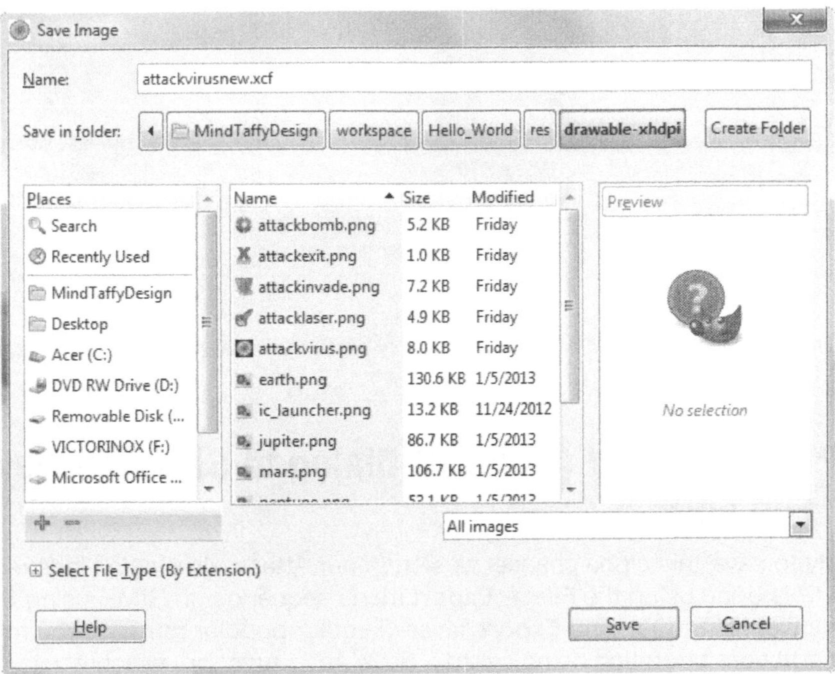

Figure 7-13. Saving the new untitled image as attackvirusnew.xcf so our work is saved

The next thing that we want to do is to put our newly masked attack virus back into the center of a 96x96 pixel image container. We need to do this before we create our other three lower resolution versions of this image asset that we will need to use in our other three resolution image folders inside our Android project resource drawable sub-folder structure.

Using the Canvas Size Tool to Re-Center Our Newly Masked Image

We will re-center our masked image using the **Image ➤ Canvas Size** menu sequence, which will invoke the Canvas Size dialog in GIMP. Assuming your newly titled attackvirusnew window in GIMP is active, let's apply the Canvas Size image operation to the 90x89 pixel image and turn it into a 96x96 pixel image.

The **Canvas Size** dialog is shown in Figure 7-14, and it allows you to enter the **target resolution** (Canvas Size), and to either set **offsets** from each X Y dimension, or allow GIMP to do this for you, by using the **Center** button on the right side of the dialog. This is what I did, as I'm that shortcut kind of guy, and thus GIMP entered values of 3 pixels in each of the X and Y fields for me when I did so.

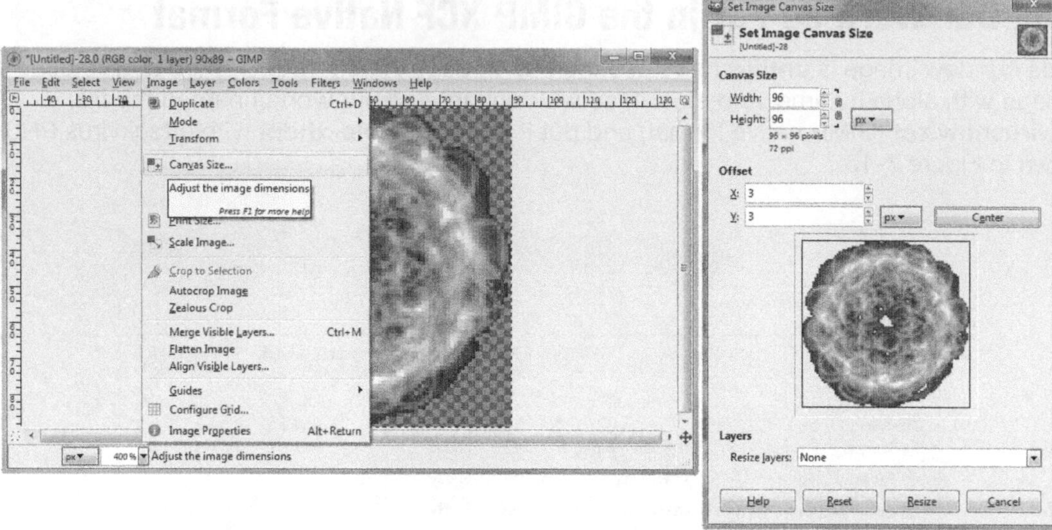

Figure 7-14. Using Image ➤ Canvas Size and a Center function to re-center the masked image in 96 pixel square

Using GIMP's File Export (Save As) Dialog to Save Our New Image in a PNG32 File Format

Now we are ready to save this alpha channel version of our Attack Virus as an indexed color PNG file, which in GIMP is done using the **File ➤ Export** menu sequence. In GIMP, using **Save** yields an **XCF** (GIMP Native) file format, and **Export** saves via other popular formats. You may be more familiar with this software operation being called a Save As... function, which it was in GIMP in version 2.6.12 and previous, and is called this in other software packages as well, so this is something you will need to get used to with GIMP 2.8 and later.

Figure 7-15 shows the Export Image dialog in GIMP where we type in our new file name of attackvirusalpha and an extension of .png to specify format.

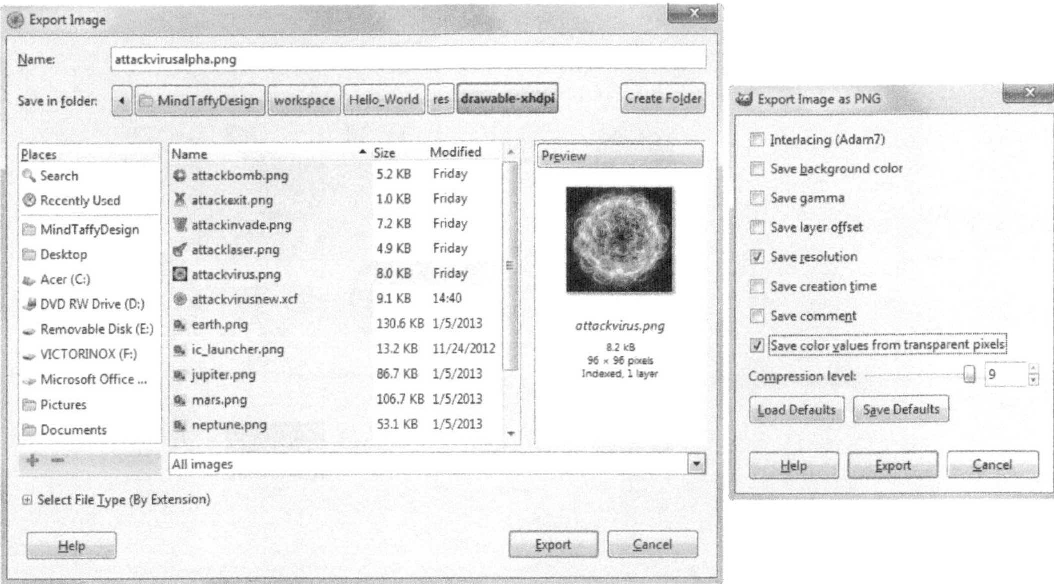

***Figure 7-15.** Using File ➤ Export Image to export a new PNG8 version of the image with an alpha channel*

In GIMP the file format is specified as part of the filename that we type in, or you can use the Select File Type (By Extension) UI element at the bottom left of the dialog if you want to see what other file types can be exported. I usually use .tif (TIFF, or Tagged Image File format) or .png as these are lossless formats and yield perfect visual results, but you can also use .jpg (JPEG, a lossy format) or even .tga (Targa, another lossless format) format, if you prefer.

Once we export our attackvirusalpha as a PNG8, we need to go into our OSes file manager (Explorer or similar), and rename some files, so that next we can access the correct (alpha) version of the graphic inside of Eclipse.

Shown in Figure 7-16 is Windows 7 Explorer, where we have renamed our old version (original) attackvirus.png to attackvirusold.png and then **renamed** the new **attackvirusalpha.png** file to the **attackvirus.png** that's referenced in our Hello World application's XML mark-up, as shown in the screenshot.

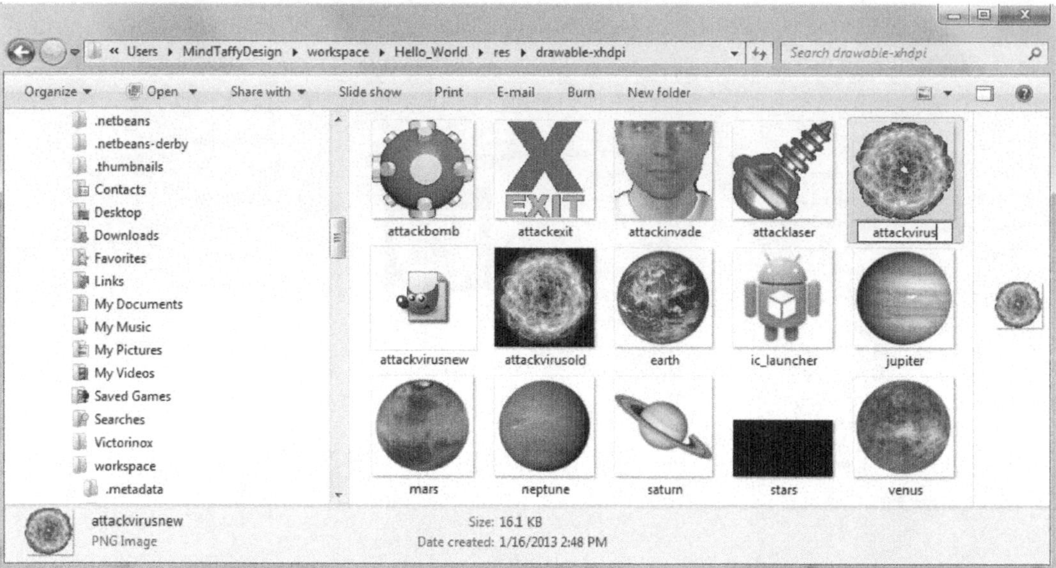

***Figure 7-16.** Using Windows Explorer to rename attackvirus to attackvirus old and attackvirusalpha to attackvirus*

Notice that our GIMP attackvirusnew.xcf working file is also now present; this will not affect our project in Eclipse, but we can delete this file later on, or move it to another folder on our hard disk drive, say, one that is used for original artwork or assets in development, if you wish.

Creating Our Other Resolution Density Image Versions Using the Image Resize Tool

Now that our highest resolution image asset has been masked, and includes an alpha channel to define its transparency, we can resize the image down to 80-pixel, 64-pixel, and 48-pixel versions, which we need for our other drawable folders inside our application project resource folder hierarchy (see Figure 7-17).

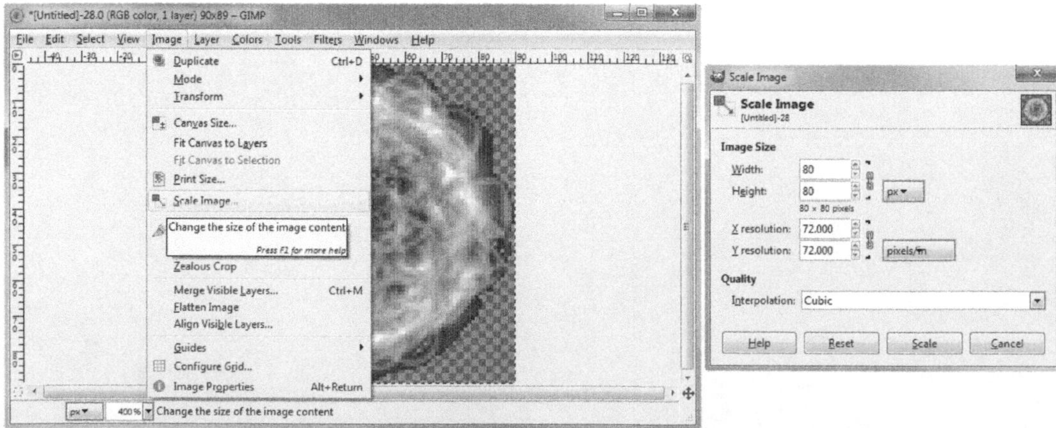

***Figure 7-17.** Resizing the 96 pixel image to 80 pixels using the Image ➤ Scale Image and Cubic Interpolation*

This work process is done via the **Image** menu and the **Scale Image** submenu, which accesses the often used Scale Image tool dialog, which is used for resizing digital imagery to different resolutions. Notice the **chain icons** that allow you to **lock** the image **aspect ratio** as we discussed previously.

Replace the **96** in the **Width** field with an **80** and then notice that when you click the Height field (or press the Enter key) that the other field auto types in 80 as well, because the aspect ratio is locked (by default). The second set of fields contain screen resolution (pixel densities), so leave these set at 72 DPI for screen work (use 300 DPI or higher for printing).

Set the **Interpolation Quality** drop-down menu to **Cubic** (known as Bi-Cubic in Photoshop) for the scaling algorithm, and then click the **Scale** button.

Now that our image is 80 by 80 pixels we need to go through the exact same work process that we did before, starting with Figure 7-13. Save your file as a GIMP .XCF in case you need it later in the drawable-ldpi folder, then export it as a **PNG8** with the name **attackvirusalpha**, and then go into your file manager so you can rename the original file to be **attackvirusold**, and rename the new one to **attackvirus**, so that the correct image data is used in your Android Hello World application after we **Refresh** our project view.

Do this work process again for the **64 pixel** image asset in **drawable-mdpi**, as well as for the **48 pixel** image asset in **drawable-ldpi**, and when you are done, you will have the practice that you need to be comfortable with this work process.

Now we are ready to go into our XML mark-up and add stars to the background of our AttackPlanet user interface screen layout container. It is important to note that when you do the image scale to 64 and 48 pixels that you should start with the 96 pixel version of your saved image in order to give the Image resizing algorithm the most data to work from, so that it can give you the best scaling result.

Launch Eclipse (if it's not open already) and click the activity_attack XML editing tab, and change your LinearLayout android:background parameter from black (#000000) to @drawable/stars.png, and don't forget the **Refresh**!

Whenever you change any filenames or file contents or add new files, you must always right-click your project folder and select **Refresh** or left-click (select) your project folder and hit the **F5** key on your keyboard.

Now let's **Run As Android Application**, and see the stars behind our second user interface screen that uses a dark background and light (color) text.

As you will see in Figure 7-18, the visual results are as incredible as we had anticipated, with our stars showing through both the icon and the text user interface elements absolutely perfectly. Notice that text elements in Android carry their own alpha channel and opacity settings, as we will see in the next chapter, when we go into far greater detail regarding our user interface element (widget) graphics design techniques.

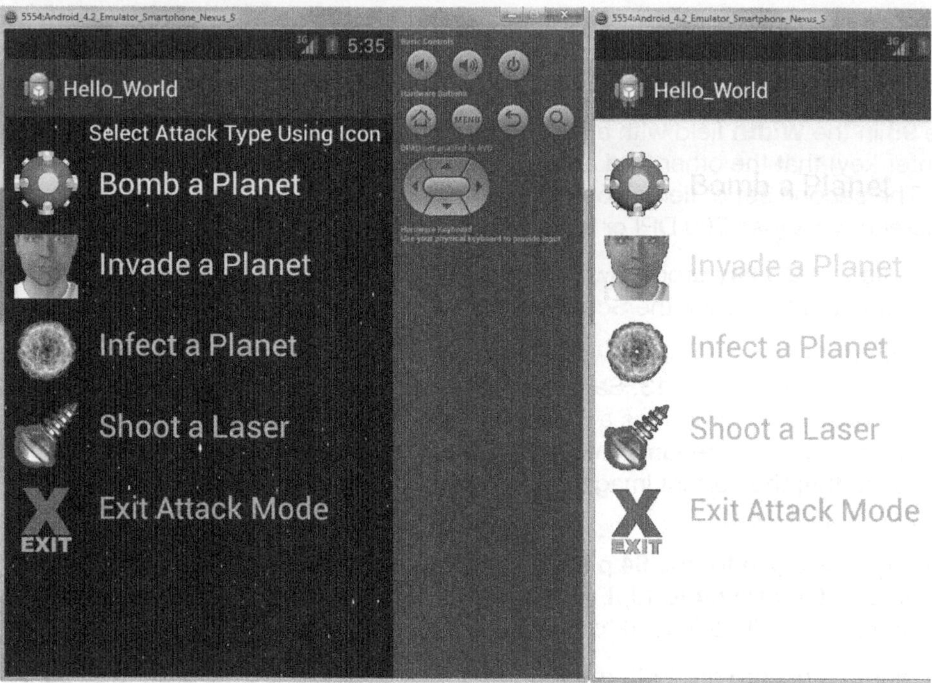

Figure 7-18. AttackPlanet UI screen showing stars background and masked virus on white background

We have made a lot of progress on the graphics design foundation for our Hello World application with half of our Activity user interface screens now exhibiting new media-based user interface elements and backgrounds. We also learned a lot of foundational principles behind digital imaging, and some digital imaging work processes regarding alpha channels and masking.

Summary

In this chapter, we learned the foundational concepts of digital imaging and of graphics design, as well as how Android assimilates these concepts into its application development infrastructure. To practice implementing these graphic design and digital imaging concepts within our Hello World application, we added starfield image background parameters to some of our Activities, and masked our AttackVirus to add an alpha channel so that the stars would seamlessly show through that UI element's transparency region.

We learned about the Android **Drawable** class and its **direct subclasses** that define all the various types of graphic design assets which we can utilize within our Android applications, including **shapes**, **colors**, **insets**, **layers**, **gradients** and **bitmaps** (bitmap imagery, also known as pixel-based imagery).

We learned about the more complicated **indirect subclasses** of Drawable, such as Animation, Image Transitions, LevelLists, and StateLists. We learned about **DrawableContainer**, and that we could create our own custom indirect multi-graphics subclasses, using that superclass as their foundation.

Next we looked at the concept of the **pixel**, which is the building block of digital imaging and digital video. We then looked at the image concepts of resolution and aspect ratio and how both are calculated using simple math.

We learned about **color theory**, and about the different color depths that are used in digital imaging and how color is represented using **hexidecimal** notation. We learned how to compute the total number of colors in an image based on its **color depth**, and about the concept of **indexed color** imagery and 256 color **palettes** which **sample** primary colors from a **truecolor** image.

We learned about image **channels** and the **RGB** color channels, and the fourth **alpha channel** that holds transparency values for pixels so that images can be used in **compositing** more complex imagery or special effects via the use of **layers** and **blending modes**. We learned about blending support in Android via the **android.graphics.PorterDuff** class and we learned about its primary blending modes, such as: **Overlay**, **Screen**, **Darken**, **Lighten**, and **XOR**.

We covered all the different graphics file formats in Android, as well as which ones were preferred for use, and why, along with which formats were lossless, and which ones were lossy. We covered the new **WebP** image format support in Android 4.0 and later, and covered the difference between **PNG8** indexed and **PNG24** truecolor and **PNG32** truecolor with alpha channel images.

Finally, we covered compression concepts and techniques, such as **dithering**, and then we applied the digital imaging concepts that we learned to our Hello World app, to add more visual design and professional features, via compositing cool icons and text with custom background starfield imagery.

In the next chapter, we will build upon this foundation of digital imaging knowledge established in this chapter and add custom UI elements.

Chapter 8

Compositing in Android: Advanced Graphical User Interface Design

In this chapter, we will take the foundational digital imaging concepts that we mastered in the previous chapter, and build more complicated digital imaging constructs to add even more advanced graphics design-based (i.e., bitmap-based) user interface elements to our Hello World application. This will help you to make your app visually spectacular, whether it is a game, business app, utility app, or (hopefully) something altogether new and never before done.

We discuss **multi-state** user interface elements, which change the images that a user sees while using the UI, and provide the end-user **visual feedback** regarding what they are touching (or are clicking), and which user interface element was the last used. We **composite** various UI elements with other graphics design elements to create advanced, seamless visual effects; effects that span several different tags and their parameter settings, but which appear to function as one single UI entity.

We also finish making each of our app Activity screen user interfaces similar in their design and look and feel, adding unique (non-standard) UI elements that make our application completely custom on all visual levels. Many Android developers implement and use only the standard user interface widgets, and thus their apps feature only the standard Android look and feel, without using any imaging-based visual modifications that would make their Android application stand far apart from the rest of the market.

Multi-State UI Elements: The Normal, Pressed, and Focused States

Let's take our **ImageButton** user interface elements that are on our Attack Planet Activity user interface screen to the next level, and change them into **multi-state** image buttons. Multi-state image buttons **interactively** change their button graphics, depending on what the user is doing (or has just done) to interact with them. Adding an interactive user interface element to your user interface design can take a user's perception of the level of professionalism exhibited by your application to an entirely new level.

The **normal** state in a multi-state image button is the graphic element that you see on the user interface screen when you first arrive at that screen. In our Attack a Planet user interface screen, the normal state for these buttons would be the button icon graphics that we already have in place. You could also call this button state the **default** button image state.

The **pressed** state in a multi-state image button reveals itself whenever a user touches that button, which means a finger-touch on a touchscreen or a navigation button down action if a user is using nav-keys. For our new AttackPlanet multi-state ImageButton **button-pressed** image element, let's add a golden hoop around the icon. In this way, when a user touches the Attack method icon on this user interface screen, a golden hoop encircles the icon, showing interactive feedback that the UI element is being touched.

The **focused** state in our multi-state button happens when the user releases (stops touching) that button and is using that user interface element. The user interface element is said to have **focus** because the user is using it, and it does not **lose focus** until the user selects another user interface element (touch another ImageButton UI element) or the operation attached to that UI element is completed, such as our Toast message currently acting as a placeholder in our Java code.

We utilize a silver hoop around our image button icons to show which one has focus, and is currently being used, and thus which one was the last one selected for use by our users. First we need to create our ImageButton source files for each of the three image states, and our normal state is already created, so we only need to create pressed and focused button states, using some advanced multi-layer compositing techniques in GIMP 2.8.

Creating Our ImageButton Multi-State Image Source Files

Let's fire up GIMP 2.8, and do that now for each of our four attack mode icons, for each of our four pixel densities required by Android. That's four attack mode image buttons times four pixel densities, times two button states, and that equals **thirty-two** different image assets that we need to create. Developing a professional Android app isn't an easy process by any stretch of the imagination, if you want to do it right.

Add the four image buttons in four pixel densities that we already have, and we're at **48** images for our four attack mode multi-state buttons. Finally, add another four pixel density assets for our Exit Attack Mode button, and you have **52** separate digital image assets that are needed to implement our Attack a Planet screen, Note that this is not including the background **stars.png** digital image, which brings the grand total for this one user interface screen to **53** digital image assets needed to create this advanced user interface screen design for each screen density. I thought this was an introductory book! Once we're at the end of this book, you will find you will have used hundreds of assets developing your Android app!

Once GIMP has launched, use the **File ➤ Open** menu sequence to find your **attackinvade** 96-pixel graphic in the **drawable-XHDPI** folder of your Android Hello_World project folder inside your workspace folder.

Let's set-up GIMP's working environment first, and use the **View ➤ Zoom ➤ 2:1** menu sequence to set the view to **200%,** as is shown in Figure 8-1.

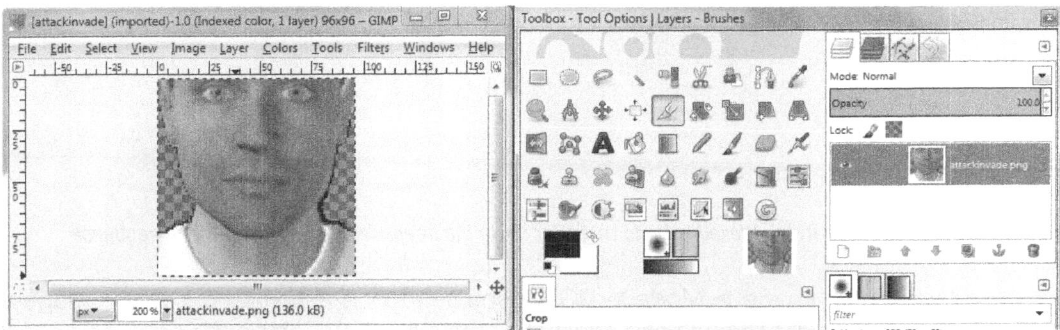

***Figure 8-1.** Launch GIMP 2.8, zoom to 200% and then click the Layers tab on the right (looks like stacked white sheets of vellum)*

Next, click the **Layers** tab at the top right (looks like stacked white vellum), so you can see that our image currently has a single layer called **attackinvade.png**, which is the indexed color PNG8 Soldier's Face icon image that we just opened.

If you click the **Channels** tab (a stacked RGB color channels icon), you will see a single indexed color channel that contains our 8-bits of image data. If we add our hoop layer while our image is in **indexed color mode**, the hoop will only have a few colors with which to use to portray its 3D metal look, and will not look photo-real the way that we want it to. What we need to do is to convert our image into **truecolor color mode** before we import the next layer for the image compositing functions we're about to perform.

In GIMP 2.8, the **color depth** that your image is currently set to use is found in the **Image** menu under the **Mode** sub-menu. If you access this **Image ➤ Mode** menu sequence, you will see several key image modes, including **RGB** (Truecolor mode), **Grayscale** (Monochrome mode) and **Indexed** color mode, which as you will see is the currently selected mode (a **dot** next to that sub-menu entry indicates the current mode).

Let's change the color mode of our image before we go any further in our work process, so that we get the highest visual results from any additional truecolor image layers that we might add during this process. To change the color depth of the current image from Indexed (8-bit) to RGB (32-bit) color mode, select the **Image ➤ Mode ➤ RGB** menu sequence shown in Figure 8-2 to change the image mode from 8-bit to 32-bit color. If we don't do this, any layer we add will use the 256 color palette for the image, which is taken from the initial image layer (data). This will constrain any future imagery (layers) imported later on to using those 256 colors; this will severely affect our visual quality, especially as we add more layers.

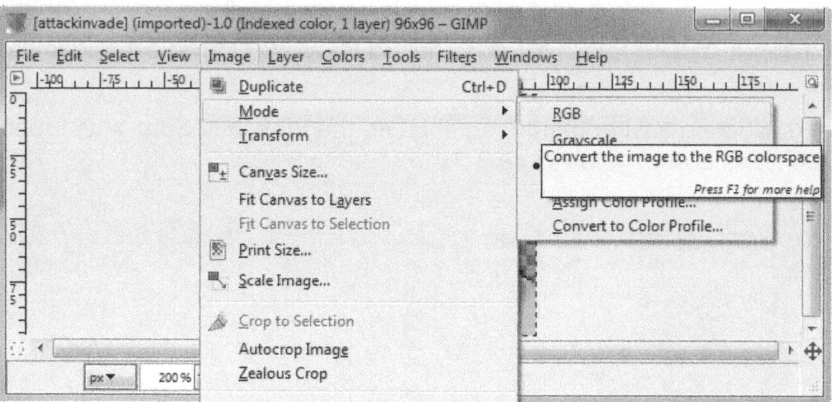

***Figure 8-2.** Convert image mode from indexed color to truecolor using the Image ➤ Mode ➤ RGB menu sequence*

Once we have invoked an Image ➤ Mode ➤ RGB menu sequence to switch our GIMP image editing environment into **Truecolor Mode**, we can again click the **Channels** tab on the right, and see that we have now gone from having one channel, with an indexed color palette of 256 colors for our image, to an image editing situation where we have four color channels (or three color channels and a transparency channel). This is shown in Figure 8-3, and since our layer was selected (highlighted in blue) for use in Figure 8-1, so too are our four channels selected to maintain this selection from the Layer Editing Mode (tab) to the Channel Editing Mode (tab).

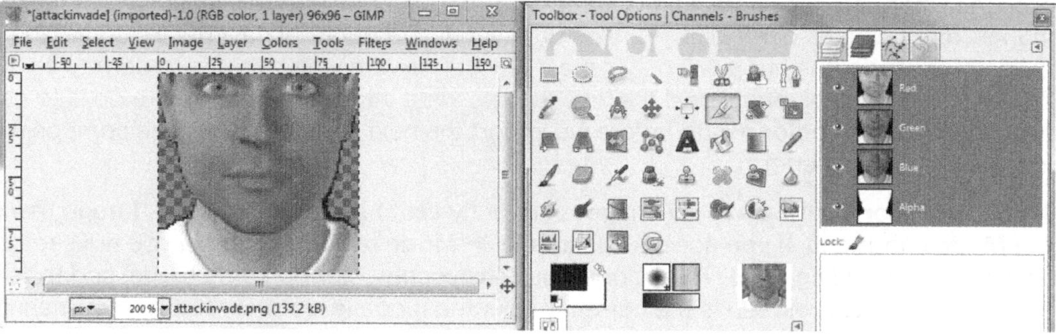

***Figure 8-3.** Click the Channels tab shown on the right to confirm there are now red, green, blue and alpha channels*

Image editing software is **modal**, that is, whatever tool, color, and editing modes are set and active at any given point affect what happens when you use the current tool on your image. Thus, if you are in **Layer Mode**, and you edit the image in **Layer Mode**, it will affect data on all the channels in your image. However, if you want to edit the data on just the **Green Channel** of the image, you can switch into **Channel Editing Mode** to do this, by clicking the Channels tab and the Green Channel before you use those editing tools (any editing tool can be used in any mode).

This modal software operation is much more powerful in its ability to combine software features into any toolset the user wants to create. Thus, it yields more professional results, but it is also far more difficult to use effectively. The user must always keep track of what modes, settings, and tools are currently active at any given time during the use of a modal software package. These editing modes, tools, and settings combine in real-time to ultimately create the exact editing function that is being used.

Importing Our Gold Hoop Image for Compositing

Now we are ready to get down to business and import our golden hoop image into its own layer to set up our image compositing operation. To do this, we are going to use GIMP's **File ➤ Open as Layer...** menu sequence, as shown in Figure 8-4. This will, as the tool-tip tells us, open up an image file as a layer in our Layers tab. Once you select this menu option, you get a dialog that lets you find the image asset named **GoldHoop96.png**, which is a truecolor **PNG32** file with an alpha channel defining transparency.

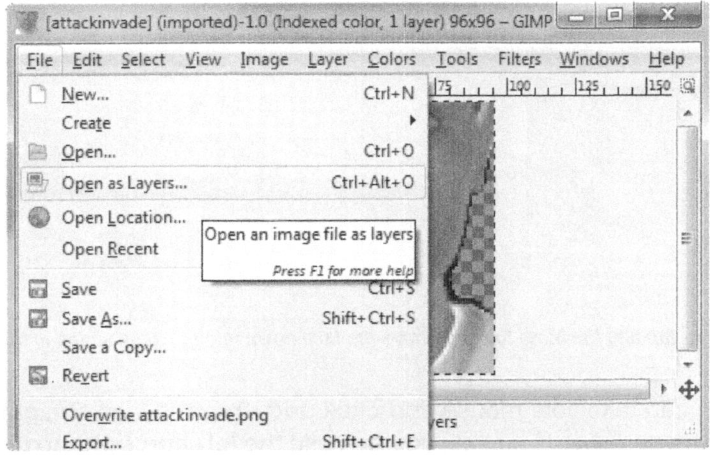

***Figure 8-4.** Importing the Hoop Layer using the File ➤ Open as Layers... menu sequence*

After you select this file to open it, it is merged into the project as its own layer in the Layers tab. The Channels tab shows the merged RGBA channel data, as shown in Figure 8-5, and your image view shows the golden hoop seamlessly composited over the soldier's face. Next, we need to move this new layer containing the soldier's face down, so that the face moves into the center of the hoop. We do this so that it looks like our soldier is looking through the hoop, and so that the eyes are not covered. It is important to note that GIMP uses RGBA channel ordering, whereas Android uses ARGB, that is, when specifying channels in hexadecimal in Android, the first two positions are the alpha value, not the last two positions, as someone who works with Photoshop or GIMP might simply assume.

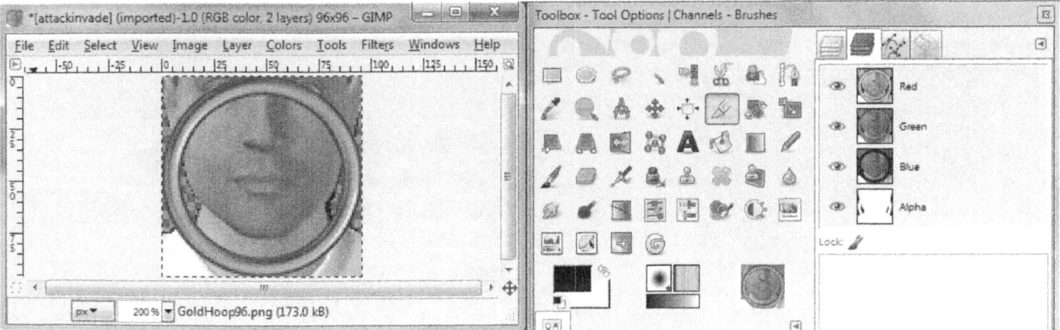

***Figure 8-5.** Hoop layer imported, and data combined in the RGBA channels, as shown on the right in the Channels tab*

Centering Our Soldier's Face in the Gold Hoop by Moving Its Layer Position

To move the face layer down into the hoop, select the lower layer with the face graphic, as shown in blue in Figure 8-6, and then also click the **Move tool** (a four-arrow cross, located in the second row, middle) to set the modal editing operation to move (move tool mode) the attackinvade layer (layer editing mode).

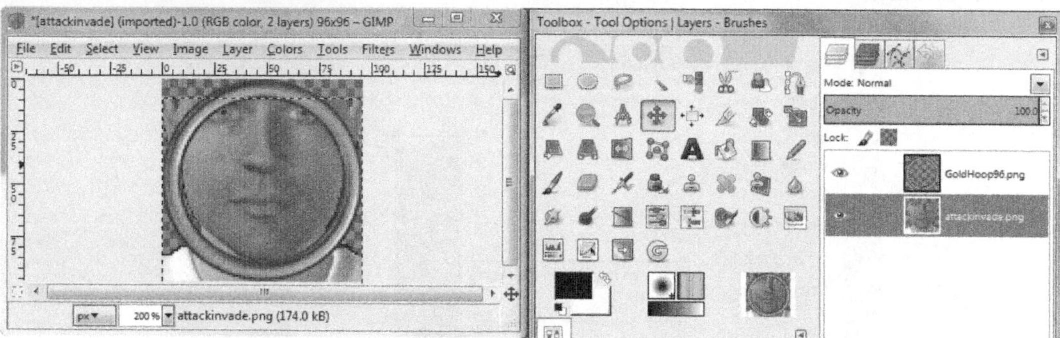

Figure 8-6. *Select the Layers tab and the Move tool and move the face down into the hoop so top is tangent to inside of hoop*

Once you do this, you can take your mouse and **click and drag** the face straight down into the center of the hoop, and then, if you like, you can use the **left and right arrow keys** on your keyboard to **nudge** the image into place, one pixel at a time. This **fine-tunes** your image centering operation, until the resulting composited image looks like it does in Figure 8-6.

Erasing the Unwanted Pixels Outside the Gold Hoop

Now, all we have to do is to select the **Eraser tool** shown in Figure 8-7 (fourth row down second icon) to put GIMP into **Erase Mode** and erase the parts of the soldier's face and shirt that are outside of the hoop. Note that we are keeping the bottom (face) layer selected, so our image editing software modes include: **Erase Tool Mode**, **RGB Truecolor Mode**, and **Layer Editing Mode** set to the attackinvade.png imagery layer (which applies Eraser tool editing to all four channels at the same time for imagery on that layer only).

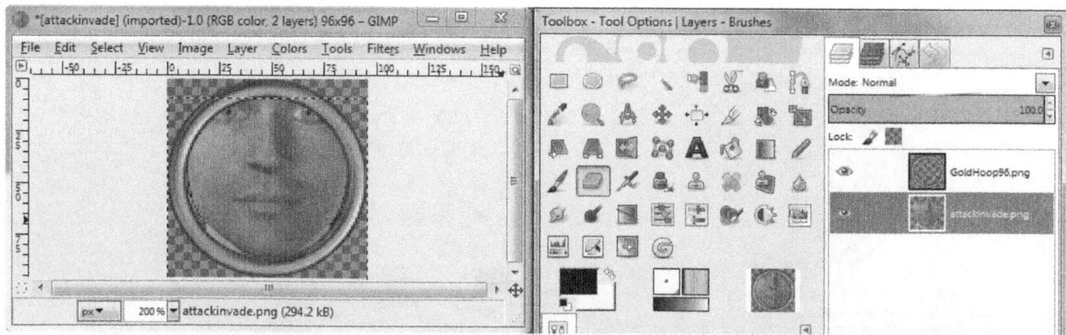

Figure 8-7. *Use the Eraser tool and remove the parts of the soldier image that fall outside of the hoop as shown*

Exporting Our attackinvadepress Button Icon State

Now, we are ready to **export** our **attackinvadepress** button icon state into our **drawable-xhdpi** folder, and two of our three image state buttons (Normal and Pressed) will be ready to implement in XML code.

To do this, we use GIMP's **File ➤ Export** menu sequence, name the file **attackinvadepress.png,** and finally, locate our **workspace/Hello_World/res/drawable-xhdpi** folder where we want to save this 96-pixel high-resolution (extra-high density pixel image) digital image file. After all this filename, folder pathname, and image type (.png extension) info has been specified in the GIMP Export Image dialog, you can then click the **Export** button to complete this operation, as shown in Figure 8-8.

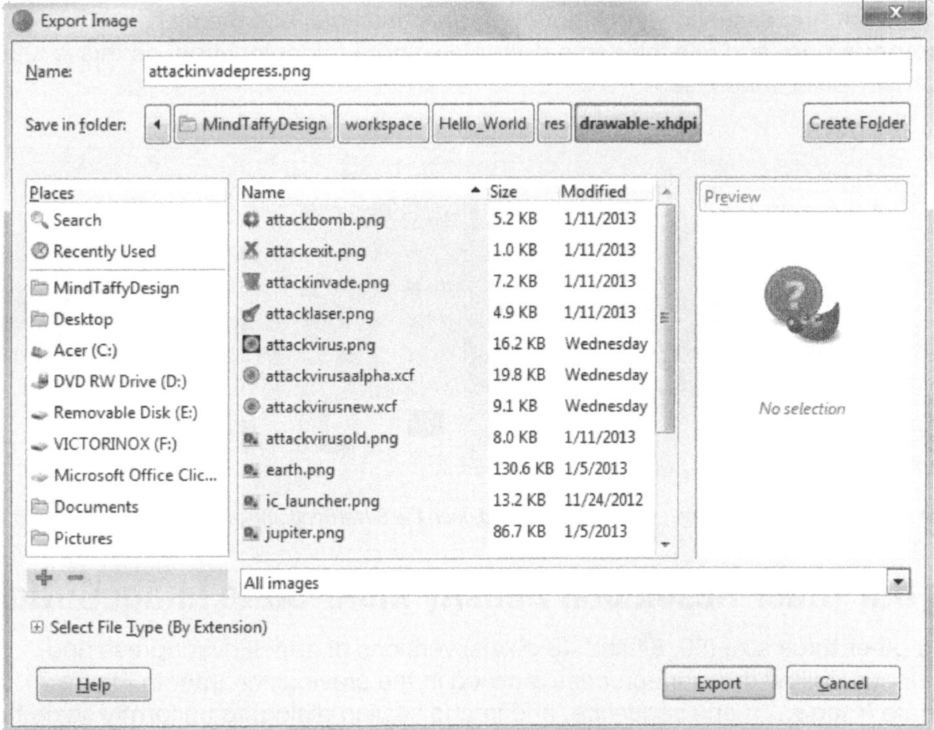

***Figure 8-8.** Using the Export Image dialog to save a truecolor .png filenamed attackinvaderpress.png in drawable-xhdpi folder*

Note that because our GIMP Color Depth Mode is set to truecolor RGB that we are now exporting **PNG32** truecolor PNG files with an alpha channel, but our file size has only doubled, from 8K to 16K, because we removed (erased) a lot of image data, and because the PNG32 compression algorithm is very efficient.

It is almost always desirable to use a PNG32 format over a PNG8 format if you can get the **data footprint** well-optimized, because the **level of quality** of the image data, as well as alpha channel, are considerably better (far more colors and more transparency values are utilized) in a PNG32 file than in a PNG8 file.

Creating Our attackinvadefocus Image Button State

Finally, we need to create our **attackinvadefocus** image button state. This is much easier, as much of our image editing work process for this third button state has already been accomplished for our **attackimagepress** image button state, including changing the image mode, moving the soldier's face, and erasing pixels outside of the hoop perimeter. All we have to do now is to add a silver hoop to show focus.

Use the **File ➤ Open as Layer...** function, shown in Figure 8-4, to add another layer to our image compositing stack, by finding the **SilverHoop96.png** image, and importing it into our GIMP 2.8.4 project.

Because the result looks great, as shown in Figure 8-9, we can proceed to again use our **File ➤ Export** work process, shown in Figure 8-8, only this time, use the filename: **attackimagefocus.png,** and use the same **drawable-xhdpi** folder location, as this is a 96-pixel extra-high density pixel image file.

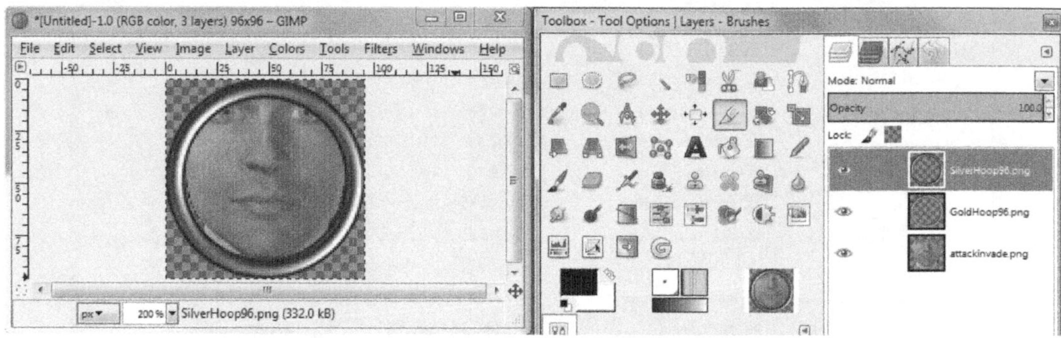

Figure 8-9. Use the File ➤ Open as Layer... menu sequence to open the SilverHoop.png and add it onto the Layer stack

Creating Our Other Resolution Density Multi-State ImageButton Icons

To create the other three size (80, 64 and 48 pixels) versions of attackinvadepress and attackinvadefocus, follow the work process outlined in the previous chapter in Figure 7-17 using the **Image ➤ Scale Image...** menu sequence, and image scaling dialog, to uniformly scale the images from 96 to 80 (and later 96 to 64 and 96 to 48) pixels. Be sure during each work process to click the **eye icon** on the SilverHoop96 layer to turn off its visibility, then use **File ➤ Export** to save the file in **drawable-hdpi** as **attackinvadepress.png**.

Once that is done, you can click the eye icon again to turn the SilverHoop96 layer visibility back on, and execute the **File ➤ Export** operation again, to create an **attackinvadefocus.png** in your **drawable-hdpi** folder. Once you have generated these two files, use the **Edit ➤ Undo** menu sequence to go back to your 96-pixel version, and do the entire work process outlined here to create 64-pixel **MDPI** and 48-pixel **LDPI** invade icon assets. It is important to note that the focus button state is not used on Android devices that have touchscreen only (such as our Nexus S emulator). This focused state is only used on Android devices that utilize a trackball, keypad, or keyboard navigation. Once a user touches the touchscreen (if the device has one), Android goes into **touch mode**, and in this mode of operation the focus button state is not used, but it is still installed and works on other Android device types (such as iTVs) that don't use touchscreen.

Implementing Multi-State Buttons in XML: Android's Selector Tag

Once you finish the work process outlined in the previous section for the other three image button icons (bomb, virus and laser), and create all 32 (4 x 4 x 2) images that we will need to implement the **pressed** and **focused** states of our multi-state ImageButton UI elements in our Attack Planet Activity screen, we can start coding the XML files (all four of them) that implement the **<selector>** tags. Selector tags allow Android to select from the three different button image state **<item>** tags from the image assets we now have in place in our drawable resource folders. Remember that our normal or default state images are already done, so this Activity user interface screen requires a total of 48 multi-state image assets, plus 4 resolution-specific images for our attackexit icon, so 52 images total, not including our stars background image,of course.

Creating a New Android XML File of Resource Type: Drawable

The first thing that we want to do is to create a **New Android XML File**. Right-click your Hello_World project's drawable-xhdpi folder, and then select the **New ➤ Android XML File** creation wizard dialog. This dialog is shown in Figure 8-10, and automates XML file creation for you.

Figure 8-10. Creating a new Android XML file with a <selector> root element

Set the **Resource Type** to **Drawable** and the **Project** to **Hello_World** and name the **File: attack_invade**. Since Android does not use file extensions in XML and Java code, be sure not to name the file attackinvade as that is our PNG8 filename. Because underscores are allowed in Android file names, use an underscore between the words attack and invade, to simulate a space character between those words.

Next, find the **Root Element** named **selector**, and select that for our parent tag (root element) container, and finally click the **Finish** button to create the **attack_invade.xml** file. It's important to note in Figure 8-11 that Android put the attack_invade.xml file in a **/res/drawable/** folder, which it created as part of the New Android XML File operation. This is because the file references multiple resolution assets, so it goes once in the **/res/drawable** folder instead of in each drawable-dpi folder.

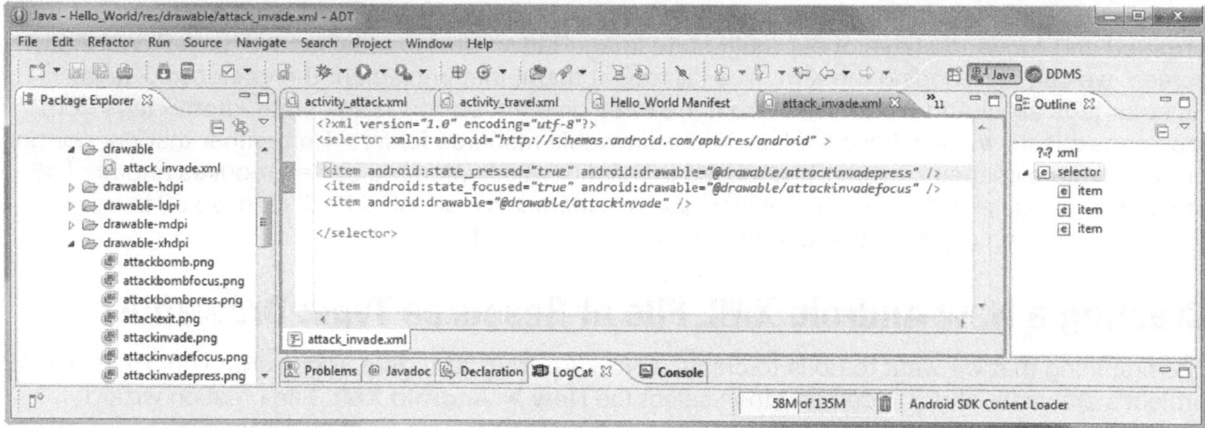

***Figure 8-11.** XML mark-up for multi-state ImageButton: adding <item> tags inside a <selector> tag in attack_invade.xml*

Adding Android <item> Tags to our attack_invade.xml Multi-State XML Definition

Now that we have our attack_invade.xml file open in our editing pane, let's add the three <item> tags that specify our three image states. The item tags contain one parameter for state definition and another for drawable asset definition. The pressed and focused multi-state item tags are coded like this:

```
<item android:state_pressed="true" android:drawable="@drawable/attackinvadepress" />
<item android:state_focused="true" android:drawable="@drawable/attackinvadefocus" />
```

The default or **normal** button state item tag does not have a multi-state parameter, it just has the image's drawable asset reference parameter, and this <item> tag is added in last, as can be seen in Figure 8-11.

The order of these <item> tags in the selector container is important in this case, because that is the order in which these items are evaluated, much like the select (case) statement we used in our Java code.

Referencing Our New Multi-State ImageButton XML Definitions from Our Activity Screen Layout XML

The last thing that we need to do is open the tab for our **activity_attack.xml** user interface screen layout definition, and change the reference for the attackinvade button to point to **attack_invade** (XML) instead of attackinvade (PNG). This is so the chain of logic that Android goes through to implement the ImageButton now includes the multi-state XML selector logic in how it processes the use of that user interface element.

To implement the other three bomb, virus, and laser attack mode multi-state buttons, we must go through the work process shown in Figures 8-10 and 8-11 three more times, adding in XML <selector> definitions for attack_bomb.xml, attack_virus.xml, and attack_laser.xml multi-state image asset definition XML files.

Each of the selector XML files must point to the proper PNG8 (normal) and PNG32 (presses and focused) digital image asset filenames in the drawable sub-folders, and then we can reference these new XML file definitions in our activity_attack XML file, instead of referencing the default image state PNG8 filename.

Once all this work process is completed for each of our four attack mode buttons, our Attack a Planet user interface screen will be fully converted to feature multi-state ImageButton user interface elements!

Remember that when you test the user interface screen next using the Nexus S emulator that the focused image state does not show, as that Android device that we are emulating is a consumer electronics product that features a touchscreen only.

Figure 8-12 shows an Eclipse IDE with the XML files in the **/res/drawable** folder in the Package Explorer pane (highlighted in blue) for the attack_bomb, attack_invade, attack_laser, and attack_virus files that we just created (also notice the tabs for these files still open at the top of the Eclipse primary editing pane).

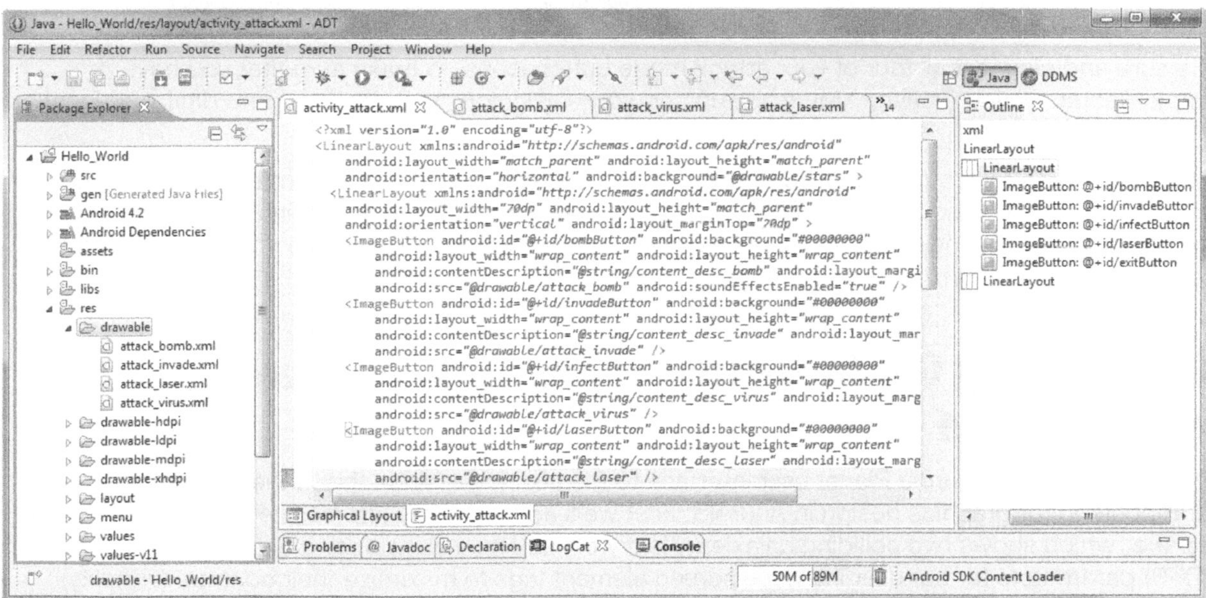

***Figure 8-12.** New XML mark-up in activity_attack.xml referencing the new multi-state image button selector XML files*

The XML mark-up for our **activity_attack** user interface screen definition in Figure 8-12 also shows that we have changed all the **android:src** parameters for each of our **ImageButton** tags to point to the XML filenames, which use an underscore in the middle of each filename, instead of pointing to the PNG8 filenames, which do not use an underscore character in the middle.

Finally, we need to test the application, and our new multi-state ImageButton user interface elements, via the **Run As Android Application** work process. Launch a Nexus S emulator and click the Soldier Face icon for Invade a Planet, and you will see that the face moves into the center of the hoop when you click and hold down (via a mouse-down operation) the left mouse button, as shown in Figure 8-13.

***Figure 8-13.** Running our app in the Nexus S emulator to test our attackinvade ImageButton multi-state image button*

Be sure and also test all four of your attack mode button icons, to make sure that you have implemented all your activity XML mark-up and your <selector> XML mark-up and digital imagery references correctly.

Now it's time to take our **Configure Planet** user interface screen to a more professional level, by adding a space-related background image, and then changing how our user interface elements composite over that new colliding galaxies image, so that we enhance the contrast ratio (readability) for this new UI Design.

Compositing Our UI Elements: Alpha, Color, Gravity, and TextStyle

Let's take our Configure a Planet user interface to the next level, since this is the chapter on compositing for graphics design in Android. First we'll add a visually impressive background called **space**, which shows two colliding galaxies. Next we'll add new compositing and desktop publishing (DTP) parameters for our user interface screen element tags to maximize their contrast (visibility) and improve the UI look and feel using the new background in conjunction with new fonts, spacing, gravity, and alpha effects.

First, let's copy the space1280x720.png, space1024x600.png, space 800x480.png, and space 480x320.png files into the XHDPI, HDPI, MDPI, and LDPI folders as we have done previously, and then rename them all once they are in place to **space.png**, which is the filename we will be referencing in our code later on.

Modifying Our activity_config XML Parameters to Composite Space Background Image with Our UI Elements

The first thing we want to do in our **activity_config.xml** file is to add an **android:background** parameter that points to our newly installed **space.png** files, using the **@drawable/space** reference parameter, as shown in Figure 8-14. If you click on the **Graphical Layout** tab at the bottom of the editing pane after you add in the new digital image background, you will see that our existing user interface elements have essentially disappeared, and so we'll have to make some fairly drastic parameter changes to our current XML mark-up to make our UI look really professional with this space background.

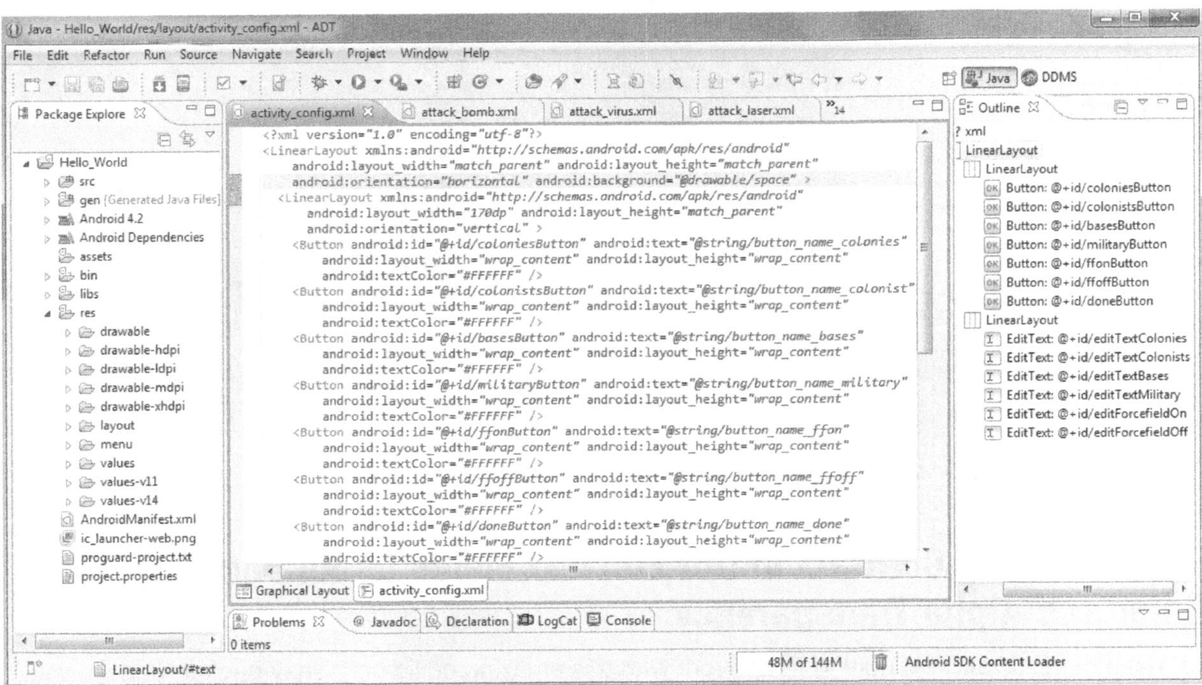

***Figure 8-14.** Editing our LinearLayout to add the space.png background and Button tags to add a white textColor value*

Let's start with the **Button** tags, and add in an **android:textColor** parameter, set to the hexadecimal value for **white** of **#FFFFFF**, as is shown in Figure 8-14. Once again, let's use the Graphical Layout tab as a quick and easy screen preview, and see if our buttons have become easier to read. As you can see in Figure 8-15 this solves the problem for the Button UI elements, and they look great. However, the **EditText** text fields are nearly impossible to discern, and these will require a number of new tag parameters to make them both readable and ultimately professional in appearance.

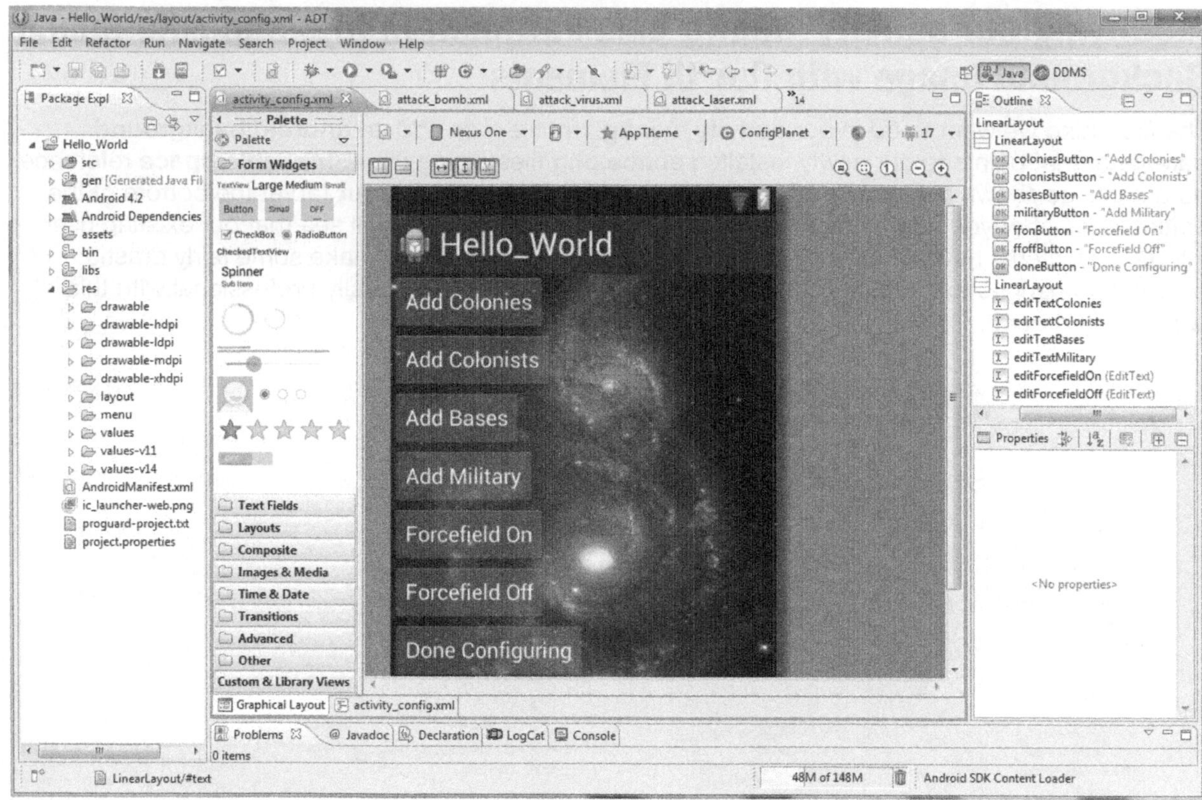

***Figure 8-15.** Previewing our new Button and Background parameters in the Graphical Layout Editor*

Improving the Contrast of Our EditText Fields Using Background Color and Alpha Transparency

To make our EditText text editing fields work with this amazing colliding galaxy background we will have to use a combination of bright background colors (white), some opacity (alpha channel) to allow the stars to shine through, and some better fonts, alignment and edit text field spacing to match (balance out) the button spacing on the opposite side of the screen layout.

The first EditText tag parameter we will want to add, so that we can see what we are doing on this dark background, is the **android:background** parameter, which we will set to the hexadecimal color value for white (#FFFFFF). To make this white background somewhat **translucent**, let's also add an **android:alpha** parameter, which controls **opacity** (alpha channel value) for the UI element using a decimal range of Zero (transparent) to One (opaque). We use a 50% transparent setting of **0.5** to start off with. Now that we can see our text fields, we can next adjust our **android:layout_marginTop** parameter to space them out.

For the first EditText tag this equates to **13dp** and the rest require an additional **10 dp**, or a final setting of **23dp**, to space them perfectly opposite each button, as you can see in the XML mark-up in Figure 8-16.

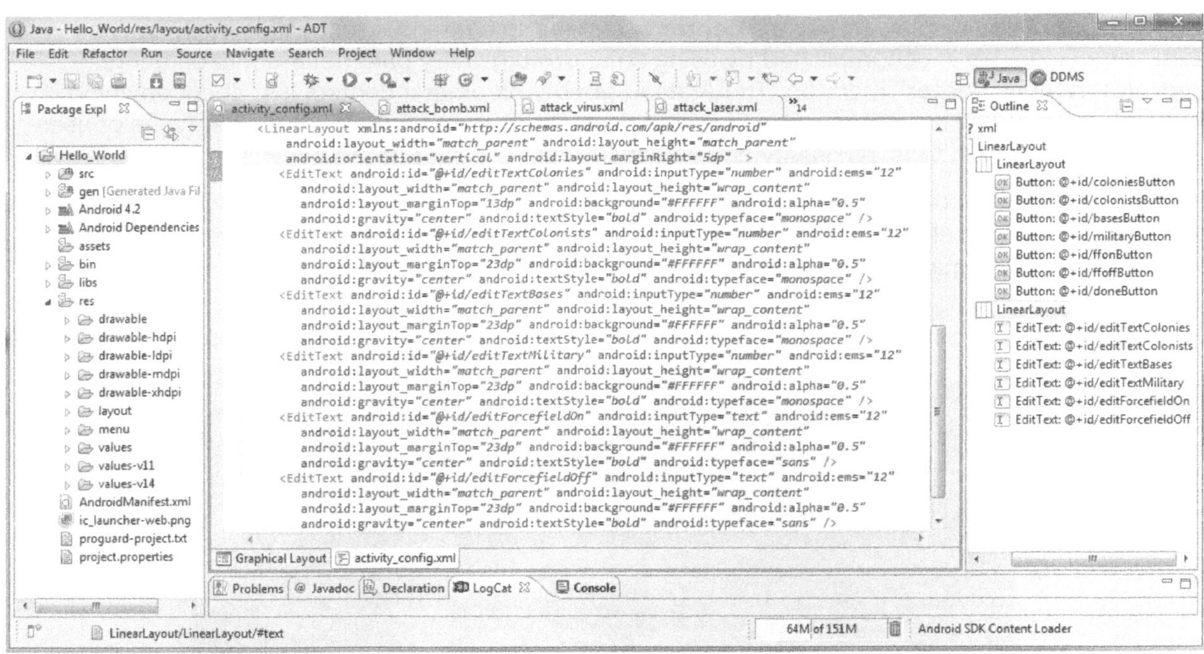

***Figure 8-16.** Editing our LinearLayout Container Tag and EditText Tags and their parameters*

So now that our text fields are perfectly spaced out from top to bottom opposite each of their respective buttons, we need to space them out from left to right. They are touching the right-hand side of the UI screen and this looks unprofessional. Let's adjust this to add some **symmetry** to the UI screen design.

Because we want to move all the EditText fields an even distance of **5dp**, similar to the spacing on our buttons on the opposite side of the screen, let's do that with a **single tag** in the **LinearLayout** container that holds them, instead of adding a half-dozen tags (one in each EditText element tag).

Once you add the **android:layout_marginRight="5dp"** as shown in Figure 8-16, hit your **Graphical Layout** tab, and see how it looks. To get an even more precise look as to how it will all line up, use the **Run As Android Application** work process and look at the current UI design in the Nexus S emulator; you will see that it is starting to look truly amazing.

Formatting the Text Characteristics Inside Our EditText UI Elements

Now that we have the EditText UI container spaced out and composited perfectly with the screen and its background image, let's set some parameters to optimize the text that is contained within that text field. For the numeric data entry text fields let's specify a **monospace** font, which makes numeric entries especially readable; this is accomplished via the **android:typeface="monospace"** parameter.

To make the text a bit more readable on the screen let's also add an **android:textStyle** parameter, setting the font to use **bold** text to make the characters thicker and easier to read on smaller displays. Finally, to make the text look evenly spaced within the text field and be symmetrical on the right side of the display, let's use a **center** parameter to center the text within each EditText data entry field. This is accomplished by using an **android:gravity** parameter set to center or **android:gravity="center"** mark-up. The Android **gravity** parameter centers just about anything in Android, not just text, so become familiar with this parameter, and look for it in other types of user interface widgets and tags, as gravity can be very useful.

Now it's time to use our **Run As Android Application** work process and to preview the outcome of all this user interface element tag parameter modification and optimization in the Nexus S emulator. As you can see in Figure 8-17, the Configure Activity user interface screen is really starting to look professional.

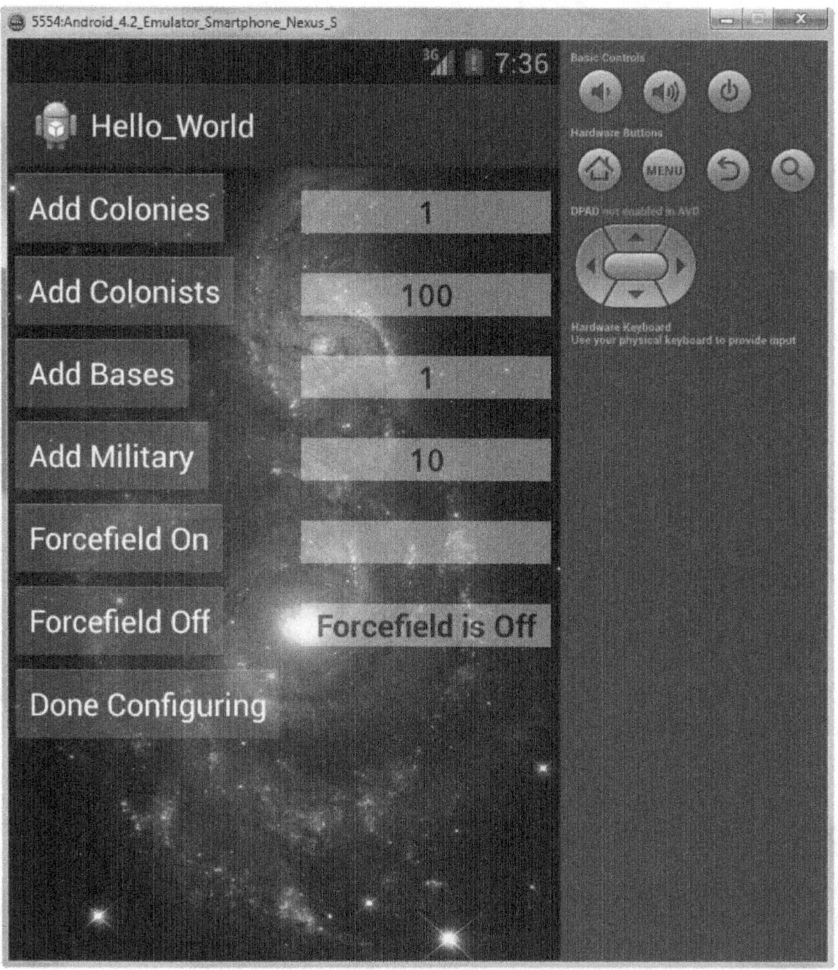

Figure 8-17. Previewing our finished Configure Activity screen in the Nexus S emulator

Next let's take our Hello World application **Home Screen** to the next level by adding custom background imagery and an **ImageView** of the planet we're on. We will customize these later on in the Animation chapters. Finally, we'll color our text to match dazzling plasma light colors in a **galaxy** background image.

Upgrading Our App Home Screen: Adding an ImageView Tag and textColor Parameters

The first thing that we need to do to set-up for our all new Home Screen is to copy the galaxy480x320.png, galaxy800x480.png, galaxy1024x600.png and galaxy1280x720.png images into their respective drawable sub-folders, as we have done several times before. Once these are inside the LDPI, MDPI, HDPI, and XHDPI folders, respectively, rename them to simply be **galaxy.png**, and we will be ready to reference them in our XML mark-up in the **activity_main.xml** file, which defines our Hello World application Home Screen user interface design. Once we do this, we can then fine-tune our UI element colors, to match the galaxy image.

Because we want this new background image to span the entire layout container, we will add the parameter **android:background** to the **RelativeLayout** container tag, and set it equal to the **@drawable/galaxy** reference path to our **galaxy.png** files, as shown at the top of Figure 8-18.

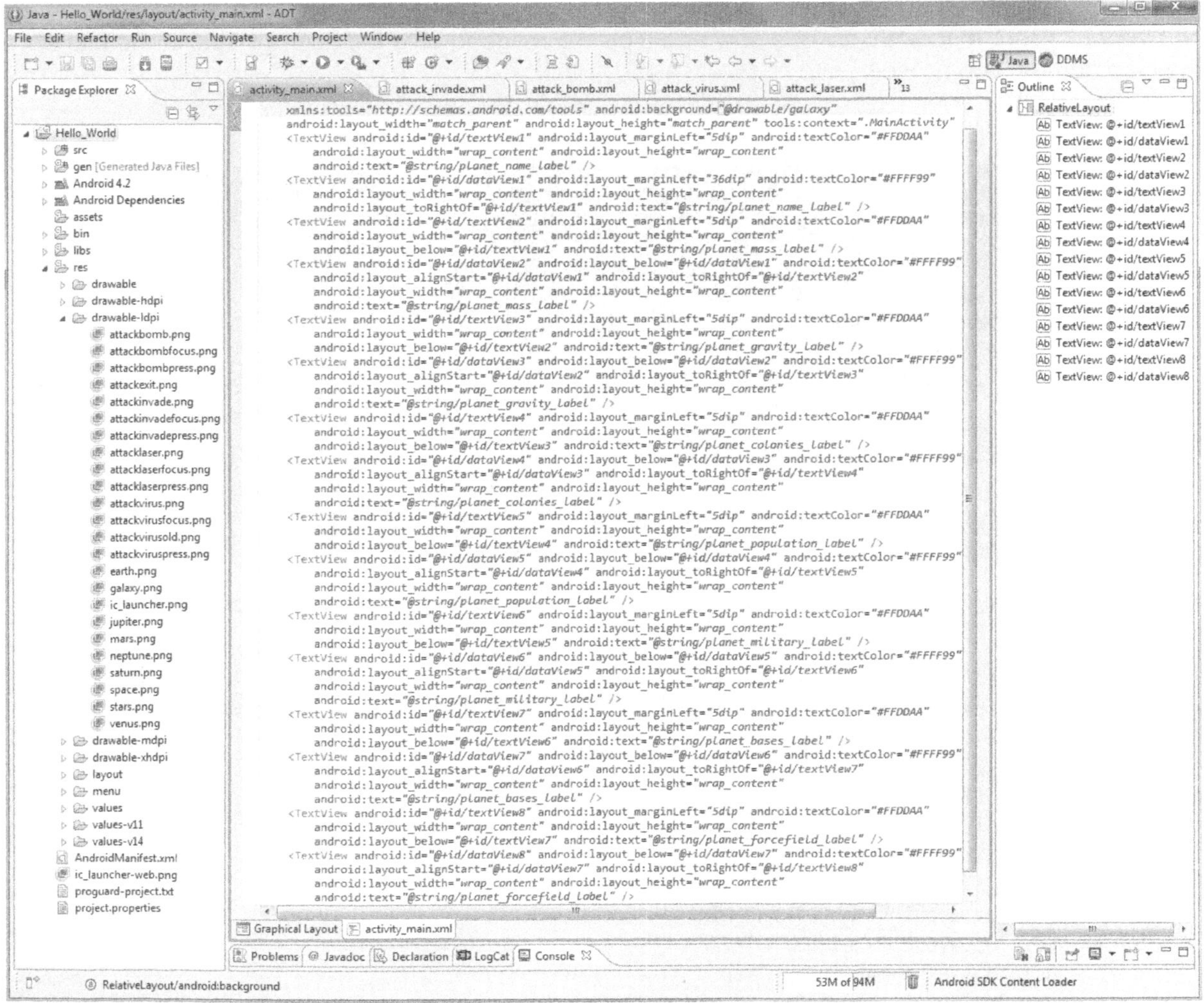

Figure 8-18. Adding galaxy.png background image; customizing textColor parameters to match plasma colors in image

Use the Graphical Layout tab to preview the image, and notice that the text now needs our attention, due to **low contrast** (readability). Let's match our new text color to the **orange** and **yellow** hues prominent in the plasma on the right and bottom part of the background image.

Let's make the label text on the left orange to balance out the orange at the top right of the background image, and the data text yellow to match the yellow plasma flares in the center of our background image. To create a matching orange color, leave the **red channels** on full intensity by using two **F** values and use less intensity in the **green channels** (remember equal red and green values result in yellow), by setting those two values to **D**, and even less intensity in the **blue channels**, by setting those two values to **A**, so the **#RRGGBB** values for a bright plasma orange are **#FFDDAA**. Since we know that equal Red and Green values yield a yellow color, we would want to use **#FFFF99** to obtain a **fully saturated** yellow color, similar to the color that is in the plasma flare in the middle of the Home Screen background image.

Change all the **android:textColor** hexadecimal values in your **activity_main.xml** mark-up, as shown in Figure 8-18, and then use the **Run As Android Application** work process to see how our new Home Screen looks at this point. As you can see in Figure 8-19, the new screen is visually arresting and very pleasant to look at, so let's now add a planet image to give the user a visual of the planet they are currently on as well.

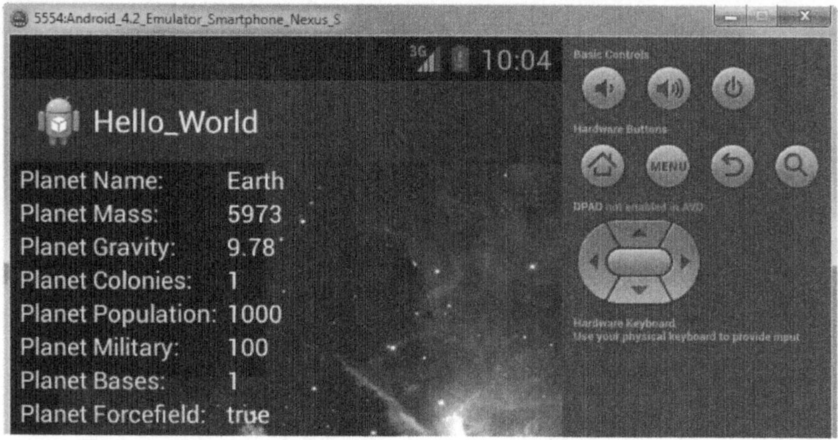

***Figure 8-19.** Previewing our new galaxy.png background image and our new text coloration in the Nexus S emulator*

To add a planet image to our UI screen, use the **ImageView** tag and RelativeLayout positioning parameters as shown in Figure 8-20. The XML mark-up for the tag and its parameters should look like the following:

```
<ImageView android:id="@+id/imageEarth"
          android:src="@drawable/earth"
          android:background="#00000000"
          android:layout_width="wrap_width"
          android:layout_height="wrap_width"
          android:layout_marginLeft="12dp"
          android:layout_marginTop="8dp"
          android:layout_below="@+id/textView8"
          android:contentDescription="@string/content_desc_earth" />
```

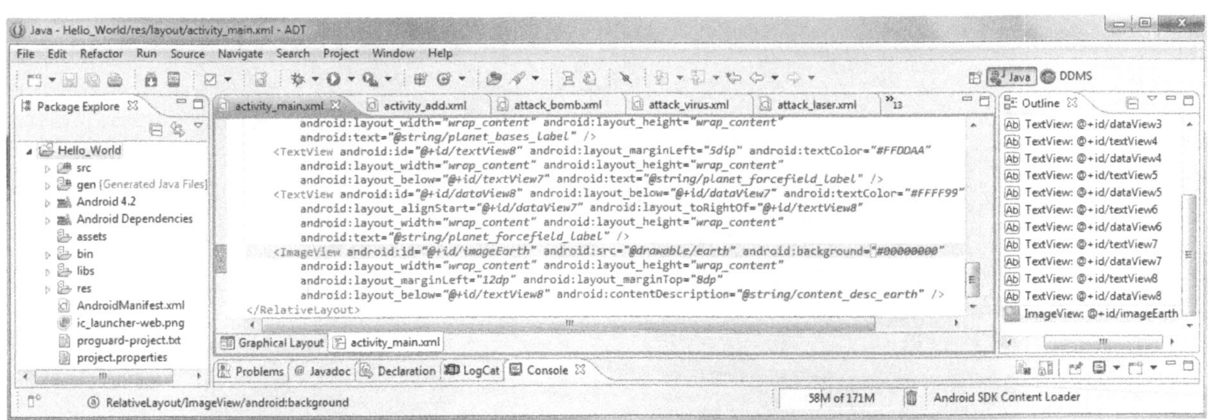

Figure 8-20. Adding an ImageView tag to hold our Planet and configuring its background alpha and margin parameters

We will reference our **earth.png** source imagery, and set an alpha channel of **#00000000** (#AARRGGBB), which is 100% transparent. We do this so that the compositing effect on our background **galaxy** image is completely seamless. Next we will use an **android:layout_below** parameter that references the TextView above it, and finally **marginLeft** and **marginTop** parameter settings of **12dp** and **8dp,** respectively, to position our planet image perfectly.

Now let's do a final preview our work in the Nexus S emulator, via the **Run As Android Application** work process, and note that we now have a visual image of our current world, as well as the characteristics and settings for that world on the primary application Home Screen as shown in Figure 8-21.

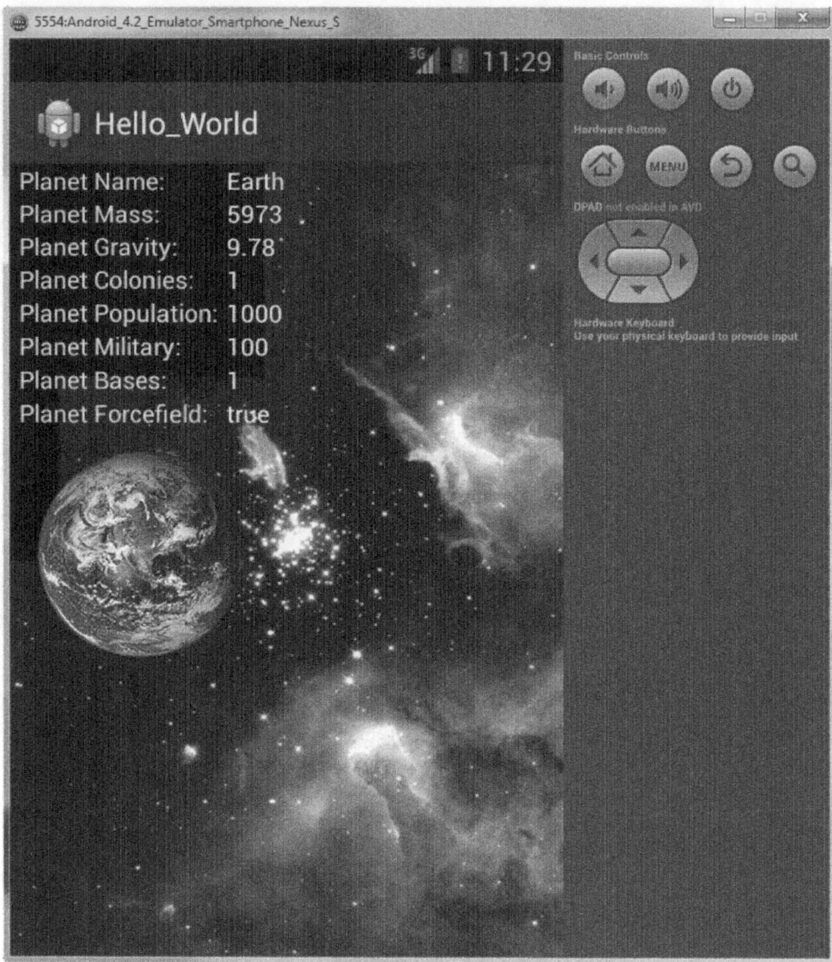

Figure 8-21. *Previewing our Hello_World app Home Screen in the Nexus S emulator*

These user interface design improvements give our user visual feedback on the current world that they are dealing with, and also make the application appearance 100% more professional.

We will be enhancing this UI screen (as well as our other user interface screens) with animation and cool special image effects in future chapters, using a couple of other techniques and tag parameters. So be aware that we will be utilizing similar compositing concepts and techniques in future chapters on Animation and Video, where compositing will logically be needed, so you'll soon have a chance to build on your recent compositing knowledge, and gain compositing experience.

Because this is the last chapter specifically addressing graphics design and compositing, I wanted to get all the primary imagery in place for this app as soon as possible, and get it seamlessly compositing with all the major user interface elements that we will be using within our "out of this world" Hello World app.

Next we will finally upgrade our Hello World application launch icon, because as we all know the devil is in the details, which not only shows on the Android device icon launch screen, but also at the top of the app.

Custom Activity Screen Title and App Icon: Details Make a Difference

The first thing we need to do is to copy the saturn36.png, saturn48.png, saturn72.png, and saturn96.png files into the LDPI, MDPI, HDPI, and XHDPI drawable folders, respectively, using the Windows Explorer file management utility, as shown in Figure 8-22. Rename ic_launcher to ic_launcher_old, and rename the saturn36.png file to **helloworldicon.png**. Later I show you how to implement a custom application icon filename, using XML mark-up in your application's **AndroidManifest.xml** file.

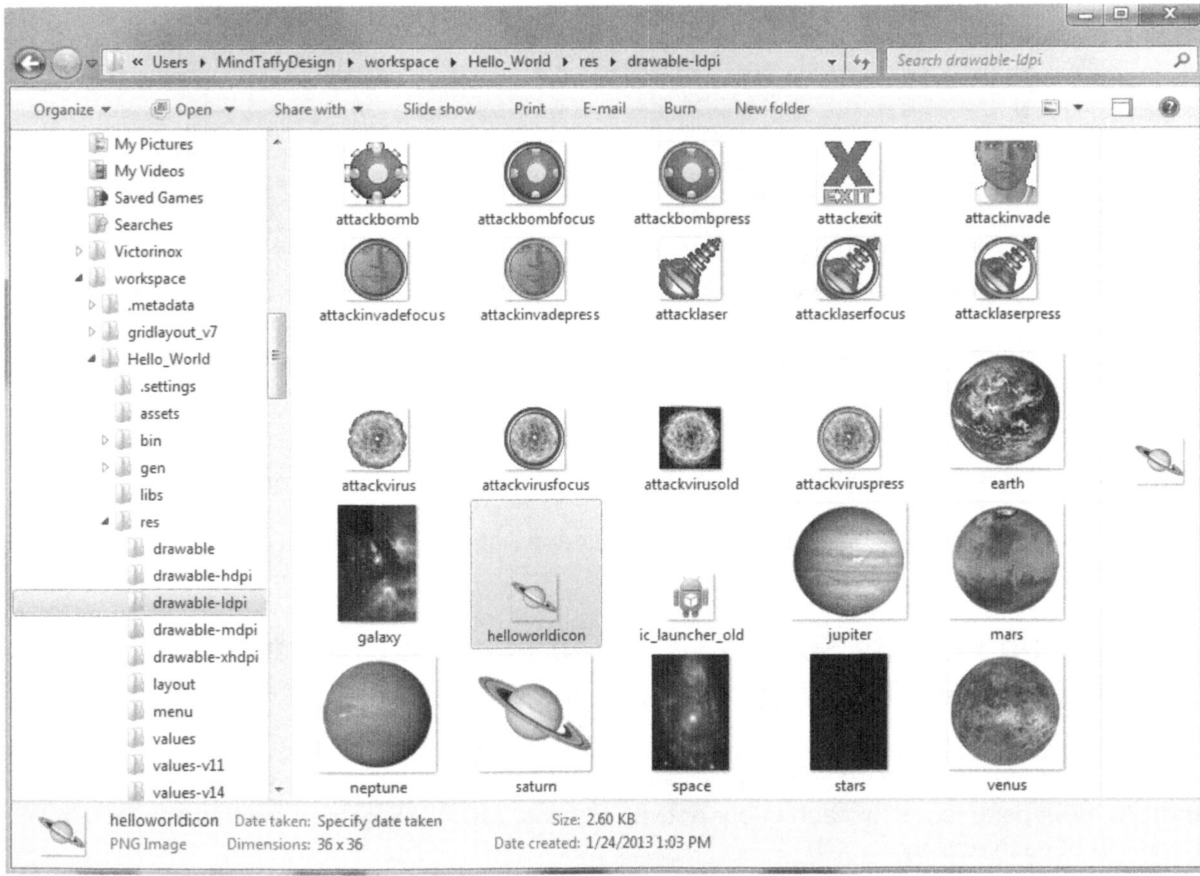

Figure 8-22. Renaming ic_launcher_old and adding a new helloworldicon.png application icon

Once your new custom application icon image files are in place in their respective drawable-dpi folders, the next thing that we need to do is to create some custom Activity user interface screen titles, known in Android as **labels**, in our **strings.xml** file in our resource values **/res/values/** folder.

Creating Our Activity Screen Title Constants in the strings.xml File

Click the number in the top right of the Eclipse central editing pane (in Figure 8-23 it is 14) to drop-down the open files menu. Next, select the **strings.xml** file for editing, and change the **app_name** text value to **Hello World - Home Screen**. Copy and paste that **<string>** tag underneath itself four more times, so we can add titles (labels) for each of our four application Activity user interface screens.

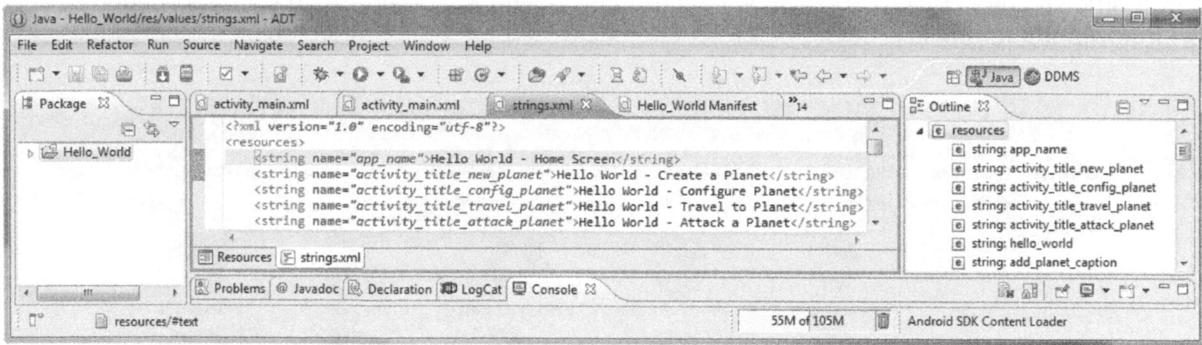

Figure 8-23. Adding <string> tag constants in strings.xml for use in our Activity user interface screens as custom titles

Name each <string> tag constant with the name="activity_title_type_planet" parameter and with the text value **Hello World - Screen Title**, for instance, a <string> tag for the NewPlanet Activity would look like:

```
<string name="activity_title_new_planet">Hello World - Create a Planet</string>
```

The five resulting **<string>** constant tags to label our app Activity screen titles can be seen in Figure 8-23.

Configuring Activity Screen Labels in Our Hello_World AndroidManifest XML File

Once we have our string constants defined and in place in the strings.xml file, we can then reference them from our **AndroidManifest.xml** file, which is where we are going to set up the **android:label** parameters for each of our Activity screens, which will install a custom screen title at the top of each Activity.

Click the number in the top right of the Eclipse central editing pane (in Figure 8-23 it is 14) to drop-down the open files menu. Next, select the **AndroidManifest.xml** file for editing and change the current **android:icon** parameter in the **<application>** tag to reference an **@drawable/helloworldicon** reference, which is the reference to our new Saturn icon image PNG file.

Next, in each of our **<activity>** tags add a new **android:label** parameter that references the new **<string>** tag constants that we just created by name via @string/activity_title, as shown in Figure 8-24.

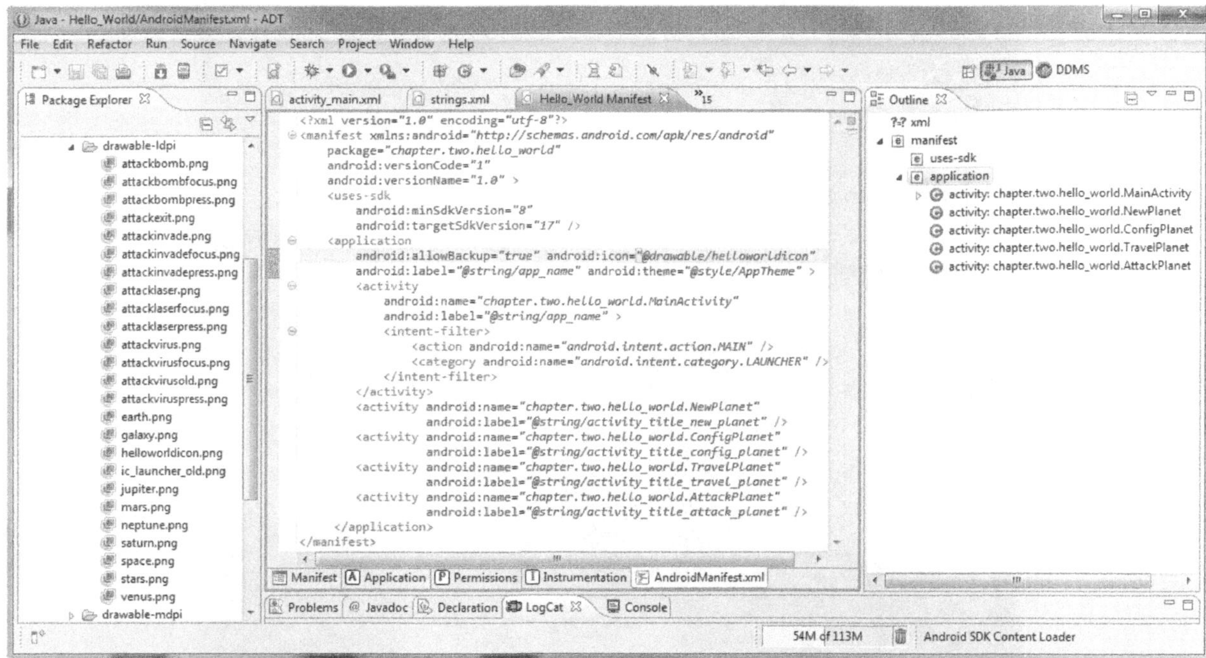

***Figure 8-24.** Adding a new application android:icon filename and android:label screen titles to our AndroidManifest.xml*

For the NewPlanet.java Activity user interface screen, the parameter to place a custom title at the top of the application is **android:label="@string/activity_title_new_planet"** which is fairly straight forward, once you know where Android wants you to put everything. So using the NewPlanet Activity <activity> tag as an example, the entire <activity> tag with the name and label parameters would look like this:

```
<activity android:name="chapter.two.hello_world.NewPlanet"
          android:label="string/activity_title_new_planet" />
```

Now let's use the Eclipse **Run As Android Application** command, and launch the Nexus S emulator and see how the new icon and screen title looks at the top of our application. As you can see in Figure 8-25 the results are professional and an improvement over the previous screen title (Hello_World) and app icon (Android Bot) as they are now more specific to what our app is and what it is doing.

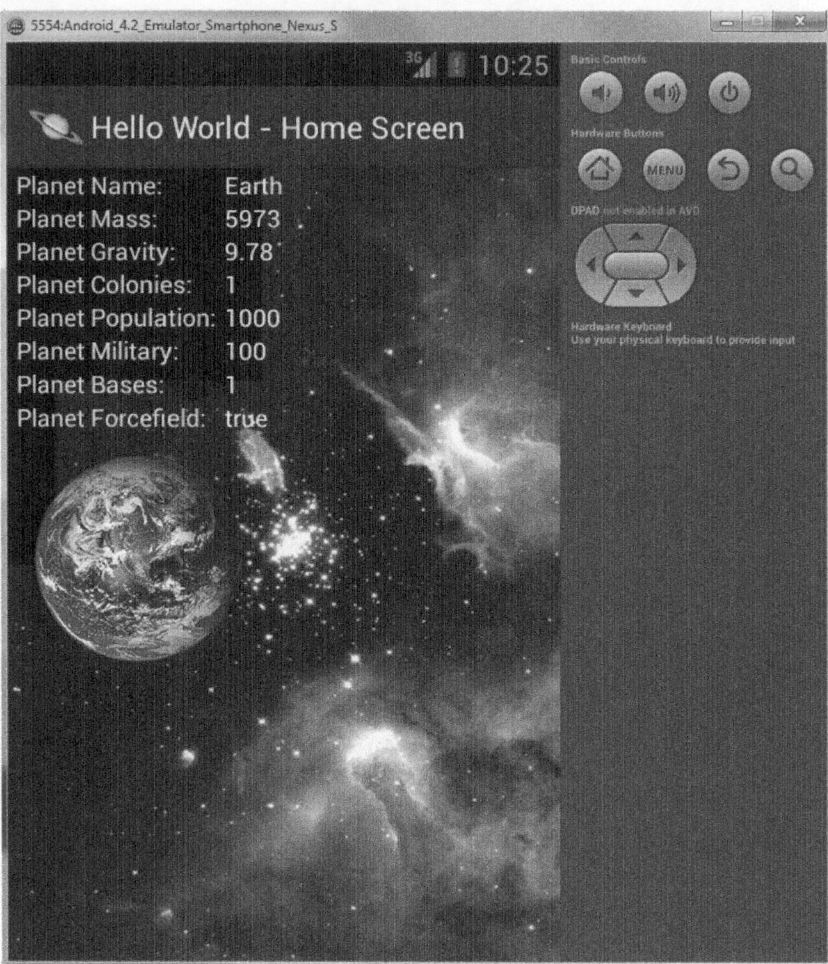

***Figure 8-25.** New Hello World Home Screen with new screen title and application icon*

Click the Menu button in the upper-right of the Nexus S emulator and let's see what our Activity UI screens look like with their new icons and screen titles. As you can see in Figure 8-26, our screens (the three that we have finished, the fourth TravelPlanet Activity screen we are going to implement in future Chapters 11 and 12 covering Digital Video) look great, and look far more custom and professional due to this attention to UI detail.

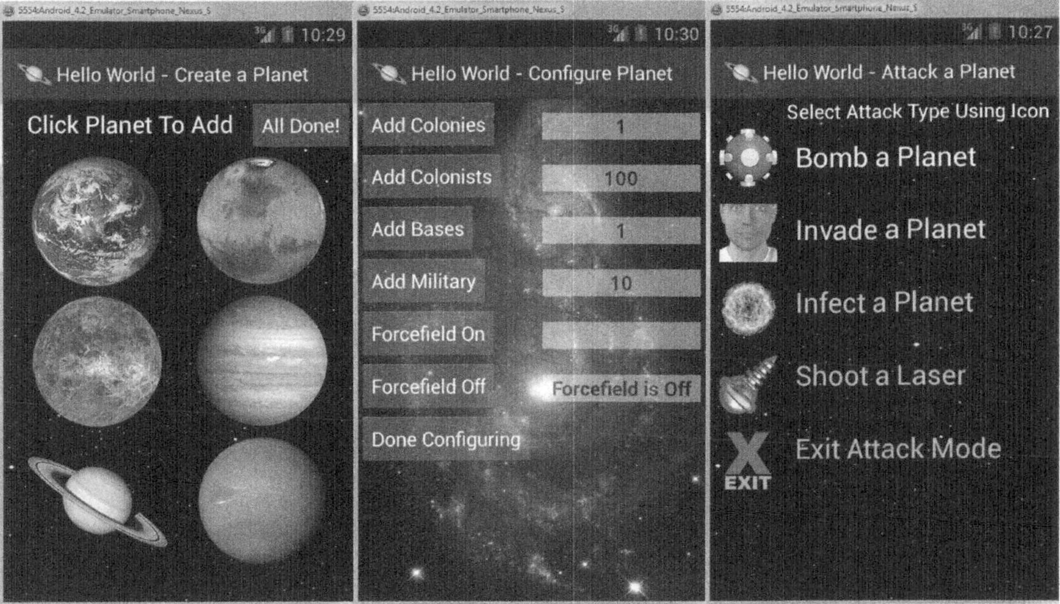

***Figure 8-26.** Previewing our Hello World application Activity screens with their new screen title labels and icons in place*

Note that by using this **android:label** parameter to create our Activity screen title, we don't have to use a TextView UI element at the top of our screen container, so we only need a TextView on two of the screens to instruct the user what to do when they get to the screen. On the Configure Planet UI screen, our button labels call the user to action, and thus we require no TextView UI elements on that screen at all.

Also notice that our Activity user interface screen titles (labels) closely match our Options Menu Labels, thus providing the user with excellent **continuity** throughout the application user interface infrastructure.

Now that we have the basic graphics elements composited together with our application's user interface elements, we can proceed to implement more advanced new media elements such as Animation, Digital Audio, and Digital Video over the next several chapters.

Summary

In this chapter, we took a closer look at some of the more advanced user interface elements and image compositing concepts to take our Hello World application user interface design to the next level visually. We learned about **multi-state** user interface elements. These elements change an image to represent the current state of a user interface element, namely its default or **normal** state versus its touched or **pressed** state, as well as its in-use or **focused** state.

We learned how to create multi-channel images using GIMP 2.8.4, and learned about advanced modal imaging software operations, as well as digital imaging color modes, editing modes, and tool modes.

We used these **modal** digital imaging tools and software settings to create multi-state image buttons for our Attack a Planet icons, and created over 50 digital image assets to be used for all the various image resolution density levels in our Android application.

We learned how to use the XML **<selector>** tag and its children **<item>** tags to define our multi-state ImageButton user interface elements using XML mark-up, so that we do not have to write any Java code whatsoever to implement multi-state user interface elements in our Android application.

We learned that all XML files that define imaging-related structures, such as our <selector> multi-image constructs, go into the **root /drawable** folder, and then reference commonly named digital image elements within the drawable-dpi subfolders located underneath that drawable folder.

We learned that the **focus** button state is not used on Android devices which have touchscreens only (such as the Nexus S emulator). The **focused state** is used on Android devices that feature a trackball, nav-keys, mini-keypads, or external keyboard navigation hardware.

We learned that once a user touches a touchscreen (if an Android device has one), that the Android OS puts itself into **touch mode**. In this touch mode of operation, the focus button state is not used, but it is still installed, and will work on other Android device types (such as iTVs) that don't use touchscreens. What this means for developers is that we still need to implement and accommodate focus button states in our Android application development.

We added new background imagery to our Activity screen user interfaces, to replace the black and white background colors. Next we added new tags and new parameters to upgrade those screens with color matching text, different fonts, text alignment, new imagery, improved margin spacing, and alpha channel-based translucency, to achieve a far more professional visual result.

We learned about the concept of **gravity** in Android, via the **android:gravity** parameter, which allows us to push or pull our user interface element into a certain orientation using gravity. User interface gravity is a concept that is certainly appropriate for us to learn about in an application regarding planets and space.

We learned about the concept of **contrast** and the need to keep a high **contrast ratio** between color **brightness** and **saturation** and the corresponding background image darkness, and learned more about 32-bit **#AARRGGBB** color theory by developing text colors for our Home Screen that matched colors in the background galaxy image. We did this by adjusting the relative **hexadecimal** color channel **intensity** via the two RR (Red), GG (Green) and BB (Blue) channel slots, which give us control over 256 levels of color intensity variation for each channel, for total color control equating to 16,777,216 color variations.

Finally, we learned how to implement our own **custom application icon,** as well as our own custom icon naming schemes by using the **android:icon** parameter inside of the **<application>** tag at the beginning of our **AndroidManifest.xml** file's mark-up. We also learned how to implement **custom Activity screen titles** by using new **android:label** parameters in the AndroidManifest.xml file, inside of our **<activity>** tags, located near the bottom of our Hello_World Manifest XML mark-up application definition logic.

In the next chapter, we will start adding bitmap or **frame-based animation** and **imaging special effects** to the user interface screens for our Hello World Android application, and yet again, we'll be using **XML** mark-up (for the most part) to define, and even implement, these animation and special effect elements.

What is a space application without a ton of cool special effects anyway? One that doesn't sell very well, would be my guess. Let's be sure that you don't fall into that trap by making sure you have a solid grip in the next chapter on implementing **raster animation** and **digital imaging special effects** by utilizing Android's built-in animation classes that have been provided to developers precisely for that purpose.

Chapter 9

Android Image Animation: Frame-Based Animation Using XML Constructs

In this chapter, we will take our already visually impressive Hello World application to the next level of New Media awareness, by adding animated visual elements to our application user interface screen using XML markup.

Android features two different types of animation, the first type, which we'll be focusing on in this chapter, is **frame-based** or **raster** animation.

Raster animation uses a **sequence of bitmaps** called **cels** (if you are in the 2D animation industry) or **frames** (if you are in the Film or digital video editing industry). The second type of animation is **procedural** or **vector** animation and we will cover that in Chapter 10, as it is completely different.

In this chapter we will cover both the theory of frame-based animation, as well as the XML logic constructs that are needed to implement the animation at all four of the different image pixel density resolutions, from LDPI to XHDPI. This will take our Hello World app to a new level of UI design.

Frame-Based Animation: Concepts and Data Optimization

Since raster or frame-based animation is comprised of bitmap images, many of the technical concepts we learned in the past two chapters on graphics design and digital imaging all hold true in this chapter as well, and each plays a part in your raster animation, so you get more practice with these digital imaging concepts in this chapter as well.

Raster animation can be created by using either indexed color or truecolor bitmap images. These images can have an alpha channel, and therefore frame-based animation can leverage transparency, which is very good news for our special effects. We can do the same compositing tricks with animation as we did with our static imagery in the previous two chapters.

Similar to our static imagery, we'll also need to provide density-matched imagery for every screen density, and as with our static imagery Android handles which pixel densities to use for which screens, as long as we support all of the different pixel density levels with our animation cels, or frames, as we have been doing religiously throughout this book.

The primary technical difference between your static imagery optimization and motion imagery (animation) optimization involves the animation's **frame rate**. Frame rates are usually described in **frames per second** or **FPS**, which is a number that defines how many images are displayed within one second, which equates to how fast image frames replace one another on the screen.

A higher (faster) frame rate gives a smoother visual appearance, but takes more image data to create, as the animation needs to have more frames, and each frame is a PNG32 image that needs to be stored in your application's drawable-dpi folders (or a PNG8 image, if it can be optimized as such).

Typical frame rates for new media assets that you're familiar with in your everyday life are digital video, which runs at **30 FPS**; motion picture film, which runs at **24 FPS**; or video games, which run at **60 FPS**. It is important to note that the **illusion of motion** can be achieved in as little as **12 FPS** and we'll be using this little known fact in our animations data footprint optimization work process later on in this chapter.

So, part of our **data footprint optimization** process for a raster animation involves not only the **color depth** of the image frames that we use for the animation, but also the **total number of image frames** that we will need to use to create the illusion of motion. Fewer PNG8 frames make a far more data-compact animation than lots of PNG32 frames make.

We will make compelling, photo-real animation in this chapter using just a few frames and indexed color images, so you can see how to make just a few kilobytes of image data go a long ways toward creating convincing special effects in your application, using very little data overhead.

The other fundamental animation concept that we will cover in this chapter is called **looping**. As you probably know, animations can be played once, or they can be **looped seamlessly** and played forever, or they can be looped and played a certain number of times by variables dictated by our XML mark-up.

There are two types of looping: **seamless looping**, where the frames play in a circle, like this **0,1,2,3,4,0,1,2,3,4** and **pong looping**, where images go back and forth, like a good game of pong, like this **0,1,2,3,4,3,2,1,0**.

We will look at both types of animation looping in this chapter, and we will see how both types are useful for different types of special effects.

Implementing Frame Animation in XML: The Animation-List Tag

The first thing we need to do before we can create our animation mark-up in XML that defines the animation frame numbers and their duration (frame rate) is to copy the drawable assets, in this case, **cels** or **frames** of the animation, into each respective drawable-dpi folder.

Find the PNG8 files named: **atackvirus96frame0** through **attackvirus96frame5**, and copy them to the **/res/drawable-xhdpi** folder, and finally rename them **attackvirus0.png** through **attackvirus5.png** for a total of six frames of animation. Note that we are using only **six** total frames here to achieve this animated virus cell effect, and that we are using optimized indexed color PNG8 files, so our total data weight to implement this animation in all four resolution densities is only **120KB** of total data, or **30KB** average per animation (which, in turn, is a data-compact **5KB** average per frame).

Creating a New Android XML File of Resource Type: Drawable for Frame Animation

Once our source image animation frame data is in place, we need to create the XML construct that references these frames and that is referenced as a single animation asset name (anim_virus). Right-click any of the project **/res/drawable** folders and select **New ➤ Android XML File** from the context-sensitive menu and open the dialog shown in Figure 9-1.

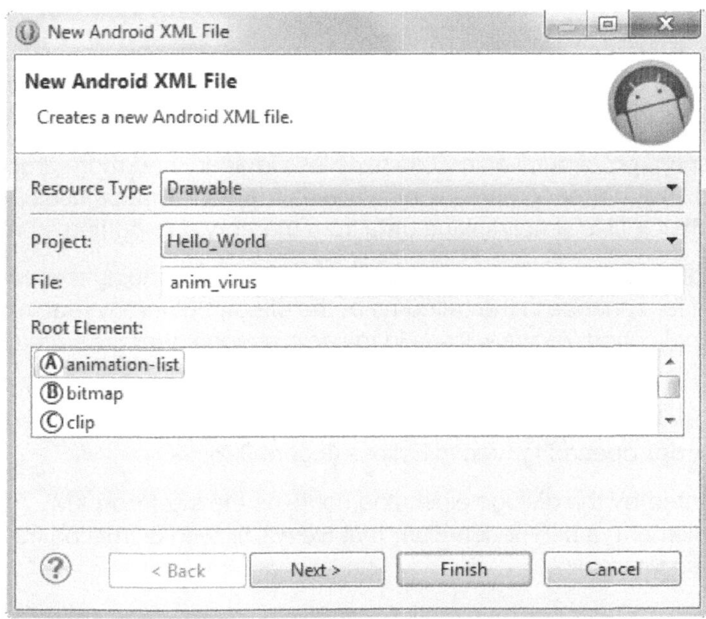

***Figure 9-1.** Creating a new Android XML file named anim_virus.xml with a root element of <animation-list>*

Select resource type of **Drawable** in the **Hello_World** project and name the file **anim_virus** and then select the root element type of **<animation-list>** from the selection box in the middle of the dialog. Note that in the drop-down menu for **Resource Type:** there are a couple of animation-related options–do not select those (until the next chapter) as they are used for procedural (vector) animation and not for frame-based (raster) animation, which utilizes only drawables (bitmap imagery).

Another thing that is important to note here, because we are touching on it now in Figures 9-1 and 9-2, is that Android keeps frame animation assets and definitions in **drawable** asset folders, whereas Android keeps procedural animation assets and definitions in **animation** asset folders.

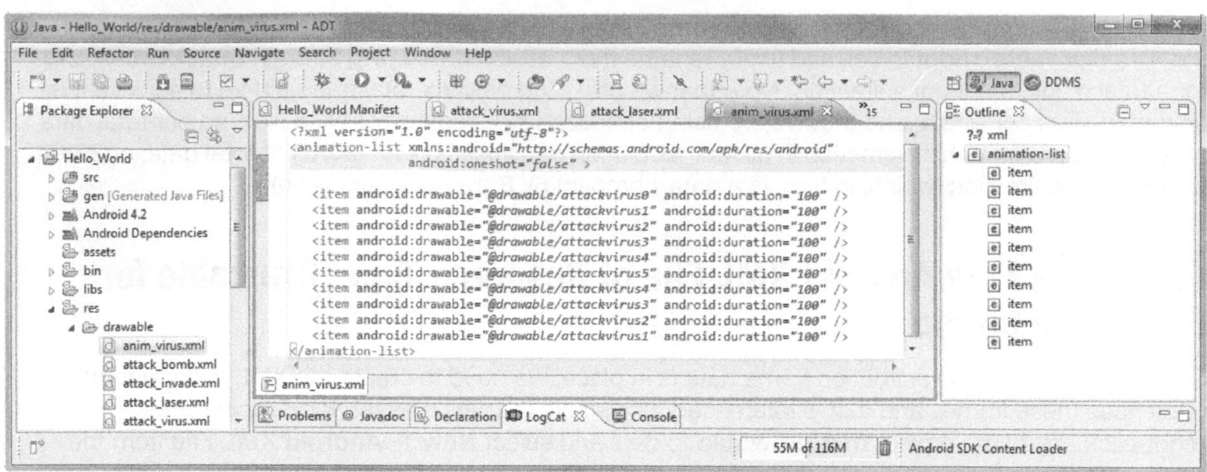

***Figure 9-2.** Adding <item> tags to the <animation-list> tag container to pong animate the virus cell imagery*

Similarly, there are also different classes and packages for each distinct type of animation in Android, so don't confuse the Android animation package, which contains classes used for procedural or vector animation, with the AnimationDrawable class that is utilized for frame-based or raster animation.

In case you are wondering, procedural animation uses less imagery and more processing power, and so yields a smaller app size (better compression), whereas frame animation uses more imagery and less processing power, as the CPU is simply taking data from memory and putting it on the screen.

Ultimately, frame animation gives you control over what every pixel is doing and where it is doing it, and leaves zero margin for variance in the outcome of the effect, but it may require a somewhat larger data footprint for the application. As we will see in the next chapter, there is a great balance that can be achieved by using the two techniques together as well.

After you clicked the Finish button in the New Android XML dialog (Figure 9-1), you should now have an anim_virus.xml **shell script** opened for you in Eclipse (Figure 9-2).

This was of course created by the dialog helper, and contains the **skeleton** XML mark-up for the **<animation-list>** tag element, a parent container that we will fill with animation frame **<item>** tags, as you may have guessed.

Before we start filling our container with animation frames via <item> tags, there is one important parameter we need to add to our parent tag called the **android:oneshot** parameter. This key parameter defines whether or not the animation **loops seamlessly** or simply **plays once** (one shot). Because we want our virus to pulsate forever, set this to **false**.

Adding Our Frame Animation <item> Tags Specifying the Animation Frames

Each **<item>** tag specifies a frame reference and duration, in this form:

```
<item android:drawable="@drawable/attackvirus0" android:duration="100" />
```

The **android:drawable** filename reference allows Android to get the proper resolution density version of each frame from the correct drawable folder.

The **android:duration** parameter specifies the length of time to display that frame on the screen, using a **milliseconds** value, in this case, **100**.

You may be wondering how this milliseconds duration value translates into the **frame rate**, or FPS, that we learned about earlier. The math is fairly simple to compute; since there are **one thousand milliseconds** within each second, we can divide the number 1000 by our milliseconds per frame value, and that yields our frames per second, or FPS, value. In this case, we are using **10 FPS** to obtain a sufficiently convincing vibrating virus cell.

From an optimization standpoint, this time it's CPU processing optimization we are talking about, the fewer frames (the lower frame rate, or the more milliseconds duration you can allocate per frame) used to create an effect the better. 20 FPS is logically twice as much work for a CPU as 10 FPS is.

This is because over time, as we add animation assets to our application, we are asking the CPU (central processing unit) to do more and more, and thus the more time we give the CPU to do each of these tasks individually, the more time the CPU will have in between doing these tasks to do other tasks which we will be asking it to do.

Referencing Our Frame Animation Definition XML File from Our attack_virus.xml File

Next, we need to reference this new animated virus cell drawable asset in our existing code for our **activity_attack.xml** user interface screen layout XML definition. We observe that our attackvirus ImageButton user interface element currently references the **attack_virus.xml** multi-state UI element definition, and so this is where our new **anim_virus.xml** file name must be referenced from to maintain the button multi-state functionality.

For this reason, we must find (and open) the tab for the **attack_virus.xml** mark-up, as shown in Figure 9-3, and change our drawable reference to now point to the new **anim_virus** XML animation definition drawable asset.

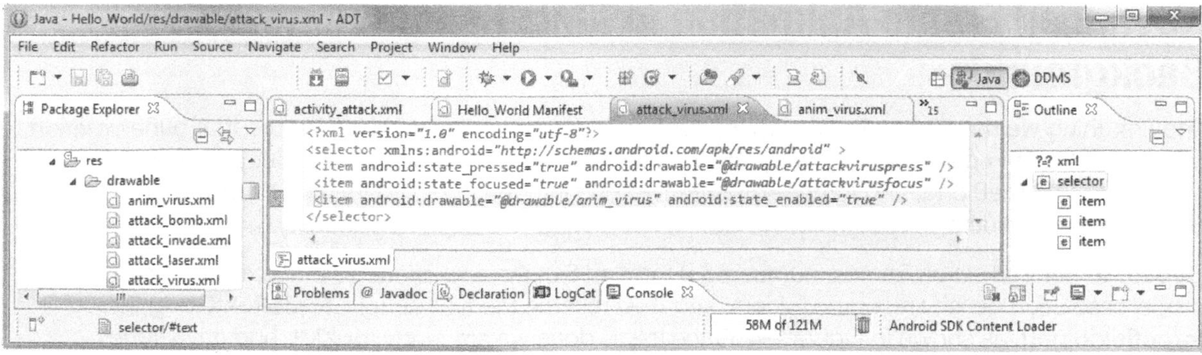

Figure 9-3. Changing the normal state of our multi-state attack_virus.xml to reference the anim_virus.xml file

Make a note of the anim_virus.xml file in the **/res/drawable** folder in Figure 9-3, as well as the new **android:drawable="@drawable/anim_virus"** parameter that is now in place. If you use the **Run As Android Application** work process now and go into the Attack a Planet UI screen, you will notice that you have to click the virus once to activate (enable) it to get the virus to start animating.

This is the default behavior for animation assets in Android, and for a very logical reason. Usually you want an animation to trigger when you click a UI element, and we will be setting up one of these animation types in this chapter as well.

Thus, in the default Android behavior for animation, when you click the UI element, the animation fires, and, if you have **oneshot** set to **true**, you have the effect that you're looking for. We will have our LaserCannon pulse once it's clicked in the next chapter, to show you this type of XML set-up as well. However, for now, we have to figure out how to make this attack virus animate all the time, even if the user does not click on it first.

Leveraging the Android state_enabled Parameter to Make Our Virus Animate on Activity Screen Launch

To make our virus animate on screen launch, we add an **android:state_enabled** parameter to our default (normal) button state item tag, specified in the **attack_virus.xml** file that is shown in Figure 9-3. This defines this button state as already being enabled when this user interface screen loads. When you **Run As Android Application** again our virus is immediately pulsating with life when the user interface screen appears.

Now that we have learned how to implement an animated source image for the ImageButton user interface element, let's get a bit more advanced and animate a background user interface element for our app's Home Planet (the home planet is shown on the app Home Screen). This shows our planet forcefield setting visually, when it is enabled and active.

We do this using **looping** animation frames, instead of **pong** animation frames (the back and forth through the frames type of frame access we used for the animated attack virus cell), so you have experience implementing both types of animation frame access order.

Advanced Frame Animation in XML: Using Animated Backgrounds

The first thing we need to do to implement our Forcefield animation is to make sure that our animation frame assets are in place, so let's copy the forcefield120frame0.png, forcefield160frame0.png, forcefield240frame0.png, and forcefield320frame0.png into the LDPI, MDPI, HDPI, and XHDPI **/res/drawable** folders, respectively. We do this via a Windows Explorer file utility.

Be sure to copy all seven frames, numbered 0 through 6 at the end of each file name, into their proper resolution density resource folders, and then rename them all simply: **forcefield0.png** through **forcefield6.png**, as shown in Figure 9-4. Once this is done we are ready for XML and Java code.

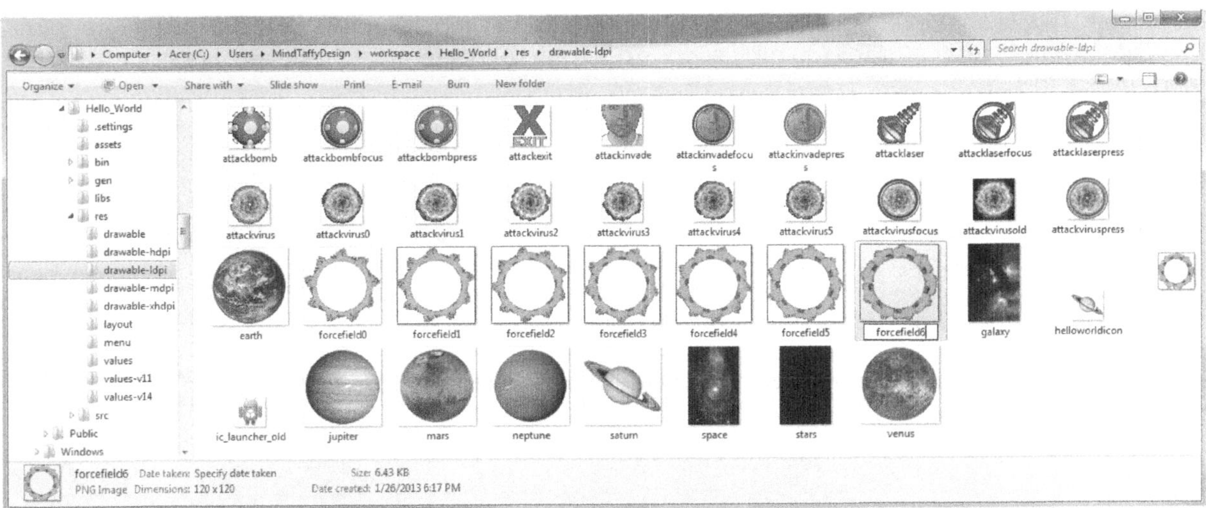

Figure 9-4. Copy and rename the forcefield animation frames into each drawable-dpi folder to prepare our assets

Now we can get some more practice implementing frame animation, this time looping rather than pong, by right-clicking the project folder and selecting New ➤ Android XML File. If you forgot what this looks like, refer to Figure 9-1 at the beginning of the chapter.

Name the file **anim_forcefield** and use **Resource Type: Drawable** and **Project: Hello_World** and **Root Element: <animation-list>** just like we did earlier.

If you are wondering about our naming convention, and why we are copying the Android activity_name naming convention, it is because when the files are sorted (alphabetized) by the OS or Eclipse, the logical files are grouped together, so all attack_names and anim_names stay grouped together in an orderly fashion.

Adding Our Animation Frame <item> Tags in Our anim_forcefield.xml File

You should now have an XML editing pane open in Eclipse that contains your new **anim_forcefield.xml** file, with a skeleton **<animation-list>** container inside where we will put our <item> child tags that specify our animation frames.

The first thing we want to do is to add the **android:oneshot="false"** parameter so that our animation loops forever. Note that **false** is the **default** value for oneshot, so if you like, you can leave this parameter out entirely. Since we will be changing looping parameters (and learning about them) at various points in this book, I am always going to code this parameter in the parent container, as it's just good programming practice.

Now we are ready to add the seven <item> tags for our animation frames, using the same android:drawable and android:duration parameters that we used previously to implement our pong animation. This is shown in Figure 9-5, and notice our frames loop seamlessly, from frame 6 to frame zero, at a frame rate of **12 FPS** (80 milliseconds goes into one second 12.5 times). Here is the XML mark-up for this:

```
<animation-list xmlns:android=http://schemas.android.com/apk/res/android
                android:oneshot="false" >
    <item android:drawable="@drawable/forcefield0" android:duration="80" />
    <item android:drawable="@drawable/forcefield1" android:duration="80" />
    <item android:drawable="@drawable/forcefield2" android:duration="80" />
    <item android:drawable="@drawable/forcefield3" android:duration="80" />
    <item android:drawable="@drawable/forcefield4" android:duration="80" />
    <item android:drawable="@drawable/forcefield5" android:duration="80" />
    <item android:drawable="@drawable/forcefield6" android:duration="80" />
</animation-list>
```

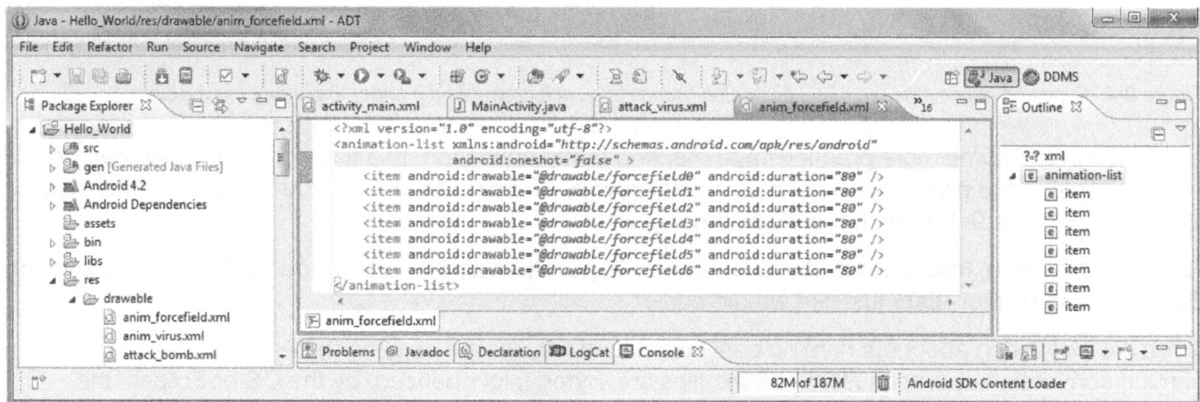

***Figure 9-5.** Add <item> tags for each forcefield animation frame to the parent <animation-list> container tag*

Next comes the new technique of using both a background image (or, in this case, an animation) and a foreground (called a source) image inside of the same user interface element container, in this case it's an ImageView tag.

Compositing Within a Single UI Element: Using Both the Source Image and Background Image Together

To accomplish this compositing we will add a couple of new parameters to the ImageView tag that is at the end of our Home Screen, which is defined via XML in the activity_main.xml file. Open this editing tab inside of Eclipse and add the parameter **android:background="@drawable/anim_forcefield"** to reference the animation-list XML that you just created so you could reference all the frames in your forcefield animation asset.

The second parameter we want to add is just as important as the background parameter, as it allows us to push out the boundaries of the ImageView container, because our background animation asset is 25% larger (125% of the size) than our planet images are. Both the foreground (source) image asset and the background animation asset utilize alpha channels; this is so that they will composite together seamlessly.

Add the **android:padding="30dp"** parameter, which adds 30 device independent pixels to the **inside** of the ImageView UI element container. Since we are pushing our Earth planet image away from the left side of the UI screen, as well as away from the text fields above it, let's also remove or delete the android:marginTop and android:marginLeft tags from this ImageView tag.

Figure 9-6 shows our new ImageView tag and its parameters, with the same number of parameters (we added two, and removed two) achieving a much more advanced special effect. If you want to adjust the amount of space between the planet and its forcefield, you can vary the android:padding DP setting anywhere from 24dp (tight fit) to 40dp (spaced far away). Remember you can use either 30dp or 30dip as your DIP parameter and Android will accept it.

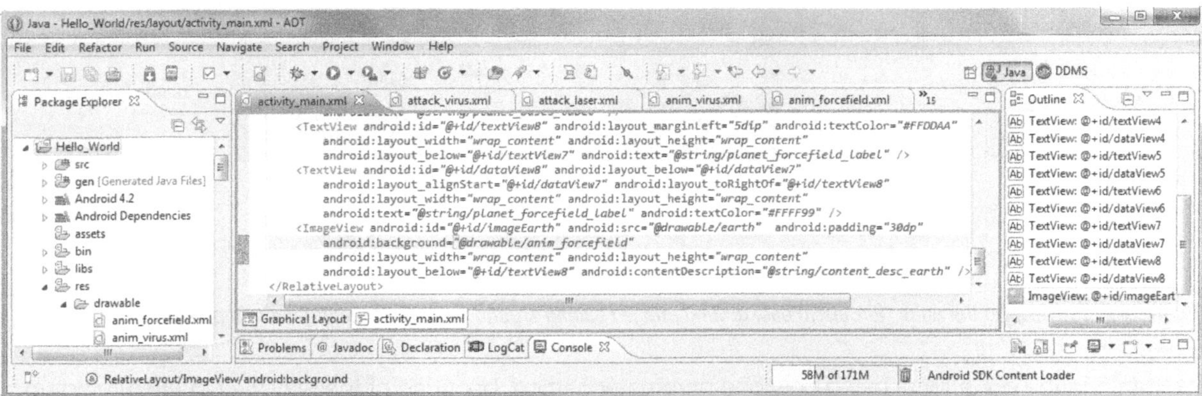

***Figure 9-6.** Reference anim_forcefield as background image for the imageEarth ImageView in activity_main.xml*

The **padding** parameter **adds space on the interior** of the UI element, rather than on the exterior, as the margin parameter does. This can be visualized really well using the Graphical Layout Editor, because the GLE gives you **guidelines** (in blue and green) to what each selected user interface element is doing relative to other user interface elements. For instance, before you deleted the margin parameters, a Graphical Layout Editor view pane showed a blue selection box close to the planet image and green arrows showing the margin setting, pushing the entire container away from the parent (the screen edge) and the text elements located above it. Now, notice in Figure 9-7 that the UI container itself has expanded to fit both our new background animation, as well as our foreground imagery.

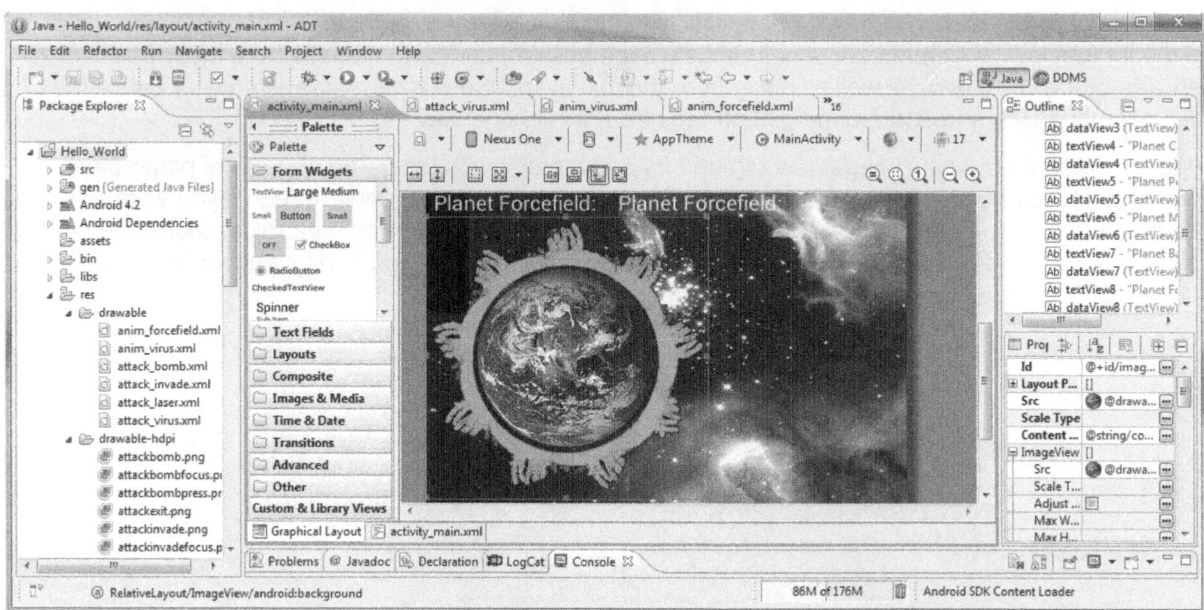

***Figure 9-7.** Previewing the anim_forcefield background image spacing around imageEarth using android:padding*

We can change our effects using only one parameter setting, because of the way we set everything up using alpha channels; in this way, no matter how we set up our padding or animation speeds, the results are professional. You could even animate this padding value in your Java code, or tie how tightly the forcefield is around the planet to the proximity of some other object to the planet, for instance.

Figure 9-7 shows the **30dp** padding setting in the Graphical Layout Editor. To set this parameter value to your own taste, switch back and forth between the activity_main.xml tab (look at the bottom of the editing pane), and the Graphical Layout Editor tab to see the results of the DIP setting on the resulting user interface element container padding values, which in this case we set up to affect how the planet centers within the forcefield animation. As of the time of writing of this book, the animation could not be played in the GLE. To see animation in action, you need to use the **Run As Android Application** work process and launch the Nexus S emulator.

Coding Our AnimationDrawable Object in Java to Implement Our Forcefield Animation

Before we can launch the emulator and see the animation in action we need to add some Java code, shown in Figure 9-8, to add our ImageView and AnimationDrawable classes and objects to our MainActivity.java class, so that Android knows they are there. Remember, designers can implement UI designs in XML, but often the programmers must make them work, using Java.

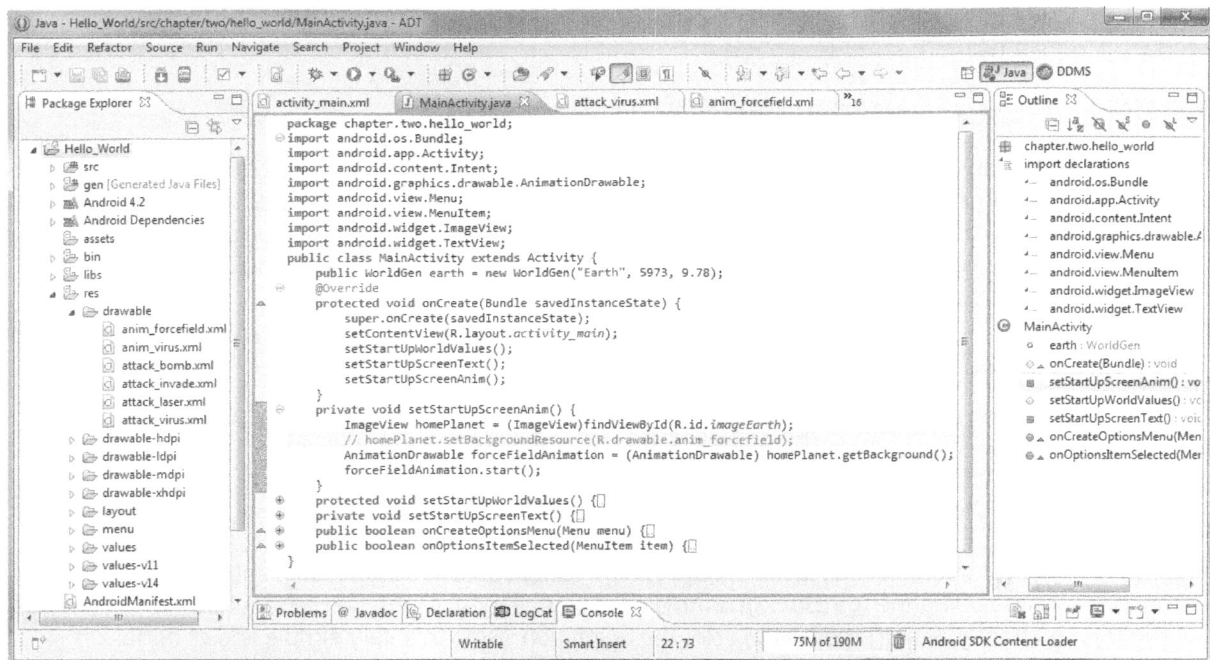

***Figure 9-8.** Coding a setStartUpScreenAnim() method to set-up our AnimationDrawable and call its start() method*

It is true that Android made it possible to implement animated **ImageButton** UI elements without having to write any Java code (I will always show the coolest and easiest to achieve tricks early on in each chapter) and only using XML mark-up. However, with **ImageView** UI elements, since they were designed more to hold image assets than to be used as UI elements, we will need to write some Java code, to make sure that the animation is playing when your application launches.

This is also fine with me because I am trying to cover some Java coding in each chapter, if I can, to keep those concepts fresh in your mind as well.

Let's create a new Java method in our MainActivity.java class called **setUpScreenAnim()** that will initialize the ImageView, set its background image, and call the AnimationDrawable class to animate the background animation asset we have set up here.

Find and open the MainActivity.java editing tab in Eclipse and collapse the setStartUpWorldValues(), SetStartUpScreenText(), onCreateOptionsMenu(), and onOptionsItemSelected() methods so that we have some room to code our new method.

Like our setStartUpScreenText() method, make the new method **private** and **void** and name it setStartUpScreenAnim. The code should look like this:

```
private void setStartUpScreenAnim() { animation code will go in here }
```

Now we have an empty method and we can write the Java code statements that will implement our ImageView and its AnimationDrawable background element.

The first thing we need to do is to declare, name, and instantiate our homePlanet ImageView user interface element using the following code:

```
ImageView homePlanet = (ImageView)findViewById(R.id.imageEarth);
```

The next line of code (it is commented out in Figure 9-8 as we don't need it, as we defined a background in XML) shows how to set up your background asset in Java. Note that because we used the **android:background** parameter in our ImageView tag, we do not need to redundantly do this in Java. However, if we did not have this XML background parameter in place, we would need this line of code. I have thus included it here for learning purposes:

```
homePlanet.setBackgroundResource(R.id.anim_forcefield); (commented out in Figure 9-8)
```

The next line of code does some heavy lifting, and sets up our forcefield animation using the Android AnimationDrawable class, using the following single line of code:

```
AnimationDrawable forceFieldAnimation = (AnimationDrawable)homePlanet.getBackground();
```

Finally, now that our **AnimationDrawable object** named **forceFieldAnimation** is set up to hold our animation resource using the **.getBackground()** method called off of the homePlanet ImageView object, we can use the handy **.start()** method to start the animation using this very simple line of code:

```
forceFieldAnimation.start();
```

Now we are ready to test our application in the Nexus S emulator using the **Run As Android Application** work process. Once we do this we can see that our forcefield animation is running on our application Home Screen and that the planet Earth is now spaced away from the left side of the screen and the text elements above it using the padding value rather than the margin values. In this way we are getting our spacing away from the other UI elements and making room for our background animation effect using the same tag parameter. This is all shown in Figure 9-9, although you'll have to run the emulator yourself, to see the forcefield animation in action!

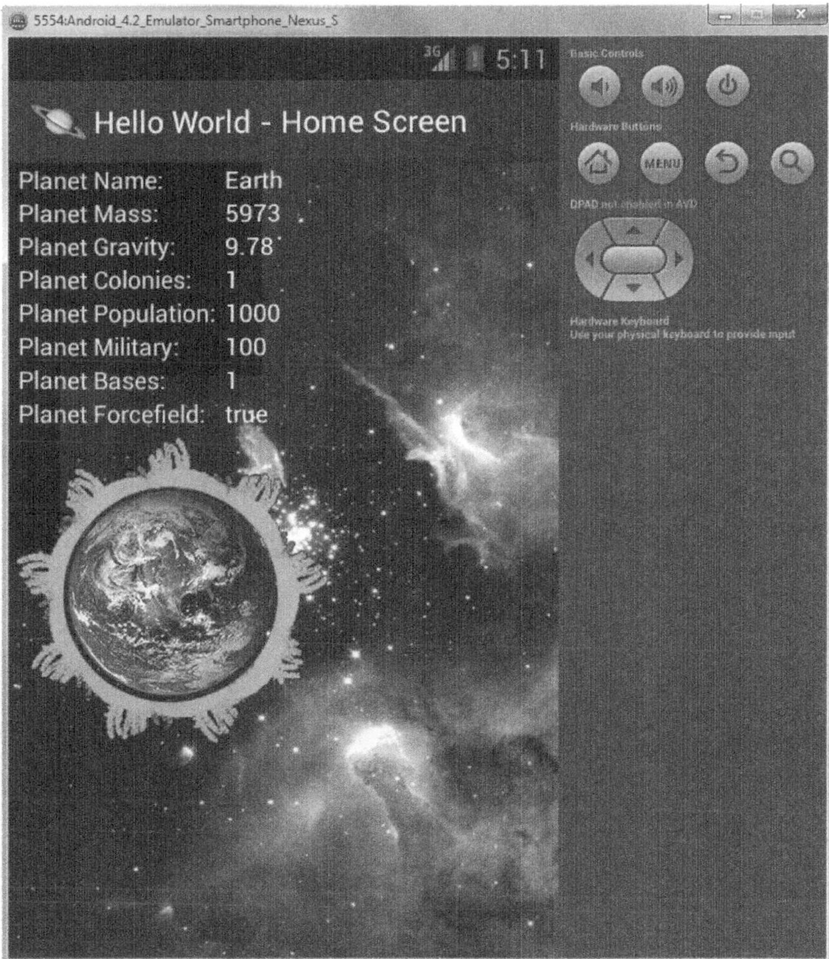

***Figure 9-9.** Running our ForcefieldAnimation ImageView UI element background in the Nexus S emulator*

In this section we implemented a seven frame animated forcefield effect in all four resolution densities using only 400KB total PNG8 image assets. That's an average of 100KB per resolution or an average of 14KB per frame.

Next, we will implement an even more impressive visual special effect, on our Configure a Planet user interface screen, so that we have added frame animation (or image based animation) special effects to each of the major user interface screens in our application where they would be appropriate.

Let's take a look at how to animate all the pixels in the image at the same time, via the built-in Android **image transition** special effect.

Image transitions are the foundation for digital imaging special effects such as **morphing**, as well as for digital imaging **cross-fade transitions**.

Full-Screen XML Frame Animation: Background Image Transitions

Let's use a different work process this time to create an **image transition** XML definition file so that you can see that there is more than one way to do this in Eclipse. Right-click your project's **/res/drawable** folder, and select the **New ➤ File** menu command sequence that brings up the **New File** dialog (creates a file containing any data type, not just XML data), shown in Figure 9-10.

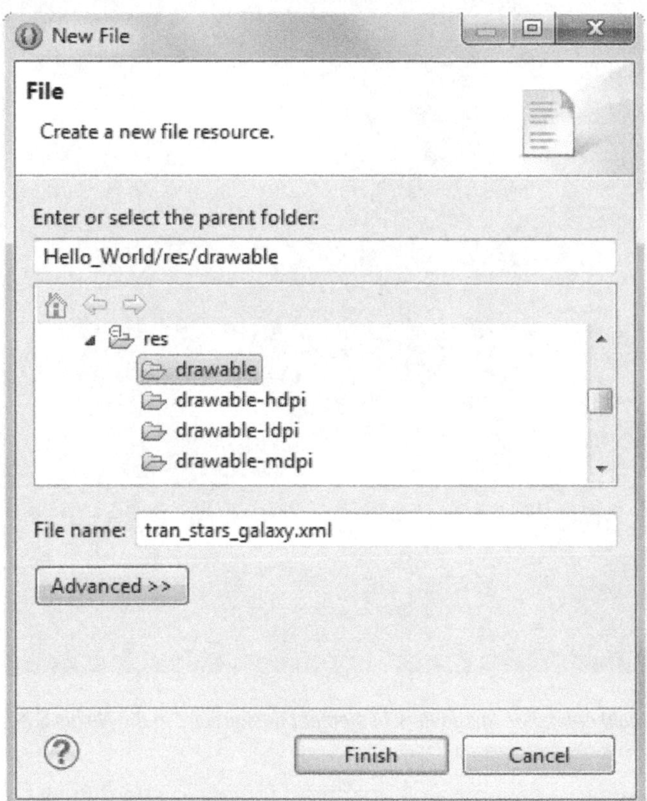

***Figure 9-10.** Creating a tran_stars_galaxy XML file using the New File dialog*

Notice that the New File dialog auto-populates with the parent folder that we right-clicked on to access the New ➤ File menu sequence, so all that we have to do now is to specify the filename. Name the file **tran_stars_galaxy**, which stands for transition from stars to galaxy.

Setting Up the <item> Tags for an Image Transition XML Definition

When the blank editing tab is opened for the **tran_stars_galaxy.xml** file in Eclipse, type in the **<transition>** parent tag that contains the **<item>** tags that define the **image drawable elements** that are a part of this image transition XML definition. The opening <transition> tag contains the XML schema address as all opening container tags do, and looks like this:

```
<transition xmlns:android="http://schemas.android.com/apk/res/android" >
```

Inside this parent image transition container, place two **<item>** tags, the first for the source image, and the second for the destination image. The <item> tags use the **android:drawable** parameter to point to the drawable image assets in the usual way, via the **@drawable/stars** reference for the source and a **@drawable/galaxy** reference for the destination image.

Once your tran_stars_galaxy.xml file looks like the mark-up that we wrote in Figure 9-11, the next thing that we need to do to prepare our existing code for the implementation of an image transition is to open our XML file named **activity_add.xml** and assign an **ID** value to our parent RelativeLayout layout container tag, using the **android:id** parameter.

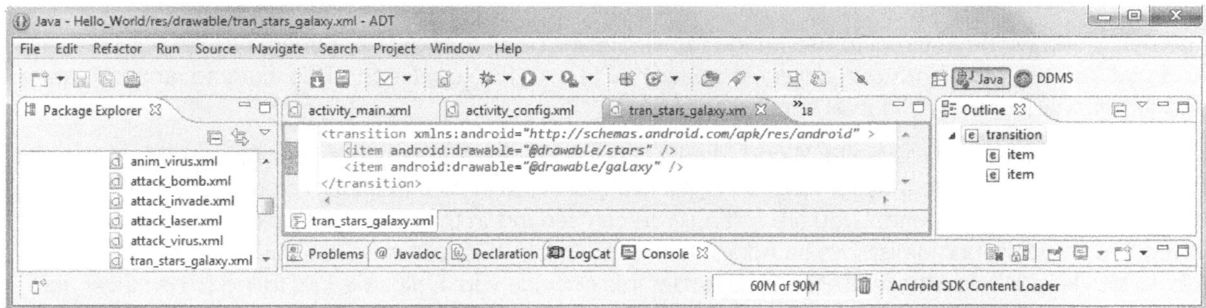

***Figure 9-11.** Using a <transition> tag parent container to define digital image transition elements via <item> tags*

The reason that we are adding this is because we need to reference, and later access, this screen layout container in our Java code. This is because this RelativeLayout container holds the background image for the user interface screen. Since this is the UI element (a background image for the RelativeLayout screen layout container) that we are trying to crossfade to a new image using an image transition object in Java, we must be able to access it via our **findViewById()** method in our Java code.

We have added the **android:id="@+id/new_planet_screen"** at the very end of our parent RelativeLayout container opening tag, as shown in Figure 9-12. Note that the order of tag parameters makes no difference; we can put the tag ID parameter first, or we can put it last in the parameter list.

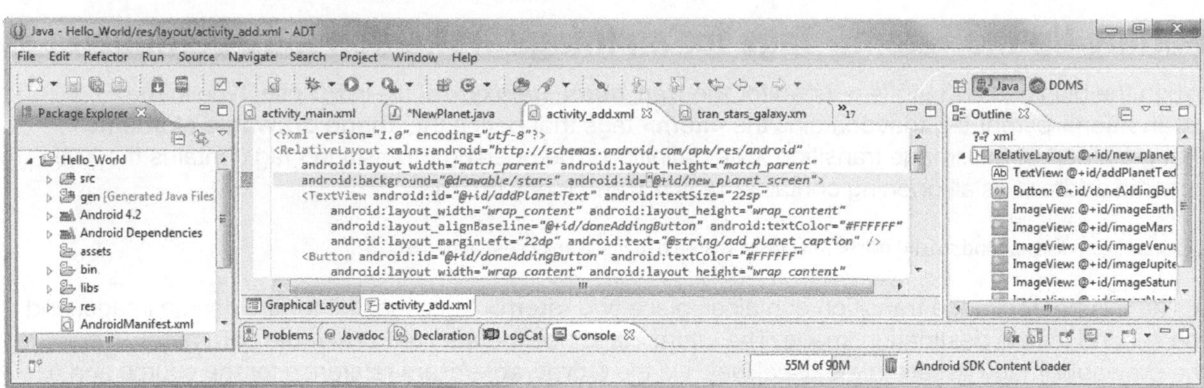

Figure 9-12. Naming the RelativeLayout container using the android:id parameter so it can be referenced in Java

Upgrading Our App API Level Support in the AndroidManifest XML for Hello_World

The next thing we have to do to use image transitions inside of a layout container is to set our AndroidManifest.xml file for our project to specify API Level 16 (Jelly Bean). This is an advanced feature and requires advanced API Level support to execute.

To accomplish this open the **Hello_World Manifest** tab in Eclipse that contains your **AndroidManifest.xml** file. It is important to note that in Figure 9-13 this is the only tab in your Eclipse project that will not simply display the exact filename that you are editing. You can see this in the Package Explorer at the bottom, where the actual filename displays as AndroidManifest.xml, but Eclipse modifies this in the editing pane tab, to be Hello_World Manifest! Please do not let this confuse you; Eclipse is just trying to be clever and advanced. Don't go thinking you can name your AndroidManifest.xml file Hello_WorldManifest.xml, or your project will not compile. Remember the Android OS is **hard-coded** to look only for (and find) a bootstrap file called AndroidManifest.xml so only use that filename.

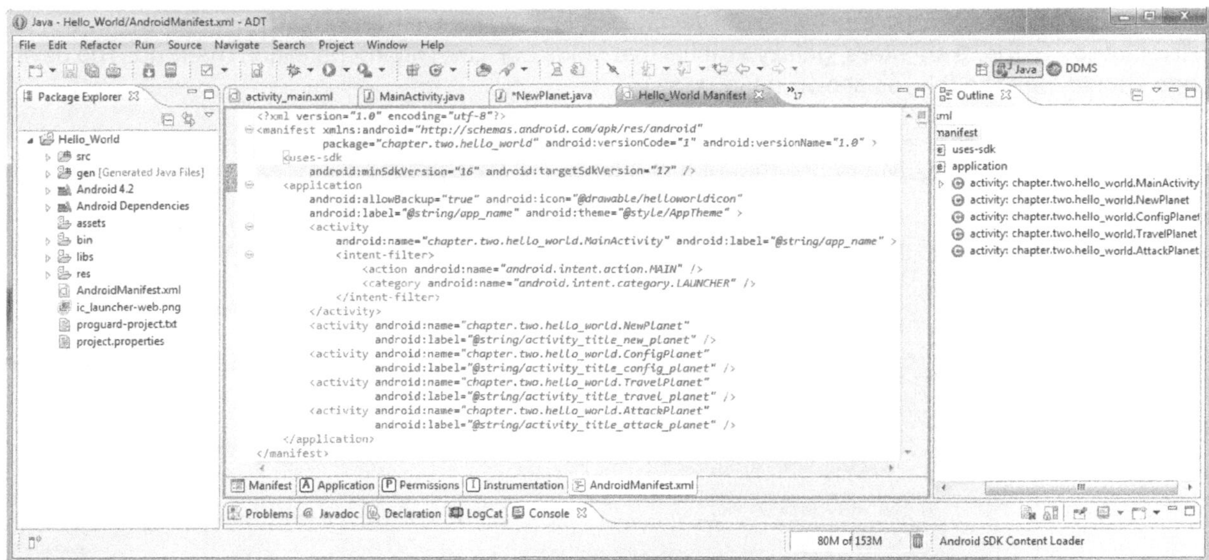

***Figure 9-13.** Adjusting our android:minSdkVersion to API Level 16 to allow screen layout background transitions*

To specify that we are using a **minimum API** support level of API 16, and a **current API** support level of 17, we adjust these tag parameters for the **<uses-sdk>** tag inside of the AndroidManifest.xml file near the top of the XML mark-up, the results of which are shown in Figure 9-13.

Set the **android:minSdkVersion** parameter to a value of **16**, which signifies **Android 4.1.2** Jelly Bean API Level 16 support. Leave the other parameter in this tag, **android:targetSdkVersion** set to the current value of **17**, or **Android 4.2.2** Jelly Bean Plus API Level 17 support. Our Manifest looks good!

You might be wondering if this will reduce your app's capability on older platforms and devices. If you remember, in the first chapter we installed an API along with everything else that **simulated** current API level support on older API level APIs. My guess would be that blending layout container backgrounds via image transitions would not be too difficult to do in any API level, so this may well work on Android 3.x and 4.0 platforms as well.

It is also the type of wow-factor application feature which, if it did not work (implement properly) on an older platform, it would simply not happen; that is, the background image transition would not occur, but the end user would not realize this, because nothing would perceptibly go wrong, unless that user had utilized the application on a platform where this background image transition was in fact supported.

Adding a TransitionDrawable Object in Our Java Code to Implement the Image Transition

Now we are ready for the fun stuff! We need to add three key lines of code to our NewPlanet.java Java class definition, I added them right after the Activity onCreate() and setContentView() method calls since we are setting up objects and wiring them together. Later in the onClick() method for our marsImage object, we will call this effect, when the user clicks on Mars.

The first line of code sets up our TransitionDrawable object, which we will name **trans**, and which we will reference to the: **tran_stars_galaxy.xml** file that holds our <transition> definition mark-up. The Java code should look like this, as shown in Figure 9-14:

```
final TransitionDrawable trans =
(TransitionDrawable)getResources().getDrawable(R.id.trans_stars_galaxy);
```

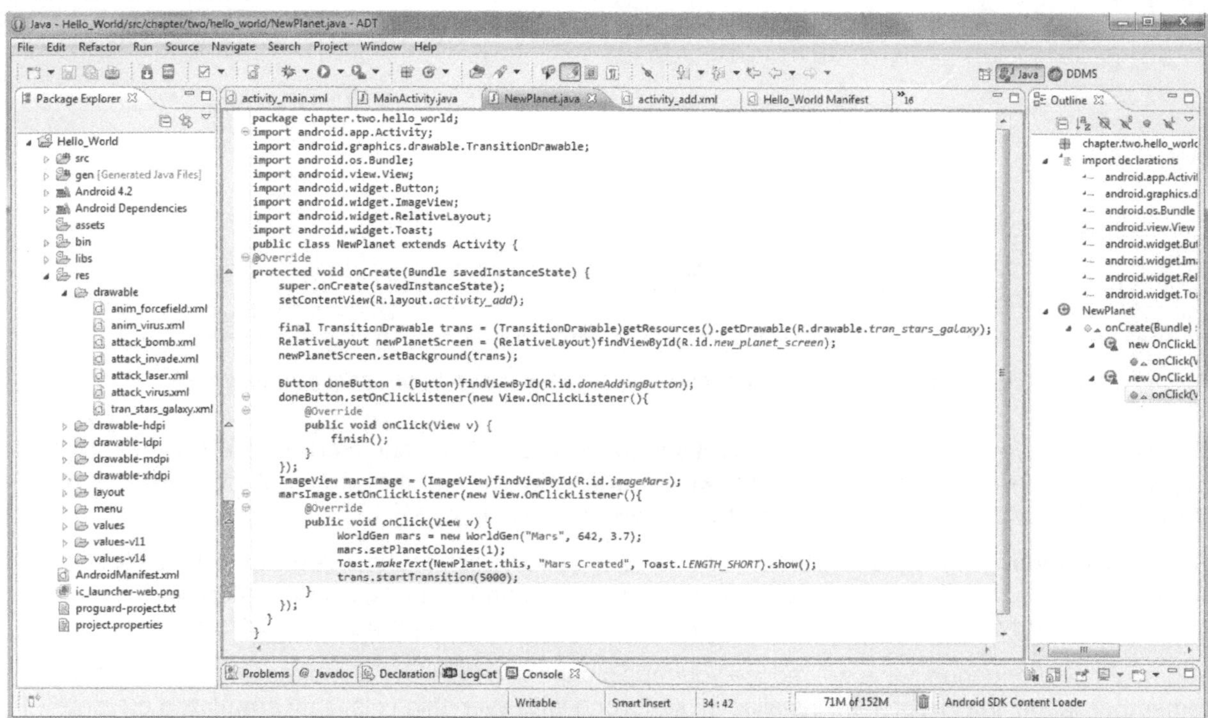

Figure 9-14. Implementing our RelativeLayout and TransitionDrawable objects in our NewPlanet.java code

We need to make our object **final** as we are referencing it from the inside of an onClick() method deeper in the class, and the final keyword prevents the trans object from ever being edited, essentially making it an object constant, which is actually what we wanted this transition effect to be–usable–and the same every time, by any method in the class that calls it.

Next, we need to instantiate our RelativeLayout container object, and name it **newPlanetScreen** and reference it to our activity_add.xml layout, where it is defined and recently given an **android:id** value of **new_planet_screen.**

This is done in the same way that we instantiate any of our user interface elements in Java, by declaring it as an object, and naming it, like this:

```
RelativeLayout newPlanetScreen = (RelativeLayout)findViewById(R.id.new_planet_screen);
```

Now that we have a **trans** TransitionDrawable object and our **newPlanetScreen** RelativeLayout object declared, the next thing that we will need to do is to wire them together, so that they can work together as a team, to create the background image transition effect that we are seeking to implement.

This is done by setting the background element (parameter) of our recent **newPlanetScreen** RelativeLayout container object to the TransitionDrawable object we created to perform our image transition. Remember we named this object **trans**, and we will accomplish this by using one simple but powerful line of Java code, which wires these two objects together (or more accurately, references the trans object inside of the newPlanetScreen object) via the **.setBackground()** method call:

```
newPlanetScreen.setBackground(trans);
```

Now that our digital imaging special effect has been implemented in XML (in three XML files), and in Java, and is ready to be triggered using the .start() method call inside our planet onClick() methods, one of which we have coded already for our **imageMars** user interface object, and thus we can now test all this new code by adding this short line of code:

```
trans.startTransition(5000);
```

This line of code calls the trans TransitionDrawable object via its **.start()** method, which starts the transition, as well as passing it a **duration variable** specified in milliseconds, in this particular case, we are using **5000 milliseconds** (or 5 seconds) to create a slow cross-fade effect between the current stars.png image to the new galaxy.png image.

All this new Java code can be seen in Figure 9-14, in the middle of the class (I put some white space around the three core lines of Java code), as well as at the bottom, in a line highlighted in light blue.

Now we are ready to right-click our Project Folder in the Package Explorer pane and select the **Run As Android Application** command to launch the Nexus S emulator and see our background image transition in action!

When the Nexus S emulator launches and the application finishes loading, click the menu button and select the New Planet first menu option, and load the New Planet Activity user interface screen. Then click the Mars planet image, and watch the stars background slowly cross-fade, becoming a galaxy background image, as shown in Figure 9-15. Because of the fact that we have been using **alpha channels** in our digital imagery so far to develop this application, the end-result is 100% professional seamless compositing, even during the fade, of our six planets on our new background imagery.

Figure 9-15. Background image transition to galaxy.png shown in Nexus S emulator

Now that we know how to implement bitmap animation and image transitions using the AnimationDrawable and TransitionDrawable classes in Android, we can take our application to an even higher level of visual effects artistry in the next chapter on procedural animation.

Using procedural animation, where we modify both static imagery as well as motion animation (yes, while it is in motion animating through its frames) using XML parameters for translation (movement), scaling, rotation, alpha channel (blending) and more, we can achieve an order of magnitude greater visual impact from our special effects.

So let's summarize what we have learned in this chapter regarding raster image-based animation, and get right into vector animation, so we can use those classes and techniques to compound the WOW! factor of our Hello World application's visual effects.

Summary

In this chapter, we took our knowledge of digital imaging concepts and the techniques that we learned in the last couple of chapters, and took these techniques into the fourth dimension of time via Android's Frame Animation capabilities, and applied them to further enhance our Hello World app.

First, we learned about some of the fundamental concepts of digital image animation, which built upon those static imaging concepts that we learned about in the two previous chapters. We learned that image-based animation is commonly called **raster animation** or **frame animation**, and that this type of animation is comprised of **cels** or **frames**, which are displayed rapidly over time to create the illusion of motion.

We learned about the core animation concept of **frame rates**, and how we can calculate the **FPS** or **frames per second** for any given animation. We learned that videogames use the fastest frame rate of **60 FPS** whereas **digital video** (television) uses half that frame rate, or **30 FPS**. Motion Pictures (Film) uses a frame rate of **24 FPS** and digital media uses frame rates even lower than that, ranging from **10 FPS** to **20 FPS**, to save on the data footprint.

We learned how to **optimize** the data footprint for our application's frame-based animation, by optimizing both the **color depth** of our imagery (using optimized indexed color imagery), as well as the **number of frames** needed to create the visual special effect that we're looking for.

We implemented several animation effects for our Hello_World application. One six frame animation used a mere 120 kilobtyes of image data across all four Android resolution density targets, or a compact **30KB** per resolution screen density. Our forcefield animation was seven frames, and used 400KB, but was a much larger effect that encompassed an entire planet, and still averaged only **100KB** of total frame(s) data per Android resolution density.

We learned about the concept of **looping** and the **android:oneshot** parameter, which controls whether an animation loops seamlessly, or whether it simply plays once and then stops. We explored the concepts of **pong looping,** where a loop **pongs back and forth** amongst its component frames. We also learned about **seamless looping**, where an animation's loop is predesigned to loop seamlessly, and thus does not need to reverse its frame direction.

We then started to implement frame-based animation inside our Hello World Android application, using the **<animation-list>** parent tag and its child **<item>** tags, which define the drawable assets for the animation frames as well as each frame duration.

We learned about Android's **AnimationDrawable** class, and how it is used to implement image-based (drawable) animation via an AnimationDrawable object declared inside of the Java code in our Android application Activities. We learned how to call the **.start()** method on our AnimationDrawable object.

We brought our attack virus icon to life on our Attack a Planet Activity user interface screen using only XML mark-up code, and implemented this pulsating virus as a pong-looping animated user interface element, using only XML tags and parameters, and zero Java code.

We accomplished this by replacing the source imagery for the ImageButton UI element with an XML-based frame animation definition and then we used an **android:state_enabled** parameter to automate the virus animation after the Activity screen had finished loading.

We then graduated to a more advanced UI technique of using our background image plate for a user interface element to hold our animation frames, and compositing them with the foreground (source) imagery for the UI element.

We implemented this intra-UI compositing technique on our application Home Screen to add a forcefield around our planet Earth by using the ImageView tag background parameter to hold our seamless looping, 7 frame forcefield animation which we again defined in an XML file using the <animation-list> parent tag, and <item> child tags.

We then investigated the Android **TransitionDrawable** class, and its ability to implement **Digital Image Transitions** within our Android applications. We created an XML file completely from scratch and implemented a **<transition>** tag parent container, and two child **<item>** tags, which defined the imagery that we wanted to transition between.

Because we wanted to get tricky (read: advanced) and use an image transition inside the background parameter (image container) of a RelativeLayout user interface screen layout container element, we needed to upgrade our app's Minimum API support to Android API Level 16 and a Target API Level of 17 in our **AndroidManifest.xml** file. Then we wired everything together using only four lines of Java code in our **MainActivity.java** class.

In the next chapter we build on our frame animation knowledge learned in this chapter by learning about **procedural** or **vector animation**, which can be used in conjunction with frame animation constructs, or with simple static imagery, or even with non-image UI elements, such as TextViews.

Chapter 10

Android Vector Animation: Procedural Animation via XML Constructs

In this second chapter covering animation, we will learn about the "other" type of animation in Android, the type that uses **code**, rather than **pixels**, to produce its magic. This type of code-based animation is commonly called **procedural animation** and involves things like **ranges** and **pivot points**.

There are several procedural animation terms used in the industry. If you hear the term **tween animation**, it is referring to a procedural way of creating animation. This is because **tweening** is actually **interpolation**, or dividing the number of frames you want your animation to span, between the start and end values, or range, for that animation's calculation.

We'll get into the math for interpolation and other procedural animation concepts such as pivot points in the next section. Another term that you may hear for procedural animation is **vector animation**. A vector is a **ray** or line, but the general concept is that the animation is created by using mathematical constructs rather than using collections of rasters (pixels).

Vector and raster are two completely different approaches; raster is **data heavy**, whereas vector is **data compact**. The reason for this is because text (math) compresses well, and arrays of pixels (and frames) simply do not. Vector uses more CPU resources (while it does the calculations), whereas raster uses more storage or bandwidth resources (transferring data). This is because a mathematical vector needs to be **rendered** to the display screen, which means the math is turned into graphical elements, usually motion graphics, or 2D animation.

So, Adobe Illustrator (or InkScape) is a vector imaging software package, whereas Adobe Photoshop (or GIMP 2) is a raster imaging software package.

Procedural Animation Concepts: Rotation, Scale, and Translation

Let's start out by learning about some of the concepts involved in vector imaging and animation. First of all, there are two primary types of vector platforms, **2D** or **two dimensional** (flat) vector graphics, such as we find in Illustrator or InkScape, and **3D** or **three dimensional** (volumetric) vector graphics, such as what we find in 3D modeling software like Blender 3D.

> **Note** Concepts that we'll cover in this section of the chapter apply to both 2D and 3D imaging and animation. Both use vectors; 2D vectors in 2D, and 3D vectors in 3D, and both 2D and 3D involve the core concepts of **translation** (movement), **rotation**, and **scaling**. In 2D these concepts involve the **X** and **Y** axes, and in 3D, these involve the **X**, **Y**, and **Z** axes.

There is a Z concept in 2D animation, but it is not a Z axis, but rather a Z order. **Z order** in 2D is more like layers in digital imaging, it involves what layer order each 2D (flat) layer is in, and whether it is front of or behind other 2D layers. Z order is a number that orders the layers in a 2D composite, and defines what is in front of, and what is behind, a given 2D layer. Changing Z order in real-time can create flip-book special effects.

Translation in 2D involves movement along the X and Y axes, and it is the most basic of the three **transformations** that can be done in 2D animation. Translation is defined by the **starting point** of the movement, the **amount** of that movement, in pixels or percentages, and the **direction** of movement, along either the **X** or the **Y** axis, or some relative combination of both.

Rotation in 2D involves the rotation around a given **pivot point**, and it is defined by **degrees**, the **direction** (positive or negative) of that rotation, and the **pivot point** (center) **location** of the rotation. Because there are **360** degrees in a full circle, rotational mathematics involves this 360 number specifically, just like FPS calculations involve the number 1000 (a number of milliseconds in a second).

Scale in 2D involves the **size** of a given shape defined by a decimal number relative to the current size of the shape. For instance, a **0.5** scale would be **half** of the current size and a **2.0** scale would be **twice** the size of the current shape. Like translation, scaling has an X and a Y component to it, if the values are the same, the scaling can be said to be **uniform scaling**, if they are not the same, the scaling is said to be **non-uniform scaling**.

Interestingly you can also define a **pivot point** in your scaling operation, which allows **skewed scaling** where your scaling operation can be **influenced** by the placement of the pivot point. On irregular shapes, this can give a more precise level of control over the resulting shape-warping effects of the scaling operation. Given that sometimes the 2D shapes being scaled are bitmap images, some very interesting results can be obtained using a pivot point placement that is not at the center point of the image.

Implementing Rotational Animation: The Attack Bomb UI Icon

Let's start out implementing procedural animation by animating a static image on our attack a planet user interface screen so that it looks like an animated icon. We'll rotate our bomb ImageButton UI element, so it is animated along with our virus ImageButton, which we frame animated in the previous chapter. Because we created an alpha channel for the bomb image, this gives us a seamless 2D effect with our space image background.

Right-click your project resource folder, then select the **New ➤ Android XML File** menu option sequence. Select a **Resource Type:** of **Tween Animation** in **Project:** set **Hello_World** and then name the file **anim_rot_bomb**, short for animation rotation bomb image. Next select the **Root Element** of **<rotate>** and finally click the **Finish** button, as shown in Figure 10-1.

***Figure 10-1.** New Android XML file for Tween Animation (rotation)*

This opens up a blank XML file with the **<rotate>** tag, which we populate with parameters for what we want our rotation process to entail.

First delete the **</rotate>** end-tag, because this is not going to be a parent (container) tag. Split the **<rotate>** opening tag into a **<rotate** on one line, and then add an **ending** or **closing** tag symbol **/>** on the next line, as shown in Figure 10-2.

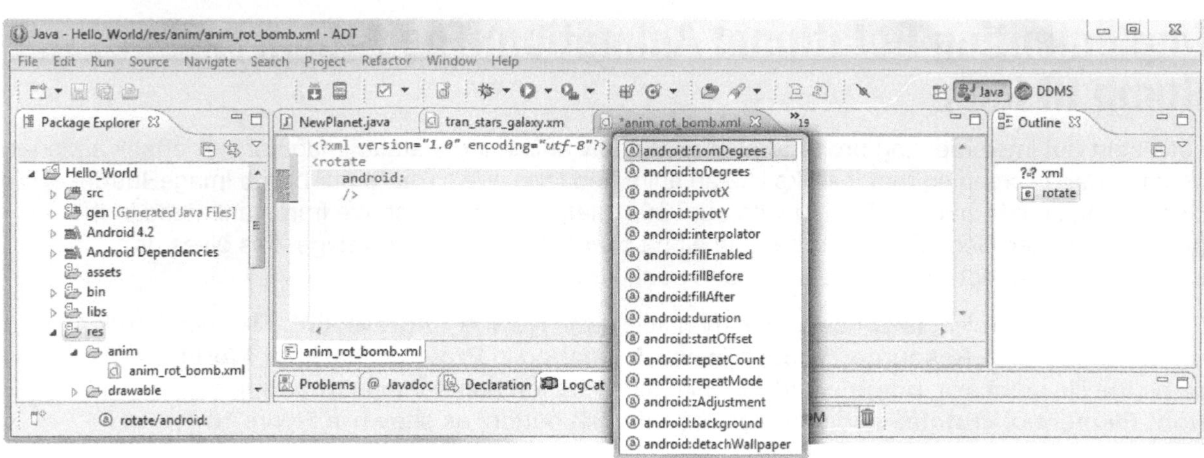

Figure 10-2. Adding rotation animation parameters via the android: parameter helper dialog inside of Eclipse

Completing the Rotate Tag

Also shown in Figure 10-2 is our little trick of typing **android:** to get a **parameter helper dialog** with a list of parameters that will be usable in the **<rotate>** tag. You should always utilize this technique to invoke and study available parameters before you use a tag, and we will try and use as many of these parameters in this example, to show you what they all will do.

The first thing we need to add is an **xmlns:android** parameter that references the **`http://schemas.android.com/apk/res/android`** URL so that any parameters that we add can be validated with the current specification that is located on the Android website. Until you add this initial XML Naming Schema (XMLNS) reference any parameter you add will be marked with a red X error because it cannot be verified as a proper parameter. This is because the android: that is appended before each parameter equates to the URL defined herein.

The most important thing to define in a rotation animation is the rotation parameters themselves, in degrees, using the **android:fromDegrees** and the **android:toDegrees** parameters. Since we want full circle seamless animation for our attack bomb icon, we will use from 0 to 360 in these settings to obtain a full seamless rotation of the bomb image.

The next two settings that we add establish the center point, or **pivot point**, of this rotation, using X and Y **coordinates**. In Android, your pivot point is established using a **percentage**, from **0%** to **100%** into the 2D image from the upper-left corner of the image. By making this a percentage it doesn't matter how many pixels our image is, and this thus accommodates the wide range of resolution images that we need to support the many types of Android devices on the market these days.

Because we want the image to rotate around its center point, we will use a setting of **50%** for the **android:pivotX** parameter, and a setting of **50%** for the **android:pivotY** parameter as well. If the image (and alpha) is not centered to the pixel perfectly, there may be some wobble. Note that this is more easily fixed in this XML mark-up (i.e., by using settings of 49% and 51% to slightly move the pivot diagonally) than by going back onto GIMP and counting border pixels above and to the side of the bomb image.

The next thing we need to do is to set an **interpolation method** for our 2D animation by using an **android:interpolator** parameter, with an **interpolator constant** that is defined in the Android OS internal resources **R.** pathway.

Currently, the Android OS supports **13** interpolator constants. Each of the interpolator constants accesses an **Interpolator** class subclass in Android.

Each of these Interpolator subclasses apply a mathematical curve to the animation frame rate that adjusts the transition speeds between each animation frame to achieve more complex and realistic motion effects.

If you want to research these **interpolator methods** in detail, there is an entire page dedicated to them on the Android Developer website located at:

```
http://developer.android.com/reference/android/view/animation/Interpolator.html
```

The interpolator that we need to use here is a **linear interpolator**, which gives us a nice **even movement** along all parts of our animation. We will be using other interpolator constants throughout this chapter, so you can see what they do and how they look when applied to your 2D animation settings. If you want to see all the **R.interpolator** constants in one place, go to:

```
http://developer.android.com/reference/android/R.interpolator.html
```

To apply an interpolator constant, we will reference it from the Android OS **resource (R)** bucket using **@android** (the OS) along with **:anim** (animation resources) and **/linear_interpolator** (the path to that constant) like this:

```
android:interpolator="@android:anim/linear_interpolator"
```

Next we need to define the **Repeat Count** for the animation. This is done via an **android:repeatCount** parameter, which takes either an **integer value** (a number of loops to complete value) or the predefined **infinite** constant.

The infinite constant is used only if there is a UI element that needs to animate forever, such as a user interface button or a UI design element.

Because our attack bomb ImageButton image icon falls into this category, we will use an **android:repeatCount="infinite"** parameter to achieve this end-result.

Finally, we need to define the **cycle duration** for the animation, that is, the time over that one loop of the procedural animation is to occur.

Animation cycle duration is defined using the **android:duration** parameter, with the exact time that each loop of the animation is to span (animation speed) defined in milliseconds. Let's start out with a fast value of **2000** milliseconds, or one second per 180 degrees of rotation, and later on, if this is too fast, we can increase its value to **8000** milliseconds or more.

Now we have implemented the **<rotate>** tag parameters that we need to define our bomb rotation 2D animation (using about half the available parameters, which are shown in Figure 10-2) and we can implement the animation in Java next. The XML tag and its parameters should contain the following mark-up:

```
<?xml version="1.0" encoding="utf-8"?>
  <rotate
    xmlns:android="http://schemas.android.com/apk/res/android"
    android:fromDegrees="0"
    android:toDegrees="360"
```

```
    android:pivotX="50%"
    android:pivotY="50%"
    android:interpolator="@android:anim/linear_interpolator"
    android:repeatCount="infinite"
    android:duration="2000"
/>
```

Figure 10-3 shows the completed anim_rot_bomb.xml file in Eclipse.

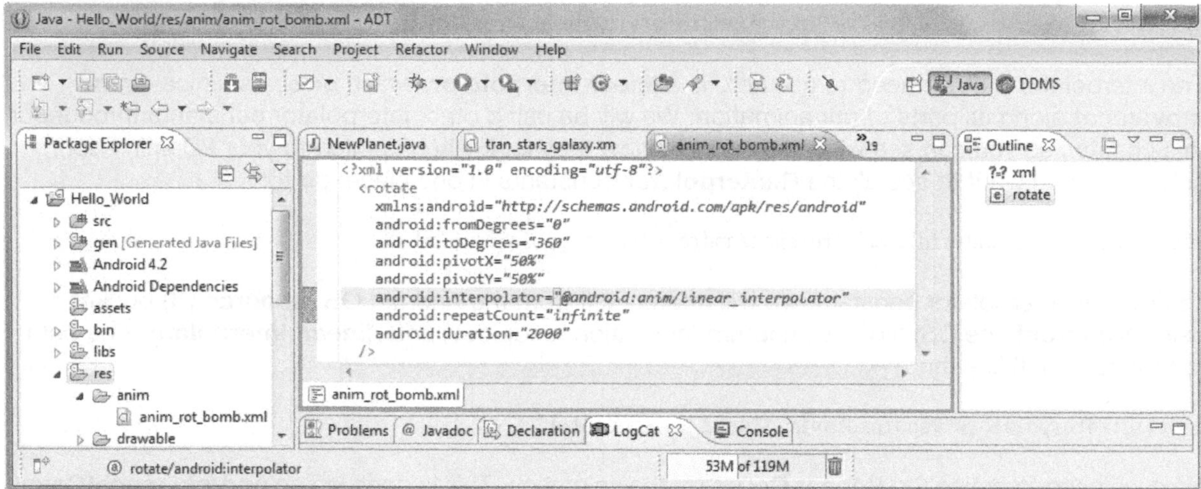

***Figure 10-3.** Configuring <rotate> tag's rotational definition parameters for the anim_rot_bomb.xml file in Eclipse*

Adding Java Code for the Rotation

Our Java code for the animation trigger is logically defined within the AttackPlanet.java file because that class controls the Activity screen for attack functions. Click the number in the top right of the Eclipse editing pane, drop down the open files menu, and select: AttackPlanet.java.

The first thing that we need to do in our Java code is to add a line of space under our `.setContentView()` method call, so that we can declare an `Animation` object, using the Android `Animation` class. Name this `Animation` object `rotateBomb` and reference the `anim_rot_bomb` XML like this:

```
Animation rotateBomb = AnimationUtils.loadAnimation(this, R.anim.anim_rot_bomb);
```

Notice that declaring an animation and loading a procedural XML definition is done a bit differently, by declaring and naming the Animation object on the left side of the equal sign, and calling the **.loadAnimation()** method via dot notation off of the **AnimationUtils** class. The AnimationUtils class uses its loadAnimation method to reference the current context (**this**) and the animation XML definition in **anim_rot_bomb.xml** in its second parameter.

When you type in this line of code, Eclipse red underlines the classes for which you need to define import statements, and you can click these and select the link that has the IDE do this for you, if you prefer.

Now that we have set up an Animation object to perform this animation for us, all we have to do is to wire it to our bombButton UI object and start the animation, which again we accomplish in one compact line of Java code.

```
bombButton.startAnimation(rotateBomb);
```

This has our `bombButton ImageButton` object call its `startAnimation` method and passes it over the `rotateBomb Animation` object that we just created in the line of code directly above it. As you can see in Figure 10-4, it only takes two very dense lines of Java code to implement a procedural animation since all the heavy lifting defining what we want the animation to do has been off-loaded to XML. This allows designers to focus on the UI and animation design so that the Java coders do not have to. Pretty genius stuff!

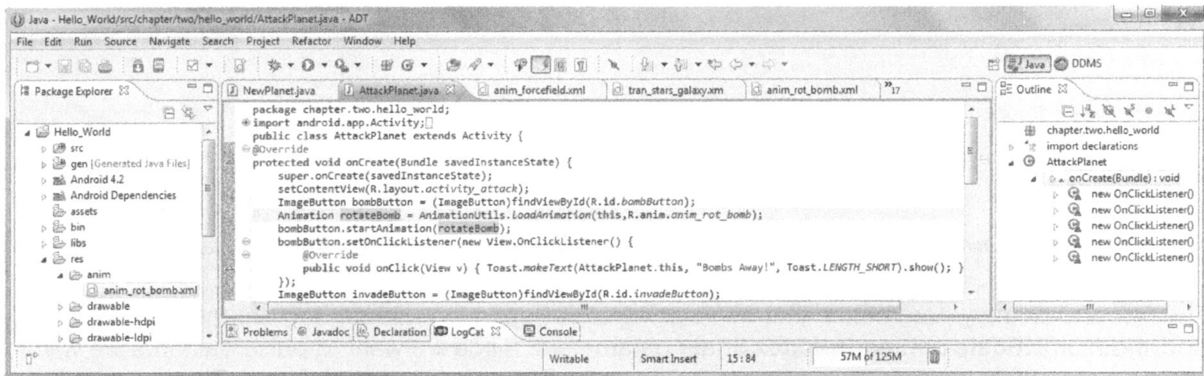

***Figure 10-4.** Adding an Animation object named rotateBomb and assigning it to bombButton via .startAnimation()*

Next, let's get a little bit more complicated, and combine some procedural (vector) animation with our existing frame-based (raster) animation in our attack virus icon ImageButton UI element. In this way, you can see how to use an optimal combination of both the vector and raster animation worlds, to obtain an advanced end-result, using a relatively small amount of Java and XML code and only a half-dozen digital image assets (frames).

Implementing Scalar Animation: The Pulsing Attack Virus UI Icon

We start out creating another procedural animation XML file just like we did back in Figure 10-1, only this time we select the **<scale>** root element for our XML file, instead of the <rotate> element. This is because we are going to make our attack virus pulse or flex, in addition to its current frame-based virus movements. Let's name this XML file **anim_scale_virus**.

Now we again separate the <scale> tag into **<scale** and **/>** and delete the </scale> closing tag, as well as add our **xmlns:android** parameter to reference the **DTD** (document type definition) online via the usual URL.

Completing the Scale Tag

Now we use the **android:** work process to bring up the Eclipse helper dialog listing all the **<scale>** element tag parameters, so we can peruse what this tag can (and will) do for us. This is all shown in Figure 10-5.

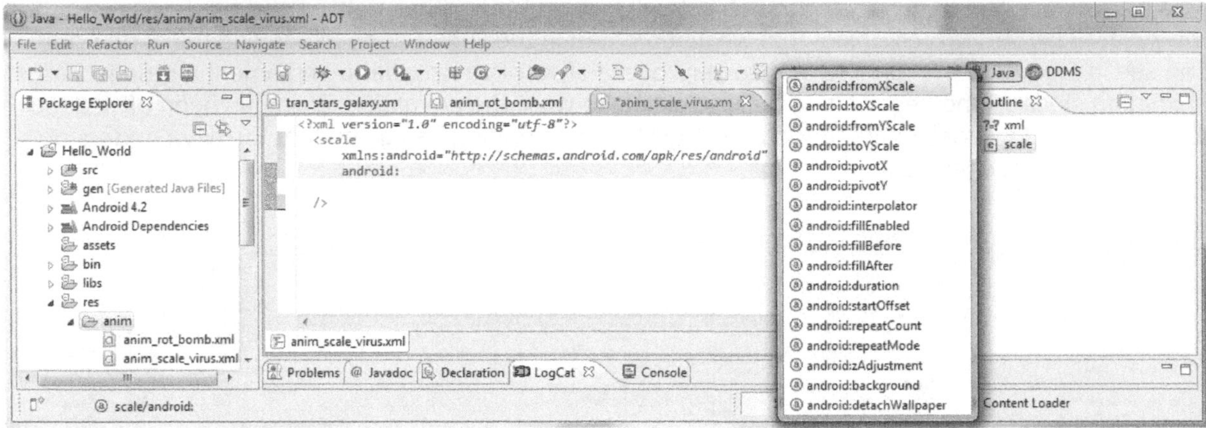

***Figure 10-5.** Creating our anim_scale_virus.xml and using the android: parameter helper dialog with <scale> parameters*

The first and primary parameters that we're going to set-up in the <scale> tag are the **android:fromXScale** and **android:toXScale** parameters. Since we want to pulse our virus we will scale it from 100% (its default or current size) down to 75%, and then back again. Thus we need to set our fromXScale parameter to **1.0** (or 100% in decimal representation), and set our toXScale parameter to **0.75** (or 75%, as expressed as a decimal representation).

Because we want to scale our virus **uniformly** or evenly across both the X and Y axes, we set our **android:fromYScale** and **android:toYScale** parameters with the exact same numeric values.

As I mentioned earlier in the chapter, scales can be made to scale with a directional **skew** by setting a pivot point X and Y values, which we set here to familiarize you with the parameter, but since we want the virus to flex evenly on its center we center our pivot point using 50% values in both the X and Y pivot parameters.

Now it's time to set an animation interpolator using **android:interpolator**, and we will use an **accelerate_decelerate** interpolator here to get a little bit more fancy, and give a little character to our virus's flexing motion.

Next we set the length of a single loop of our scale animation using the **android:duration parameter** set to 3000 milliseconds, or 3 seconds. We need a smooth, slow scale so this should be a good starting value that we can tweak (increase) later if needed for a more realistic effect.

Now all we have to do is set our **repeat parameters** and we will be ready to implement the scale animation definition in our Java code. There are two repeat parameters that we are going to use for this scale animation, the **android:repeatCount**, which we have seen before and we are going to again set to **infinite**, and the **android:repeatMode** which is new to us and which we are going to set to **reverse**.

RepeatMode has two constants in Android, the **reverse** constant we are using here, which causes a **pong** animation effect and makes our virus flex, and the **restart** constant, which creates a seamless loop and is the default value or setting. Thus, if you leave the android:repeatMode parameter out, or undeclared, your animation will loop seamlessly, if you have included an android:repeatCount parameter set to infinite. Your XML mark-up should look like this:

```
<?xml version="1.0" encoding="utf-8"?>
  <scale
    xmlns:android="http://schemas.android.com/apk/res/android"
    android:fromXScale="1.0"
    android:toXScale="0.75"
    android:fromYScale="1.0"
    android:toYScale="0.75"
    android:pivotX="50%"
    android:pivotY="50%"
    android:interpolator="@android:anim/accelerate_decelerate_interpolator"
    android:duration="3000"
    android:repeatCount="infinite"
    android:repeatMode="reverse"
  />
```

Figure 10-6 shows the completed tag.

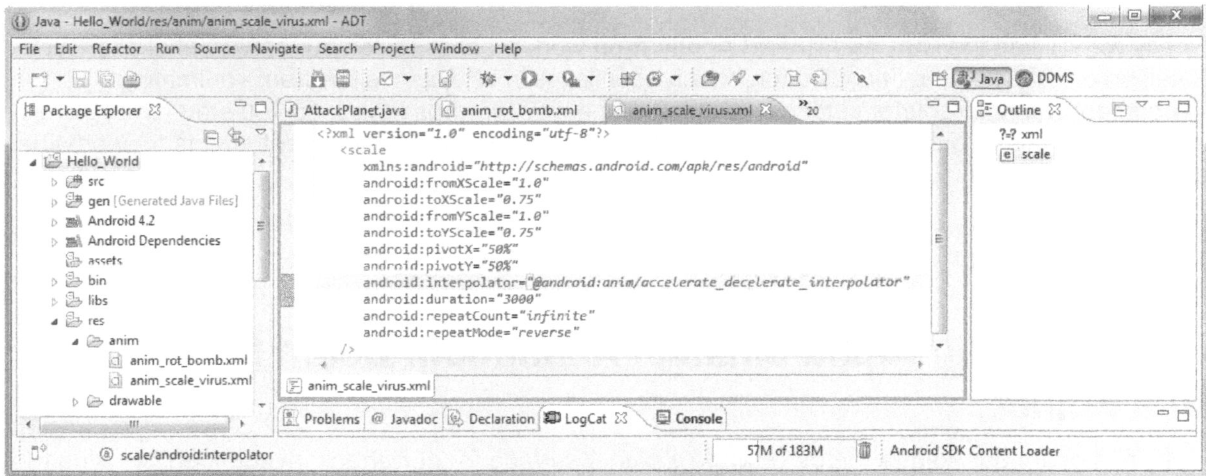

***Figure 10-6.** Configuring <scale> tag's scaling definition parameters for the anim_scale_virus.xml file in Eclipse*

Adding Java Code for the Scaling

Now it's time to implement the scale Animation object in our AttackPlanet Java code. Add a line of space under the infectButton ImageButton object declaration and copy the two lines of code above it, Animation rotateBomb and bombButton.startAnimation() and paste them into that space.

Next change the Animation name to **scaleVirus** and set the infectButton startAnimation() method to call this scaleVirus Animation object, using the following two lines of Java code:

```
Animation scaleVirus = AnimationUtils.loadAnimation(this, R.anim.anim_scale_virus);
infectButton.startAnimation(scaleVirus);
```

This Java code implementing the scaleVirus is shown in Figure 10-7.

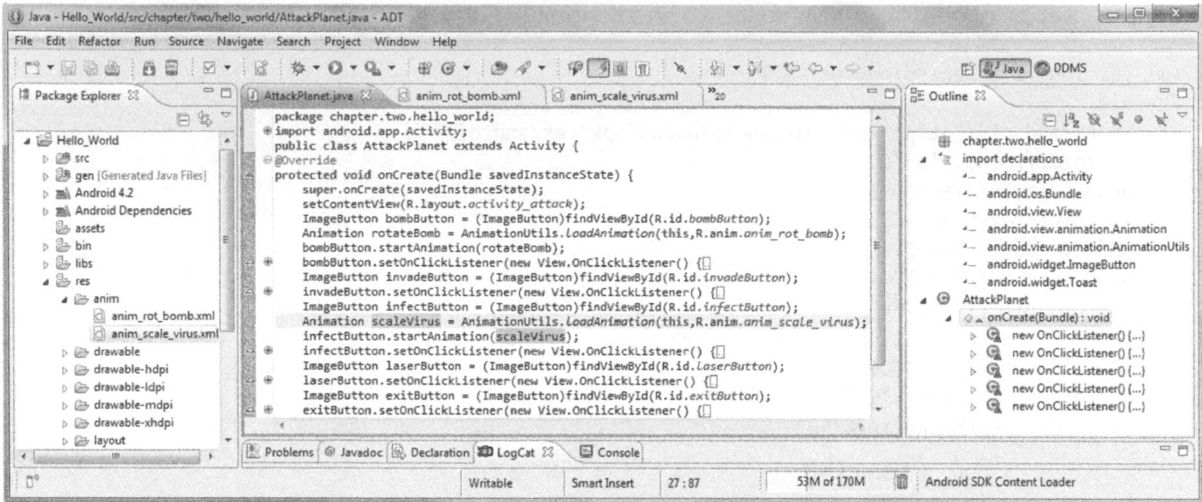

Figure 10-7. Adding an Animation object named scaleVirus and assigning it to infectButton via .startAnimation()

Finally we will use the **Run As Android Application** work process to see our new level of animation detail on our attack virus ImageButton, which now flexes in size, as well as frame animating. Experiment with interpolator settings and change the way the virus flexes, so you start to familiarize yourself with the 13 different interpolator constants in Android, and the different effects they provide on the motion curves within your animation.

Next, we will animate the alpha channel for our soldier, so that we can beam him down to the planet surface to properly invade the planet.

Implementing Alpha Channel Animation: Beam Me Over to a Planet

Next let's beam our soldier forces down to a planet surface for our attack invade icon by using the **<alpha>** root element shown in the Tween Animation XML dialog, which is shown in Figure 10-1. Right-click on your Hello_World project folder, and select the **New ➤ Android XML File** dialog, and name the new XML file: **anim_alpha_invade**, after selecting: **Tween Animation** from the Resource Type: drop-down menu and setting the **Hello_World** project and then selecting the <**alpha> root element**.

Completing the Alpha Tag

Once you set everything, and click the **Finish** button, you will get the open XML file in Eclipse, and you can set up your <alpha> tag. Just like we did before for the <rotate> and <scale> tags, let's set up the tag to take our parameters by splitting the tag into **<alpha** and **/>** components, and adding your **xmlns:android** parameter and URL, as shown in Figure 10-8. Then, to see what parameters the <alpha> tag provides us, type in **android:** and pop up the parameter helper dialog.

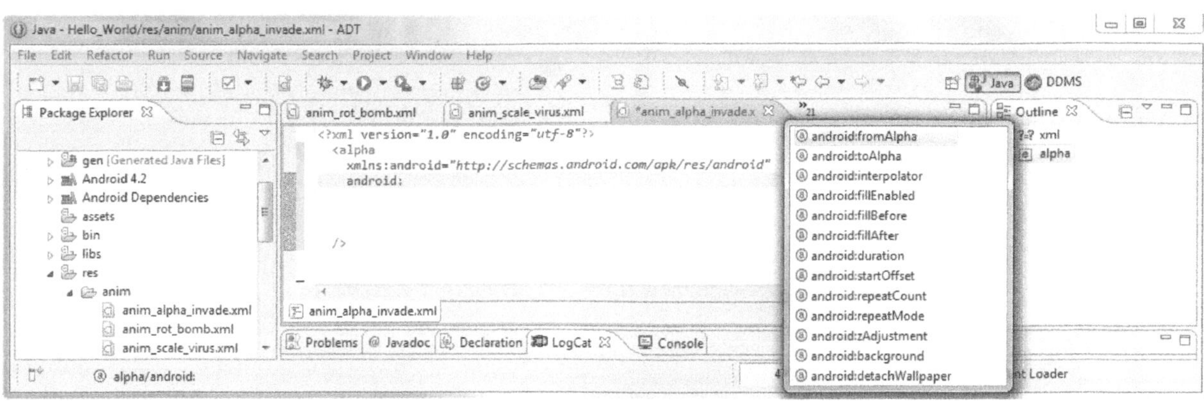

***Figure 10-8.** Creating our anim_alpha_invade.xml and android: parameter helper dialog with <alpha> parameters*

The first alpha parameter that we want to add is the **android:fromAlpha** parameter, which takes an integer value between 1 (100%, or opaque) and 0 (0%, or completely transparent). Because we want to animate our soldier visibility from opaque to transparent, we'll set the initial value to **1.0**.

Next, we'll add the **android:toAlpha** parameter, which specifies what alpha value we want to animate to. We will set this to 0, which indicates fully transparent, just like a **#AARRGGBB** setting of 0 does in the A channel.

Next, we need to specify a method of frame motion interpolation, using the now familiar **android:interpolator** parameter, which we will also set to the **accelerate_decelerate** setting, to achieve a realistic fade-out transporter effect. If you like, you can play around with some of the other 12 motion curve constant settings to better familiarize yourself with them.

Next, let's set the **android:duration** parameter to **4000** milliseconds (or 4 seconds), to give us a nice slow fade-out. Since we don't want the soldier fading in and out constantly, we're going to try out a new parameter, the **android:startOffset** parameter, set to **5000** milliseconds, to add in a five second delay on each animation cycle, so that the soldier remains visible (solid), for more time than he is transparent (transported to the planet). You can set these two parameters to taste, to fine-tune the effect timing.

Next, we set our alpha channel animation **repeat** parameters, with the **android:repeatCount** again set to **infinite**, and the **android:repeatMode** set to **reverse**, so that the soldier fades back in (return from the planet) in much the same way that he faded out, as shown in the following mark-up:

```
<?xml version="1.0" encoding="utf-8"?>
  <alpha
    xmlns:android="http://schemas.android.com/apk/res/android"
    android:fromAlpha="1.0"
    android:toAlpha="0.0"
    android:interpolator="@android:anim/accelerate_decelerate_interpolator"
    android:duration="4000"
    android:startOffset="5000"
    android:repeatCount="infinite"
    android:repeatMode="reverse"
  />
```

This is also shown in the Eclipse IDE code editor in Figure 10-9.

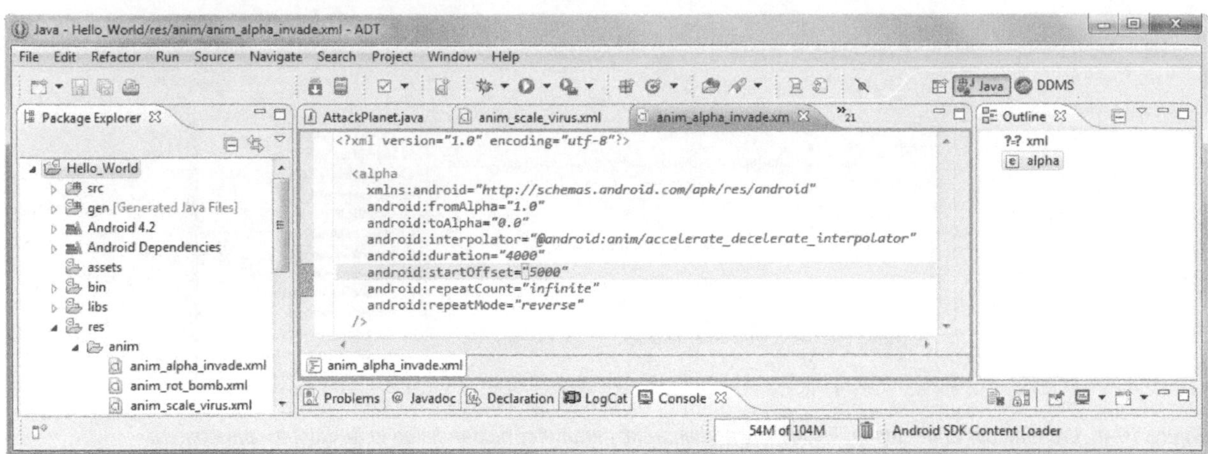

Figure 10-9. Configuring <alpha> tag's alpha fade definition parameters for anim_alpha_invade.xml file in Eclipse

Adding Java Code for the Alpha Animation

Now it's time to add in your Java code that creates the needed **alphaInvade** Animation object and wires it up to the invadeButton via a .startAnimation method. This is done via the following line of code:

```
Animation alphaInvade = AnimationUtils.loadAnimation(this, R.anim.anim_alpha_invade);
```

As we have seen before, this dense line of Java code declares an **Animation** object, names it **alphaInvade**, and then loads it with our **anim_alpha_invade** XML <alpha> animation definition via a call to the **.loadAnimation()** method that is accessed off the **AnimationUtils** object using dot notation.

Now all we have to do is to wire the alphaInvade Animation object into the invadeButton UI object via the **.startAnimation()** method, which is now done using the following simple but powerful line of Java programming code:

```
invadeButton.startAnimation(alphaInvade);
```

Note that you could have also done all this coding by using a copy and paste operation on the two lines of code we already wrote for one of the other attack icon UI elements and Animation object calls above this one.

Now that all our XML mark-up has been assimilated into our Java coding, as shown in Figure 10-10, it is time to use our **Run As Android Application** work process, and see our attack soldier fade into space and come back.

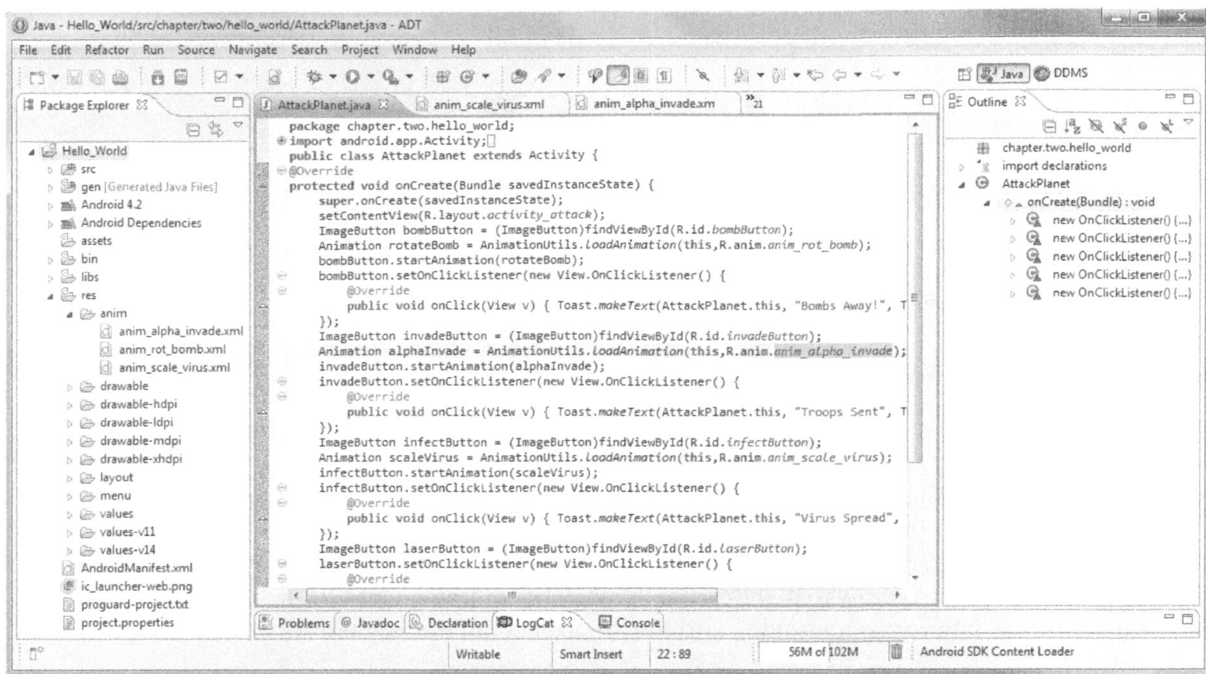

***Figure 10-10.** Adding Animation object named alphaInvade, and assigning it to invadeButton via .startAnimation()*

Although this is pretty cool in and of itself, I'm not satisfied with it, because what's a transporter beam effect, without the beam part? So we need to take this effect to the next level, which means doing what we did with our attack virus by combining both bitmap (frame or raster) and procedural (vector or code-based) animation together to create a more robust effect.

Combining Bitmap and Procedural Animation

To produce a convincing animation (one where the repeating or looping part cannot be easily noticed by the viewer) we need to use about a dozen frame bitmaps which I named beam64frame0.png through beam64frame11.png and also optimized to PNG8 indexed color so that all 48 resolution DPI version frames total only 190KB or an average of less than 4KB per frame.

We left an alpha channel on both sides of the animation, so that the beams animation can play behind the soldier (optimally inside a background layer of the ImageButton UI element) and not show through the alpha channel (the transparent areas) of the soldier image, which will be held inside the foreground layer (android:src). In this way, when we alpha-fade out the image of the soldier, this beams animation special effect shows, both as part of the soldier fade-out process, and as its own effect once the soldier image is gone (and while the soldier image is not there).

The first thing we need to do is to copy all our four dozen beam frame animation assets into their proper /res/drawable-dpi/ project folders, as shown in Figure 10-11.

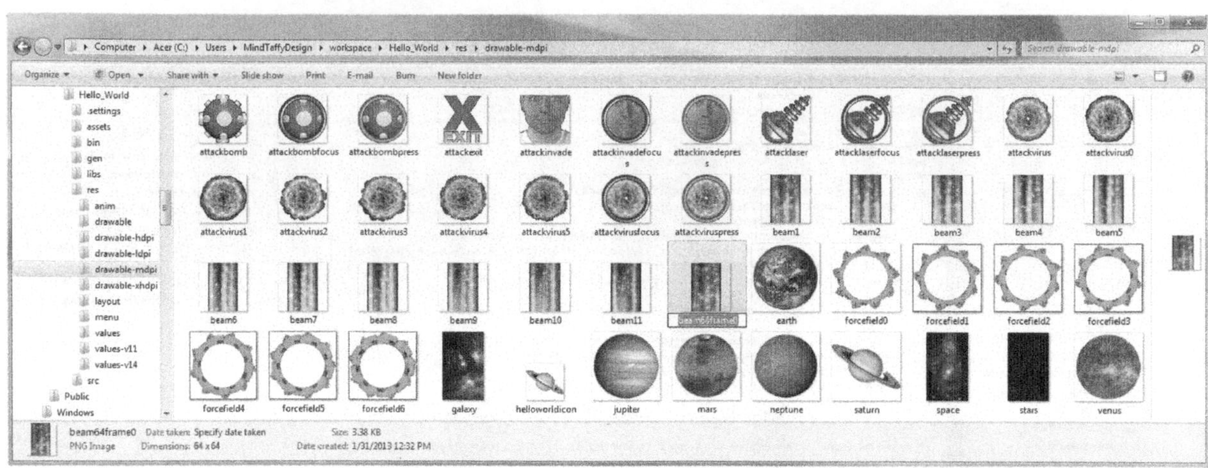

Figure 10-11. *Copying our transporter special effect animation frames into our drawable-dpi folder and renaming*

This work process should be familiar to you by now, so let's get a bit more practice at it, and copy your 96 pixel frames into /drawable-xhdpi, the 80 pixel beam frames into /drawable-hdpi, the 64 pixel beam frames into /drawable-mdpi, and the 48 pixel beam frames into /drawable-ldpi.

Next we will rename these files to be **beam0.png** through **beam11.png** so we have a simpler filename to reference in our XML. We do this by removing the resolution indicator number and the word frame for each of the 48 files (12 in each of the resolution density folders).

Next, we need to right-click the project resource drawable folder, and use our New > Android XML File helper dialog work process shown earlier in the chapter in Figure 10-1, as well as in Chapter 9, in Figure 9-1. Don't forget to use the F5 or Refresh work process once you have added these files outside of the Eclipse environment, so that your project can "see" them.

Set your **Resource Type:** to **Drawable**, and then select the **Root Element:** of **<animation-list>**, and finally, name the file **anim_effect_beam**, as that is what it is going to be, an animation effect named beam, and click **Finish**.

Next, add the frames for this transporter beam effect to the XML file that is created for us.

Configuring the Animation in XML

We want the effect to be seamless so we are going to use a pong animation effect and bounce back and forth between frame zero and frame 11, so frames 1 through 10 will all be used twice in the XML code.

Note that we are not duplicating frames zero or eleven as this would cause a pause in the animation, and give away its frame boundaries to the viewer by a playback hesitation during the seamless animation loop. We want to utilize a fairly slow **frame rate** of **8 FPS** to get a slow shimmering effect, and since 8 divides into 1000 a total of 125 times, our android:duration value will be 125 milliseconds, denoted in XML as **android:duration="125"**.

The XML mark-up for one of the <item> tags is shown here. All 22 <item> tag lines of XML mark-up will follow the same format as the following:

```
<item android:drawable="@drawable/beam0" android:duration="125" />
```

The XML code that configures our beam animation frame access and order is shown in Figure 10-12. We start with beam0, and go through beam11 and then back down to beam1, using an 8 FPS setting for each. This set-up gives us a nice, even, seamless transporter beam pong animation special effect.

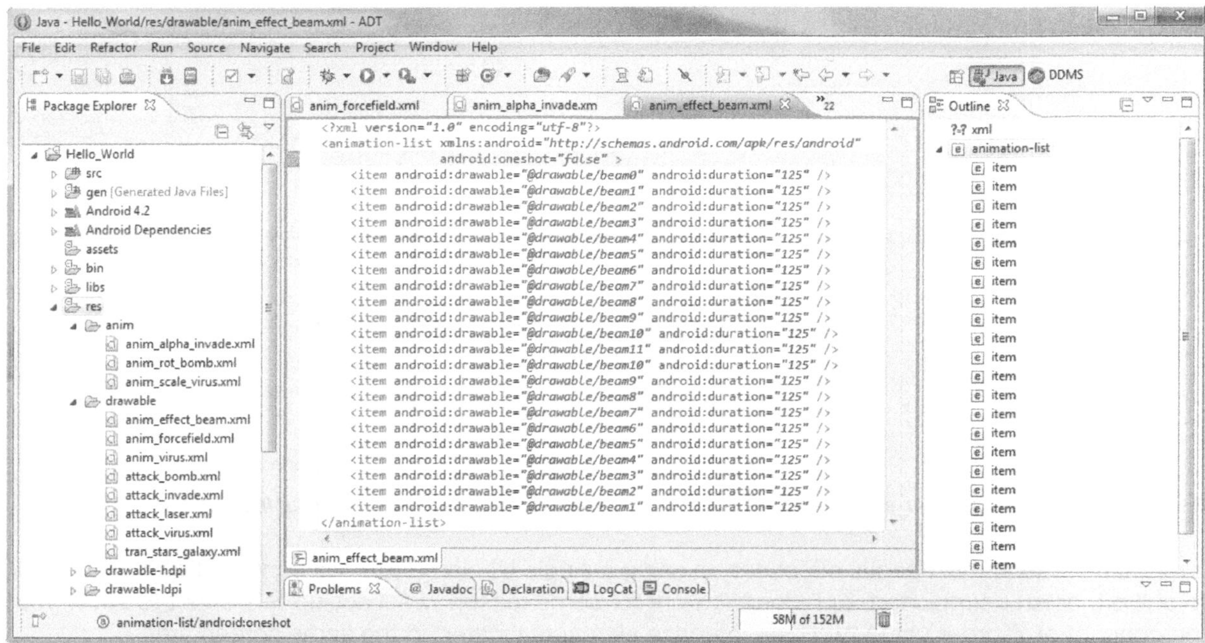

Figure 10-12. ***Adding transporter beam special effect frames in a pong configuration to anim_effect_beam.xml***

Next, we need to reference the anim_effect_beam.xml file, via the first part of its name in the **android:background** parameter of our attack invade ImageButton, so that it animates behind the foreground source image inside that UI element. Because we have crafted our alpha channels carefully, the background effect will only be visible when the foreground image fades out, as well as during the fade created by the <alpha>. This creates a transporting effect that we are looking for, by combining these two key types of animation in Android, along with a minimal amount of digital image assets.

Remember that the foreground source image is actually a multi-state image XML definition file that we named **attack_invade.xml**, referenced inside of the **android:src** parameter. This shows that we're waxing pretty complicated here, using an XML-based frame animation compositing special effect in our UI element background plate, along with XML-based multi-state image button definitions in our UI element foreground plate, as shown in Figure 10-13. Here is the XML mark-up for the invadeButton that is shown in the figure:

```
<ImageButton
  android:id="@+id/invadeButton"
  android:background="@drawable/anim_effect_beam"
  android:layout_width="wrap_content"
  android:layout_height="wrap_content"
  android:contentDescription="@string/content_desc_invade"
  android:layout_margin="8dp"
  android:src="@drawable/attack_invade" />
```

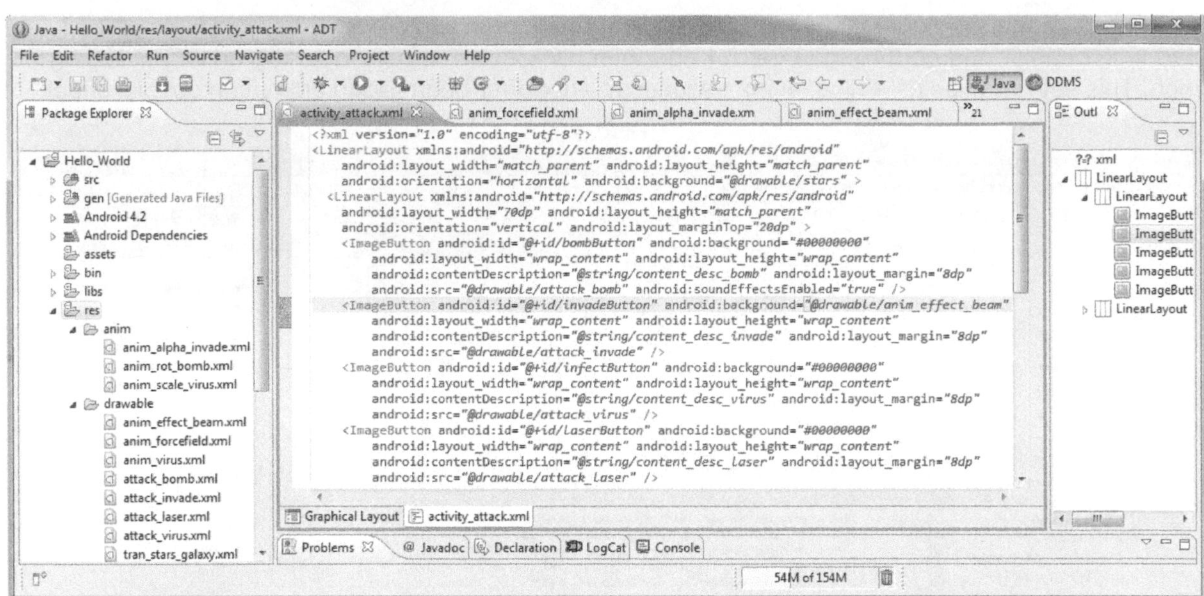

Figure 10-13. Inserting an anim_effect_beam reference into the android:background element of our ImageButton

If for some reason this special effect set-up using a single UI element is too complicated for Android to pull off, or isn't supported, or it doesn't work for some reason, we'll set-up this effect to show you the concept of Z-order using two user interface elements located in the same screen area.

Let's take a look at our effect using the **Run As Android Application** work process. Once the application launches, click the menu button, and select the Attack a Planet Activity screen, and then watch the Invade icon.

Notice the soldier fades to black as before, but the background animation is not visible, so either it is not supported, or more likely, the alpha fade is being applied to the entire user interface element, and not just to its foreground image component.

Implementing a Background Behind a Fade

The next thing we should try is to use the **android:background** parameter, which is part of the <alpha> tag's parameters, shown in Figure 10-8. This parameter should allow us to implement a background behind our fade, so add this parameter to the parameters we show in Figure 10-9, and set it to reference the anim_effect_beam and remove the android:background parameter from the ImageButton tag parameters shown in Figure 10-13.

Use the **Run As Android Application** work process again, and test the effect yet again in the Attack a Planet Activity screen. Because the background effect does not remain after the soldier fades out, we will need to implement it via a separate UI element, an ImageView, which is used to hold images for just such a purpose.

Add an ImageView tag before the invadeButton ImageButton tag and set it to an **android:id** of **invadeEffect** and set its **android:background** parameter to the **anim_effect_beam** to reference our frame animation special effect. Be sure to add the **android:layout_width** and **android:layout_height** parameters set to **wrap content** and the **android:layout_marginLeft** set to **8dp** to align.

The 8dp left margin pushes your background image into place behind the invadeButton UI element, so the effect lines up with the soldier. Be sure and include an **android:contentDescription** parameter set to reference the **@string/content_desc_invade** constant, or Eclipse will give you a warning.

Once you have added this ImageView tag between the first two ImageButtons, we must change and add a couple of parameters in our invadeButton, because a LinearLayout, as you might remember, lines things up in rows or columns, and for this reason, this ImageView will push our ImageButton UI elements down one notch each, unless we make parameter changes to adjust for this.

The alternate option to these UI parameter changes is to recode the entire screen layout container as a **RelativeLayout** container, which, as you will soon see in the next section, makes Z-ordering alpha channel compatible UI elements much easier. For now, we'll do this the easier of the two ways.

The most critical thing that we need to adjust is the pixel spacing of the invade icon ImageButton, so it covers up the invadeEffect ImageView. We do this so our transporter effect plays behind our multi-state ImageButton.

Remove the **android:layout_margin="8dp"** that had put 8dp of pixel spacing around our button, and add an **android:layout_marginLeft="8dp"** that pushes the ImageButton out from the side of the screen, lining it up with those other ImageButton icons.

Next, add an **android:layout_marginTop** parameter, set to –54,–yes, that's **negative** fifty-four as shown in Figure 10-14. This pushes our invade icon ImageButton up and over the top of our invadeEffect ImageView, which contains our transporter beam special effect animation. Here is what the XML mark-up will look like for this <ImageButton> tag at this point:

```
<ImageButton
  android:id="@+id/invadeButton"
  android:background="#00000000"
  android:layout_marginTop="-54dp"
  android:layout_width="wrap_content"
  android:layout_height="wrap_content"
  android:src="@drawable/attack_invade"
  android:contentDescription="@string/content_desc_invade"
  android:layout_marginLeft="8dp" />
```

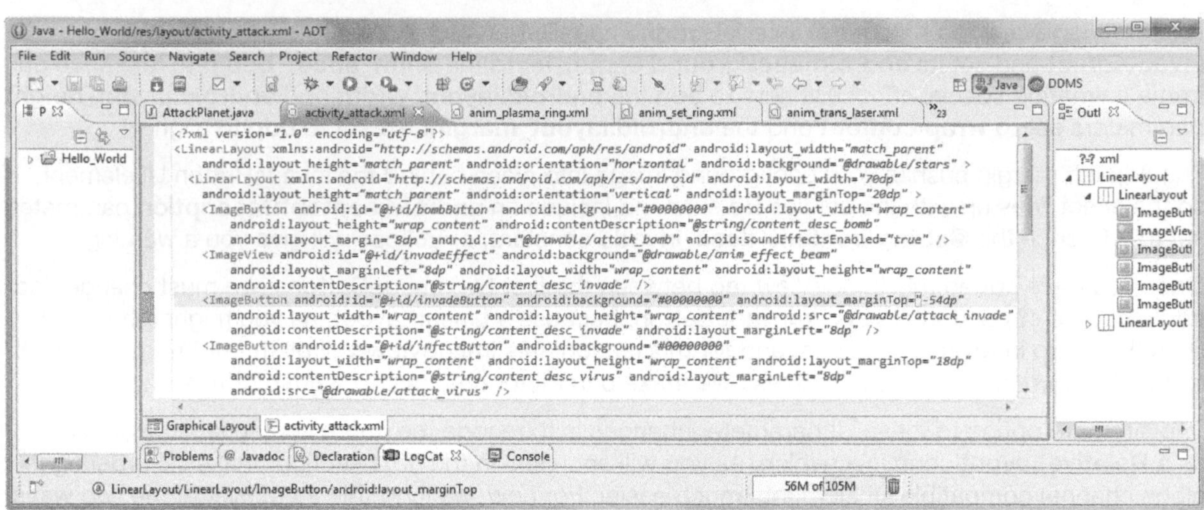

***Figure 10-14.** Adding an ImageView UI element to our activity_attack.xml to hold our transporter beam effect*

The final Eclipse editing pane content for the new <ImageButton> XML mark-up is shown in Figure 10-14.

To pull the rest of the ImageButton icons up, and back into place, remove the android:layout_margin="8dp" from the infectButton ImageButton tag just below the invadeButton and add an **android:layout_MarginTop="18dp"**, to space the other icons back down, and an **android:layout_marginLeft="8dp"** as well.

Adding Java Code for the Animation

Now it's time to implement the ImageView object and the AnimationDrawable object in our Java code, so that we can implement our transporter effect.

Declare an ImageView object named **invadeEffect**, and set it equal to the invadeEffect UI tag defined in our XML file, by using the **findViewById()** method, using the following line of Java code, as shown in Figure 10-15:

```
ImageView invadeEffect = (ImageView)findViewById(R.id.invadeEffect);
```

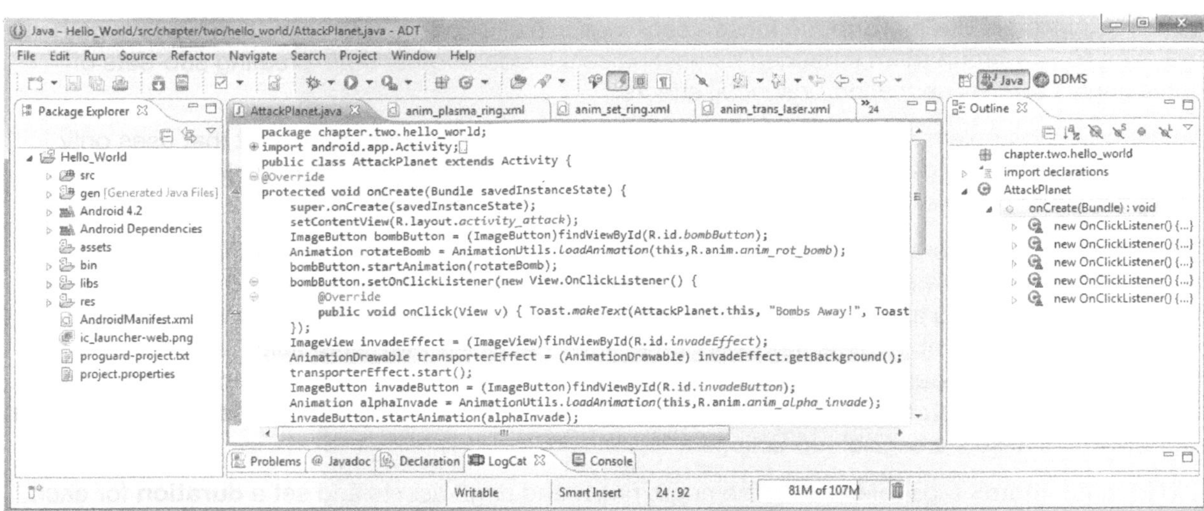

***Figure 10-15.** Adding the invadeEffect ImageView and transporterEffect AnimationDrawable to AttackPlanet.java*

Then declare an **AnimationDrawable** object named **transporterEffect** using the **.getbackground()** method by using the following line of Java code:

```
AnimationDrawable transporterEffect = (AnimationDrawable) invadeEffect.getBackground();
```

Next, call the **.start()** method for the **transporterEffect** AnimationDrawable object by using the following line of Java code:

```
transporterEffect.start();
```

Now we are ready to see our final effect implemented in our application, by using the **Run As Android Application** work process. Fire up the Nexus S emulator, and click the menu button, and select the Attack a Planet menu selection that takes you to our Activity screen.

As you can see, when our soldier now fades out, via our <alpha> procedural animation there is a transporter beam frame animation that is incorporated into this special effect, making it a much more realistic transporter beam space travel effect.

Note that we accomplished this using only 190KB of total assets along with a few lines of Java code and a couple dozen lines of XML mark-up. If we had to do this effect via digital video or frame animation alone, it would have taken ten times more data footprint to pull off with similar quality.

Implementing Complex Animation: XML <set> Parameter Grouping

The next thing we're going to do is to create a **complex animation** by using rotate, scale, and alpha tags together, in a single **animation set**. This is done using the **<set>** tag, as you might have guessed, since you've already seen this <set> root element option in several screen shots before.

An animation set is like a **group**, so these <set> tags allows you to group ani[illegible] and even to sub-group them if needed by nesting sets inside of other sets, cr[illegible] increasingly complex animation or special effects.

We are going to implement a much simpler forcefield animation around our p[illegible] three frames of 2D image animation and then rotate, scale, and fade this ras[illegible] produce a more complex and data compact planet forcefield effect.

To do this, we must first copy and rename the ring320frame0.png through ri[illegible] (and other resolution density versions) into the drawable-dpi folders, and re[illegible] through ring2.png using the usual work process shown in Figure 10-11. After [illegible] right-click on the drawable folder, and select the **New > Android XML File** [illegible] **Drawable** XML container with an **<animation-list>** root element, and name [illegible] and finally hit the **Finish** button. Don't forget to utilize the F5 or Refresh wo[illegible] your drawable assets are visible to Eclipse.

Add in three **<item>** tags referencing the ring0, ring1, and ring2 assets an[illegible] of **166** milliseconds, which animates your forcefield ring twice each second [illegible] Each <item> tag that you add should have the following XML mark-up for[illegible]

```
<item android:drawable="@drawable/ring0" android:duration="166" />
```

The final XML mark-up is shown in the Eclipse XML editing pane in Figure 10-16.

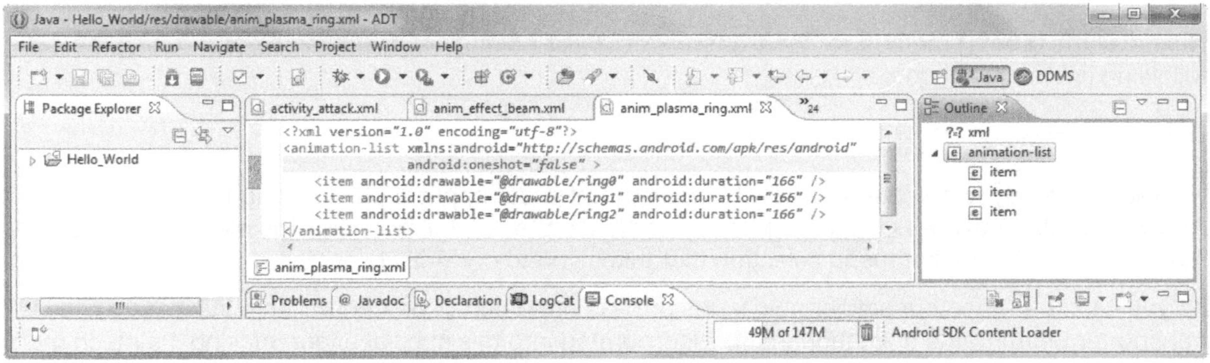

***Figure 10-16.** Creating an anim_plasma_ring frame animation XML definition for use with our complex animation*

Then go into your **activity_main.xml** file, and change your ImageView tag android:background parameter to reference @drawable/anim_plasma_ring as shown in the following XML mark-up:

```
<ImageView
  android:id="@+id/imageEarth"
  android:src="@drawable/earth"
  android:padding="24dp"
  android:background="@drawable/anim_plasma_ring"
  android:layout_width="wrap_content"
  android:layout_height="wrap_content"
  android:layout_below="@+id/textView8"
  android:contentDescription="@string/content_desc_invade" />
```

This is shown in Figure 10-17, and once you change your XML mark-up to include the new android:background parameter referencing your new anim_plasma_ring drawable, we will be ready to implement our animation set, which will further rotate your background as it animates, and scale it in and out around the planet, while the entire animation fades in and out slightly.

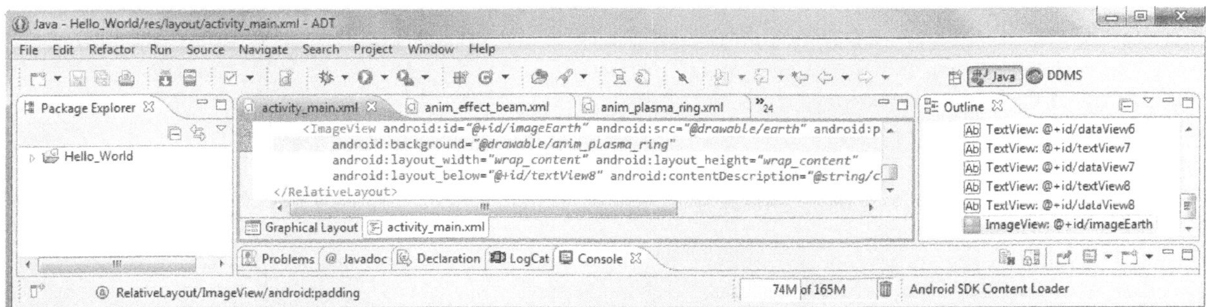

***Figure 10-17.** Referencing the new anim_plasma_ring frame animation in our activity_main.xml file ImageView*

Now we can right-click the drawable folder and select our New ➤ Android XML File menu sequence and create a **Tween Animation** XML Resource Type, and name it **anim_set_ring** and then select the **<set>** root element and click the **Finish** button as shown in Figure 10-18.

New Android XML File

New Android XML File

Creates a new Android XML file.

Resource Type: Tween Animation

Project: Hello_World

File: anim_set_ring

Root Element:

alpha
rotate
scale
set
translate

< Back | Next > | Finish | Cancel

***Figure 10-18.** Creating an anim_set_ring <set> complex animation structure using the New Android XML File dialog*

Configuring the Set Tag

Next, go into the empty <set> animation file, and type the **<** character as shown in Figure 10-19. This brings up the **tag selector dialog**, and we can then select the **<rotate>** tag for its inclusion in our animation <set>, since we will set-up our rotational animation parameters first. Order does not matter as a <set> serves to group the animations together so that they are processed in **parallel**, or all at the same time as each other, and not in order, which would be called **serial** animation (or one after the other).

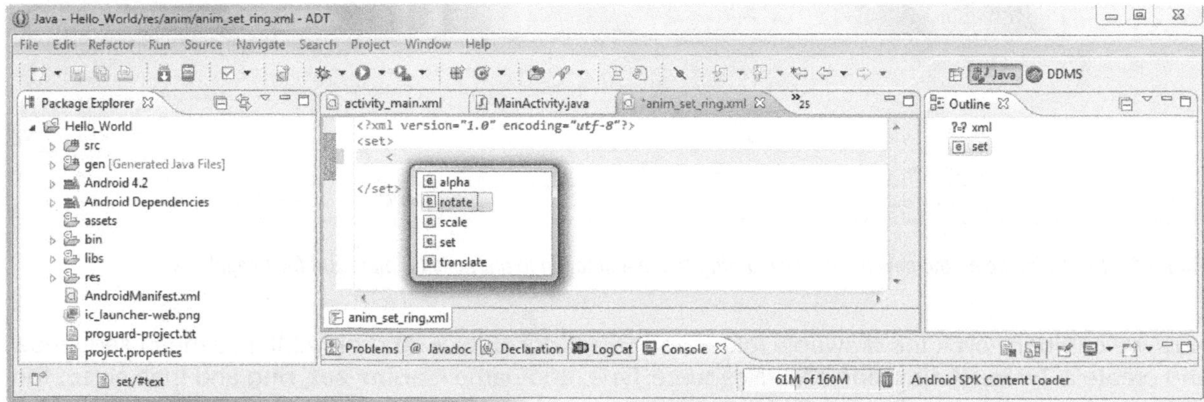

***Figure 10-19.** Adding a <rotate> child tag to our <set> parent tag using the helper dialog accessed via the < key*

Be sure and add the **xmlns:android** parameter to your <set> tag to reference the `http://schemas.android.com/apk/res/android` URL, so that all these tags and parameters that we put inside of our <set> tag validate and do not **throw** Red-X errors inside of the Eclipse XML editing pane.

Let's set our rotation **android:fromDegrees** parameter to **0 (zero)**, and set our **android:toDegrees** parameter to **360**, so we get a seamless ring rotation.

Next let's set our **android:pivotX** and **android:pivotY** parameters to **50%** to center our rotation in the center of the animated ring element. We will use a nice even linear interpolation since we are looping the animation, and a slow duration of 10,000 milliseconds, or 10 seconds total rotation.

For our repeat parameters, we will use the **android:repeatCount="infinite"** and the **android:repeatMode="restart"** parameters so that we can achieve a seamless loop that continues forever.

We can turn this forcefield effect on and off using **visibility** parameters later on in our Java code, so we want our forcefield to animate forever, as far as all these animation set parameters are concerned. The XML mark-up for the <rotate> tag inside of the parent <set> tag should look like the following:

```
<?xml version="1.0" encoding="utf-8"?>
<set xmlns:android="http://schemas.android.com/apk/res/android">
  <rotate android:fromDegrees="0"
          android:toDegrees="360"
          android:pivotX="50%"
          android:pivotY="50%"
          android:interpolator="@android:anim/linear_interpolator"
```

```
        android:duration="10000"
        android:repeatCount="infinite"
        android:repeatMode="restart"  />
</set>
```

You can see our completed <rotate> tag parameters shown in Figure 10-20.

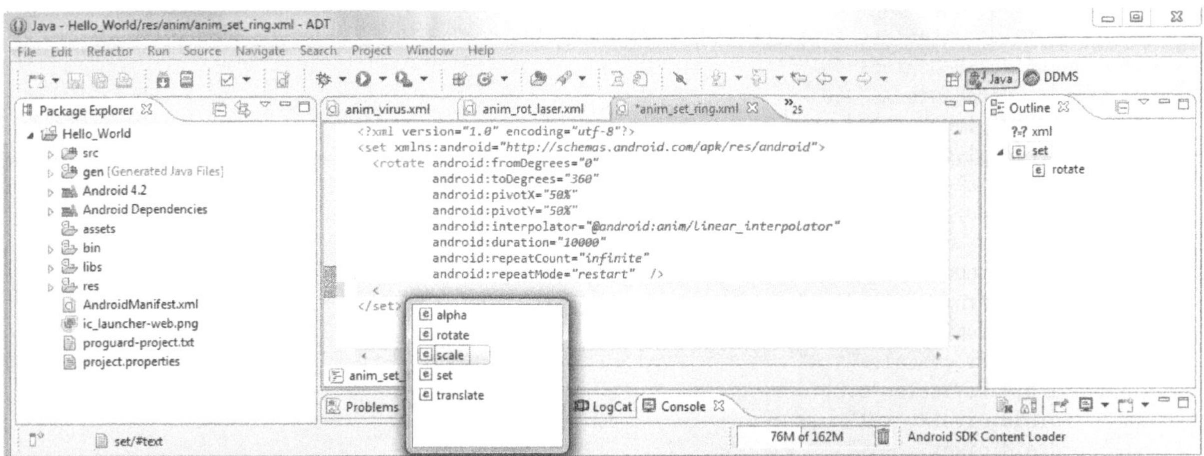

***Figure 10-20.** Adding a <scale> child tag to our <set> parent tag using the helper dialog accessed via the < key*

As you can see in Figure 10-20, we have again utilized the **<** key to bring up the tag selector dialog, and we are now selecting a **<scale>** tag to add in our scaling parameters to add image scaling this complex animation set.

Adding Image Scaling

We will start with the most important **android:fromXScale="1.0"**, or, full scale (original bitmap graphics elements pixel dimension), and scale down to an **android:toXScale="0.75"** or three-quarters of original size scaling.

Because we want a **uniform** (aspect ratio maintained) scaling, we will use the same parameters for the **android:fromYScale** and **android:toYScale** parameters as well. As we learned previously in the book, aspect ratio is maintained, and spacial distortion is reduced, by scaling an image or animation frames by an equal amount on both of our X and Y axes or dimension (H & W sides).

Since we want to scale the forcefield ring evenly in and out, we set our **android:pivotX** and **android:pivotY** parameters to a value of 50%, which puts the scaling origin directly in the center of the bitmap image (or in this case, a frame-based raster animation) that we are scaling down and then back up again using the next four parameters that we're going to add.

Because we want to scale smoothly and evenly, we want to add a linear interpolator via the **android:interpolator="@android:anim/linear_interpolator"** parameter. To get a slow scaling effect, we set our **android:duration** parameter to **10,000 milliseconds** (10 seconds) to obtain a more realistic effect.

Finally we set our repeat parameters to define how our scaling will perform over time. We want the effect to continue forever, so we set the **android:repeatCount** parameter to **infinite**. Because we want the scaling effect to pulsate slowly in and out around each planet, we set the **android:repeatMode** to **reverse**, so that the scaling reverses itself.

The XML mark-up so far should look like the tags and parameters shown here:

```
<?xml version="1.0" encoding="utf-8"?>
<set xmlns:android="http://schemas.android.com/apk/res/android">
  <rotate android:fromDegrees="0"
          android:toDegrees="360"
          android:pivotX="50%"
          android:pivotY="50%"
          android:interpolator="@android:anim/linear_interpolator"
          android:duration="10000"
          android:repeatCount="infinite"
          android:repeatMode="restart"  />
  <scale  android:fromXScale="1.0"
          android:toXScale="0.8"
          android:fromYScale="1.0"
          android:toYScale="0.8"
          android:pivotX="50%"
          android:pivotY="50%"
          android:interpolator="@android:anim/linear_interpolator"
          android:duration="10000"
          android:repeatCount="infinite"
          android:repeatMode="reverse"  />
</set>
```

The final scale tag is shown in Figure 10-21.

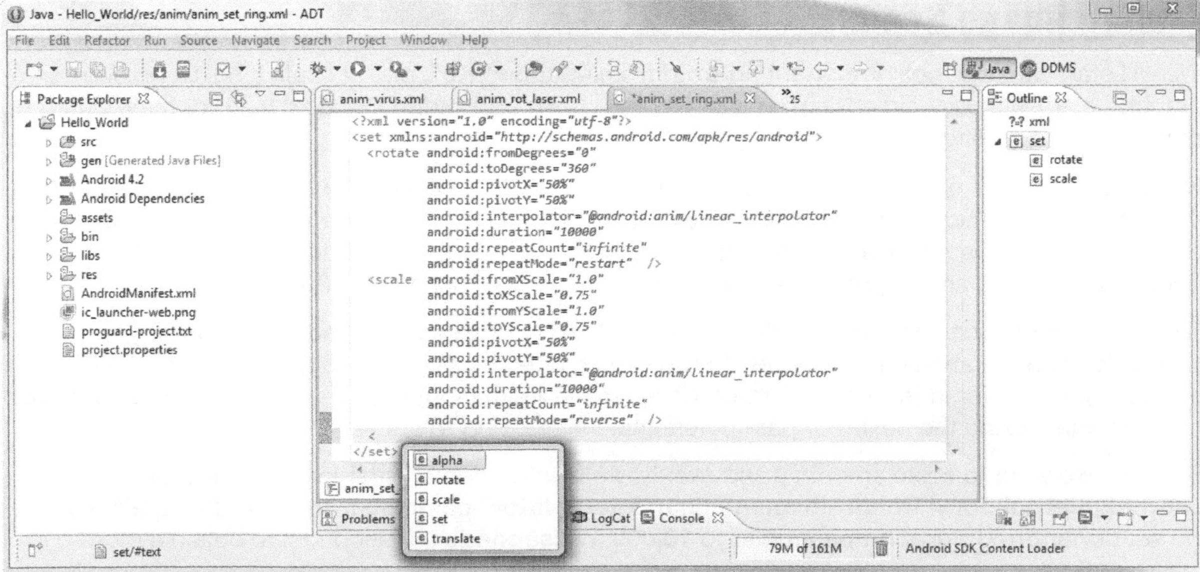

***Figure 10-21.** Adding an <alpha> child tag to our <set> parent tag using the helper dialog accessed via the < key*

Finally, we add our **<alpha>** procedural animation tag using the **<** key, as shown in Figure 10-21, along with our completed <scale> tag parameters.

Adding an Alpha Procedural Animation

The <alpha> tag has the fewest total parameters, as it is just controlling a fade effect, in this case from 100% opaque to 50% transparent or halfway there, to show some of the stars or galaxy background imagery. Since forcefields are usually somewhat transparent, why break with convention!

Start by using the **android:fromAlpha** parameter, to set our source imagery (or animation in this case) transparency level to 100% by using a value of **1.0**. Next use the **android:toAlpha** set to a value of **0.5** or 50% transparent to get a realistic translucency effect for our forcefield ring animation.

Next let's set our **android:interpolator** parameter to **linear**, to give us a nice smooth even linear interpolation for our fade (blend) alpha values. This is a parameter that you could probably play around with interpolator constants with and try to get a more dynamic transparency changing effect.

Because we want to match the duration of this effect to the other two scale and rotation effects, we will use an **android:duration** parameter and set it to **10000** milliseconds. Again, since a fading effect does not need to sync as closely with the rotate and scale effects, you could also play around with this numeric value, to get a more realistic forcefield pulse effect.

Finally we set our repeat parameters, setting the **android:repeatCount** parameter to **infinite** and the **android:repeatMode** parameter to **reverse**, so that this fade-out turns around and becomes a fade-in after it gets to the end of the animation cycle. The XML markup should look like the following:

```
<?xml version="1.0" encoding="utf-8"?>
<set xmlns:android="http://schemas.android.com/apk/res/android">
  <rotate android:fromDegrees="0"
          android:toDegrees="360"
          android:pivotX="50%"
          android:pivotY="50%"
          android:interpolator="@android:anim/linear_interpolator"
          android:duration="10000"
          android:repeatCount="infinite"
          android:repeatMode="restart"  />
  <scale  android:fromXScale="1.0"
          android:toXScale="0.8"
          android:fromYScale="1.0"
          android:toYScale="0.8"
          android:pivotX="50%"
          android:pivotY="50%"
          android:interpolator="@android:anim/linear_interpolator"
          android:duration="10000"
          android:repeatCount="infinite"
          android:repeatMode="reverse"  />
  <alpha  android:fromAlpha="1.0"
          android:toAlpha="0.5"
          android:interpolator="@android:anim/linear_interpolator"
```

```
        android:duration="10000"
        android:repeatCount="infinite"
        android:repeatMode="reverse"  />
</set>
```

The XML editing pane in Eclipse should look like the screen shown in Figure 10-22.

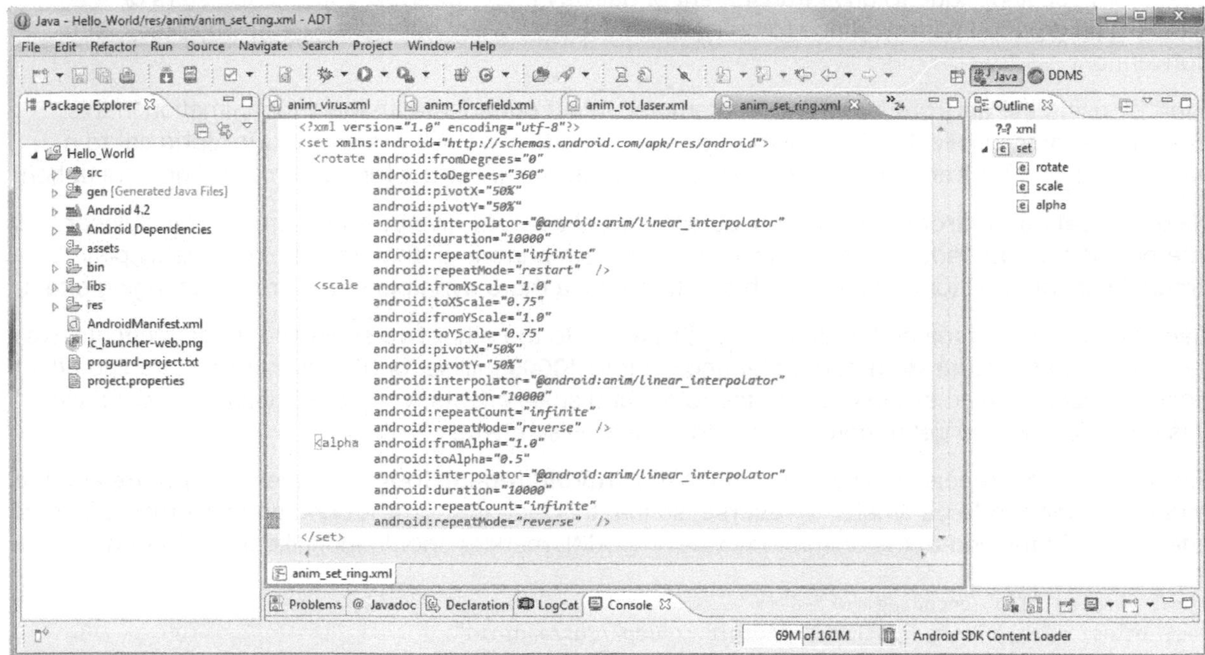

***Figure 10-22.** Completing our <set> parent tag containing complex animation parameters for rotate, scale, alpha*

Next, we need to implement this new forcefield animation into our Home Screen user interface screen via the current XML RelativeLayout container. We give this animated user interface element its own ImageView tag, using an **android:id** parameter set to **planetEffect**.

We are setting it up this way because if we apply this scale animation to our original imageEarth ImageView with the anim_plasma_ring.xml referenced as its background component, the entire UI element will be rotated, scaled, and blended, and in this case, we want the planet image to be left alone.

In fact we saw this same consideration in the previous section of the book where we needed to separate our procedural animation effect to process its own UI element container for much the same reasons.

Next, include the required **android:layout_height** and **android:layout_width** parameters, both set to **wrap_content**, and the **android:contentDescription** parameter, which is also required by Android for any image-related tag.

Next we'll add our relative positioning tag, **android:layout_below**, and we will reference the **@+id/textView8** that our imageEarth ImageView references as we want this planetEffect ImageView to be in the exact screen location that the imageEarth ImageView occupies. Also be sure that your

android:src parameter references the **@drawable/anim_plasma_ring** XML file that contains our <set> complex procedural animation definition. The XML mark-up looks like the following:

```
<ImageView
        android:id="@+id/planetEffect"
        android:src="@drawable/anim_plasma_ring"
        android:layout_width="wrap_content"
        android:layout_height="wrap_content"
        android:layout_below="@+id/textView8"
        android:contentDescription="@string/content_desc_earth"
/>
```

The final XML is shown in Figure 10-23.

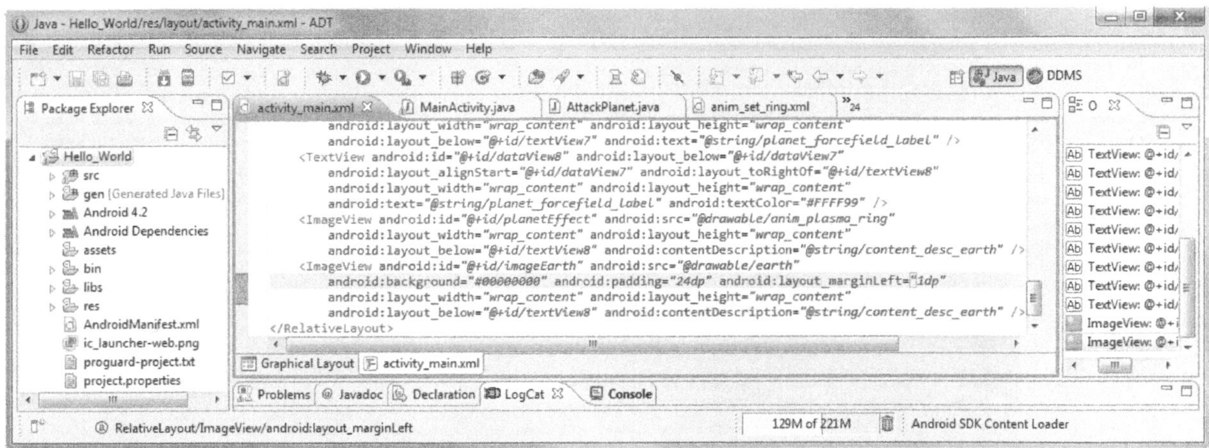

***Figure 10-23.** Add ImageView XML tag with an ID of planetEffect and anim_plasma_ring source reference*

Now let's adjust our imageEarth ImageView tag parameters to make sure that the planet imagery both lines up with, and composites with, our procedural animation contained inside the planetEffect ImageView UI element. Set your **android:padding** to **24dp** and fine-tune the centering of the planet image in the effect using your **android:layout_marginLeft** parameter set to **1dp**. Make sure the ImageView is transparent by using an **android:background** parameter set to **#00000000** as shown in the following XML mark-up:

```
<ImageView
        android:id="@+id/imageEarth"
        android:src="@drawable/earth"
        android:background="#00000000"
        android:padding="24dp"
        android:layout_marginLeft="1dp"
        android:layout_width="wrap_content"
        android:layout_height="wrap_content"
        android:layout_below="@+id/textView8"
        android:contentDescription="@string/content_desc_earth"
/>
```

The results are shown in Figure 10-23, and we'll be ready to write our Java code that implements these ImageView UI elements together to create a planet forcefield effect using only 200KB of digital image data footprint.

Adding Java Code for the Animation

Now all we have to do to implement this new forcefield animation scenario is to change our Java code to implement the new ImageView holding our forcefield ring animation and to remove the ImageView object that was holding the old forcefield animation, as shown in Figure 10-24.

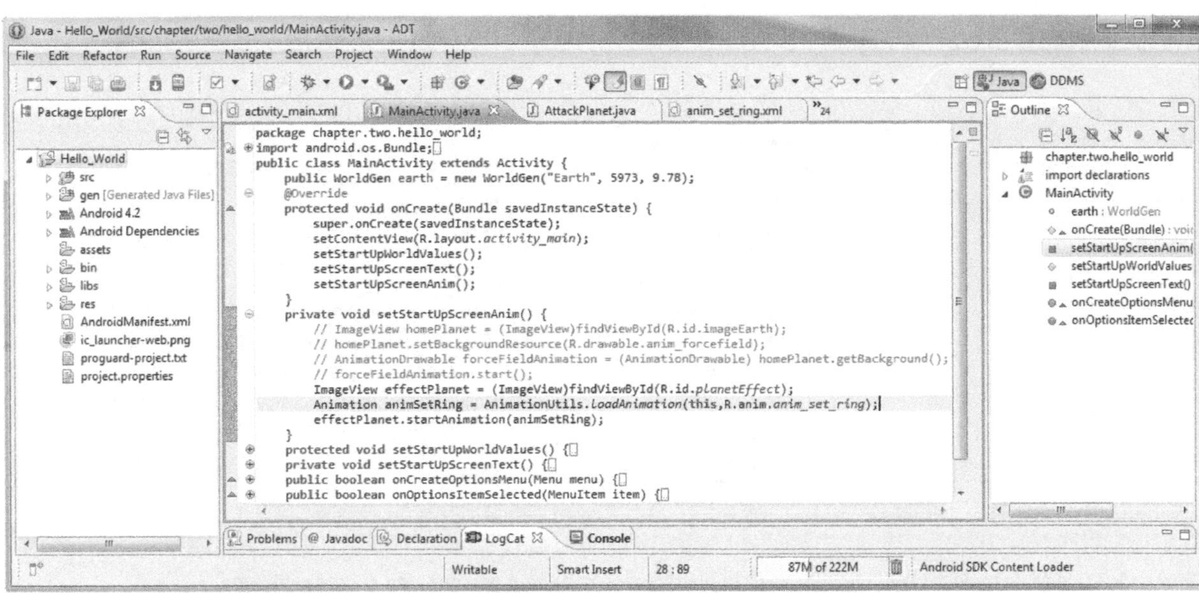

***Figure 10-24.** Add effectPlanet ImageView, set it to reference animSetRing Animation object via .startAnimation()*

As you can see in the old Java code in Figure 10-24, which I left by using the double-slash commenting feature, to eliminate these lines of code from consideration by the compiler, but to also remain for our own use (a handy use of this feature you may wish to consider using yourself) as a learning reference so that you can compare the before and after Java code scenario.

The first line of code is essentially the same as it was before; declaring the **effectPlanet** ImageView object and then setting it to an XML definition using the **findViewById()** method. The Java code should look as follows:

```
Imageview effectPlanet = (ImageView)findViewById(R.id.planetEffect);
```

The rest we get done in only two lines of code, one which declares the procedural animation object and another that wires it to the effectPlanet ImageView and starts the animation running.

To declare a procedural animation object we will use the Android **Animation** class, and instantiate an Animation object and name it in the same line of code that we utilize to load it with an XML animation definition using the **.loadAnimation()** method that is called off an **AnimationUtils** object by using dot notation. This can be done in one line of Java code, as follows:

```
Animation animSetRing = AnimationUtils.loadAnimation(this,R.anim.anim_set_ring);
```

What this is saying to the Android OS and compiler is: I'd like to create an Animation object named animSetRing and, in the current context, load it using the AnimationUtils class with the animation data that I have defined in the anim_set_ring.xml file. Once this is done, we start the animation.

The **.startAnimation()** method is called off the **effectPlanet** ImageView object, which we set-up two lines of Java code preceding, and is passed over an Animation object, that we also just created, using one short line of code:

```
effectPlanet.startAnimation(animSetRing);
```

Now it's time to see our new planetary forcefield in action. Right-click the project folder and use the **Run As Android Application** work process to launch the Hello World Android application in your Nexus S emulator.

Once the application is running, you can see the planet Earth ImageView at the bottom of the Home Screen along with the new forcefield animated user interface element, as shown in Figure 10-25. The forcefield animated user interface element is now animating between the three different image composite frames, as well as rotating, scaling, and fading all at the same time, using procedural animation XML mark-up that we have written to control dozens of attributes of this user interface element.

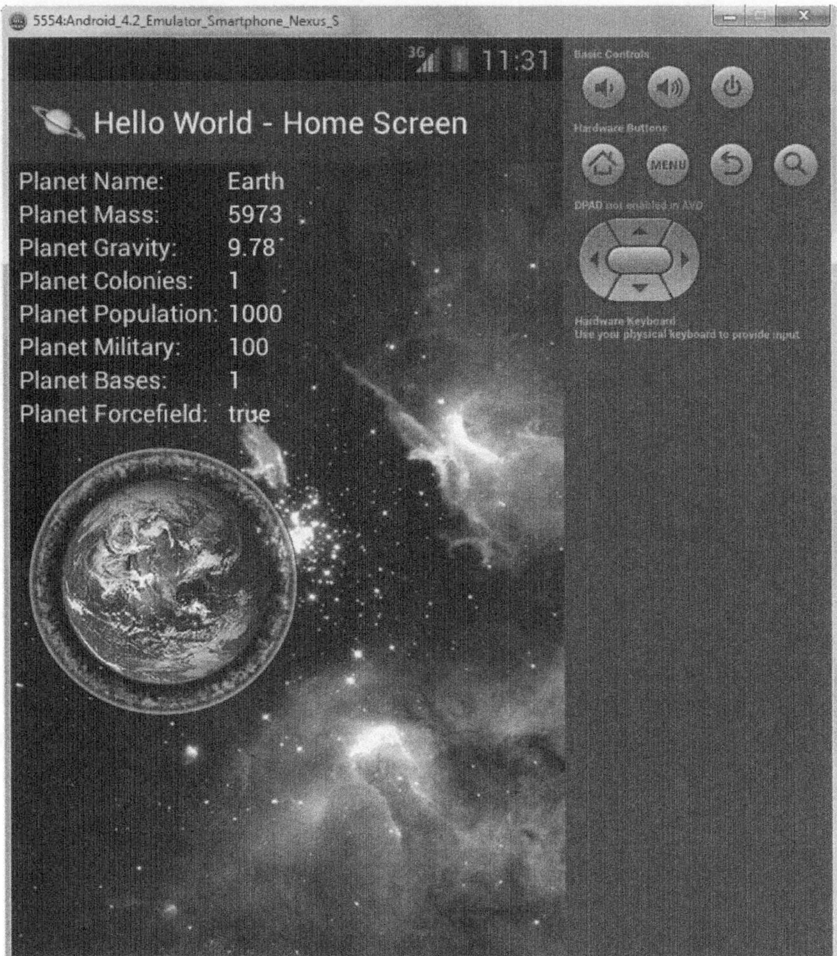

Figure 10-25. Running our new Home Screen and special effects

Next, we'll finish up by implementing procedural animation for the last of our Attack Planet ImageButton icons: the deadly but beautiful LaserCannon.

Implementing Motion Animation: The XML <translate> Parameter

Finally, just to make sure all the root elements in Android which are utilized for procedural animation are covered using hands-on examples in this chapter, we will now create a realistic **firing kickback pulse** for our LaserCannon ImageButton icon in our Attack Planet Activity user interface.

Let's right-click on our drawable folder and select **New ➤ Android XML File** and create a new **Tween Animation** XML container named **anim_trans_laser**, and then select a translate option, so it contains a **<translate>** root element.

Since the XML file is only going to have one tag, follow the work process where we delete the </translate> closing tag and then turn the <translate> opening tag into a **<translate** and **/>** to prepare this tag for the addition of parameters that configure our translation animation operation.

If you like, you can type **android:** to see all the 15 possible parameter options for the <translate> tag, as shown here in Figure 10-26.

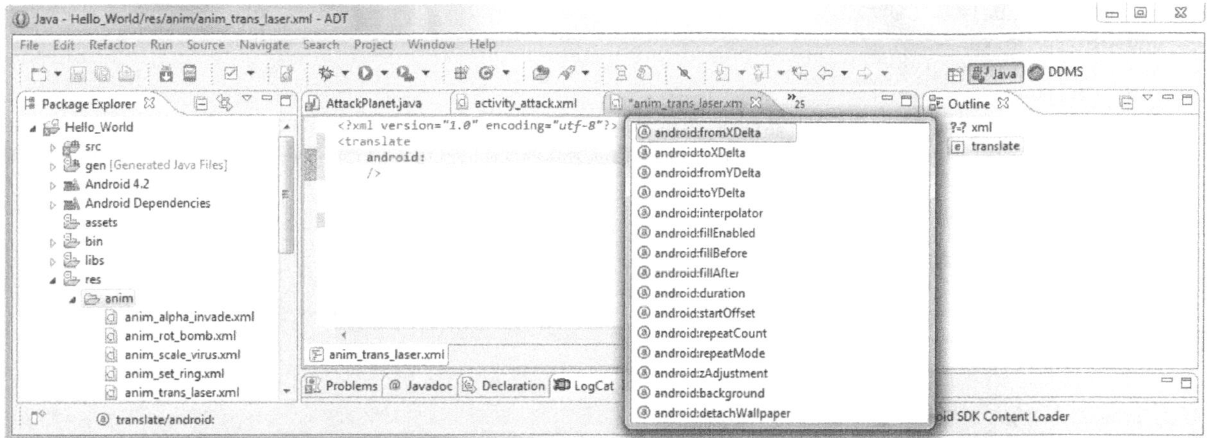

***Figure 10-26.** Adding a <translate> root element to our anim_trans_laser and invoking parameter helper dialog*

Configuring the Translate Tag

Our most important parameters are the ones that tell our animation how to move the object on the screen: the **android:fromXDelta** and **android:toXDelta** parameters. These Delta parameters take percentage values, and because we're just going to simulate a short, pulsing backfire for our laser cannon, we will set these two parameters to go from 0% (defines where they're located currently) to –10% (a short distance backward along the negative X axis).

Because we want our movement to be along a diagonal line, we will also set our Y axis parameters to 0% and 10%, so that the amount of movement will be equal, and perfectly diagonal (45 degrees, just like our laser cannon).

You can play around with these four values to adjust the magnitude and the direction of the effect, and to get a feel for how the parameters operate.

Next, we want to set up our interpolator, which, for a pulsing LaserCannon kickback is an important attribute. Fortunately, there is a perfect **bounce** interpolator for just this sort of effect application, so let's add in our **android:interpolator="@android:anim/bounce_interpolator"** so that we can get this realistic motion curve effect put into place.

Because this animation is going to feature a short, quick burst of motion energy, we will use an **android:duration** parameter of only **80** milliseconds, so that the movement is quick and sharp. On the other hand, we don't want the LaserCannon firing that often, so we will use the **android:startOffset** parameter set to **8000** milliseconds, so that the LaserCannon does not pulse too often, and end up disturbing our end-users visually.

Finally, we will need to set our repeat parameters, so let's set up the **android:repeatCount** to **infinite** and the **android:repeatMode** to **restart** so that the LaserCannon pulses a kickback burst in the same way every time. The XML mark-up for the tag should look like the following:

```
<?xml version="1.0" encoding="utf-8"?>
<translate
    xmlns:android="http://schemas.android.com/apk/res/android"
    android:fromXDelta="0%"
    android:toXDelta="-10%"
    android:fromYDelta="0%"
    android:toYDelta="10%"
    android:interpolator="@android:anim/bounce_interpolator"
    android:duration="80"
    android:startOffset="8000"
    android:repeatCount="infinite"
    android:repeatMode="restart"
/>
```

The final tag is shown in Figure 10-27.

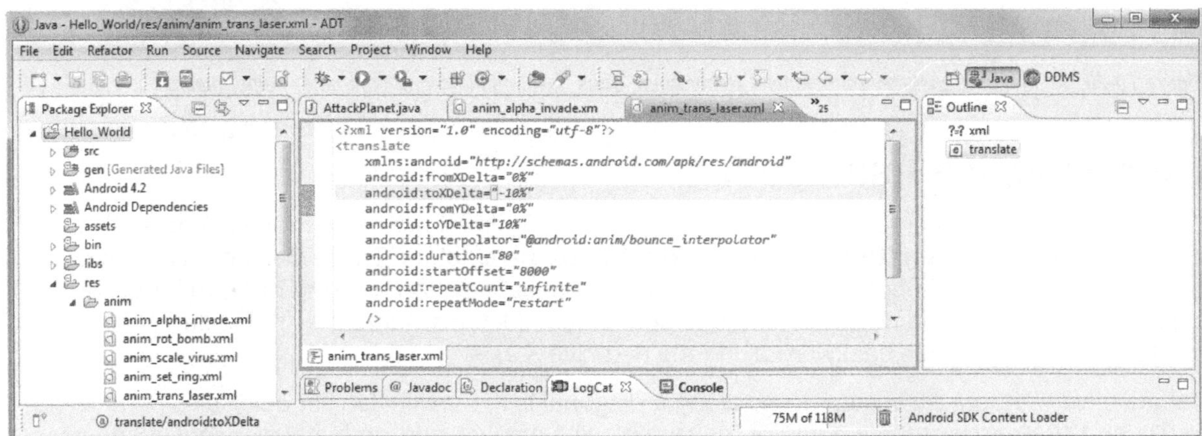

***Figure 10-27.** Adding the translation animation parameters to our XML file to make the laser cannon pulse fire*

Finally, we need to go into our AttackPlanet.java Activity class and add in the Java code that will set all this into motion (no pun intended).

Adding Java Code for the Translation

This should all be getting pretty familiar by now, after all, practice makes perfect, so let's begin by instantiating our Animation object and naming it translateLaser and then loading our animation from the XML file named anim_trans_laser.xml using the AnimationUtils class loadAnimation() method via the following line of Java code, as shown in Figure 10-28:

```
Animation translateLaser = AnimationUtils.loadAnimation(this,R.anim.anim_trans_laser);
```

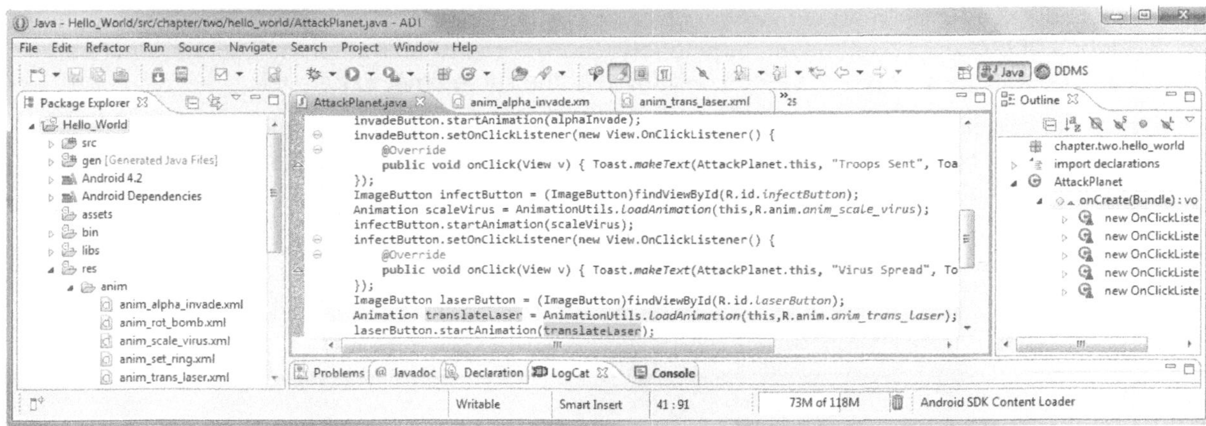

***Figure 10-28.** Coding translateLaser Animation object and using .startAnimation() method to wire it to laserButton*

Then we can call the **.startAnimation()** method with **translateLaser** off of our **laserButton** ImageButton object, using the following line of Java code:

```
laserButton.startAnimation(translateLaser);
```

Once this is all in place (see Figure 10-28) we can use our **Run As Android Application** work process and launch our Nexus S emulator and see our LaserCannon pulsing!

Once the application starts, hit the menu button, and select the Attack a Planet menu option, and go into your user interface screen, and watch the LaserCannon kickback, recoiling from its laser firing sequence. Remember that due to the **startOffset** parameter, you will have to wait 8 seconds for the first translation animation to "kick in!" Now our Attack a Planet UI screen is fully animated, and is ready for end-user consumption.

Summary

In this chapter, we learned about how to implement **procedural animation** in Android. We learned that this type of animation uses code and algorithms, rather than bitmaps, just like frame-based animation uses, and we learned about the major concepts and components of **vector animation**, and vector imagery for that matter, **rotation**, **translation** and **scale**. We also took a look at how to animate **alpha channel** values.

We then proceeded (no pun intended) to add procedural animation to both static and animated bitmap imagery in our current Hello World application, adding scale to make our virus pulse more realistically, rotation to our bomb image to make it animated, alpha channel blending to our invasion soldier to implement an impressive transporter beam effect and translation to our laser cannon to make it recoil as if it had shot out a laser pulse.

We also looked at how to create a more complex animation set, by using a **<set>** tag to group the various types of procedural animation tags to form more complex animation definitions, where all these components are being processed by Android at the same time, in parallel.

In the next section of the book, we will learn about and implement more complex new media elements, such as digital audio and digital video, into our Hello_World application. In the next chapter we'll learn about digital video concepts, digital video editing, and digital video compression.

Chapter 11

An Introduction to Video: Concepts and Optimization

In this chapter, we will give you the foundational knowledge that you will need to understand how digital video works, as well as to be able to work competently with digital video inside your Android applications.

This chapter includes a number of advanced concepts that will build on top of all the knowledge regarding digital imaging concepts and techniques that you learned about back in Chapters 7 and 8.

This new media asset is more difficult to understand and optimize because digital video is essentially a moving collection of static digital images. Because digital video is always moving, it introduces the fourth dimension, or time, into the equation. This, along with the complexities introduced by today's powerful but complicated digital video encoding and decoding algorithms makes digital video inherently more difficult to learn about than digital imaging, and even more difficult than procedural animation.

Optimizing a digital video is also complicated, primarily because digital video applies compression across all the frames within the video, which requires even more advanced mathematics, and therefore a far more advanced knowledge of what exactly is going on during the compression process, to implement those compression algorithms effectively.

We are going to look at all this within a context of how it applies to creating an optimal user experience for your Android application end-user.

This means not only learning about underlying principles of digital video editing and its data footprint optimization, but also about which digital video formats are best to use for Android, as well as what resolutions to use them in. These topics are so advanced that we are going to utilize two chapters to effectively cover everything thoroughly, so that you will have an excellent handle on digital video, and how to optimize it for Android.

The Foundation of Digital Video: Pixels, Frames, FPS, and Codecs

All the concepts that you learned about in Chapter 7 that apply to your digital imagery (pixels, resolution, aspect ratio, color depth, alpha channels, layers, blending, and compositing) will apply equally as well to digital video, and they are equally important for you to consider when you are working with digital video, if not more so.

Some of the concepts that you learned about back in Chapter 9 regarding frame-based animation are also applicable to digital video. This is due to the fact that digital video, like raster animation, is frame-based content that is rapidly displayed over time. For this reason, the concept of frame rate, expressed as frames per second, or FPS, is also quite important when it comes to your digital video data footprint optimization work process.

Digital video files are created using a piece of software called a digital video **codec**, which is short for **co**de-**dec**ode. The DV codec is a collection of complex algorithms that both **encode** and **decode** a container (file) full of digital video frames, so that they can be stored, transmitted, and later viewed by your end-users. Note that your end-users must have access to the same codec that encoded the video frames to be able to decode them; this is usually done via an OS (Android) or a browser (Chrome or Firefox).

Because the same codec (algorithm) that encodes any given digital video data file must also be utilized to decode that digital video data, this proves that each digital video codec has an encoding component, or side, as well as a decoding component or side that can decipher what its encoder wrote.

For this reason, MPEG4 H.264 encoded digital video files can only be read (decoded) using the MPEG4 H.264 codec, which is a part of your Android OS. Similarly digital video frames encoded by the VP8 codec can only be played back (decoded) using the VP8 codec, which is also supported by Android OS.

Digital video files have different types of **file extensions** that tell the developer and Android OS what type of digital video data is inside that file, and thus, which type of codec (decoder) to use to read (decode) that type of video data. The **MPEG4 H.264** file we mentioned earlier has an **.mp4** file extension, so our Mars Travel video would be called **mars.mp4** if we were to use this particular video codec to encode that video data.

Different types of digital video codecs exhibit different capabilities and performance specifications. Thus, the key thing that we want to look at is the **quality to file size ratio** that any given codec gives us. Some digital video codecs such as MPEG4's H.263 codec are of lower quality and suitable for applications such as low-resolution video conferencing, whereas others such as MPEG4 H.264 and VP8 were developed more for higher quality content, such as movies and television programs. At the time this book was written, an MPEG4 H.268 codec had also been released, but was not yet adopted. Why? Because: the H.268 codec would have to be present to decode H.268 content!

Important Digital Video Attributes: SD, HD, Streaming, and Bit-Rates

So, now we know that video codecs turn the pixels in the frames into math; where does resolution come into play and how is video stored and accessed?

Storing Video: Resolution

The original video resolution used before HD became popular was called **SD**, or **Standard Definition** digital video. In the United States, SD video originally used **480** lines of resolution in height, so 4:3 aspect ratio was VGA resolution or 640 by 480 and wide-screen aspect ratio SD video was 720 by 480. In Europe, SD video uses 576 lines of resolution in height, so 4:3 SD video in the EU would be 768 by 576 and wide-screen aspect ratio SD video in Europe would be 1024 by 576.

Recently **High Definition (HD)** digital video has become popular and uses the wide-screen **16:9** aspect ratio. There are two HD resolutions, the first was **1280 by 720** pixels, which I call **Pseudo HD** resolution, and the second, and now more common HD resolution, is **1920 by 1080** pixels, which is called **True HD** in the video industry.

Interestingly, all these resolutions are very close to common screen sizes found on Android consumer electronics devices. There are entry-level Android phones with 640 by 480 VGA screens, and mainstream Android phones with 800 by 480 WVGA screens, which are close to the 720 by 480 wide SD standard resolution. There are also 1024 by 600 entry-level (a smaller form factor) Android tablets, which are close to the European wide SD resolution of 1024 by 576.

The newer Android HD phones are 1280 by 720, or Pseudo HD, and the newest Android tablets are True HD 1920 by 1080. This is pretty convenient, as we can use the broadcast resolution standards for our video content and still hit most of the popular Android screen resolutions pixel for pixel.

Accessing Digital Video Data: Captive and Streaming

So, how do Android devices access digital video data in the first place? This can be done in one of two ways. The digital video data (file) can be **captive** within your application itself, in which case, it is a new media asset in your resource folder, just like your images and animation data.

The second way that digital video can be accessed is via a concept called **streaming**, where a digital video file is decoded (played) from an **external video server** outside your Android devices and applications.

The upside to streaming digital video data is that it can greatly reduce the data footprint of your application. This is because you do not have to include all that heavy new media digital video data in your .APK file.

The downside to streaming digital video is that if your user's connection (or the video server) goes down, your video file may not always be present for your end-users to play and enjoy; thus **reliability** and **availability** of video content is a factor to be considered on the other side of this coin.

One of the central concepts in streaming digital video is the **bit-rate** of the digital video data. Bit-rate is defined during the compression process and thus we will be getting into that in more detail in future sections of this chapter, but let's define it here as it's an important video concept.

Bit-rate essentially defines how much compression your digital video data is going to have applied to it. The bit-rate is defined during the digital video compression process, which is why I am going to cover it in greater detail in the section of this chapter on data footprint optimization.

Digital video files that feature lower (small number) bit-rates are going to have more compression applied to the data, which will result in a lower level of quality, but which will play back more smoothly, across a greater number of consumer electronics devices.

This is because the bit-rate is a measure of the **bits per second**, or **BPS**, that can be processed or transmitted effectively. As a computer processor gets faster it can process more bits per second, and similarly, as a data bandwidth connection gets faster it can comfortably send or receive more bits per second as well.

So as you can see, bit/s is important not only for streaming digital video content, due to what will fit through the bandwidth, but also once it gets to the Android device it also affects what can be processed (decoded) fast enough to allow smooth playback by processors inside an Android device. Thus, the bit-rate is important for two reasons with regards to streaming video, and important only in one regard (the decoder processing speed) to captive (imbedded) video files inside your Android application.

Thus, with a **captive** or **imbedded** video inside an Android app, the lower the bit-rate that a video asset has, the more Android devices that can decode that video asset smoothly (without dropping frames).

The reason for this is fairly obvious, as fewer bits per second of digital video data to process will obviously lead to a reduced processing load on your processor. This results in superior performance, not only for the video playback, but for the Android application as a whole, and everything else that is going on inside that Android device, for that matter.

For this reason, our data footprint optimization for digital video is very important, and getting good video image quality at lower bit-rates becomes our ultimate goal, which is why we want to use the best codec available.

A bit per second is written in the video industry as: **bit/s** and it usually includes a size modifier, like **kbit/s** in front of it. This **k** would signify **kilobits per second**, which means thousands of bits per second. Most video compression bit-rates are set between **256 kbit/s** (**256kbps**) and **768 kbit/s**, although we are going to try and optimize our digital video data for our Android app to a lower range, between 192 kbit/s and 384 kbit/s, and still obtain great image quality. If we can do this, our digital video will play smoothly, and will look great across all the different types of Android consumer electronics devices. That is why this chapter is very important.

Digital Video Formats: Support for Digital Video Codecs in Android

There are three primary digital video data formats supported in Android: **MPEG4 H.263**, which is the lowest quality (poorest performance) codec, and can have a **.3gp** or an **.mp4** file extension; **MPEG4 H.264 AVC**, which can have an **.3gp** or **.mp4** file extension; and **VP8**, which can have a **.webm** or an **.mkv** file extension, and is supported in Android 2.3.3 (and later) for **captive** playback, and in Android 4.0 (and later) for video **streaming** playback.

The first codec MPEG4 H.263 is primarily for video conferencing, so we are going to focus more on the higher quality and more common and far reaching codecs, MPEG4 H.264 AVC and VP8. AVC stands for: **Advanced Video Coding**.

Both of these popular codecs are well supported in HTML5, and thus in all popular browsers. MPEG4 H.264 AVC is supported in all versions of Android for playback, and in Android 3.0 (and later) for encoding video using the digital camera hardware, if the Android device includes one, that is.

VP8, also known as WebM, is included in Android 2.3.3 for the playback of captive digital video files, and in Android 4.0 and later for the playback of streaming digital video files. Current versions of Android do not support the encoding of camera data into the VP8 format, but maybe that feature will be a part of Android 5.0, it should be interesting to see.

Because we are focusing on the decoding of digital video for our Hello World app, and we are optimizing for and using captive or imbedded digital video files in our project resource folder, we're going to focus on optimization for MPEG4 H.264 AVC and VP8 in this chapter, since those are currently the superior codecs which are available to us.

The most common digital video codec of these two is the MPEG4 H.264 AVC codec, and for that reason most of the digital video editing software in the market, software such as Final Cut Pro or After Effects, can encode digital video into this format. This is because almost everyone on the internet is currently using HTML5 for their digital video, so H.264 codec support is included in most popular digital video editing packages.

I am going to be using the open source Lightworks digital video editing software package from EditShare in London, England. EditShare was gracious enough to make their formerly six-figure non-linear digital video editing software package open source a couple years ago, and the new version 11 should be released by the time this book publishes, and they have just added H.264 support in version 11.1 that I recently downloaded. We are also going to take a look at digital video encoding using the popular Sorenson Squeeze Pro software, the industry standard for Internet 2.0 video encoding.

VP8 codec support is a little bit newer, and not currently in Lightworks, so I am going to use the popular Sorenson Squeeze video encoding software package in this book, so that you can see an encoding package that supports all of the formats currently supported in Android.

Digital Video Optimization: Playback Across Devices and Resolution

Now that we have decided which of the supported digital video codecs that are included in the Android OS would be the most optimal for our usage in our Hello World application, we now need to determine which resolutions we are going to support for different density-level Android device screens.

We need to select three or four key resolutions that are spread far enough apart to perfectly hit the wide array of screen sizes from the entry-level 320 by 480 pre-paid el-cheapo phone all the way up to the new mega-tablets and iTVs that support True HD 1920 by 1080 or even higher resolutions.

If we're going to support **True HD** at a native **XXHDPI** resolution of 1920 by 1080, then we should have four different resolutions (and bit-rates) one of which would be that one. I would use **VP8** in this circumstance because each frame of video would have 1920 (width) times 1080 (height) times 3 (R,G,B) or **6,220,800** pixel values per frame to compress. If we want a fast, **30 FPS** frame rate, we need to multiply that value by 30, giving us a total amount of pixel data per second to compress of 186,624,000 pixels per second.

The next resolution level that is logical to support is the **Pseudo HD** 1280 by 720 **XHDPI** resolution level, used on HD smartphones, on most tablets and on some iTVs. If you are only going to use three target resolutions, this one would become the top level, and could be **scaled up** to fit 1920 by 1080 displays, and still look relatively decent, given that you did a great job getting a lot of quality out of the codec settings. This would actually be quite possible using VP8, which can yield an amazing level of quality, and a great data footprint, at low bit-rates, if you know what you are doing.

The next target resolution level which would be logical to support is also a popular broadcast resolution, the American **Wide SD** format, or 720 by 480 pixels for **HDPI** screens. So far, three of our four target resolutions are also very common target video broadcast resolutions, so your work process in preparing digital video files for your Android application support can conveniently also provide optimized digital video assets for other mediums and purposes as well, all with zero loss of effort. This target resolution will work well on Android devices that feature the 800 by 480 and 854 by 480 screen resolutions, primarily mid-level smartphones and mini-tablets.

The final target resolution that would be logical to support is **Quarter HD,** which is 480 by 270 pixels for **MDPI** screens. This fits the original smartphone resolution of 480 by 320 because there are inexpensive pre-paid smartphones still in production that use this resolution.

Note that 480 by 270 is exactly one-quarter of HD (thus the QHD or Quarter HD), and that scaling down resolution by a factor or 2 or 4 gives the most optimal quality results. As long as we do a great job of video compression optimization, we should be able to get this MPDI into a 192 kbps bit-rate. Then we will target a 384 kbps bit-rate for HDPI and a 768 kbps for XHDPI.

Digital Video Creation: Creating our Mars Planet Surface Fly-Over

Before we can actually go into a video compression software package, such as **Sorenson Squeeze Pro**, we need to create a fly-over of our planet surface. Since Mars is popular these days, we'll use the popular terrain editing software package called **Bryce 7 Professional** to create 900 frames of video content. We'll create this video content at 15 frames per second, giving us one minute of fly-over of a red planet surface which we can use to learn about some of the concepts of digital video optimization.

If you don't have it already, go to the DAZ 3D website and download Bryce 7.1 or Google "Bryce 7 Download" and go to one of the sites that has a download hosted for this software. Install the software and launch it, and you will see the Bryce 7 Pro start-up screen shown in Figure 11-1.

Figure 11-1. Bryce 7 Pro from DAZ 3D is terrain generation software

Go to the Bryce folder in the resource .zip file for this book and open the Mars.br7 file there. This is a simple surface terrain, mapped with Mars-like material, with some thin orange clouds, horizon haze, and a yellow sun. I have placed a camera near the surface that shows the ground as well as the sky and sun, and animated that camera in a straight line to simulate flying rapidly over a planet surface.

Generating Uncompressed Frames

In the next chapter, where we will get into using some more advanced Media Player controls via Java code, we can adjust our playback speed. For now, we will generate the uncompressed frames that we need inside an .AVI file format Squeeze can read to practice video compression.

1. Once Bryce has launched, use the **File ➤ Open** menu sequence, and locate the book resources folder and the Bryce sub-folder, and then open the **Mars.br7** file, as shown in Figure 11-2. Notice the 3D data is only 77 KB.

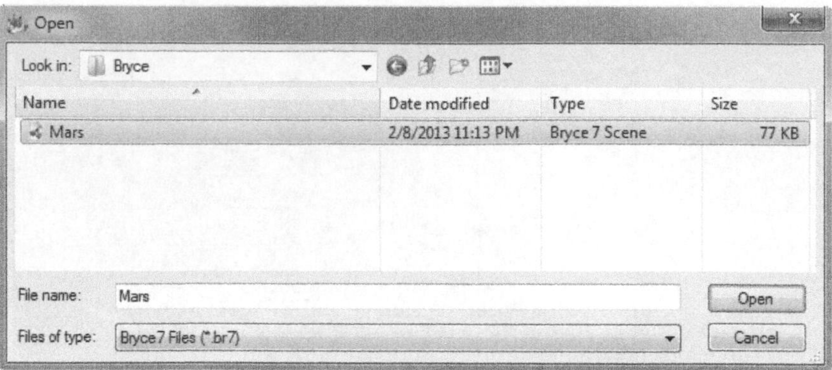

***Figure 11-2.** Using the File ➤ Open menu sequence in Bryce 7.1 to open Mars file*

2. Once this file is open, you will see a flat land terrain mesh and horizon line; you won't see the image this will generate until you **render** this 3D scene. If you want to render the first frame of the 3D Mars scene, you can click the larger (lowest centered) green sphere, in the left UI panel.

3. Next, we use the **File ➤ Animation Setup...** menu sequence to set-up our 3D animation parameters, including the Current start time or frame number, Duration, or ending time or frame number, our frame rate using FPS, and our playback parameters and type of frame display (Frame Count or SMPTE Time).

4. Set the **Current** time to **0:00:00.00** Frame Number **0** and the **Duration** time to **0:01:00.00** Frame Number **900** and set the **FPS** to **15** as shown in Figure 11-3.

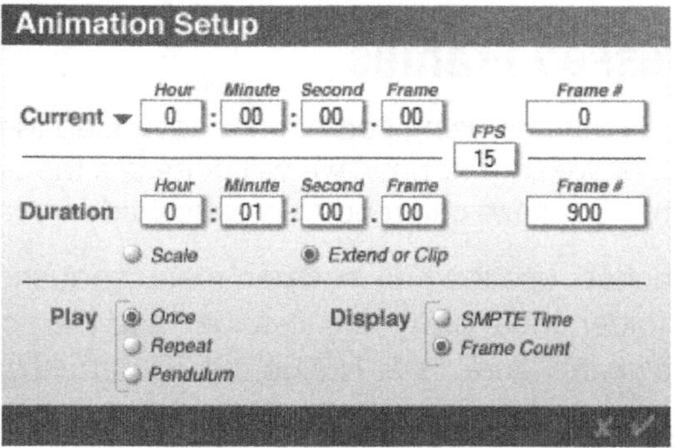

***Figure 11-3.** Setting animation parameters*

> **Note** Notice that Bryce describes Pong animation using the term: **Pendulum** animation!

5. I guess Pendulum animation is a clever improvement on the Pong animation description, but we are going to set our animation to **Play Once** and control any other playback parameter in Android. Also, set the **Display** parameter to **Frame Count**, so you will be able to see which frame is currently rendering in Bryce, once you actually render this Mars animation. First, we must configure our rendering engine.

Configuring the Render Engine

Next let's set up our Render Options. These control 3D features, determining how long each frame of video takes to render, as shown in Figure 11-4.

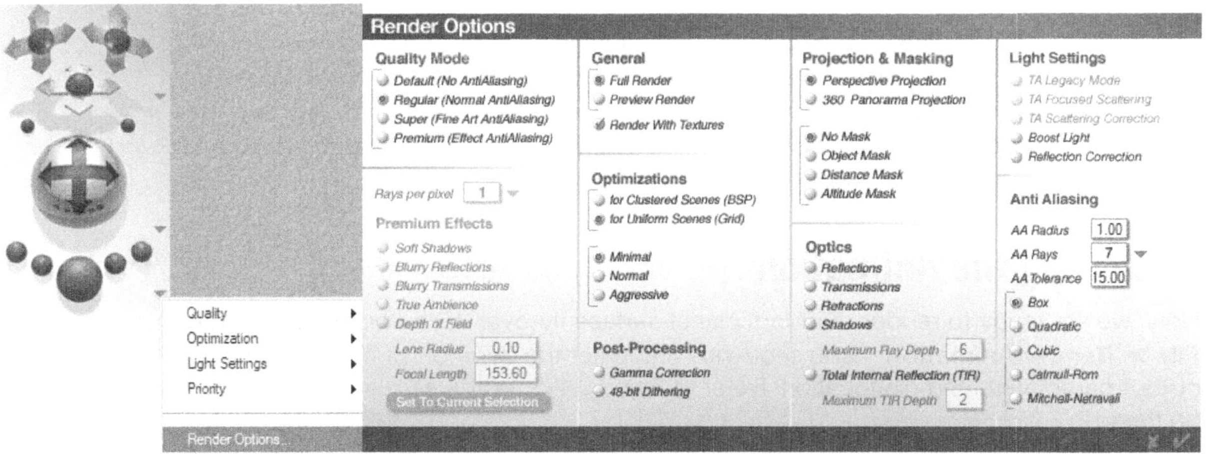

***Figure 11-4.** Setting our Mars 3D animation rendering options for the Mars planet surface fly-over animation*

1. Access the Render Options dialog by clicking the down-arrow next to the Render Sphere, opening a menu, and selecting **Render Options**.
2. The main determination of rendering time (or speed of frame rendering) for our Mars animation at each resolution level is set using Quality Mode settings. The more Anti-Aliasing **passes** we do on each frame, the longer it takes to render. To get top-quality video and a reasonable render time use the **Regular** setting shown in the upper-left corner of the dialog.
3. We do a **Full Render** on each frame, and **Render With Textures** so that our Mars planet surface has its reddish-rock look. We also Optimize for **Uniform Scenes** and **Minimal Optimizations** to save on per-frame render time.
4. We turn all the **Post-Processing** options **off**, because we do not need **Gamma Correction**, and we do not want the extra **noise** introduced into each frame via **48-bit Dithering**, as that option makes our file size larger, as learned previously in this book.

5. We are using **Perspective Projection** (a normal camera lens) and **No Masking** as we are not using any alpha channels. Finally, we will turn off all the "expensive" calculation intensive options under **Optics** and **Light Settings**, as these are not needed for this simple planet surface fly-over, and mostly involve scenes with water, and there's not too much water on Mars.

6. The final section, on the lower-right section of the dialog, controls the **Anti-Aliasing** settings, as well as the type of **algorithms** used to perform the Anti-Aliasing function on each frame of the 3D animation video we are creating. The algorithms get more complex (and time consuming) from top to bottom, but provide a better result, at the expense of processing cycles.

7. Finally, the **AA Radius** defines the number of pixels surrounding each pixel that need to be anti-aliased. Leave this set for: **1.0**. **AA Rays** determines the number of rays or the number of ray-tracing calculations if you will that the rendering engine uses to do its anti-aliasing. Higher AA Rays values yield longer rendering times. Finally, leave **AA Tolerance** set to **15**, and the **algorithm** set to the **Box** algorithm, as the other algorithms use far more processing time and increase your render times.

Rendering the Animation

Now, we are ready to render our Mars planet surface fly-over 3D animation, so drop-down the **File ➤ Render Animation** menu sequence and enter the duration of the animation and specify output parameters and file location. Refer to Figure 11-5 for the sequence we are about to go through.

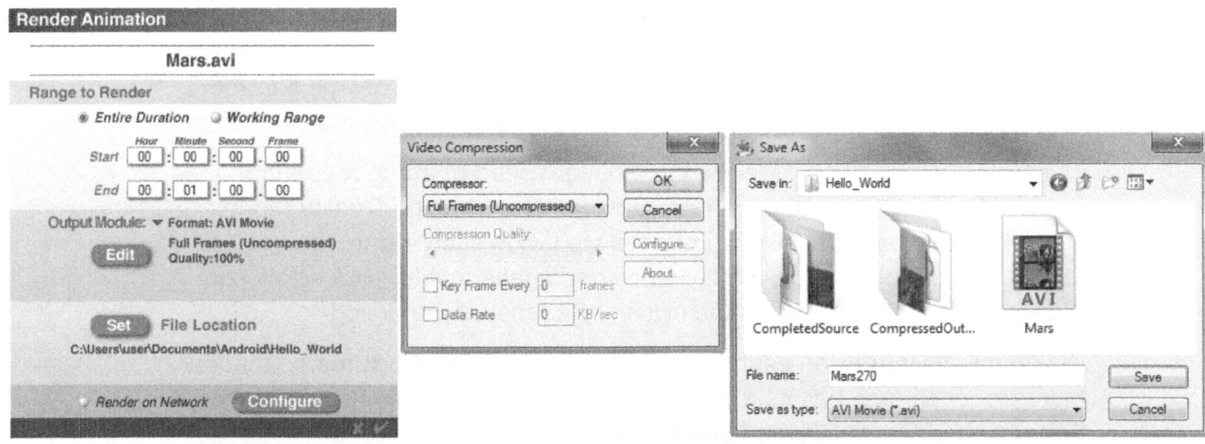

Figure 11-5. Render Animation dialog and sub-dialogs for Edit button (center) and the Set button (right)

1. Select the Entire Duration option, which shows the information that we entered in the Animation Setup dialog, shown in Figure 11-3.
2. Next click the Edit button, and select the Full Frames (Uncompressed) setting for our video data, and store it in an AVI (Audio Video Interleaved) container. This means we don't have to use numbered files, which can get a bit tedious with 900 frames, as you might well imagine.
3. Next click the Set button, and specify a file location for our Mars.avi file, in your User folder, under Documents. Create a folder called Android if you don't have one already, and then a Hello_World sub-folder inside that for this particular application's work-in-process data files.
4. If you have a network set up and want to render across all the machines on your network, then you will need to install Bryce 7.1 Pro across all your workstations. Once this is done, you can use the **Configure** button at the bottom of the dialog to configure your **render farm**. Then, all you have to do is select the **Render on Network** radio button to enable this feature.
5. Once everything in this dialog is configured, as shown in Figure 11-5, you can click the check mark at the bottom right of the dialog, and the rendering of the 900 frame Mars surface animation video will commence. On a Hexa-Core 64-bit workstation at 1080×1920 resolution it took 8 hours.

Creating the Resolution Files

The next step in the work process is to create the other three resolution source files for the 270 by 480 (MDPI), 480 by 854 (HDPI), and 720 by 1280 (XHDPI) Android device resolution densities. This is done in the **Document Setup** dialog, which as you already know is accessed by double-clicking the green Bryce Render Sphere, as shown in the left side of Figure 11-4.

1. For each of our target DPI resolutions, we need to enter our desired target resolution into a Document Resolution field in this Document Setup (see Figure 11-6).

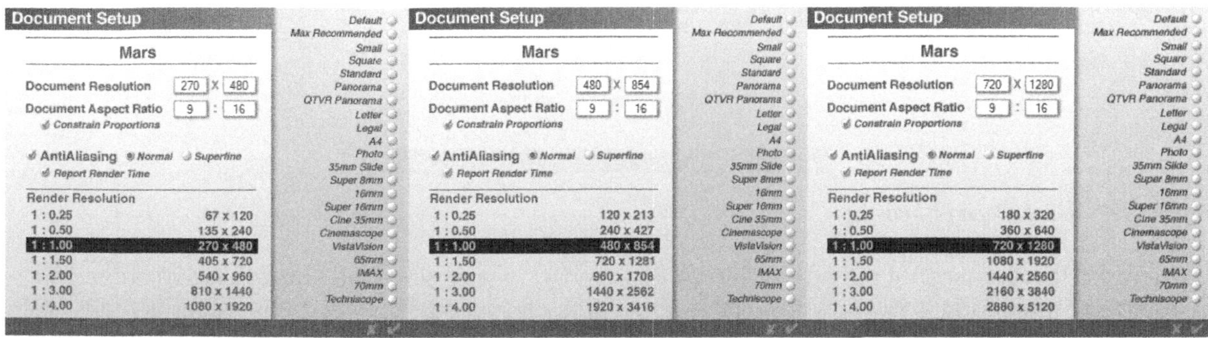

***Figure 11-6.** Setting Document Resolution, Aspect Ratio, Anti-Aliasing, and Report Render Time options in Bryce*

2. Make sure that your Document Aspect Ratio is 9:16 widescreen (in this case our app is utilized in portrait mode, or using a vertical orientation) and that the exact Android device screen resolutions shown above are utilized.
3. If your resolution is off by one pixel, uncheck your Constrain Proportions option (this keeps your aspect ratio locked), and change the pixel by one, and then re-check that same Constrain Proportions radio button to turn it back on again once you have made the change. As you know, we are trying to hit these mainstream (common) Android device screen resolutions pixel-for-pixel when we play our video full-screen to obtain the best quality by not needing Android to scale the data for us, which can introduce artifacts. The one thing Android is not currently really good at is scaling images and video.
4. When you click the check mark at the bottom of the dialog, shown in Figure 11-6 each time you set one of the target resolutions, you will notice that Bryce 7 scales your viewport to that number of pixels in resolution.

Next, repeat the work process shown in Figures 11-3 through 11-5 to render the three smaller resolutions, and name the files **Mars270.avi**, **Mars480.avi**, and **Mars720.avi**, respectively.

Notice that in Figure 11-5, the **Mars.avi** High Definition HD digital video file (1080 by 1920 resolution) has already been rendered, and that we are setting the filename for our **Mars270.avi** file in the dialog on the right-side of this screen shot. Also notice that we selected an option to **Report Render Time**, so that we can see what the rendering engine is doing, from a mathematical standpoint. This is shown in Figure 11-7 and I included it so we can see why our 3D rendering process is taking so much time on each of the 900 frames of digital video that we are generating.

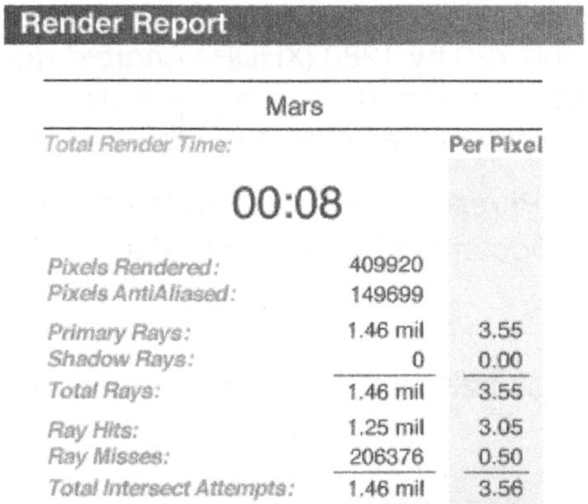

Render Report

Mars

Total Render Time:	00:08	**Per Pixel**
Pixels Rendered:	409920	
Pixels AntiAliased:	149699	
Primary Rays:	1.46 mil	3.55
Shadow Rays:	0	0.00
Total Rays:	1.46 mil	3.55
Ray Hits:	1.25 mil	3.05
Ray Misses:	206376	0.50
Total Intersect Attempts:	1.46 mil	3.56

***Figure 11-7.** Render Report information*

I generated this screenshot during the 480 by 854 rendering, and since we know that 480 times 854 is 409,920, we already know how this first number was calculated. The second number is the number of pixels that were anti-aliased, and we already know that means that there are 149,699 pixels in the image where there are drastic color changes between two pixels (which simply equates to **edges** between different objects or colors in the image).

The rendering engine cast out 1.46 million rays to be able to define the color values for each pixel in this image, or an average of 3.55 rays per pixel. If you want the exact number, 3.55 times 409,920 yields 1,455,216.

Because we turned shadows off there are no shadow rays cast by the rendering engine; as you can imagine, that saved us some rendering time! Of the 1.46 million rays cast, 1.25 million of them hit something, and 206,376 did not hit anything, and thus were not used to create pixel data values with.

Digital Video Compression: Key Concepts and Techniques

Now that we have one of our source planet's (Mars) fly-over animation data rendered in 3D we can use it to create digital video files that we can use in the next chapter, where we'll be learning how to implement this digital video content, as well as how to control it in our Android Hello World app via the Android VideoView and MediaPlayer classes.

Before we can do this, we must optimize these files that we have rendered in the previous section, as they range from 400MB to 4GB in file size, and our .APK file can only be 50MB, so we must learn about digital video codec settings and digital video compression concepts, settings and techniques.

The best software to use for optimizing digital video is called Sorenson Squeeze. If you have ever developed for the Adobe Flash platform, you may be familiar with this software package, now in its ninth revision.

The first thing we want to do is to launch **Sorenson Squeeze Pro**, version 8.5.1. When you do, you will see a start-up screen as shown in Figure 11-8.

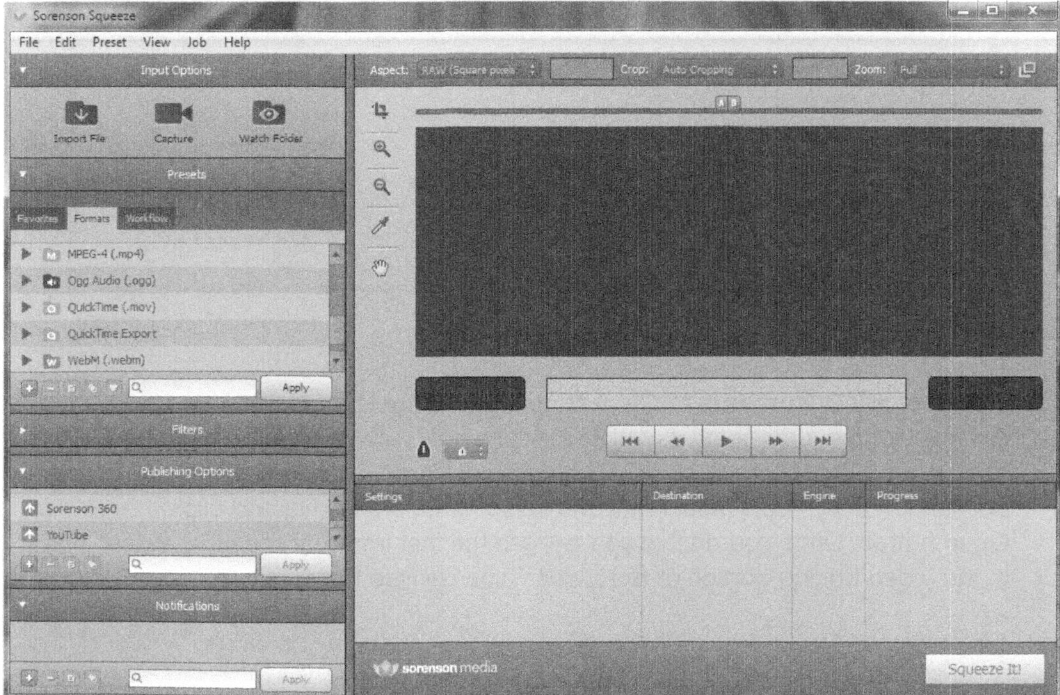

***Figure 11-8.** Launching Sorenson Squeeze Pro to compress and optimize our MPEG4 and WebM video files*

There are seven primary areas of this video compression software tool, as you can see above in Figure 11-8, including Input Options, Codec Presets, Effects Filters, Publishing Platforms, Notifications, a Sequencer Window (bottom right) and a Video Editing Window (top right).

Importing the Video

The first thing that we need to do is to import our digital video AVI full frames uncompressed format file.

1. This is done by clicking the icon on the upper right labeled **Import File**. This opens a file navigation dialog window, shown in Figure 11-9, which allows us to navigate through the hard disk drive, and find the 3D **Mars.avi** source digital video files that we created earlier in Bryce 7.1 Pro.

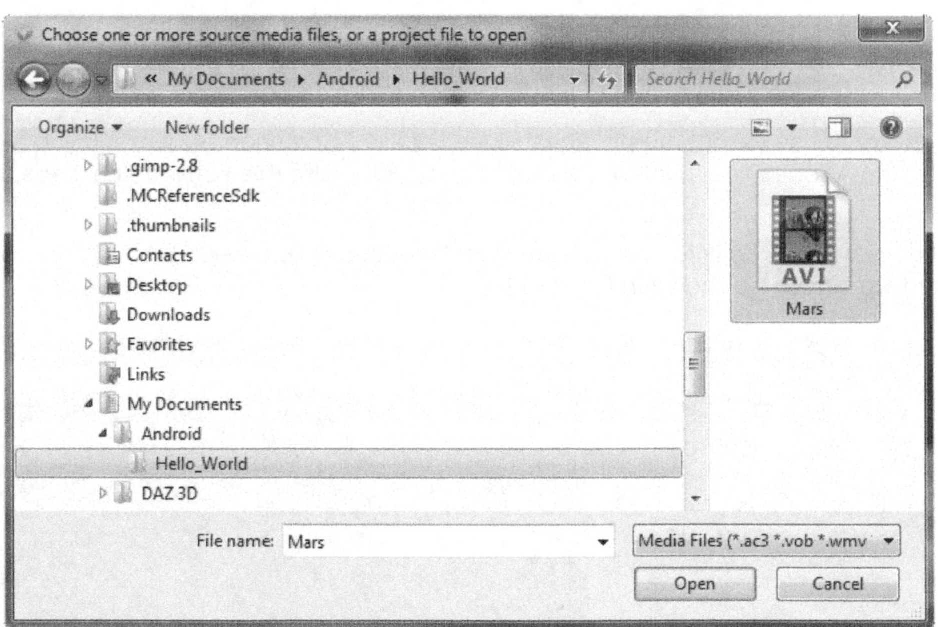

***Figure 11-9.** Using the Import File dialog to locate our Mars.avi source file*

2. Find your **My Documents** folder (it should be in your Users folder) and the **Android** folder underneath it, which contains your Android related working assets. Find the sub-folder that you created earlier for your **Hello_World** application new media resources, and select the Mars.avi file and click the Open button. Once you do this you will see the first frame of the Mars video in the Video Editing portion of Sorenson Squeeze (see Figure 11-11).

3. Locate the **+** icon on the left at the bottom of the Presets Pane, and click it to open a new presets dialog, so that we can develop a codec that is Android specific, as shown in Figure 11-10. Type **Android 1080x1920 15 FPS** in the **Name:** and **Desc:** fields, to label our custom settings, which will be saved for future use with other digital video. The **Format Constraints** are set to **None**, and the **Stream Type** is set to **Non-Streaming** as we are optimizing to a .MP4 file. The best **Codec** to use for H.264 is **MainConcept**.

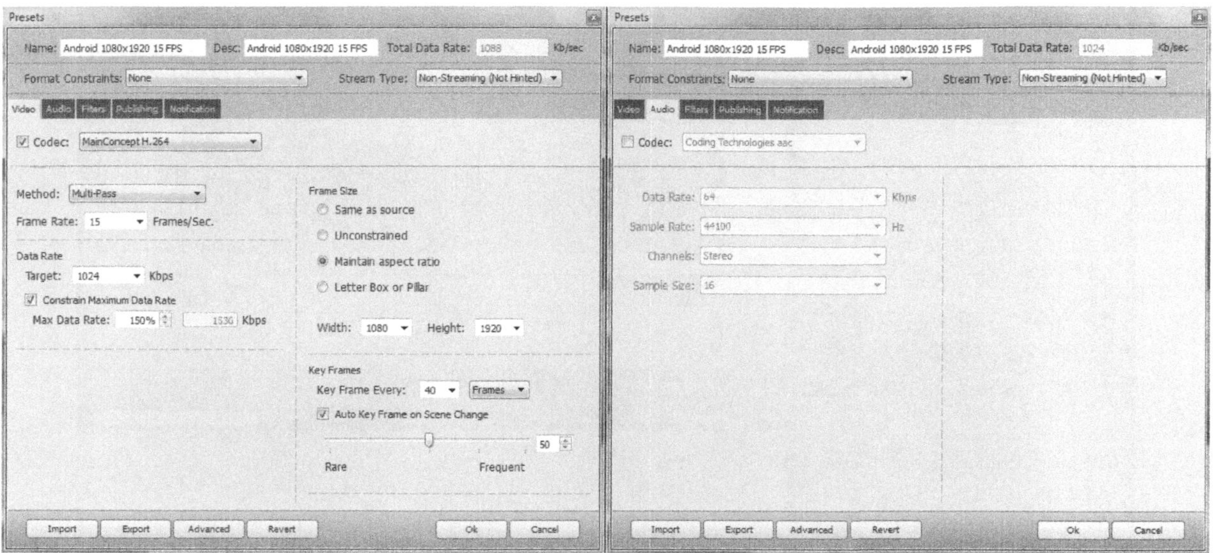

Figure 11-10. Creating a 1080×1920 Android video compression settings preset for 15 FPS and 1 Mbps data rate

4. The reason we are using the **MainConcept H.264 codec** is because it is the most advanced, and features a **Multi-Pass Method**, which makes several passes over the video data to achieve the best quality to file size ratio possible. This takes more time, but I assume here that you have at least a quad-core workstation (if not an octa-core), and that quality is your ultimate concern. Once you select **Multi-Pass** set the **Frame Rate:** to **15 FPS** and set a **Target Data Rate** of **1024 Kbps** (which is also 1 Mbps).

5. Select **Constrain Maximum Data Rate** and set the **Max Data Rate** to **150%** of 1024 Kbps, which is **1536** Kbps. This allows some wiggle room for our data to **burst,** if it needs a little more headroom on any given frame.

6. Set the **Frame Size** to **1080 by 1920** to prevent scaling and **Maintain Aspect Ratio** and let's make sure the codec looks at **KeyFrames** every **40** frames. Finally, select **Auto KeyFrame on Scene Change**, and select an average keyframe frequency of 50 to start with, for this compression setting preset.

7. Once everything is set click the OK button shown in Figure 11-10 and you will be returned to the main Squeeze Pro program screen where you can now click the Apply button in the top left panel to apply these settings (see Figure 11-11).

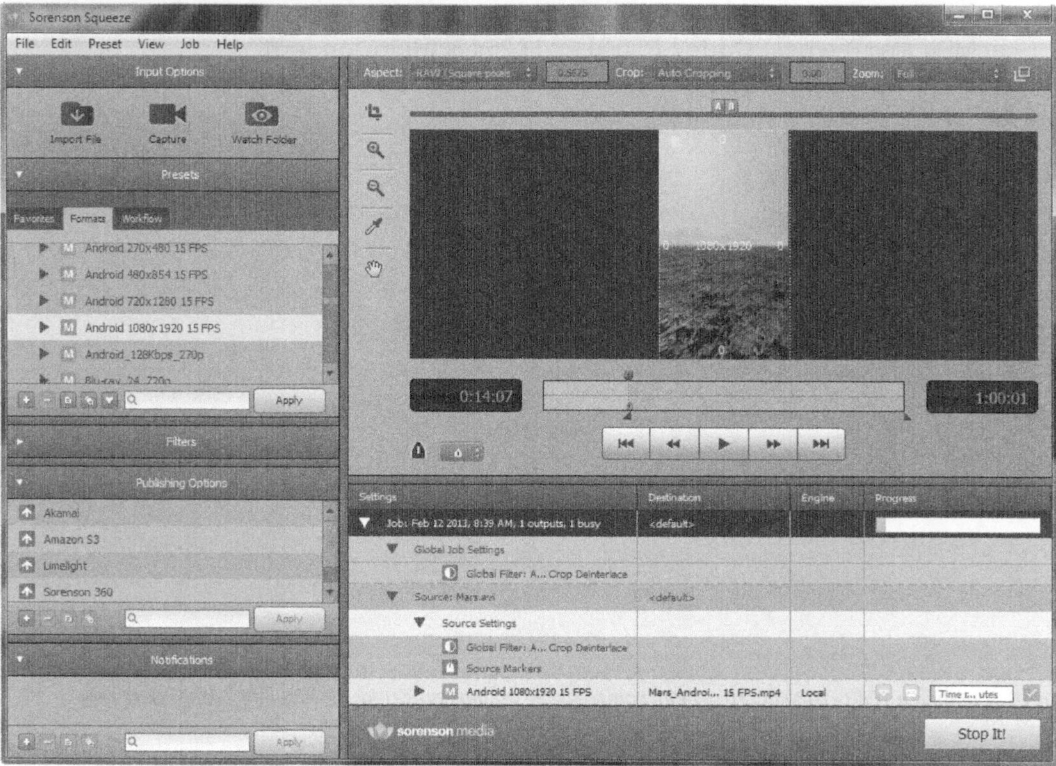

***Figure 11-11.** Applying the Android 1080×1920 15 FPS video compression preset to the imported Mars.avi file*

8. Finally, we can click the **Squeeze It!** button, on the lower-right of the software screen, and start our video compression process.

While your video data is compressing, we will talk a little bit about what **keyframes** are, and what exactly they do in the overall video compression process.

A keyframe is a frame of your animation data that the codec looks at to store an entire image of your video at that exact frame in time, which is why, of course, it is called a "keyframe!"

The way that a codec saves space (reduces data footprint) for your video is to not have to save every single frame in the digital video, in this case, it's a 3D animation of a fly-over of the surface of Mars.

This is done via some of the most complex mathematics in new media algorithms today, and beyond the scope of a *Learn Android* book to be sure. It is essentially going into the fourth dimension (time) and looking at frames after each keyframe that it encodes to see what has changed on the next frame, relative to the **keyframe** that it just **sampled**.

The codec then encodes only the changed data from frame to frame, and this can save a significant amount of encoding data in many video scenarios. A great example of this would be **talking head** videos, for example a teacher or a politician. If the person remains calm, still, and fixed in place, then only their mouth (speech) movements would change from frame to frame.

In this case, because that area of pixels that contains the mouth represents only a very small percentage of the entire video frame's pixels, the codec could end up encoding only those pixels from frame to frame instead of the entire image. Much of the video frame's pixels are frozen over time in this type of scenario, and that is something that a codec can turn into reduced data footprint, which is the name of the game where codecs are concerned.

Thus, a very still (zero head movements) talking person encodes very well, as long as the background behind them is not too noisy or does not have a lot of fast-paced movement that the codec would need to address. So a talking head in a busy newsroom would thus not encode as well as a talking head on a special set with a solid color, evenly lit background.

The things that codecs cannot **transcode** (code across frames) very well are noise, just like with static image codecs, and full-frame movement. Full frame movement is where every pixel in a video frame changes its location on each frame of video. Examples of this would include a very rapid camera panning, such as is used in the filming of car racing; camera zooming in or out, such as is used in the filming of nature documentaries; and camera fly-throughs, such as are used in action films and in our Mars fly-overs.

By now your digital video should be finished encoding and you will see a playable video icon in the bottom of the Squeeze Pro working area on the bottom right of the software screen, as shown in Figure 11-12.

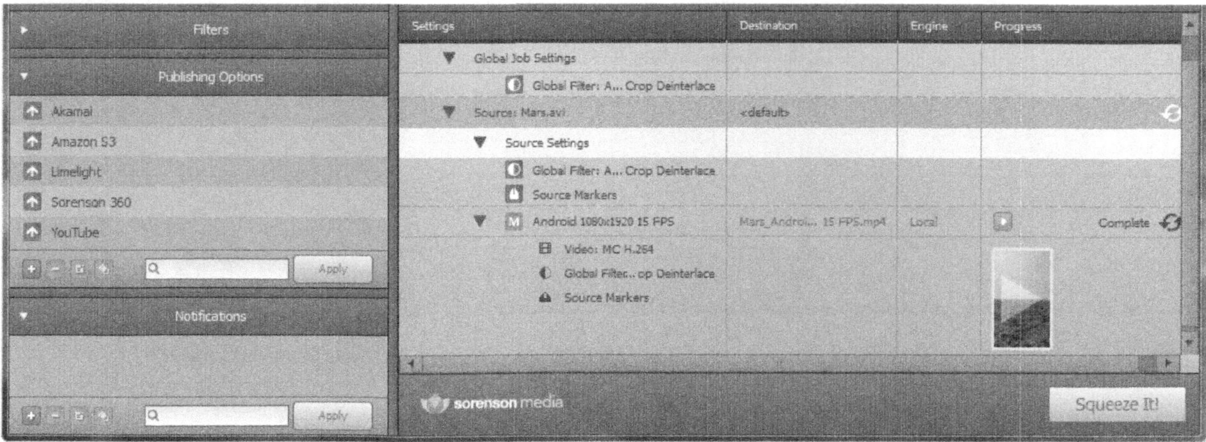

Figure 11-12. Finished video compression (bottom area of screen shot only) showing MP4 video ready to play

Compressing the Video

Next, we need to compress our MDPI resolution Android screen's video asset:

1. Use **File ➤ Save** to save your Squeeze Pro environment as it sits now. Next use **File ➤ New** to set out a new blank canvas, so we can use the **Import File** button to bring in our **Mars270.avi** raw video data file to compress into H.264 MPEG-4 data, as shown in Figure 11-13.

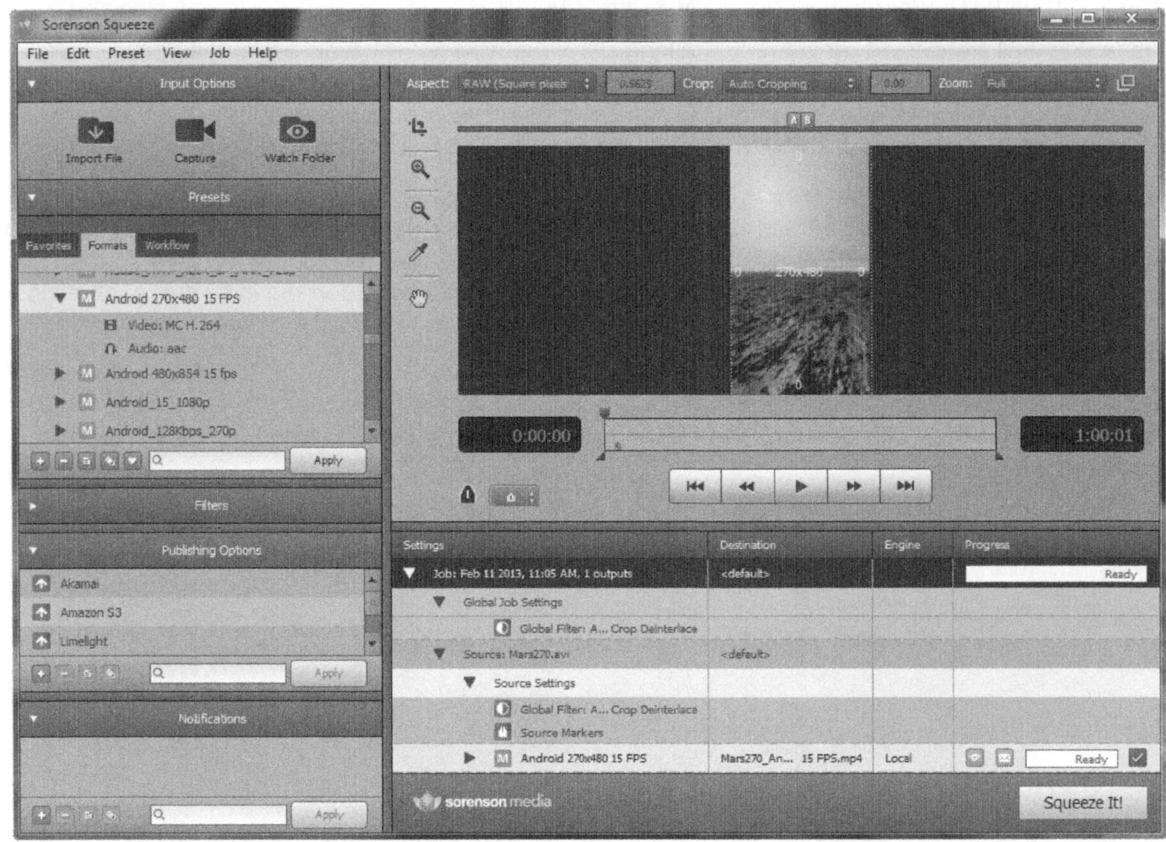

Figure 11-13. Compressing 270×480 digital video source at 15FPS in Squeeze using 192 Kbps Multi-Pass H.264

2. Follow the same work process that we did for the 1080 version and click the + button in the Presets Panel and set up a preset for our 270 by 480 resolution video that uses a **Target Data Rate** of **192 Kbps** and a **Max Data Rate** of **256 Kbps**, or a 133% burst data rate ceiling. Keep **KeyFrames** every **30** frames (30 total per 900 frames), and be sure to lock in the resolution by specifying it, and then using **Maintain Aspect Ratio**, or **Same as Source**, as shown in Figure 11-14.

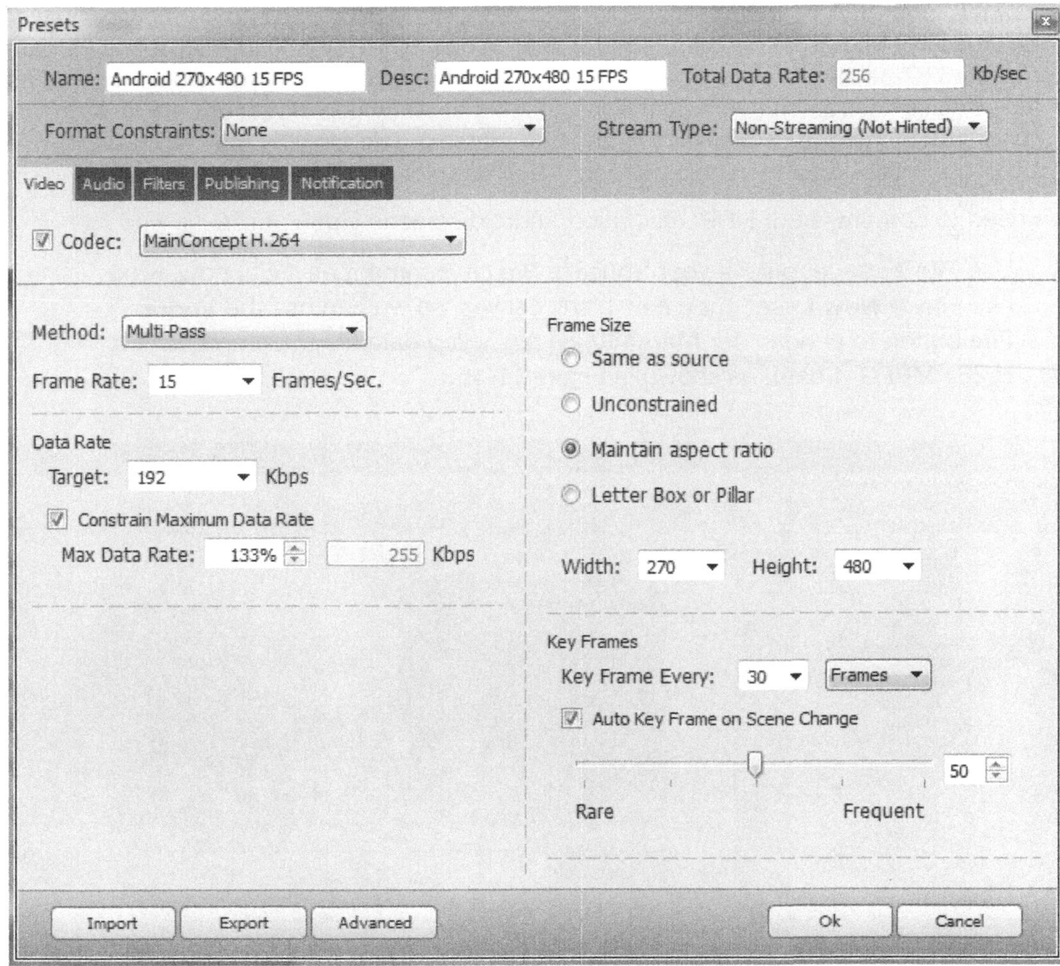

Figure 11-14. Setting the codec settings for our 270×480 video file output

3. Be sure to label your new MDPI codec settings using the Name and Desc fields at the top; I used the label Android 270×480 15 FPS as it was short and descriptive and would fit well in the Presets Pane. Once everything is configured click the **OK** button and then select the new codec definition in the Presets Pane and click the **Apply** button to apply it to your Mars project settings window. Now, you are ready to click the **Squeeze It!** button, and compress your full frames uncompressed .AVI into an MP4 file.

The MPEG-4 file that was created was only 1.3 megabytes, so we obtained some amazing compression with these settings, given that our source (raw) data in the .AVI file was close to 342 megabytes. As we learned earlier, this gives us a 263:1 compression, and it takes the amount of data that an Android device has to deal with processing from a couple hundred megabytes in one minute, to not much more than one megabyte processed over the span of one minute, which an Android device processor should be able to handle.

It is important to note that optimizing video is never a one-time process, and if you find the video plays back smoothly across all devices, you can add in quality, by specifying a higher data rate. For example **256 Kbps** with a 384 Kbps ceiling would be the next setting you would try, and more keyframes, say, use keyframes every **20** frames, instead of 30 (which would equate to 45 keyframes sampled and stored, instead of 30 over the total 900 frames). The file size goes up, as will the visual quality of the video data, and there will be more video data for the processor to decode and display.

Next, we need to compress our HDPI resolution Android screens video asset:

1. Use **File ➤ Save** to save your Squeeze Pro environment as it sits now. Next use **File ➤ New** to set out a new blank canvas, so we can use the **Import File** button to bring in our **Mars480.avi** raw video data file to compress into H.264 MPEG-4 data, as shown in Figure 11-15.

Figure 11-15. Compressing 480×854 digital video source at 15FPS in Squeeze using 384 Kbps Multi-Pass H.264

2. Follow the same work process that we did for the 1080 version, and click the + button in the Presets Panel, and set up a preset for our 480 by 854 resolution video that uses the **Target Data Rate** of **384 Kbps** and a **Max Data Rate** of **512 Kbps**, or a **133%** burst data rate ceiling. Keep

KeyFrames every **30** frames (a total of 30 per 900 frames), and be sure you lock in the resolution, by either specifying it and using **Maintain Aspect Ratio**, or by using the **Same as Source option** instead, as shown in Figure 11-16.

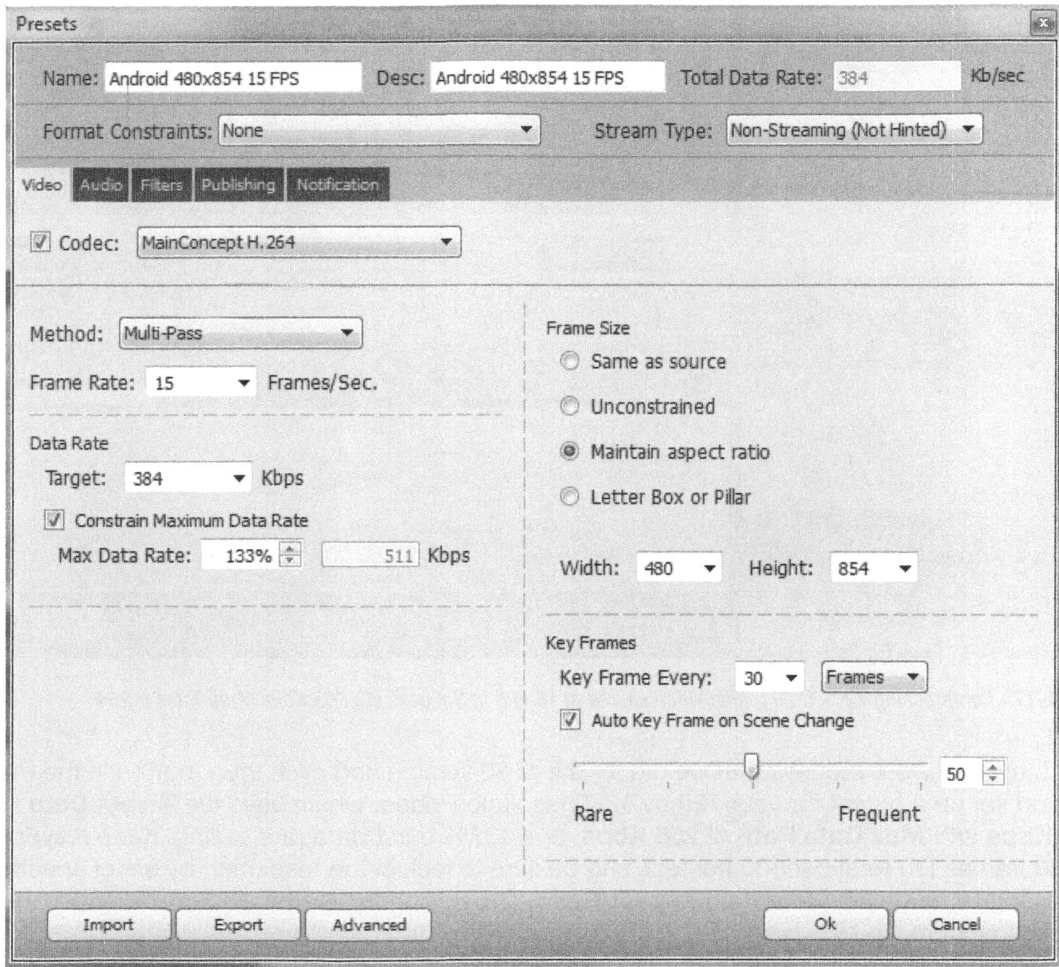

Figure 11-16. Setting the codec settings for our 480×854 video file output

3. Finally, we need to compress our XHDPI target resolution Android screen's video asset, so again, use **File ➤ Save** to save your previous Squeeze Pro environment. Next use **File ➤ New** to set out a new blank canvas, so we can use the **Import File** button to bring in our **Mars720.avi** raw video data file to compress into an H.264 MPEG-4 MP4 data file, as shown in Figure 11-17.

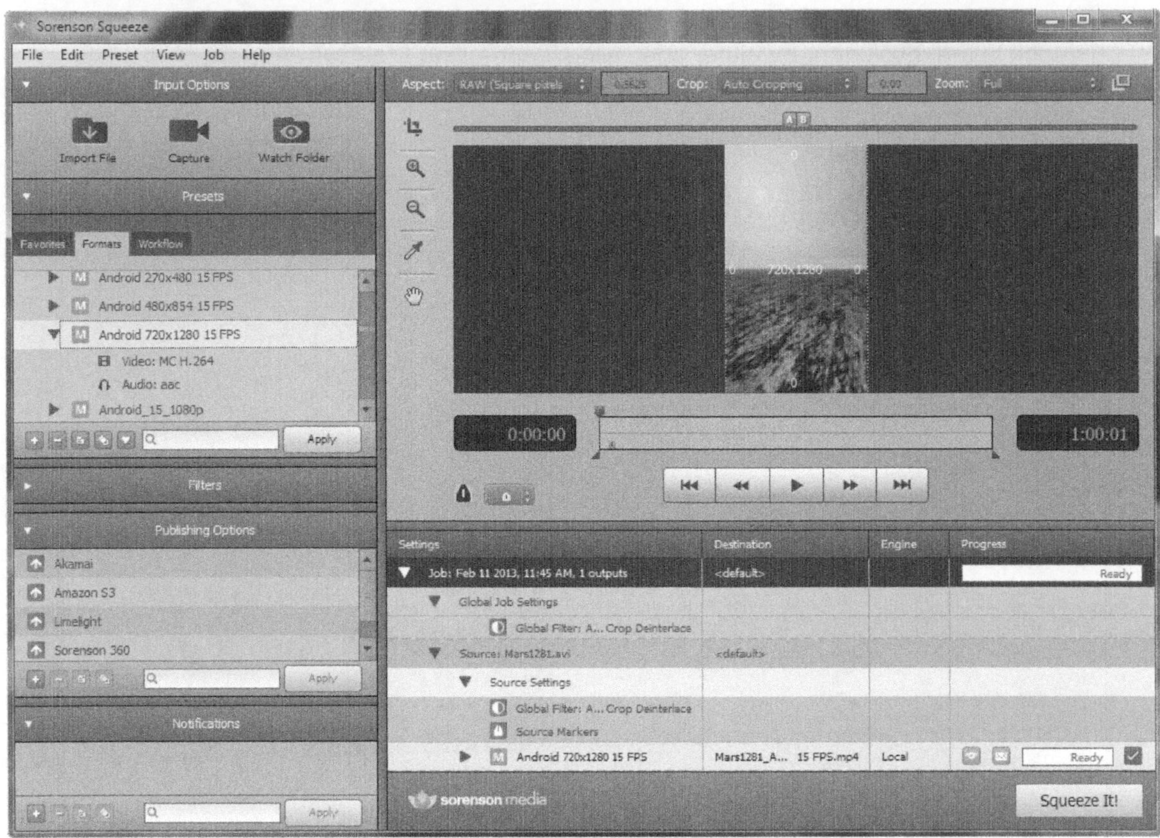

***Figure 11-17.** Compressing 720×1280 digital video source at 15 FPS in Squeeze via 768 Kbps Multi-Pass H.264*

Follow the same work process that we did for the 1080 version and click the + button in the Presets Panel and set up a preset for your 720 by 1280 resolution video, which uses the **Target Data Rate** of **192 Kbps** and **Max Data Rate** of **256 Kbps**, or a 133% burst data rate ceiling. Keep **KeyFrames** every **30** frames (30 total per 900 frames), and be sure to lock in the resolution by either specifying it in the dialog UI, and using **Maintain Aspect Ratio**, or by using the **Same as Source** option instead, as shown in Figure 11-18.

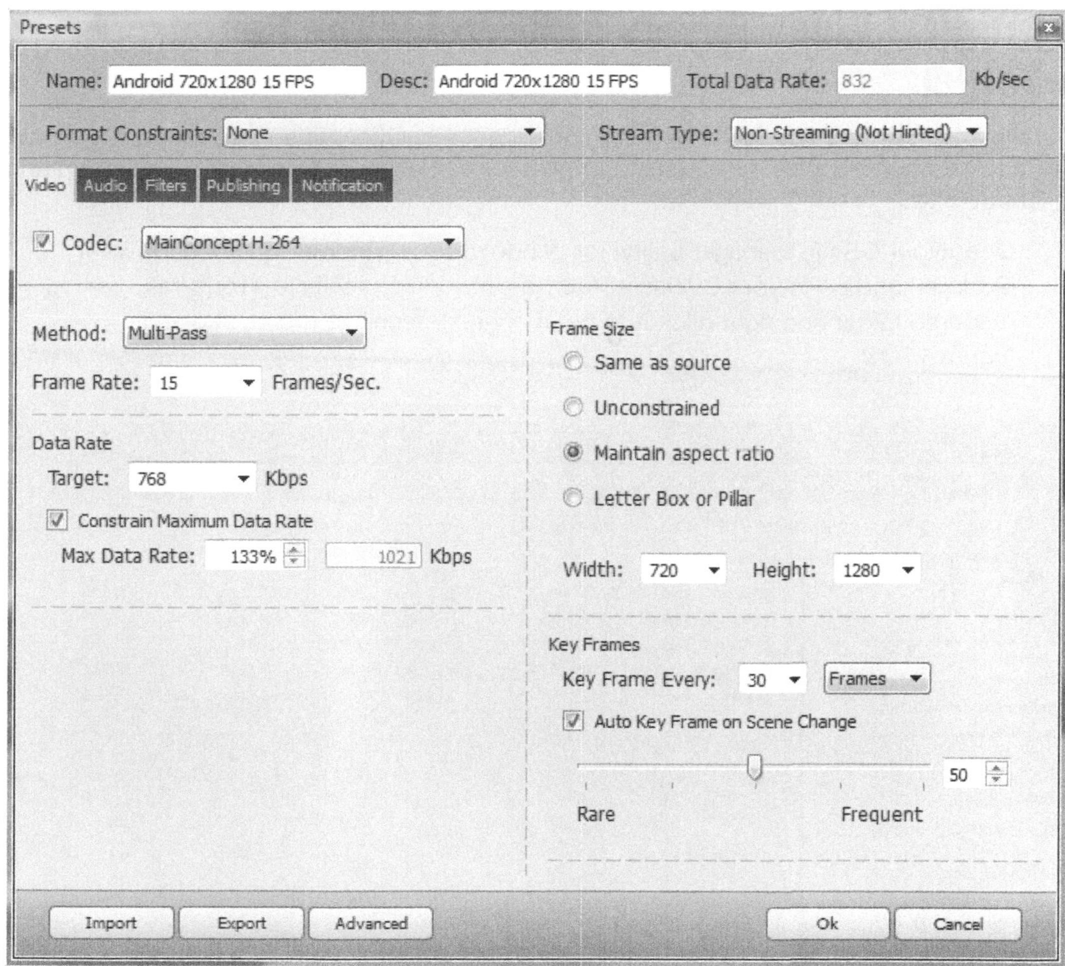

Figure 11-18. *Setting the codec settings for our 720×1280 video file output*

Next we need to put the MPEG-4 H.264 video assets we have created into the proper Hello_World project resource folder, or **Hello_World/res/raw** for raw video data files that have already been optimized, and do not need to be further optimized by Android. This is a concept we covered earlier in the book, and that we will now go into in detail in the next section of the book. Once this is done, our video data will be ready to utilize.

Using Digital Video Assets in Android: The Resource's Raw Folder

Now that we have our four resolution density (DPI) target resolution video files created, we can copy them into their proper resource sub-folder, and then we can access them via XML mark-up and Java code in Chapter 12.

1. Open your OS file manager utility, for Windows 7 or Windows 8 it's Windows Explorer, and go to your C:/Users/YourName/workspace/Hello_World/res resource folder and right-click it to get a context-sensitive menu, shown in Figure 11-19.

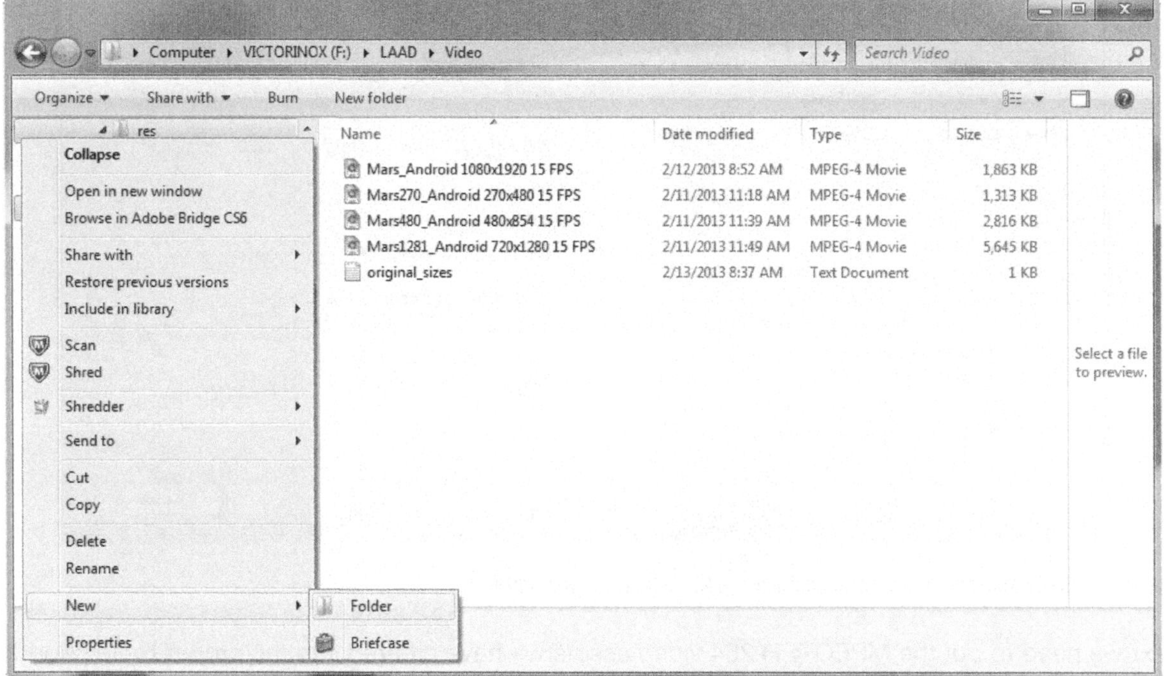

***Figure 11-19.** Creating a New ➤ Folder under Hello_World resources (res) folder named /raw to hold video files*

2. At the bottom of this menu, select the **New ➤ Folder** sub-menu sequence to create a new folder under the res (resource) folder and name it **raw**. Once created, the folder shows up under your menu sub-folder (see Figure 11-20).

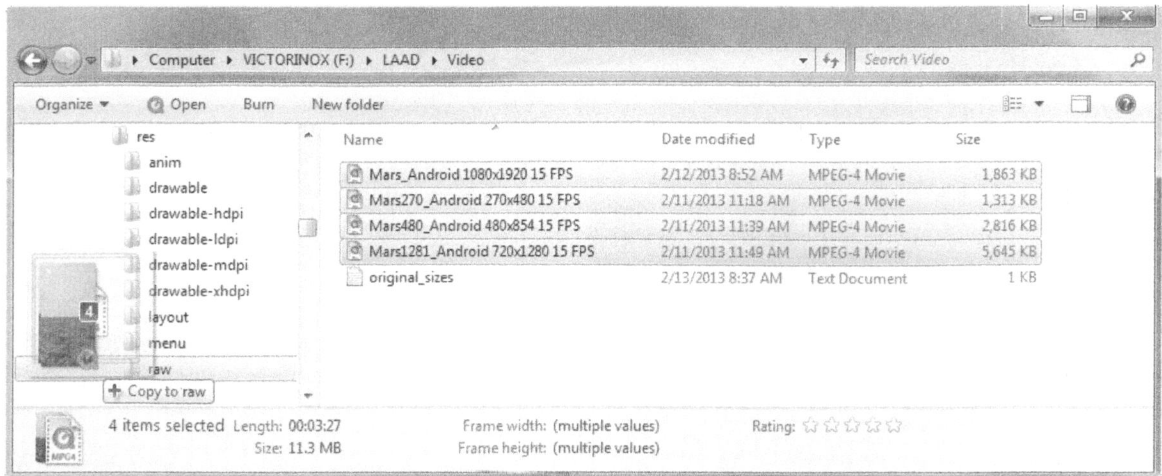

***Figure 11-20.** Drag and drop the four DPI resolution versions of our Mars planet surface fly-over into /raw*

> **Note** As I mentioned earlier in this book, this raw resource sub-folder is used in Android to contain new media assets that have already been optimized by the developer, and which do not require any further optimization or other intervention by the Android OS. Essentially new media assets in the /raw folder are assets that we are telling Android to store in the .APK file for our application, and access and use them as-is within the application code without further alteration of any kind.

3. Once the /raw folder is created and showing in the left pane of the file management utility, select the first of the four files and then hold down the Shift key and select the last file in the group. This serve to group-select the entire group of files, and you can then drag and drop all four files onto, and into, the **/res/raw** folder, as shown in Figure 11-17.
4. Next, we need to go into the **/res/raw** folder, and use the file manager to rename all the files from the detailed names assigned by Squeeze Pro to use simpler filenames, as we've been doing previously in this book. This process is shown in Figure 11-21 showing our new lower-case names and the raw folder.

> **Note** As we have done in the past, we will follow Android's lowercase letters and numbers asset naming convention, use planet name (in this case, mars) and the horizontal resolution of the digital video in pixels as our video file naming convention.

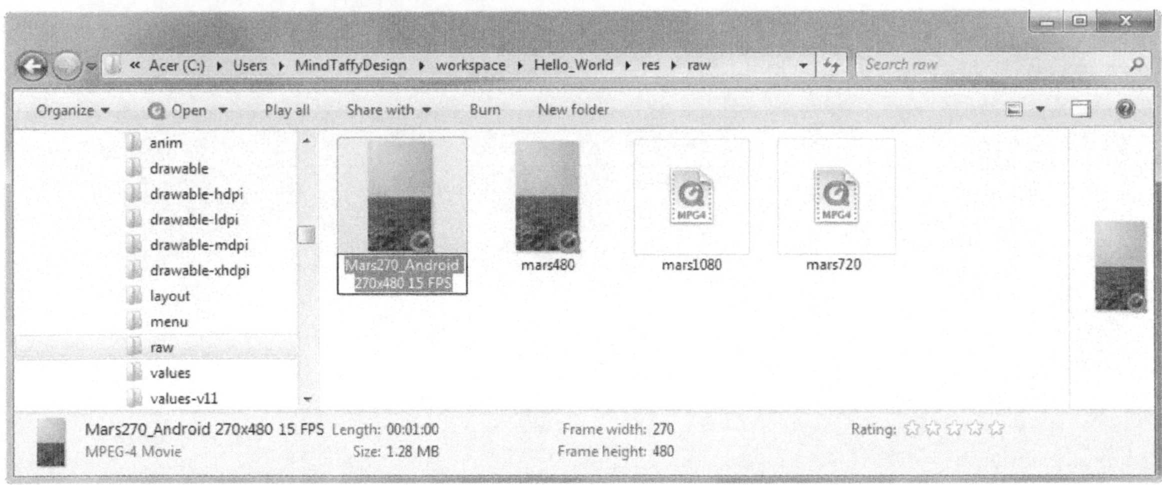

Figure 11-21. Renaming the four resolution versions for Mars video to: mars270, mars480, mars720, mars1080

5. Now let's launch our Eclipse ADT IDE, and make sure that we did everything correctly and that our digital video assets are in place and ready for use in our next chapter covering how to code Java and XML mark-up to implement digital video in our Android application. As you can see in Figure 11-22, we now have our /raw folder in our Android Hello_World project resource folder and it has four MPEG-4 files inside it that we can use to play video in our Travel to Planet Activity screen. If you already had Eclipse running, be sure and use the F5 (or Refresh) work process.

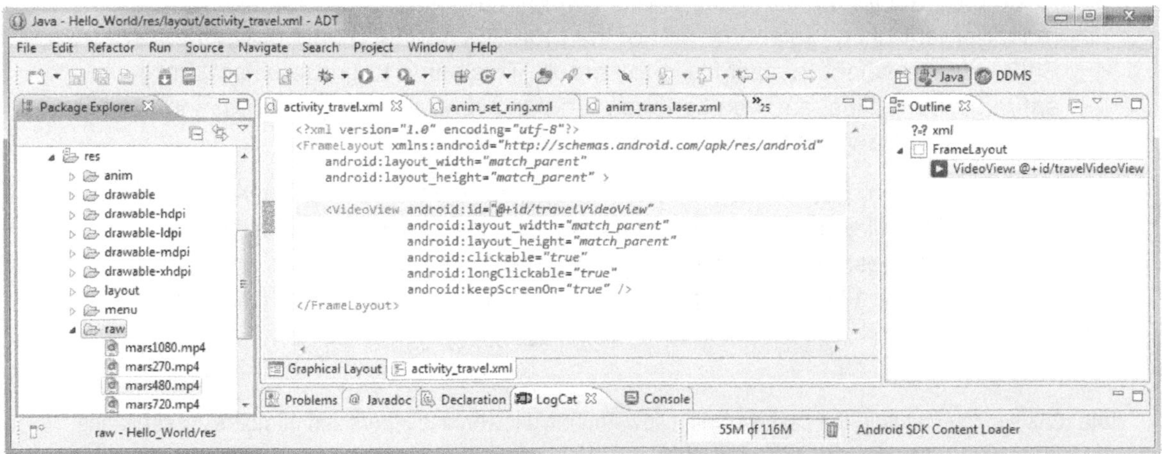

Figure 11-22. View of the four resolution versions of the digital video MPEG-4 files in the project's /res/raw/ folder

Next, we'll talk a little bit about the Android VideoView class, which we will utillze in the Chapter 12 to hold and play our digital video assets and then we'll have the foundational knowledge that we will need to begin coding our digital video assets into our Hello_World Android application.

Playing Digital Video in the UI Design: Android's VideoView Class

Android has designed a user interface widget that makes the digital video playback inside our application a fairly straightforward proposition.

It is called the **VideoView** class, and it uses the **<VideoView>** tag in XML to implement its UI properties via various parameters, as we have already seen in earlier chapters in this book when we implemented our TravelPlanet Activity class in Java and XML.

The Android VideoView class is a subclass of the **SurfaceView** class, which is itself a subclass of the **View** class, which as we know, is a subclass of the Java **Object** class.

The VideoView class implements the **MediaPlayerControl** interface so that we have access to methods relating to controlling our digital video playback.

This interface is provided by the **android.widget.MediaController** package, so its full path is **android.widget.MediaController.MediaPlayerControl** and thus we'll be able to **play** or **pause** our video in our Java code if we want to.

In fact, implementing the VideoView and MediaPlayer functionality in XML and Java is what our next chapter on Digital Video in Android is all about, now that we have the foundational knowledge to know what exactly we are talking about regarding digital video concepts, codecs, features, and playback.

Summary

In this chapter, we built up a solid foundation for understanding digital video new media assets, so that we can implement them optimally within an Android application.

We learned how pixels, the video frames they live in, and the codecs that compress and decompress them into usable files all work together to make a huge amount of moving digital image data more manageable and usable.

Then we learned about some important concepts and standards in the digital video world, such as Standard Resolution SD video and its native resolution and about the newer HD video and its two common resolution specifications. We learned the digital video in Android can be **captive**, or held in a resource folder and included inside our application .APK file or that it can be **streaming video** and served up remotely, via a video server.

We talked about the important concept of bit-rate and bits per second and how this measurement was used in the data footprint optimization process for digital video. We also learned that the bit-rate not only determined what types of bandwidth speed environments can accommodate digital video but also what types of Android device data processing (CPU) capabilities can decode that video stream once it actually gets across that bandwidth.

We discovered that even with captive video files inside an Android .APK container, that the bit-rate and quality levels were the key components to obtaining crystal clear video that played smoothly without dropping frames to try and keep up with the frame rate required by the digital video file.

Next we took a look at digital video codecs and formats that are supported in Android, such as the MPEG4 H.263 and H.264 codecs, as well as VP8, and how these codecs differ in their level of support both inside Android OS, as well as outside of Android OS, and as part of the HTML5 specification.

We also looked at the optimal digital video resolutions that we will need to support across all Android consumer electronics devices, and discovered that the major broadcast resolutions for SD and HD digital video, in both the United States and Europe, match up exceptionally well with most current Android device screen resolutions.

We learned how to use Bryce 7 Pro and created our basic Mars planet surface animations. We practiced implementing digital video file asset generation, for some of the key Android device resolutions using 3D terrain generation software. We learned some basic concepts about 3D rendering as well.

Next we covered the key concepts in digital video optimization and learned about the types of things besides resolution that affect video compression, such as panning and zooming, as well as things that introduce noise into the frame image data, such as previous compression artifacts.

We learned about keyframes and bit-rates by actually using these settings in the MainConcept H.264 codec inside Sorenson Squeeze Pro, to optimize our digital video from a native, uncompressed, raw data state into a highly compressed digital video asset that we can use in our Hello_World app.

We practiced this compression process by optimizing video assets for four target resolution density levels, ranging from a medium resolution (MDPI) 480 pixel screen, to a high resolution (HDPI) 800 pixel screen to an extra high resolution (XHDPI) Pseudo HD 1280 pixel screen, all the way up to an ultra-high resolution (XXHDPI) True HD 1920 pixel screen density.

We then copied these four optimized digital video assets into the resource folder, into a /raw sub-folder that we created to hold these digital video assets inside our Hello_World project folder. We renamed these files, for easier access within our code, and then entered Eclipse ADT, to make sure everything was in place and ready for us to start coding, implementing and testing these digital video assets inside our application.

To learn how digital video is implemented in our Hello World Android app, we learned about the user interface widget VideoView, which we initially implemented earlier in the book in our TravelPlanet Activity screen user interface.

We learned about the Android VideoView class hierarchy, and corresponding <VideoView> tag elements in XML. We learned that VideoView was actually a SurfaceView container that was connected to the MediaPlayer class and next we will learn how to implement it within our TravelPlanet.java Activity class.

In the next chapter we will get more advanced with digital video new media elements, by getting deeper into the XML and Java coding needed to implement digital video using the Android VideoView and MediaPlayer classes and their methods. We will also build Java code that controls our VideoView XML UI definition and ultimately the user experience.

Chapter 12

Digital Video in Android: Using the VideoView Class

In this chapter, we will take our newfound knowledge of Digital Video concepts, techniques, and formats that we learned in the previous chapter and apply that to actually implement digital video assets in our own Hello_World Android Application.

We will add in new Java code to our TravelPlanet.java Activity subclass to instantiate a MediaController object, so that we can play our video in the VideoView user interface element that we set up in our activity_travel.xml screen layout definition earlier on in this book.

We will cover how to play video that is a different aspect ratio than the source video and how to create and add video transport control user interface elements.

Using Android MediaController Class to Play Video

Because we have already added and configured our VideoView user interface element in our activity_travel.xml file inside of a FrameLayout container, let's open up our TravelPlanet.java Activity class we created earlier in the book and add the code to actually play our video now that we have the files in the correct resource folder, /res/raw, ready to be played.

The first thing that we need to do to set the stage for playing video is to define a path to where our video files are being stored so that the Android MediaController class can find them, and eventually, play them.

This is done via a **Uniform Resource Identifier** (**URI**). URIs are so important in Android development that there is a special class just for defining and utilizing them, called **Uri**, like the Russian name.

Uri is in the **`android.net`** package, since URIs are so often used to access data over the Internet, usually via that **HTTP://** moniker we are all used to using. As you will soon see, to access something in Android's Resource folder, we will be using the **android.resource://** path access definition.

The Uri class is a subclass of the java.lang.Object class, so a Uri object path in Java goes through **android.net.Uri** up through java.lang.Object. You can find out more information about the Uri class if you are interested on the Android Developer website reference section, at the following URL:

```
http://developer.android.com/reference/android/net/Uri.html
```

So, let's define our URI for our digital video file, using the Uri class's **parse()** method, along with the **getpackageName()** method, which is a part of the Android **Context** class, which is also subclassed from java.lang.Object.

Creating a Java videoUri Object in the TravelPlanet Activity

Let's get into adding the code to our TravelPlanet.java Activity class, by adding our first line of Java code that sets up the URI that will be used to reference our video data.

Let's put the first line of code defining our video's URI right underneath our Activity's **setContentView(R.layout.activity_travel)** method call, which references our Travel to a Planet user interface screen layout definition.

The line of Java code that sets up our Uri object is structured like this:

```
Uri videoUri = Uri.parse("android.resource://"+getpackageName()+"/"+R.raw.mars270);
```

This fairly dense line of code defines our **Uri object**, names it **videoUri**, and sets it equal to the URI for our **mars270.mp4** file, which is located in our **/res/raw** folder.

It does this via the Uri class **.parse()** method, which is used to construct valid URI objects that the Android OS can understand, and thus implement.

The **Uri.parse()** method outlined here is passed a concatenation (which is done via the Java language + operator) of the location of the file located in **android.resource://** with our Hello_World package name and context that is obtained by the **getpackageName()** method, and a path level definer, also known as a **forward slash** character, and finally, our resource identifier, **R.raw.mars270,** which is our filename (first part only is used in Android), and the /raw sub-folder, which is under the /res Resource (R) folder.

You can see this line of code in Figure 12-1, its right before the line of code that we already had written in our Activity to define our VideoView.

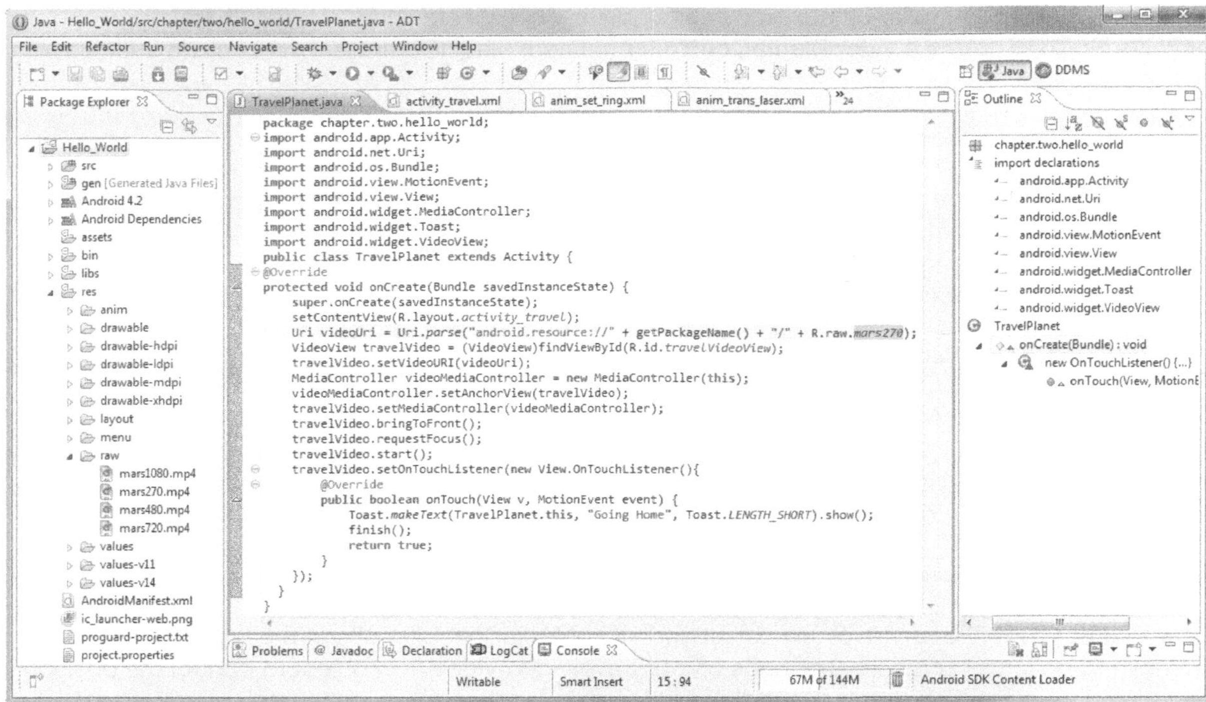

Figure 12-1. Adding Java code to our TravelPlanet.java Activity to implement MediaController for our VideoView

Because we already have our **travelVideo** VideoView object defined as well as referenced to our **travelVideoView** XML user interface element definition, we can use the **.setVideoURI()** method to wire up our newly created **videoUri** object to our travelVideo VideoView object via the following line of code:

```
travelVideo.setVideoURI(videoUri);
```

This is fairly straightforward, we are passing the **videoUri** object to the **travelVideo** VideoView object, via its **.setVideoURI()** method, and thereby defining which digital video data file to use for our VideoView as well as where this digital video file is located within our Android project.

Next we need to set up an Android MediaController object to accomplish the digital video file playback, so let's do that next.

Creating a MediaController Object to Play Our Digital Video

To playback our digital video files in Android we will utilize the Android **MediaController** class, which is a subclass of Android's **FrameLayout** class.

Note that we are using a FrameLayout to contain our VideoView UI element (widget) and remember that the FrameLayout class is subclassed from the ViewGroup class which is itself subclassed from the View class that is subclassed from the java.lang.Object master class.

To create a MediaController object, let's use our usual object instancing Java code structure, and the **new** keyword, to create a **videoMediaController** (named) MediaController object using the following line of Java code:

```
MediaController videoMediaController = new MediaController(this);
```

The next thing we have to do is to tell our MediaController object where we want it to play our video. This is done via the **.setAnchorView()** method that defines which Android View object, in this case our VideoView object named **travelVideo** to which we want to **anchor** this MediaController object's functionality. This is accomplished via the following line of Java code:

```
videoMediaController.setAnchorView(travelVideo);
```

Now we have told our MediaController object where we want it to play our digital video data, but we still need to tell our travelVideo VideoView object which MediaController object to access to play back the digital video data. This is done via the .setMediaController() method, which is called off the travelVideo VideoView object using the following code:

```
travelVideo.setMediaController(videoMediaController);
```

Now that our travelVideo VideoView object and videoMediaController object are wired together, all we have to do is call some key methods off our travelVideo VideoView object to control the position (Z-order), Focus, and playback of our digital video data, and we are all done implementing basic video playback inside our Android application.

Controlling Video Playback in Our travelVideo VideoView

Now that our VideoView object and MediaController object are interfaced to each other, we can call some key methods off our travelVideo object to make sure our digital video data is displayed at the front (top) of the screen layer stack, has focus so it can be played, and start the playback.

The first method that we need to invoke, by using dot notation off our travelVideo object, is the **.bringToFront()** method. This ensures that our VideoView is on top of any other user interface elements that may be defined along with the VideoView in its layout container. The Java code to accomplish this looks like this:

```
travelVideo.bringToFront();
```

The next thing that we need to do before we start the video playback is to make sure that the VideoView has the Focus, a concept we covered earlier in the book. This is done via the .requestFocus() method, which makes sure that the VideoView has Focus by requesting the Focus. In this way, even if the VideoView currently has the Focus, calling this method assures us that we have the focus. This is done via the following line of Java code:

```
travelVideo.requestFocus();
```

Finally, we are ready to start the playback of our digital video data, using the .start() method, as you may have guessed. This is done via the following line of code called off the travelVideo object via dot notation:

```
travelVideo.start();
```

Now it is time to fire up our Nexus S emulator, and test our digital video file playback inside the Android software emulator. Note that it is always better to test digital video file playback on the actual Android hardware devices; however, for this Android book it is not feasible as there are literally thousands of different manufacturers and models out there, which any one of you readers might have.

Because the only baseline that we all have is the latest Eclipse ADT and its various software emulators, we'll have to use that solution for our tests.

Testing Video Playback in Eclipse ADT's Nexus S Emulator

Let's fire up our Nexus S emulator, and when your Hello World Home Screen comes up, click the Menu button in the emulator on the right, and then select the Travel to Planet Activity screen so that we can see our digital video file playback, the result of which is shown in Figure 12-2.

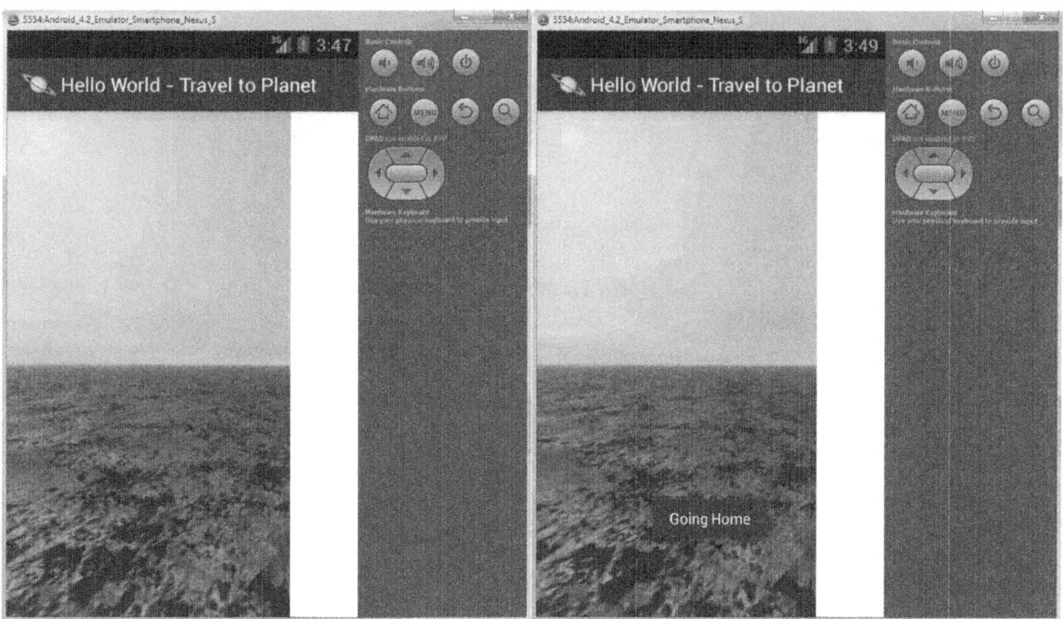

***Figure 12-2.** Playing the Mars digital video in the Nexus S emulator and testing whether onTouch() event still works*

As you can see, our digital video retains its 16:9 aspect ratio, even in a 5:3 aspect ratio emulator screen, and when we click the video screen, we are returned to our app Home Screen, with the Going Home Toast message.

So, we now know that our existing Java code from the previous chapters is still working as well. You may have noticed that there is a white strip at the right side of the screen; this is because the background color of the layout container is unconfigured, and defaults to a #FFFFFF or White value. You already know how to change this to a Black color value via the android:background="#000000" parameter inside of the FrameLayout tag.

You may be wondering: What if I wanted to scale this digital video data to fit the entire display screen? This might be an option, depending on what type of data it is and how sensitive the subject matter would be to uneven scaling, or scaling where the aspect ratio is **unlocked**.

This planet surface data of Mars that we are using could be scaled without the user detecting a change in the subject material, whereas a full screen face or talking head might look distorted (fat or coneheaded).

There is a way to accomplish this end-result in Android, by putting the VideoView user interface element inside of the **RelativeLayout** container, instead of using a Framelayout container, which maintains aspect ratio.

The reason that this can be done with the RelativeLayout container and not the FrameLayout container is because these two different layout containers support completely different **android:layout** parameters.

Scaling a VideoView to Fit a Screen Using a RelativeLayout

Go into your **activity_travel.xml** file and change the **FrameLayout** container tag to a **RelativeLayout** container tag, as shown in Figure 12-3.

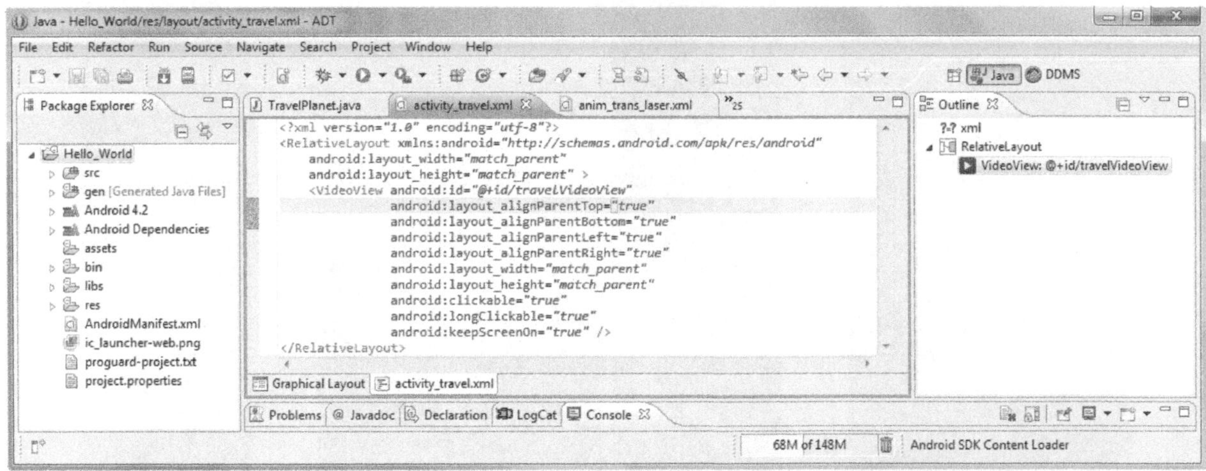

Figure 12-3. Changing our activity_travel.xml screen layout to use Relativelatout container and layout_alignParent tags

The key to making this work in a RelativeLayout container is using the **android:layout** parameters that align the four different sides of your digital video file with the **Parent Container**, in this case, a Relative Layout. I have added these four parameters to our VideoView tag, right after the **android:id** parameter, as shown in Figure 12-3.

The trick is to set all four of the **android:layout_alignParent** parameters to a value of **true**, as shown in the following XML mark-up code:

```
android:layout_alignParentTop="true"
android:layout_alignParentBottom="true"
android:layout_alignParentLeft="true"
android:layout_alignParentRight="true"
```

This stretches each side of the VideoView container to match the sides of the RelativeLayout container. Because the RelativeLayout tag is set to **match_parent** in android:layout_width and android:layout_height parameters, the VideoView thus is forced by parameter settings to fill the screen regardless of the correct tendency of Android OS to try to maintain (lock) the digital video aspect ratio. The result is shown in Figure 12-4.

***Figure 12-4.** Testing our RelativeLayout layout_alignParent tags in Nexus S*

Next, we need to test the Travel to a Planet Activity in the Nexus S emulator to be sure everything is working correctly. The digital video plays full screen and touching the screen takes our end-user back to the Home Screen, just as we have coded this functionality earlier in the book.

However there is one significant problem that may not be readily apparent to the Android neophyte, and that is, that touching the video is supposed to bring up the MediaController **Transport**. A Video Transport is a bank of basic user controls for playing, pausing, or navigating through the digital video content.

Currently, our onTouch() event handling is blocking our end-user's ability to access this Media Controller transport UI element, so, we need to add a Button UI element to our UI and wire it up with an onClick() event handler to free up the touchscreen. In this way, Android's MediaController can display its transport utility when the screen is touched.

Modifying Our UI to Support the MediaController Transport

So, the first thing we need to do is to remove the onTouch() Java code, to make sure we can access the MediaController transport controls. The simple way to do this is to use the **double forward slash** code commenting ability in Java and temporarily comment out this code block, the first line of code looks like this:

```
// travelVideo.setOnTouchListener(new View.OnTouchListener() {
```

This is shown in Figure 12-5 along with the other commented code.

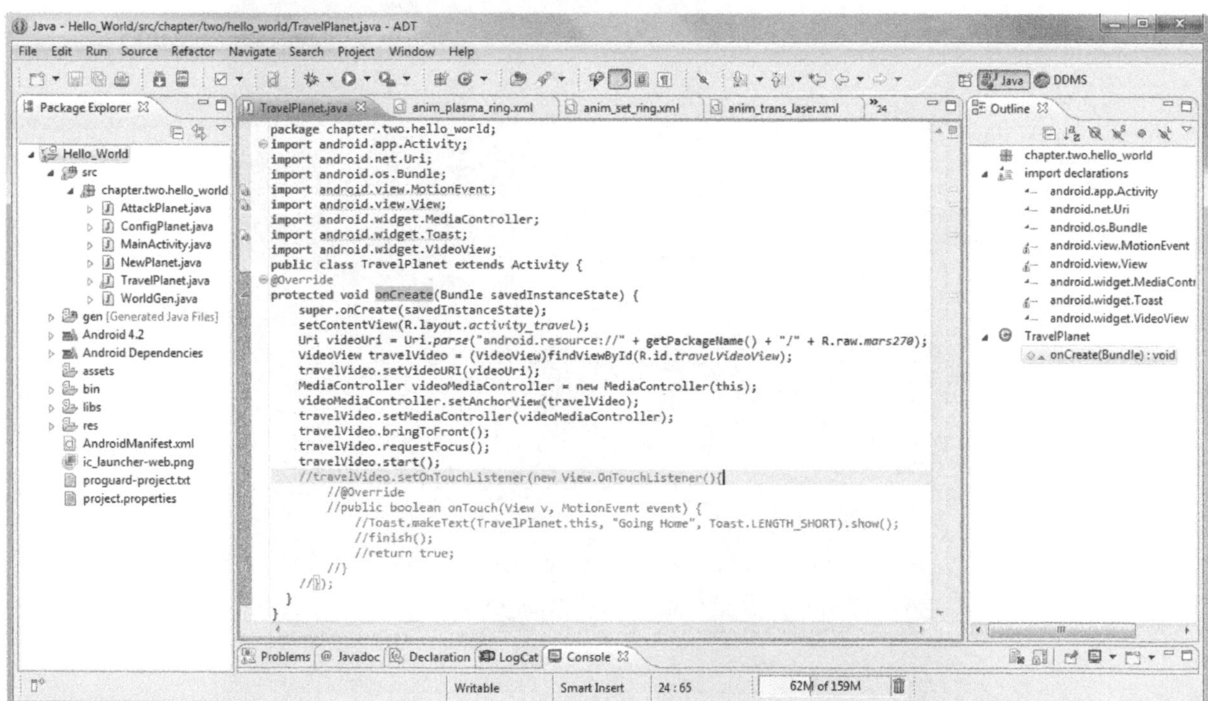

***Figure 12-5.** Remove the onTouch() event handling that is interfering with MediaController Transport UI element*

As you can see, Eclipse immediately displays warning flags next to the three import statements that are no longer needed, because the commenting of this code has removed it from the "view" of the Eclipse Java compiler.

Because a warning in Eclipse doesn't prevent us from running our application in the Nexus S emulator, let's use the familiar Run As Android Application work process, and see if we can get the Media Controller Transport to show up when we touch our video screen.

As you can see in Figure 12-6, we can now access video transport controls, when we touch the screen in our emulator. However, we now have no way to get back to our Home Screen, so we need to add a user interface element to be able to do this. Fortunately, we are only in testing mode in an Android emulator that has a red X close icon in the upper right we can use to exit!

***Figure 12-6.** Clicking or touching the screen now brings up the MediaController Transport*

Next, let's add a Button user interface element on top of our video at the top right of the screen, which allows our user to exit the Travel to Planet Activity screen and return to our Hello World application Home Screen.

Adding a Button UI Element to Return Us to Home Screen

Find and open your **activity_travel.xml** editing tab in Eclipse, and add a line of white space under the **<VideoView>** tag, and then press the **<** key to invoke the **Add a New Tag** helper dialog. Find the **Button** tag, as shown in Figure 12-7, and double-click it to add the tag to the <RelativeLayout> container. Now we're ready to add parameters to configure our Button tag.

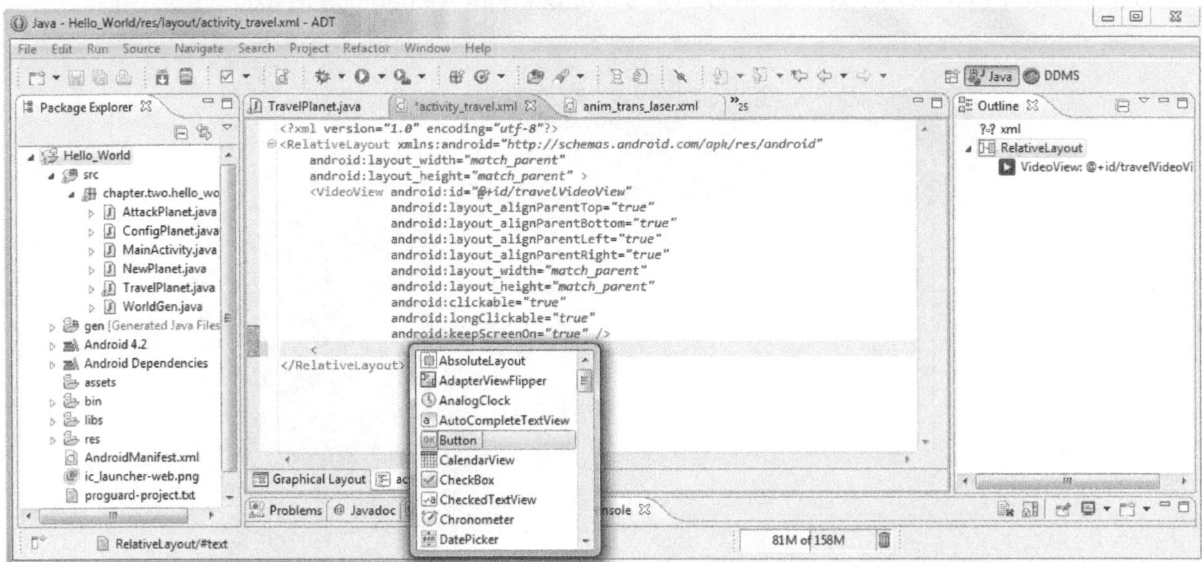

Figure 12-7. Adding a Button user interface element tag to our activity_travel.xml screen layout definition file

First we need to give our Button UI element an ID so that we can reference it in our Java code, so use the android:id parameter and name the button travelButton via the android:id="@+id/travelButton" parameter mark-up.

Next find your **strings.xml** file and add a **<string>** constant for the button named **travel_button_caption** with a value **Return to Home Screen** as follows:

```
<string name="travel_button_caption">Return to Home Screen</string>
```

Use the **android:text** parameter to reference this string constant, and also be sure to add the required **android:layout_width** and **android:layout_height** parameters, both set to the **wrap_content** constant value.

Because we want the button at the top right of the screen, out of the way of our video content, let's use the **android:alignParentTop="true"**, as well as the **android:alignParentRight="true"** parameters to achieve this end result.

Finally, let's make our Button background color White and give it a semitransparent alpha value by using an eight character (AARRGGBB) Hexadecimal value for the android:background parameter as follows:

```
android:background="99FFFFFF"
```

The XML mark-up for our Button tag so far should look like the following:

```
<Button android:id="@+id/travelButton"
        android:text="@string/travel_button_caption"
        android:layout_width="wrap_content"
        android:layout_height="wrap_content"
        android:alignParentTop="true"
        android:alignParentRight="true"
        android:background="#99FFFFFF" />
```

The entire RelativeLayout XML container mark-up is shown in Figure 12-8.

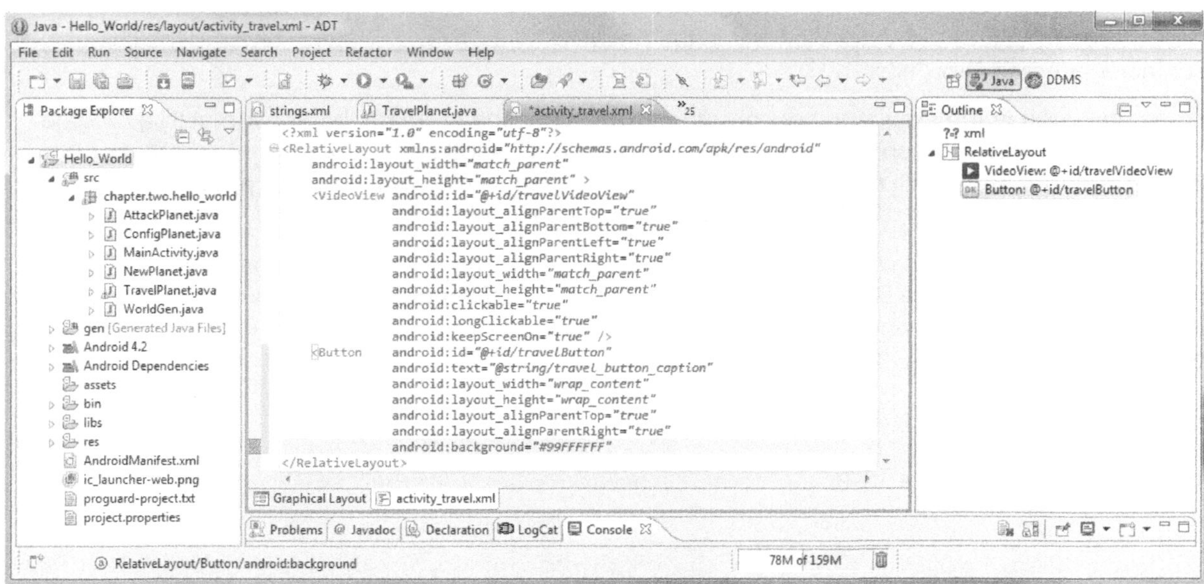

Figure 12-8. ***Configuring our Button tag parameters to place a UI button on top right of screen and be transparent***

Now it's time to test our application again using the Nexus S emulator and see if we have both a Media Controller Transport UI element, as well as an exit button UI element for our Travel to a Planet Activity screen.

Invoke the **Run As Android Application** menu sequence and launch the Nexus S emulator. When your application launches, click the Menu button and select the Travel to Planet option, and go to that Activity screen.

As you can see in Figure 12-6 (no need to duplicate screenshots here) the video plays and a click or touch on the screen brings up the transport controls, but the Button UI element is not overlayed on the top-right corner of the video, so something is amiss.

The first thing I did, to see if I could rectify this problem, was to type in **android:** in the Button tag, to see if I could find a **z-order parameter.**

A z-order parameter would bring the button to the top of the layer order, so that the button displays on top of the video, like we want it to. Alas, there is no such parameter currently, so we'll have to figure out another way to get close to the UI results we are looking for with some clever tag parameter work, most likely in both the <Button> and the <VideoView> tags.

Troubleshooting Our VideoView User Interface Design

Let's take a look at our code and see what can be done to get our top-mounted button visible over the top of our digital video asset. It looks like the android:layout_alignParentTop parameter is pulling the VideoView UI element up to the top of the screen and over the Button UI element.

Because there is no android:z-order parameter available the first thing I tried was to cut and paste the Button tag before the VideoView tag in the RelativeLayout to see whether order in the layout container affected Z-order.

When I tested it in the emulator, not only did this not solve the problem, but it generated a runtime error. I then restored the previous tag order, and looked for another way around this problem. If I can't put this Button UI element over the top of a VideoView, I will next try to put it directly above, and connected to, the top of the VideoView UI element instead.

The next thing that I tried was to **move** the **android:layout_alignParentTop** parameter from the VideoView tag over to the Button tag, and then added an **android:layout_below** parameter to the VideoView, in the space where I had removed the alignParentTop parameter, so look for the following parameter in <VideoView>:"

```
android:layout_below="@+id/travelButton"
```

This is all shown in Figure 12-9.

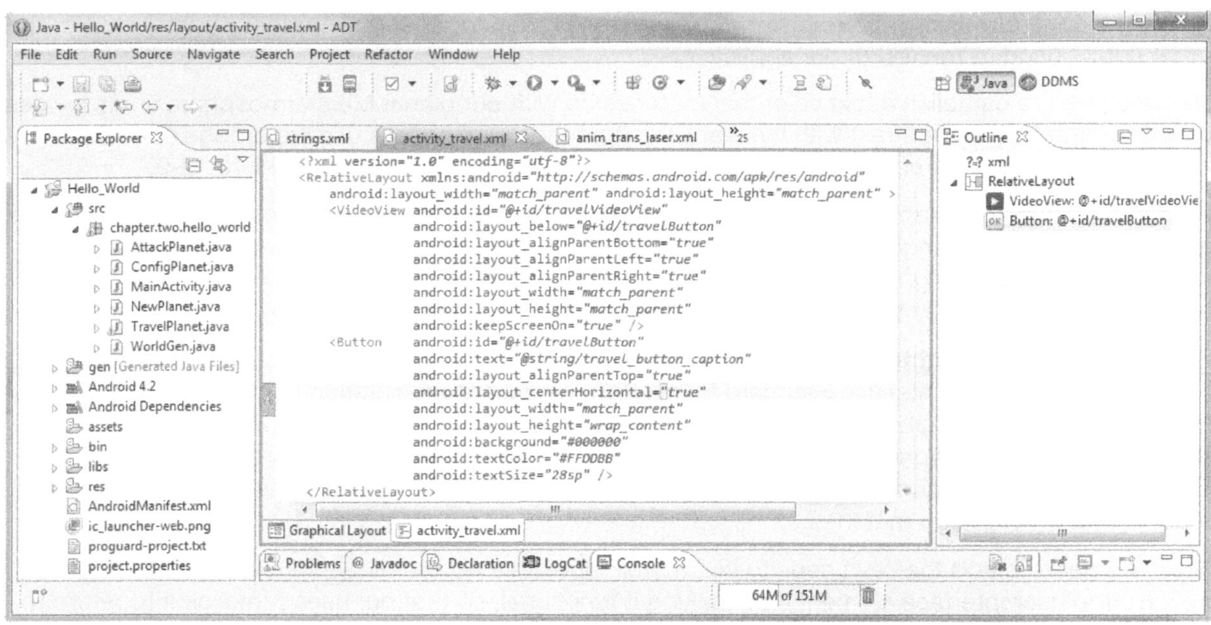

Figure 12-9. Adding Button tag parameters to place button element at top of screen and center it over VideoView

I then again used my **Run As Android Application** work process to launch the Nexus S Emulator and see whether that solved the problem, which, as you can see on the left-side of Figure 12-10 it did. However, now our background color and transparency settings don't match up with the look and feel of our UI.

Figure 12-10. Testing and refining our Travel to Planet UI screen Button element over the VideoView UI element

So let's change our **android:background** parameter to black or **#000000**, so that it matches with the other colors used at the top of our application.

Next we need to establish a text color that matches up with our planet Mars atmosphere and provides us with a high level of contrast with the black background color, so let's use the orange color value #FFDDBB that we used earlier in an android:textColor parameter as shown in Figure 12-9.

Be sure to utilize the Graphical Layout Editor tab, located at the bottom of your XML Editor in Eclipse as you make these changes, so that you can get an idea of what each of these is doing to and for your user interface design. You will notice at this point, for instance, that our text, now that we can actually see it, is actually too small and needs to be larger.

So, let's add an **android:textSize="28sp"** parameter, and make sure our text is nice and large. Remember that text (fonts) use Standard Pixels (SP), as their representation in XML tags, not Density Pixels (DP) as other graphic or user interface elements do. Now we are ready to use our **Run As Android Application** work process and to check out our new user interface screen in the Nexus emulator. The result is shown on the right side of Figure 12-10, and as you can see our text is now readable and the design matches.

Next, we need to add the Java code to our TravelPlanet.java Activity class so we can instantiate the new Button user interface element thus making it functional, so that our user can click it to return to the Home Screen.

Adding the Return to Home Planet Button to the Java Code

Let's add a new line of code under our **travelVideo.start()** method call and instantiate our Button user interface element. We'll name it **travelButton** and reference it to our XML parameters using the following line of code:

```
Button travelButton = (Button)findViewById(R.id.travelButton);
```

Next we're going to modify the commented-out code in our TravelPlanet.java Activity to change it from a onTouch() event handling scenario attached to our VideoView UI element, to an onClick() event handling scenario attached to our Button UI element. The commented-out code was shown in Figure 12-5, whereas all the modified code is shown in Figure 12-11.

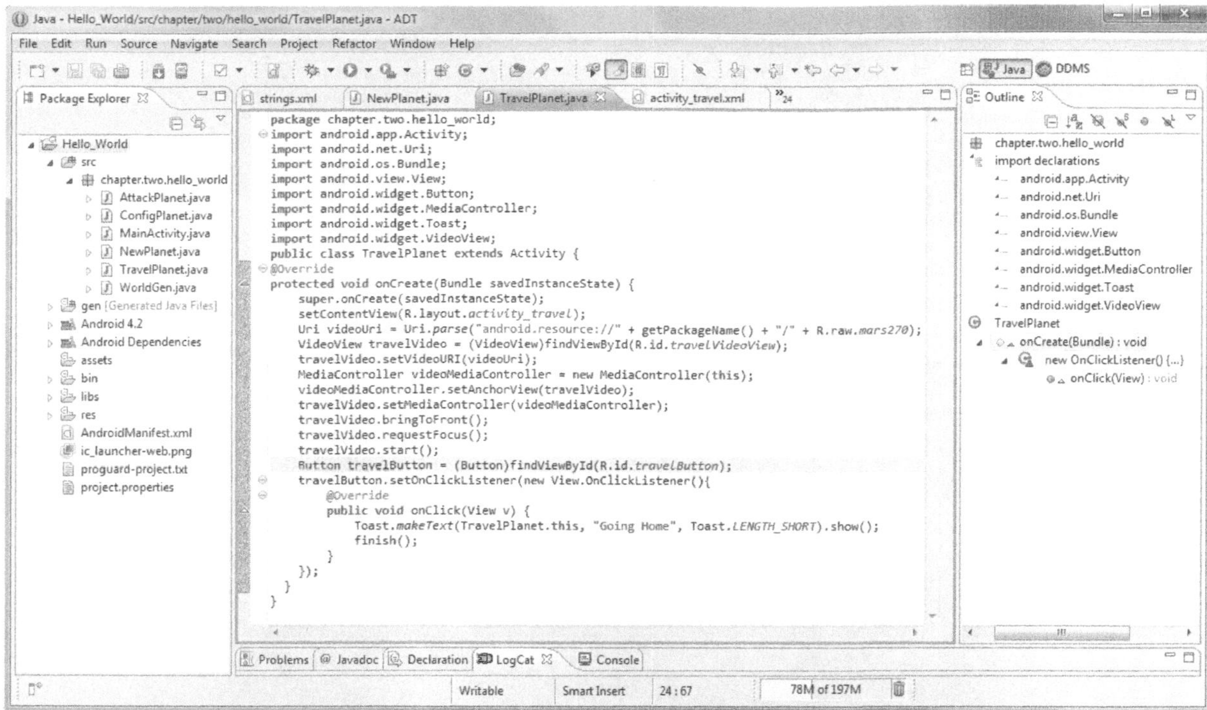

Figure 12-11. Adding our travelButton Java code to instantiate a button UI element and attach onClick() handler

So, change your **travelVideo.setOnTouchListener()** method call a **travelButton.setOnClickListener()** method call, using the following code:

```
travelButton.setOnClickListener(new View.OnClickListener() {new code goes in here}
```

The next thing that we need to do is remove the rest of those double slash commenting characters so we can modify the inside of the **OnClickListener()** method, changing our **onTouch()** method and its contents an onClick() method instead. The new **onClick()** code should look like the following:

```
@Override
public void onClick(View v) {
        Toast.makeToast(TravelPlanet.this, "Going Home", Toast.LENGTH_SHORT).show();
        finish();
}
```

Notice that two of the three warning highlights shown in the Figure 12-5 screenshot have disappeared, now that we have utilized the **View** and **Toast** class objects in our new onClick() Java code. Because the MotionEvent class is used with the onTouch() event handling that we have since removed, you can go ahead and delete this import statement, and your Java code will now be error and warning free, and ready to test in your Nexus S emulator. Use the **Run As Android Application** menu sequence to run your Hello_World app in the Nexus S emulator, and test the functions, as shown in Figure 12-12.

Figure 12-12. Testing our Button user interface element and MediaController transport

The only problem I can see now with the Travel to a Planet Activity user interface screen is a problem (issue) with the User Experience UX Design.

The problem is that the Button UI element we have added at the top of the screen looks like a heading for the screen rather than a Button that can be clicked. This may seem minor to you, but to some users who assume that the top part of the screen is a heading and not a button, this assumption will serve to trap them on this screen with no way to get back to the Home Screen. So let's fix this one last UX issue, and we'll be finished here!

Fine-Tuning Our Travel to Planet User Experience Design

To highlight our top-centered Button as being a button and not a caption, we need to put a **border** around it so that it looks more like a button. The first thing I did was to type in **android:** inside my Button tag and to look for an android:border parameter in the list of available parameters in the helper dialog. Surprisingly, there was no such option, so I had to instead get creative, and figure something else out that would serve to achieve the same visual end-result. The XML mark-up code is shown in Figure 12-13.

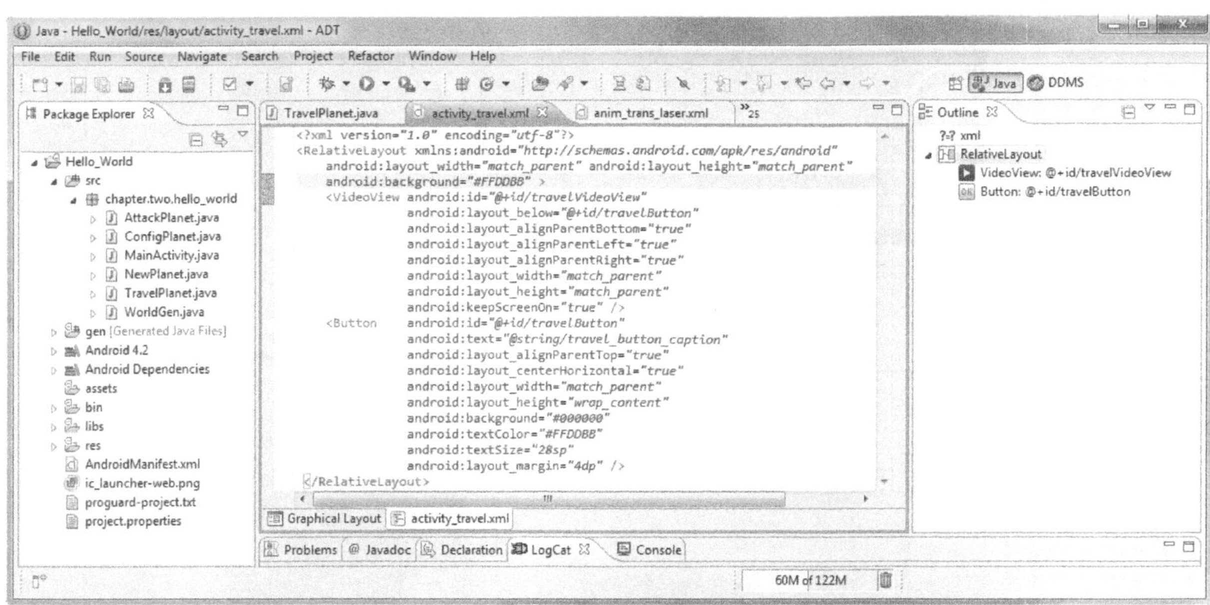

***Figure 12-13.** Create a Button border effect, using a RelativeLayout background with a Button margin parameter*

What I did was to set an **android:background="#FFDDBB"** tag parameter for the parent RelativeLayout container. Because our VideoView UI element fills the screen, I can effectively use the background color (which I matched to the android:textColor parameter value) to create a nice border around the button, by also using an **android:layout_margin="4dp"** parameter to pull in the black background of the Button UI element enough to let this Relative Layout background color show through, and become a border for my Button!

Now let's use the **Run As Android Application** work process, and see whether our button looks and acts more like a button now, instead of a screen caption.

As you can see in Figure 12-14, the button at the top of the Activity user interface screen now looks more like it is a button than a screen caption, and a click on the Button returns the user to the Home Screen, and a click on the digital video shows an Android Media Controller Transport Control Bar, so both are now working perfectly.

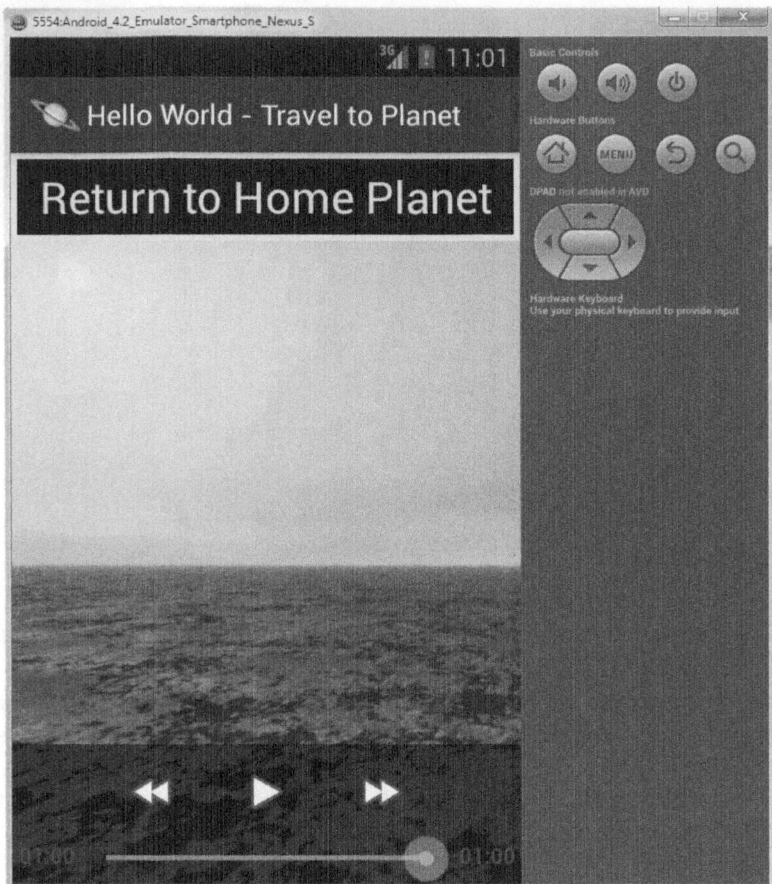

Figure 12-14. Testing the Travel to Planet UI Screen and Button with Margin Border

In Chapter 13 we will learn about the other part of video, that is, audio, and how to create, manipulate, compress, encode, optimize, and work with audio for your Android application. After we learn the basic concepts and techniques regarding audio, we'll start to incorporate it into our app.

Summary

In this chapter covering digital video, we took a closer look at how to incorporate the digital video concepts and assets that we learned about in the previous chapter in our Hello World Android application XML and Java code and user interface and user experience designs.

We learned about the Android MediaController class, which is used to play digital video files in our Android application. We learned how to create a **Uniform Resource Identifier** object, or URI object, using the **Uri** class and the **Uri.parse()** method along with the **getPackageName()** method.

Then we wrote the Java code for our TravelPlanet.java Activity class that implemented the **MediaController** class by instantiating a new object named **videoMediaController**, and then anchored the MediaController object to the travelVideo VideoView object by using the **.setAnchorView()** method.

We then completed wiring the MediaController to the VideoView by calling the **.setMediaController()** method off our travelView VideoView object using the videoMediaController object reference. Once that was completed, we were ready to set up our digital video playback, using our travelView object.

We called several View class methods to set up our digital video playback, first bringing the View to the forefront, using the **.bringToFront()** method and then making sure it had Focus, by calling the **.requestFocus()** method. Then we started the playback of our MPEG4 digital video file using the **.start()** method and tested our program logic in the Nexus S emulator.

Next, we did some troubleshooting to see why we were not getting the MediaController transport bar on the bottom of our VideoView UI element.

We needed to replace our onTouch() event handling with a Button UI element and implement onClick() event handling so that our VideoView could trap an onTouch() event and bring up the MediaController Transport Control widget.

Finally, we did some fine-tuning to our user interface design, to add some parameters affecting our button coloration, to increase the contrast, and to match the look and feel of the application. We also added a thin border around our Button UI object, so that it did not appear to our end-users as a screen caption, which would have been a user experience design mistake.

In the next chapter, we will learn about the other primary new media genre supported in the Android OS: digital audio. We will learn the core digital audio concepts, design principles, and production techniques behind digital audio, and the file formats and codecs that are used to implement digital audio in our Android Applications. We will learn about the open source audio editing software package Audacity and how to use it to create audio assets for use in our Hello World Android application.

Chapter 13

An Introduction to Audio: Concepts and Optimization

In this chapter, we will give you the foundational knowledge that you will need to understand how digital audio works, as well as to be able to work competently with digital audio within your Android application.

Digital audio is one of those new media assets that is more difficult to understand and optimize because digital audio is essentially a collection of digitally sampled sound waves, and, on top of that, they are invisible to the naked eye. Thus, we have to rely on our ears rather than our eyes, and most of us are not used to doing production using our ears, unless we are audio engineers, songwriters, musicians or opera singers!

Because digital audio data plays back in real-time it introduces that fourth dimension, time, into the equation, just like digital video does. This, along with the complexities introduced by today's powerful but complicated digital audio editing software and encoding and decoding algorithms, can make digital audio as difficult to learn about as digital video is.

We are going to look at all this within a context of how it applies to creating an optimal user experience for your Android application end-user.

This means not only learning about underlying principles of digital audio editing and its data footprint optimization, but also about which digital audio formats are best to use for Android, as well as what sample rates to use with them. These topics are advanced, so we are going to utilize three chapters to effectively cover everything thoroughly, so that you will have an excellent handle on digital audio, and how to optimize it for Android.

The Foundation of Analog Audio: Sound Waves and Air

As those of you who are stereo buffs already know, sounds are created by sound waves pulsing through air, which is why sub-woofers are huge 12-inch to 24-inch cones that are rapidly pushed out via magnetic pulses throwing major sound waves into that audience of 100,000 fans at rock concerts.

Before digital audio existed analog audio was a major consumer electronics industry. In fact, it still is today, where sound waves are controlled by complex analog electronics composed of capacitors, resistors, oscillators, crystals, tubes, circuit boards, speaker cones, cardioid microphones, and similar analog technologies. As I said, digital audio is complex, and part of this complexity comes from the need to bridge analog audio and digital audio technologies.

Just as sounds are generated by speaker cones of various sizes, which are essentially just membranes made of one material or another, which generate sound waves by pulsing or vibrating them into existence, so too do our ears receive and then hear these sound waves, by receiving those pulses of air or vibrations and turning them back into data that our brain can process.

Sound waves generate different **tones**, depending on the **frequency** of the sound wave. A wide or infrequent (long) wave produces a lower (bass) tone, whereas a more frequent (short) wavelength produces a higher (treble) tone. It is quite interesting to note that different frequencies of light will produce different colors, so there's a very close correlation between analog sound (audio or music) and analog light (color or photography) that carries through into the digital realm.

The **volume** of a sound wave will be predicated on the **amplitude** of that sound wave, or the height (or size) if it. So, the frequency is how close together the waves are spaced, along the **X axis** in 2D, and the amplitude is how tall the waves are as measured along the **Y axis**.

Sound waves themselves can be shaped differently, to carry different sound effects; the baseline type of wave is called a **sine wave**, which we learned about in high school math with our sine, cosine, and tangent math functions.

Those of you well-versed in audio synthesis are aware that there are other types of core sound waves in sound design, such as the **saw wave** that looks like the edge of a saw (hence its name), or a **pulse wave**, which is shaped using right angles (resulting in immediate on and off sounds, or pulses).

Even random wave forms, such as **noise**, are used in sound design to obtain an edgy sound result. As you may have guessed from your previous learning about data footprint optimization in this book, the more chaos or noise that is present in your sound wave, the harder it will be to compress for the codec, and the larger the resulting digital audio file will be for that particular sound. Next we're going to take a closer look at how these analog audio sound waves are turned into digital audio data, via a process called **sampling**, which is a core tool of sound design and music synthesis.

The Foundation of Digital Audio: Sampling, Sample Resolution, and Sampling Frequency

The process of turning analog audio sound waves into digital audio data is called **sampling**. You may have heard about a type of keyboard or rack-mount equipment, if you are in the music industry, which is called a **sampler**.

Sampling is a process of **slicing** the audio waves, usually complex sine waves, into **segments** and storing their shape and any other wave attributes (i.e., noise) data in a digital format (zeroes and ones).

These digital segments of an audio sound wave are called **samples**, as they take a sample of the sound wave at any given point in time. The precision of a sample is determined by how much data is used to define each wave slice, and like in digital imaging, this precision is termed the resolution, or the **sampling resolution** and is usually defined as 8-bit, 16-bit, or 24-bit.

In digital imaging (and digital video) the resolution is quantified in the number of colors, and in digital audio, this resolution is quantified in how many bits of data are used to define each of the audio samples taken.

As you may have surmised, a higher sampling resolution, or more data taken to reproduce a given sound wave sample, will yield a higher audio playback resolution, and thus a higher sound quality result. This is the reason why 16-bit (also termed: **CD quality**) audio sounds far better than 8-bit audio, just like a 24-bit color image looks better than an 8-bit color image.

In digital audio, we now have a 24-bit data sampling, known in the digital audio realm as: **HD digital audio**. HD digital broadcast radio uses a 24-bit sample resolution, so each audio sample or slice of a sound wave, contains 16,777,216 units of sample resolution. Some newer Android devices will also support HD audio, such as those smartphones you see advertised, with super high-quality (HD) audio, which means they have 24-bit audio hardware support onboard.

Besides the digital audio sample resolution, we also have a digital audio **sampling frequency**, or how many samples at that particular resolution are taken over one second of time. In digital imaging, the sampling frequency would be analogous to the number of pixels within the image that we use.

Sampling frequency can also be called the **sampling rate**, and you might be familiar with CD quality audio, which is defined as using a **16-bit** sample resolution and a **44.1 kHz** sampling rate, which takes **44,100** samples, each of which will contain 16-bits of data, or 65,536 units of total data within each sample.

Let's do the math, and find out how many samples of data are used to provide one second of **raw** (uncompressed) digital audio data. This is accomplished by multiplying 65,536 units by 44,100 samples to get a data value of **2,890,137,600** samples used to represent one second of CD quality audio.

So to figure out **raw data** in an audio file, you would multiply the sampling bit-rate decimal value by the sampling frequency by the number of seconds in that audio snippet. Rest assured it will be a large number, but relax; audio codecs are really great at optimizing this data down to an amazingly small data footprint with very little (audible) loss in quality.

So the exact same trade-off that we have in digital imaging and in digital video exists with digital audio as well. The more data we include the more (high) quality results that we will get, but, at the cost of a larger data footprint. In the visual medium, this is defined using color depth, pixels and (with digital video) frames, and in the aural medium, it's defined via the **sample resolution** in combination with the **sampling rate**.

Common sampling rates in the digital audio industry include: 22 kHz, 32 kHz, 44.1 kHz, 48 kHz, 96 kHz, 192 kHz, and recently 384 kHz. Lower sampling rates, such as 22 kHz or 32 kHz, would be adequate for sampling voice-based digital audio, such as movie dialog or narration track for an eBook, for instance.

Higher sampling rates would be more appropriate for music, and other sound effects that need a high dynamic range (high fidelity) that allows an audio reproduction that exhibits excellent "Hi-Fi" sound quality.

Some sound effects, such as the ones that we will use in our Hello World app, can get away with using a lower 32 kHz sampling rate, as long as the sampling resolution used is 16-bit quality.

Key Digital Audio Attributes: CD Audio, HD Audio, Audio Streaming, and Audio Bit-Rates

As we mentioned already, the **industry baseline** for superior audio quality is known as the **CD audio standard,** which is defined as **16-bit** data sampling resolution at a **44.1 kHz** data sampling frequency. This is what was used to produce audio CD-ROMs during the 20th Century, and it is still used today.

There is also a much more recent **HD audio standard** of **24-bit** data sampling at a **48 kHz** (or even at 96 kHz) sample frequency, which is used today in HD radio and in HD audio compatible Android devices such as Hi-Fi smartphones.

If you are going to use HD audio in your Android applications, you need to make sure that your target end-user is going to own the HD audio standard compatible hardware that will be required to utilize this higher level of audio fidelity.

Just like with your digital video data, your digital audio data can either be **captive** within your application (data files in the /raw folder), or can be streamed from a remote digital audio file streaming data server.

The up-side to streaming digital audio data is that it can reduce the data footprint of your application, just as streaming digital video data can do the same. Many of the same concepts apply equally well to audio and video.

Streaming audio saves data footprint because you do not have to include all that heavy new media digital audio data in your .APK file, so if you are planning on coding a Jukebox application, you may want to consider streaming your digital audio data. Otherwise try and optimize your digital audio data, so that you can include it inside the .APK file. In this way, it will always available to your application's users when they need it.

The down-side to streaming digital audio is that if your user's connection (or the audio server) goes down, your audio file may not always be present for your end-users to play and listen to! The reliability and availability of your digital audio data is the key factor to be considered on the other side of this streaming audio versus captive digital audio data coin.

Just like with digital video, one of the primary concepts in regards to streaming your digital audio is the bit-rate of that digital audio data.

As we have learned previously, bit-rate is defined during the compression process, and we will be getting into this, as it relates to digital audio, in further detail in later sections of this chapter. However let's revisit it here just to make sure you understand it because it's a fundamental concept.

Bit-rates define how much compression your digital audio data is going to have applied to it. A bit-rate is going to be defined during the digital audio file compression process, which is why I am going to cover it in far greater detail in a later section of this chapter that covers digital audio data footprint optimization.

Digital audio files that feature lower (small number) bit-rates are going to have more compression applied to the data, which results in a lower level of quality, but which plays back more smoothly, across a greater number of consumer electronics devices.

As you know the bit-rate is a measure of the bits per second, or BPS, that can be processed or transmitted effectively. As a computer processor gets faster, it can process more BPS; similarly, as a data bandwidth connection gets faster, it can more comfortably send or receive more bits per second.

So, to reiterate, bit/s is important not only for streaming digital audio content, due to what will fit through the bandwidth, but also once it gets to your Android devices, bit-rates affect what can be processed (decoded) fast enough to allow smooth playback by processors inside Android devices.

For this reason, the bit-rate is important for two reasons with regards to streaming audio, and important only in one regard (the decoding CPU's processing speed) in regard to captive (imbedded) digital audio files, which are held as captive files inside of your Android application resource /raw folder.

Thus, with a captive or imbedded audio inside of an Android app, the lower the bit-rate that an audio asset has, the more Android devices that can decode that audio asset smoothly (without dropping audio samples). Next, we need to take a look at digital audio file formats and codecs that are supported in Android and learn which ones to use and when to use them.

Digital Audio Formats: Support for Popular Digital Audio Codecs in Android

There are far more digital audio codecs in Android than there are digital video codecs (MPEG-4 and VP8). Android supports **.MP3** (MPEG-3) files, Wave (PCM or Pulse Code Modulated) **.WAV** files, **.MP4** (or .M4A) MPEG-4 audio, OGG Vorbis (**.OGG**) audio files, Matroska (**.MKS**) audio files, FLAC (**.FLAC**) audio files, and even MIDI (.MID, .MXMF and .XMF) files, which technically aren't really even digital audio data at all. Let's get MIDI out of the way first since it's not something we are going to use in our Hello World app.

MIDI stands for **Musical Instrument Data Interface**, and it is one of the very first ways that digital audio and computers worked together, dating all the way back to the 1980s. The first computer to feature a MIDI port was the Atari ST-1040, and it allowed you to plug a **keyboard synthesizer**, such as the Yamaha DX-7, into that MIDI port, and to play and record MIDI data into the computer using audio software called a **MIDI sequencer**.

A MIDI file contains no sample data, that is, it contains no audio, only **performance data**. MIDI keeps track of which keys on the keyboard were pressed and when, along with the key press duration, how hard the key was pressed (termed: after-touch) and similar performance features. When a MIDI file is played back through the synthesizer, it replicates the performance of the player even though the player is no longer playing that **track**.

A track in music production jargon is one section or part of a song composition or performance. In a recording studio, different instrument and vocal performances are kept on different tracks, so that they can be "mixed-down" more precisely by an Engineer in Post-Production.

The way this was used in MIDI sequencing software was that you could play one instrument track, record it as MIDI data, and the sequencer would play it back for you while you played another instrument track alongside of it. This enabled digital songwriters to assemble complex arrangements by using the computer, instead of a studio full of musicians.

Android supports playback of MIDI files, but does not implement a MIDI class, so it would not be an easy task to code a MIDI sequencer for Android, although some on the code forums are talking about it. For that reason it is beyond the scope of this book and I mention it here only to educate you on the history and scope of digital audio, as MIDI played an important role in the evolution of digital audio.

The most common format supported by Android is the **MP3** digital audio file format. Most of us are familiar with MP3 files, due to music download websites like Napster, and most of us collect songs in this format to use on popular MP3 players and via CD-ROM and DVD-ROM based music collections.

The reason MP3 digital audio file format is so popular is because it has a good compression to quality ratio, and because the codec needed to play it back can be found almost anywhere, even in the Android OS. MP3 would be an acceptable format to use in an Android application, as long as you get the best quality level out of it, by using an optimal encoding work process.

It is important to note that MP3 is a **lossy** audio file format, like JPEG is for imaging, where some of the audio data (and thus quality) is thrown away during the compression process, and cannot later be recovered. Thus, if you are going to use MP3 audio, make sure to save your original uncompressed audio data files.

Android does have a **lossless** audio compression codec, called: **FLAC**, which stands for **Free Lossless Audio Codec**. FLAC is an open source audio codec, whose support is virtually as widespread as MP3, due to the free nature of the software decoder. So it would be possible to use completely lossless new media assets in your Android application using PNG32 and FLAC.

FLAC is also very fast (very tightly coded), supports HD (24-bit) audio, and there are no patent concerns for using it. This is a great audio codec to use if you need high-quality audio within a reasonable data footprint.

FLAC supports a wide range of sample resolutions, from 4-bits per sample up to 32-bits per sample. It also supports a very wide range of sampling frequency, from 1Hz to 655350Hz (65 kHz) in 1Hz increments, so it is very flexible. From an audio playback hardware standpoint, I'd suggest using a 16-bit sample resolution and either a 44.1 kHz or 48 kHz sample frequency.

FLAC is supported in Android 3.1 and later, so if your end-users are using modern Android devices, you should be able to safely utilize a FLAC codec.

Another open source digital audio codec supported by Android is the **Vorbis** codec, a **lossy** audio codec from the **Xiph.Org Foundation**. The Vorbis codec data is most often held in an **.OGG** data file container, and thus Vorbis is commonly called the **Ogg Vorbis** digital audio data format.

Ogg Vorbis supports sampling rates from **8 kHz** up to **192 kHz**, and up to **255** discrete channels of digital audio (as we now know, this represents 8-bits worth of audio channels). Vorbis is supported in all versions of Android.

Vorbis is quickly approaching the quality of HE-AAC and WMA (Windows Media Audio) Professional, and is superior in quality to MP3, AAC-LC, and WMA. It is a lossy format, so FLAC would still have a higher quality level than Ogg Vorbis, as it contains all the original digital audio sample data.

Android supports most popular MPEG4 **AAC**, or **Advanced Audio Coding**, codecs, including **AAC-LC**, **HE-AAC**, and **AAC-ELD**. These can all be contained in MPEG4 containers (.3gp, .mp4, .m4a), and played back in all versions of Android, except for AAC-ELD, which is only supported after Android 4.1. **ELD** stands for **Enhanced Low Delay**, and this codec is intended for use in a real-time two-way communications application, such as a digital walkie-talkie.

The simplest AAC codec is the AAC-LC or **Low Complexity** codec, which is the most widely used and should be sufficient for most applications. An AAC-LC should yield a higher-quality result, at a lower data footprint, than MP3.

The next most complicated AAC codec is the HE-AAC or **High Efficiency** AAC codec. This codec supports sampling rates from 8 kHz to 48 kHz and both Stereo and Dolby 5.1 channel encoding. Android supports decoding both the v1 and v2 levels of this codec, and also encodes audio in the HE-AAC v1 codec, in Android devices later than version 4.1 (Jelly Bean).

For encoding speech, which usually features a different type of sound wave than music does, there are also two other **AMR** or **Adaptive Multi-Rate** audio codecs that are highly efficient for encoding things like speech or short-burst sound effects that do not need high-quality reproduction (such as, a bomb blast sound effect).

There is an **AMR-WB**, or **Adaptive Multi-Rate Wide-Band** standard in Android, which supports 9 discrete settings from **6.6 to 23.85 kbps** audio bit-rates sampled at 16 kHz, which is a high sample rate where voice is concerned. This would be the codec to use for a Narrator track, if you were creating an interactive eBook application, for instance.

There is also an **AMR-NB**, or **Adaptive Multi-Rate Narrow-Band**, standard in Android, which supports 8 discrete settings from **4.75 to 12.2 kbps** audio bit-rates sampled at 8 kHz, which is an adequate sample rate, if the data going into the codec is of high quality, or the resulting audio sample does not require high quality due to its noisy nature (bomb blast).

Finally, we have **PCM** or **Pulse Code Modulated** audio, commonly known as the **WAVE** or **.WAV** audio format. Many of you are familiar with this format, as it is the original audio format used for the Windows operating system.

PCM audio is also commonly used for CD-ROM and DVD-ROM content, as well as telephony applications. This is because PCM Wave audio is an **uncompressed** digital audio format, and it has no computationally intensive compression algorithms applied to its data stream, and thus decoding (CPU overhead) is not an issue for telephone equipment or CD-ROM or DVD-ROM players.

For this reason, as you will soon see, when we start compressing digital audio assets into the various formats, we can use PCM as a baseline, but probably won't put it into our .APK file, because there are other formats, like FLAC and AAC, which will give us the same quality, using an order of magnitude less data.

Ultimately, the only way to really find out which audio formats in Android have the best digital audio codec for any given audio data instance is to actually encode your digital audio in the primary codecs that we know are well supported and efficient, and observe the data footprint results, and then listen to audio playback quality to make our final decision.

Digital Audio Optimization: Playback Across Devices

Optimizing our digital audio assets for playback across the wide range of Android devices in the market is going to be much easier than optimizing our digital video or even our digital imagery across Android devices was.

This is because there is a much wider disparity of screen resolutions and display aspect ratios than there is a disparity of digital audio playback hardware support across Android devices. This is because user's ears can't perceive the same quality difference in audio that the eye can with video.

Generally, there are three primary "sweet spots" of digital audio support across all Android devices, which we should support for our high-quality audio. Lower-quality audio such as narration tracks or short sound effects can use 22 kHz or 32 kHz sampling with 8-bit, 12-bit, or 16-bit resolution.

These high-quality audio targets include CD quality audio, also known as 16-bit data sampling at 44.1 kHz, HD quality audio is at the other end of this audio spectrum, also known as **24-bit** data sampling at **48 kHz** sampling rate, and an unnamed "somewhere in the middle" specification, using 16-bit data sampling at a 48 kHz sampling rate. The last option in the right hands can yield results similar to THX quality audio that was used in theaters.

Thus, our work process for optimizing our digital audio assets across all the Android devices is going to be to create 16-bit assets at 44.1 kHz and at 48 kHz, and then optimize (compress) them in the different formats supported in Android, and see which ones provide the highest quality audio playback with the lowest possible data footprint.

We will do this using the recently released **Audacity 2.0.3** digital audio editing and engineering software package. This software package is open source, and thus is accessible to all our readers and available on all popular OS platforms, including Windows, Macintosh, and Linux.

Setting Up Audacity 2 with Plug-Ins and Codec Libraries

If you haven't downloaded the latest version of Audacity (currently 2.0.3 as of the writing of this book) as yet, go to **audacity.sourceforge.net** and get your free copy now and install it.

Be sure that you also install the latest Audacity 2 plug-ins, FF-MPEG and LAME codecs, so that you can export the very latest and most up to date digital audio encoding algorithms for the digital audio file formats.

It is important to note here that the encoder side of a codec can be made more efficient without changing the decoder side of the codec; so getting the latest encoders at any given time does not mean that Android needs to update their decoder support in their OS API libraries for you to be able to gain a quality-to-filesize benefit from any particular codec.

Once you download and install the latest Audacity, you can enhance it with all of the new plug-ins and codecs by going to the **Download** tab (page) for Audacity and clicking the **Plug-Ins and Libraries** link.

To install the more than 90 free LADSPA plug-ins, find and then click on the link that says: "set of over 90 LADSPA plug-ins." This triggers a download on an .EXE file (in the case of Windows) that you should be sure to install in Audacity's **Plug-Ins** folder, as shown in a **Select Destination Location** stage of the LADSPA Plug-Ins Setup dialog in Figure 13-1. If you don't put these plug-ins in the right folder, they won't load in Audacity.

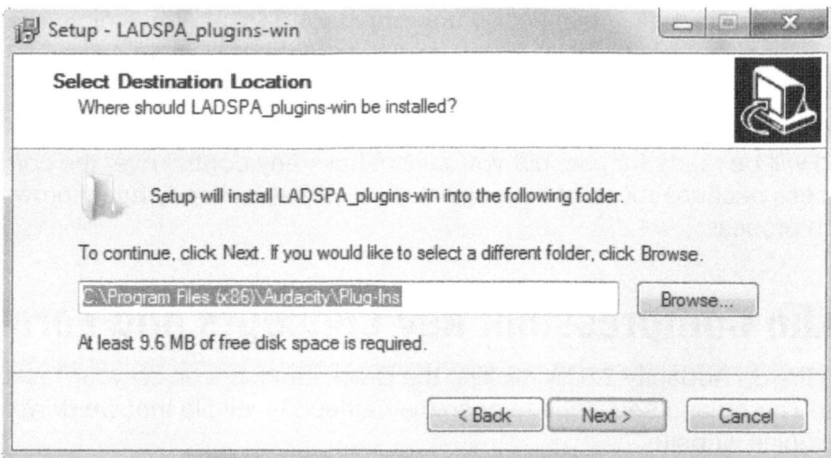

***Figure 13-1.** Select Destination Location Setup dialog for LADSPA Plug-Ins specifying \Audacity\Plug-Ins Folder*

If you like, you can also install the Nyquist and VST plug-ins, listed on this page as well, although they are not needed for this book as we are not going to go quite that deep into digital audio engineering at this time!

Next scroll to the bottom of the page and right-click the **LAME FAQ** link and open up the LAME MP3 encoder page, and then click the **download page** link at the top. Scroll halfway down and click the text link for the .EXE file that reads **Lame_v.3.99.3_for_Windows.exe** and download and install the .EXE file into its default directory location.

Next, scroll to the bottom of the page, and right-click the **FFmpeg FAQ** link and open up the FFmpeg Import Export Library page, and then click the **download page** link at the top. Scroll down two links underneath the LAME link, and then click the text link for the .EXE file **FFmpeg_v0.6.2_for_Audacity_on_Windows.exe** and download and install that .EXE file into its default directory location as well.

Once you have installed all these plug-ins and codecs onto your content production workstation, you can then launch Audacity, and it will find and install the latest digital audio codec library support and plug-ins during its start-up initialization routine.

Digital Audio Creation: Finding Hello World Sound Effects

To find some free for commercial use audio samples, I'm going to use the **Google search engine**, and type in a query, for Free Audio Samples, or Free Digital Studio Samples, or Free Audio Files, or Free Digital Audio Files, and similar Google search term combinations.

Note that each of these Google searches turns up completely different results, due to **keywords** used in each of the different websites that offer these digital audio assets.

There are dozens of good websites all of which fit the bill for our needs, so be sure and investigate these further, when you have the spare time. Make sure that the ones that you use for your application development are **free for commercial use**, and do not have any royalties, usage, or copyright restrictions.

What we want to look for is the highest quality **uncompressed PCM** (Wave or .wav audio file format) samples, using 16-bit or better (24-bit or 32-bit) format, and hopefully a 44.1 kHz or 48 kHz sampling frequency.

Note that if you download and use .MP3 files (which most also offer) they will already have been compressed, and will be ready for use, but you will not have any control over the compression and optimization process because much of the original data will have already been thrown away during their compression process.

Digital Audio Compression: Key Concepts and Formats

First you need to fire up Audacity 2.0 by clicking the Quick Launch icon on your Taskbar and use the **File ➤ Open** menu command sequence to open the battle003.wav file that we downloaded from the free audio samples website.

The first time you open a Wave file you will get the Warning dialog shown in Figure 13-2. Select the **Make a Copy** radio button option, and check the **Don't warn again** checkbox and finally click on the **OK** button to load the audio sample into Audacity.

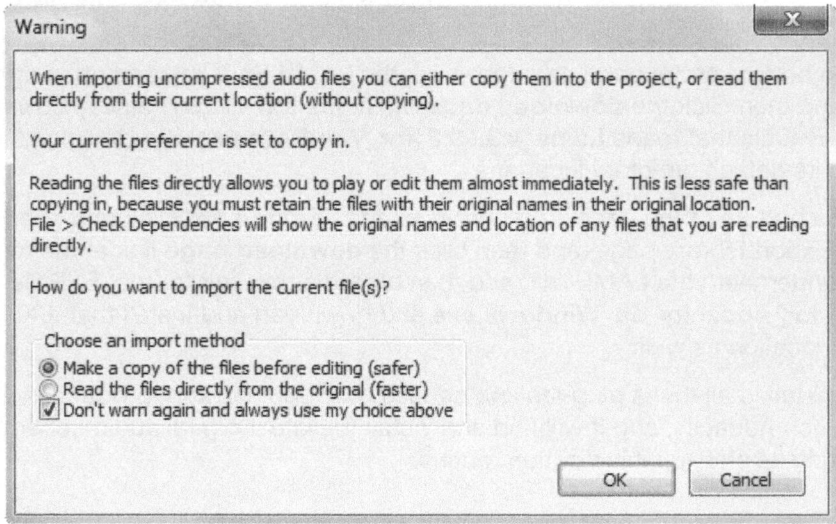

Figure 13-2. Import audio file warning and proper Make a copy settings

Using these audio file import settings (using a copy of the file, instead of the actual file itself) is called **non-destructive audio editing**, and is common practice in the digital audio editing and effects industry.

The reason for this is because if you mess up in your audio **sweetening** and special effects application, and damage the audio data, you can always go back to square one, by going back and loading the original audio data.

Once the battle003.wav sample data is loaded into Audacity 2, you will see a screen exactly like the one shown in Figure 13-3. The upper-left corner contains the audio transport controls, including pause, play, stop, back, forward, and record. Right next to that are the editing tools and on the far right are the level meters that will show green, yellow, and red signal peak indicators when your audio is playing. Underneath these are settings for speaker and microphone volume as well as system audio setting selector drop-downs. On the bottom of the Audacity window you will find the project sample rate in Hz, and hours, minutes, seconds, and millisecond display for Selection Start, End or Length, and Audio Position, for micro-fine-tuning.

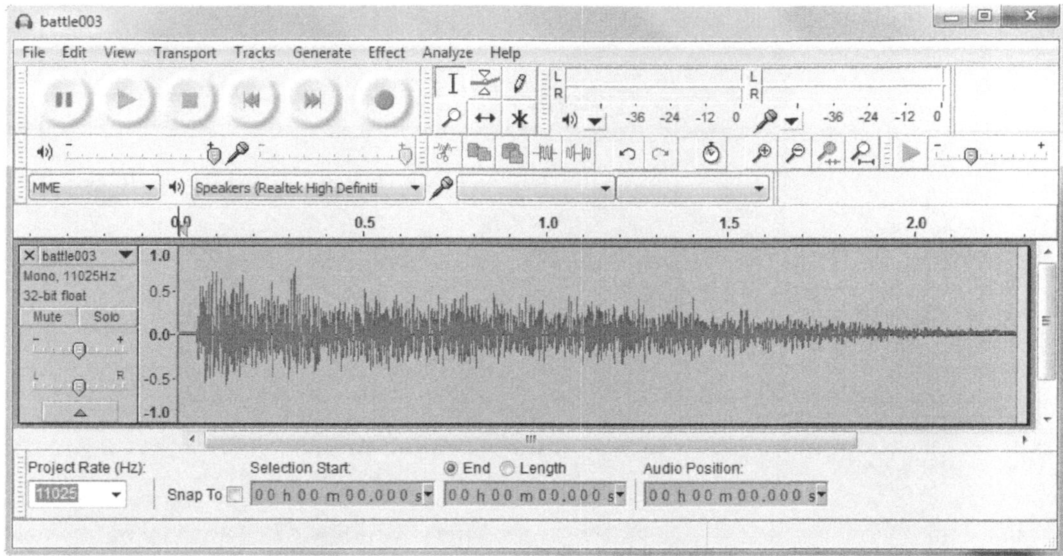

Figure 13-3. Audacity 2.0 main editing screen showing the 32-bit floating point 11 kHz sample data for battle003

The first thing that we want to do is to make sure our sample resolution and sample rate are set correctly, before we start to export to the various digital audio formats that we have learned about, so we can see the actual compression result that each audio codec can offer to our Android project.

Setting Sample Rate and Sample Resolution in Audacity

In the blue-gray control panel located to the left of the visual display of our audio sample, you will see the **battle003** sample (file) name, and a down-facing arrow next to it. Click this arrow to drop-down an options menu, and select the **Set Sample Format** option, and then select the **16-bit PCM** option from its sub-menu, shown in Figure 13-4. This ensures that we're exporting to the 16-bit sample resolution supported across Android.

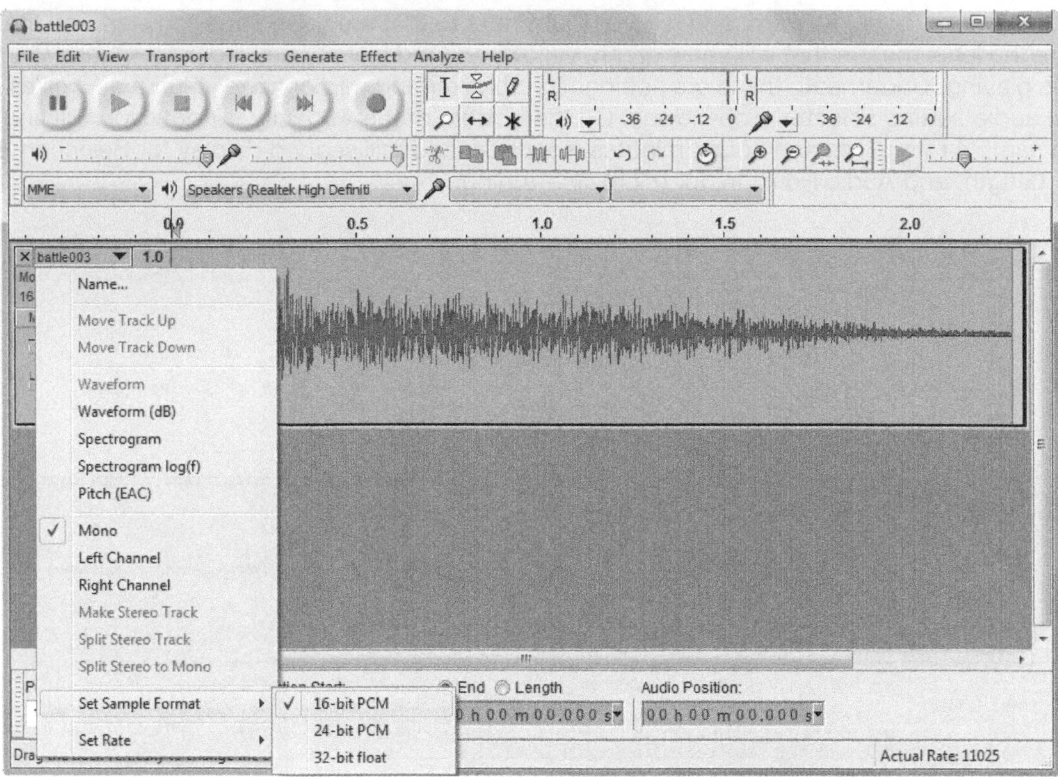

***Figure 13-4.** Setting audio sample resolution to 16-bit PCM (uncompressed) before export to various formats*

Now we can export our **baseline** 16-bit uncompressed Wave audio .wav file format, to use to see what the largest file size would be for this 16-bit 11.025 kHz audio sample of a 2.5 second bomb explosion.

It should be very similar in file size to the original file that we opened (imported) into the Audacity 2 software, but we will name it **blast.wav**, as that is the simpler name that we are going to use for this audio asset (in our Android Java code we will be writing in the next chapter).

Export an Uncompressed PCM Baseline .WAV Format File

To export a file in Audacity, we'll use the **File ➤ Export** menu sequence to open the **Export File** dialog, shown in Figure 13-5. This dialog has several key areas, including the **Save In:** folder specifier, which we have pointing to our **Audio** assets folder, the **File List Pane**, which shows our original battle003.wav file, the **File name:** data entry field where we will name our file, in this case **blast**, and underneath that, the **Save as type:** drop-down selector, which contains all the file formats that Audacity will export to (given that we have correctly installed the LAME and FFmpeg libraries). Note we have the dialog set to export **blast.wav** in **.wav 16-bit PCM** format, which is why we **do not need to specify** the .wav part of this filename.

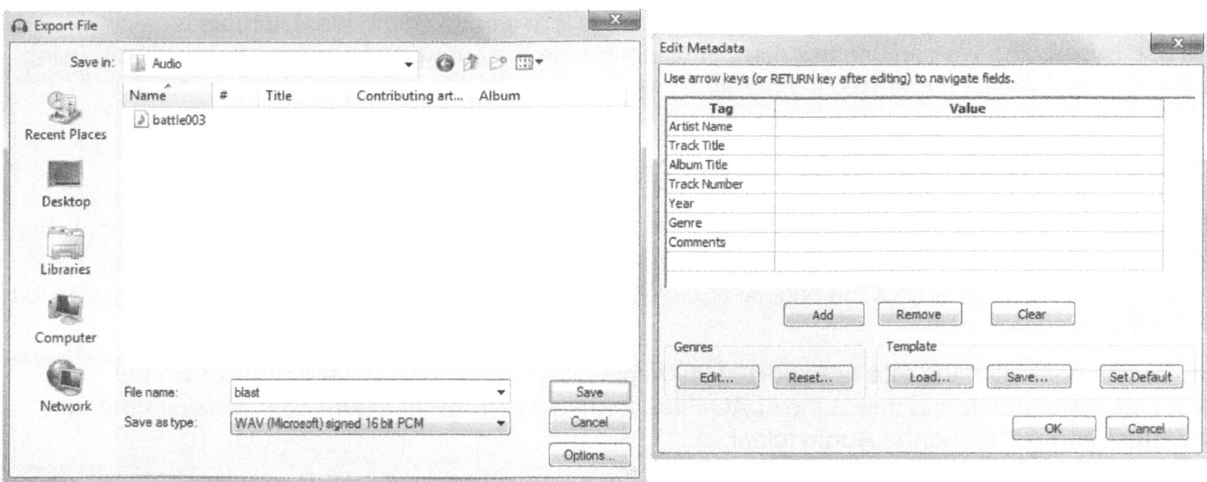

Figure 13-5. Exporting our baseline 16-bit PCM .wav format file, and the Edit Metadata dialog shown on exports

If you click the **Options** button, which is shown at the bottom-right of the Export File dialog, you will see that for the Wave audio file format, you will get a dialog that informs you that there are no encoding options for the PCM format.

If you think about it, this is logical, as the PCM Wave is an uncompressed audio format, and thus the data is not encoded at all, and for this reason there would be no audio encoding parameters or options.

Once you click the **Save** button, another **Edit Metadata** dialog then appears, as shown on the right in Figure 13-5. This dialog has data fields for text values for Artist Name, Track Title, Album Title, Track Number, Year, Genre, and Comments.

Because I am optimizing here for the smallest possible data footprint, and our application does not require audio metadata, I am leaving these fields blank for now, so that we can get an accurate read on what the compression is on just our audio data.

If you are wondering if Android could read and support metadata even if we did put this data into our audio files, the answer is a resounding **yes!** In fact, Android even has a **MediaMetadataRetriever** class that developers can utilize exactly for this specific purpose.

If for some reason your audio application needs to leverage metadata, you can use the Edit Metadata dialog, which shows itself every single time you save any type of audio file format in Audacity, along with the Android MediaMetadataRetriever class, which you can research and learn all about at the following URL:

`http://developer.android.com/reference/android/media/MediaMetadataRetriever.html`

If you look at the blast.wav 16-bit PCM file that we just saved you will see that the file size is the same as the original battle003.wav file.

What we can infer from this is that even though Audacity told us that this was encoded in 32-bit sample resolution at 11.025 kHzi that in fact it was actually 16-bit data, inside of a 32-bit data container (or lots of unused headroom) because the file size was identical right down to the last byte.

So our baseline uncompressed data footprint for this 2.5 second bomb blast sample is **50,380 bytes**, and we can use this number to determine the amount of compression we'll get using all the major formats supported in Android.

Export a Lossless .FLAC Open Source Audio Format File

The first format I am going to try out is the FLAC audio codec, because it uses lossless compression. This will give us an idea of what kind of data footprint reduction we can get using compression that does not throw away any of the original audio data, and thus will give us as perfect a result as 16-bit PCM Wave audio does.

To do this again use the **File ➤ Export** menu sequence and this time we will drop-down the **Save as type:** menu and select the **FLAC Files** format, as shown in Figure 13-6. Again name the file **blast** and put it into the **Audio** folder.

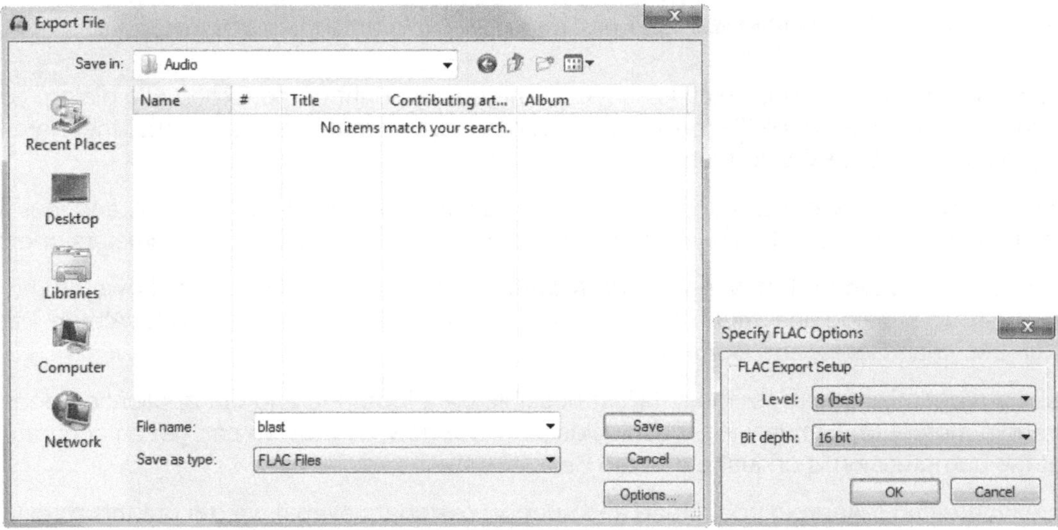

***Figure 13-6.** Exporting FLAC audio file named blast.flac with Level 8 (best) quality and 16-bit sample bit depth*

Notice that there are no other files listed within the center area of this dialog; this is because now that we have selected a FLAC file format type, that region is showing only FLAC files, and currently there are none in the Audio folder. This is another good example of **modal software operation** only this time it is in our audio engineering software, instead of digital imaging software.

To set our FLAC codec options, click the Options button, and set the quality level to **8 (best)** and the Bit depth to **16-bit**. Note under the Bit depth drop-down that we can also use FLAC for a lossless 24-bit HD audio.

Once you have output your **blast.flac** audio asset, go into your file manager and take a look at the file size. You will see that it is **33,537** bytes, or reduced by **one-third** (33,537 divided by 50,380 is 0.66568 or two-thirds).

Next let's take a look at the other open source format, Vorbis, and see whether it can give us an even smaller data footprint. Since Ogg Vorbis is a lossy file format it should give us an even smaller file than FLAC did.

Export Lossy Ogg Vorbis Open Source .OGG Format Files

Use the **File ➤ Export** work process, as before to open the Export File dialog, and select the **Ogg Vorbis Files** from the **Save as type:** drop-down menu. Name the file: **blast** (which will produce a blast.ogg filename) and put it into the **Audio** folder.

Click the **Options** button, and select a **Quality** setting level between 0 and 10. I used the default setting of 5 to start with; during a real data footprint optimization, you would try several settings to see how the data footprint to quality trade-off was affected.

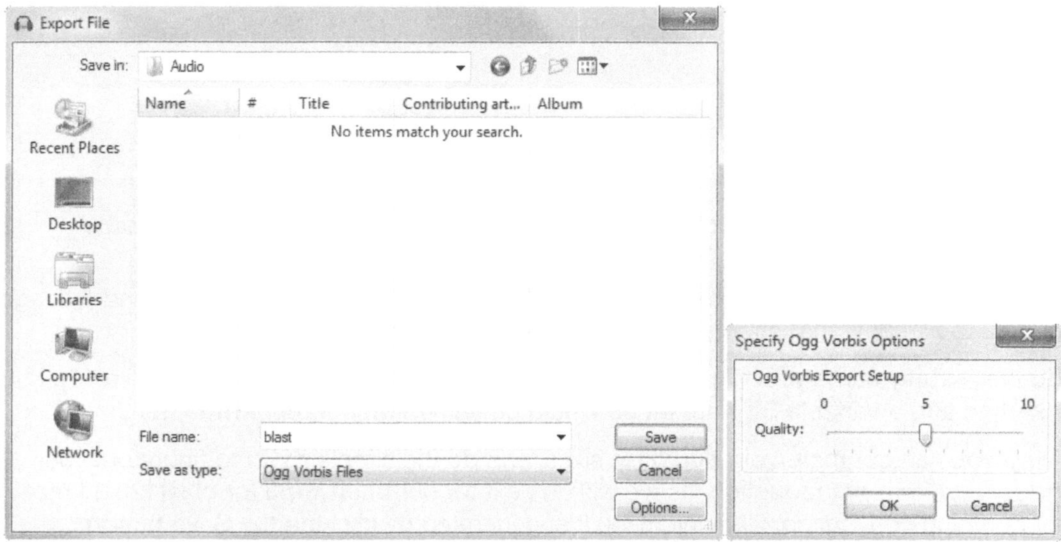

Figure 13-7. Exporting Ogg Vorbis audio file named blast.ogg with Level 5 (default) quality and 16-bit sampling

Once you have output your **blast.ogg** audio asset, go into your file manager and take a look at the file size. You will see that it is **12,995** bytes, or reduced by **three-fourths** (12,995 divided by 50,380 is 0.25794, or equal to one-fourth). This is a significant size reduction and the audio sounds the same as it did before (then again, it's just a basic blast) compression.

Next, let's take a look at MP3, the most common lossy audio format on the market. It should be interesting to see whether MP3 can give us an even smaller data footprint than the Ogg Vorbis open source codec did.

Exporting to a Lossy MPEG-3 Format .MP3 Audio File

Use the **File ➤ Export** work process again, to bring up the Audacity Export File dialog, and set the Save as type: drop-down selector to **MP3 Files**.

Name the file **blast** and select the **Audio** folder, and then click the MP3 Options button to open up the **Specify MP3 Options** dialog that is shown on the right side of Figure 13-8. I used the default Quality Bit-rate setting of **128 kbps**, which is fairly high for audio data, and a **Constant Bit Rate Mode** setting and a **Joint Stereo Channel Mode**, because the file is in Mono.

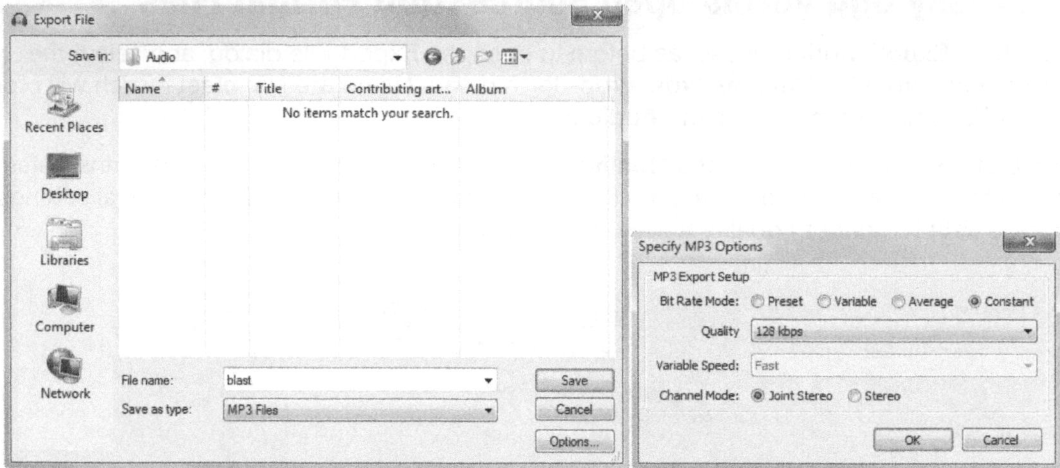

***Figure 13-8.** Exporting MP3 audio file named blast.mp3 with a 128 kbps Constant Rate (Bit Rate Mode) encoding*

If you like, you can try several different Quality bit-rate settings, as well as Variable and Average Bit Rate Modes, to see how that affects your audio file data footprint.

If you do this, simply name your file with the settings in the filename. Thus, a file with a 128 kbps Quality setting and a Variable Bit Rate Mode would be named **blast128vbr.mp3**, for instance.

In this way, you can compare your audio file sizes, and do the simple math to figure out your percentage data footprint reduction, as we will do next for our **blast.mp3** (or blast128cbr.mp3, if we follow our naming convention) file, which you just generated by clicking the Save button.

The blast.mp3 file size is 19,643 bytes, representing a **61%** data footprint reduction. To figure this out, 19,643 divided by 50,380 is **0.3898**, which is 39% of the original, uncompressed file size. 100% minus 39% equals the 61% file size reduction.

Now that we have seen that our .MP3 file size is not that impressive, not even as good as Ogg Vorbis, let's see how MPEG4, or MP4, data compression has improved over MPEG3. Because MPEG-4 is a more recent and advanced codec technology, it should provide us a much better file size to quality ratio.

Exporting to a Lossy MPEG-4 Format .M4A Audio File

Follow the previous **File ➤ Export** work process to invoke the Audacity Export File dialog and select the **M4A (AAC) Files (FFmpeg)** from the **Save as type:** drop-down menu selector. As usual name the file **blast** (which will be named blast.m4a by the Exporter after you click Save) in the Audio directory and then click the **Options** button to open the **Specify AAC Options** dialog as shown in Figure 13-9. I chose to ratchet up the Quality setting to 500, to see what a resulting MPEG4 file size would be when using a maximum quality level setting. Click the Save button and export the blast.m4a file now.

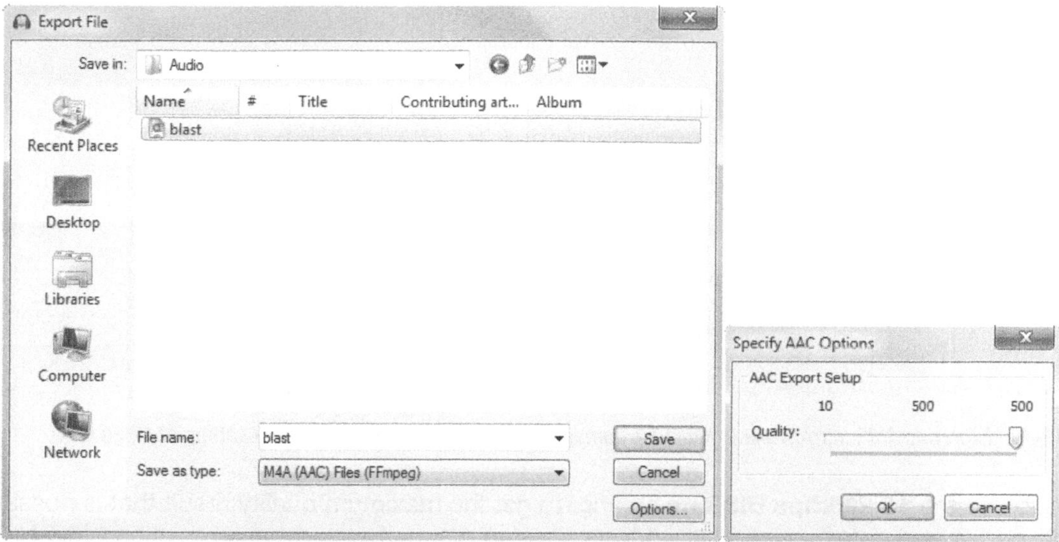

***Figure 13-9.** Exporting our MP4 AAC audio file named blast.m4a with a maximum quality setting of 500*

The blast.m4a file size is 10,513 bytes, representing a **79%** data footprint reduction. To figure this out, 10,513 divided by 50,380 is **0.2087** which is 21% of the original, uncompressed file size. 100% minus 21% equals the 79% file size reduction.

Now that we've seen that our M4A AAC file size is the most impressive thus far, let's see if the more specialized AMR-NB Narrow Band data compression codec will give us any further data footprint improvements over MPEG4 AAC.

Even though the MPEG-4 AMR-NB codec and format was designed and optimized specifically for voice applications, there may be some other applications, such as certain short-burst sound effects, which might obtain good results from this codec.

After all, any codec is simply a complex mathematical equation implemented as software, and does not discriminate, so the only way to really find out is to run your original uncompressed audio data through the codec, and see what happens. Let's do that next; then we will be finished comparing audio codecs that are supported in Android and are also available in Audacity.

Exporting a Narrow Band MPEG-4 Format .AMR Audio File

Follow the **File ➤ Export** work process to invoke the Audacity Export File dialog and select the **AMR (narrow band) Files (FFmpeg)** from the **Save as type:** drop-down menu selector.

As usual, let's name the file **blast** (which will be named blast.amr by the Exporter, after you click on the Save button) in the **Audio** directory, and then click the **Options** button to open the **AMR-NB Export Setup** dialog as shown in Figure 13-10.

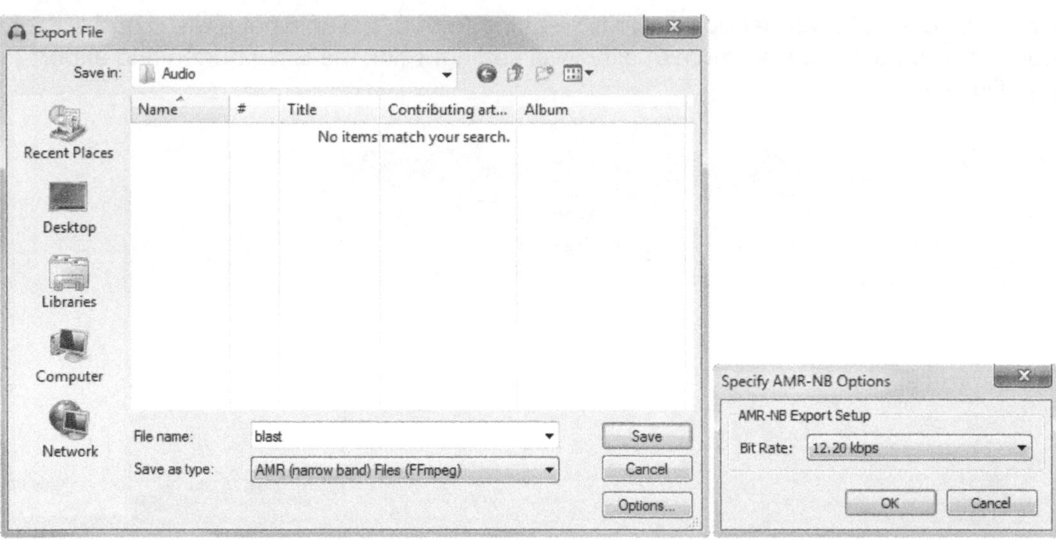

***Figure 13-10.** Exporting AMR (narrow band) audio file named blast.3gp with maximum bit-rate setting of 12.20 kbps*

I chose to use the **12.20 kbps Bit Rate** setting, to get the maximum quality result that is possible with this codec and data format. This work process allows me to see what a resulting AMR-NB file size would be when using a maximum quality level setting.

Let's click the **Save** button, and export our **blast.amr** audio file now. As you can see, this is the smallest data footprint that we have obtained thus far, and yet when we play it back it still sounds very much like a bomb explosion.

The blast.amr file size is 3,686 bytes, representing a **93%** data footprint reduction. To figure this out, 3,686 divided by 50,380 is **0.0732** which is 7% of the original, uncompressed file size. 100% minus 7% equals the 93% file size reduction.

The only problem we have now, and fortunately only with this last very niche codec and file format, is that Audacity wants to output AMR-NB files with an .AMR file extension, whereas Android wants to see AMR-NB audio files using a .3GP file extension. It's always something, isn't it? Let's hope that in a future version of the Android OS, maybe 5.0, that Android decides to play nice and accept .amr file name extensions!

So we go back to the drawing board and look at the Audacity documentation.

The Audacity manual File Export dialog section tells us that we should be able to specify certain non-standard file extensions and get away with it, so let's go back into Audacity and try it!

Follow the usual **File ➤ Export** work process to invoke the Audacity Export File dialog and select the **AMR (narrow band) Files (FFmpeg)** from the **Save as type:** drop-down menu selector.

This time, let's name the file **blast.3gp** in the **Audio** directory, and then click on the **Options** button, and set the 12.20 kbps quality option in the **AMR-NB Export Setup** dialog as shown in Figure 13-10.

Once you click the Save button you will see the Warning dialog shown in Figure 13-11. Click the **Yes** button, and save the file as blast.3gp, and we will shortly ascertain (in the next chapter) if the blast.3gp file will play in our Android application.

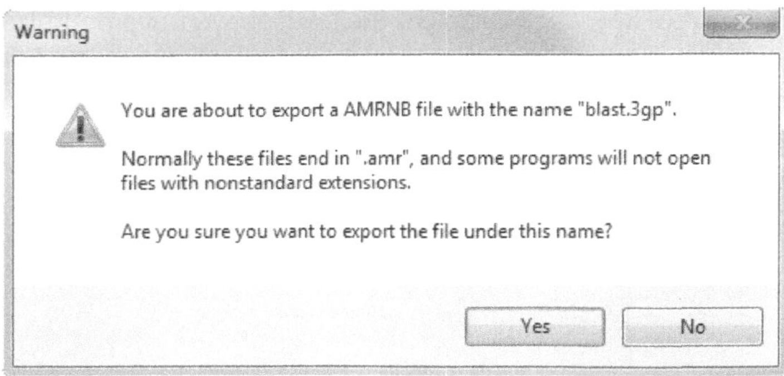

***Figure 13-11.** Warning dialog shown in Audacity on File ➤ Export of blast AMR-NB file with a .3GP file extension*

Next we are going to place these optimized digital audio assets into their proper asset location in our Android Project resource folder hierarchy, so that we can access them in our Java code in the next chapter.

Using Digital Audio Assets in Android: The Project Resource Raw Folder

Now let's open up our operating system's file management software and copy the half-dozen digital audio file formats which we have optimized thus far into our **/res/raw** sub-folder in our Android Hello_World Project folder.

Go into your digital audio assets production folder, in my case, it is on one of my quad-core workstations in a **Book ➤ Audio** folder under the Users folder inside of the MindTaffyDesign folder, as is shown at the top of Figure 13-12.

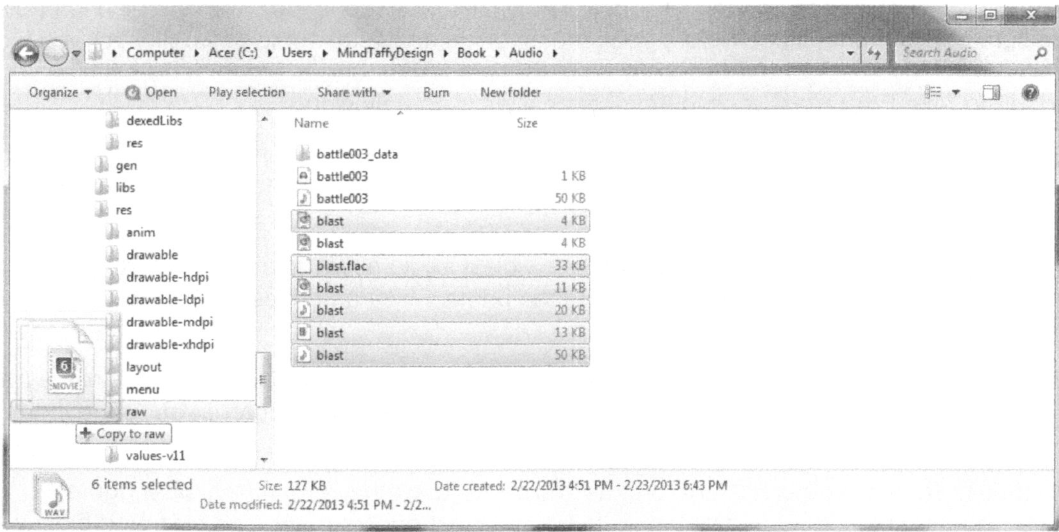

***Figure 13-12.** Select our six optimized blast digital audio files and drag them over to the /res/raw folder*

While holding down the Control key, click to select the six files we have optimized and drag them over to the /res/raw subfolder in your Hello_World Android project folder, as is also shown in Figure 13-12.

Once these are all in the /res/raw folder, as shown in Figure 13-13 we can rename them so that Android knows which one to use when we reference **blast** in our Java code.

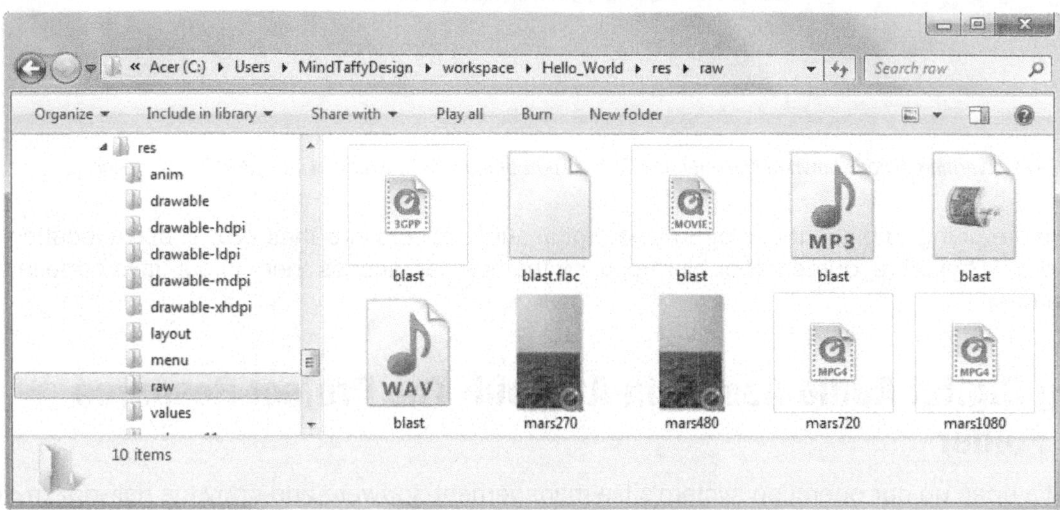

***Figure 13-13.** Our blast files showing in the /res/raw folder*

If we do not rename these files before we launch Eclipse, as we will do in the next step, we will see a number of errors in the **Problems** tab, which is located at the bottom left of the main editing pane in Eclipse ADT.

If you want to actually see what these errors are now, just for experience sake, then launch Eclipse now. Be sure and launch Eclipse before you rename all these digital audio asset files, or you won't see these errors. If you select the **Problems** tab, you will see around a dozen or so blast errors outlined in red text. Error messages in Eclipse are always an ugly sight!

What these errors will tell you is that there is already a blast asset, so Android will take the first blast digital audio asset that it finds as the one to implement and will then generate errors for the other assets.

These errors will specify that Android already has a blast audio asset to utilize, and so you will have to remove any other audio assets that start with the primary file name blast, which we are about to do next.

Now let's go into your operating system file management utility, and we'll rename all these audio assets so that only one, blast.flac, which we will start within the next chapter in our code, can be seen by the Android OS.

This process is shown in Figure 13-14, and as you can see, we have renamed blast.3gp as blast_3gp.3gp, and blast.m4a as blast_m4a.m4a, and blast.ogg as blast_ogg.ogg, and blast.wav as blast_wav.wav, and finally blast.mp3 as blast_mp3.mp3, and so on according to our digital audio asset placeholder naming convention that gets us around these errors in Android.

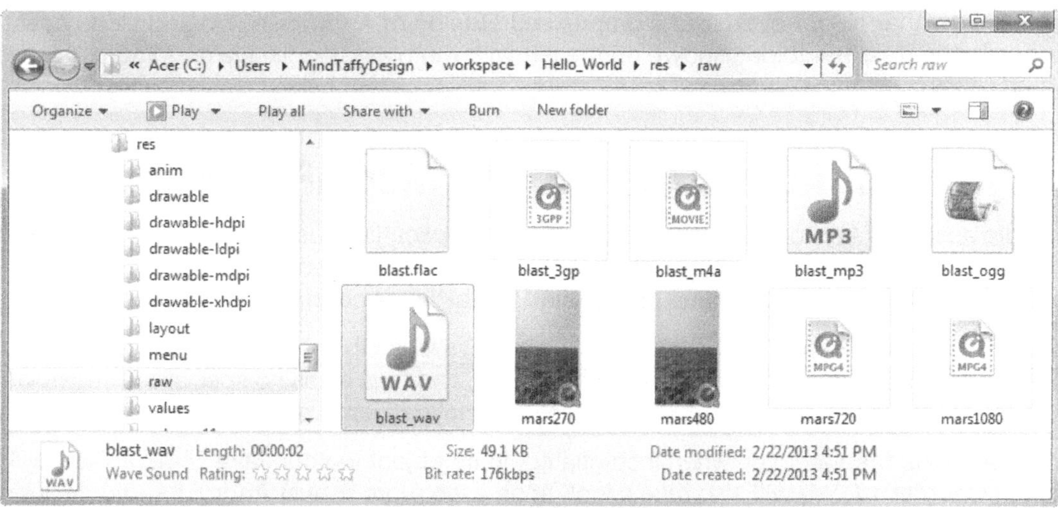

Figure 13-14. ***Renaming the blast digital audio files with their codec types so there is only one named blast***

Later, when we want to implement any given digital audio file format in Android, we will rename blast.flac to blast_flac.flac and then rename the codec we want to use, say blast_m4a.m4a to be simply blast.m4a so that Android then sees the MPEG4 AAC codec version of the audio asset blast. Finally, remember to use **only lowercase letters and numbers** in your filenames; this is a filename **convention** in Android that needs to be followed.

Now let's launch Eclipse, or if you have already launched it to see all of those juicy errors, then use the right-click on project folder and **Refresh** work process, so that we can see that we now have a clean, error-free, IDE software development working environment, as shown in Figure 13-15.

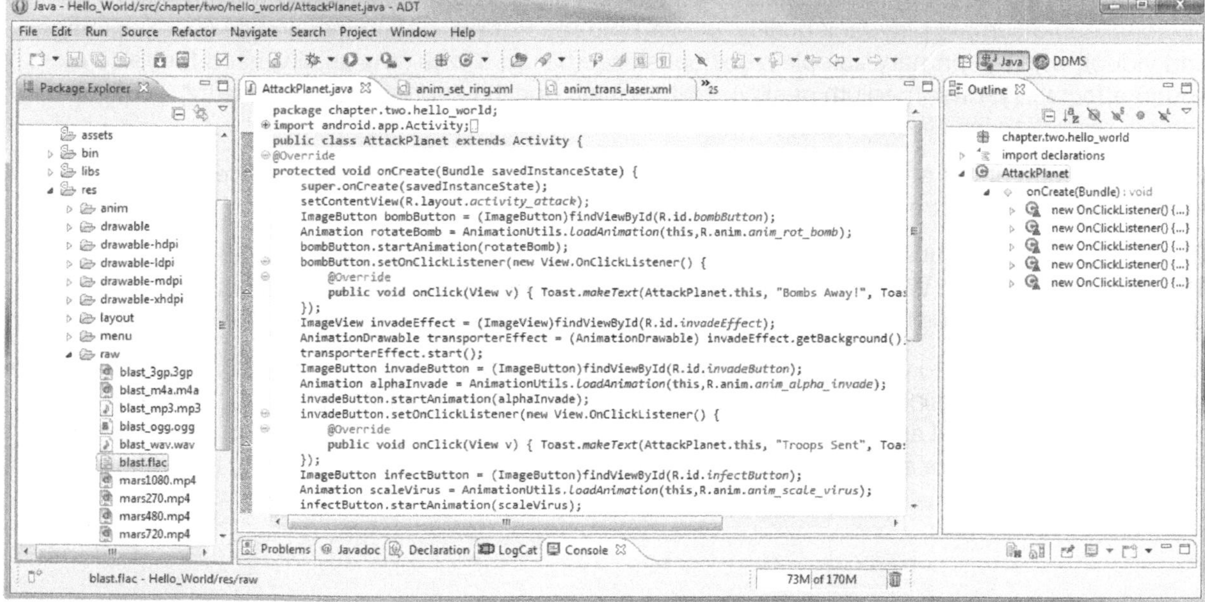

Figure 13-15. ***Our blast digital audio assets shown in the /res/raw folder inside the Eclipse ADT IDE***

You can see now that all our optimized (compressed outside of Android) audio and video assets are all together, in the /res/raw folder, shown on the left with the blast.flac file we're going to access first highlighted.

Playing Digital Audio: The Android MediaPlayer Class

Digital audio assets in Android are played back in your applications using the Android **MediaPlayer** class. Not surprisingly, the MediaPlayer class is part of Android's **media** package, so it will be imported using the familiar import **android.media.MediaPlayer** code statement.

As you know, the MediaPlayer class is a subclass of the java.lang.Object class, as it is its own specialized class, for playing back audio and video new media assets, and thus it has no specialized superclasses that it is subclassed from other than Object class in Java that defines everything as an object.

This is because the MediaPlayer, when instantiated, in an object in your Java code, as you will soon see in Chapter 14. We will also take a look at an even more robust Android **audio sequencing** class in Chapter 15 called the **SoundPool** class, so lots of audio asset coding to learn over the next couple of chapters, which should be a **blast!**

Summary

In this chapter, we learned all about digital audio concepts, techniques, popular codecs, and support for these inside the Android operating system.

We started out with the fundamentals of analog audio and sound waves, and we learned about the core audio concepts of **frequency** and **amplitude**, as well as tones and waves and the role that noise plays in **audio sampling**.

Next we took a look at digital audio **samples** and the process of sampling and the core determinants of digital audio sample playback quality, the **sample resolution**, determined in bits (just like images and video), with the primary sample resolutions used being: **8-bits** (low quality, used for voice or sound effects), **12-bits** (medium quality), **16-bits** (high quality) and **24-bits** (HD quality). A 32-bit sample resolution is seldom required.

We also learned about **sample frequency**, or how many time-slices are taken to define a given analog waveform, to turn it into digital data.

Common sampling frequencies include 8 kHz, 11 kHz, 22 kHz, 32 kHz, 44.1 kHz, 48 kHz, 96 kHz, 192 kHz, and 384 kHz. We learned for our Android development we should be using a reasonable range of quality and thus to use sample rates between 11 kHz (medium quality) and 48 kHz (HD quality).

Next, we learned how to optimize our digital audio bomb blast asset, using Audacity 2 (after we made sure that the latest version of the software and its plug-ins were installed correctly). We took a look at all the primary digital audio formats that are supported in Android, and are also on the Audacity **File Export** dialog **Save as Type:** drop-down menu, which is just about all of them, fortunately.

We exported our **baseline** PCM uncompressed Wave audio to all these major Android supported audio formats and codecs and we did the math to find out which ones gave us the smallest data footprint while still reproducing the audio effect that we were looking for. We found our lossless FLAC format gave us a 33% reduction in data footprint with zero loss of quality, and that the lossy codecs yielded us a 61% to 93% reduction in data overhead.

We then copied the half-dozen optimized files that we created to the **/raw** folder in our Android project and renamed the files so that there was only one **blast.flac** audio asset visible to Eclipse, so that we did not have any **duplicate audio asset errors** in our Eclipse ADT IDE.

Finally, we took a look at the Android MediaPlayer class, which we will be utilizing over the next couple of chapters, to play back our digital audio assets. We learned MediaPlayer is in the **android.media.MediaPlayer** package and a subclass of the **java.lang.Object** master class. In this next chapter on the Android MediaPlayer, we will learn exactly how to implement all these digital audio assets in the Java code that currently exist inside of your Hello_World Android application. That's going to be very exciting!

Chapter 14

Playing Audio in Android: The MediaPlayer Class

In this chapter, we will take the digital audio assets that we optimized in the previous chapter and teach you how to implement them for playback in your Hello_World AttackPlanet.java Activity event handling code.

We'll add sound effects to the Attack a Planet user interface ImageButton elements, so that when users click these animated buttons the digital audio will playback, adding to the already impressive visual effects we created in the graphics design and animation chapters previously.

Now that you know how to optimize audio for use in Android, we'll also use some higher-quality audio from world-renowned sound designer and music composer **Frank Serafine**, who is a friend of mine and was gracious enough to give me a few audio samples for us to use for this book.

These sound effects, background music, and ambient environment sounds will allow us to greatly enhance our other Activity screens to yet again take our user interface and user experience to an entirely new level.

We will also take a look at some more concepts in digital audio playback, which are very similar to those which we observed in the digital video and the frame and vector animation chapters, such as seamless audio looping, where you can't tell where the background audio loop (seam) is in the audio playback cycle.

Since we've already gone over the basic origins of the Android MediaPlayer class in the previous chapter, we will now go ahead and cover the various Java methods that are available in this advanced class. We will do this in the first part of this chapter, and then we'll get into writing some code that implements some of these core MediaPlayer functions. Once we do this, we'll be able to give some of our user interface elements and our Activity screens some really cool digital audio features thanks to Mr. Serafine.

The Android Media Player: Methods and the State Engine

In Android, the MediaPlayer class is what could be termed a **state machine**, that is, a digital file playback entity that has certain **states** that it is in at any given time. I have generously included the **state machine diagram** from the `developer.android.com` website in this section (see Figure 14-1), so that you can reference it here, along with the text in this section, which discusses it in detail. You can find it on the developer website here:

`http://developer.android.com/reference/android/media/MediaPlayer.html`

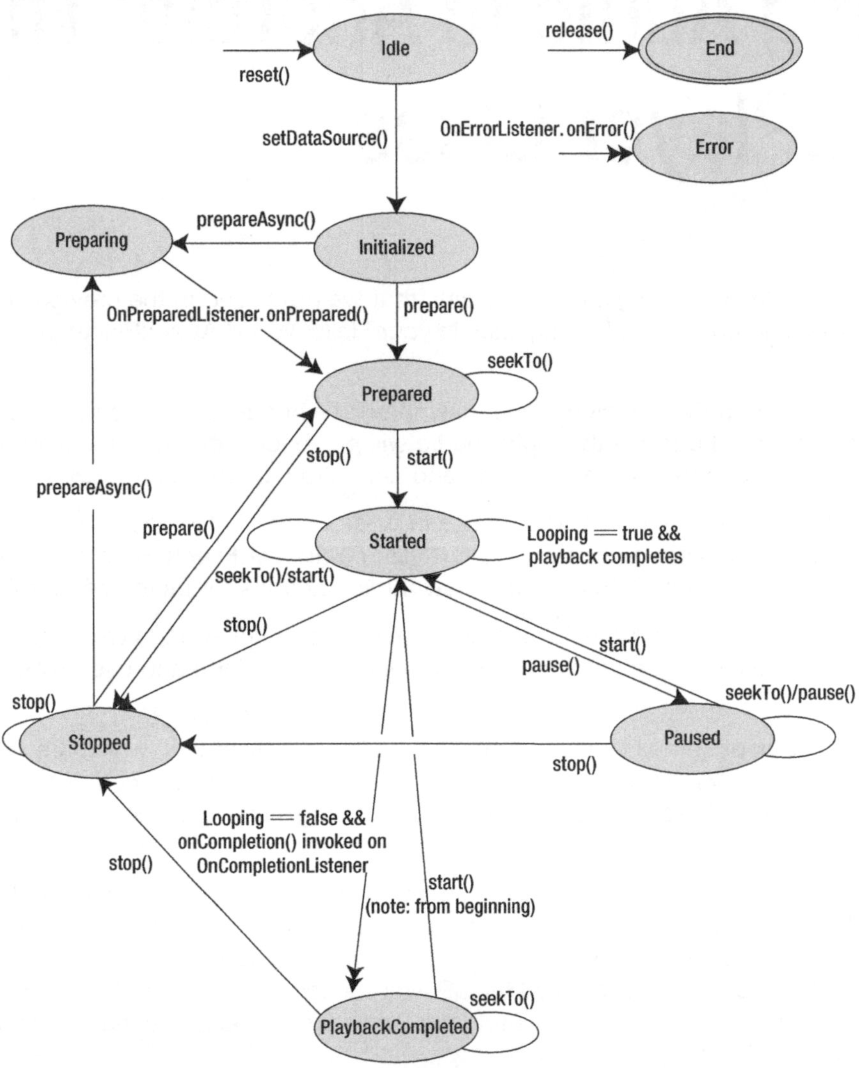

***Figure 14-1.** Diagram of MediaPlayer State Engine (from the MediaPlayer Class page on `developer.android.com`)*[1]

[1]Portions of this page are reproduced from work created and shared by the Android Open Source Project and used according to terms described in the Creative Commons 2.5 Attribution License. `http://developer.android.com/reference/android/media/MediaPlayer.html`

We learned about **states** in one of the earliest chapters in this book, when we reviewed our Java programming principles. Your Android MediaPlayer will always be in one of these following states: **Idle**, **Initialized** (loaded with your audio or video data), **Preparing**, **Prepared**, **Started** (Playing), **Paused**, **Completed** (Playback has Completed), and **Stopped**.

There are also **End** and **Error** MediaPlayer states. Let's cover these two special states first and get them out of the way. End happens once the MediaPlayer object has been released from the memory needed to use it in the first place, and Error is used for when something goes wrong with the media playback process.

The MediaPlayer End state comes about when the Java method **.release()** is called. So if our MediaPlayer object is named **bombPlayer**, as it will be, for our bombButton ImageButton object in the next section of this chapter, you would release the MediaPlayer from memory using this code statement:

```
bombPlayer.release();
```

This clears the MediaPlayer object named bombPlayer from main memory, so that this memory can be utilized for other purposes.

The MediaPlayer **Error** state comes about when the **OnErrorListener** interface **.onError()** method is called via the following Java callback construct **public abstract boolean onError (MediaPlayer mp, int what, int extra)**.

The **mp** parameter contains the **name** of the MediaPlayer object, for instance bombPlayer, the **what** parameter contains the **type of error constant,** and the **extra** parameter contains the **error-specific code constant**.

What constants include MEDIA_ERROR_UNKNOWN and MEDIA_ERROR_SERVER_DIED and extra constants can include MEDIA_ERROR_IO, MEDIA_ERROR_MALFORMED, MEDIA_ERROR_TIMED_OUT, and MEDIA_ERROR_UNSUPPORTED.

Information on the **OnErrorListener** public static interface is located at:

```
developer.android.com/reference/android/media/MediaPlayer.OnErrorListener.html
```

Now let's start at the top of the MediaPlayer state engine diagram, shown in Figure 14-1, and work our way down the state tree logic diagram by one state at a time, starting with the **Idle** state and its **reset()** Java method.

If you use the **.reset()** method via a **bombPlayer.reset();** line of code, the MediaPlayer object resets itself (simulates its initial launch) and goes into Idle state or mode. The next mode after Idle is the **Initialized** state or mode; this is achieved by using the **.setDataSource()** method to set the data source reference to the media file you want to use.

For data resources in the **/res/raw** folder, you should use the **.onCreate()** method (which we will implement in the next section), and specify the data file resource path using the second parameter in the format **R.raw.filename**.

The **Preparing** state is utilized when accessing data files from an external server, and is used in conjunction with an external server URL, parsed by the familiar **Uri.parse()** method. Even though we are using internal media data assets in our application, I will show you the code to do this here, to be complete in my coverage of this MediaPlayer state diagram.

You'd use an **.setOnPreparedListener()** that calls **new OnPreparedListener(),** with a Java code block that uses the **onPrepared()** method something like the following:

```
MediaPlayer mp = MediaPlayer.create(this,Uri.parse("http://www.url.com/file.mp3"));
     player.setOnPreparedListener(new OnPreparedListener() {
          @Override
          public void onPrepared(MediaPlayer mp) {
               mp.start();
          }
     });
```

Once the MediaPlayer has reached the **Prepared** state, by using either the **.onCreate()** method or something similar to the above specified code block, you can then call the **.start()** method to put the MediaPlayer state into the **Started** state (or mode, if you'd rather look at it modally).

Note that these states are similar to the modes which we discussed earlier in this book, except that with the modes we discussed, there were multiple digital imaging modes that needed to be considered all at the same time when using GIMP 2.

The next level down in the diagram are the **Paused** and **Stopped** states, which depend on whether the **.pause()** method is called or whether the **.stop()** method is called. As you can see in the state diagram, once a MediaPlayer object is **Paused**, you can use the **.start()** method to restart your media playback.

The **Playback Completed** state is reached (or is set) when your media file finishes its playback. If the **Looping** flag is set to **false** (its default), then an **onCompletion()** method is invoked (if you have code defined inside it) by the **OnCompletionListener**, and those tasks would then be performed.

Notice that once your MediaPlayer reaches the **Initialized** or the **Stopped** state, that a **.prepareAsync()** method can be used to put your MediaPlayer object into the **Preparing** state.

This Preparing state is usually taking place while your media data file is being fetched (transferred) from a remote location, usually a media server of some sort, such as Amazon S3 or Akamai or your own custom data server.

Note that if you are going to center your application functionality around the MediaPlayer class, rather than just using it to play an audio or video asset, that you should review the MediaPlayer developer page referenced at the beginning of this section.

Using the MediaPlayer class to create your own advanced Media Player is beyond the scope of an introductory book on Android such as this one, as the MediaPlayer functionality in Android is complex enough to have its own book written about it.

There is another **digital audio sequencing** class inside Android called the **SoundPool** class, which might actually be more optimal for use if your app uses a lot of sounds, and these need to be mixed and matched in real time, such as you would do in a game or animated eBook or similarly robust new media application.

This Android SoundPool class will be covered in the next chapter, so rest assured that you will be exposed to the key, primary digital audio classes and work processes in Android within this section of the book.

Setting Up a MediaPlayer Object and Loading It with Digital Audio Data

The first thing that we need to do in implementing our MediaPlayer object is to declare it at the top of our AttackPlanet.java Activity subclass in a line of code that declares it as a **private** access object and sets it to a **null** value for now (until we use it later on) via the following code:

```
private MediaPlayer bombPlayer = null;
```

You will notice that Eclipse ADT red underlines your code with a wavy line under the word MediaPlayer. This is because we have not imported its library at the top of our code as yet. Place your mouse over this wavy red underline and select the **Import android.media.MediaPlayer** package reference link, and let's have Eclipse write this code for us.

This import statement and the MediaPlayer object declaration can be seen in Figure 14-2.

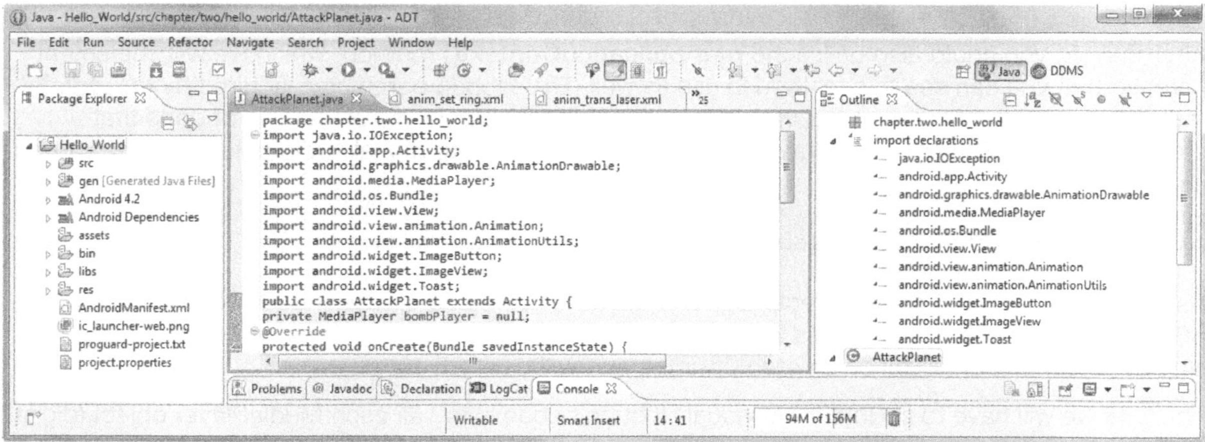

***Figure 14-2.** Declaring a MediaPlayer Object named bombPlayer and setting its value to null*

Next, we need to write a method that sets up our MediaPlayer objects for use in our Attack a Planet user interface ImageButton icons. We will do this so that a different sound effect is played back when each button is clicked.

Writing Our Custom setAudioPlayers() Java Method

Let's call this custom Java method **setAudioPlayers()** and add in our first bombPlayer MediaPlayer Object, which plays back our **blast** audio asset.

First, let's add in the line of code that invokes our new method at the top of our AttackPlanet Activity right after the setContentView() method, using the following Java method call statement:

```
setAudioPlayers();
```

Next we need to write the setAudioPlayers() method itself, and we will do this at the very bottom of the editing screen, just after all our other ImageView, ImageButton, Animation, and AnimationDrawawble object(s) code.

We declare the setAudioPlayers() method as **private** as it is used only by this class to set up all the MediaPlayer objects for our digital audio samples, and as **void**, as it does not return any values when it is called.

Inside of the two curly braces we add our MediaPlayer object creation code, using the **.create()** method from the MediaPlayer class. This method requires the current context, which could be written as follows:

```
AttackPlanet.this
```

Alternatively, you could also utilize the **getApplicationContext()** method, which we will implement here, so that you can see this method in use as well. The second parameter required by the .create() method is the asset file reference, which we know is **R.raw.blast**, and so our line of code that creates our bombPlayer MediaPlayer object and loads it with our digital audio data would be written as follows:

```
bombPlayer = MediaPlayer.create(getApplicationContext(), R.raw.blast);
```

As we add in our other sound effects digital audio assets, we add similar lines of code for each of these inside this method. In this way, when this method is called on our Activity start-up, the MediaPlayer objects will all be created up-front, and will be ready for use.

Then, all we will have to do in our individual UI button code is to call each MediaPlayer object (digital audio sample) from our event handling code at the time that respective button is clicked by our end-user. The new method call and the body of the method with its first MediaPlayer object already coded are shown in Figure 14-3.

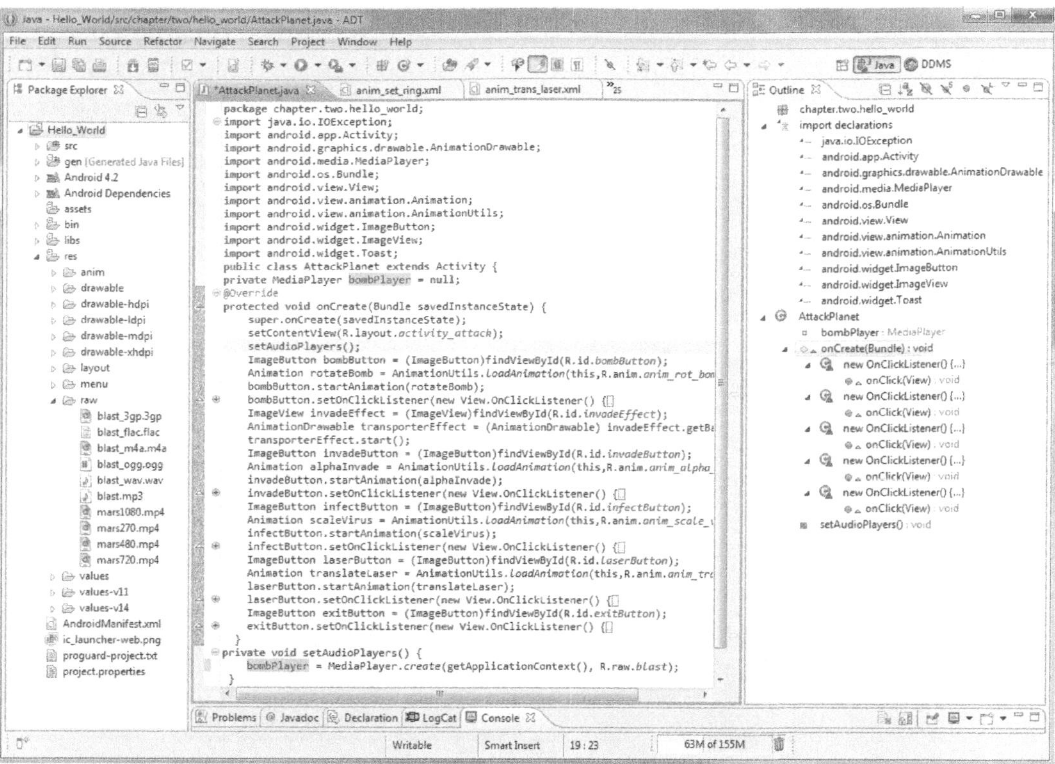

Figure 14-3. Creating a setAudioPlayers() method to set up and create our MediaPlayer objects for sound effects

Next we will add the programming logic that is needed to **start** (play) the MediaPlayer object. This Java code exists inside each onClick() event handler routine in each of the ImageButton objects. Let's write that code next for the bombButton ImageButton object so that you know how the basic format for this is coded and what method to use.

Using Our Media Player Object: Starting Audio Playback Using the .start() Method

Click on the **+ icon** (in the left margin, beside your bombButton object) in Eclipse and expand that block of Java code (if it is not expanded for view already). Inside this block of code you have your onClick() event handling method that contains your Toast object and soon we will add the code that triggers the audio sample when the button is clicked as well.

Add a line of code underneath your Toast.makeText() method call (or above it, if you prefer) that references the bombPlayer MediaPlayer object that we created inside our setAudioPlayers() method, which is shown at the very bottom of Figure 14-4. Use Java dot notation to append the .start() method call to your bombPlayer MediaPlayer object, by using the following line of Java code:

```
bombPlayer.start();
```

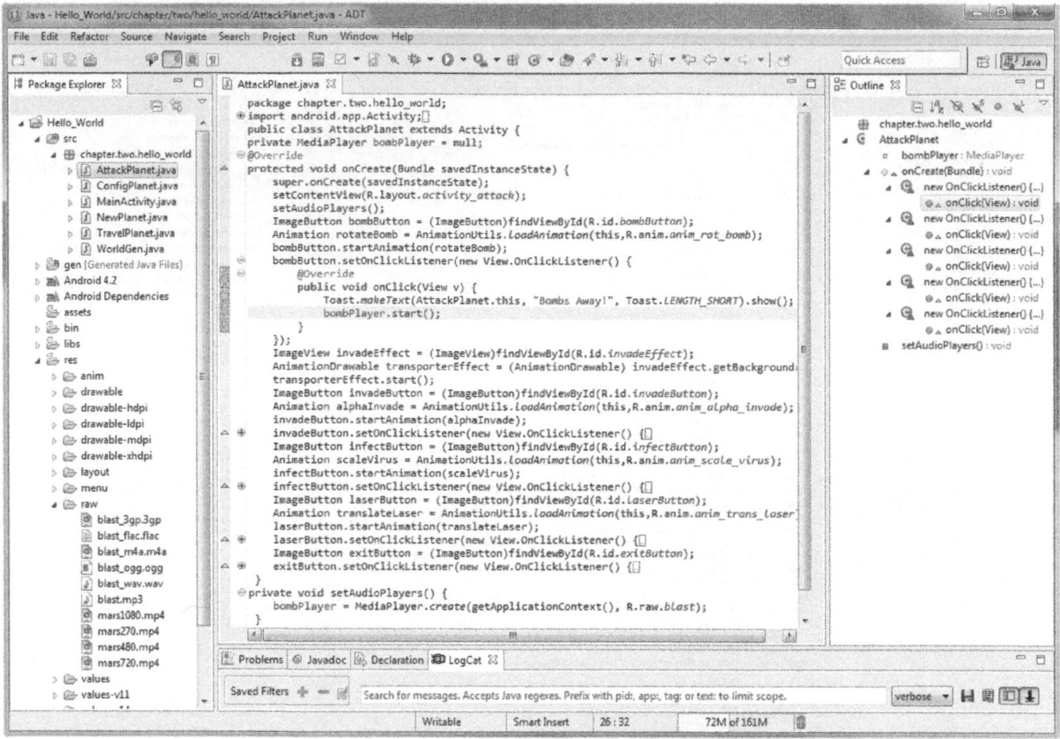

***Figure 14-4.** Adding bombPlayer MediaPlayer Object start() method call to bombButton onClick() event handler method*

This **starts**, or more accurately, **plays**, your **blast** digital audio sample, which is referenced in your **.create()** method call in the **setAudioPlayers()** method.

Now we have created the MediaPlayer object that contains our blast digital audio sample, and we've wired it up to the audio data file that we placed into our Hello_World project's /res/raw folder in the previous chapter, and finally triggered the audio sample for playback within our onClick() event handling method for the bomb button that we want to play that audio sound effect.

We have imported the Android MediaPlayer library and class, coded a custom setAudioPlayers() Java method, wired the MediaPlayer object to our digital audio sample, and triggered it for playback using only a half-dozen lines of Java code.

Now all we have to do for our other three sound effects is add them to our setAudioPlayers() method, and then use the start() method in our onClick() handler methods to start the audio playback when each of our UI buttons is clicked.

Coding the Other Special Effect Audio MediaPlayer Objects

Copy the **private MediaPlayer bombPlayer = null;** line of code at the top of your AttackPlanet class, and paste it underneath itself three more times. Change your MediaPlayer object names from bombPlayer to **transportPlayer**, **virusPlayer**, and **laserPlayer**, respectively, as shown at the top of Figure 14-5.

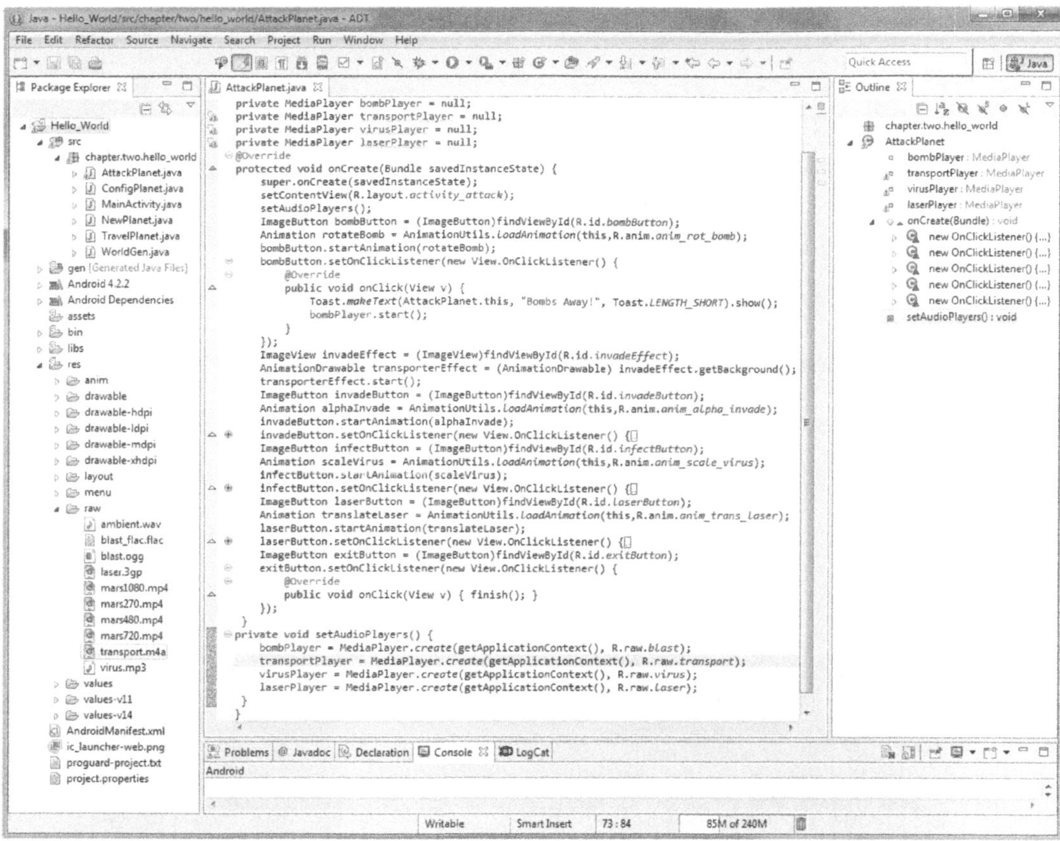

Figure 14-5. Completing our setAudioPlayers() method and declaring our other sound effect MediaPlayer objects

Next, copy the **bombPlayer** object and **MediaPlayer.create()** method call from the first line of your **setAudioPlayers()** method, then paste it underneath itself three more times. Again change the object names from bombPlayer to transportPlayer, virusPlayer, and laserPlayer, respectively.

Now we are ready to add a MediaPlayer object **.start()** method call in each ImageButton onClick() event handling code block, as shown in Figure 14-6.

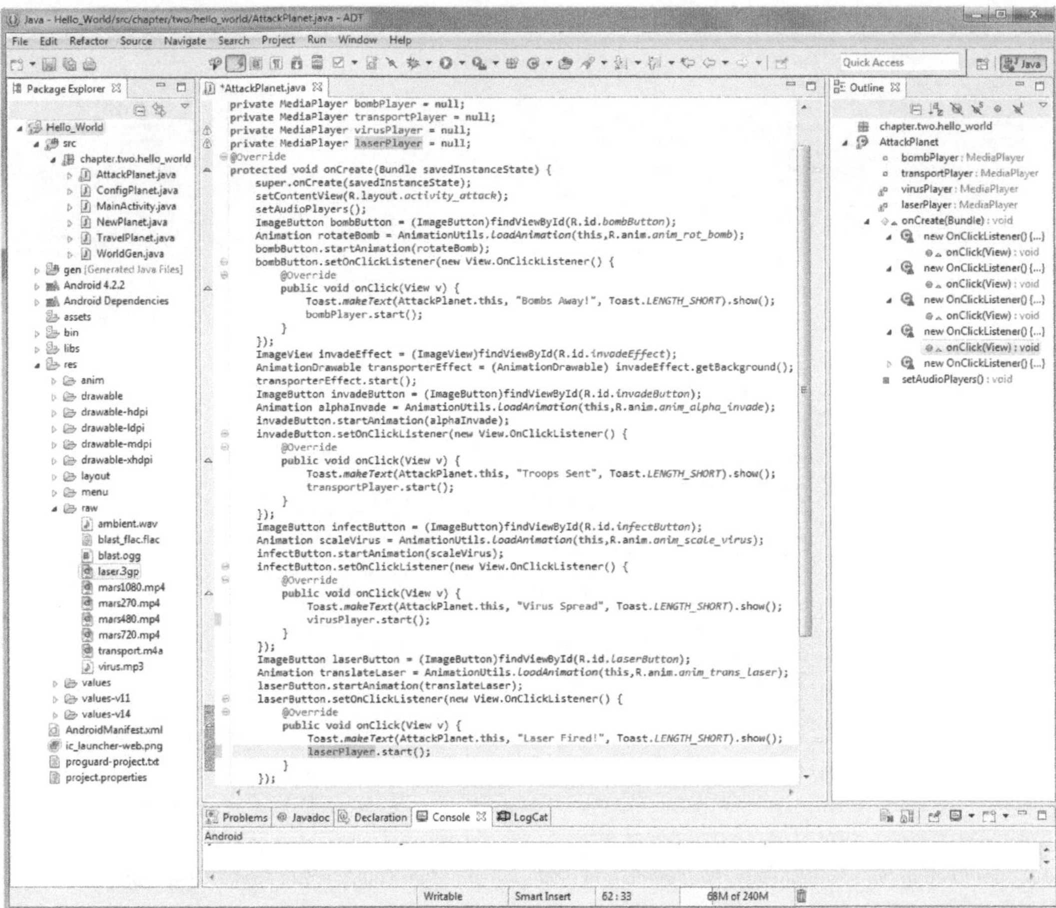

Figure 14-6. Adding the MediaPlayer .start() method calls to our other three ImageButton UI elements

Next we need to take a look at how to add seamlessly looping audio to our Home Screen MainActivity.java Activity subclass. In that scenario, we can simply write one setStartUpScreenAudio() method that will do everything on Activity launch, such as declare an object, set loop parameters and start.

Looping Background Ambient Audio for Our MainActivity

Add a line of code into the top part of your MainActivity class, in the **onCreate()** method, so that your audio MediaPlayer object is initialized along with your World object values, screen text, and screen animations.

Let's call our new method **setStartUpScreenAudio()**, and notice than when you type in the setStartUpScreenAudio(); line of code that Eclipse underlines it with a wavy red line. Place your mouse over the red-underlined text and the Eclipse helper dialog pops up and offers to write your new method for you. Select the last link of the three that are shown, Create method setStartUpScreenAudio(), and voila instant method (see Figure 14-7)!

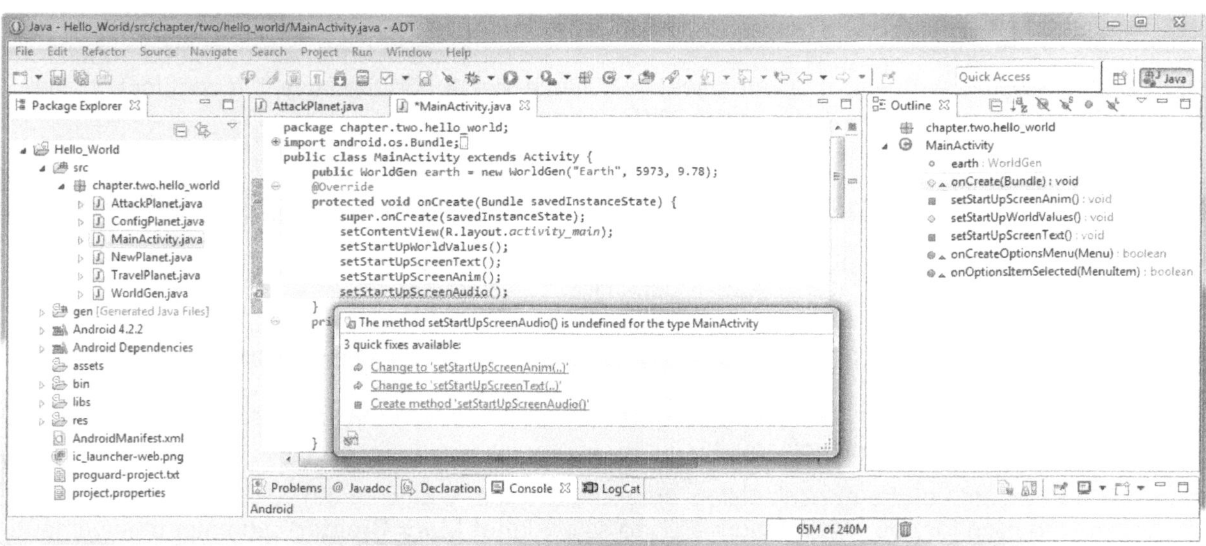

Figure 14-7. Creating our setStartUpAudio() method for our MainActivity.java Home Screen to play an audio loop

Next, we will fill in the interior of the setStartUpScreenAudio() method with three statements. The first will instantiate, name, and .create() our new **audioPlayer** MediaPlayer object, and the second will use the new object to call the **.setLooping()** method to a true (looping) state, and the third will call the looping audio to play back in the background using the .start() method, which we will also call off of the new audioPlayer object. These three new lines of Java code will look like this:

```
MediaPlayer audioPlayer=MediaPlayer.create(getApplicationContext(), R.raw.ambient);
audioPlayer.setLooping(true);
audioPlayer.start();
```

The final code inside the Eclipse IDE can be seen below in Figure 14-8. Notice that we set the .setLooping() method to a value of true **after** the MediaPlayer is instantiated, but **before** it is called for use via .start().

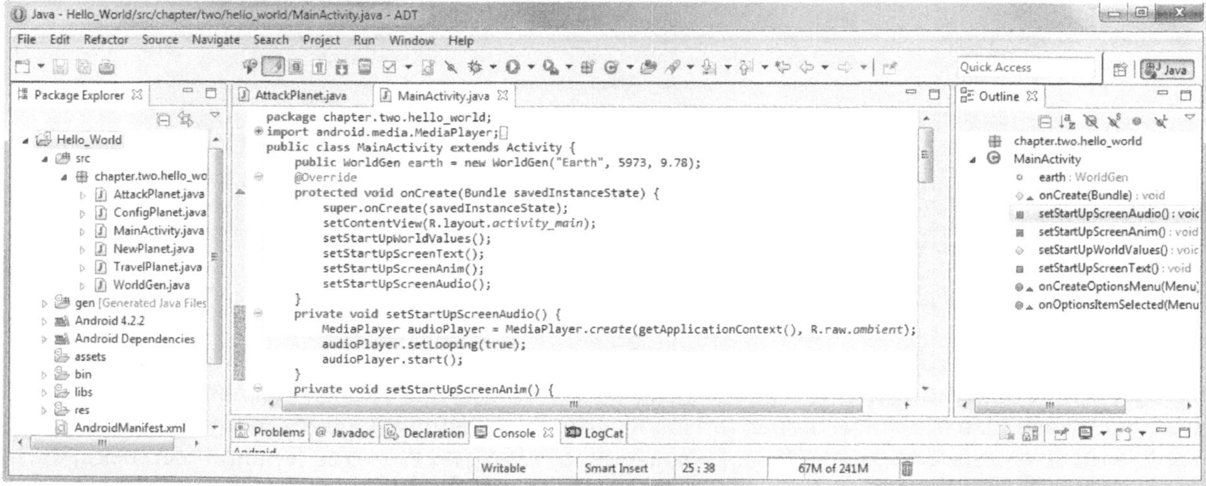

Figure 14-8. Coding audioPlayer MediaPlayer object and .setLooping() and .start() methods in setStartUpScreenAudio()

Next we need to add a cool alien voice to our Add a Planet Activity so the user can get some audio feedback when they click the Planet Mars to create it. We do this by getting set up with a popular open source speech synthesis software package called **eSpeak** and then use it in conjunction with Audacity to create an alien phrase in under 60KB of data.

Creating Voice Synthesis for Our NewPlanet.java Add a Planet Activity

Let's go to SourceForge and download the eSpeak Voice Synthesizer, or TTS (Text To Speech) technology software. It is located at the following URL:

`http://espeak.sourceforge.net/`

Once you finish downloading the version needed for your OS, install the software, and then launch it, so that we can create our alien voiceover.

In the top-center area of the eSpeak dialog, enter the text that you want the voice synthesizer to speak or synthesize for you. We want our alien to say "**Planet Mars Created**" so enter that (without the quotes) into the text field area, as shown in Figure 14-9 as highlighted in blue.

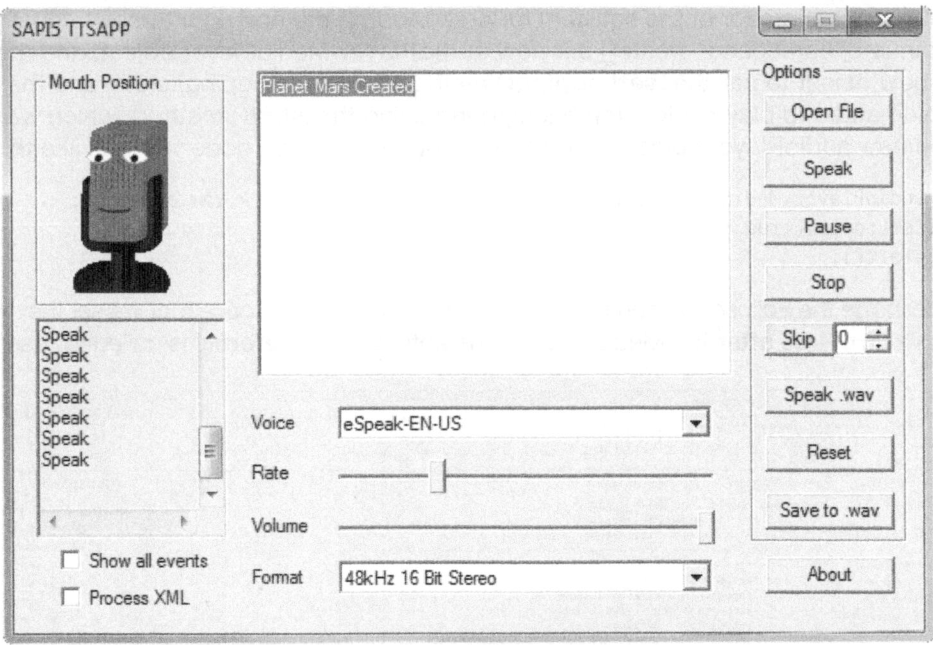

***Figure 14-9.** Running the eSpeak open source application to generate an alien voiceover*

To test your alien voice, utilize the **Speak** button, which is located on the top-right of the eSpeak dialog, second button down. If you would like to change the current speech synthesis **voice font** to a different voice, use the **Voice** drop-down menu, it's right underneath the text entry area. You can use this menu to select and test different voice fonts by changing the voice font and then using the Speak button to test each one.

Similarly, if you want to fine-tune your voice, there are sliders at the bottom middle of the eSpeak dialog for **speech rate** and **volume** (amplitude).

Now that we have fine-tuned all our settings, let's generate a digital audio data file. At the very bottom of eSpeak's dialog, there is a drop-down selector that we will use for selecting our target audio sample rate and our target audio sample frequency.

I selected the highest quality possible, **48kHz 16-bit Stereo**, so that we could go into Audacity and see what kind of data footprint reduction we could get using stereo (two tracks) audio at a full 16-bit resolution and 48 kHz professional level sampling rate.

Finally, we need to click the **Save to .wav** button, to save our alien voiceover audio sample in a 48 kHz uncompressed 16-bit PCM Wave sample format.

When the Save Dialog appears, navigate to the same Audio folder that we have been using for our audio assets and save the file with a **mars.wav** filename. Next we'll use our Audacity audio editing and optimization software to take this sample size from nearly 300KB down to less than 60KB and yet still have the maximum quality maintained for our application.

Optimizing Our Alien Voiceover Audio Sample Using Audacity 2.0

Let's launch Audacity now, and use the **File ➤ Open** menu sequence to find and open our **mars.wav** digital audio file, which we just created previously using eSpeak. As you can see in Figure 14-10, there are two audio samples.

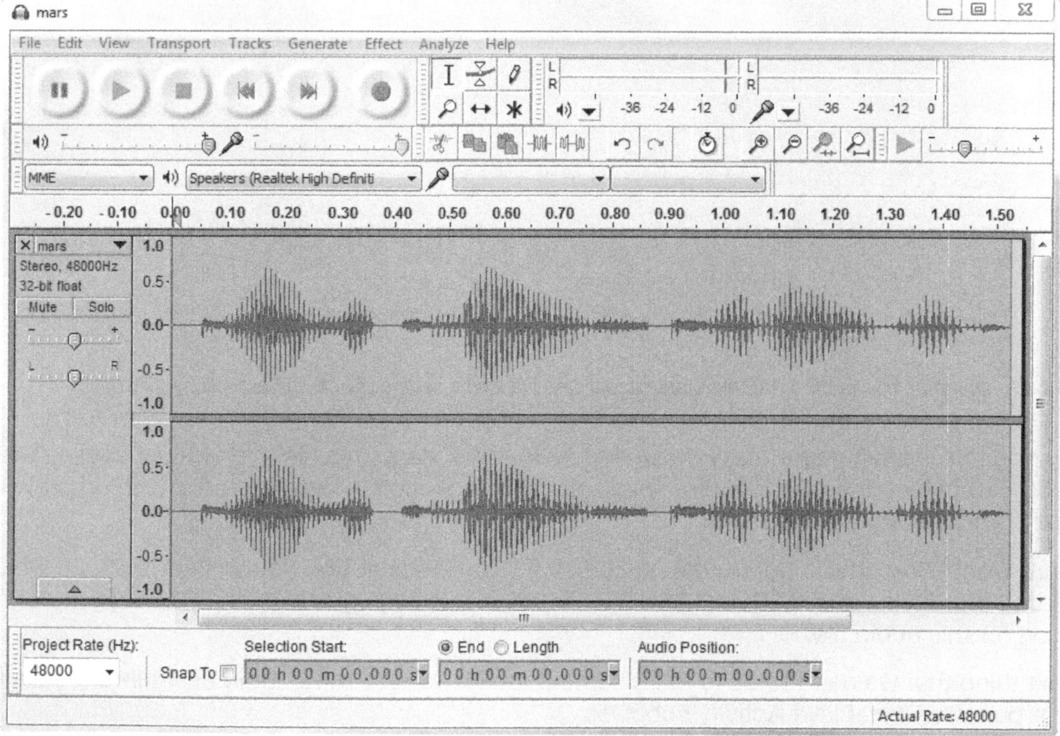

Figure 14-10. Opening our synthesized voice sample in Audacity to optimize an MPEG-4 AAC data file

The reason there are two samples is because this is a **Stereo** audio sample, which means that we now have **left channel** and **right channel** audio samples.

This also means that there is twice as much audio data, so, if you can use **Mono** samples, such as we have in our sound effects, you will obtain a much more compact data footprint in the end.

Let's see what kind of data footprint optimization we can get on this alien voiceover. As we remember from the previous chapter, MPEG-4 AAC gave us the best data footprint reduction, even when we used the highest (500) quality setting, so let's use that here, and see what happens.

If you look at our mars.wav uncompressed audio sample in your operating system file management utility, you will see that the original data size is 293,894 bytes of data, or close to 300 kilobytes of raw audio data.

Let's use the Audacity **File ➤ Export** menu sequence to open the **Export File** dialog, shown in Figure 14-11, and select the drop-down to: **M4A AAC FFmpeg** codec selection. Then click the **Options** button, and select the highest quality level of **500** and let's see just how efficient this MPEG-4 codec is at compressing professional quality 48 kHz 16-bit stereo audio samples.

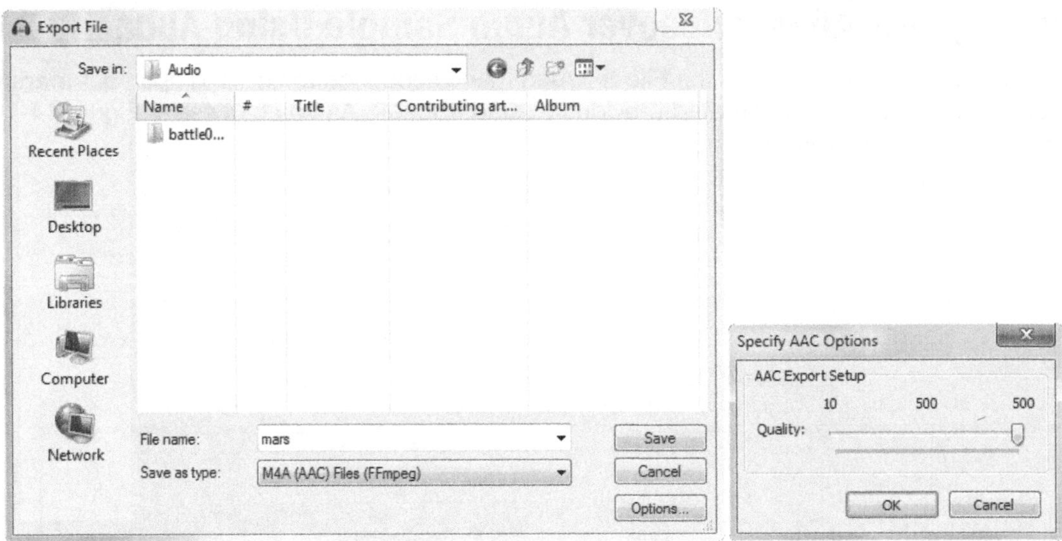

***Figure 14-11.** Exporting our MPEG-4 AAC mars.m4a audio data file with a setting of 500 highest quality (59KB)*

Go into your file management utility again and look at the mars.m4a file that we just saved. The file size is 60,638 bytes, or 59.2 kilobytes. This is an 80% reduction in data footprint with no audible loss of quality, which is a great result.

If you are wondering how I figured that, divide 60,638 by 293,894 and you will get .206326 which means that 60,638 is around 20% of 293,894. 100% minus 20% gives us an 80% data footprint reduction for this audio file.

The next thing that we need to do is to implement this new **mars.m4a** audio asset into the Java code for our NewPlanet.java Activity subclass.

Fire up Eclipse, if it's not open already, and open the NewPlanet.java tab in the central editing pane. At the top of the Activity class, add a line of code that declares the MediaPlayer object as **private** and also names it **marsPlayer** and sets it to **null**. The line of code should look like this:

```
private MediaPlayer marsPlayer = null;
```

Next, we need to create the MediaPlayer, in the **onCreate()** method of our Activity class, so that the MediaPlayer functionality has been created for our marsPlayer MediaPlayer object. That line of code looks like this:

```
marsPlayer = MediaPlayer.create(this, R.raw.mars);
```

Notice that I used **this** to reference the current context in this example, just to show you both ways that the context can be referenced, either by using the keyword **this**, or by using the **getApplicationContext()** method.

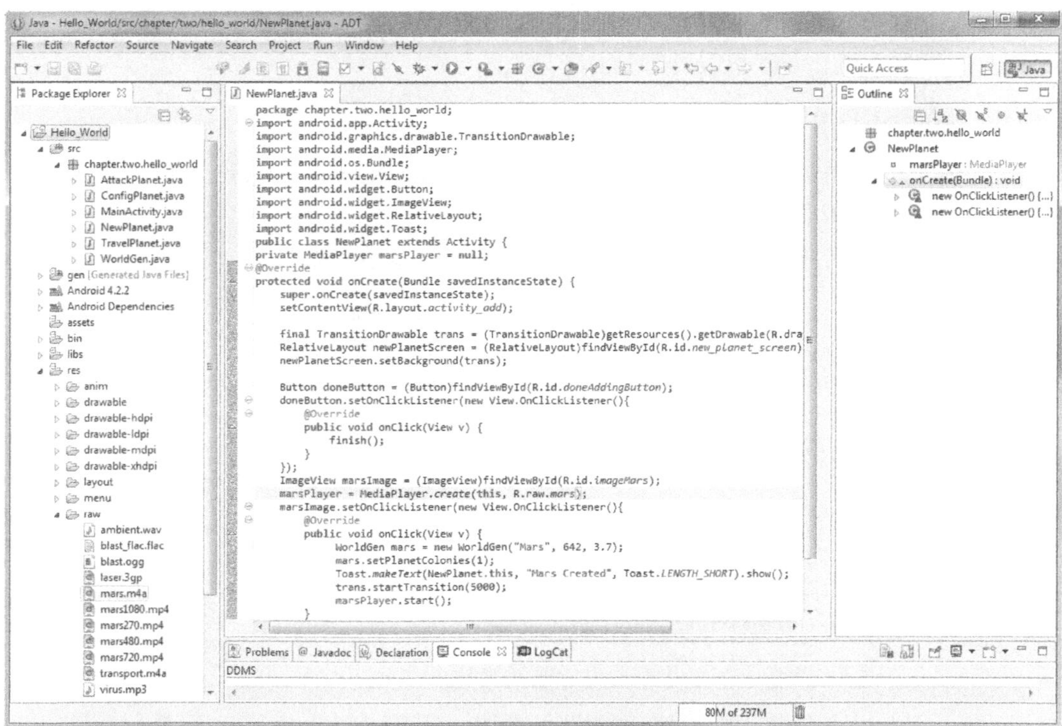

***Figure 14-12.** Creating the Java code to implement our synthetic voice to speak "Planet Mars Created" in onClick()*

Next, we're going to go into our marsImage ImageView object's onClick() event handling method, and add in the line of code that starts up our marsPlayer MediaPlayer object. This line of Java code will look like this:

```
marsPlayer.start();
```

Now we should be ready to use the **Run As Android Application** work process, and test all of the audio work that we have done thus far in this chapter inside of the Android Nexus S emulator.

Once your emulator launches, you should hear the ambient background audio loop on the Home Screen. Next, click the menu button on the emulator, and go into the Attack a Planet Activity, and click on each of the ImageButton icon buttons to hear the cool audio effects that each of these trigger.

Exit the Attack a Planet screen and go back to the Home Screen and again use the menu button in the emulator to go to the Add a New Planet Activity and click the Planet Mars and listen to our alien voiceover say "Planet Mars Created" and as you can see all of our audio assets are implemented!

Creating Button Click Audio FX for Our Configure a Planet Activity

Next let's add a user interface button feedback audio effect; so that you have experience in this chapter with implementing all the different types of audio, for all the different reasons you would use audio, within your user interface designs or user experience designs, for your Hello World Android applications development or any other application for that matter.

Let's start by declaring a **private** MediaPlayer object, name it **clickPlayer** and set it to a **null** value for now, using the following line of Java code:

```
private MediaPlayer clickPlayer = null;
```

Next we need to initialize our clickPlayer MediaPlayer object by using the .create() method with our context and data resource reference, as follows:

```
clickPlayer = MediaPlayer.create(getApplicationContext(), R.raw.click);
```

As you can see in Figure 14-13, we're creating our clickPlayer MediaPlayer object at the very top (first line) of our ConfigPlanet Activity, and we are initializing our MediaPlayer object using the .create() method right after we set our Activity content view using the setContentView() method.

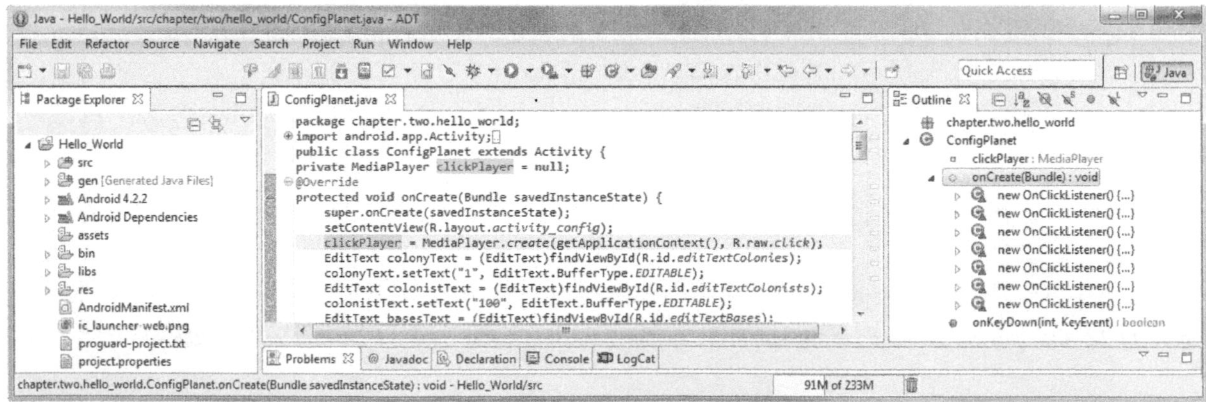

***Figure 14-13.** Adding the clickPlayer MediaPlayer object to our ConfigPlanet.java Activity and invoking .create()*

Next, we need to add in the code that starts up the MediaPlayer object in each of our user interface Button objects onClick() event handling method code blocks, using the following line of Java code:

```
clickPlayer.start();
```

We need to add this line of Java code for all seven of our Button objects, as is shown in Figure 14-14. Once we have completed this, we can test our Hello_World Android application in the Nexus S emulator, and then we will be finished implementing audio in each of our primary Activities.

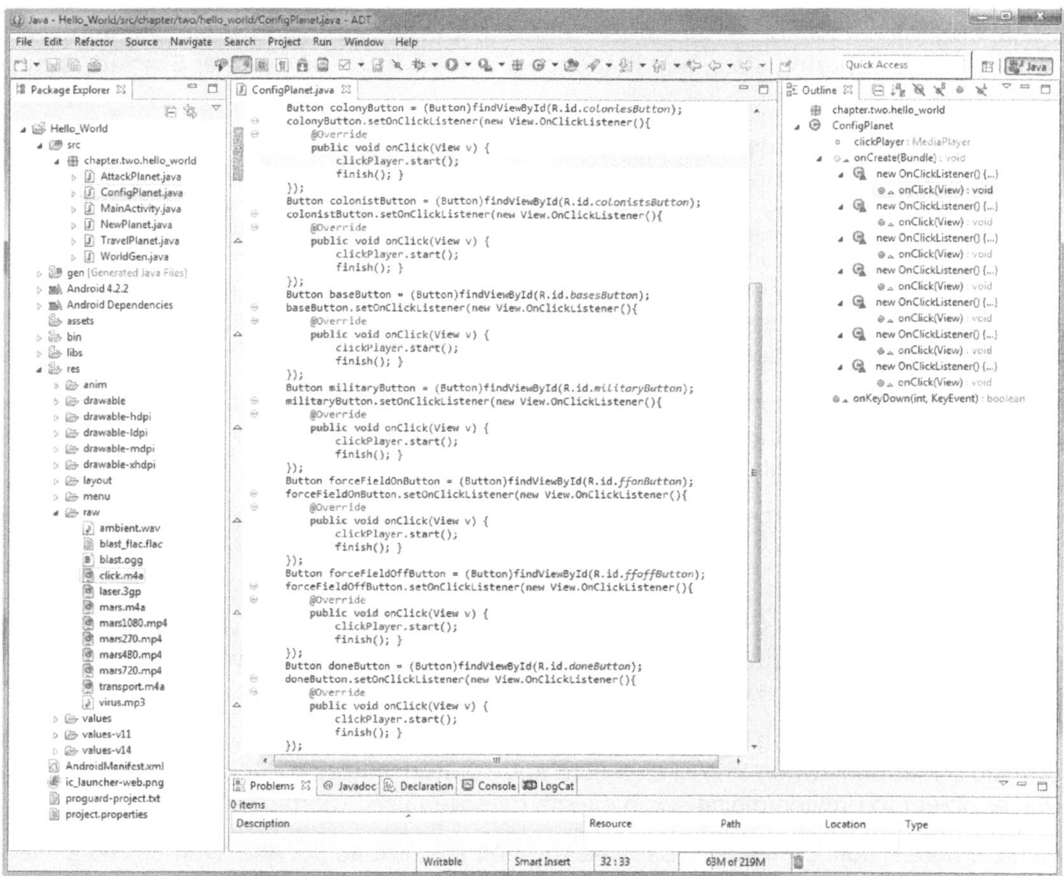

***Figure 14-14.** Adding the clickPlayer.start() method to the Button UI element onClick() event handling methods*

This code set-up is more highly optimized than the others we have put in place so far in the chapter in the sense that we only have to create one object and initialize it, but seven of our user interface elements can leverage the object and the MediaPlayer functionality via one short line of Java code in the their event handling method.

Use the **Run As Android Application** work process to launch your Android ADT Nexus S emulator, then click the menu button, and select your Configure a Planet menu option and click each of the user interface buttons to make sure that they work properly.

Summary

In this chapter, we took a closer look at the Android MediaPlayer class, which can be used to play back audio samples, implement sound effects for our user interface buttons, and play looping ambient background audio or looping background music.

We took a close look at the MediaPlayer **state engine diagram** that is on the Android Developer website, and we went through it from top to bottom, state by state, method by method, to get a good feel for exactly what the MediaPlayer is capable of.

We learned that the MediaPlayer is **Idle** until **Initialized**, that it needs to be **Prepared** by using the **.prepareAsync()** (streaming) or the **.create()** method (captive), that during streaming from a remote server it will be in a **Preparing** state, and that once prepared, it can be in either **Started**, **Stopped,** or **Paused** states.

We took a look at which **methods**, **interfaces,** and **callbacks** are implemented to control those various states for the MediaPlayer, either for playing a captive audio data file from your /res/raw folder, or for streaming audio into your apps, from a remote audio media server of some kind or another.

We then wrote a custom method called **setAudioPlayers()** for our Attack a Planet Activity subclass, so that we could implement several short burst audio sound effects for our user interface buttons. We did this so that when our user clicks an animated button there's an audio representation of what that animated object actually sounds like.

We then wrote a custom method called **setStartUpScreenAudio()**, for our Main Activity Home Screen, and set the **.setLooping()** method to **true**, so that we could loop ambient space background audio for a special audio effect.

Next, we utilized an open source TTS technology voice synthesizer software package called **eSpeak** to create an alien voice for our NewPlanet.java Planet Mars creation tasks in our Add a Planet Activity subclass.

We then learned how to use eSpeak to synthesize, and fine-tune, our alien voice sample, and we then optimized this audio data that we created using Audacity. Finally, we wrote the Java code necessary to implement this cool alien voiceover inside of our Add a Planet Activity.

Finally, we added a click button sound effect to our Configure a Planet Activity user interface, to give our users audio feedback when they click a data entry button. In this instance we utilized a single MediaPlayer object to provide digital audio effects for seven user interface elements.

Thus we have added sound effects, clicks, background ambient audio, and synthesized alien voiceovers to our Hello World Android application. I think that pretty much covers the gamut of digital audio use fairly well.

In the next chapter, we will take a look at a more advanced audio playback class called **SoundPool**, which can be utilized as an **audio sequencer**. Audio sequencing and real-time mixing is the audio equivalent of the compositing that we learned about earlier in the book in our digital imaging, bitmap (frame-based) and procedural vector animation, and digital video chapters.

Android SoundPool can store, trigger, and mix, in real-time, a ton of audio samples (not really, as audio doesn't weigh a whole lot). This audio class is utilized for more advanced applications, such as a game. It could also be used for other advanced audio applications that might require more granular management of a large number of samples, without having to create an Android MediaPlayer object for each of them, which, as we have see, could get unwieldy with a lot of digital audio samples.

Chapter 15

Audio Sequencing: Android SoundPool Class

In this chapter, we will take a look at a more specialized audio playback class in Android called: **SoundPool**. This class is significantly different from the Android MediaPlayer class, enough so that I have decided to put a specific chapter into this book that covers this useful audio class.

This chapter delves deeply into Android SoundPool, as well as defining what makes it different from MediaPlayer, and in what types of situations each of these classes should be utilized for digital audio asset playback.

In a nutshell, what makes SoundPool so special is that it allows the audio equivalent of image compositing (layering and blending). This means, like with image compositing, that audio-related new media assets can be broken down into their component parts and controlled individually.

Using SoundPool, these component parts can later be attached to, and even manipulated with, Java code. This allows developers to present these rich media digital asset components to the user as a single finished work, when in fact they are actually being seamlessly composited (or in popular audio terminology: mixed-down, pitch-shifted and sequenced) by your application.

This allows the Android developer to inject interactivity into their new media assets, whereas in the past, traditional media assets such as music, film, or television were just one long linear performance; repeatable but always the same, and thus, eventually, end-users tire of their user experience.

In this chapter, we will first cover the foundational principles of **audio synthesis** and **sequencing**, and then we will review the SoundPool class and what it can do, much as we did with the MediaPlayer class in the previous chapter. Then we will implement the SoundPool class in our Hello_World app and see how it can make our sounds play more quickly as well as giving us the flexibility to combine them and to change the way they sound.

MIDI and Audio Sequencing: Concepts and Principles

The earliest forms of audio sequencing utilized MIDI, which we learned in the previous chapter stands for Musical Instrument Digital Interface, and which allows performance data to be recorded and played back via computer.

The early computers that did this were the Amiga, the Atari ST-1040 and Apple Macintosh, and ran software packages called **MIDI sequencers** from software companies like Opcode (Vision), Steinberg (CuBase), Cakewalk (Sonar), Mark of the Unicorn (Performer), PropellerHead (Reason), and eMagic (Logic).

Most of these MIDI sequencer software packages are still around (a couple were acquired by other companies as well) and all remain extremely popular to this day with digital audio musicians worldwide.

MIDI sequencers allowed **performance data sequencing**, where one composer could play each instrumental part into the computer using a synthesizer set to that given instrument sample, say a guitar or a piano sample, and then the computer would play back this performance data later while the composer accompanied the computer-replayed version of his performance.

While the computer **played out** the composition **tracks** that had been created thus far, the composer would **play in** the next **part** or track, using the next instrument needed in that song, score, or jingle arrangement.

Eventually MIDI sequencers added digital audio capabilities, alongside the MIDI playback capabilities, as increased computer processing power as well as specialized digital audio adapters, such as Creative Labs' SoundBlaster and X-Fi, became widely available at affordable prices.

It turns out that the concept of **audio sequencing** can be applied equally well to digital audio samples manipulated directly by the computer as it can to MIDI performance data sequencing. As computers became more powerful more digital audio could be sampled and played back, although not quite as easily as MIDI, since MIDI is performance data (note on, note off) only.

Computers kept getting more powerful, came with more memory to hold more samples (an issue with SoundPool as we'll soon see), added more processors (64-bit multi-cores now allow 4/6/8/16 CPU cores per processor) and faster processing speed, 64-bit audio adapters and multi-core DSP (Digital Signal Processor) capabilities are all now both available and affordable.

For this reason, audio sequencers now allow a thousand times more options than the early MIDI sequencers of the 1980s, although they still support and play MIDI performance data right alongside of the audio sampling data. This is because MIDI is so very efficient, and it allows the samples to be played back using the synthesizer keyboard if the composer prefers to work that way. Audio sequencers then added a plethora of features usually found only in synthesizers; we'll cover these features, terms, and concepts next.

Digital Audio Synthesis: Basic Concepts and Principles

Some of the first MIDI keyboards were really just digital audio samplers, which recorded and played back digital audio samples using various sample rates and sample frequencies. We learned about samples in the previous couple of chapters in the book, so what we're going to focus on here is how those samples are taken to the next level, via further **audio synthesis** of those samples, or even of just a raw waveform, such as a sine wave or saw wave.

Synthesizers take wave audio, whether it's a generated wave, born out of an **oscillator** on a circuit board in in a consumer electronics device, or a more complex sampled waveform, such as a sample of a plucked instrument string for instance, and then applies further waveform manipulations to that waveform in order to create new and different tonality, sound or even special effects. We're all familiar with the new synthesized instrument sounds in today's popular music; all that is done using math and code!

One of the core mathematical manipulations that can be applied to an audio waveform within the digital audio domain is called **pitch-shifting**, which can take a sound or a tone up or down an **octave** (or a small fraction of an octave, known as **pitch** or **key**), to provide us with a **range** of that sample much as though we were playing it up and down the keys of a synthesizer keyboard.

As we learned previously, the **tone** of a waveform can be determined by the **frequency** of that waveform itself, so it becomes a fairly straightforward mathematical computation to be able to accurately shift that pitch (wave) up an octave, by cutting that wavelength in half, or shift the pitch down an octave, by doubling that wavelength. Any fraction thereof would change the pitch, which is how we get different notes along the keyboard using a single sampled waveform. Digital audio synthesis is pretty amazing stuff!

SoundPool can do this (which is why we are learning about these concepts here in the first place) so it does have some audio synthesis capabilities and will probably add even more in future versions of the Android OS. You need to know these concepts to leverage what it can do effectively and optimally, which is why we are going over all this here at this level of detail, so that if you need to wield SoundPool, you will know how to do it correctly, and why you need to do it that way in the first place.

Another core audio synthesis mathematical manipulation is the **combination** (**compositing**) of two waveforms together, that is, playing two sounds at the same time out of a single **oscillator** hardware (speaker) scenario. Like with digital imaging or video compositing, here we're adding two different sample data values together to achieve the final audible result.

Today's audio hardware does have fairly impressive multi-channel support, and may have the capability to play **stereo** (two channels) or **quadrophonic** (four channels) of individual sounds (effects, music, vocal tracks, etc.) directly out of the audio hardware inside the consumer electronics device.

What if we want to combine 8 or 16 tracks of digital audio in real-time, like a sequencer does? This is where SoundPool can give you **digital audio sequencing** capabilities right inside your application.

What's important, if you are going to attempt real-time audio compositing of 8 to 16 audio samples, is that each of these samples is very well optimized. This makes what we learned about in Chapter 13 regarding digital audio data optimization extremely important when it comes to using Android SoundPool. So you see, there's a method to my madness!

For instance, if you don't really need HD (24-bit sample resolution) audio to get the quality result that you can get in CD (16-bit) quality audio, you are saving a ton of memory while achieving the same end result.

Similarly, if you can get the same audio quality using a 32 kHz sample rate instead of a 48 kHz sample rate, you are using 50% less samples (memory) to do this. For voiceovers or sound effects, memory savings are there for the taking, as often you can sample a bomb or laser blast effectively by using 8-bit resolution with an 11 kHz sample rate and you won't be able to detect any difference over a 16-bit 48 kHz sound effect, but you will be using 8.7 times less memory (16 times 48 divided by 8 times 11).

Just like with digital imaging and digital video playback, optimizing your digital audio assets is important for two completely different but related reasons. With digital audio samples, especially in regard to using Android SoundPool, it is the amount of your system's memory that is needed to hold each sample once it has been decompressed by the codec, and put in its raw uncompressed state into your Android device's memory, ready for playback.

The second reason that well-optimized audio is important is the processing part of the equation. It's pretty obvious that with less audio to process, even if it's just sending that audio to the audio hardware, there are less CPU cycles used. Thus, if you can get the same basic audio quality results using less sample resolution (fewer bits per slice of audio) or using less sample frequency (fewer slices of the waveform per second), you are saving on both your system memory resources and CPU processing cycle resources.

This becomes more and more important, where SoundPool is concerned, as the number of digital audio samples that you will require for use within your application increases. This is again true for both the system memory and the system processing cycle usage considerations, because as you add samples both of these resources are utilized more and more, and don't forget that you have other things that your application is doing as well, such as user interface rendering, imaging, video, and possibly even 3D.

Another reason highly optimized digital audio samples are so important when using the SoundPool class specifically is because there is currently a **one megabyte** limit on digital audio sample data when using SoundPool. Although this limit might be increased in future Android API revisions of this audio class, it's still always best practice to optimize any digital audio assets effectively and efficiently.

An Introduction to SoundPool: Class Rules and Methods

The Android SoundPool class is a direct subclass of the **java.lang.Object** class and is not a subclass of the MediaPlayer class, as one might assume.

Like the MediaPlayer class, it is a part of the **android.media** package, and thus the complete path to the class (as used in an import statement) would be: **android.media.SoundPool**.

Because SoundPool is a subclass of java.lang.Object we can infer that it is its own scratch-coded creation, if you will. It is also important to note that a SoundPool object (i.e., a SoundPool class) and a MediaPlayer object (i.e., a MediaPlayer class) can be utilized at the same time, if needed.

In fact, there are distinct applications for both of these audio playback classes. MediaPlayer is best used for **long form** audio and video data, such as songs, albums, or movies. SoundPool is best used for lots of **short form** audio snippets, especially when they need to be played in rapid succession and (or) combined, such as in a game or a gamified application.

A SoundPool collection of samples can be loaded into memory from one of two places. The first and most common would be from inside the .APK file, which I call captive new media assets, in which case, they would live in your /res/raw project folder. The second place samples can be loaded from is an SD card or similar static memory storage location (what one would term the Android OS file system).

The SoundPool internally uses the Android MediaPlayer Service to decode an audio asset into memory. It does this using uncompressed, 16-bit, PCM mono or stereo audio streams. For this reason, make sure to optimize your audio using a 16-bit sampling resolution, because, if you use 8-bit, and Android up-samples this to 16-bit, you'll end up with wasted headroom. So optimize your sample frequency well, and don't use stereo samples unless you really have to. It's very important to conform your work process to how SoundPool works, to get the most optimal results, across the largest number of Android consumer electronics devices.

When a SoundPool object is constructed in Java, as we will be doing later on in this chapter, the developer can set a **maxStreams** integer parameter. This parameter determines how many audio streams can be composited, or rendered, at the same time. To use the digital image compositing analogy, this would equate to the number of image layers that would be allowed in a digital image composite.

Setting this maximum number of streams parameter to as small a number as possible is a good standard practice. This is because doing so will help to minimize the CPU cycles used on processing audio, and will thus reduce any likelihood that your SoundPool audio mixing will impact other areas of your application performance such as 3D, image visuals, or UI performance.

The SoundPool engine tracks the number of active streams to make sure that it does not exceed the maxStreams setting. If this maximum number of audio streams is ever exceeded, SoundPool will abort a previously playing stream. It does this based primarily on a sample **priority value** that you can set for each audio sample.

If SoundPool finds two or more audio samples with an equal priority value, it will then make a decision regarding which sample to stop playing based on sample age, which means the sample that has been playing the longest is the one that gets killed. I like to call it the *Logan's Run* principle.

Priority level values are evaluated from low to high numeric values. This means that higher (larger) numbers represent a higher priority level. Priority is evaluated when a call to the SoundPool **.play()** method causes a number of active streams to exceed the value established by the **maxStreams** parameter that was set when the SoundPool object was created.

In this case, the SoundPool **stream allocator** stops the lowest priority audio stream. As I mentioned, if there are multiple streams with the same low priority, SoundPool chooses the oldest stream to stop. In the case where the priority of the new stream is lower than all the active streams, the new sound **will not play** and the play() function will return a **streamID** of zero, so be sure that your app Java code keeps track of exactly what is going on with your audio sample priority level settings at all times.

Samples are looped in SoundPool by setting any non-zero looping value. The exception to this is that a value of **-1** causes samples to loop forever and under this circumstance, your application code must make a call to the SoundPool .stop() method to stop the looping sample. So a non-zero integer value causes a sample to repeat itself that specified number of times, thus a value of 7 causes your sample to play back a total of 8 times, as computers start counting using the number 0 instead of 1.

Each sample playback rate can be changed by SoundPool, which, as mentioned makes this class into an audio synthesis tool. Thus a sample playback rate equal to **1.0** causes your sample to play at an original frequency level (resampled, if necessary, to match up with the hardware output frequency).

A sample playback rate of **2.0** causes the sample to be played at twice its original frequency, which sounds like a full octave higher if it is a musical instrument note. Similarly, a sample playback rate set to **0.5** causes SoundPool to play that sample at half of its original frequency, which sounds like a full octave lower.

The sample playback rate range of SoundPool is currently somewhat limited at 0.5 to 2.0, but this could be upgraded in a future API revision to say, 0.25 to 4, which would give developers a four octave sample playback range.

Next we'll go over a few caveats regarding the use of SoundPool, or rather how **not** to use SoundPool, and then we'll dive into some fairly robust Java coding, so that we can implement this SoundPool audio engine in our Hello World Android application, inside our Attack a Planet Activity subclass.

Android Digital Audio Synthesis and Sequencing Caveats

Digital audio synthesis and sequencing using SoundPool in an Android app is a balancing act, both within the device that you are testing it on at the moment, as well as across all devices that your app will ever be run on. If a given hardware platform (smartphone, tablet, eReader, iTV) cannot handle playing a given audio data load, then it simply will not play back.

As we have learned up to this point, digital audio synthesis, sequencing, and compositing is heavily predicated on the speed of the processor, the number of processor cores available, and the amount of memory available to hold all the digital audio samples needed in their uncompressed format.

So bottom-line, you need to be extremely smart in how you are doing things in SoundPool. Not as much in how you write your code, although, certainly, that is important, but also in how you set-up your audio samples, so that they use less memory and can be leveraged farther within your application.

The primary mistake make by Android developers in regards to SoundPool is trying to use it more as an audio sequencer than as an audio synthesizer.

Users focus on SoundPool's ability to load multiple audio file waveforms, but do not leverage its capability of creating a myriad of new waveforms by using those waveforms with the SoundPool pitch-shifting capability.

If you use SoundPool as an audio sequencer, system memory could overload, and this can shut down SoundPool's functionality. Android developers must thus harness SoundPool features optimally and also optimize their samples.

Here's a good example of this. SoundPool allows pitch-shifting across two full octaves, from a setting of **0.5** (down one full octave, or half of your original sample waveform) up to **2.0** (up one full octave, or twice of your original waveform width). Remember waveform width equates to frequency or pitch.

Most users don't even use this pitch-shifting feature, but instead, will use different samples to achieve different notes, which fills up memory, and the result is the app works less and less well across older devices.

The correct way to use SoundPool is to take your samples, say a one string pluck from a guitar, one horn blow from a saxophone, one piano key strike, and one drum beat, and using only four 16-bit 32 kHz high-quality samples, you could make a basic synthesizer that had the four basic instruments.

Using this basic synthesizer set-up, your user could play instruments up and down two full octaves. This application would use only a megabyte of memory to hold these 16-bit 32 kHz uncompressed samples. If you use a high-quality microphone for your sampling, you would be amazed at the high-quality result that can be obtained these days using a 16-bit 32 kHz sampling format. Try it sometime, and see if you can hear any real difference between 16-bit 44 kHz CD quality audio and 16-bit 32 kHz audio.

Using SoundPool for Our Attack a Planet Activity

The logical area within our Hello_World app to leverage Android SoundPool is inside of our Attack a Planet activity, as this uses a number of audio samples, and these samples should trigger rapidly when our user clicks the icon ImageButtons to provide the most professional user experience.

The first things that we need to do are open up Eclipse, and then open our AttackPlanet.java class in an editing tab so that we can add our new code.

Let's remove the code we wrote in the previous chapter declaring, creating, and starting the MediaPlayer objects. So, delete the statements at the top of the class, declaring the four special effects MediaPlayer objects, and then delete the **setAudioPlayers()** method we wrote and its method call, so that we are back to having no audio implementation in this Activity class.

Now we are ready to add in our all new audio processing Java code, using a single SoundPool class loaded with all of our sound effects samples rather than using four MediaPlayer objects. This should be far more efficient for this particular Activity class due to the number of sound effects that we need to implement within our animated user interface ImageButton elements.

Setting Up SoundPool: The SoundPool Object

The first thing that we need to do at the top of our AttackPlanet Activity class, to prepare our SoundPool audio engine for use is to instantiate the SoundPool object. We'll declare it via classname, name it **soundPoolFX**, and apply **private** access control using the following single line of Java code:

```
private SoundPool soundPoolFX;
```

As you can see in Figure 15-1, when we write this line of code under our class declaration line of code, Eclipse underlines the SoundPool object with a wavy red line.

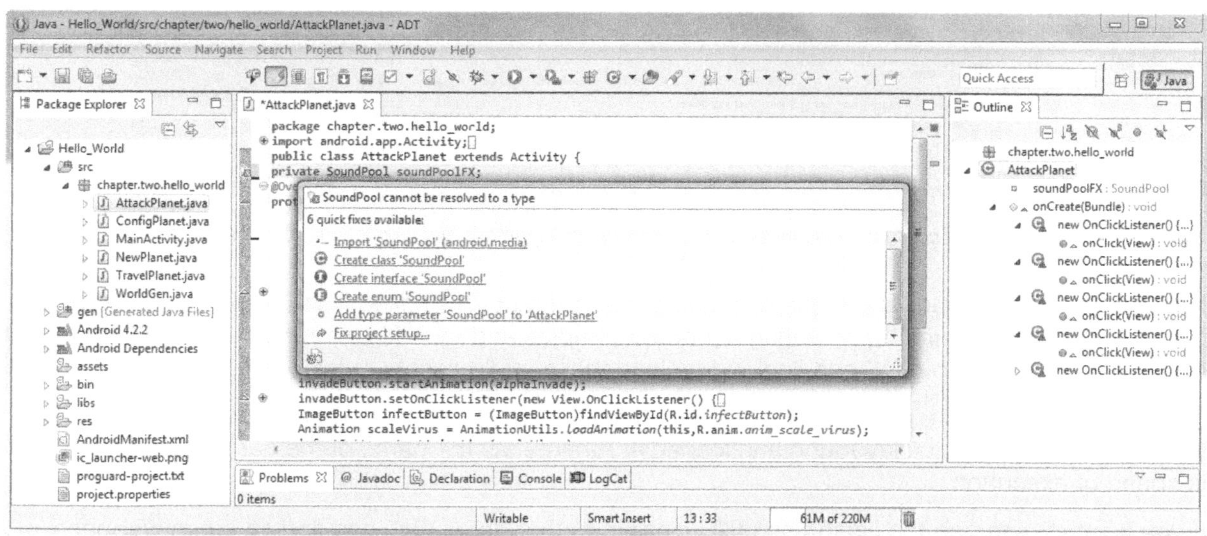

***Figure 15-1.** Declaring a private SoundPool object named soundPoolFX and using Eclipse helper to add import*

Place your mouse over this error highlighting, and pop up the Eclipse ADT helper dialog. This dialog gives us several options for removing this error flag within our code.

Select the first option, **Import "SoundPool" (android.media package)** as the solution that you want to select and Eclipse then writes in our import statement for us.

Open up the import statement code block, located at the top of the editing pane, above the class declaration, but below the package declaration, and make sure that the **import android.media.MediaPlayer;**

code statement has been removed. We do not need to explicitly declare (import) the MediaPlayer class for use with SoundPool, even though we know that the SoundPool engine uses Android's MediaPlayer Service behind the scenes, so to speak, to play our digital audio samples.

Now that we have imported the SoundPool library for use you will notice that Eclipse has yellow underlined a warning under our SoundPool object name, soundPoolFX. Let's place our mouse over this and find out what Eclipse thinks that the issue is with our code now.

As you can see in Figure 15-2, Eclipse pops up a helper dialog that tells us that our new SoundPool object named **soundPoolFX** isn't being used. Well of course we know that, so we will not worry about this warning demarcation for now, and we will proceed and continue to declare our other classes and audio sample instance integer variables that we will need to implement this new SoundPool audio sequencing engine in the Java code for our AttackPlanet.java Activity subclass.

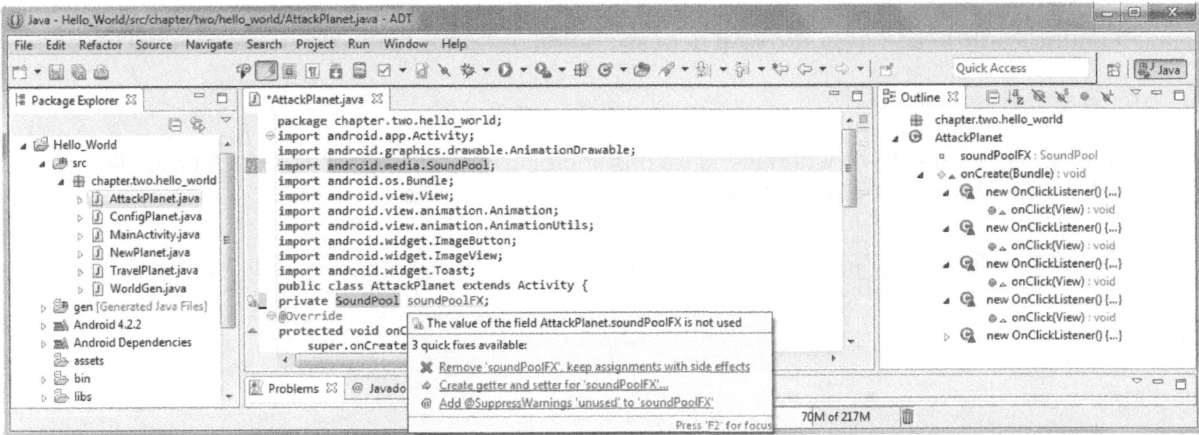

***Figure 15-2.** Checking our Eclipse warning message and showing an import android.media.SoundPool statement*

Next, we need to declare and implement an Android **utility class** called **HashMap**, which we use to hold our data value pairs, representing our audio samples and their file reference URI data. This is done so that the Android OS can find and preload these audio assets quickly and easily.

SoundPool uses a more complicated data structure to do this audio content loading; this is so that your samples can be quickly found and loaded at runtime, as the name of the game with SoundPool is speed of execution.

If you want to research the HashMap utility class in further detail, you can find an entire webpage devoted to it located at the following Android Developer website URL:

```
http://developer.android.com/reference/java/util/HashMap.html
```

Now let's take a look at how to implement a HashMap in our SoundPool code.

Loading the SoundPool Data: The Android HashMap Class

The first thing that we need to do at the top of our AttackPlanet Activity to prepare our HashMap utility for use is to instantiate a HashMap object. We'll declare it via classname, name it **soundPoolMap**, and apply a **private** access control to the HashMap using the following short line of Java code:

```
private HashMap<Integer, Integer> soundPoolMap;
```

As you can see in Figure 15-3, when we write this line of code under our class declaration line of code, Eclipse underlines this HashMap object with a wavy red line. Place your mouse over the error highlighting, and pop up the Eclipse ADT helper dialog. This dialog gives us several options for removing this error flag within our code.

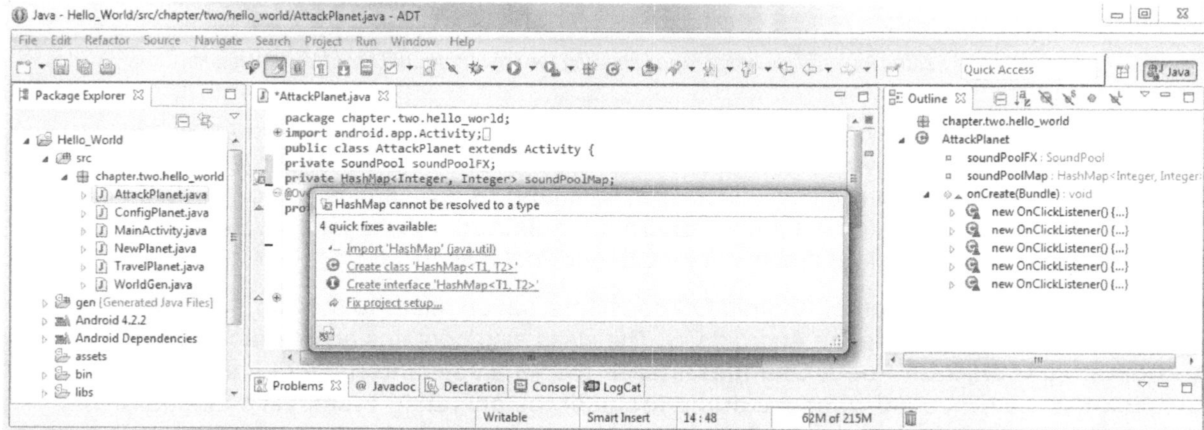

***Figure 15-3.** Declaring a private HashMap object named soundPoolMap and using Eclipse helper to add import statement*

Select the first quick fix option, **Import "HashMap" (java.util package)**, as the solution that you want to select, and Eclipse proceeds to write in our **import java.util.HashMap;** Java code import statement for us.

Next we need to declare four integer variables to hold our sample numbers that we will be using in SoundPool by using the following lines of Java code:

```
int sample1 = 1;
int sample2 = 2;
int sample3 = 3;
int sample4 = 4;
```

Now we have our SoundPool object, HashMap object and sample integers declared at the top of our Activity, before our onCreate() method, as shown in Figure 15-4. Now we are ready to use the new keyword and create a new SoundPool object for use sequencing audio in our Activity.

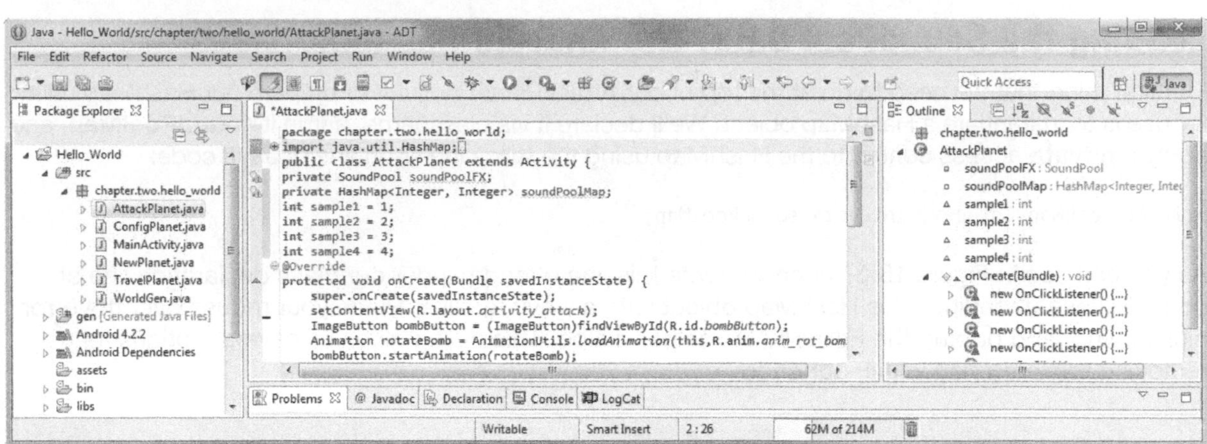

Figure 15-4. *Declaring and Setting four sample integers and showing the import java.util.HashMap statement*

Next we are going to learn about the Android **AudioManager** class, which, as you may have guessed, is used to access **volume**, as well as the **ringer mode** control, in your Android applications. AudioManager is also a subclass of **java.lang.Object**, and is part of the Android Media package, with an import statement path of **android.media.AudioManager** as we will see in the next section of this chapter when we create our new SoundPool object.

AudioManager is a collection of Android OS constants, which relate to the state of different audio-related features inside the Android OS. The class also contains an interface called: **AudioManager.onAudioFocusChangeListener** that is a Java Interface definition for a callback that gets invoked when the **audio focus** of the operating system is changed or updated at any time.

If you want to study the AudioManager class in greater detail, and see for yourself which of these AudioManager SCO, Vibrate, and Bluetooth constants have been deprecated, and in which of the API levels they were deprecated, the Android developer website has a webpage dedicated to it, at this URL:

```
http://developer.android.com/reference/android/media/AudioManager.html
```

Configuring the SoundPool: Using Android AudioManager

We need to create a new instance of the SoundPool object in our Activity's onCreate() method that specifies the number of sounds that can be played at the same time, as well as the type of audio and the quality level. This is done via the SoundPool constructor, which takes the following format:

```
public SoundPool (int maxStreams, int streamType, int srcQuality);
```

So let's add a line of space after our setContentView() method call, and **construct** a **new** SoundPool object, named **soundPoolFX**, using the following single line of Java code:

```
soundPoolFX = new SoundPool(4, AudioManager.STREAM_MUSIC, 100);
```

Notice that once you type this line of code into the Eclipse editing pane, that Eclipse red underlines the AudioManager class reference. So let's get rid of this error by placing the mouse over the error highlighting and selecting the **Import "AudioManager" (android.media package)** option so that Eclipse writes the needed import android.media.AudioManager statement for you, as shown in Figure 15-5.

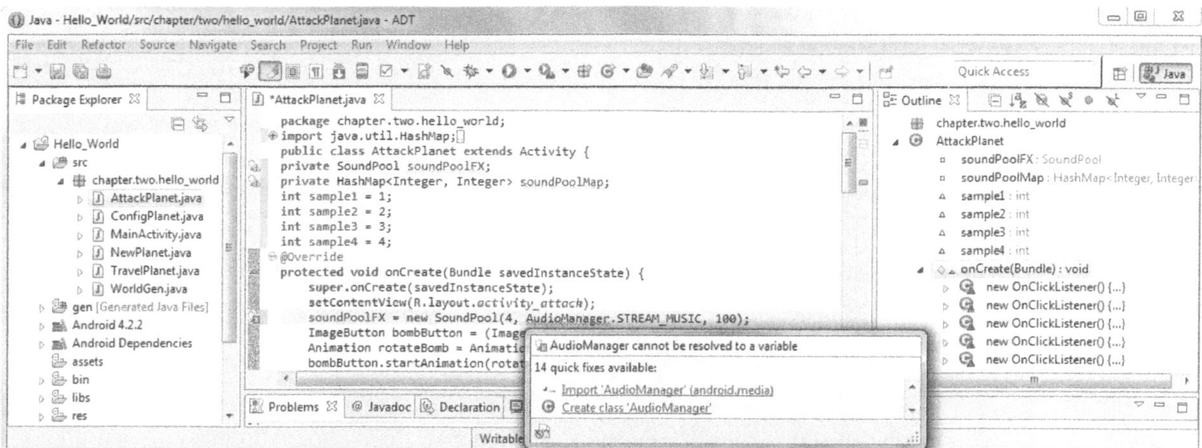

Figure 15-5. *Configuring a SoundPool object and using the Eclipse helper to import the AudioManager package*

Next, we need to do the same work process for the HashMap object, and call its constructor method, using the **new** keyword. If you've forgotten what a Hash table or a Hash map is, here's a short overview.

Hash tables, also known as **hash maps**, are two-dimensional data structures. These specialized data structures are utilized to implement an associative array, which is a data structure that can rapidly map keys to values. Hash tables leverage a **hash function** to compute an **index** into an array of data entry slots, from which the correct value can be quickly found.

Configuring Your HashMap: Using the .put() Method

Let's add a line of space under the soundPoolFX constructor that we just wrote and we'll write our soundPoolMap HashMap constructor Java code next.

The constructor line of code to create an empty Hash table, which takes an integer key and an integer data value pair, would be coded as follows:

```
soundPoolMap = new HashMap<Integer, Integer>();
```

Now that we have an empty Hash table structure defined and created, it is time to load it with the audio data that we will be using in our SoundPool engine. This is done via the HashMap class **.put()** method, which allows us to put (insert) a data pair into the empty Hash table structure, which we now need to **populate** with audio asset data, as shown in Figure 15-6.

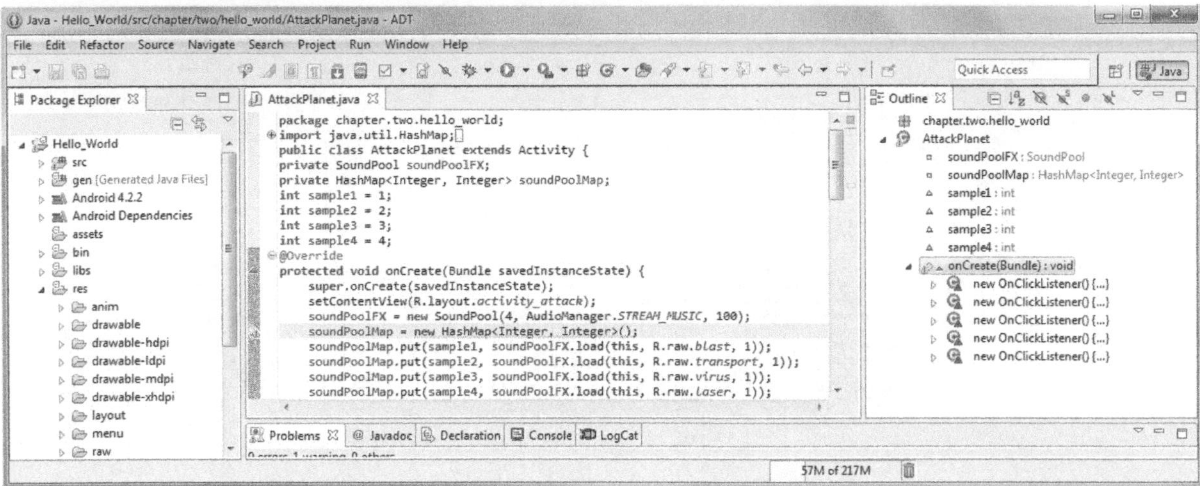

***Figure 15-6.** Using the .put() method to populate our soundPoolMap HashMap object*

We'll use four lines of Java code underneath our HashMap constructor that will leverage dot notation to call the .put() method from the soundPoolMap HashMap object.

The .put() method passes our sample1 through sample4 integer variables, along with the .load() function call to our soundPoolFX SoundPool object, which will pass over the **current context**, a R.raw **reference data path** to each of our digital audio asset files, and a sample **priority** value of 1.

These four soundPoolMap.put() method calls should look something like the following four lines of Java code:

```
soundPoolMap.put(sample1, soundPoolFX.load(this, R.raw.blast, 1));
soundPoolMap.put(sample1, soundPoolFX.load(this, R.raw.blast, 1));
soundPoolMap.put(sample1, soundPoolFX.load(this, R.raw.blast, 1));
soundPoolMap.put(sample1, soundPoolFX.load(this, R.raw.blast, 1));
```

Now we have created our soundPoolFX SoundPool object and our soundPoolMap HashMap object and wired the two together for each of the four samples, which are now loaded into the HashMap and ready for rapid access by the Android SoundPool audio engine.

Next, we'll write a method which will allow us to configure and play our SoundPool audio engine using a single method and two parameters specifying the sample to play, and the pitch shifting value to shift the pitch by.

Coding a playSample() Method: Using SoundPool .play()

Next we are going to write a method called playSample() that we will use to control our usage of the SoundPool engine. This method creates a manageAudio AudioManager object to get the AUDIO_SERVICE system service and uses this object to get current and maximum volume settings from the OS and then uses these data values to set the volume settings for our .play() method call for our soundPoolFX SoundPool object, as shown in Figure 15-7.

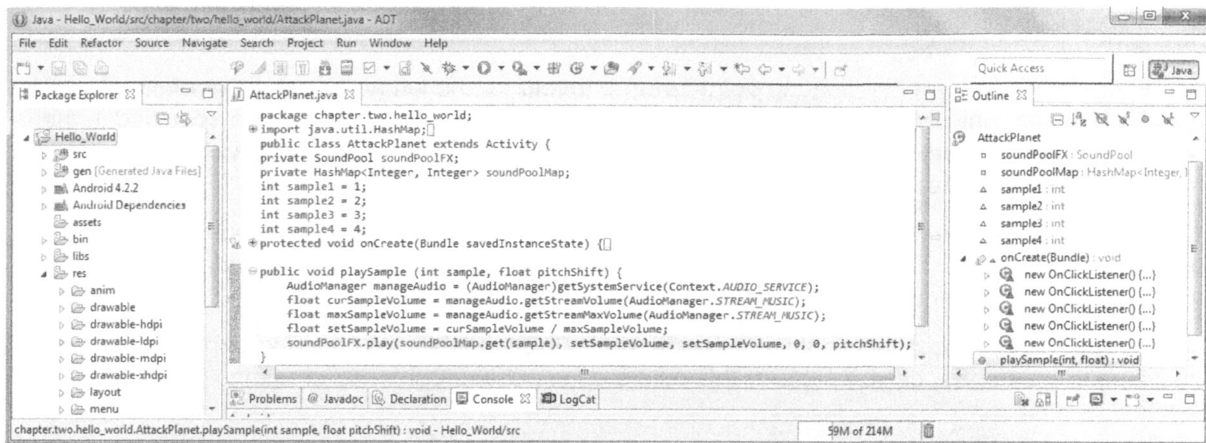

***Figure 15-7.** Coding a playSample() method that sets up and then calls our SoundPool object .play() method*

The first line of Java code in our playSample() method creates an AudioManager object named **manageAudio** and sets it equal to a call to the **getSystemService()** method passing over the **Context.AUDIO_SERVICE** constant. This is done using the following line of Java code:

```
AudioManager manageAudio = (AudioManager)getSystemService(Context.AUDIO_SERVICE);
```

The next three lines of code create **float** variables. We set the first two float variables, **curSampleVolume** and **maxSampleVolume**, to the current audio stream volume and maximum audio stream volume data values, which we obtain via the manageAudio AudioManager object that we created in our first line of code. These two float variables are set using the following Java code:

```
float curSampleVolume = manageAudio.getStreamVolume(AudioManager.STREAM_MUSIC);
float maxSampleVolume = manageAudio.getStreamMaxVolume(AudioManager.STREAM_MUSIC);
```

We then use these two float variable data values to calculate our third float variable data value, using the following line of Java code, which calculates the **setSampleVolume** volume setting that we need to pass to the SoundPool engine by dividing the current volume by the maximum volume:

```
float setSampleVolume = curSampleVolume / maxSampleVolume;
```

Finally we are going to call the SoundPool **.play()** method on our SoundPool object, and configure it with these float volume variables, as well as the data that we passed into the playSample() method, which this final line of code is contained in. The single line of Java code should look like this:

```
soundPoolFX.play(soundPoolMap.get(sample),setSampleVolume,setSampleVolume,0,0,pitchShift);
```

So now a .play() method is called off our soundPoolFX SoundPool object, and passes over the sample **soundID** that is pulled out of the soundPoolMap HashMap object, based on which sample variable (the sample number is the key used to index which sample data we want) is passed over in the method parameter list.

The other parameters are the floating point **volume levels** for the left and right audio channels, specified by our final float calculation held in the **setSampleVolume** variable. Also specified in the .play() parameter list are the **playback priority**, the number of times to play **loop value**, and finally the **pitch shifting factor**, from 0.5 through 2.0, in floating point format.

Notice that in our code this pitch shifting factor that we're passing over is specified using a **lowercase f** after each number. In our code currently this is written as **1.0f**. This f stands for **float** and specifies the decimal number as a floating point value.

While we're talking about this float value for our **pitchShift** variable, be sure and experiment with this value in your code, as you perform this next step in our work process of testing this code in the Nexus S emulator.

Fire up the Nexus S emulator using the **Run As Android Application** work process and use the menu key to go into the Attack a Planet Activity and click the ImageButton icons and trigger some of your samples. Notice that they play quickly and smoothly, almost like your user interface is a video game. This is what is known in the industry as UI **gamification**.

The last thing that we need to do is to address a warning highlight in our Eclipse editor, which is saying there is a better class to use for storing and accessing data pairs than a HashMap class. We'll address this warning, now that we've shown you how to use HashMap and still gotten our code to work despite a warning message in our IDE editor. We'll look into this warning in detail in the next section, as it's asking us to change our Java code.

Android SparseIntArrays: Using the SparseIntArray Class

Open up the **.onCreate()** method contents by clicking the + symbol in the left margin of the IDE editing pane, and notice that there is still one wavy yellow underline highlighting your **new HashMap<Integer, Integer>();** portion of your Java code statement constructing your soundPoolMap HashMap object. Place your mouse over this warning highlight and pop up the helper dialog in Eclipse, as shown in Figure 15-8.

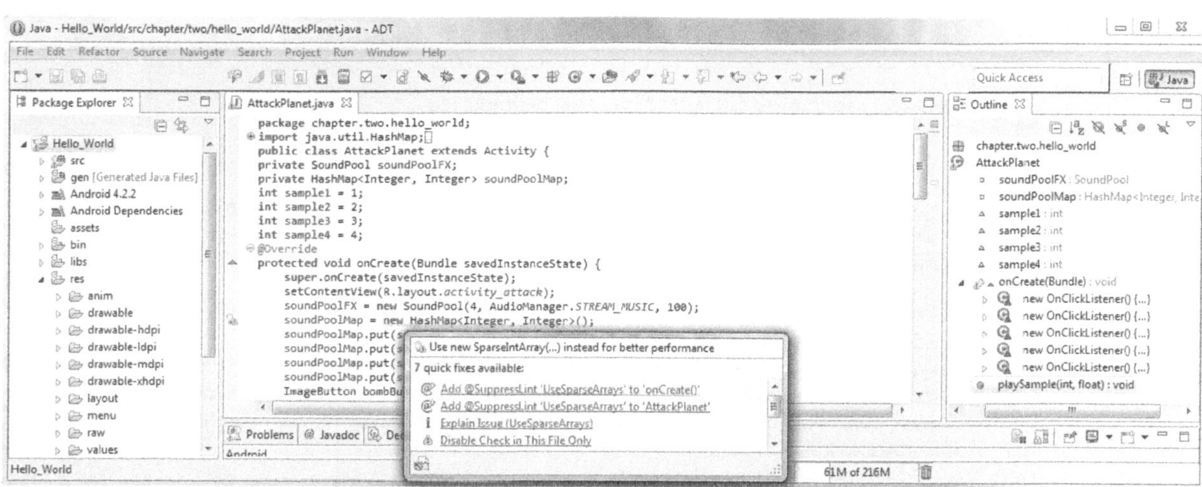

***Figure 15-8.** Examining warning message in Eclipse regarding HashMap and selecting the Explain Issue option*

Notice that one of the options says: **Explain Issue (Use SparseArrays)**. It looks like Eclipse is offering to teach us something that it knows about using SparseArrays instead of HashMaps in this particular implementation.

Let's go ahead and click this option, and see what information Eclipse ADT has to offer us. Note that this particular information is coming more from the Android ADT plug-in portion of Eclipse, than it is from the core Eclipse IDE itself. We know this because the information in the dialog is relating to the use of Android Classes, and not to using the IDE functions themselves.

Once we click this **Explain Issue** link, it opens up yet another dialog, called **More Info**. This dialog tells us that there is an alternate class to HashMap called **SparseIntArray** that would be more efficient for us to use for our purpose of storing and accessing integer key values for the SoundPool audio engine.

The **Issue Explanation** essentially says that the Android SparseArray API is more efficient than the Android HashMap API because HashMap auto-boxes int values from int to Integer, whereas SparseArrays do not. You can see all this issue explanation text in Figure 15-9.

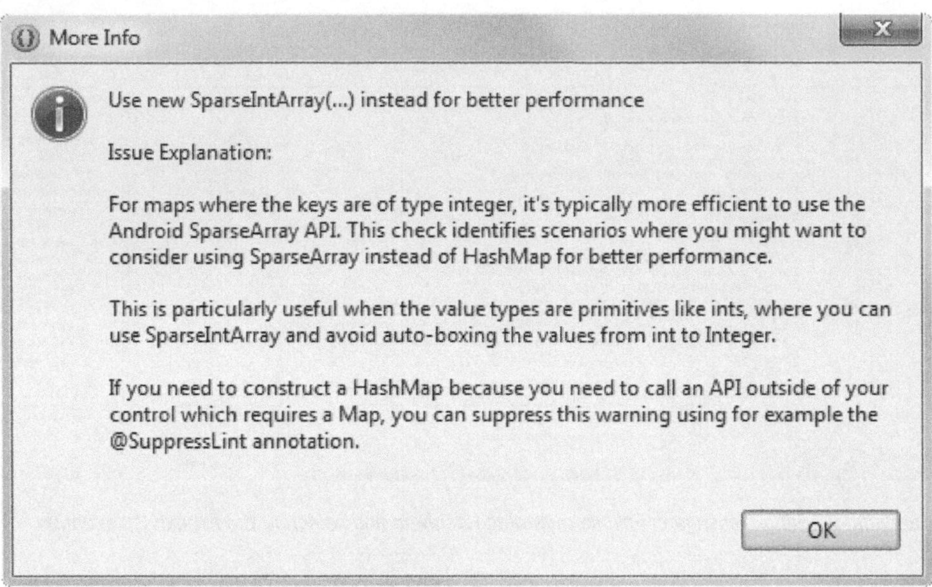

***Figure 15-9.** Viewing a SparseIntArray Issue Explanation in the More Info dialog*

This switch can save processing time when using larger arrays, according to more detailed information found on the Android developer website. For this reason, and to expose you to the SparseArrays API, we will go ahead and upgrade our Attack a Planet Activity subclass Java code to utilize the SparseIntArray class instead of using the HashMap class.

If you want to read the more detailed information available regarding this SparseIntArray class on the Android developer website, it has its own page dedicated to the subject, which can be found at the following URL:

```
http://developer.android.com/reference/android/util/SparseIntArray.html
```

To make this change in our current Java code, we will need to remove the current line of code constructing our HashMap object, and replace it with a new line of code constructing a SparseIntArray object instead.

Let's name our SparseIntArray soundPoolMap also, and call its constructor method using the **new** keyword, using the following line of Java code:

```
soundPoolMap = new SparseIntArray(4);
```

Notice that we are specifying the number of index values in this table, making the table hard-coded and thus more memory and processing efficient.

This is because there are two ways to construct SparseIntArrays, according to the developer website. One is to simply construct **SparseIntArray()** and the other is to construct **SparseIntArray(int initialCapacity)**.

The second method of construction will create a **new** SparseIntArray() that initially contains no mappings, but which will not require any additional memory allocation to store this specified number of mappings, because by specifying this number, the API knows exactly how much memory to allocate.

In our case, we know exactly how many digital audio samples we are going to utilize with the SoundPool engine, so we select the more efficient option for our soundPoolMap SparseIntArray object construction in our Java code.

Once we type in the constructor method call via the new keyword we see that Eclipse gives us an error wavy red underline under our SparseIntArray that we know is a pathway to having Eclipse write some more code for us.

So let's place our mouse over this error highlighting and pop up the helper dialog and select the **Import SparseIntArray (android.util package)** option and make that error highlighting in our code vanish forever.

Now that our soundPoolMap is constructed as a SparseIntArray, as Android wants it to be, we can modify the next four lines of code to use the proper method calls that need to be used for a SparseIntArray object.

This means changing the **.put()** method call, which is used with the HashMap object and shown in Figure 15-10, over to an **.append()** method call, which is the proper method call to use with a SparseIntArray object.

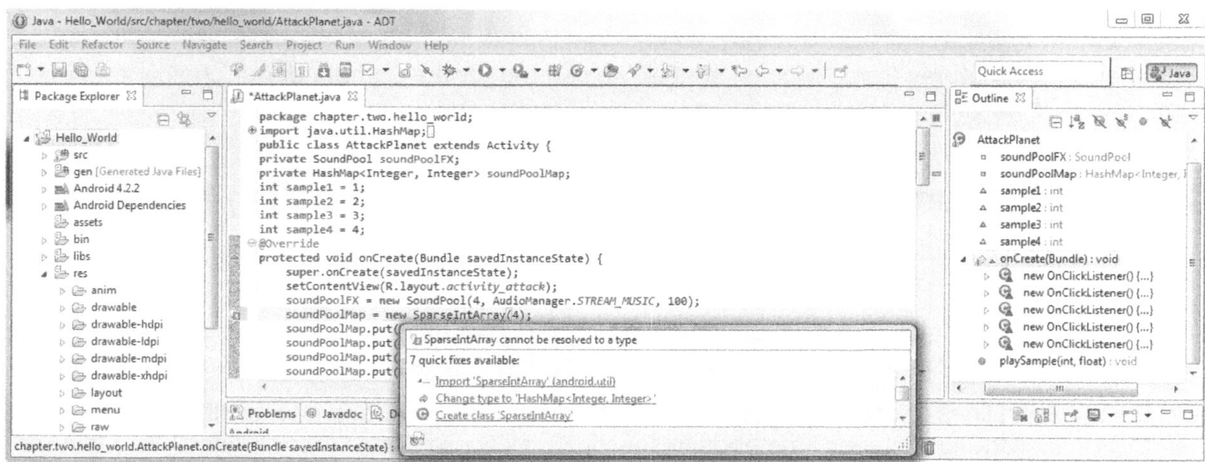

***Figure 15-10.** Changing HashMap object over to a SparseIntArray object and using Eclipse helper to add import statement*

Fortunately, this is a fairly simple modification to our existing Java code, and so our four modified lines of Java code will look like this:

```
soundPoolMap.append(sample1, soundPoolFX.load(this, R.raw.blast, 1));
soundPoolMap.append(sample1, soundPoolFX.load(this, R.raw.blast, 1));
soundPoolMap.append(sample1, soundPoolFX.load(this, R.raw.blast, 1));
soundPoolMap.append(sample1, soundPoolFX.load(this, R.raw.blast, 1));
```

The new soundPoolMap SparseIntArray object is now completely implemented within our SoundPool engine logic, and our IDE is showing zero errors or warnings, as shown in Figure 15-11.

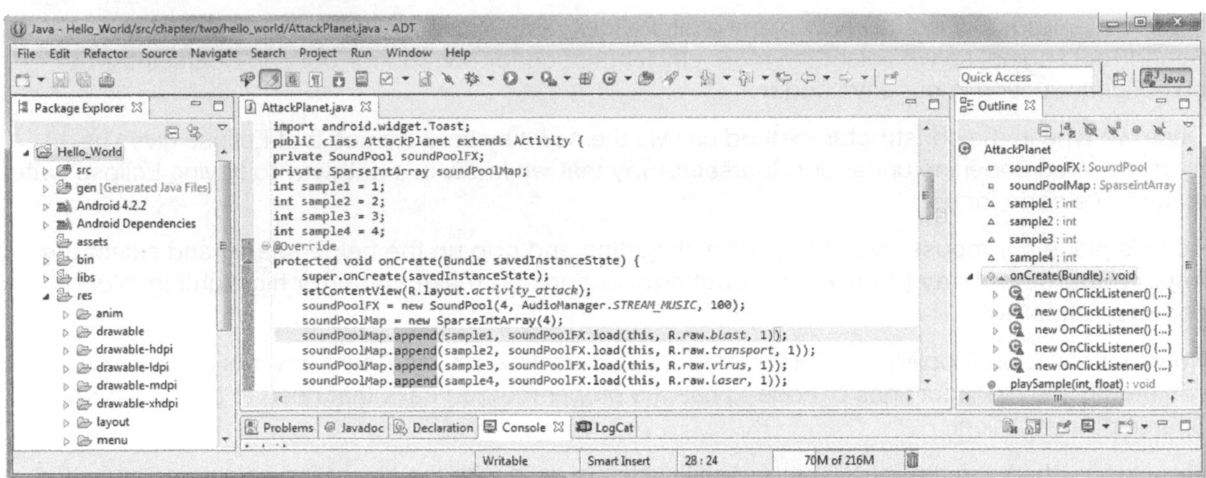

***Figure 15-11.** Changing our soundPoolMap.put() HashMap method calls over to soundPoolMap.append() SparseIntArray method calls*

Finally we are ready to call our SoundPool engine inside our ImageButton onClick() event handling logic structures (code blocks) so that we can trigger the sample of our choice, and even pitch shift it, if we like.

Calling Our SoundPool Objects: Using Our playSample() Method

Let's call our **playSample(int sample, float pitchShift)** method, which we wrote earlier in this chapter, inside of each of our ImageButton onClick() event handler methods next.

This involves a fairly simple line of code to be placed in each of four ImageButton onClick() event handler methods, right after (or before, if you prefer) the Toast.makeToast() object and method call.

Add the following lines of code to each of the bombButton, invadeButton, infectButton, and laserButton .setOnClickListener() methods, respectively, as shown in the following four lines of code (one goes in each handler):

```
playSample (sample1, 1.0f);
playSample (sample2, 1.0f);
playSample (sample3, 1.0f);
playSample (sample4, 1.0f);
```

The placement of these four lines of code inside each of the ImageButton onClick() event handing method code blocks is shown in Figure 15-12.

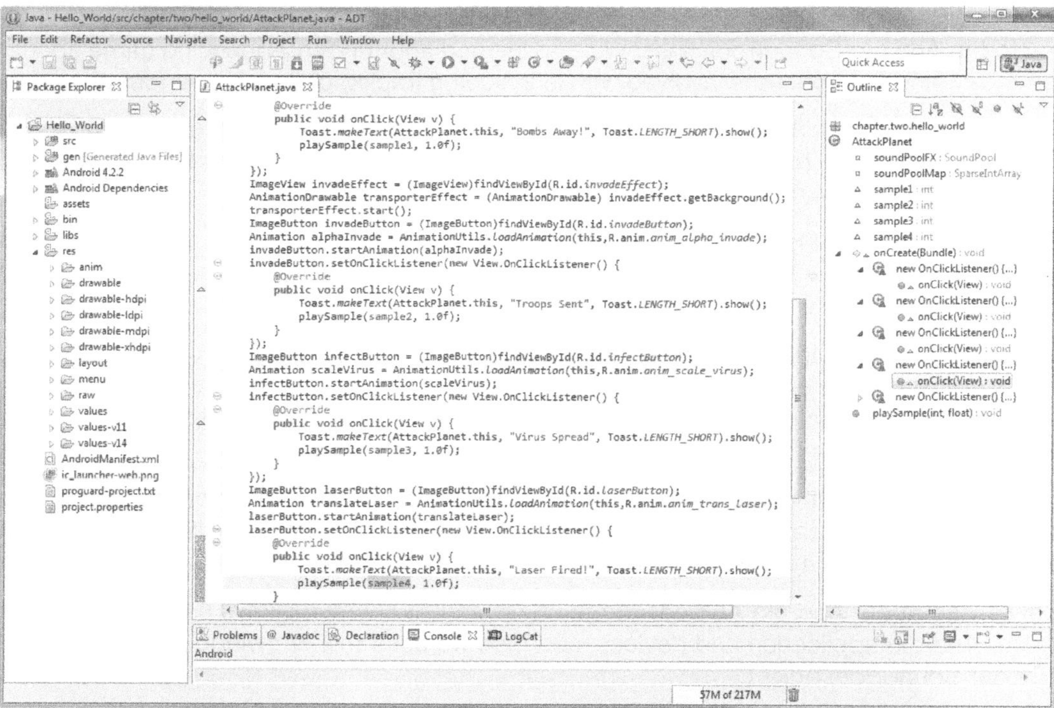

***Figure 15-12.** Calling our playSample() method with sample name and pitch shift parameter to play a SoundPool sample*

Now that all the Java code constructs that would be needed to implement our soundPoolFX SoundPool object audio engine within our AttackPlanet.java Activity subclass are in place, it is time to utilize our **Run As Android Application** work process, and test all our code in the Nexus S emulator.

Once the Nexus S emulator launches, click the menu button, and select the Attack a Planet menu option, and launch the Activity subclass that we have just implemented SoundPool in. Click the animated ImageButton user interface elements, and trigger some digital audio samples. Pretty cool.

Now notice that your samples trigger immediately as SoundPool now has them preloaded into memory. Also note that you can now click the buttons in rapid succession, triggering audio in a more game-like fashion. Responsive feedback is important for this type of multimedia user interface design, which we've implemented in this Activity during the past several chapters.

This activity now implements a plethora of "trick" new media user interface elements, including: 3D multi-state image buttons, frame-based animation, vector or procedural animation, digital image and animation compositing, and an audio sample engine, all seamlessly integrated with great results.

Summary

In this final chapter covering digital audio in Android, we took a closer look at audio sequencing and audio synthesis concepts, as they relate to the powerful Android SoundPool digital audio engine class and API.

We started out by learning about the concept of MIDI and audio sequencers and sequencing, which is central to the Android SoundPool class. We also learned about how sequencing came about, where it is used today, and the concepts involved with it, including tracks, parts, and performance data.

Next we took a closer look at digital audio synthesis, including the basic concepts of waves, tones, pitch, octaves, oscillators, pitch shifting, and many of those fundamental concepts that need to be understood to turn the SoundPool class API into an audio synthesis engine.

Next we looked at the SoundPool class and API specifically, examining how it works and its methods and memory requirements. We took a closer look at the SoundPool **maxStreams** parameter as well as how it handles **priority** when the maxStreams sample streams number has been exceeded.

The next logical step was for us to look at some of the **caveats** regarding the use of a digital audio sequencing and synthesis engine, which happens to be very memory and processing intensive, and thus, if we are going to implement this in our application, there are certain factors that we must take into account, and optimize for, within our code and new media assets.

Finally, we were ready to implement a SoundPool audio engine in one of the Activity subclasses in our Hello_World Android application. We set-up our SoundPool object, loaded it with our audio sample data, and learned about the Android **HashMap** class API that allows us to create Hash tables.

Then we learned about Android **AudioManager** class and API, which allows us to manage audio focus in our Android application and devices, and then we used this knowledge to allow us to construct our SoundPool object.

Next we wrote a custom **playSample()** method, so that we could pass sample data parameters to our SoundPool, such as the samples we wanted to play and how much we wanted to pitch-shift those samples.

To get rid of a pesky warning flag in Eclipse we replaced our HashMap with a **SparseIntArray** object and learned about the differences between the two Android utilities. Then we implemented calls to our playSample() method in our ImageButton onClick() event handlers, and SoundPool was implemented.

In the next chapter, we will start learning about Android **Services**, and using background processing to off-load computationally intensive tasks, so that they don't affect the responsiveness of our user interface designs or our application user experience in any way.

Chapter 16

Android Intents: Inter-Application Programming

In this chapter, we will delve deeper into Android **Intents**. Intents are utilized by developers to process inter-module communications or instructions within four primary functional areas comprising Android Application Development: **Activities**, **Services**, **Broadcast Receivers** and **Content Providers**.

We have learned all about Activities, since those contain the front-end of your Android application, including your designs, content, new media, user interface, and so on. In the next three chapters, we're going to cover the other three primary functional areas for Android: Services (Processing), Broadcast Receivers (Messaging), and Content Providers (Data Storage).

To be able to cover these three more advanced areas in Android application development, we first need to cover the vast subject of **Intents** and **Intent Filters**. This is because Intents are more heavily utilized in implementing these more complicated "behind the scenes" Android application components.

Intents can also be utilized with Activities, and because we are well-versed with Activities we will learn about how to use Intents with our Activities and, during the next three chapters, we'll also learn how to leverage them using Services, Broadcast Receivers, and finally, with Content Providers.

In this chapter, we are going to look closely at both the Android Intent and Intent Filter class, and all the various characteristics of Android Intents, as well as how these features, functions, settings, constants, and similar characteristics are declared for use in your Android application.

We will take a closer look at Intent Filters, which allow you to automate how your Intents are utilized in your application when it is used by other applications. As you may have surmised, declaring Intent Filters for usage is done via your **AndroidManifest.xml** file, using the **<intent-filter>** tag.

This is one of the more complex and involved topics in Android, because it involves intermodule communications, messaging, AndroidManifest, filters, and similarly advanced programming topics in both Java and XML formats.

Android Intent Messaging: First, the Global Overview

Intent messaging is an Android OS facility providing **late runtime binding** between **application components** within the same or different applications.

An Android Intent object is instantiated using the **android.content.Intent** class, which is a subclass of **java.lang.Object**. This means that Intent was developed solely for its own unique purpose and is not subclassed from any other type of Android class. It's packaged in the Android **Content** package, as you can clearly see from the package name designation outlined previously.

The reason that it is packaged with the **android.content** package is because Intents can be used to quickly access and to manipulate content providers (databases), which we will learn all about in a future chapter. The usage of an Intent object is much broader than just database access, as it can be used with Android Services, Activities, and Broadcast Receivers as well.

The Android Developer Reference defines Intents as **abstract descriptions** of an operation to be performed. This means that Android designed Intents with the purpose of creating a Java object type that can be utilized to easily accomplish tasks that would normally take complex programming code.

So an Intent is essentially a programming shortcut, which has been built in to the Android OS and programming environment to make things easier in the long-run. I say "in the long-run" because first we need to learn how to use Intents and Intent Filters, and then they will become powerful to us once we understand them, making us more advanced Android programmers.

An Intent object structure is known to be a **passive** data structure object, because it is simply a passive collection of data, and instructions, which are bundled together in one comprehensive Java object, which can easily be passed around between the various functional modules of your application.

An Intent **object data structure** should contain a description that contains standard operating system or developer created "**actions**" that need to be executed, and additionally passes over the **data** upon which those actions need to process. This is passed to the Java code module via its **component name**, specifying which class is the **target** for (receiving) the Intent.

We will be learning all about these Intent object data structure formats later on in this chapter. In addition to these specific actions and data, an Android Intent object can also specify **data type** (MIME) specifications, as well as **category constants**, **flags**, and even **extra** data pairs, which are related to the primary data packet that is needed by the Intent action for processing. We will be learning all about these various functional areas of Intent objects in great detail throughout the remainder of the chapter.

Android Intent Implementation: Three Different Types of Intent Usage

There are three different uses for Intent objects, each of which can be utilized within the Android operating system to invoke your intermodule communications between your Activities, Services, and Broadcast Receivers.

However one type of Intent, the Intent object, can be used with each of three specific areas of the OS. None of the different classification types of Intent object usage are allowed to be used interchangeably, to avoid processing errors.

Of course, you can name your Intent object anything that you like, but it is the type of Intent processing method calls that you utilize to pass your Intent object around your application modules that will ultimately determine what type of usage that Intent object will involve, regardless of what you may name the Intent object when you construct it. It is the type of use that the Intent is used for that determines what type of Intent (or more precisely, what type of objective that Intent is leveraged for) it is.

Different Intent object method calls are used to guarantee that these different uses of Intent objects do not get confused amongst each other, that is, that they do not ever intersect with, interfere with, collide with, or mistakenly get used with or by, any of the other implementation of an Intent object.

For instance, **startActivity()** uses an Intent object to start an Activity, whereas **startService()** uses an Intent object to start a Service. To send an Intent object to a Broadcast Receiver one would use the **broadcastIntent()** method, and so the method used to distribute the Intent object determines its implementation.

For this reason, we will cover each usage scenario of Intent objects separately, so that we can see how intent-based communication with Activities, Services, and Broadcast Receiver messages differ from each other.

In this final section of the book we will also practice using Intent objects within each of those four major areas of the Android OS. Because you are already a pro at Activities, in this chapter we will look at code examples using Intent objects with Activity subclasses. Over the next three chapters regarding Android Services, Broadcast Receivers, and Content Providers, we will also see how Intent objects are used to initiate and control these other functional areas within Android as well.

Activities

An Intent object to be used with **Activities** can be passed to each Activity using the **Context.startActivity()** or the **Activity.startActivityForResult()** to launch the Activity, or to ask an existing Activity to perform some application specific programming task.

Intents can be passed back using the **Activity.setResult()** method to return information to the calling Activity that originated Intent communications by using the Activity.startActivityForResult() method in the first place.

Android Services

An Intent object to be used with Android **Services** is passed to the Service subclass using the **Context.startService()** method call to initiate an Android Service, or deliver new instructions to a **started** Service. We will be learning all about Services in the next chapter in this book.

An Intent object can also be passed using the **Context.bindService()** method to establish a connection (bind) between the calling application component and **bound** Service. Intents can also initiate bound Services if the Service is not already **started** and running.

We will be covering **bound** Services in the next chapter of this book, as well as **started** Services and **hybrid** Services. We will cover how Intents are utilized in this context, and thus, I am covering them here for the purposes of context and overview regarding the different types of Intents.

Broadcast Receivers

Intent objects passed to any of the Android **Broadcast Receiver** methods are delivered to all interested Android Broadcast Receivers. A large number of Android operating system broadcasts will originate from the Android system code, as might well be expected in complex, full versions of the Linux OS.

Broadcast Receiver specific versions of Intent method calls include the **Context.sendBroadcast()** method, the **Context.sendOrderedBroadcast()** method, and the **Context.sendStickyBroadcast()** method which we cover in Chapter 18.

Because each type of Intent has a unique calling method, the Android system can easily locate the appropriate application Activity, Service, or Broadcast Receiver that needs to respond to each particular Intent object.

Because of the way that the Android Intent system is set up, there is zero overlap between these Intent messaging systems. Broadcast Receiver Intents are delivered only to Broadcast Receivers, never to Android Activities or to Services. An Intent object that is passed over using a **.startActivity()** method is delivered only to an Activity subclass, and never delivered to a Service subclass or a Broadcast Receiver subclass, and so on and so forth.

Android Intent Structure: Anatomy of an Android Intent

An Intent object contains a **bundle** of information. You are familiar with Android **Bundle** objects from the very first time that you had Eclipse ADT generate your Android app for you, as Bundle objects are utilized in every single Android application, used to save instance state information for an Activity subclass. Maybe you remember seeing this following line of code:

```
public void onCreate(Bundle savedInstanceState) {onCreate Method Logic is in here}
```

Intents contain information that is of interest to application components which receive that Intent. This includes information such as the **action** to be taken by the receiving application components, as well as the **data** that needs to be acted upon. An Intent can also include information that is of interest to the Android operating system itself, such as which **category** of the receiving component should handle the Intent, or even instructions, on how to launch the target activity.

An Android Intent can contain the following seven functional parts:

1. **Component Name:** Fully qualified class name of target component
2. **Action:** String naming an action or a predefined ACTION constant
3. **Data:** The URI of a data object (file) which is to be acted on
4. **Category:** String naming category, or Android CATEGORY constant

5. **Data (MIME) Type:** MIME Type of the data that is to be acted on
6. **Extras:** Key-value pairs for additional information for Intent
7. **Flags:** Flags of various sorts defined within the Intent class

Let's go into each of these seven areas that are so important to specify within an Intent object, and see why each is important in their own right, and how these areas of an Intent object would be implemented inside of the different types of Android Intent objects.

Intent Object Components: Specify a Component Name Parameter

The most important thing that you can specify for your Intent object is the **component name** of the application component that you are explicitly designating to **handle** that Intent object.

When you specify this component name in your Intent object, you are also creating an **explicit Intent** object by doing so. We will be discussing this Explicit Intent in far greater detail within the next few sections of this chapter.

This field within the Intent object is a **ComponentName** object, and it contains a combination of the fully-qualified class name of your target component. In the case of our Hello World application, this might be "chapter.two.Hello_World.AttackPlanet" for the Attack a Planet Activity subclass.

Note that the package name is set in the AndroidManifest XML file for each application where the component resides. The package part of the component name and the package name set in the AndroidManifest.xml don't necessarily have to match if you are calling a component that lives inside a different application. Intents are flexible enough to be able to communicate across disparate applications, as well as inside of just a single application.

It is important to note here that the component name is **optional**. If it is set, your Intent object will be delivered to an instance of the designated class. If a component name is not specified, Android will look at all the other information in your Intent object to locate a suitable target.

Under this scenario, the Intent becomes an **implicit Intent** because Android must **imply** how to apply the Intent, by **inferring** which component to apply it to. This is accomplished by looking at all the other information in the Intent and deducing where to process the Intent. Sherlock Holmes would surely have been proud to be an Android developer.

In your Intent object, if you want to specify a component name, it would be set by using the **.setComponent()** method, or, by using the **.setClass()** method, or using the **.setClassName()** method.

On the other side of the coin, the component name could be read from an Intent object by using the Intent class's **.getComponent()** method. This is used to extract the component name information from the Intent object, so that it can be matched up with a given application component and processed if there is a match.

Intent Object Actions: Specifying an Action Parameter

An Intent **action** parameter is specified using a **string** naming an action to be performed, or an **ACTION_ constant** used to specify those actions already defined inside of the Android operating system. Action constants that are defined for all Android Activity subclasses include the following actions:

```
ACTION_MAIN
ACTION_VIEW
ACTION_ATTACH_DATA
ACTION_EDIT
ACTION_PICK
ACTION_CHOOSER
ACTION_GET_CONTENT
ACTION_DIAL
ACTION_CALL
ACTION_SEND
ACTION_SENDTO
ACTION_ANSWER
ACTION_INSERT
ACTION_DELETE
ACTION_RUN
ACTION_SYNC
ACTION_PICK_ACTIVITY
ACTION_SEARCH
ACTION_WEB_SEARCH
ACTION_FACTORY_TEST
```

In the case of Intents used with Broadcast Receivers, the action actually specifies an action that took place in the past (already has happened) and is thus being reported rather than requested. The Intent class has defined a number of Broadcast Receiver action constants, including the following:

```
ACTION_TIME_TICK
ACTION_TIME_CHANGED
ACTION_TIMEZONE_CHANGED
ACTION_BOOT_COMPLETED
ACTION_PACKAGE_ADDED
ACTION_PACKAGE_CHANGED
ACTION_PACKAGE_REMOVED
ACTION_PACKAGE_RESTARTED
ACTION_PACKAGE_DATA_CLEARED
ACTION_UID_REMOVED
ACTION_BATTERY_CHANGED
ACTION_POWER_CONNECTED
ACTION_POWER_DISCONNECTED
ACTION_SHUTDOWN
```

It's important to note that you can also define your own customized action strings for activating your own custom components within your application. This allows you to develop your own custom Intent system within your apps.

The actions that you design and name yourself should include an application package as a prefix and then the action constant that you create for your own usage. As an example from our own Hello World application, you might use the following full path name to your action:

```
chapter.two.hello_world.ACTION_SHOW_PLANET_STATUS
```

The Intent action parameter is extremely significant in the determination of how the remaining information parameters of your Intent are structured.

For this reason, its best practice to use an action constant that is as specific as possible. You should also associate your action constants as tightly with the other information fields of your Intent object, such as the data, category, data type, and flags, as is possible in your design.

What you want to try to do is, instead of defining an action in isolation, define an entire protocol and set of constants for the Intent objects that your custom application components will be handling.

The action constant or string value in your Intent object should be set by using a **.setAction()** method. Conversely, an action constant or string value should be read from an Intent object by using a **.getAction()** method.

Intent Object Data: Sending Data for the Action to Act Upon

The Intent object **data** parameter contains a **URI** object for the data to be processed using the action specified. As you may have guessed, various types of actions are used together with a logically corresponding type of data specification that would fit well with the action parameter passed.

For instance if the action passed to the Intent object's action parameter is an **ACTION_DIAL** constant, then a data parameter would contain the phone number to display in the dial area of the smartphone.

If the Intent action constant parameter was an **ACTION_CALL**, then the data parameter would be a **URI** object containing the **tel:** prefix reference with the telephone number that your application wants to place as a phone call.

If the Intent action constant was **ACTION_VIEW** and the data parameter used was an **http:** URI, the receiving activity would be called on to download and display whatever data that URI reference was referring to be viewed.

Intent Object Category: Using a Category Constant Parameter

An Intent object's **category** parameter contains a **string** object that specifies additional information regarding the kind of component to handle the Intent. Any number of category descriptions can be placed inside the Intent object to help the receiving component.

The Android Intent class also defines a number of **category constants**, just like it defines ACTION_ constants for Activities and Broadcast Receivers. These category constants all begin with the word CATEGORY_ and include:

```
CATEGORY_DEFAULT
CATEGORY_BROWSABLE
CATEGORY_TAB
CATEGORY_ALTERNATIVE
CATEGORY_SELECTED_ALTERNATIVE
CATEGORY_LAUNCHER
CATEGORY_INFO
CATEGORY_HOME
CATEGORY_PREFERENCE
CATEGORY_TEST
CATEGORY_CAR_DOCK
CATEGORY_DESK_DOCK
CATEGORY_LE_DESK_DOCK
CATEGORY_HE_DESK_DOCK
CATEGORY_CAR_MODE
CATEGORY_APP_MARKET
```

The Intent class has several methods that allow you to work with category parameters, including the **.addCategory()** method, which adds a category in an Intent object, the **.removeCategory(),** which removes a category once it has been added, and the **.getCategories(),** which retrieves the set of all the categories that are currently contained within the Intent object.

Intent Object Data Types: Setting a MIME Data Type Parameter

When matching up your Intent to components that are capable of handling a given **data type**, it is usually very important to know which classification or type of data value (the data's **MIME** type) that you are dealing with (in addition, of course, to the URI location for that data).

MIME stands for **MultiPurpose Internet Mail Extension** and it was originally developed for use with e-mail servers to define their support for different types of data.

MIME has now been extended to other platform definitions of supported data and content types, and to communication protocols (such as HTTP) data type definitions, and also to Android OS, to define content data types here, as well. Suffice it to say that MIME has become a major standard for defining content data types in a myriad of computing environments. Examples of MIME data type definitions include the following commonly used Content-Types:

- `Content-Type: text/html        (HTML Data)`
- `Content-Type: video/mp4        (MPEG Data)`
- `Content-Type: image/png        (PNG8 Data)`
- `Content-Type: audio/mp3        (MPEG Data)`
- `Content-Type: application/pdf  (.PDF Data)`
- `Content-Type: multipart/x-zip  (.ZIP Data)`

To give an example of why one would declare a MIME data type in an Intent object, you may want to make sure that an application component that is supposed to display video data is not mistakenly called upon to play an audio file, just as you would not want an application component that plays audio, like our playSample() method, to be mistakenly called and passed a video or image data file for playback.

In most cases your data type can be inferred from the URI that is passed. This is especially true for Android **content://** URIs, which indicate where the data is located on your device, and which are controlled by a content provider. We will be covering Android Content Providers in a later chapter in this final section of this book.

The data type can be **explicitly set** in your Intent object as well. Using the Intent object **.setData()** method specifies the data only, as a URI, whereas using the **.setType()** method call specifies the data solely using a MIME type.

A third method called **.setDataAndType()** combines these two methods and specifies the data as both a URI and a MIME type. The URI can be read using the Intent object **.getData()** method and the data type can be read by using the Intent object **.getType()** method.

Intent Object Extras: Using Extras in Your Intent Object

An Intent object can also include extras (data) in the form of key-value pairs. These are used to deliver additional information that should be included to facilitate proper component handling of the Intent object.

The Android Intent class also defines a number of **extra constants**, just like it defines ACTION_ constants for Activities and Broadcast Receivers, and CATEGORY_ constants, as we saw in the previous section. These extra constants always begin with the word EXTRA and include the following:

```
EXTRA_ALARM_COUNT
EXTRA_BCC
EXTRA_CC
EXTRA_CHANGED_COMPONENT_NAME
EXTRA_DATA_REMOVED
EXTRA_DOCK_STATE
EXTRA_DOCK_STATE_HE_DESK
EXTRA_DOCK_STATE_LE_DESK
EXTRA_DOCK_STATE_CAR
EXTRA_DOCK_STATE_DESK
EXTRA_DOCK_STATE_UNDOCKED
EXTRA_DONT_KILL_APP
EXTRA_EMAIL
EXTRA_INITIAL_INTENTS
EXTRA_INTENT
EXTRA_KEY_EVENT
EXTRA_ORIGINATING_URI
EXTRA_PHONE_NUMBER
EXTRA_REFERRER
EXTRA_REMOTE_INTENT_TOKEN
EXTRA_REPLACING
```

```
EXTRA_SHORTCUT_ICON
EXTRA_SHORTCUT_ICON_RESOURCE
EXTRA_SHORTCUT_INTENT
EXTRA_STREAM
EXTRA_SHORTCUT_NAME
EXTRA_SUBJECT
EXTRA_TEMPLATE
EXTRA_TEXT
EXTRA_TITLE
EXTRA_UID
```

We have seen that some actions are paired with certain types of data URIs; similarly, some actions are commonly paired with certain types of extras.

For example, an ACTION_TIMEZONE_CHANGED Intent object action parameter has a "time-zone" extra that identifies the new time zone, and ACTION_HEADSET_PLUG has a "state" extra indicating whether the headset is now plugged in or unplugged, as well as a "name" extra for the type of headset.

If you were to invent an ACTION_SHOW_PLANET_STATUS action, then the planet status value would be set using an EXTRA_STATUS_PLANET key-value pair.

The Intent object has a series of **.putExtra()** methods for inserting various types of extra data parameters and a similar set of **.getExtra()** methods for reading the extra data parameters. It is interesting to note that these Java methods also parallel those methods utilized with Bundle objects.

It is important to note that these key-value pair extras can be installed and read as an Android **Bundle** object by using the **.putExtras()** method and the **.getExtras()** methods. If you are using a large number of extras this may be the most efficient way of setting things, up, after all, this is what the Bundle object was intended to be used for in the first place.

Intent Object Flags: Using Flags with Your Intent Object

The final type of parameter that can be contained in an Android Intent object is called a **flag** parameter. Flags are boolean values that as a programmer you are probably quite familiar with. Flags are very useful for setting states and switches in a highly data-compact fashion.

Where an Intent object is concerned, most flag parameters would instruct the Android system how to launch or handle that activity in some fashion or possibly how to treat the Intent after its launched. However, Intent object flag parameters are open and flexible enough for you to use them in any creative way that you see fit for your application, so get creative!

Explicit Versus Implicit Intents: Which Intent Type to Use

There are two classifications of Android Intent objects: **Explicit Intents** and **Implicit Intents**. Explicit Intents are the easier of the two to work with and utilize within your application, whereas Implicit Intents are far more complicated, and via **Intent Filters** you can allow other developers to work with your application components implicitly via their Intent objects.

Explicit Intents

Explicit Intents objects specify a target application component using the component name parameter, as I mentioned earlier. This is termed explicit due to the fact that your component (class) naming schema is not going to be generally available to developers of other applications, so if they are going to be allowed to access your code using Intent objects, they must be given the class names to call via the component name parameter.

For this reason, Explicit Intents are typically utilized primarily for intra-application messaging (or internal application messaging). A good example of this would be an Activity starting a subordinate Service class or launching a related Activity, which we will see later in this chapter.

Android always delivers an explicit Intent to the instance of the designated target class specified in component name. When you utilize an explicit Intent, nothing in the Intent object other than the component name matters for determining which application component gets the Intent.

Implicit intents, on the other hand, do not name the target (the component name parameter in the Intent object is blank).

Implicit Intents

Implicit intents are often used to activate components in other applications or more generalized features or functions in the Android OS where it's easy to infer what is desired, such as dialing or calling a telephone number for your user via your application user interface rather than through an OS phone dialer utility.

A different approach entirely needs to be followed when an implicit Intent object is received. With a clearly designated target not having been specified, the Android operating system must ascertain the best application component with which to handle that Intent object.

This is termed **Intent Resolution**, as the Android OS is resolving your Intent object for you. The Intent object resolution might result in the launching an Activity class to display a new user interface, or a starting of a Service class to perform the requested actions, or even activating an Android Broadcast Receiver, to respond to your broadcast announcements.

Intent resolution can be performed in a couple of different ways. If the contents of the Intent make it obvious what needs to be done, say in the instance that you have an action parameter of ACTION_MAIN and a category parameter constant of CATEGORY_HOME in your Intent object, the Home Screen will be launched on your Android device's screen. The other way to resolve Intents containing more customized actions is by using an **Intent Filter**, which developers can define to help other apps send Intents to their proper component for processing.

Implicit Intent Resolution: Introducing Intent Filters

In the absence of an Intent object filled with Android specified Intent constants, which we have gone over in detail earlier in this chapter, **implicit Intent resolution** is usually performed by comparing the entire contents of any submitted Intent object to the existing intent filter definitions within that application's AndroidManifest.xml file.

Intent Filters are complex logic structures that are created inside your AndroidManifest using **XML mark-up** tag/parameter logic. They are associated with your application's components that can potentially receive Intents.

Intent Filters perform a couple of important functions where Intent objects are concerned. First, they outline the functional capabilities that your application component embodies, and second, they serve to specify the characteristics and limitations of the Intents it can handle.

Intent filter XML definitions open up your application components to a much higher probability of successfully receiving implicit intents of a designated type. In the next section we will go over the tags that can be used to define **Intent Filter Resolution Structures** for your application.

Note that if your application component does not have any intent filters defined in your AndroidManifest.xml file, it will only be able to **receive** explicit intents. Your application can of course continue to **send** implicit intents using the Android OS Intent constants which we covered earlier, as these are defined using Intent Filter structures that are part of the OS.

A component with intent filters defined for it can receive both explicit and implicit intents.

There are three primary parameters of an Intent object that are analyzed when that Intent object is tested against the Intent Filter. These are the ACTION (or action constant), the DATA (URI and MIME) and the CATEGORY.

If you think about it, there is quite a bit of information in these three mainstream Intent parameters as we have learned previously, so with these and an Intent Filter structure (definition) to tell us how to apply these information parameters, the OS should be able to resolve any and all Intent objects successfully.

It is also interesting to note that the extras and flags parameters in an Intent object play absolutely no part in the Intent resolution process that determines which application component receives a given Intent.

Next, let's take a closer look at the Android **<intent-filter>** tag and its parameters and child (nested) tags so that we can see how an Intent Filter is specified in your AndroidManifest.xml file. More detailed information regarding the <intent-filter> tag structure, parameters and child tags can be found on the Android developer website, located at the following URL:

`http://developer.android.com/guide/topics/manifest/intent-filter-element.html`

Creating Intent Filters: Using the <intent-filter> XML Tag

While the coding of custom Intent Filter structures is beyond the scope of this introductory book covering Android application development, I'm going to give you an overview of these <intent-filter> tags and structure within this section, so that you understand how these structures are implemented, using XML mark-up in your AndroidManifest.xml application bootstrap file.

An <intent-filter> tag structure or hierarchy is utilized to specify the types of Intent objects that an Activity, Service, or Broadcast Receiver subclass can respond to within your application.

An <intent-filter> tag declares its capabilities within the context of its parent component tag container, which is going to be an **<activity>** tag, a **<service>** tag, or a **<receiver>** tag, since those are the primary application component subclasses under which you can design your custom Intent Filter hierarchy structure. We will be learning about these tags during the next three chapters on Services, Broadcast Receivers, and Content Providers.

The <intent-filter> tag located inside of its parent tag defines what an Intent object can do for that <activity> or <service> as well as which types of broadcasts a <receiver> component class can handle.

The <intent-filter> tag structure defines the component tag that it is contained within so that it knows it can receive Intents of the specified type, and allows the OS to filter-out those Intents which are not going to be meaningful for that particular component XML definition.

As you have seen already in this book with our <activity> XML declarations in previous chapters, and which you will soon see, using the <service> and the broadcast <receiver> components, all the categories of core Android components are always defined inside the AndroidManifest.xml file.

So as you can see, this approach works efficiently and seamlessly with the way that components are set-up and configured for your Android application in the first place. Thus, if you need to add an <intent-filter> hierarchy, you simply code it modularly, nested inside of one of your component tags, right underneath the existing component tag's child tags and parameters.

Most of the contents of the <intent-filter> tag are described by its child tags, including the **<action>** tags, the **<category>** tags, and the **<data>** tag elements. As you might imagine these child tags of the <intent-filter> tag contain the definition of what to look for in each of these parameter slots within any given Intent object.

The only one of these three child tags that is absolutely required in the **<action>** tag, which will define what action or actions are to be taken to resolve (to complete) the Intent object's message or mission. The <intent-filter> tag can also have three basic parameters itself; one for an **icon graphic**, one for a **text label**, and one giving it a **priority value**.

Next let's actually implement an Intent object in our Hello_World Android application to see how all this works together within our existing app.

Using an Intent Object to Launch an Activity in Hello World

Let's create a new Activity subclass called **TimePlanet** that we can call using an Intent object from our ConfigPlanet Activity subclass. We will create a new Activity subclass, create a new XML user interface screen layout for it, add it to our AndroidManifest.xml file so the Android OS knows that it is there for use, add user interface elements to our Configure a Planet Activity to call the new TimePlanet Activity and then write the Java code that implements the Intent object and uses it to call (start) the TimePlanet Activity and its Atomic Clock user interface.

Open up Eclipse, and then open your Hello World project folder, and right-click on the chapter.two. hello_world package name folder, and finally select the **New ➤ Class** menu sequence as shown in Figure 16-1.

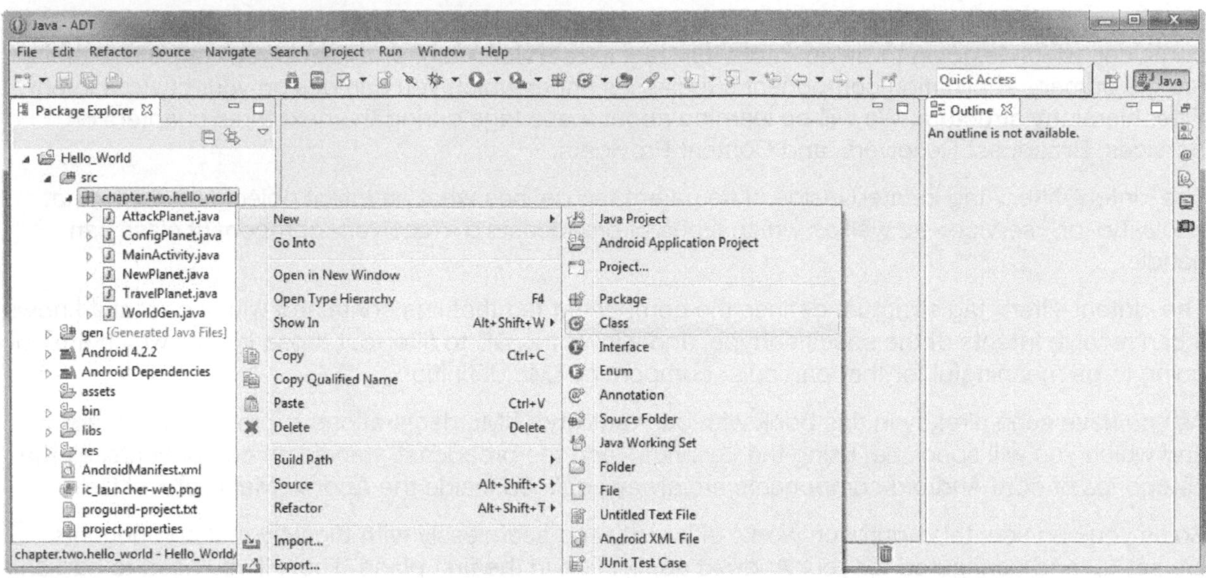

Figure 16-1. Creating a New ➤ Class in Eclipse to hold our TimePlanet.java Activity subclass Java code

This opens the New Java Class dialog, shown in Figure 16-2, and we can fill out all those necessary parameters to create precisely the type of Java class that we want Eclipse to generate for us, in this case, it's an Activity subclass that will hold our Planet Time user interface elements.

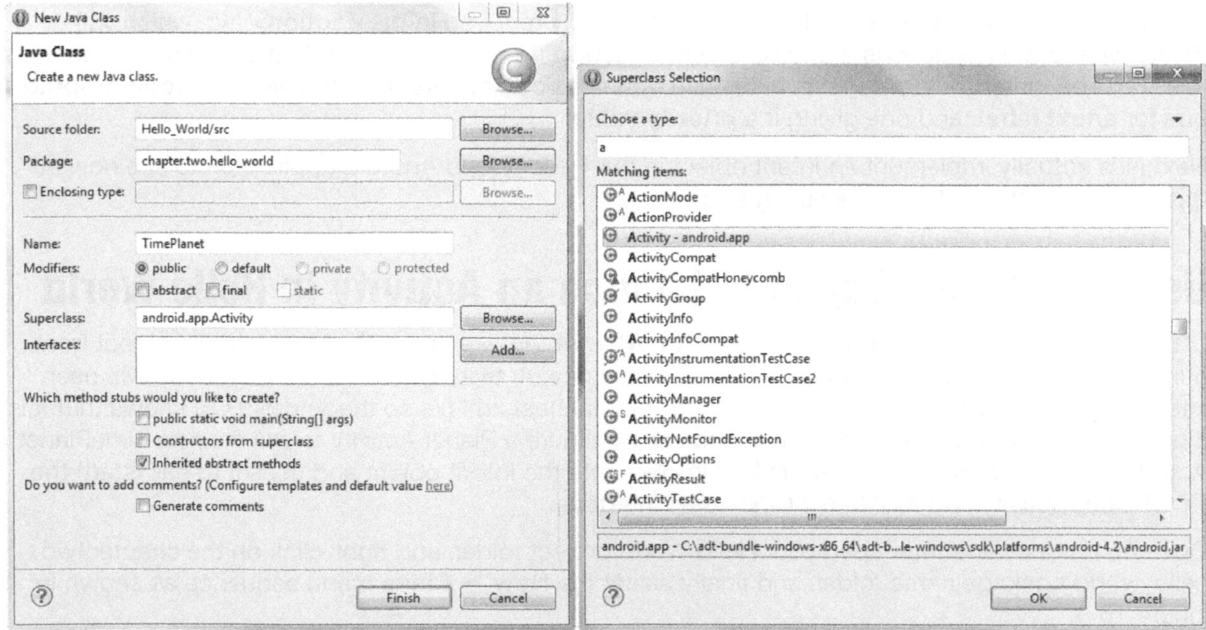

Figure 16-2. Naming our TimePlanet.java class, selecting an android.app.Activity Superclass and public Modifier

The **Source folder:** field should have your **Hello_World/src** project source code folder already in it. Because you right-clicked the package folder to invoke this New Java Class dialog, Eclipse inferred that folder information for you. Similarly the **Package:** field should have auto-filled with your **chapter.two.hello_world** package name as well.

Next place your **TimePlanet** class name into the **Name:** field, and then click the **Browse...** button located on the right side of the **Superclass:** field, so that we can select what type of class we want to subclass our new class from, in this case, we want to use the Activity class.

When the **Superclass Selection** dialog shown on the right in Figure 16-2 has opened up, type an "**a**" character in the **Choose a type:** field and after you do select the **Activity - android.app** selection option, and click the **OK** button. Once you're back in New Java Class dialog click the **Finish** button.

Once you finish this New Java Class work process, Eclipse ADT should have opened up a new editing tab for you in the central part of the IDE editing pane called TimePlanet.java (see Figure 16-3).

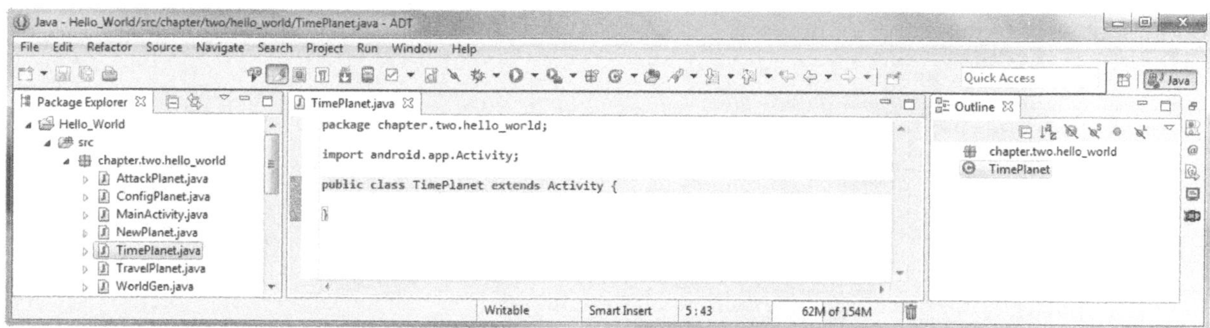

***Figure 16-3.** Opening a newly created TimePlanet.java Activity subclass inside Eclipse showing import statement*

There should be four lines of Java code already written for you, as follows:

```
package chapter.two.hello_world;
import android.app.Activity;
public class TimePlanet extends Activity {
}
```

These declare the chapter.two.hello_world package name as well as an import statement, importing an android.app.Activity package, and its associated classes for your usage inside of your TimePlanet.java Activity subclass that you are about to write.

Your public class, named TimePlanet, should also be declared for you, and should use the **extends** keyword to subclass the Activity class as well as have the infrastructure in place for you to start writing your Java code.

Let's write the standard code that will create our Activity screen and set its content view to the XML user interface design document, which we are about to write next.

First we write our protected class onCreate() with the Android Bundle object named savedInstanceState, inside of which we call the onCreate() method from the parent Activity Superclass using the super keyword and passing the savedInstanceState variable inside of the onCreate() method call, using the following line of Java code:

```
super.onCreate(savedInstanceState);
```

Next we will want to use the **setContentView()** Activity class method to set our content view to an XML file that we are going to create next that will hold our user interface definition using XML mark-up.

This setContentView() method call line of Java code reads as follows:

```
setContentView(R.layout.activity_time);
```

Notice in Figure 16-4 that the Eclipse IDE has error flagged the activity_time.xml file reference; this is because we have not yet created this file, and since we are going to be doing that next, we can ignore that error highlighting for now.

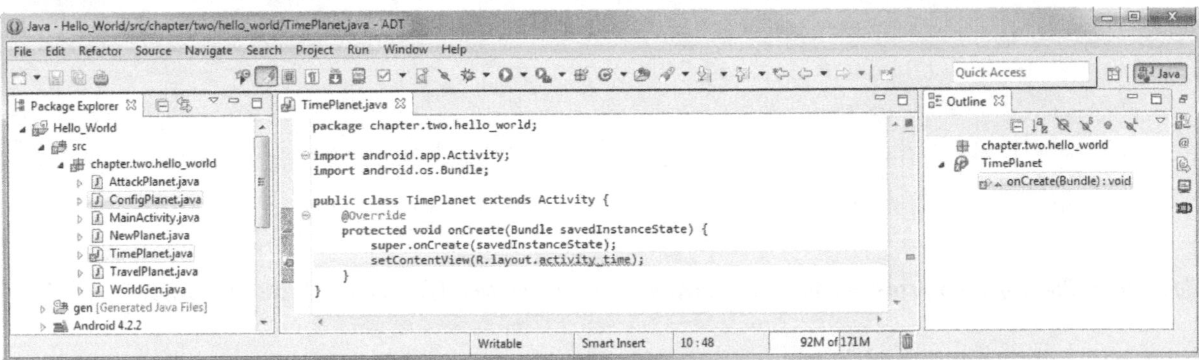

Figure 16-4. Coding our onCreate() method and setContentView() method to access our activity_time.xml UI layout

Next we are going to create our XML user interface, so we can resolve this error, and then once that is done we will return to this editing tab and write the code implementing our Intent object.

Creating the LinearLayout XML for Our TimePlanet.java Activity

The next thing that we'll need to do is to right-click the now familiar **/res/layout** folder inside the project resources folder, and then select the **New ➤ Android XML File** menu command sequence to launch the New Android XML File dialog shown in Figure 16-5.

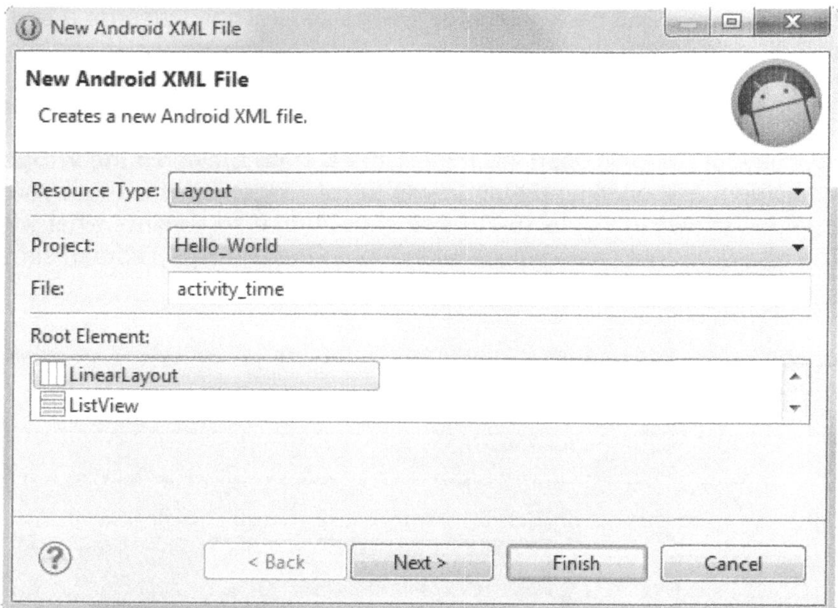

***Figure 16-5.** Creating a New ➤ Android XML File and LinearLayout Root Element*

Select a **Resource Type:** of **Layout** and **Project:** name **Hello_World** and name the file **activity_time** to match our activity XML file naming convention.

Next, select the **Root Element:** type of **LinearLayout**, and then click the **Finish** button, which creates our **activity_time.xml** file, along with a parent LinearLayout tag. Once you click Finish, Eclipse automatically opens up an editing pane in the center portion of the IDE, showing the XML mark-up that it has written for you, as shown in Figure 16-6.

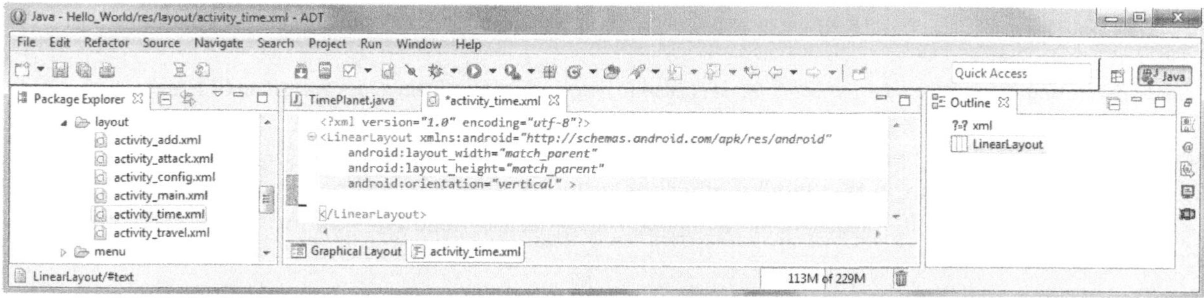

***Figure 16-6.** Opening our activity_time.xml layout XML file in Eclipse and editing the <LinearLayout> tag*

Now we can add our LinearLayout parameters, as well as several child tags for a text caption element, an analog clock element, and a button user interface element, which returns us to the Configure a Planet Activity when we are finished using the Planet Time Activity. Next, let's click the Graphical Layout Editor tab at the bottom of the IDE so that we can add an **AnalogClock** UI widget.

Once the Graphical Layout Editor is open, click the **Time & Date** drawer in the **Widget Palette** on the left side of the screen, and open it up that drawer full of widget icons, so that you can see the analog clock widget, as shown in Figure 16-7. I also show in that screenshot what your screen looks like when you drag and drop that analog clock widget onto the blank app screen simulation that is shown in the central working area of Eclipse.

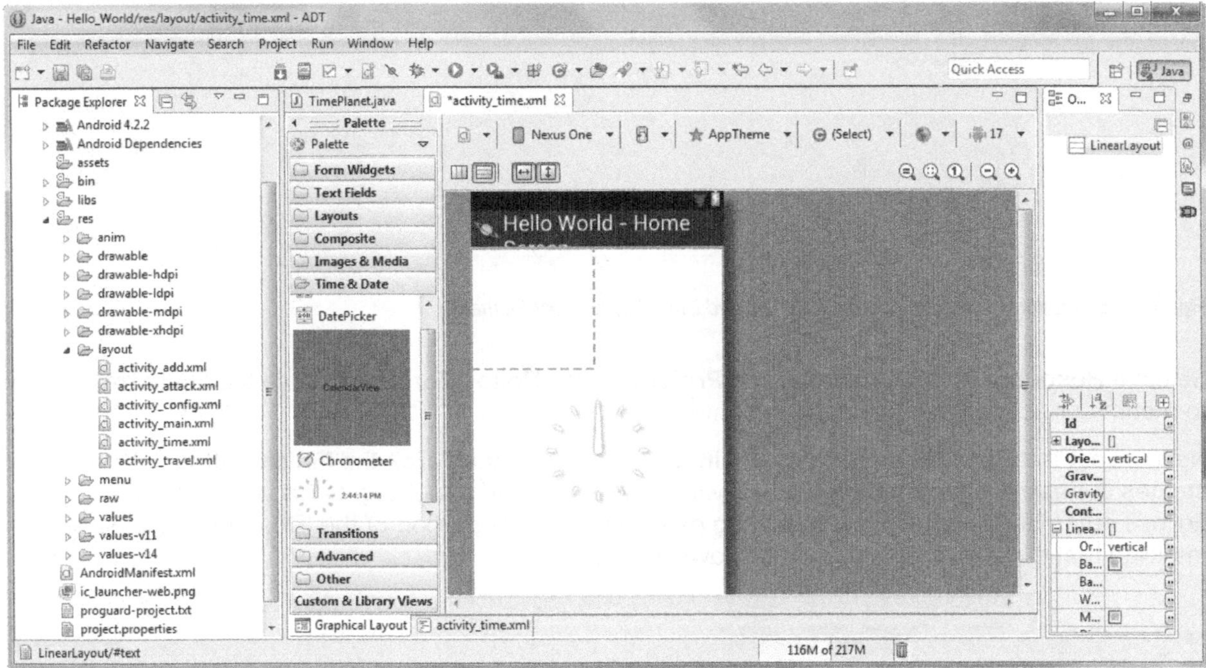

***Figure 16-7.** Using the Graphical Layout Editor tab in Eclipse to drag and drop an AnalogClock widget on UI screen*

Next we need to create two string constant data values for the Planet Time Screen, a caption (heading text) as well as the text label that will be on the button that will be underneath the analog clock widget, as shown in Figure 16-8. The XML mark-up for these two <string> constants should look like the following:

```
<string name="time_caption_value">Home Planet Earth Time</string>
<string name="time_button_value">Return to Planet Configuration</string>
```

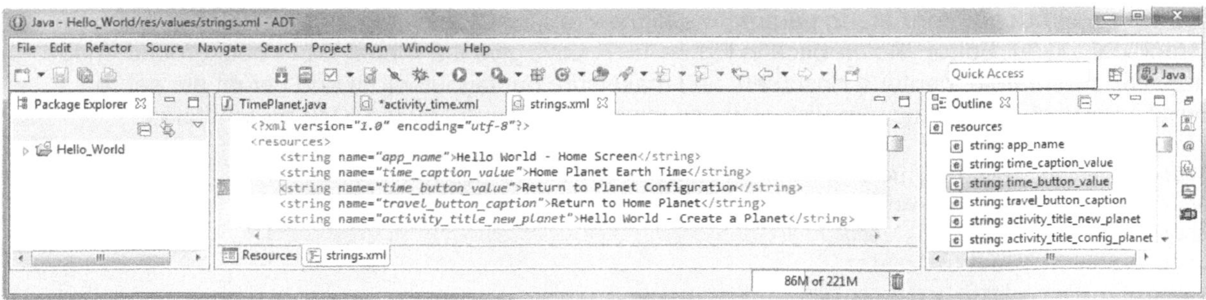

***Figure 16-8.** Adding the two string constants needed for our activity_time.xml file to our strings.xml file*

We will use the button to return us to the Configure a Planet Activity, after we are finished using the Planet's Atomic Clock feature.

Now, we are ready to configure our LinearLayout parent tag and child tags in our activity_time.xml user interface XML specification. First, we need to add two parameters to the LinearLayout tag itself that will allow us to control it from our Java code (android:id) and to give it our spectacular background image (android:background) that we created earlier in the book.

Add the following two parameters to LinearLayout, as shown in Figure 16-9:

```
android:id="@+id/timePlanetScreen"
android:background="@drawable/trans_stars_galaxy"
```

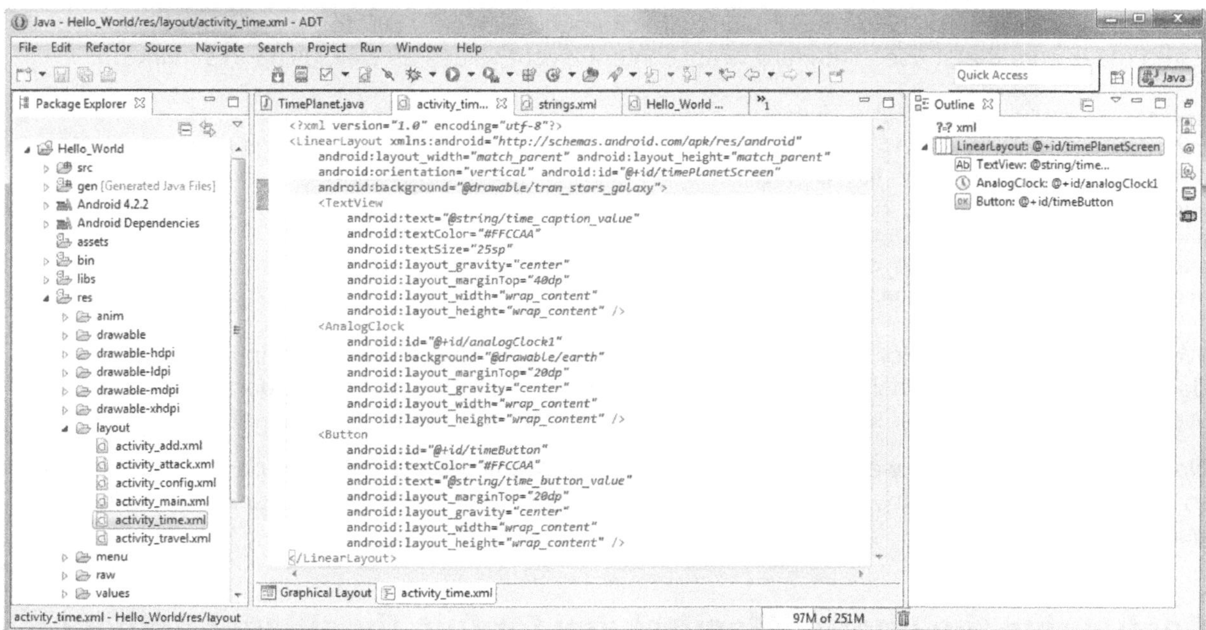

***Figure 16-9.** Adding layout and text parameters for our TextView, AnalogClock, Button, and LinearLayout tags*

Next we need to add formatting parameters to the **<AnalogClock>** tag that we created using the Graphical Layout Editor shown back in Figure 16-7. Let's give it a Planet Earth background image, a 20 DIP top margin, center it onscreen, and make sure our layout width and height are set to **wrap_content**. We can accomplish all these things using the following XML parameters:

```
android:id="@+id/analogClock1"
android:background="@drawable/earth"
android:layout_marginTop="20dp"
android:layout_gravity="center"
android:layout_width="wrap_content"
android:layout_height="wrap_content"
```

Next let's add our **<TextView>** user interface element, either in the GLE or an XML Editor and configure it to match the color of our plasma background with a large 25sp text size and a 40 DIP top margin and also center it and make sure that it uses a wrap_content value as well, using this mark-up:

```
android:text="@string/time_caption_value"
android:textColor="#FFCCAA"
android:textSize="25sp"
android:layout_gravity="center"
android:layout_marginTop="40dp"
android:layout_width="wrap_content"
android:layout_height="wrap_content"
```

Finally, we need to add a **<Button>** user interface element, either in the GLE or in an XML Editor and configure it to match the color of our plasma background with a 20 DIP top margin, and also center it and make sure that it uses standard wrap_content layout values as well, using this mark-up:

```
android:id="@+id/timeButton"
android:textColor="#FFCCAA"
android:text="@string/time_button_value"
android:layout_marginTop="20dp"
android:layout_gravity="center"
android:layout_width="wrap_content"
android:layout_height="wrap_content"
```

We have matched our color, spacing, and size values to our other Activity user interface screen designs, to maintain a consistent look and feel across all the user interface screens in this Hello World app. The entire user interface design XML mark-up can be seen in Figure 16-9.

Next we will look at what we need to do in our **AndroidManifest.xml** file to prepare our application to support this new Activity, and to put a custom screen caption at the top of our Activity screen using a label parameter.

Configuring the AndroidManifest.xml for Our TimePlanet Activity

Before we start adding mark-up tags to our AndroidManifest.xml file, we will need to create a string constant value named: **activity_title_time_planet**, as shown in Figure 16-10.

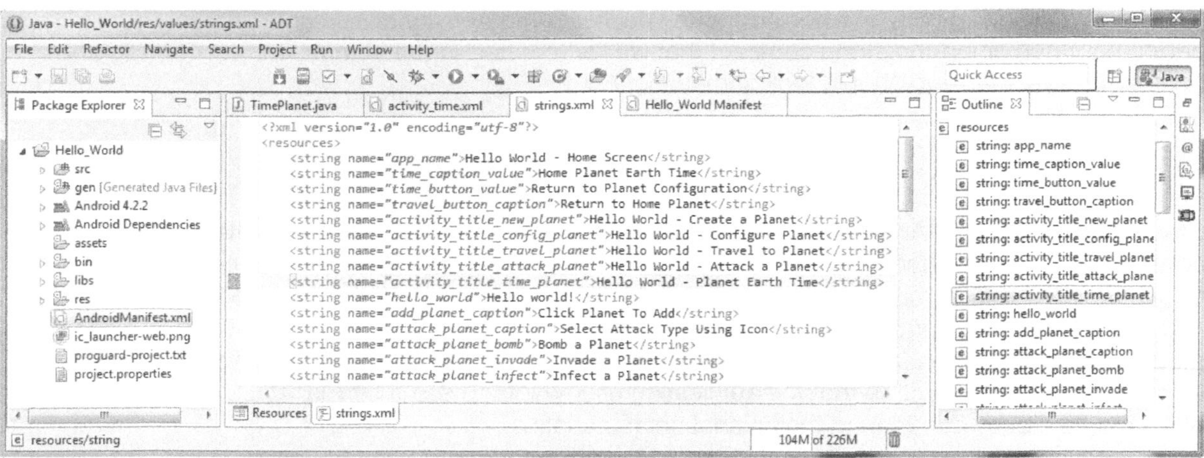

***Figure 16-10.** Adding a <string> tag and parameters for a screen label for the TimePlanet.java Activity*

Open up the **strings.xml** file in an editing tab in Eclipse, and add in a new **<string>** tag, with the following name value and text data value:

```
<string name="activity_title_time_planet">Hello World - Planet Earth Time</string>
```

Next we will add the <activity> tag for our TimePlanet Activity subclass into our app's AndroidManifest.xml file. Right-click the Android Manifest file shown in Figure 16-11 at the bottom of the Package Explorer pane, and select **Open** from the menu, so that we can edit the file's contents in an Editing pane, also shown in the middle part of Figure 16-11.

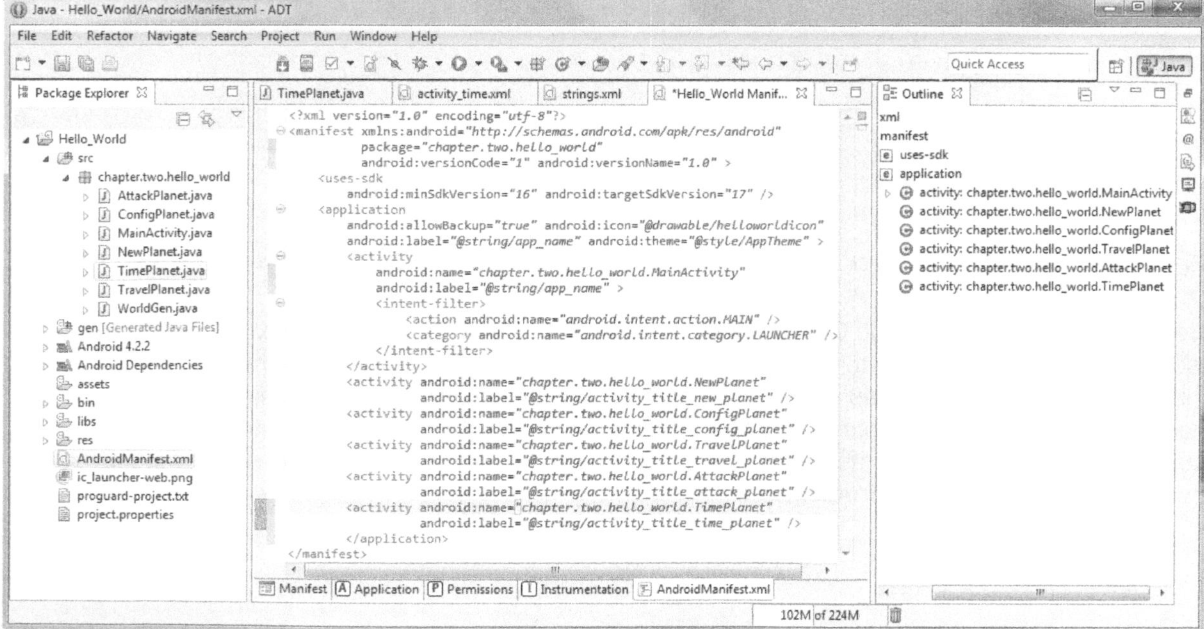

***Figure 16-11.** Adding an <activity> tag and parameters for the new TimePlanet.java Activity subclass*

Add an <activity> tag with an **android:name** specifying the Activity class name and an **android:label** parameter referencing the string constant that we just created in the strings.xml file. The tag and parameter XML mark-up should look something like this:

```
<activity      android:name="chapter.two.hello_world.TimePlanet"
               android:label="@string/activity_title_time_planet" />
```

Now that we have told Android OS about our new Activity in our application Manifest, we need to add a Button user interface element to our Configure a Planet Activity screen. Once we add this XML to our activity_config.xml user interface screen definition, we can add the Java code that declares and instantiates this Button element. Once that has been done, then we can add the event handling method that contains the Intent object that we need to send to our TimePlanet.java Activity, to launch that Activity any time that the application user wants to see their Planet Earth Atomic Clock while they are busy configuring their planet characteristics.

Adding an Atomic Clock Button Tag to Our activity_config.xml File

The first thing that we need to do is to create our <string> constant value for our Atomic Clock Button user interface element that we add to our activity_config.xml UI XML definition. Let's name the string constant **button_name_time** and then set its value to **Atomic Clock**, as shown in Figure 16-12. Now we can add our XML Button UI element mark-up that references this string constant in our **activity_config.xml** file.

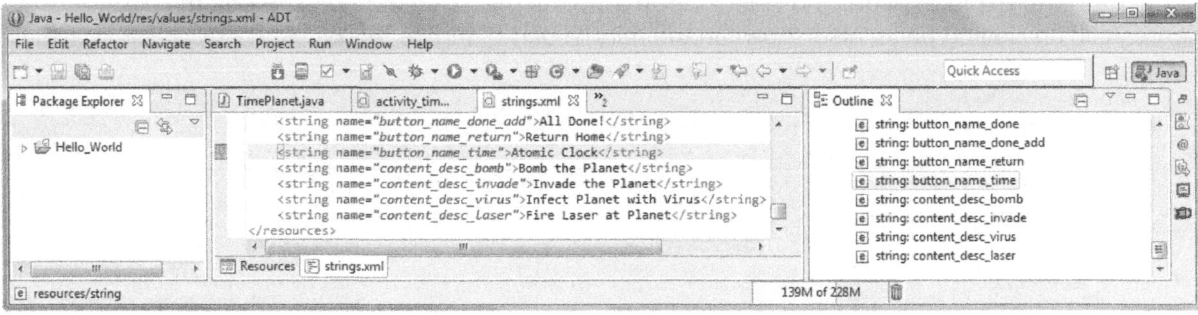

***Figure 16-12.** Adding an Atomic Clock button label string constant named button_name_time to the strings.xml file*

Because we want the Atomic Clock UI Button element to be underneath the text data entry fields (so that it is not confused with the configuration user interface buttons) we will put it in the second LinearLayout container tag as shown in Figure 16-13. This way we have less parameters that are needed to put it into its proper place, only a MarginTop and a MarginLeft and a textColor to make sure it matches our space plasma and screen text caption color. We also reference our string constant and set the **ID** to **timeButton**.

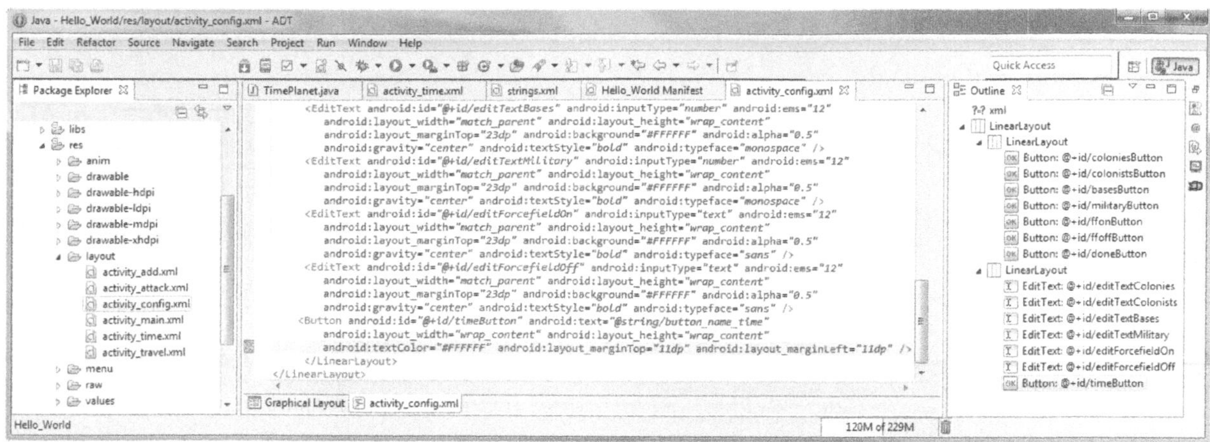

Figure 16-13. Adding a Button tag to the bottom of our second LinearLayout container in our activity_config.xml

The XML mark-up for our timeButton Button element should look like this:

```
<Button android:id="@+id/timeButton"
        android:text="@string/button_name_time"
        android:layout_width="wrap_content"
        android:layout_height="wrap_content"
        android:textColor="#FFFFFF"
        android:layout_marginTop="11dp"
        android:layout_marginLeft="11dp" />
```

Now that we have added an Atomic Clock UI Button object in our Configure a Planet Activity, it is time to go into our Java code, and instantiate that Button object so we can add event handling code that allows us to send an Intent object over to our TimePlanet.java Activity class and launch it!

Coding an Intent Object in Java for Our ConfigPlanet.java Activity

Let's collapse the other Button object code blocks as shown by the plus symbols shown in Figure 16-14 and instantiate a new timeButton object and reference it to our XML using the following line of Java code:

```
Button timeButton = (Button) findViewById(R.id.timeButton);
```

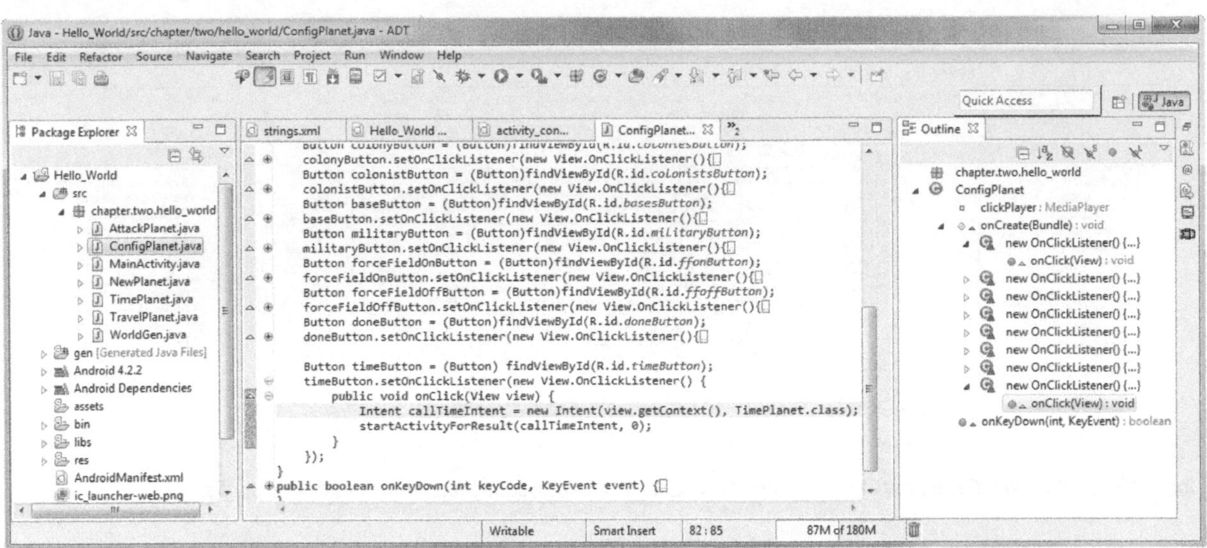

***Figure 16-14.** Coding our callTimeIntent Intent Object in a timeButton event handler in our ConfigPlanet Activity*

Next we need to attach an event listener to the Button object, using the **.setOnClickListener()** method, and creating a **new View.OnClickListener()** event handling method using the four lines of code shown in Figure 16-14:

```
timeButton.setOnClickListener(new View.OnClickListener() {
    public void onClick(View view) {
        Intent callTimeIntent = new Intent(view.getContext(), TimePlanet.class);
        startActivityForResult(callTimeIntent, 0);
    }
});
```

As you can see, we construct our Intent object inside our onClick() event handling method, using the following line of Java code:

```
Intent callTimeIntent = new Intent(view.getContext(), TimePlanet.class);
```

This declares the **Intent**, names it **callTimeIntent** and uses the **new** keyword to construct the Intent, passing it over the two required parameters, the current context, represented by a **view.getContext()** method, and the **target** of the Intent, the **TimePlanet.class** Activity proper name.

The next line of code starts a TimePlanet Activity, using a **callTimeIntent** object that we just created, using the following line of code:

```
startActivityForResult(callTimeIntent, 0);
```

The first parameter is the Intent object, the second is a code, where zero means no code, and any non-zero positive number being a code that is returned in an **.onActivityResult()** method called when the Activity exits.

Coding an Intent Object in Java for Our TimePlanet.java Activity

Next, we will need to add our Intent handling code to our TimePlanet.java Activity subclass so that we can return an Intent result when we exit the Activity using our Return to Planet Configuration button. The Java code we need to add is

```
Button returnFromTimeButton = (Button) findViewById(R.id.timeButton);
returnFromTimeButton.setOnClickListener(new view.OnClickListener() {
    public void onClick(View view) {
          Intent returnIntent = new Intent();
          setResult(RESULT_OK, returnIntent);
          finish();
    }
});
```

First we need to instantiate our returnFromTimeButton Button object, and then set it to handle an OnClickListener() event, using the .setOnClickListener() method. This invokes the new View.OnClickListener() method, which then contains our onClick() event handler that finally contains our Intent object declaration and our setResult() method call and ultimately our finish() method call, returning us to ConfigPlanet, as shown in Figure 16-15.

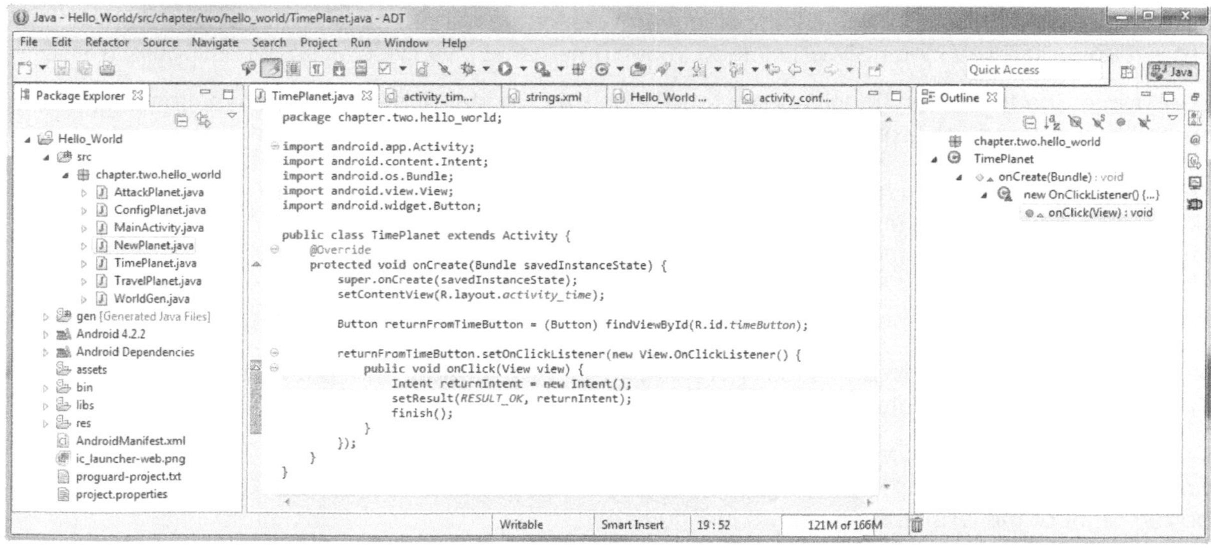

***Figure 16-15.** Coding a returnIntent Intent Object in a returnFromTimeButton handler in our TimePlanet Activity*

Now the only thing we need to do is to add in our wow factor background image fade Java code for the tran_stars_galaxy drawable XML file that we specified in our activity_time.xml file, as shown in Figure 16-16.

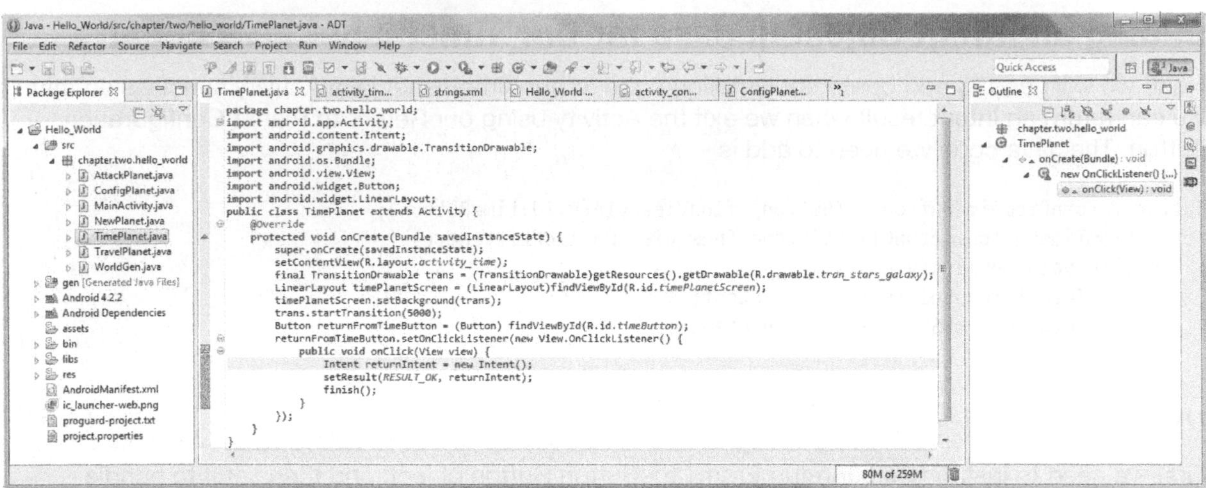

Figure 16-16. Adding the Java code for our TransitionDrawable user interface screen background fade-out effect

We do this because we have already done all the work in a previous chapter setting up that special effect, so why not utilize it on an Atomic Clock screen for an added dose of special effects!

Let's copy the TransitionDrawable trans object and related code from our NewPlanet.java Activity and paste it under the setContentView() method in our TimePlanet.java class as shown in Figure 16-16.

Don't forget the trans.startTransition() method code that will start the transition animation when we enter the user interface screen. The final Java code block should look like this:

```
final TransitionDrawable trans = (TransitionDrawable)getResources().getDrawable
(R.drawable.tran_stars_galaxy);
LinearLayout timePlanetScreen = (LinearLayout)findViewById(R.id.timePlanetScreen);
timePlanetScreen.setBackground(trans);
trans.startTransition(5000);
```

Now we are finally ready to utilize the **Run As Android Application** work process, and test our new TimePlanet Activity and Intent handling code.

Once the Nexus S emulator launches, click the Menu button and select the Configure Planet option from the menu and launch the ConfigPlanet.java Activity. Then click the Atomic Clock button on the bottom right of the UI screen as shown in Figure 16-17.

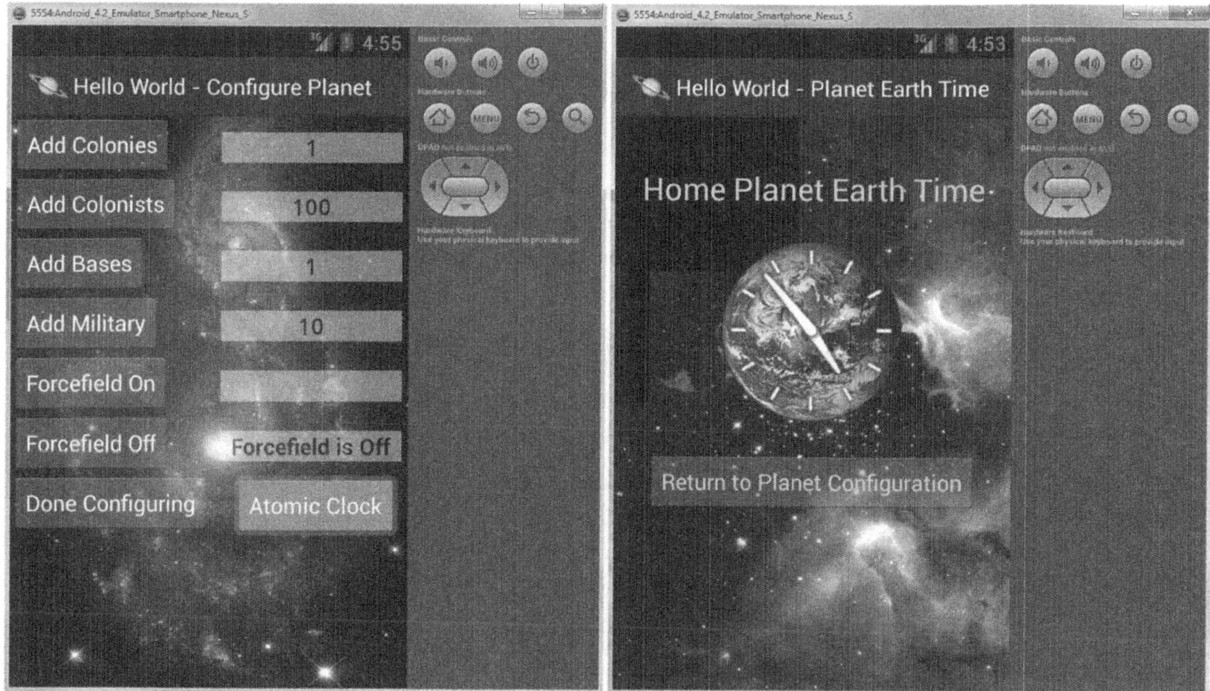

Figure 16-17. Testing our TimePlanet.java Activity and Intent Object calls in the Nexus S emulator in Eclipse

As you can see, our new Planet Earth Time Screen launches smoothly, and an animated transition, from a stars background to a plasma space background, occurs smoothly behind an impressive Analog Clock that we made out of the Planet Earth, and as is shown on the right side of Figure 16-17.

At the bottom of the Planet Earth Time Activity Screen is your Return to Planet Configuration button, click this, and it will return you to the Configure a Planet Activity.

To test our Intent objects and their effectiveness, click the Atomic Clock and Return to Planet Configuration Buttons several more times to make absolutely sure that we can go back and forth between these two Activity screens as many times as we want or need to. Congratulations, you have now used an Intent object to switch between two application Activity screens!

Summary

In this chapter, we took a closer look at Android Intent objects as well as Android Intent Filters. We looked at how they work, and the different types of Intents, so that we can use them in the next few chapters where they are used to launch Services and invoke Broadcast Receivers.

We learned about what information is contained within an Intent object, about actions, data, category, extras, and their constants that are specified in the Android OS, as well as flags, data types (MIME), and component name attributes that are usually specified within an Intent.

We learned about the difference between explicit Intents that specify the component name so that the target of the Intent object is known and does not need to be inferred, and we looked at implicit Intents where the component name is not known and the target is inferred via the action, data and category.

We learned about how it is possible to create your own Intent Filters in your application AndroidManifest.xml file that can provide the inference engine for resolving implied Intent objects (those without component names specified) and under what conditions these Intent Filters would need to be utilized to provide other applications compatibility to other developers using your application's components via Intents.

Finally, we added an Atomic Clock TimePlanet.java Activity to our Hello World application so we could show how to use Intent objects to switch between Activities within an application. We will be learning how to use Intent objects with Services and Broadcast Receivers in the next two chapters in the book, so we are not covering examples of those in this chapter.

In the next chapter we will take a closer look at Android Services, and learn about started and bound Services, and learn how they can help our applications work more smoothly and efficiently.

Chapter 17

Android Services: Using Background Processing

In this chapter, we will delve into Android **Services**, which are utilized by developers to perform background **asynchronous** operations, which can process data streams or computations on their own, without having to **synchronize** with the application user interface design, or sync-up with the application content (the on-going user experience) in any way.

Services are generally utilized to handle things that need to be going on in the **background** of your app user experience, in **parallel** with an Android user's real-time usage of your application, but not directly synchronized or connected in real-time with that application's user experience design.

Examples of uses of Android Services would include: the playback of long-form digital audio (say, album music tracks) while the user is using your application, talking to some sort of server or database in the background, downloading data, managing file input-output streams, streaming new media content, such as digital video streams or digital audio streams, handling networking (SMTP or HTTP) protocol transactions, handling payment gateway transactions, real-time processing of GPS data, and similar complex tasks.

Tasks that are generally delegated to an Android Service class are those tasks that should not be tied to the user interface and user experience, because forcing concurrent (synchronized) processing might cause that user experience to become stilted or jerky (i.e., to not portray a smooth user interface response, and thereby a smooth and enjoyable user experience).

Tasks that are delegated to an Android Service also are very processor intensive, so keep your end-user's battery life in mind, while you are developing processor intensive applications. As you might guess, the two primary power drains on an Android battery are prolonged processing, and keeping the display screen lit (on) for long periods of time (which we covered earlier in the Video chapters).

In this chapter we are going to look closely at the Android Service class, and all the various characteristics of Android Services, as well as how these features, functions, settings, constants, and similar characteristics are declared for use in your Android application. As you may have guessed already, declaring Services for use is done in an **AndroidManifest.xml** file.

This is one of the more complex and involved topics in Android, because it inherently involves binding, synchronization, processes, processor cycles, threads, access control, permissions, and similarly advanced OS topics.

Android Service Basics: The Rules and Characteristics

A Service is defined as an Android application component that can perform processing intensive functions in the background, without needing any user interface design or any Activity display screen and that does not require any user interaction with the processing that needs to be accomplished.

An Android application component can start a Service class using an Intent object and the Service will continue to process in the background, even if that Android device user switches over to a different Android application.

An Android application component can **bind** to a Service to interact with it, and even perform **inter-process communications**, which you may also know as **IPC**. We will be taking a closer look at processes and threads in the next section of this chapter after this overview of Android Services.

Binding is an advanced programming concept involving establishing a real-time connection between two separate application component processes, where these processes will alert each other when something has changed and when an update needs to be made between their logical **bind** connection.

An Android Service usually takes one of two formats, **bound** or **started**. An Android Service becomes **started** when an application component (such as an Activity) starts the Service by calling the **.startService()** method.

Once started, a Service can run in the background indefinitely, even in a scenario where the component that started that Service gets subsequently destroyed, either by the application program logic, or by the Android OS.

A **started** Service performs one single operation, and does not return a result to the calling entity, much like a method that is declared as void.

For example, a started Service might download or upload a data file over a network. Best practices dictates that when a started Service operation is completed, that service should automatically stop itself, to help optimize Android operating system resources such as processor cycles or memory use.

A **bound** Service is created when an Android application component **binds** to a Service. This is accomplished by calling the **.bindService()** method. The bound service offers a client-server interface, which allows components to interact with the bound Service, to send requests, to get results, and to even do this across processes, by using interprocess communication (IPC).

Bound Services exist in Android system memory only for as long as any other Android application components are bound to it. Multiple application components can bind to this Service at the same time, however, when all these **unbind**, the service is then **destroyed** (removed from system memory).

We will take a look at both of these types of Service formats, as well as a **hybrid** approach, wherein your Services can work in both of these ways at the same time. What this means is that you can start your Service (so that it is a **started** Service, and can run indefinitely) and also allow **binding**.

Whether an Android Service is specified as a **started Service** or as a **bound Service** is determined by whether or not you have implemented a couple of the more useful Service class callback methods. For instance, the Service class **.onStartCommand()** method allows components to start a Service, and the **.onBind()** method allows binding to that Service. We will cover methods of the Service class in detail in a later section of this chapter.

Regardless of whether your application's Service is started, bound, or is both started and bound, any other application component can use a Service, even from a separate application. This is similar to the way that any of your application components can start an Activity, by starting it with an Intent. We covered using Intent objects in detail in the previous chapter, and we will cover how to use Intent objects with Services in this chapter.

It is important to note that Services run with a **higher priority** than inactive Activities and because of this it is less likely that the Android operating system will terminate a Service class than an Activity class.

It is also important to note that you can declare your Service as **private**, in the Manifest XML file, and block access from other applications, which is often times what individual developers will do with their applications.

A Service, by default, will always run inside the **main thread** of the host application's primary **process**. Services which run inside of this primary process of your application are often termed **Local Services**.

A common misconception amongst programmers is that an Android Service will always run on its own separate thread. Although this is certainly possible if you set it up that way, as a default, the Service does **not** in fact by default create its own thread, and thus does not run in a separate thread unless you specify otherwise. We will be going into processes and threads in the next section of this chapter as it is a very closely related topic.

What this means is that if your Service is going to do any extremely CPU intensive work (such as decoding streaming data in real-time) or blocking operations (such as real-time network access over busy network protocols), you should additionally create a new thread within your service to do that type of processing.

It is important to note that you may not need to use another thread for your service class apart from the one it is on (using already), for instance, in our example in this chapter we play a music file using the MediaPlayer in a Service without needing to spawn another thread.

The only way to really determine if this is needed is to first try using a Service class for your background processing, and then, if it affects your user experience, consider implementing a Thread class and object if needed.

Processes or Threads: Valuable Foundational Information

When one of your Android application's components, say, your MainActivity class, starts, and your application does not have any components currently running, the Android operating system will start a brand new Linux **process** for your application, using a single **thread** of execution, called the **UI thread**. A **Process** can generate or launch (or **spawn**) more than one **thread**.

As a rule, all your Android application components will run inside the same initial process and thread. This is generally termed **the main thread**.

If one of your Android application components starts up and Android sees that a process already exists for your application, due to the fact that another component from your application already exists, then that component will also be started within that same application process and will also uses that same thread. So essentially to start your own thread, you must do so specifically in your Java code.

However, you can arrange for different components in your application to run in separate processes, and, you can create additional threads for any process. This is what's usually done with Android Services as we will see.

How to Specify a Process: Using android:process XML Parameters

As a default in the Android OS, all your application components will be run in the same process, and most basic Android applications will not need to change this setup unless there's a very compelling reason for doing so.

For advanced applications (which we are not covering in this book, but we will cover this concept here, to be thorough regarding Android Processes) if you happen to find yourself in a situation where you absolutely need to control which Android process a certain application component belongs to, you can specify this in, you guessed it, your AndroidManifest.xml file.

Your AndroidManifest.xml component tags for each major type of application component, whether it is an Activity <activity> tag, a Service <service> tag, a Broadcast Receiver <receiver> tag, or a Content Provider <provider> tag, will include an optional **android:process** parameter.

This process parameter can be used to specify the process under which that application component needs to run. You can set up the process parameter such that each of your application components run inside its own process, or mix and match in such a way that some of your application components will share a process while others will not share that process.

If you want to get really complex, you can also set these android:process parameters so that components from totally different Android applications can execute together inside of the same Android process.

This can only be accomplished when those particular applications share the same Linux User ID, and which are signed with the same certificates.

It is also interesting to note that the global **<application>** tag in your AndroidManifest XML file will also accept the android:process parameter.

Using the android:process parameter inside of your <application> tag will set a default process value for your application which would subsequently be applied to all of your application's components in your XML application component definition (nested) hierarchy. Of course, this would not include those application components which do not then utilize the android:process parameter to specify a different process for that particular application component than the one that you set as the default process for application use via the android:process parameter inside of your <application> tag.

It is important to note that Android has the option to shut down a process at any time, for instance, when memory is running low, or if memory used by your process is required by other processes that have a higher priority or are receiving more usage (attention) from the end-user.

Application components running inside of a process that gets **terminated** are subsequently **destroyed**, or removed from memory. Not to worry, as any of these processes can be restarted again at a later time for any of those application components that require something be accomplished for a user.

When deciding which processes to kill, the Android system weighs their relative importance to the user. For example, it more readily shuts down a process hosting activities that are no longer visible on-screen, compared to a process hosting visible activities. The decision whether to terminate a process, therefore, depends on the state of the components running in that process. The rules used to decide which processes to terminate is discussed next.

The Android Process Lifespan: How to Keep Your Processes Alive

Android tries to keep your application process in its system memory for as long as it can, but sometimes the need arises to destroy the older processes running in the OS. This is done to reclaim the system's memory resources for newer or higher priority processes.

After all, most Android devices today only ship with one or two gigabytes of main system memory, and this can fill up fairly quickly, as users play games, launch apps, read eBooks, stream music, place phone calls, and so on, and so forth.

Even when devices start to ship with three gigabytes of main memory you will still have memory management issues, and using processes and threads are at the core of these memory management issues, so it is important that we understand how processes are handled in the Android OS.

The way that the Android OS determines which of its processes to keep and which of its processes to terminate is via a **priority hierarchy**. Android places each running process into this priority hierarchy, which is based on each of the components running in the process queue, as well as the current status (running, idle, stopped, etc.) of those components.

The way that memory is cleared from the Android device is that the process with the lowest priority (importance) is terminated first, and then the next lowest priority process is terminated, and so on and so forth, until the system resources that are needed for higher priority processes have been recovered for use.

There are five process priority levels within this priority hierarchy. Once you see what they are you will realize how logically this process priority hierarchy is set up and you will also have a good knowledge of how Services (asynchronous processing or heavy lifting) and Activities (user interface screens) fit into this overall process priority schema, which is very important to understand. Get ready for some Aha moments!

The highest priority process level is the **foreground process**, which is the primary process that's currently running (processing) and is thus required for the application task that the user is currently engaging in.

A process is considered to be in the foreground if it contains an Activity (user interface screen) that the user is currently interfacing with, or if it hosts a Service that is currently **bound** to an Activity which that user is interfacing with.

A process is also considered to be a foreground process if it is currently executing a Service that is running in the foreground, which means that the Service object has called the **.startForeground()** method.

If a Service is currently executing one of its onCreate(), onDestroy(), or onStart() **Service lifecycle callbacks**, which we will be learning about in this chapter, or currently broadcasting a BroadcastReceiver object, which happens to be calling its **onReceive()** method, it will also be given a top foreground process priority level status by the Android OS.

In an optimal Android operating scenario, only a few foreground processes will be running at any given time. These processes are terminated only as a last resort, for instance, if the system memory gets scarce enough that the OS or its applications cannot continue to run effectively.

The next highest priority process level is the **visible process**, which is a process which does not contain any foreground process components but which still can affect what the user is seeing on their device display.

A process is considered to be visible if it contains an Activity that is not in the foreground, but that is still visible on the user's display screen, for instance an Activity whose **.onPause()** method has been invoked.

A great example of this would be a foreground process Activity that has started a dialog that permits the calling Activity to be seen in the background.

A process that contains a Service class that has been bound to a visible Activity would also gain visible process priority. Visible processes are considered almost as important as foreground processes are, and thus they will not be terminated unless absolutely required to keep all foreground processes running in system memory.

The middle priority process level of the five levels is a **Service process**, which is a process that contains a Service that has been started using the **.startService()** method but which Android does not classify in either of the two highest process priority categories.

Because the Service processes have no user interface screen, and are running asynchronously in a background process, are not directly tied to anything that the user sees on their display. However, Services are still performing tasks that the end-user wants to proceed (for instance playing an album of music in the background or downloading data over the network). For this reason, Android keeps them processing, unless there is not enough memory to support them along with foreground and visible processes.

The second lowest priority process level is the **background process**, which is a process that contains an Activity that is not currently visible to the end-user, for instance, the Activity **.onStop()** method has been called.

Because these background processes have no detectible impact on the user experience, Android terminates them whenever it is necessary to recover system memory for higher priority level (foreground, visible, or service) processes.

There are often quite a few background processes running, and Android keeps background processes in what is termed an LRU (Least Recently Used) list. This serves to guarantee that the process with the Activity that was most recently utilized by the user is the last process terminated.

It is important to note that if your Activities implement their lifecycle methods correctly, and save their current states, then terminating that Activity's process will not have any effect on your end-user experience.

This is due to the fact that when your user navigates back to the user interface screen for the Activity, the Activity restores all its visible states (remember your Bundle savedInstanceState code).

The lowest priority process level is the **empty process**, which is a process that does not hold any currently active application components. If you are wondering why an empty process would be kept in system memory at all, the strategic reason to keep an empty process alive is for **caching** optimization, which would improve start-up times the next time a component needs to run inside that process.

The Android operating system often terminates these empty processes in an attempt to try and balance the overall system memory resources, between the various process caches, and with its underlying Linux kernel caches.

Finally, a process priority level rank might be increased because another process is dependent on that process. Any Android process that's currently servicing another process will never be ranked lower than that process it is currently servicing.

Say that a Content Provider (Database or Datastore) contained in Process 01 is busy servicing a user interface Activity in Process 02, or, if the Service in Process 01 is bound to an application component in Process 02, Process 01 is always considered at least as important as Process 02.

Next, we will take a look at **threads**, which are much lower level and used within processes to schedule processor intensive and user interface tasks.

Some Caveats Regarding Threads: Don't Interfere with a UI Thread

After an Android OS launches your application via your AndroidManifest.xml file, its operating system **spawns** a **thread of execution** that is usually termed the **main thread**. The main thread is in charge of **dispatching** and managing events, which we learned about in an early chapter in this book, between the operating system and your user interface widgets.

The main thread also controls **drawing** your graphics, video, and animation (drawable) assets to the Activity display screen, so it is doing a lot of heavy lifting right off the bat, which is the reason you might need to spawn your own thread, if something that you want to do with your Android application might overload this already heavy workload that is on the main (or primary) thread, which is essentially running your entire application.

The main or primary thread is also often referred to as the **UI thread**, or **user interface thread**, because it is the thread inside of which your application components interact with components in Android's UI toolkit. Android UI Toolkit includes all the components (classes) from the **android.widget** and **android.view** packages, which we have learned about extensively in the first three parts of this book.

All the Android UI toolkit components that run in the main process are instantiated inside of this UI thread, and operating system calls to each required component are dispatched from this UI thread.

For this reason, methods that respond to your system callbacks, such as the **.onKeyDown()** event handler, used to report user interface interaction, or one of the lifecycle callback methods, such as an **.start()** method, or a **.pause()** method, or even a **.destroy()** method, always run inside the UI thread contained within the main process for your Android application.

When an application dispatches intensive processing in response to a user interface interaction, the single thread model can result in a slow user experience performance, which is why you must utilize threads properly.

The reason for this is obvious; if lots of processing is happening in the UI thread, then performing long-winded operations, such as network access, complex calculations, or SQL database queries will block the entire user interface response by taking away those processing cycles and essentially **blocking** the UI related events from being smoothly (quickly) processed.

When a thread is **blocked** in this way, UI events cannot be dispatched for handling, and this includes drawing graphics (drawable) elements to the screen. From a user experience perspective, your application thus appears to "hang" or pause for an undesirable length of time.

It is important to note that if your application blocks the UI thread for more than a few seconds (for more than five seconds) your user will be shown a dialog containing the exceptionally undesirable (from a user experience standpoint at least) "The Application is Not Responding" (or ANR) dialog.

It is also important to note that the Android UI toolkit is not currently what is known as "**thread-safe**." For this reason, you must not at any time manipulate your application user interface elements from a **worker thread**.

A worker thread is any non-UI thread, and is also commonly referred to as a **background thread**. In other words, it is a thread that you have spawned within your application Java code, to off-load intensive "worker" background processing, so that your UI will continue to function smoothly.

So remember, the first key rule in Android thread processing is that you must do all manipulation to your user interface elements from the inside your UI thread, which remember is the main or primary thread for your Android application.

The second rule is more generalized, and it is simply to not block the UI thread at any time for any reason. This is why you have worker threads, so that if you need to do something that would cause the UI thread to become blocked, you can spawn a worker thread in your code to do that processing, streaming, database access, or other tasks that represent heavy processor use and probably advanced application programming as well.

Should My Android Application Use Services or Threads?

An Android Service is simply a component that can run in the background, even when the user is not interacting with your application. If you need to perform work outside of your main UI thread, but only while the user is interacting with your application's user interface, then you should create a new Android Thread object within that class of your application, using a **HandlerThread** object or an **AsyncTask** object, and not go to the trouble of coding (and declaring in the Manifest) an entire Android Service subclass.

Let's say that you wanted to stream some music from a music service while your Activity is running. What you would want to do is to **create** a thread using an **.onCreate()** method, start it running using the **.onStart()** method, and finally stop it by using an **.onStop()** method.

As I mentioned before, you will probably want to utilize the more refined Android Thread subclasses that are named **AsyncTask** and (or) **HandlerThread** instead of the more generalized Thread class, at least until you become a more advanced Android programmer.

So, when would one want to use a Service subclass over spawning a Thread object in an existing class, you might be wondering. If you remember from the previous section, an Android process that contains a Service subclass will always be prioritized (ranked) higher than a process which utilizes a background processing activity (thread).

If your application is going to undertake an extensive processing, access, or streaming operation, you may want to start a Service component (class) for this operation, rather than simply creating a worker thread.

This is an especially relevant consideration if the background function is most likely going to outlast your Activity. For example, the Activity that is uploading a video that you created using the Android Camera class to a web server would want to utilize a Service class to perform this upload so that this upload process would be able to continue in the background, even if your user leaves the current Activity.

Thus the reason that you would want to use a Service class over a Thread object is because using the Service component will guarantee that your processing operation will have at least a Service process priority level, regardless of what happens to your Activity subclass.

Next, let's learn how to write our Service subclass, and how to call it by using an Intent object. We will do this using the TimePlanet.java Activity subclass, which we created in the previous chapter on Intents.

We will implement our Android Service class lifecycle by creating a music player background service component named MusicService.java. This will be a Service subclass which will utilize the **extends** keyword inside the class declaration in order to subclass the Android Service class.

After we set up new user interface elements needed to access these Service lifecycle methods, we will then code the Service class lifecycle methods using Java code, including **onCreate()**, **onStart()** and **onDestroy()** methods. We will even leverage an Android Intent object in one of them to start our background Service, which will play background music for our Planet Time Atomic Clock Activity which we created within the previous chapter of this book covering Intents.

Finally, we will also look at how to add a **<service>** tag to our AndroidManifest.xml file, and we will test our background music Service subclass inside of our Nexus S emulator, just to make absolutely sure everything is working in exactly the way that it is supposed to be.

Implementing a Music Service in Our TimePlanet Activity

The first thing that we will need to do is to create Start Music Service and Stop Music Service user interface Button objects that will control our Music Service. These go in our TimePlanet.java Activity class and XML definition file. The first thing we need to set up to do this is the string constants that are needed for the Button UI element labels, so add two <string> constant definitions in your project's strings.xml file, in the /res/values folder, by using the following XML mark-up:

```
<string name="start_button_value">Start Music Service</string>
<string name="stop_button_value">Stop Music Service</string>
```

This is shown in Figure 17-1. Now we are ready to add the two Button tags, which add the two user interface elements to our existing UI design. These control our MusicService background music component.

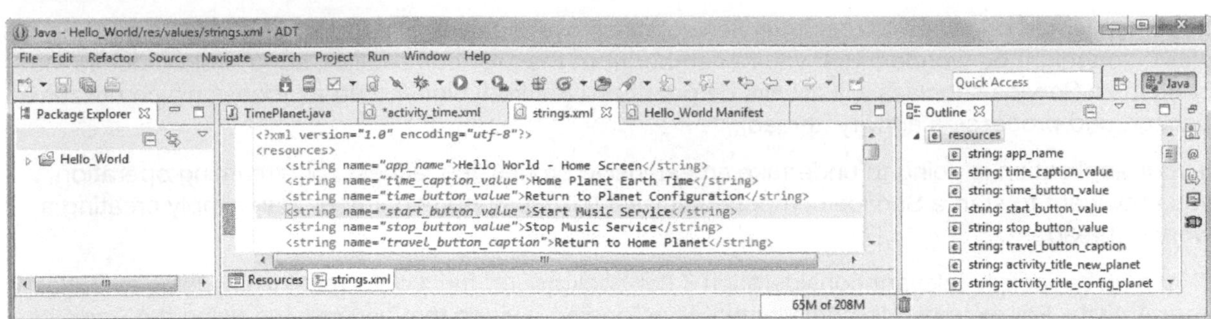

***Figure 17-1.** Adding the start_button_value and stop_button_value string constant to our strings.xml file*

Open up your **activity_time.xml** file in the Eclipse editing area, and copy the **timeButton** user interface component, which we created in the previous chapter, two more times underneath itself. Leave the third (bottom) Button tag as the timeButton, and change the first Button android:id parameter to read **startServiceButton** and the second Button android:id parameter to read **stopServiceButton**, as shown in Figure 17-2.

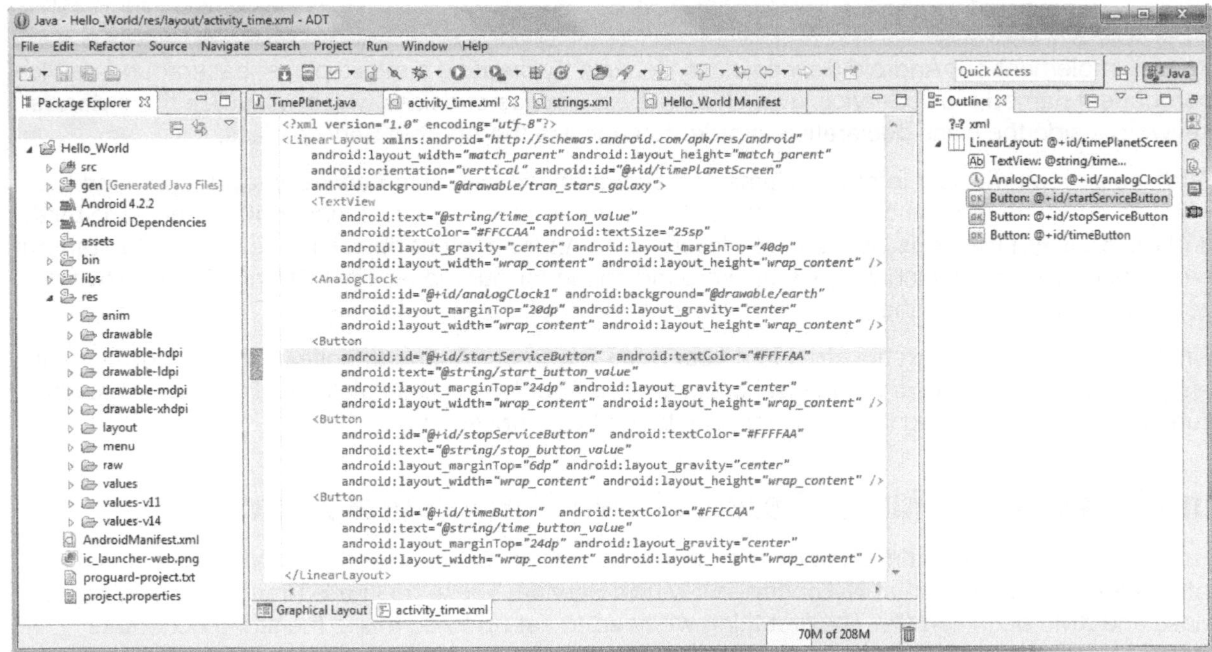

***Figure 17-2.** Add a startServiceButton and a stopServiceButton Button user interface element to activity_time.xml*

Next, let's change the **android:textColor** parameters for both of these new Button objects to **#FFAAAA**, or a nice bright **yellow** color to differentiate the Music Service Button elements from the Return to Configuration Button element, which is a light orange color to match the plasma background.

Next, change the **android:text** parameter so it points to the correct string constant values that we set-up in Figure 17-1; so change time_button_value to start_button_value, for the first Button tag, and stop_button_value for the second Button tag. We are almost done parameterizing our new Buttons!

Next, let's change our **android:marginTop** parameter in both of the Button tags spacing them close together and set apart from the other UI elements.

To accomplish this we set a startServiceButton marginTop parameter of 24 DIP (24dp) that pushes your Start Music Service Button element away from the AnalogClock UI element. Then set the stopServiceButton UI element marginTop parameter to 6 DIP (6dp) to place the Stop Music Service Button element right underneath the Start Music Service Button element.

Finally, because our startServiceButton is 24 DIP underneath our AnalogClock set the marginTop parameter for our timeButton UI element to be the same exact value. This results in Music Service Button UI elements that center attractively within the existing user interface Design that we created in the previous chapter. The final markup is shown in Figure 17-2.

```
<Button android:id="@+id/startServiceButton"
        android:textColor="#FFFFAA"
        android:text="@string/start_button_value"
        android:layout_marginTop="24dp"
        android:layout_gravity="center"
        android:layout_width="wrap_content"
        android:layout_height="wrap_content" />
<Button android:id="@+id/stopServiceButton"
        android:textColor="#FFFFAA"
        android:text="@string/stop_button_value"
        android:layout_marginTop="6dp"
        android:layout_gravity="center"
        android:layout_width="wrap_content"
        android:layout_height="wrap_content" />
```

To get a better idea of how this new TimePlanet.java Activity screen user interface design will look, click the **Graphical Layout Editor** tab, on the bottom-left side of the XML editing pane. As you can see, the screen UI design is evenly spaced out and the Music Service buttons are functionally grouped together.

To see how the user interface design really looks you will need to use the **Run As Android Application** work process, because as we know from our past experience, the Graphical Layout Editor utility in Eclipse does not always show the margin spacing parameters in exactly the way that they'll render on the Android device screen.

Now that our Planet Time user interface screen has our Music Service user interface elements on it, it is time to edit our AndroidManifest.xml file.

Configuring Our AndroidManifest file to Add a <service> Component

When you add an Android Activity, Service or Broadcast Receiver component to your Android application, you must declare it for use inside your AndroidManifest XML file, which is utilized to launch your application.

Let's do that now, by opening up your AndroidManifest.xml file, inside the central editing pane of Eclipse. At the bottom of the existing XML mark-up add a **<service>** tag before the closing </application> tag but after the last <activity> tag for TimePlanet which we added in the previous chapter.

This <service> tag should implement an **android:enabled="true"** parameter, which will enable this Service component for use inside your app, as well as an **android:name=".MusicService"** parameter, which is used to reference the MusicService.java class name. We create this Service class in the next section of the chapter. The tag mark-up should look like this:

```
<service android:enabled="true" android:name=".MusicService" />
```

The finished AndroidManifest.xml file and mark-up is shown in Figure 17-3.

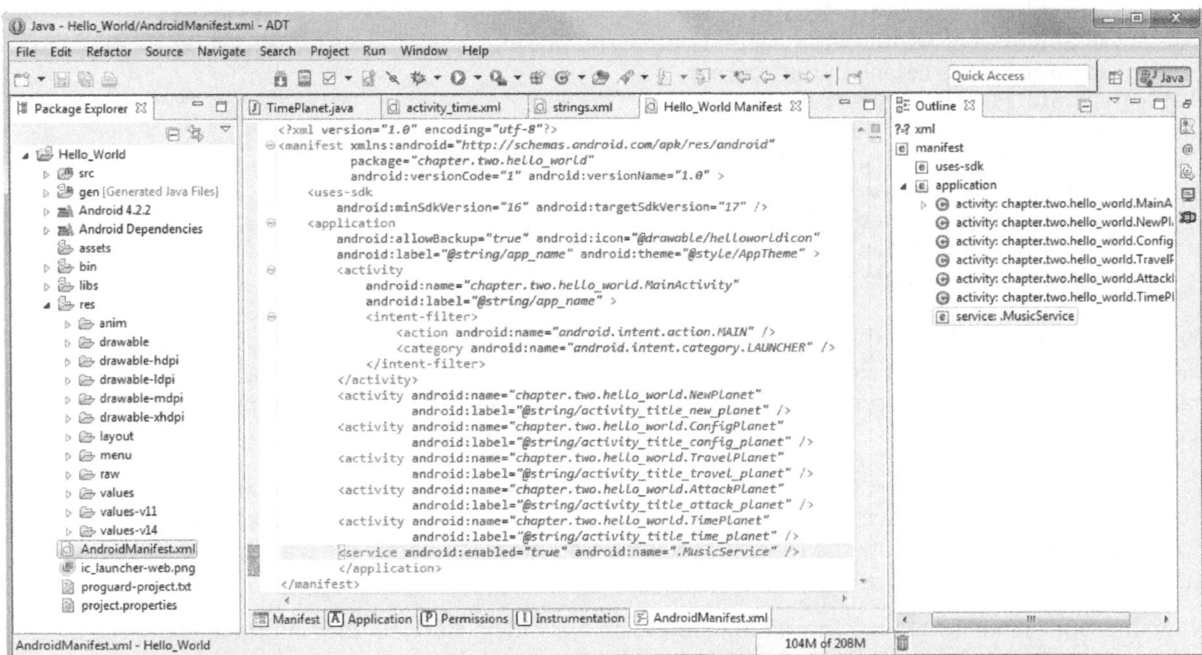

***Figure 17-3.** Adding our <service> tag and parameters to our AndroidManifest.xml file for our MusicService class*

Now we are ready to write the Java code that implements the user interface design elements that we created in the previous section of this chapter.

Writing Java Code in Our TimePlanet Activity to Launch the Service

Open up the **TimePlanet.java** Activity class in the central editing pane of Eclipse, and copy the Button instantiation and event handling method Java code structure for the **returnFromTimeButton** Button object two more times underneath itself. We do this so that we don't have to write all this Java code again from scratch, as we are implementing two very similar Button objects, along with their event handling infrastructure.

Name (rename) the first copied Button object **startMusicServiceButton**, and reference its ID as **startButton**. Delete the Java code statements in the interior of the onClick(View view) method call, so that we can add our new Service class related method calls.

Next, rename the second copied Button object: **stopMusicServiceButton**, and reference its ID as: **stopButton**. Delete the Java code statements in the interior of the onClick(View view) method call, so that we can add our new Service class related method calls.

Inside of our startMusicServiceButton onClick() event handler method let's add a **startService()** method call to start our MusicService component using an Intent object that references our current class context using the code:

```
startService(new Intent(this, MusicService.class));
```

This method call starts our Service using an Intent object that we create inside of the startService() method call using the Java **new** keyword that constructs a new Intent object using the current context and our MusicService class name reference as parameters, as is shown in the preceding line of Java code.

Next, inside our stopMusicServiceButton onClick() event handler method, let's add the **stopService()** method call, which stops and destroys our MusicService component, using an Intent object that references our current class context using the code:

```
stopService(new Intent(this, MusicService.class));
```

This method call destroys our Service using an Intent object that we create inside of the stopService() method call itself using the Java **new** keyword that constructs a new Intent object using the current context and our MusicService class name reference as parameters, as is shown in the preceding line of Java code.

Note in the Eclipse editor that both of these MusicService subclass method calls that we have put inside of our two onClick() event handling methods have been error flagged, using wavy red underline highlighting, as shown in Figure 17-4.

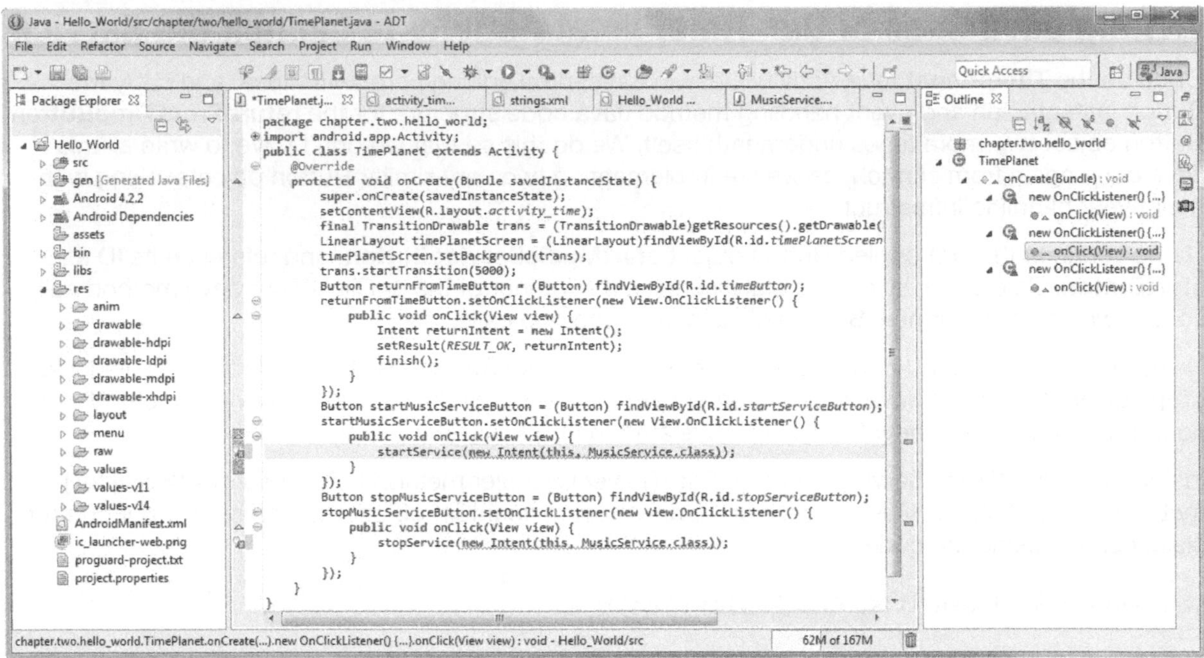

Figure 17-4. Adding the calls to .startService() and .stopService() and new Intent objects to TimePlanet.java

The reason for the wavy red underline is because we have not yet created our MusicService.java Service subclass, which as you can see is referenced in an Intent object parameter, as the class that this Intent object needs to be passed over to.

Let's create the MusicService Service subclass now so that we can get rid of this error in Eclipse, and more importantly, because it is the next step in our work process in implementing this Service component anyway!

Creating a New Service Subclass for Our MusicService.java Class

Let's take a look at another way to create a new Java Class in Eclipse by placing our mouse over the wavy red underline that we see in our current editing pane for our TimePlanet.java Activity subclass, and then select an option shown in the helper dialog that pops up that reads: **Create class "MusicService"** to launch the New Java Class dialog inside of Eclipse.

This helper dialog is shown in Figure 17-5 and is another way for us to invoke the New Java Class dialog and the Superclass Selection dialog.

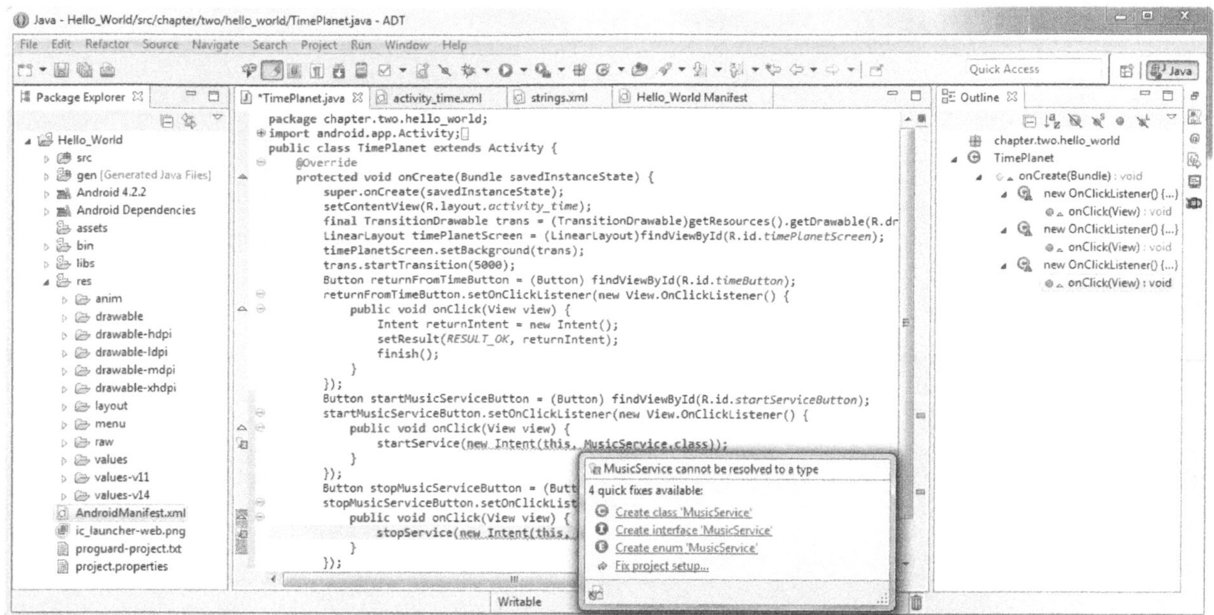

***Figure 17-5.** Using the Eclipse Error Dialog to invoke a New > Class dialog so we can create MusicService class*

The other way that we have seen to accomplish this same work process is to right-click the package name sub-folder in the Eclipse Package Explorer pane, and to then select the now familiar **New ➤ Class** menu sequence, which then accesses these same New Java Class creation dialogs for us.

Next let's fill out the New Java Class and Superclass Selection dialogs to specify our new Service subclass named MusicService.java as a public class in our chapter.two.hello_world package in our Hello_World/src source code folder.

As you can see in Figure 17-6, the first five fields have been filled out for us, so just click the **Browse** button to open a Superclass Selection dialog, type in an "s" character and select the android.app. Service class.

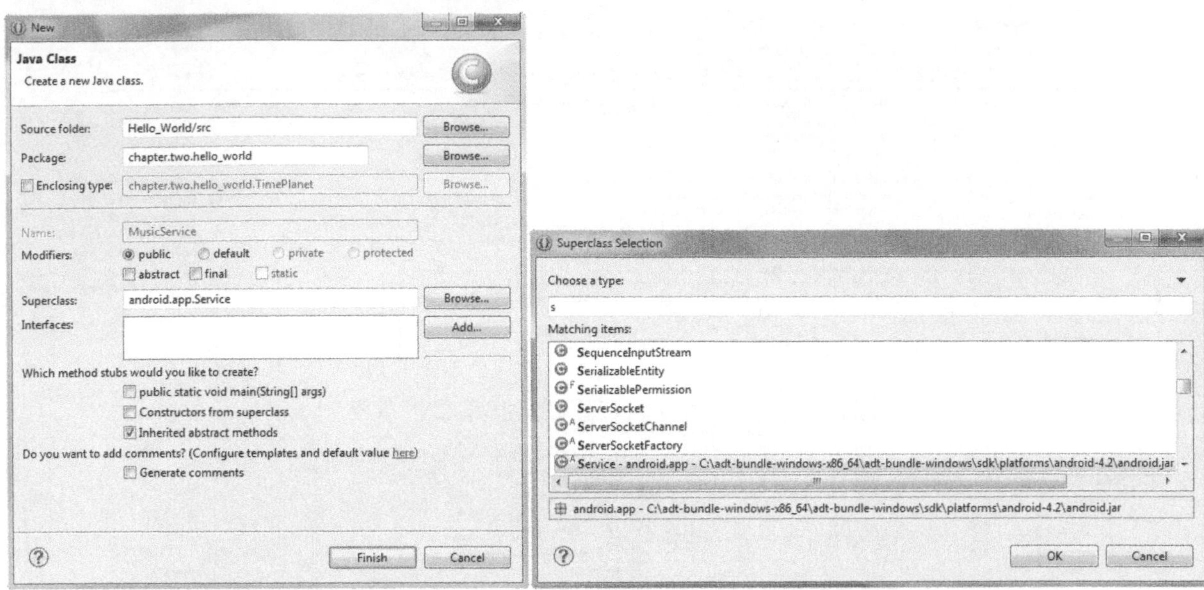

Figure 17-6. *Using the New Java Class dialog and Superclass Selection dialog to specify our MusicService class*

After you click the **OK** and **Finish** buttons in these two dialogs, you will then see your **public class MusicService extends Service** (subclass) Java code that Eclipse has written for you, as is shown in the following code and in Figure 17-7.

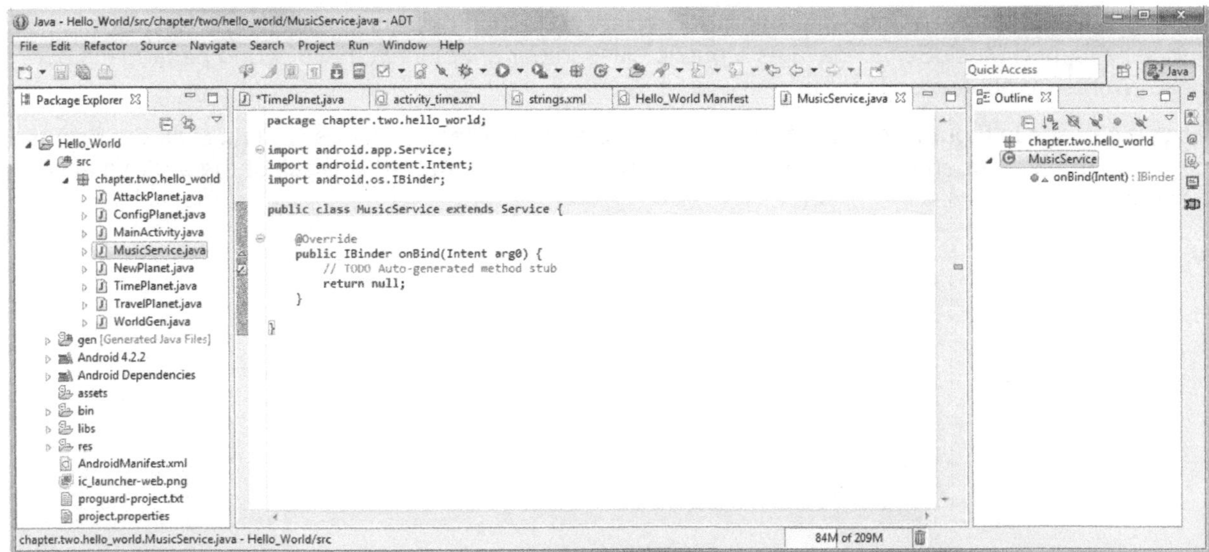

Figure 17-7. *New Service subclass MusicService with IBinder() method and import statements coded for us*

```
public class MusicService extends Service {
    @Override
    public IBinder onBind(Intent arg0) {
        // TO DO: Auto-generated method stub
        return null;
    }
}
```

Now all that we have to do is to add our Service class lifecycle method calls to implement our MediaPlayer based Music Playback Service, and we will be ready to test our application in the Nexus S emulator.

Coding Our MusicService Class Service Lifecycle Methods in Java

Now that our MusicService.java class is created and open for editing let's start by adding a MediaPlayer object named musicPlayer at the top of our class that we can use in our three lifecycle callback methods, which we are going to code next. This would involve the following line of Java code:

```
MediaPlayer musicPlayer;
```

The first method that we code is the first accessed when the Service class is called, and that's the **onCreate()** method. This method creates a MediaPlayer object and sets it up for use, as well as setting any parameters, in this case a looping parameter, as shown in Figure 17-8.

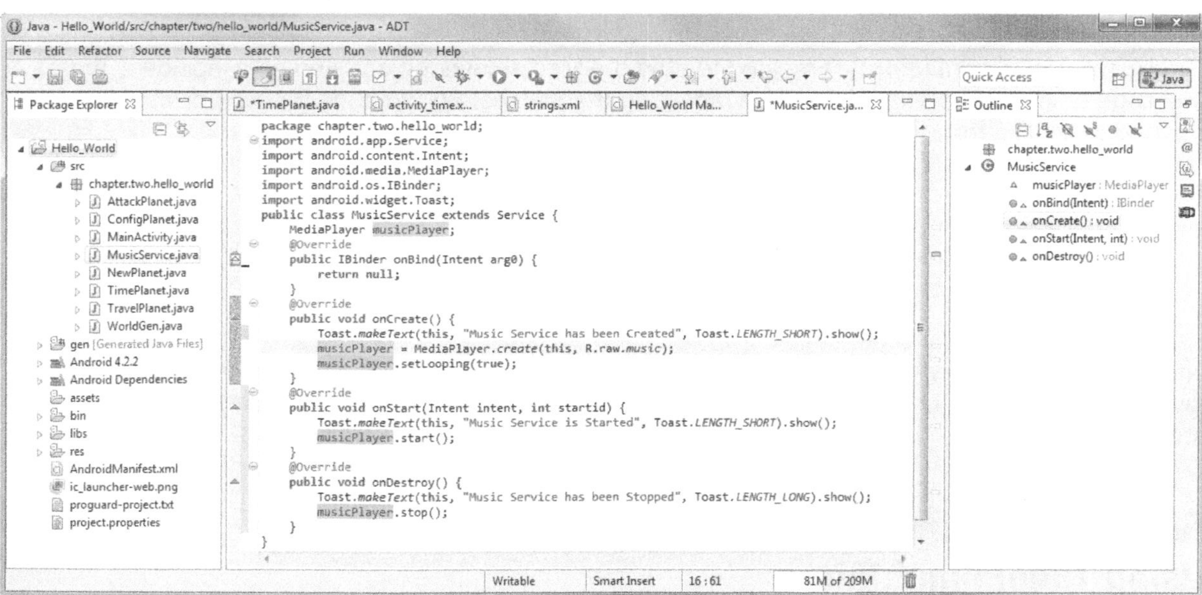

***Figure 17-8.** Coding our onCreate(), onStart(), and onDestroy Service lifecycle methods to control MediaPlayer*

We also use a Toast object and a **.makeText()** method call to show us what the OS is doing regarding creating our Service for us. The onCreate() method would be declared as public so any class can access it and void as it returns no value, and the method declaration and the three lines of Java code that we will need to put inside of the method to accomplish our MediaPlayer set-up and configuration this would look like the following:

```
@Override
public void onCreate( ) {
    Toast.makeText(this, "Music Service has been Created", Toast.LENGTH_SHORT).show( );
    musicPlayer = MediaPlayer.create(this, R.raw.music);
    musicPlayer.setLooping(true);
}
```

Next, we will code our **onStart()** method, as that would be the next method in the lifecycle that will be called when our Service is started. Remember that when a Service is called, the onCreate() method is called to create and to set-up the Service, and then the onStart() method is called, to start it running. Thus, we would utilize our onStart() method to start up the MediaPlayer object for our music playback, and again, also include another Toast message to let us see what exactly is going on regarding the Service process. So the code for an onStart() method looks like this:

```
@Override
public void onStart( ) {
    Toast.makeText(this, "Music Service is Started", Toast.LENGTH_SHORT).show( );
    musicPlayer.start( );
}
```

Finally, we use our **onDestroy()** method to stop the MediaPlayer object, and also include a Toast message to let us see what is going on regarding the Service. So the code for our onDestroy() method looks like this:

```
@Override
public void onDestroy( ) {
    Toast.makeText(this, "Music Service has been Stopped", Toast.LENGTH_SHORT).show( );
    musicPlayer.stop( );
}
```

Now that our MusicService.java Service subclass has been coded let's go back into our TimePlanet.java Activity subclass by clicking the tab at the top of Eclipse that's labeled TimePlanet.java as shown in Figure 17-8.

Refining Our TimePlanet Class Context Reference Using TimePlanet.this

When you enter the TimePlanet.java editing tab you will notice that your startService() and stopService() method calls are still red wavy underlined using Eclipse error level highlighting elements. This is because the first (context) parameter for your Intent object needs to refer to the TimePlanet class context, and it is currently referring to the **View** class that it is inside of, rather than the **Activity** class that is at the top of our current class's food chain.

So, we need to modify this code to allow this context to “see” all the way to the top of our class. To do this, we need to modify the first **this** parameter in the Intent object in the startService() and the stopService() methods, and make this parameter read: **TimePlanet.this** so that the Intent object references the TimePlanet class’s current context. As you can see in Figure 17-9, this eradicates any and all errors in our Java code, and we are now ready to compile and run our Service component savvy app in the Nexus S emulator so that we can test it to see how well it works.

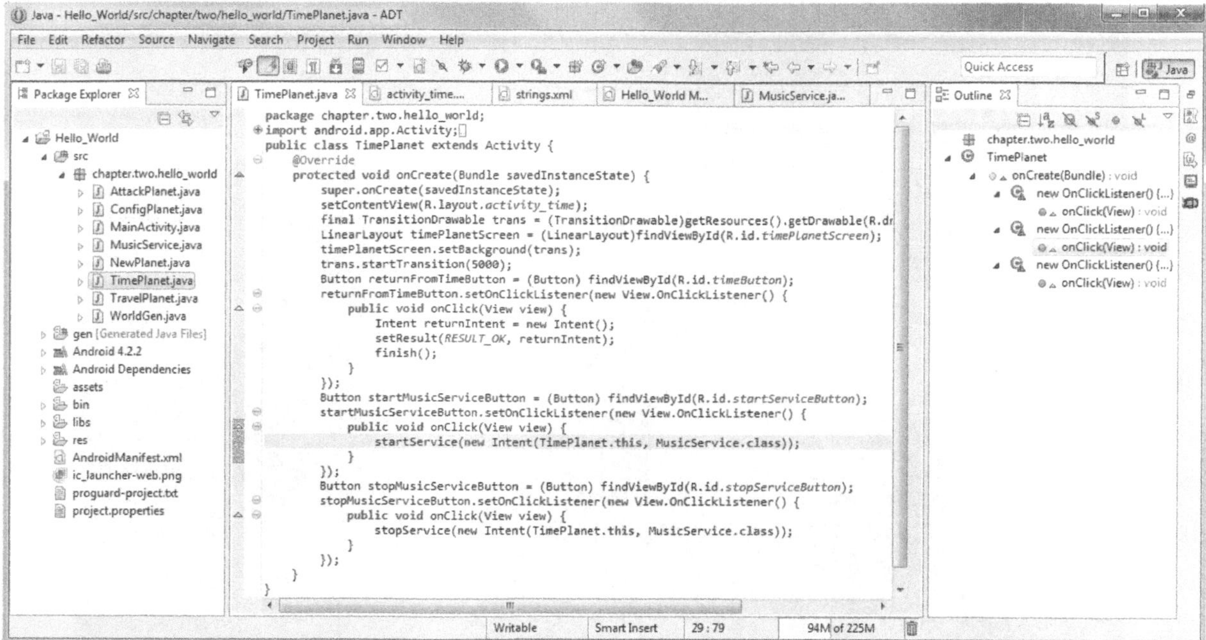

***Figure 17-9.** Error-free TimePlanet code once MusicPlayer class is in place and TimePlanet.this reference added*

Right-click your project folder and use the **Run As Android Application** work process to launch the Nexus S emulator, and when the app launches, click the menu button and select the Configure a Planet Activity, and once that appears on the screen, click the Atomic Clock button to get into the Planet Earth Time Activity screen that is shown in Figure 17-10.

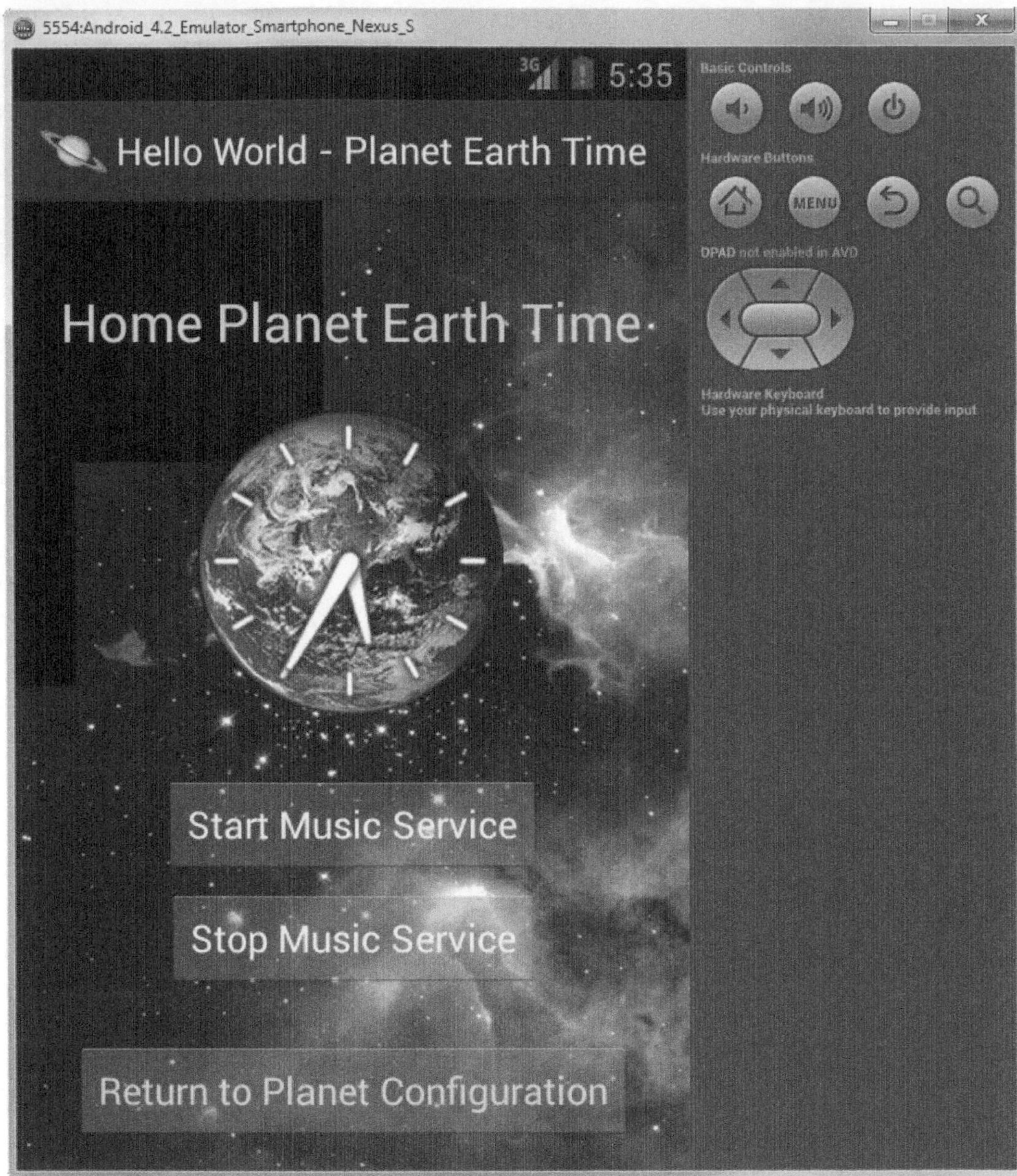

Figure 17-10. TimePlanetActivity running in the Nexus S emulator with MusicService Buttons

Testing the MusicService Component

Now it is time to test our new MusicService component that subclasses the Android Service class, and see how well it works. Click the Start Music Service button and listen to the beautiful music play back seamlessly. A Toast message should come on the screen telling you when the Service was created and when it was started.

At any time, click the Stop Music Service button, and notice the music stops playing and that a Toast message comes on the screen telling you that the Music Service has been stopped. Go ahead and click each button a few more times to make sure that the application has no bugs and that the Service and the MediaPlayer object can be started and stopped at any time.

Summary

In this chapter, we took a closer look at some of the more complex Android operating system features and concepts, including Services, Processes, and Threads. We learned how these related to each other, as well as how they differed from each other, and when to use each of them in our application.

First we took a look at Android Services and their basic forms and rules, including the difference between **started** Services and **bound** Services. We looked at some of the key methods such as startService(), stopService(), and bindService(), which we later implemented in a Service class of our own. We learned about the Service class lifecycle and how it's played out.

We then took a close look at Android Processes and Threads, as this topic is closely related to Services, and important for an Android Developer to understand. We looked at how you specify a process in your Android Manifest XML file and at the process lifespan.

We learned about the different types of processes and how they are ranked in order of importance by the Android operating system and we learned about how different types of Android components such as Activities and Services fit into the priority ranking system used with Android Processes.

We looked at the tradeoffs between using Threads within an existing class and creating a new Service subclass to do background processing. We also learned about the HandlerThread and AsyncTask classes, which you use if you decide to get more advanced in your Android Programming and utilize Threads in your application components.

Finally, we wrote our own Service subclass, called MusicService.java from scratch. We added user interface elements to our TimePlanet Activity so that we could control the Music Service from our Atomic Clock display screen, which needed some background music anyway.

We learned how to add a <service> XML tag to our AndroidManifest.xml file to declare our Service component for use, and then wrote the Java code to implement the Service class lifecycles methods that were needed to implement our MediaPlayer object and its lifecycle methods that we used to control our background music playback engine.

In the next chapter, we will learn all about the Broadcast Receiver, which can be utilized to send important applications and system related messages around to your Android application components as well as others.

Chapter 18

Broadcast Receivers: Android Inter-Application Communication

In this chapter, we will take a close look at Android's **Broadcast Receiver** classes. This class is used specifically for communications between Android components, each of which will be in the form of a subclass of the primary Android class (Activity, Service, BroadcastReceiver, etc.) as we have seen in our Java coding experiences within this book.

This can include communication between your own application components, but is more widely used for communications between unrelated application components. This would mean communication with other applications. In fact it is even more commonly used to communicate between your application and the components that are included with the Android operating system.

If you think about it, the most used components (applications) on anyone's Android phone are the components that come included with the phone and are thus an integrated part of the Android OS. No one can argue that folks use their Android device's phone dialer, calendar, alarm clock, timers, e-mail client, browser, screen savers, wallpapers, ringtones, and so on to a very large extent in their day to day use of their Android device, whether that is a smartphone, tablet, e-Reader, watch, set-top box or iTV set.

In this chapter, I am going to try and show you the various ways that you can implement Broadcast Receivers, often called simply Receivers, in your Android application, and in this case in our Hello World app. That said, this particular Android topic travels somewhat outside of the contained systems (Eclipse IDE and its emulator) that we have needed to stay within to make sure that each of our readers can follow along in lock-step.

This is because each of our readers has different Android device hardware, and are working with different developers and applications once we start getting into broadcasting (using BroadcastReceivers) between different Android device features and different external applications.

For this reason, I have to choose my Java code examples for this chapter very carefully, as they will need to support device features that every type and model of Android device on the market is guaranteed to support.

Luckily, this is an introductory book on Android, and so I can cover the theory and rules of the BroadcastReceiver class in this chapter.

We will learn how to implement Broadcast Receiver methods (Java) and tags (XML) in such as way that you will get a general idea regarding how these work, and where to start, in implementing Broadcast Receivers within your own Android applications.

Android BroadcastReceivers: Basic Concepts and Types

Android's BroadcastReceiver class is a direct subclass of java.lang.Object, which means that it is at the top of the Android class hierarchy, as might be expected from a major operating system function.

It is a part of the **android.content** package, so its full path for usage in an import statement would be **android.content.BroadcastReceiver** as we see in our Java coding later on in the chapter.

Just like there are two different types of Android Services (started and bound) there are also different types of Broadcasts which can be received: **Normal Broadcasts** and **Ordered Broadcasts**.

Normal Broadcasts are **asynchronous** and are thus free floating and not tied down (synced) to anything else in the operating system environment. Any of your receiver methods that subscribe to a normal broadcast is thus free to run in any undefined order.

Because Android is a multi-threaded and thus multi-tasking operating system, this also means that Normal Broadcasts can be processed via their receiver methods at exactly same time (in parallel).

This means that normal broadcasts are inherently more efficient, because they are not predicated upon any other system event, and the operating system has the latitude to process them in the most optimal fashion.

However, this also means that normal broadcasts cannot utilize any returned results (returned values of any type), or terminate any API or components.

Normal Broadcasts are sent by using the **Context.sendBroadcast()** method, as we will see later on in the chapter, when we get into Java coding for the Broadcast Receivers we add to our Hello World application infrastructure.

Ordered Broadcasts, on the other hand, are delivered **in order**, to a single receiver at a time. As each receiver executes an Ordered Broadcast, it can propagate a result to the next receiver. Alternatively, it can also choose to abort the broadcast at any given receiver object, so that the broadcast won't be passed over to any of the other receivers. As programmers you may see a parallel in this as to how events "bubble" up the processing chain.

The order that Broadcast Receivers process in can be controlled using the **android:priority** attribute of the <intent-filter> inside that <receiver> tag in your AndroidManifest.xml where you will define your Broadcast Receivers. At this point that is probably no surprise to you, as most component critical application infrastructure will be defined in your AndroidManifest so that the Android OS can set up those processes and memory spaces when it starts up your application.

It is important to note that <receiver> tags and <intent-filter> tags that specify the exact same priority levels will be run in an arbitrary order.

Ordered Broadcasts are sent by using the **Context.sendOrderedBroadcast()** method.

It is important to note that even in certain scenarios involving normal broadcasts that the Android operating system might revert to delivering your normal broadcast one receiver at a time, as if it were an ordered broadcast. This could happen if the Android OS decides that this method of broadcasting will provide a more processing or memory optimized result to or within the current operating environment configuration.

Another important consideration is Broadcast Receivers that may require the creation of a process. Only one of these Broadcast Receivers should be run at one time, so that the OS can avoid overloading the operating system with new processes, each of which takes memory and processing resources.

In this situation, those non-ordered (normal receiver) broadcast semantics will always hold true; these process-creating Broadcast Receivers will not be able to return any results, or to abort their broadcast components.

In summary, your BroadcastReceiver class, after it is launched as an app component through your AndroidManifest.xml <receiver> tag, will become an important part of your Android application's overall lifecycle.

If you need to review this basic Android application lifecycle and related information at any time (which is a great idea to do every once in a while when you are learning the Android OS and how it operates), you can always find this information on the Android Developer site, at the following URL:

```
http://developer.android.com/guide/components/fundamentals.html
```

Next we'll review why we need to keep our Activity Intent objects and our BroadcastReceiver Intent objects separated, and then, we'll get into the issues of security, Broadcast Receiver lifecycles, and Broadcast Receiver processing (processes) within the Android Operating System infrastructure. Once we have learned about all these things we can start coding!

Broadcasting Your Intent: Activity versus Broadcast Receiver Intents

We are using the Intent class and Intent objects to send and receive these broadcasts. As I mentioned in Chapter 16 on Intents, the Intent Broadcast Receiver engine is completely separate from Intents that are used to start your Activities using the Context.startActivity() method.

Thus there is no way for a BroadcastReceiver to process an Intent that is utilized with a **.startActivity()** method. In fact, your Broadcast Receiver does not even perceive that an Activity Intent exists! Similarly, when you broadcast your BroadcastReceiver Intents, those Intent objects will never encounter, and thus will never be able to start, any Activity subclasses.

The primary reason that the Android OS needs to keep these types of Intents so far apart is because these two types of components and the operations that they invoke utilize two very different types of Android processes.

Starting an Activity with an Intent is, as we know, a foreground process operation that takes place in the primary or main UI process and thread. That type of Android process directly modifies what the user is currently interacting with in real-time.

Broadcast receiving an Intent, on the other hand, is a background process operation, which the user is not aware of, and which is thus not as high a priority within the process priority ranking that we learned about in the previous chapter. As you can see I had a good reason for getting into all that technical information on processes and threads as it applies to more than just utilizing Services in Android.

Secure Broadcasts: BroadcastReceiver Security Considerations

BroadcastReceivers as you may have noticed in the previous sections are used via the Android Context Class API, for instance to call a Broadcast Receiver you would use their method calls off the Context object/class as follows: **Context.sendBroadcast()** or **Context.sendOrderedBroadcast()**.

Therefore Broadcast Receivers are by their core access a cross-application implementation, and as such, you would be very wise to consider how other applications external to your own can abuse your implementation of Android Broadcast Receivers. This section effectively outlines some of the primary issues that you may want to keep in mind while working with Broadcast Receivers inside your Android applications.

First of all, the Android Intent namespace is global. For this reason, you will want to assure that your Intent **action names**, as well as other string constants, are encapsulated inside namespaces which you own. If you do not follow this rule, you may inadvertently conflict with other applications.

Whenever implementing a .registerReceiver(BroadcastReceiver, IntentFilter) method, be aware that any other Android application could send broadcasts to that registered BroadcastReceiver. You can, in fact, control exactly who can send broadcasts to your registered Receiver object through the use of BroadcastReceiver permissions, which we will be covering soon.

When you publish a <receiver> in your application AndroidManifest.xml file definition and then additionally specify <intent-filter> structures in it, you need to realize that any other Android application can send broadcasts into this structure, regardless of the <intent-filter> constructs which you might specify.

There is a way to prevent other applications from sending broadcasts into your application's <intent-filter> structure in your <receiver> tag. The way to do this is to make your BroadcastReceiver unavailable to them by using an **android:exported="false"** parameter in your <receiver> tag. Note that this parameter can also be utilized in <service> and <activity> tags.

If you decide to utilize the **.sendBroadcast(Intent)** method, or its related methods, be aware that any other application can receive these broadcasts.

You can control who can receive a broadcast by using **permissions**. If you are using Android 4 (Ice Cream Sandwich) or later, you can also restrict your broadcast to any single application by using the **Intent.setPackage()** method call.

It is important to note here that none of these security issues exist when you are using the **LocalBroadcastManager**, which we are covering in a future section of this chapter, since an Intent broadcast using this class never travels outside of your current process.

Broadcast access permissions can be enforced on either the sender side or on the receiver side of that broadcast. The way to enforce permissions on the sending side of the equation is that you supply a **non-null permission argument** using **.sendBroadcast(Intent, String)** or, if you are using ordered broadcasts, by using the following: **.sendOrderedBroadcast(Intent, String, BroadcastReceiver, android.os.Handler, int, String, Bundle)** method call.

Only Broadcast Receivers who have been granted this permission constant by requesting it via the **<uses-permission>** tag in their AndroidManifest.xml file will be able to receive your secure permissioned broadcast.

The way that you enforce permissions when you are receiving a broadcast is that you again supply a **non-null permission** when registering the receiver.

This is done when you call your Java **.registerReceiver(BroadcastReceiver, IntentFilter, String, android.os.Handler)** method, or alternatively, in the static **<receiver>** tag in your AndroidManifest.xml file.

Only BroadcastReceivers that have been previously granted this permission can send an Intent object to that receiver object. Permissions may be granted by requesting those permissions using the **<uses-permission>** tag option in the AndroidManifest.xml file for that Android application.

The BroadcastReceiver Lifecycle: Rules and Regulations

A BroadcastReceiver object is only valid for the duration of that receiver call to the **.onReceive(Context, Intent)** method. Once the Java code returns from this .onReceive() method functionality the operating system will then consider that object to be finished, and it will no longer be active.

This Broadcast Receiver processing cycle has important implications as to what exactly you can do inside your **.onReceive(Context, Intent)** method call implementation.

Any Java code that you write that would require asynchronous operation is not allowed. This is because you would need to return from the function to handle that asynchronous operation. However, at that point, your BroadcastReceiver would no longer be active, and thus the system would be free to terminate the process before the asynchronous operation completed.

Additionally, you will not be able to display any dialogs, and you will not be able to bind to any Service class from within a BroadcastReceiver.

If you need to display a dialog in this situation you can still accomplish this objective by using the Android **NotificationManager** class from the android.app package. The android.app.NotificationManager is a subclass of java.lang.Object and this class notifies your user of events that happen in the background. Notifications can take three different formats: one is a persistent icon that lives in the status bar, and is accessible through your launcher; the next is by turning on or flashing an LED on your user's Android device; or finally, alerting your users by flashing the backlight, or by playing a sound, or even by vibrating a device. More information on the Android Notification Manager class can be found at the following URL:

```
http://developer.android.com/reference/android/app/NotificationManager.html
```

If you need to start a Service class, as we saw in the previous chapter, you must utilize the **Context.startService()** method call to send a command to the Service subclass.

Processing Broadcasts: How a Broadcast Affects an Android Process

An Android process that is currently executing a BroadcastReceiver object is going to be running the Java code inside that BroadcastReceiver's .onReceive(Context, Intent) method. This is considered by the Android operating system to be a high-priority foreground process, and thus it will be kept active and processing by the operating system except possibly under the case of extreme memory resource shortages.

Once your Java code returns from completing the .onReceive() method call, that Broadcast Receiver is then no longer active, and its hosting process rank is recalibrated so that it is as important as the other application components that are running in that process, but not more important.

This is especially notable because if that process was only created for the purpose of hosting your BroadcastReceiver, which is usually the case, for applications which the user has never interacted with, or has not even recently interacted with, then upon returning from the .onReceive() method execution, the operating system will consider that process to be an **empty** process priority.

As we learned about the empty process priority in the previous chapter, this means that the Android OS will most likely aggressively terminate that process, so that the operating system resources are available for other more important processes.

What this means is that for long-running operations, you should oftentimes utilize a Service in conjunction with a BroadcastReceiver to keep that containing process active for the entire duration of your function's operation.

Broadcasting Inside Your Application: The LocalBroadcastManager

If you don't need to send BroadcastReceivers between two different Android applications, you might be better off utilizing the BroadcastReceiver function using the **LocalBroadcastManager** class, instead of using the global approach described in the preceding sections. Note that if you need to support the Android OSes prior to 3.0 (such as 2.3.7 for the original Amazon Kindle Fire) that these do not support the LocalBroadcastManager class.

The LocalBroadcastManager class gives a more efficient local broadcast implementation, as no inter-process communications is required. This also relieves you from considering all the various security issues that are related to other Android applications receiving or sending your broadcasts.

The reason for this is that by utilizing this LocalBroadcastManager class you will know that the data which you are broadcasting inside your app will not leave the confines of your application, and as such, you will not need to be concerned about the leaking of any of your private data.

Secondly, by using LocalBroadcastManager it becomes impossible for other applications to send any broadcasts into your app, so you also don't need to worry about having any security windows in your application which other programmers can exploit.

Finally, using the LocalBroadcastManager class is far more efficient, as far as memory and processing is concerned, than sending a global broadcast throughout the Android operating system.

Registering a Broadcast Receiver: Dynamic versus Static Registration

There are two completely different ways to register your Android BroadcastReceiver object for use within your Android application.

One form of registration is called a **static** method of BroadcastReceiver registration, and this method is the format that you are most familiar with, and involves using the **<receiver>** tag to register the Broadcast Receiver "up-front" for use (which is why it is termed **static registration**) inside your AndroidManifest.xml file.

The other way is called **dynamic** BroadcastReceiver registration, and this is done using Java code rather than XML mark-up. The reason it is called dynamic is because it is done in your Java code at the same time as you are doing everything else in regards to the BroadcastReceiver class that you are implementing, and not up-front (static) in the AndroidManifest.xml application bootstrap file.

If you wanted to utilize dynamic BroadcastReceiver registration, the way in which you would dynamically register an instance of a BroadcastReceiver class is by utilizing the **Context.registerReceiver()** method call.

It is important to note that if you are registering a BroadcastReceiver in your **Activity.onResume()** method code, you should remember to **unregister** it in your **Activity.onPause()** method code as well.

The reason for this is to reduce wasted system resources because you don't want to receive any Intent objects when your Activity is paused, so you add an onPause() method and unregister the receiver so you don't have the operating system trying to send Intent objects to an Activity that is not actively being used.

Be sure not to make the common mistake of unregistering BroadcastReceivers inside of the Activity.onSaveInstanceState() method, because this method will not be called if the user moves backward within the history stack.

Now it's about time to try our hand at implementing the BroadcastReceiver class and methods within our very own Hello World Android application.

Implementing a Broadcast Receiver in Our Application

The first thing we need to do is to lay some groundwork for implementing a BroadcastReceiver in our Hello World application, such as: creating string constants, XML user interface design, AndroidManifest entries, and so on.

Our BroadcastReceiver will send a message when an Alarm function which we will add to our TimePlanet.java Activity is triggered and the alarm goes off. Because a Timer is time-related we will add this functionality to the UI screen where it is most logical to add it—our Planet Time UI screen!

Let's add our new string constants now, so that we can label our Button UI element that will start the Alarm countdown and our TextEdit field so that it has a hint inside of it that will tell our end-users exactly what type of information we want them to enter into this data field.

We'll label the Button object: **Start Timer Countdown**, and we'll make our hint say: **Enter Number of Seconds**, by writing the following XML mark-up:

```
<string name="timer_hint_value">Enter Number of Seconds</string>
<string name="timer_button_value">Start Timer Countdown</string>
```

These two new string constants go into our strings.xml file, which is in the /res/values folder under our project folder, shown in Figure 18-1.

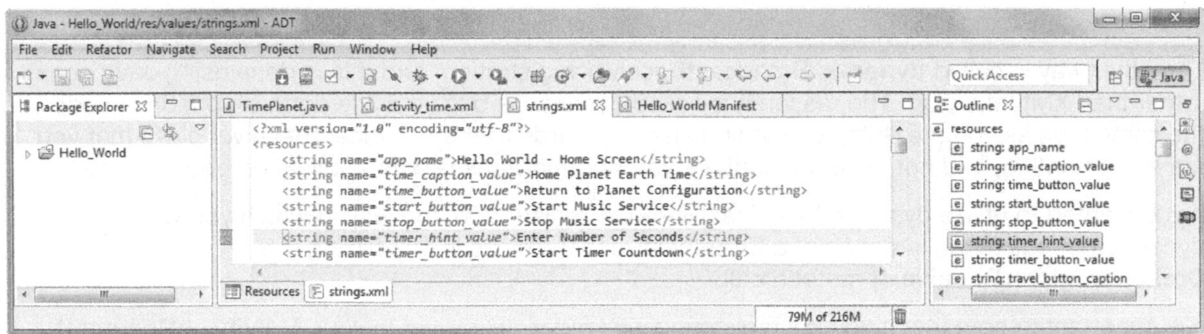

***Figure 18-1.** Adding our Button UI element label string constant and EditText UI element hint string constant*

Now that we can reference these string constants in our new UI Design for our TimePlanet.java Activity, it is time to add these new UI elements to our activity_time.xml file.

Designing Our Alarm Broadcast Receiver User Interface Using XML

Open up the **activity_time.xml** file in an editing pane in the central area of Eclipse, by right-clicking the filename in the /res/layout folder, and selecting Open (or use the F3 function key if you prefer).

We will put our **setAlarm** EditText user interface widget right underneath our Analog Clock so that all our Button UI elements on the screen will stay grouped together. Add an **<EditText>** tag under the <AnalogClock> tag and add in parameters that will configure it similarly to the EditText fields that we created for our activity_config.xml user interface screen.

Let's use an alpha value of **0.75** transparency, a text size of **12 ems,** a background color of white or **#FFFFFF,** and textStyle of a **bold** font.

Use the **android:layout_gravity="center"** to center the data entry field in the UI Design and **android:layout_marginTop="10dp"** to space our data field away from the AnalogClock UI element a bit.

Finally, let's specify our **android:typeface** parameter to be **monospace**, and an **android:inputType** of **numberDecimal** for the number of seconds to count down for our Timer.

The final EditText XML mark-up should contain the following parameters:

```
<EditText       android:id="@+id/setAlarm"
                android:hint="@string/timer_hint_value"
                android:inputType="numberDecimal"
                android:ems="12"
                android:alpha="0.75"
                android:layout_marginTop="10dp"
                android:background="#FFFFFF"
                android:textStyle="bold"
                android:layout_gravity="center"
                android:typeface="monospace"
                android:layout_width="wrap_content"
                android:layout_height="wrap_content"
/>
```

In the Eclipse XML editor we put two to three parameters on each line to save space, so we could see all our XML code for our user interface screen definition on one screen, as shown in Figure 18-2.

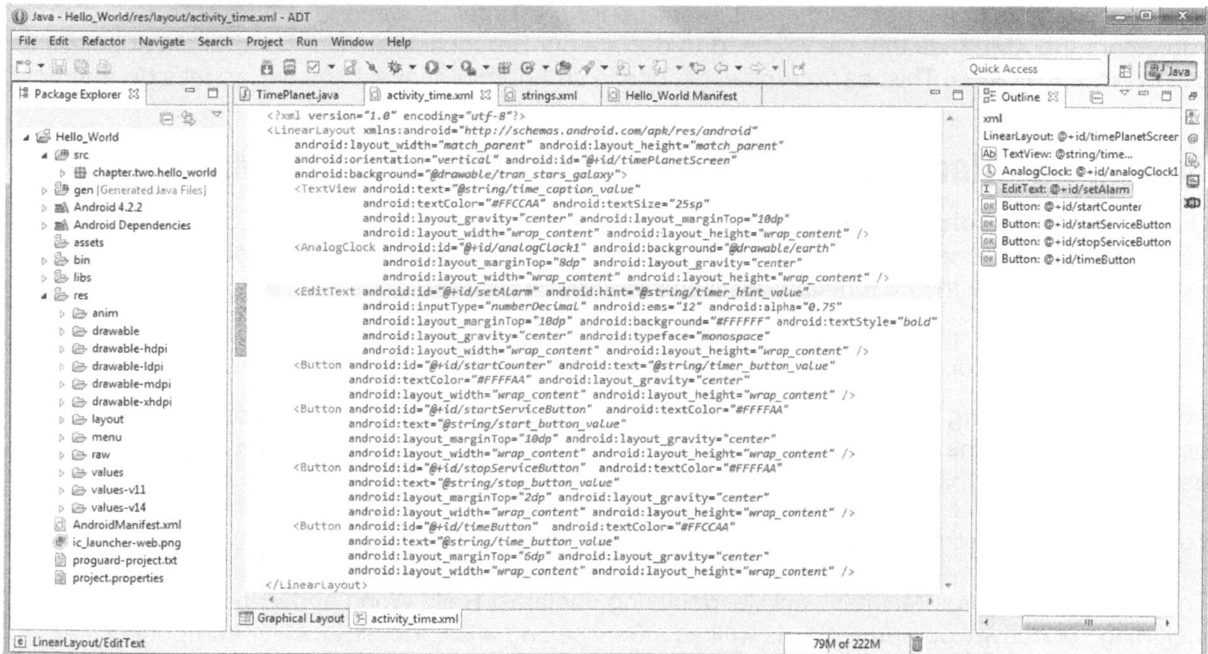

***Figure 18-2.** Adding our Button and EditText tags and configuring their parameters fo use in the UI design*

Next we need to add our **startCounter** Button object underneath our setAlarm EditText element, so that the Button element that our user clicks to start our timer running once they add the duration value is right underneath it.

Add a **<Button>** tag under the <EditText> tag and add in the parameters that will configure this Button similar to the three Button fields that we have already created right underneath it for our current user interface screen.

Let's set the android:id parameter to **startCounter** that we will reference in our Java code and set the android:text parameter to reference the string constant that we created earlier, named **timer_button_value**.

Let's use a background color of yellow or **#FFFFAA** and centering parameter of **android:layout_gravity="center"** to center the data entry field in the UI Design and make sure that the required android:layout_width and the android:layout_height parameters are included and set to **wrap_content**.

The final Button tag XML mark-up should contain the following parameters:

```
<Button android:id="@+id/startCounter"
        android:text="@string/timer_button_value"
        android:textColor="#FFFFAA"
        android:layout_gravity="center"
        android:layout_width="wrap_content"
        android:layout_height="wrap_content"
/>
```

Now that we have implemented the XML mark-up for our Timer user interface elements, let's also implement the XML tags that we will need to declare our BroadcastReceiver component subclass for use in our application. This, as you know, is done in an AndroidManifest.xml file, so let's do that now.

Adding Our AlarmReceiver BroadcastReceiver Android Manifest XML

Open up your **Androidmanifest.xml** file in an editing pane in the central area of Eclipse by right-clicking the filename in the bottom of your Hello_World project folder, and selecting the **Open** menu option (or use the F3 function key, if you prefer).

Let's add a line under the <service> tag at the bottom of our Manifest right above the closing </application> tag for our application components definition block of XML mark-up.

Add a **<receiver>** tag for our new BroadcastReceiver subclass, which we are about to code in Java next, and use a **name** parameter to reference the full pathname to the application component name, using the following mark-up:

```
<receiver name="chapter.two.hello_world.AlarmReceiver" />
```

The completed AndroidManifest.xml file, declaring our latest Hello World application components, including six Activity components, as well as a Service and a BroadcastReceiver component, is shown in Figure 18-3.

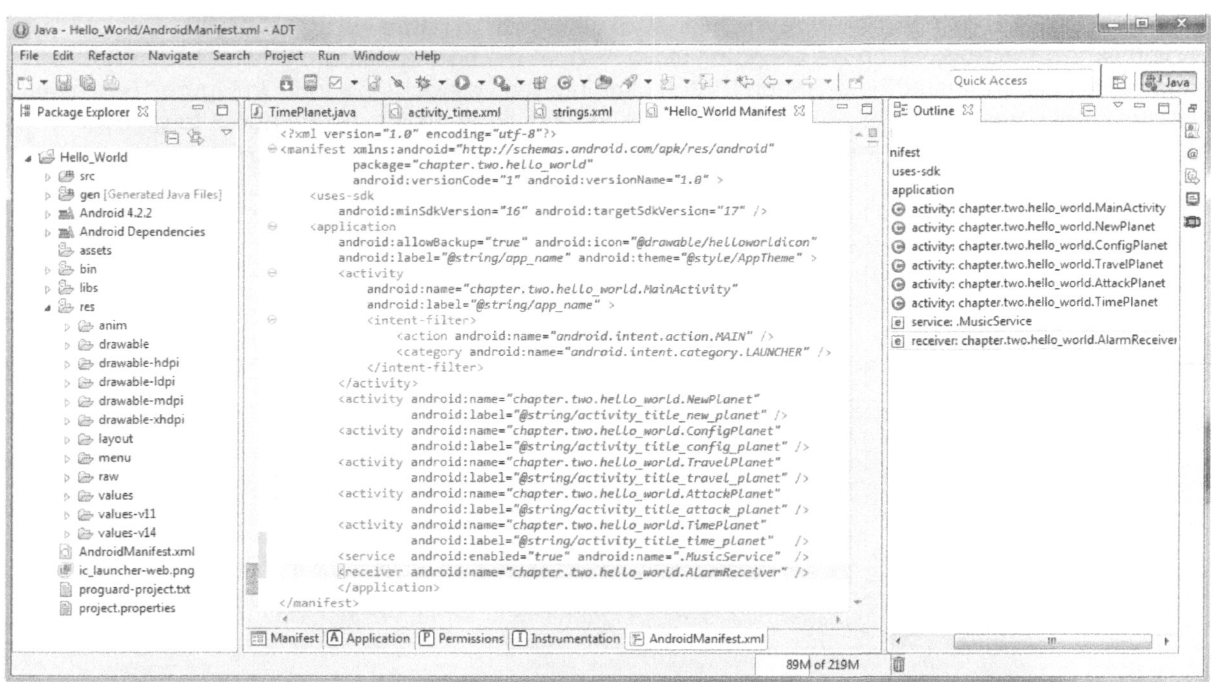

***Figure 18-3.** Adding a <receiver> tag for our AlarmReceiver BroadcastReceiver subclass to AndroidManifest.xml*

Now that we have our Alarm user interface elements designed and our Broadcast Receiver declared in our Manifest the time has come to code our Alarm Control user interface elements and methods using Java code in our TimePlanet.java Activity subclass where they will be displayed.

Coding Our startTimerButton and startTimer() Method Using Java

Let's take a programmer's short-cut, and implement our **startTimerButton** Button UI object the easy way! Copy and paste the startMusicServiceButton lines of code (all six of them) again underneath themselves to start with.

Next change the startMusicServiceButton name to startTimerButton, and the UI XML ID reference from R.id.startServiceButton to R.id.startCounter, and finally, change the startService(new Intent(this,class)) method call to be a **startTimer(view);** method call.

For now, Eclipse is going to red error highlight this new method name we are using, at least until we code this new method, which we are going to do next, at the bottom of our Activity. The new event handling code for the startTimerButton Button user interface element is shown in Figure 18-4, along with the **public void startTimer(View view)** method Java code, which we are about to go over in great detail next. The startTimerButton Java code block should look like the following:

```
startTimerButton.setOnClickListener(new View.OnClickListener() {
        public void onClick(View view) {
                startTimer(view);
        }
}
```

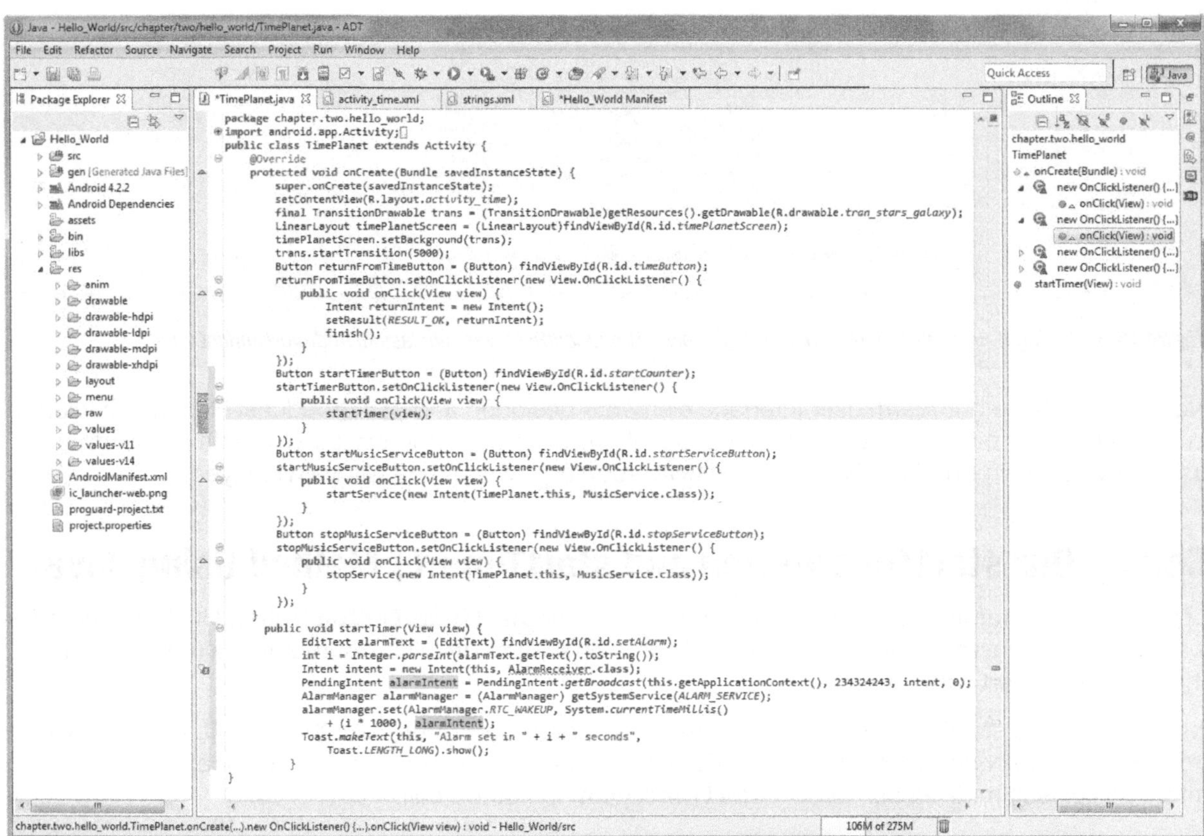

Figure 18-4. Coding our user interface button and startTimer() method in our TimePlanet.java Activity subclass

We will declare our startTimer() method with **public** access, so it is available for public usage, and with a **void** return value as it returns nothing to the calling entity, in this case, a click on the startTimerButton UI object.

Coding Our startTimer() Java Method

Next, we will declare our EditText user interface element for usage, and we will name it **alarmText** and use the **findViewById()** method to reference it to point to our **setAlarm** EditText tag XML definition via **R.id.setAlarm**.

Notice that if you have not imported the EditText class for use, that this code will have red underline highlighting, and that you can mouse-over it, and have Eclipse write this import statement Java code for you.

Next we declare an integer variable named **i** and set it equal to an Integer object, off of which we call the **.parseInt()** method. This method parses an integer value, by calling the **.toString()** conversion method, off of the **.getText()** method, which is called off of the **alarmText** EditText object to retrieve the text value that the user has entered into the data field. This is all done in a line of Java code that is written as follows:

```
int i = Integer.parseInt(alarmText.getText().toString());
```

Next, we declare an Intent object named **intent**, and construct a new Intent object, using the **new** keyword, using the current context **this** and a target component of the **AlarmReceiver.class** that we are going to code in the next section. For now, Eclipse red underline highlights this reference, as we have not as of yet created and coded this BroadcastReceiver subclass.

Next, we are going to create an Android **PendingIntent** object which we will name **alarmIntent**, and load with the Android alarm function, by calling the **.getBroadcast()** method off of the **pendingIntent** class using the parameters which configure our **alarmIntent** with the **current context**, an alarm **request code**, our **intent** Intent object that we just created in a previous line of code, and a **zero** value for the **flags** parameter, because at this time we are passing no flag values to this particular **.getBroadcast()** method call.

Notice that if you have not imported the PendingIntent class for use, that this code will have red underline highlighting, and that you should mouse-over it, and have Eclipse write the import statement Java code for you. If you want to research this PendingIntent class in further detail, you can find information on the Android Developer website, at the following URL:

```
http://developer.android.com/reference/android/app/PendingIntent.html
```

Next, we are going to create an Android **AlarmManager** object, which we will name **alarmManager**, and load this object using a **getSystemService()** method, which is called off of the AlarmManager class and passed the **ALARM_SERVICE** constant value as a parameter. This sets up an alarm function for us to use that is one of the many Android operating system functions that we can call, in that case by using the AlarmManager API.

Notice that if you have not imported the AlarmManager class for use, that this code will have red underline highlighting, and that you should mouse-over it, and have Eclipse write the import statement Java code for you. If you want to research this AlarmManager class in further detail, you can find information on the Android Developer website, at the following URL:

```
http://developer.android.com/reference/android/app/AlarmManager.html
```

Next we need to configure the **alarmManager** object we just created by using the AlarmManager class's **.set()** method. We will pass the .set() method the three parameters it requires, an Integer (in this case a system constant), which represents the **type** of Alarm, a **trigger time in milliseconds**, which is represented by a **long** value, and a **PendingIntent** operation, in our case the **alarmIntent** that we created two lines of Java code previous to this.

```
AlarmManager.set(AlarmManager.RTC_WAKEUP, System.currentTimeMillis() + (I * 1000), alarmIntent);
```

Notice that we calculate the alarm trigger time in milliseconds inside the .set() method call, using the **System.currentTimeMillis()** method, which obtains a **current system time** in milliseconds, and adds that to the number of seconds, which the user entered in our EditText UI element, times 1000, to convert that seconds value to milliseconds, giving us the trigger time!

The final line of Java code in our startTimer() method uses an Android Toast object and a .makeText() method call to post our alarm setting confirmation message to the Activity screen using the following Java code:

```
Toast.makeText(this, "Alarm set in " + i + "seconds", Toast.LENGTH_SHORT).show();
```

Again we are using string value concatenation with our integer value i to display a Toast message that tells the user Alarm set in X seconds with the value that they entered, and then using method chaining at the end to append a .show() method call to the .makeText() method call to have the entire Toast object construct use only a single line of Java code.

We're ready to create and code our **AlarmReceiver** class that will implement our **onReceive()** BroadcastReceiver method to make everything work together.

Creating Our AlarmReceiver BroadcastReceiver Subclass

Place your mouse over the red wavy underline error highlighting shown in Figure 18-4, and then select the **Create AlarmReceiver Class** option to have Eclipse create the New Java Class dialogs shown in Figure 18-5.

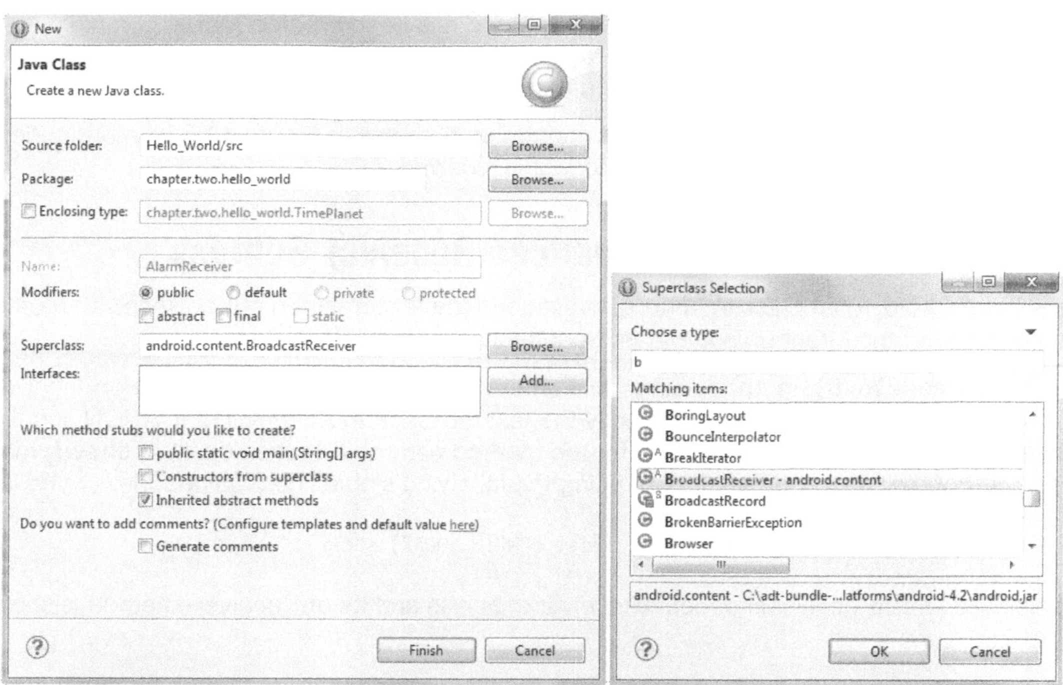

Figure 18-5. Having Eclipse create a New Java Class called AlarmReceiver using a Superclass Selection dialog

Because the Source folder:, Package:, and Name: data fields have already been filled in for us, simply click the **Browse** button, and type a "**b**" in the **Choose a type:** field located at the top of the **Superclass Selection** dialog and then scroll down to the **BroadcastReceiver - android.content** selection, found in the **Matching items:** section of the dialog, and select it as shown in Figure 18-5.

Finally, click the **OK** button, to return to the **New Java Class** dialog, and then click the **Finish** button in order to create your AlarmReceiver BroadcastReceiver subclass, which is shown in Figure 18-6.

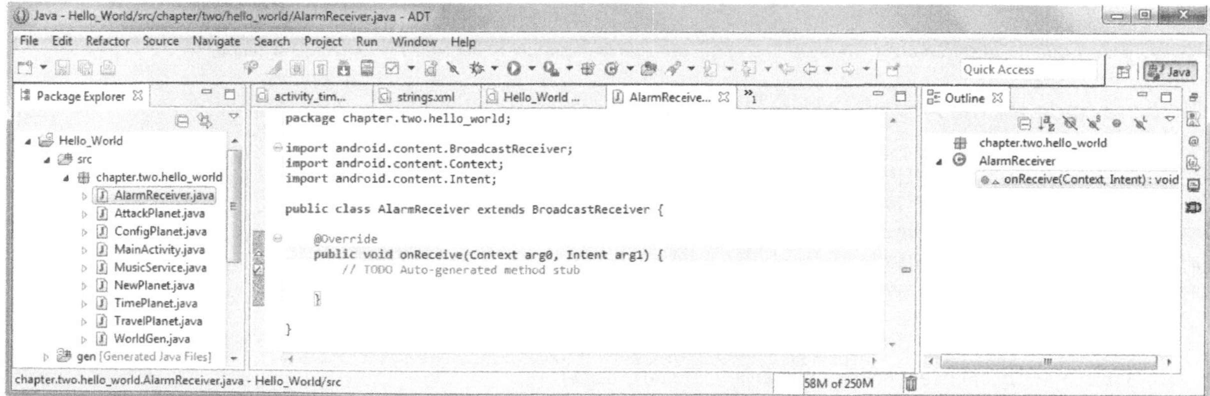

Figure 18-6. Our AlarmReceiver.java BroadcastReceiver subclass infrastructure showing an onReceive() method

Notice that the **onReceive()** BroadcastReceiver method has been created for us, complete with access control and parameters in place and ready for us to write our Java code which will implement our BroadcastReceiver method's alarm related functions.

Next we'll replace the TODO Auto-generated method stub shown in Figure 18-6 with our code to send a message to the screen once our Broadcast is received.

Coding Our AlarmReceiver BroadcastReceiver Sublass

Let's use the Android Toast class to send a message to the screen when our onReceive() method is called and received the Intent object that is broadcast over to it.

Use the Toast **.makeText()**, method using the Context object that is passed into the onReceive() method as its first parameter and then specify the text message ALARM NOTIFICATION and finally a Toast.LENGTH_SHORT duration constant for the method parameters, then chain a **.show()** method call at the end of the Java code statement using the following single line of java code:

```
Toast.makeText(arg0, "ALARM NOTIFICATION", Toast.LENGTH_SHORT).show();
```

The completed AlarmReceiver BroadcastReceiver subclass and its onReceive() method is shown in Figure 18-7.

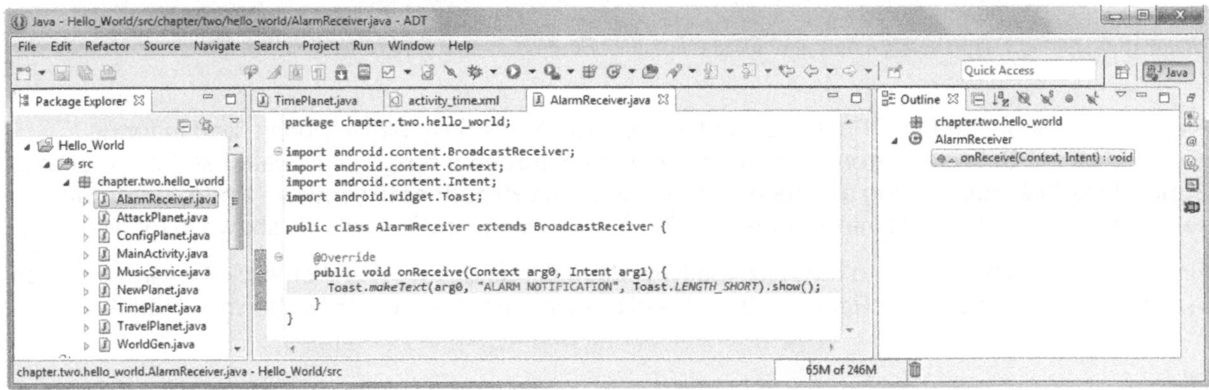

***Figure 18-7.** Coding our onReceive() method to display our Alarm Message in the AlarmReceiver.java class*

The Java code for the AlarmReceiver BroadcastReceiver subclass looks like this:

```
package chapter.two.hello_world;
import android.content.BroadcastRcceiver;
import android.content.Context;
import android.content.Intent;
import android.widget.Toast;
public class AlarmReceiver extends BroadcastReceiver  {
      @Override
      public void onReceive(Context arg0, Intent arg1) {
          Toast.makeText(arg0, "ALARM NOTIFICATION", Toast.LENGTH_SHORT).show();
      }
}
```

Now it is time to test our Broadcast Receiver implementation inside the Android Nexus S emulator, to see if all this XML and Java code that we wrote over the course of this chapter is working properly together.

Right-click the Hello_World project folder and select the **Run As Android Application** menu sequence to start up the Nexus S emulator so we can test our latest application revision.

When the Home Screen appears, click the Menu button to launch the Options Menu, and then select the Configure a Planet menu option to launch the Configure a Planet Activity screen.

At the bottom right of the screen, click the Atomic Clock button to launch your TimePlanet.java Activity user interface screen, and enter a timer duration value in seconds into the text data field under the Planet Earth Analog Clock user interface element.

Next, click the **Start Timer Countdown** button, which is located underneath the Enter Number of Seconds data entry field to send the Broadcast and start the AlarmManager object. The user interface for this screen is shown in Figure 18-8.

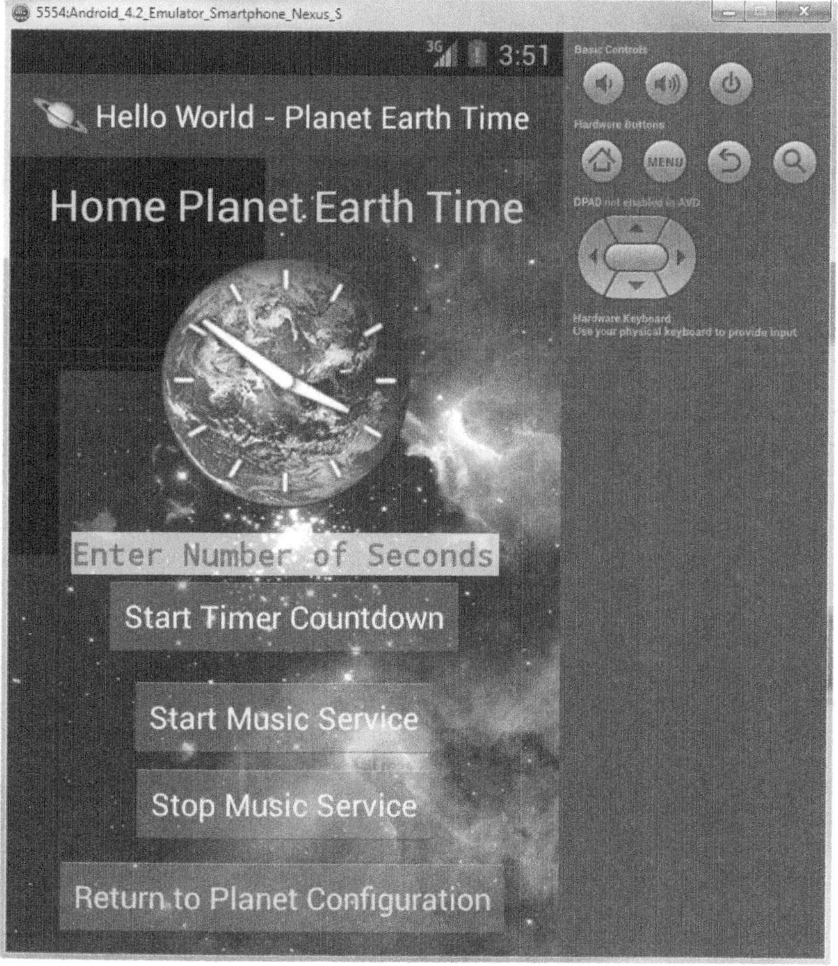

***Figure 18-8.** Testing our AlarmReceiver BroadcastReceiver subclass running in the Nexus S emulator*

As you see, the BroadcastReceiver application component that we have now implemented works perfectly, and after that Toast message specifying our number of seconds to countdown appears, our ALARM NOTIFICATION Toast message subsequently appears on-screen after the number of seconds that we specified for our Alarm function have transpired, of course.

Congratulations! You have successfully implemented the three primary types of Android components: Activities, Services, and Broadcast Receivers! Cool! Take a break and grab a cool drink, and kick back for a bit and relax!

Now we have successfully implemented a Broadcast Receiver in our Android application, and the only type of component that we need to learn how to implement is a Content Provider, which we will learn about in the next chapter when we add content provider capabilities to our Hello World Android application!

Summary

In this chapter, we took a close look at the Android **BroadcastReceiver** Class and its **onReceive()** method.

We looked at the two different types of Broadcast Receiver broadcasts, normal broadcasts and ordered broadcasts, and we learned the difference between them, and when you would want to implement each type of broadcast.

Next we looked at the security considerations for Broadcast Receivers that stem from the fact that Broadcast Receivers are sent outside of your application and also allow other developer's code inside of your application by their very nature.

Then we looked at the BroadcastReceiver lifecycle, and the basic rules and regulations regarding how you are allowed to use your onReceive() method call and Java code functions to process various types of Java programming objectives.

Next, we took a closer look at how the Android operating system processes Broadcast Receivers and how your use of them will affect your application process priority levels, which we learned about in Chapter 17.

We took a close look at the LocalBroadcastManager class used for localized broadcasting within an enclosed application environment, as well as how to dynamically (in Java method calls) and statically (in our Android Manifest XML mark-up) register broadcasts inside the Android operating system.

Finally, we took the plunge and implemented a Broadcast Receiver in our own Hello World application to implement a Timer function in our TimePlanet Activity. We added UI elements to our activity_time.xml file, added a new <receiver> tag to our AndroidMainfest.xml file, and finally implemented an AlarmReceiver BroadcastReceiver subclass and an onReceive() method.

In the next chapter we will learn all about Content Providers in Android, as well as the SQLite database engine. We saved the most complicated subjects for last so that you would have the maximum experience with Android before we dove into something as complex as building a DBMS engine using Android's Content Provider APIs. Hold on to your hats! Here we go!

Chapter 19

Android Content Providers: Access to Datastores

In this chapter, we will learn about one of the more advanced topics involving the Android operating system: Content Providers. Content Provider means: DataStore. We are familiar with the **android.content** package, having worked with its classes before, and we are about to get more familiar with the **android.database** package, as well as the **android.provider** package.

One of the most prolific Content Providers in the Android operating system is the **SQLite** database API, which is an integral part of Android. As such, this chapter is also going to cover an inherently advanced topic of SQLite Database Engine, Design Principles and overview of Android Content Provider API implementation.

The reason that this particular chapter's topic is more advanced than the other topics we have learned about in the previous chapters is the fact that this chapter contains information on two different advanced topics.

The first is SQL and SQLite Database Design concepts, on which Android's internal ContentProvider is based, and the second covers all the different types of Content Providers that are currently available in Android.

First, we will cover database design concepts at a fairly high level, so that you have the foundational knowledge regarding what we are going to be doing in the rest of the chapter.

Then we will go over the different types of Android Content Providers, as well as their concepts and techniques, and how they need to be accessed via Uniform Resource Identifier (URI) path constructs.

Next we will take a look at the SQL database engine and the Android SQLite database packages and APIs. Finally, we will implement an Android Content Provider in our Hello World application, to see how it all works together.

Database Fundamentals: Concepts and Terminology

As most programmers know already, a **database management system**, or **DBMS**, is a highly structured data storage system, or "engine," which can store valuable data in a tabular format that can be easily accessed and updated. One of the most popular open source DBMS database programming languages in the world is called **SQL**, which stands for **Structured Query Language**.

The **structured** part comes from the fact that databases are arranged into a tabular format, and the **query** part comes from the fact that these tables of data are designed to be **searched** for a certain data value. The **language** part comes from the fact that SQL has evolved into a database programming language that is so complex and involved that there are probably far more books regarding this ageless RDBMS (Relational Database Management System) topic than there are on the Android OS.

For those readers who have never worked with database technology I will go over the fundamentals here, so that we can all be using the same knowledge base. Popular database software packages that you may be familiar with may include Access and FileMaker, and many of you have probably used Excel to store data in tabular format, much like a database does, only more visual.

Data in a relational database such as MySQL is stored using **tables**, which support both **rows** and **columns** of data. This is similar to a spreadsheet like Excel except that databases aren't usually all visible at once as in a spreadsheet, although you can generate reports that will achieve this end result if you wish once we learn all the programming involved!

Each relational database table **column** will always contain a similar data type and classification of data within your database record structure, and this is generally called a database **field**.

This means that conversely, each **row** in your database table would thus represent one entire data **record**. So generally when you are writing a database record you will write one entire row or record of data when you first add that record, but when you search a database for information you are generally looking through one of the columns or fields for specific piece of data or information.

If you have a huge amount of data fields (columns) in your database table, you will probably want to have more than one database (table of data) in your database design approach.

In a real world database design, the theory of which is largely beyond the scope of an introductory book, you will want to have more than one single database structure, for both access (search) performance, as well as for organizational reasons. In fact the Android OS uses more than one database structure for its end-user information storage and access, as we will soon see later on in this chapter.

The way to have multiple databases is to have a unique **key** (unique index) for each record in each of the databases (tables). In that way information for a single data record can span more than one database table, using that key. In Android, this key is called an **ID** and is always designated via the constant **"_ID"** in Android's SQLite databases. For instance, if your key or _ID value is 137, your e-mail information and phone information could be in two different tables but stored under that same key (index) value and thus accurately associated with your Android user account.

MySQL and SQLite: An Open Source Database Engine

MySQL is currently one of the most popular Open Source Relational Database Management System (RDBMS) Engines in the world. If you own your own server hardware, you can download and install MySQL, using the `MySQL.com` website, and then you could host massive databases of information, with very little software purchasing expenditure.

SQLite is a far smaller version of the MySQL RDBMS Engine designed to work well in embedded hardware such as tablets, smartphones, eBook readers, iTV sets, watches, car dashboards, set-top boxes, home media centers, and other consumer electronics devices commonly referred to as Internet 2.0. It is also interesting to note that SQLite is also in all the HTML5 browsers.

SQLite stands for **Structured Query Language Lite**, and is the Open Source Database Engine that is included as part of the Android operating system. There is a SQLite API (package) in Android which contains all of the RDBMS functions needed to implement the SQLite API. These are contained within a series of classes and methods in the **android.database.sqlite** package.

SQLite is designed specifically for embedded systems use similar to JavaME (Micro Edition), and as such, has only a **quarter megabyte** memory footprint (256KB), which is used to host a relational database engine implementation.

SQLite supports the minimum, standard set of relational database functions and features such as common SQL syntax, database transactions, and prepared statements, which is enough to provide robust database support to Android.

SQLite supports three different data types: **TEXT** (known as a **String** value in Java), **INTEGER** (known as a **long** value in Java), and a **REAL** (known as a **double** value in Java) data type.

When working with SQLite, all other data types must be converted into one of these compatible data types before saving them in the database field.

It is important to note that SQLite does not itself validate any data type that may be written to its fields (table columns) as being actually of a defined data type. This means that you can write an integer into a string column and vice versa. If you want to research SQLite in greater detail, you can do so at the SQLite site, which is located at the following URL:

```
http://www.sqlite.org/
```

To use SQLite in Android you construct your SQLite statements for creating and updating your database, which will then be managed for you by Android. When your app creates a database, the database will be kept in a directory that will always utilize the following Android OS database path address:

```
DATA/data/YOUR_APPLICATION_NAME/databases/YOUR_DATABASE_FILE_NAME
```

Next we will take a look at the many different types of Android Content Providers as well as how they are accessed via the Android operating system and its **android.content** package and its classes and methods.

Android Content Providers and Content Resolvers: An Introduction

An Android Content Provider object manages your application's data access. Android Content Providers are what you would want to use if you wanted to share data across or between different Android applications.

This is usually some sort of structured data set in a **database** or in a **file** in system memory, or on the device's **SD Card** data storage device, or in **preferences** (name-value pairs), or even on an external network **server**.

The general purpose of an Android Content Provider is to encapsulate data in a standardized fashion, while at the same time, providing the Android Developer with some sort of mechanism for enforcing their data security.

Content Providers are the standard Android interface that connects the data in one system process with the Java code running in another process. If you want to access data that is inside a Content Provider, you would use a **ContentResolver** object within your current application **Context** to communicate with that Content Provider as a database client.

The ContentResolver class is subclassed from **java.lang.Object**, and it is a part of the **android.content** package. If you want to research more detailed information on this class and its constants, constructors, and methods, you can find an entire webpage dedicated to this information at the following URL within the Android Developer website:

```
http://developer.android.com/reference/android/content/ContentResolver.html
```

An Android ContentResolver object communicates with a Content Provider object, which as we know would be an instance of a class that implements Android's ContentProvider superclass.

The Content Provider object is kind of like Android having its own custom database engine that receives data requests from an application component client, and then performs the requested data resolution action inside its own process, returning the result if the requested data can be located.

It's important to note that developers will not need to code their very own Content Provider subclasses if they do not need to share their data outside their application, which most applications do not need to do.

Scenarios under which you will need to subclass your own Content Provider would include providing custom search suggestions in an application or if you need to copy or paste complex data between your application and other Android applications.

Android includes application specific operating system Content Providers that manage common types of new media data such as audio, video, images, as well as text data such as personal contact information.

You can take a look at the Android predefined Content Provider classes on the developer webpage, which provides the reference documentation for the **android.provider** package. It is located at the following URL:

```
http://developer.android.com/reference/android/provider/package-summary.html
```

The Android OS comes pre-installed with these Content Provider databases. These assist Android users by storing everyday data, such as an end-user's contact information, daily calendar, phone numbers, and multimedia files.

These application-specific Content Provider classes provide developers with pre-built methods for writing or reading data values to and from these customized Content Providers.

With some restrictions, outlined in the AndroidManifest.xml file as usual, these pre-built Content Provider classes are readily accessible to Android application developers for use in their application features or functions.

Addressing the Content Provider: Using a Content URI

If you want to be able to tell the Android OS what Content Provider you want to access, it is important that you understand the concept of the **Content URI**. We have used URI objects before, so you are familiar with the function they play in accurately referencing data (content) pathways in Android apps. Content Providers have a special path format, just like HTTP has a special format HTTP:// so too does content have a special format that is very similar (and thus easy for us to remember) and this is:

```
content://
```

A complete URI for an Android Content Provider follows this format:

```
content://Authority/Path/ID
```

As an example, here is an (imaginary) Hello World Content URI:

```
content://com.helloworld.universedatabase/planets/earth/1337
```

In this URI, **com.helloworld.universedatabase** would be the Data Authority, **planets/earth/** is the Data Path, and **1337** is the ID for the Data Record.

A Content URI always contains four necessary parts: The schema to use, in this case, **content://;** an authority; an optional path to the data; and the ID of the data record that you want to access.

The schema for Content Providers is always the word "**content**" and a colon and a double forward slash "**://**" are always attached to the front of the URI and serve to separate the data schema from the data authority.

The next part of the URI is known as the **authority** for a Content Provider. As you might have expected, an authority for each Content Provider must be unique. An authority naming convention usually follows Java package naming conventions.

Many organizations choose to use a backward dot com domain name of their organization, plus a data qualifier for each content provider that you may publish, so our preceding example would assume that we own the `helloworld.com` domain name, which, of course, we do not.

Because the Android developer documentation recommends that you utilize the fully qualified class name of your ContentProvider subclass, we might then name our ContentProvider subclass UniverseDatabase.java if we are following this example Content URI.

The third part of the URI standard is the **path** to the Data, which although optional, use of which is a fairly standard practice, for organizational purposes. We would not put our data in the root folder of our server, but instead we would place it in a **planets** folder, using sub-folders for each of our planet databases. In the case of our example, a subfolder is **Earth**.

The Content Provider for Android's **MediaStore** database (which we will look at next), for example, uses different path names to make sure that the audio, image, and video files are kept in separate data type locations.

By using different path names, one single Content Provider can accommodate many different types of data that are in some way related, such as the New Media content types, for example, kept in the MediaStore Content Provider.

For totally unrelated data types, it is standard programming practice that you would want to utilize a different Content Provider subclass, as well as different data authority (and path, for that matter) for each database.

The last URI reference specification component is the **ID**, which as you may have surmised, needs to be numeric. The ID, or **_ID** in Android, is utilized whenever you want to access a single database record. So as you can see the URI reference specification progresses from the most general or high-level (content://) specification through the authority (server name) down through the pathway to the data (directory path), and ultimately, to the data record itself (ID). This is the logical way to set up any data path in the first place, so I don't really anticipate you having any problems at all understanding the URI reference specification and its construction.

Android OS Content Providers: Databases That Are Part of the OS

Android provides an **android.provider** package that contains Java **interfaces** for all the primary database types that are standard in the Android OS.

These include the databases that are most often used by the Android user, such as the **Contacts** databases, the **Calendar** databases, and the **MediaStore** databases. We'll go over these and their component parts in this section.

These are used for things like personal management, time management, and multimedia management, the three most often accessed tasks on an Android device, whether it be a smartphone, tablet, eBook eReader or iTV set.

As we learned in the section on database design, these databases are split into logical sub-databases, and referenced as if they were one single data store, by using a key or an index **_ID** value. As we know, this is done for system performance (memory usage), as well as data access speed and ease of database access reasons.

The Android MediaStore Databases

The **MediaStore** databases include 9 different new media asset databases, the **CalendarContract** databases include 11 different Calendar component databases, and the **ContactsContract** databases include the most databases, with 21 functional databases.

The MediaStore databases include five audio data related databases and one image and one video related database. Table 19-1 shows the MediaStore data provider interfaces, as well as the types of data they access (reference).

Table 19-1. MediaStore Databases in the Android Provider Package and the Type of Data They Contain

Database	Description
MediaStore.Audio.AlbumColumns	Database Columns that represent an album
MediaStore.Audio.ArtistColumns	Database Columns that represent an artist
MediaStore.Audio.AudioColumns	Database Columns which represent audio files which span more than one database
MediaStore.Audio.GenresColumns	Database Columns that represent a genre
MediaStore.Audio.PlaylistsColumns	Database Columns that represent playlists
MediaStore.Images.ImageColumns	Database Columns that represent an Image
MediaStore.Video.VideoColumns	Database Columns that represent a Video
MediaStore.Files.FileColumns	Columns for a Master Table for all Media
MediaStore.MediaColumns	Common Columns for MediaProvider Tables

The Android CalendarContract Databases

The **CalendarContract** databases include 11 Calendar-related databases, each supporting various Calendar functions such as Events, Attendees, Alerts, Reminders, and other similar Calendar-related data support functions.

The reason that the Android operating system provides pre-built support, via its android.provider package for the Android Calendar database access is because it would be logical for applications that want to access these Calendar features to be able to add cool new capabilities to the existing Android Calendar feature set.

Table 19-2 shows the CalendarContract data provider interfaces, as well as the different types of Calendar function data that they access (and thus, which they will allow you to reference directly using a Content Provider).

Table 19-2. CalendarContract Databases in the Android Provider Package and the Type of Data They Contain

Database	Description
CalendarContract.CalendarAlertsColumns	Data Used for Calendar Alerts Function
CalendarContract.CalendarCacheColumns	Data Used for Calendar Cache Function
CalendarContract.CalendarColumns	Calendar Columns that other URI can query
CalendarContract.CalendarSyncColumns	Generic Columns for use by Sync Adapters
CalendarContract.ColorsColumns	Data Used for Calendar Colors Function
CalendarContract.EventDaysColumns	Data Used for Calendar Event Day Function
CalendarContract.EventsColumns	Columns (Joined) from the Events Database
CalendarContract.ExtendedPropertiesColumns	Data Used in Calendar Extended Properties
CalendarContract.RemindersColumns	Data Used for Calendar Reminders Function
CalendarContract.SyncColumns	Sync Info Columns Used by Other Databases

Next we will take a look at the new Android Contacts database structures, which are now referenced via the ContactsContract moniker (instead of just using Contacts), as of the Android 2.1 (Éclair) operating system version.

The Android ContactsContract Databases

The **ContactsContract** databases include a whopping 21 Contact data related database tables, which is not so surprising, as these days Contact management includes a myriad of information such as name, phone number, e-mail address, social media presence, status, display name, and so on. Table 19-3 shows the ContactsContract data provider interfaces, as well as the types of data that they access (and thus, which they will reference).

Table 19-3. ContactsContract Databases in the Android Provider Package and the Type of Data They Contain

Database	Description
ContactsContract.CommonDataKinds.BaseTypes	BaseTypes all Typed DataTypes support
ContactsContract.CommonDataKinds.CommonColumns	Common Columns across Specific Types
ContactsContract.ContactNameColumns	Contact Name & Contact Name MetaData columns, in the RawContacts Database
ContactsContract.ContactOptionsColumns	Columns of ContactsContract.Contacts that track the user preference for, or interaction with, the Contact
ContactsContract.ContactsColumns	Columns of ContactsContract.Contacts refer to intrinsic Contact properties

(continued)

Table 19-3. (*continued*)

Database	Description
ContactsContract.ContactStatusColumns	Data Used for Contact's Status Info
ContactsContract.DataColumns	Columns (Joined) from the Data Table
ContactsContract.DataColumnsWithJoins	Combines all Join Columns returned by ContactsContract.Data Table Queries
ContactsContract.DisplayNameSources	DataType used to produce Display Name
ContactsContract.FullNameStyle	Constant for Combining into Full Name
ContactsContract.GroupsColumns	Data Used for Contact's Grouping Info
ContactsContract.PhoneLookupColumns	Data Used for Contact's Phone Lookups
ContactsContract.PhoneticNameStyle	Constants for Pronunciation of a Name
ContactsContract.PresenceColumns	Additional DataLink Back to _ID Entry
ContactsContract.RawContactsColumns	Data Used for the RawContact Database
ContactsContract.SettingsColumns	Data Used for Contact's OS Settings
ContactsContract.StatusColumns	Data Used for Social Status Updates
ContactsContract.StreamItemPhotosColumns	Columns in the StreamItemPhotos Table
ContactsContract.StreamItemsColumns	Data Columns in the StreamItems Table
ContactsContract.SyncColumns	Columns that appear when each row of table belongs to a specific account

Next, we will take a look at the concept of deprecation, as it relates to Android databases, since some of you may need to use the old Contacts data structures to support ancient users of Android 2.0, or even 1.5 and 1.6.

Deprecated Content Providers: Deprecated Database Structures

As an Android (and any other type, for that matter) Developer, you need to be highly aware of the concept of **deprecation**. As you probably know by now deprecation happens when features, including classes, methods, interfaces, constants, or, in this case, databases, in a programming language (and, in this case, in an OS) have been discontinued in favor of newer features and general progress in the feature set (and subsequently, development power) of the programming environment over long periods of time.

The Contacts database is a great example of deprecation, so I am going to cover this topic in its own section just to make sure you understand how important it is to accommodate deprecated features in your programming work process.

If you reviewed the link to the Android Provider package in the previous section, you may have noticed when reviewing all that information that the original Android Contacts database structure was overhauled after API Level 5.

The nine databases that comprised the original Android Contacts database structure were replaced after API 5 with a new database structure called **ContactsContract** that we covered in the previous section.

Note that you can still use these databases if your Android app OS support goes far enough back, as the API Level 5 is equivalent to Android 2. There is a really informative section in the Android Developer website, which is called the **dashboards**. This shows you what **API Levels**, **OS Versions**, and even the **Percentage of Current Market Share** for each, so be sure and check this out when you have a moment, it is located at the following URL:

```
http://developer.android.com/about/dashboards/index.html
```

What this all means is that if you are supporting any Android device that came out before Android 2.1, that is, any Android 2.0, 1.6, or 1.5 device, then you would need to auto-detect your end-user's OS version, and provide code that uses the 9 Contacts databases instead of the 21 ContactsContract databases.

If you look at the dashboard in the previous link, you will also note that this support is **two-tenths of one percent** of the current market share, and that it may well not be worth the coding time and effort that is involved!

Content Provider Access: Adding Permissions in Manifest

The rest of the Android Content Provider information we will learn in the context of our Hello World project, as that is more fun, more productive and gets us working in Eclipse rather than just reading a book.

Open up your Hello_World Android project in Eclipse and right-click and Open the **AndroidManifest.xml** file, located near the bottom of your Package Explorer pane, as shown highlighted in Figure 19-1. In the central XML editing area click the **Permissions** tab at the bottom to open up the **Android Manifest Permissions Visual Editor**, shown in Figure 19-1 before we add permissions.

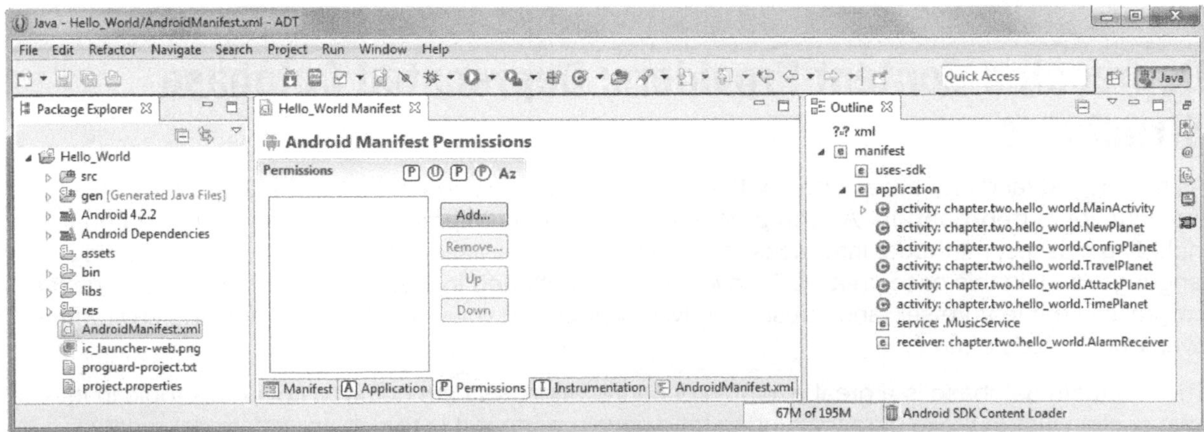

Figure 19-1. Using the Eclipse Permissions Editor tab to access the Android Manifest Permissions Editor

Click the **Add...** button to open up the dialog shown in Figure 19-2 that allows you to select the type of Permission tag that you want to add to your AndroidManifest.xml file. Select the **Uses Permission** option and click the **OK** button to close the dialog and return to the **Permissions Editor**.

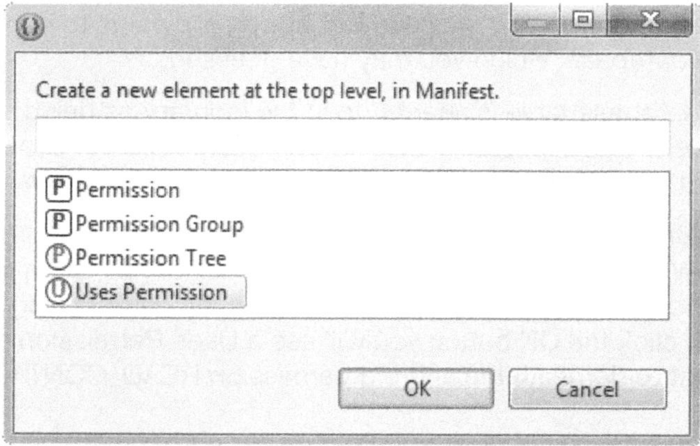

***Figure 19-2.** The Add Permissions dialog with Permission Types*

Now that we have the Uses Permission tag showing in the Permissions Column as shown in Figure 19-3, we want to configure that Uses Permission tag using the **Attribute for Uses Permission** column on the right. Find the **Name** drop-down menu and click the down-facing arrow and find and select the **android.permission.READ_CONTACTS** constant, as shown in Figure 19-3.

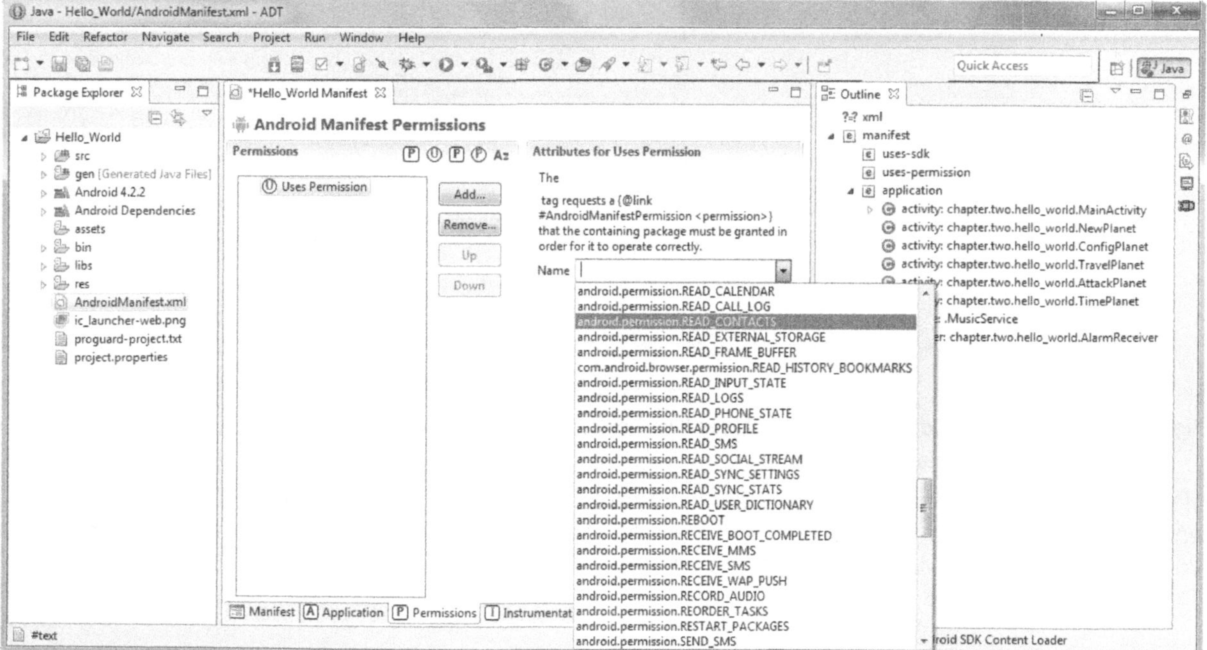

***Figure 19-3.** Adding READ_CONTACTS Uses Permission Attribute to Uses Permission tag via drop-down menu*

Once you select the **android.permission.READ_CONTACTS** constant you will see that the entry in the Permissions column, on the left side of the screen, will change to reflect the **<uses-permission>** tag's new **name parameter**. At any time, you can see what XML code is being written for you, by clicking the AndroidManifest.xml tab at the bottom of the central XML editing pane.

The **READ_CONTACTS** permission that we have just added allows us to perform READ ACCESS on the Android CONTACTS database, which you may have guessed.

A READ operation on a database table is referred to in the industry as being a **non-destructive** database access operation. This is because a READ operation does not change any data within the database, it just "looks at" the data (reads it), and possibly takes the read data and displays it in a user interface, depending on the Java code involved.

Next, we want to add a **WRITE_CONTACTS** database permission, so again click the **Add...** button, and select yet another **<uses-permission>** tag from the same dialog which we saw back in Figure 19-2. Once you click the OK button you will see a Uses Permission tag appear in the Permissions column, right underneath the android.permission.READ_CONTACTS, as shown in Figure 19-4.

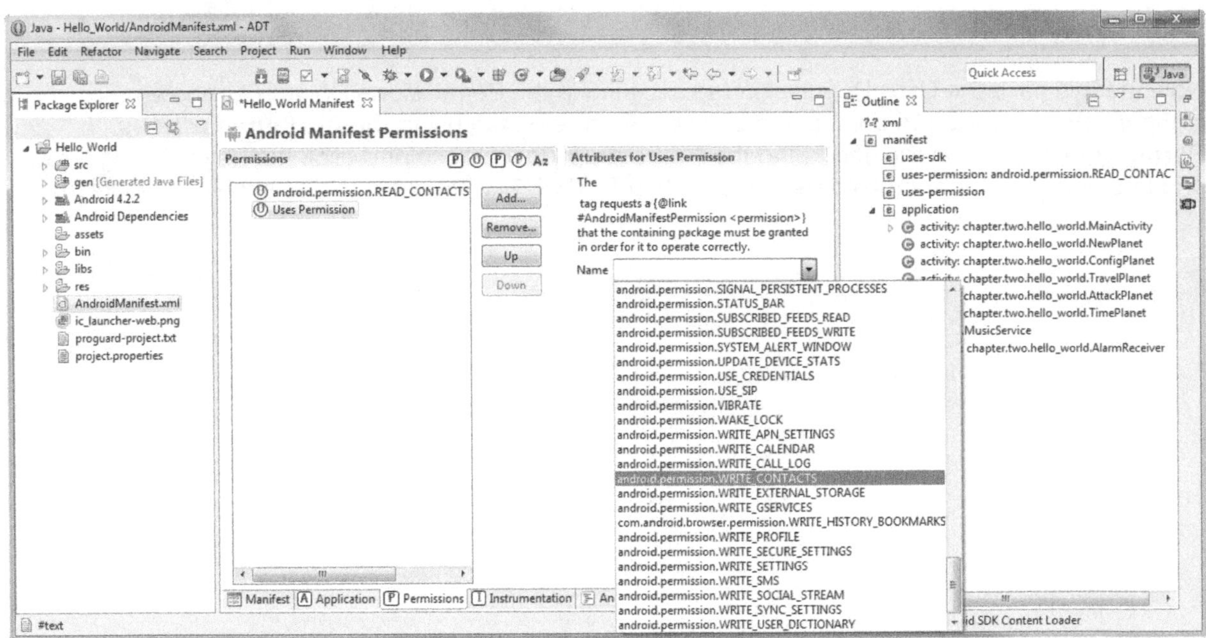

***Figure 19-4.** Adding a second WRITE_CONTACTS Uses Permission Attribute via the Name drop-down menu*

Next drop-down the Name menu and find an **android.permission.WRITE_CONTACTS** parameter and select that for your second <uses-permission> tag. To see the XML code that was written for you, click the AndroidManifest.xml tab shown in Figure 19-5.

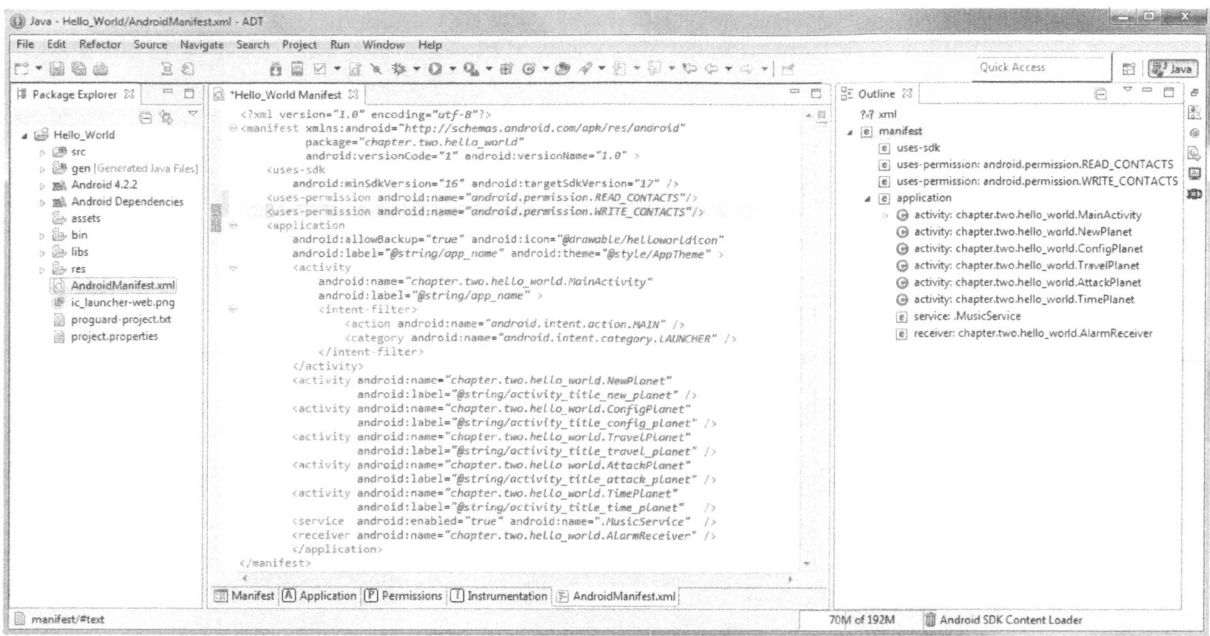

***Figure 19-5.** The AndroidManifest.xml file tab showing the XML mark-up for the two uses-permission tags*

It is important to note that to get the Permissions column to update from the Uses Permission icon to the WRITE_CONTACTS parameter, you must either click the Add… button, if you are adding more permissions, or click the AndroidManifest.xml tab, and then click the Permissions tab again to refresh the Permissions Editor Visual Editor and show the correct entry in the Permissions column on the left as shown in Figure 19-6.

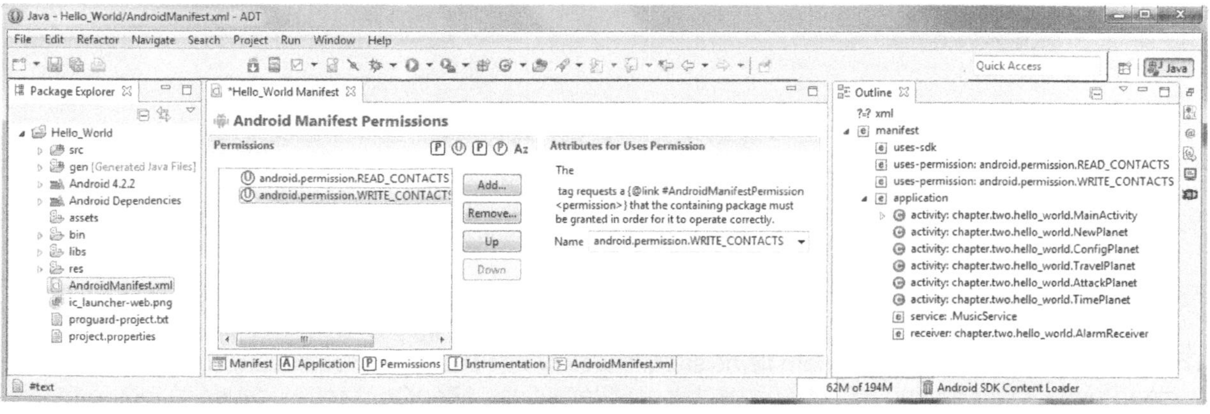

***Figure 19-6.** Eclipse Android Manifest Permissions Visual Editor showing the twp database access permissions*

Now that we have set-up our Permissions to Read and Write to the Contacts database, we can create our AlienContact.java Activity subclass that will hold our user interface design and our Make Alien Contact functionality.

Content Provider Activity: Creating an AlienContact Class

Let's create our tenth (and final) Java class in our Hello_World Android application, by right-clicking the project source (/src) folder, and selecting the **New ➤ Class** menu sequence to bring up the familiar New Java Class helper dialog inside Eclipse as shown in Figure 19-7.

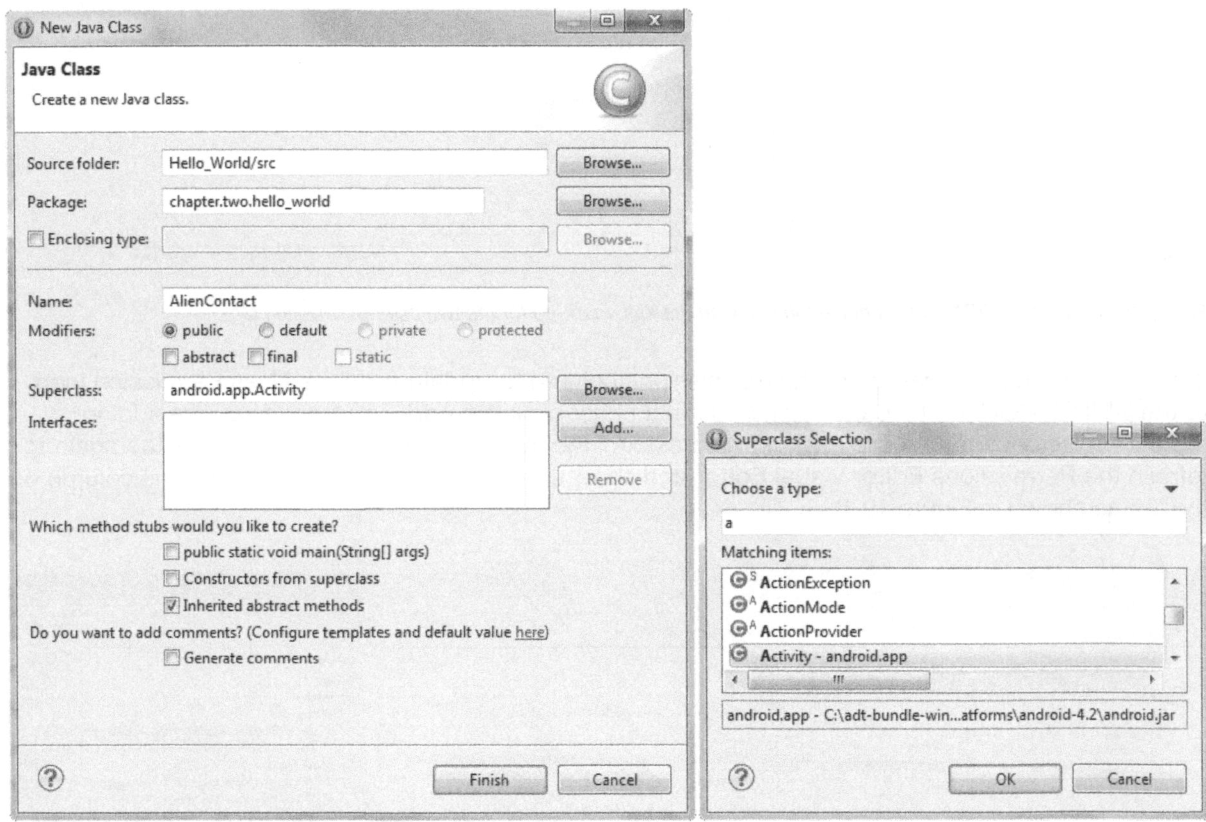

Figure 19-7. Creating a New Java Class called AlienContact.java with a Superclass type of android.app.Activity

The source folder and package data fields should already be filled out for you using your current Android project information, so let's name this new Java class **AlienContact**, because it's going to use the Contacts database to allow us to keep track of our Alien Contact on any new world we encounter.

Next click the **Browse...** button next to the Superclass field, so that we can specify an Activity Superclass type for our AlienContact.java Activity subclass. Once the Superclass Selection dialog appears, you can type in an "**a**" character in the top **Choose a type** field, and then find the **Activity - android.app** entry in the **Matching items** section of the dialog.

Once you click the **OK** button, your Superclass field should be set to the **android.app.Activity** package of classes, which implements all these Android Activity features in your new Java class. Once this is set you can click the **Finish** button to generate the code in Eclipse.

Next we will add our **.onCreate()** method basic code to create the Activity, and use the **.setContentView()** method to define a new **activity_contact.xml** user interface XML definition we will write to define our Activity screen.

We'll also define our Activity inside of our **AndroidManifest.xml** file, and give it an **android:label** parameter so that it has an Activity screen title.

Content Provider Activity: Prepare the AlienContact Class

Add your usual **protected void onCreate(Bundle savedInstanceState)** method with a call to **super.onCreate(savedInstanceState);** as we have done in previous chapters, and then also add a setContentView() method referencing the activity_contact.xml file, which we will create next. Here's the code:

```
@Override
protected void onCreate(Bundle savedInstanceState) {
    super.onCreate(savedInstanceState);
    setContentView(R.layout.activity_contact);
}
```

The new AlienContact.java Activity subclass and onCreate() method is shown in Figure 19-8. Notice the reference to our activity_contact.xml UI definition, which we are going to create next, is red error highlighted. Because we know that this reference is going to be defined and put in place soon, we can safely ignore this error in our Java code in Eclipse for now.

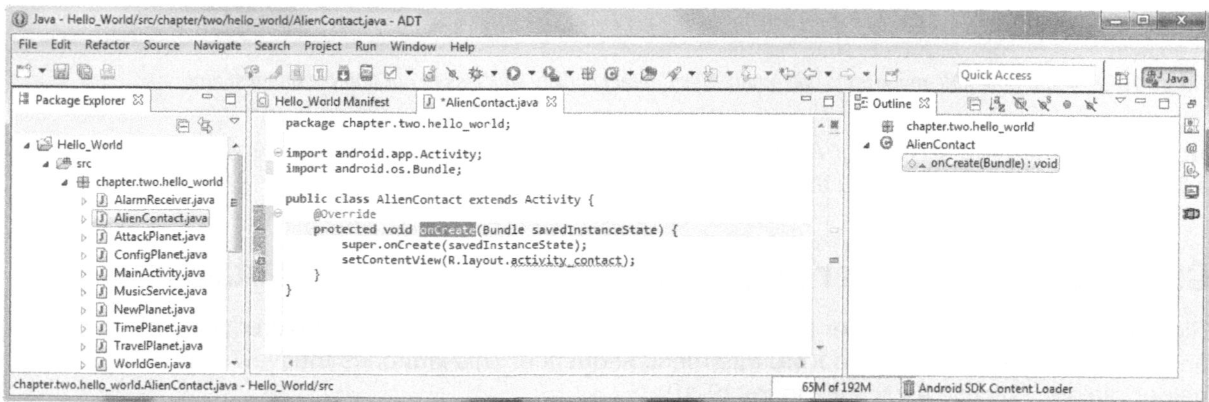

***Figure 19-8.** Creating our onCreate() method and referencing an activity_contact.xml UI layout container definition*

Next, we need to define our AlienContact Activity in our Android Manifest XML file, using an **<activity>** tag and **android:label** parameter, as we have done before to give our UI screen a title, as shown in Figure 19-9. Here is the XML mark-up that we will be adding at the bottom of our AndroidManifest.xml file:

```
<activity android:name="chapter.two.hello_world.AlienContact"
          android:label="@string/activity_title_alien_contact"   />
```

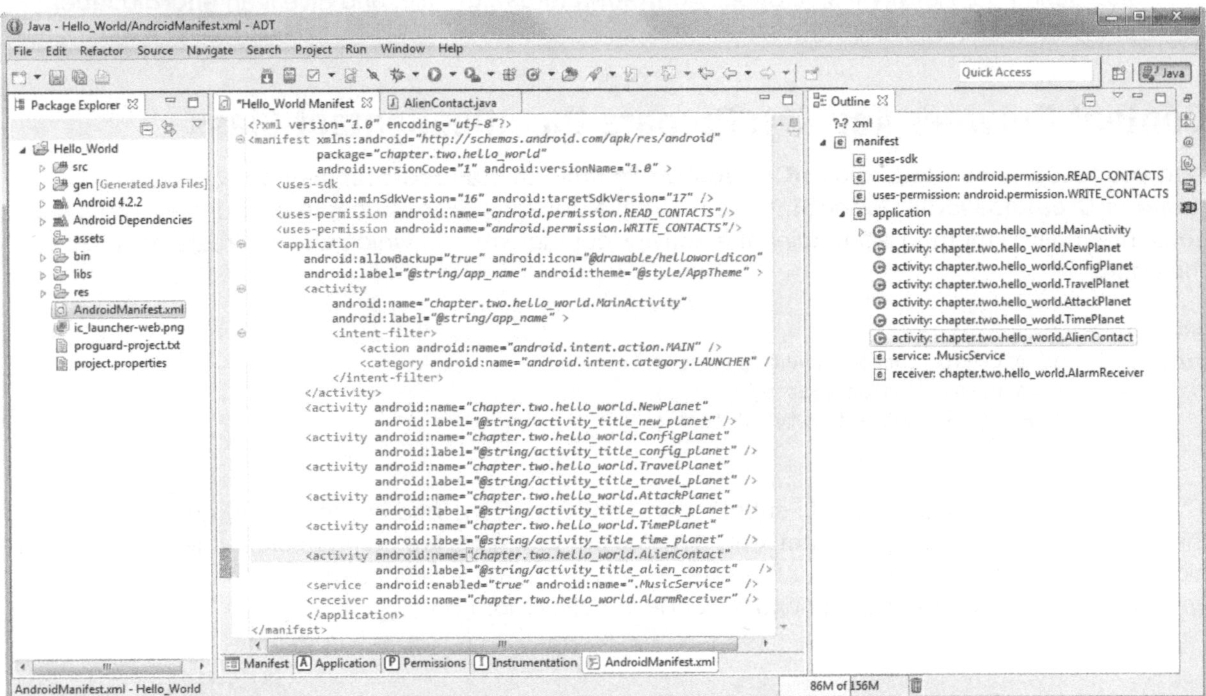

***Figure 19-9.** Adding the XML mark-up to add a new AlienContact Activity subclass to our AndroidManifest.xml*

Now we are ready to create our Activity user interface screen XML file, which we will call **activity_contact.xml** following the Android convention.

Content Provider User Interface: Creating activity_contact.xml

Right-click the /res/layout folder in your project hierarchy in the Package Explorer pane of Eclipse, and select the **New ➤ Android XML File** menu sequence. This launches the New Android XML File helper dialog, which is shown in Figure 19-10.

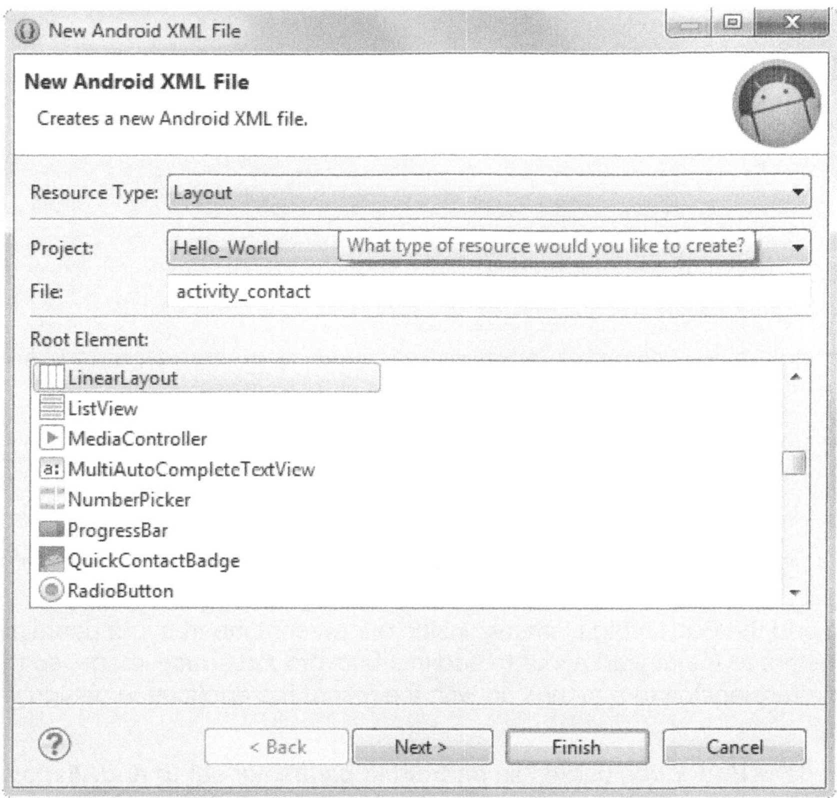

***Figure 19-10.** Using a New Android XML File dialog to create our activity_contact.xml file*

Select a Resource Type of **Layout** and a Project setting of **Hello_World**, and then name the file **activity_contact** and finally select a Root Element type of **LinearLayout** for your user interface design container.

The next thing that we will need to do is to add some string constants to our strings.xml file using the <string> tag. First, let's add the Activity screen title (label) string tag using the following XML mark-up:

```
<string name="activity_title_alien_contact">Hello World - Alien Contacts</string>
```

Next, let's add the three Alien Contact UI Button labels that we need to reference in our XML UI mark-up that we are going to write next. These would be written as follows and are shown at the top part of Figure 19-11.

```
<string name="find_alien_button_value">List Aliens in this Galaxy</string>
<string name="add_spock_button_value">Add Spock to my Alliance</string>
<string name="add_worf_button_value">Add Worf to my Alliance</string>
```

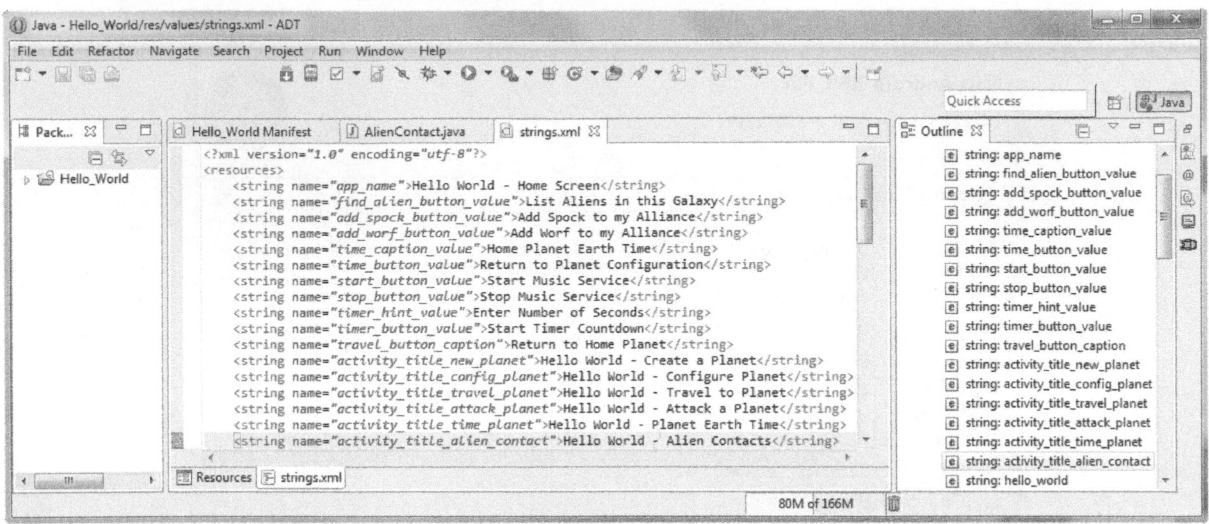

***Figure 19-11.** Adding the Activity screen title and user interface Button element <string> tags in strings.xml file*

Next we need to add the Button tag elements inside our parent LinearLayout container tag as well as adding parameters to the LinearLayout to add in a background space image, so that our user interface looks professional, and matches up with the rest of the application design we have used thus far.

The first user interface Button tag utilizes an **android:id** parameter set to **findAliens**, and features a text color of yellow or **#FFFFAA** and references the string constant that we created previously.

Additionally, we utilize an **android:layout_marginTop** parameter set to **40dp** to push our UI elements down from the top of the UI screen design a little bit, and an **android:layout_gravity** parameter set to **center** so that our UI elements center nicely in the middle of the screen design.

Finally, make sure that you have your default **android:layout_width** and **height** parameter set to **wrap_content**. Your Button XML looks like this:

```
<Button android:id="@+id/findAliens"
        android:text="@string/find_alien_button_value"
        android:textColor="#FFFFAA"
        android:layout_marginTop="40dp"
        android:layout_gravity="center"
        android:layout_width="wrap_content"
        android:layout_height="wrap_content" />
```

This first user interface Button element, as well as the next three, which we are going to generate using copy and paste operations to quickly create the remainder of our XML mark-up for this user interface design, are shown in Figure 19-12. Once we copy this XML definition and paste it three more times underneath itself we can modify the parameters to create new UI element tags for our buttons that will Add Aliens and Exit the Activity.

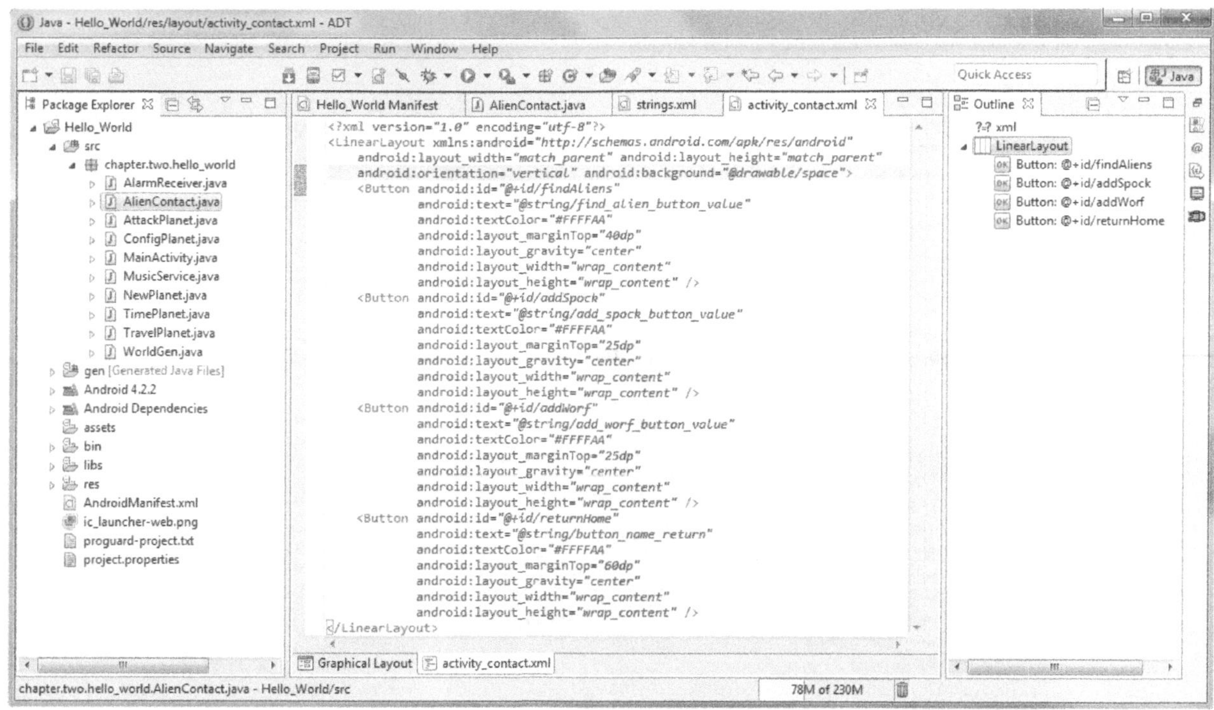

Figure 19-12. ***Writing XML mark-up to add four Button user interface elements into our LinearLayout container***

Let's do that now; copy and paste the **findAliens** (ID) Button tag three more times underneath itself, and change the **android:id** parameter from findAliens to **addSpock**, **addWorf**, and **returnHome**, respectively.

Next, change the **android:layout_marginTop** parameter to be **25dp** for the addSpock and addWorf Button tags, and to **60dp** for the returnHome Button.

We will leave the **android:textColor** parameter set to **#FFFFAA** or Yellow, and the **android:layout_gravity** parameter set to **center** and finally, the android:layout_width and height parameters set to **wrap_content** so that all our Button user interface elements are formatted uniformly.

Next let's use the **Graphical Layout Editor** tab at the bottom of the XML editing pane and see how our new user interface design looks. Because our last Button element that we edited was the returnHome Button, it should be selected in the view because that is where our cursor is in the XML text editing tab.

The visual results can be seen in Figure 19-13, and our design seems to look quite professional, and matches up well with our other five Activity screen designs. That means we are done with our XML user interface design mark-up, and we can proceed to work on our Java code to implement the functionality of our user interface design. We will be using Button objects along with their event handling methods, which will eventually contain our Java code which will access the Contact database structures stored inside of the Android operating system.

***Figure 19-13.** Previewing our activity_contact.xml user interface design in the Eclipse Graphical Layout Editor*

Next let's go back into our AlienContacts.java editing tab in Eclipse and add in the lines of code to instantiate each Button object and then attach event handling logic to it so we have a framework to trigger our database operations with.

Coding User Interface Elements in the AlienContact Class

First we need to write our first aliensButton Button object Java code for object creation and event handling and then we can copy it three more times underneath itself and create the other three user interface buttons.

The Java code to do this is shown in Figure 19-14 and has been copied to create Button objects for our aliensButton, spockButton, worfButton, and homeButton user interface elements, using the following Java code block:

```
Button aliensButton = (Button)findViewById(R.id.findAliens);
aliensButton.setOnClickListener(new View.OnClickListener() {
   @Override
   public void onClick(View v) {
      finish();
   }
}
```

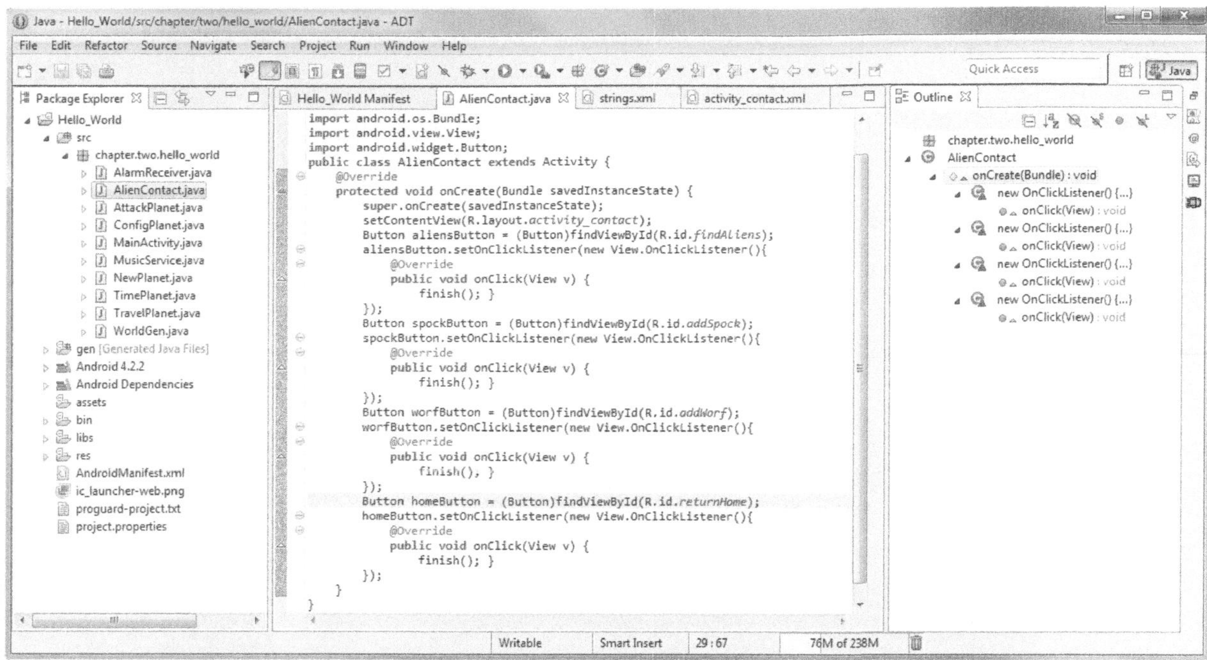

***Figure 19-14.** Adding Java code for our Button UI elements and their onClick() event handling methods*

We are using a finish() method call inside our onClick() event handling code block so that each button has a function (returns us to Home Screen) until we replace it with database related code later on in the chapter. This makes testing the Java code as we go along easier and error-free.

If you like you can use your **Run As Android Application** work process to launch the Nexus S emulator and see the user interface screen in all its glory and click each button to return to the app Home Screen.

Next we will code the aliensButton object so that it calls a **listAliens()** method which lists all the aliens in our Galaxy using the Toast class, so that all the alien names are broadcast to our user interface screen.

Using a ContentResolver: Coding Our listAliens() Method

The first thing that we need to do is to replace the finish() method call in our aliensButton event handling code block with a listAliens() method call. When you do this Eclipse uses a wavy red underline to highlight the fact that this method does not exist, as is shown in Figure 19-15.

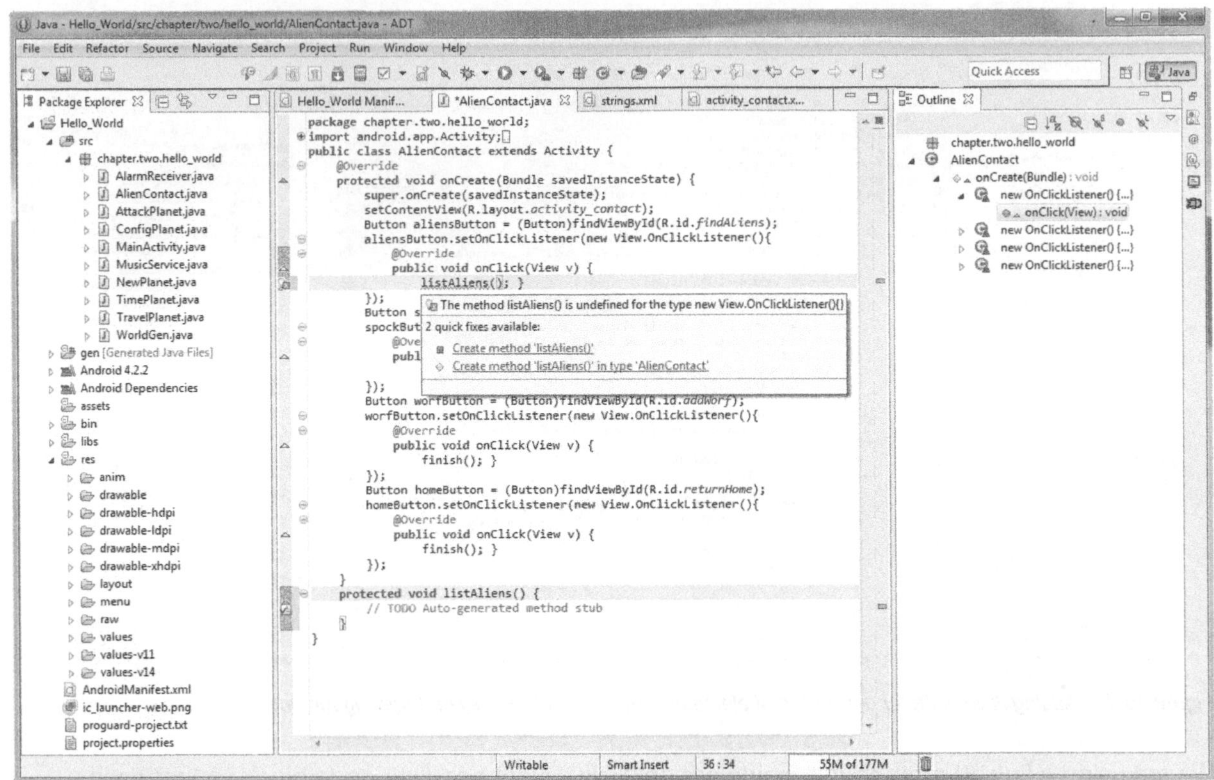

***Figure 19-15.** Adding listAliens() method call and Create method 'listAliens()' in type 'AlienContact' helper option*

Also shown in Figure 19-15 is the helper dialog that comes up when your mouse is held over this error highlighting, as well as the empty method that Eclipse writes for you when you select the second option named **Create method 'findAliens()' in type 'AlienContact'** and voila! Look at the bottom of your editing screen: the empty **listAliens()** method has appeared!

Now it is time to write our first database related Java code to access the Contacts database that we have requested permission to use in our Android Manifest XML file. In this case we'll initially be using the **READ_CONTACTS** permission, because we are going to read the Contacts database and then list all the Aliens in our Galaxy Alliance on the user interface screen.

First we use the Android Cursor class, used to navigate through database tables, and create a Cursor object named AlienCur (I was tempted to name this object alienCurse but resisted). In the same line of code we can load this Cursor object with the database table we want to traverse using the **getContentResolver()** method, using the following single line of Java code:

```
Cursor alienCur = getContentResolver().query(ContactsContract.Contacts.CONTENT_URI, null, null,
null, null);
```

This calls the ContentResolver class **getContentResolver().query()** method, which accepts parameters for the database URI that you want to query, as well as **projection**, **selection**, **arguments**, and **sort order**. Since we are just reading through the entire Contacts database, we are not going to use any of these other database access specifier parameters, and thus we use the **null** value (which serves as an unused indicator) in that parameter slot.

Now that we have created our alienCur Cursor object and loaded it with the database content that we want it to traverse and read, we can construct a Java **while statement** to read through all the records (fields) in this database table. Because we want the Cursor object to **.moveToNext()** or move to the next record while the while loop is still valid, we start off with:

```
while (alienCur.moveToNext()) { our while loop processing Java code goes in here }
```

Inside of the while loop, we have two Java statements, which process the database contents during the time that the while loop is running (valid). This is defined by the while loop's **condition**, which specifies that the contents of the while loop should be executed while the loop can still MoveToNext (while there is another record to READ in the database table).

The first line of code creates a String object named alienName to hold the data we are about to read and then sets it equal to the operation that actually reads the data from the database table using the Cursor object we created in the first line of code. The Java code to do this is as follows:

```
String alienName =
alienCur.getString(alienCur.getColumnIndex (ContactsContract.Contacts.DISPLAY_NAME_PRIMARY));
```

We set our **alienName** String object equal to a result from the **.getString()** method, called on the **alienCur** Cursor object, which gets its results from the **.getColumnIndex()** method that is called on the alienCur Cursor object.

As you can see, the parameter given to the Cursor object .getColumnIndex() method call specifies the data column (field) held in the primary display name database record. This is referenced by using the **DISPLAY_NAME_PRIMARY** constant, which is itself referenced via the **ContactsContract** database, and is located in the **Contacts** table. This is shown in Figure 19-16.

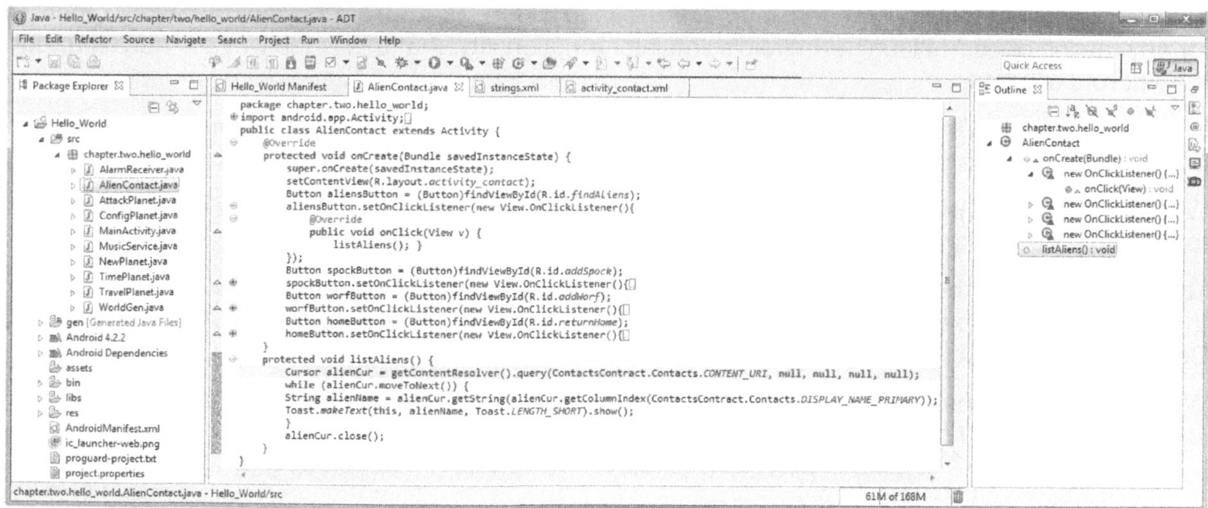

***Figure 19-16.** Coding a listAliens() method accessing the ContactContracts database using getContentResolver()*

Now that we have the data that we want to display, in the String format that we need it to be in, we can simply call the Toast object, via its .makeText() method, and display the data to our new user interface screen.

We will do this by using the following familiar line of Java code, which **chains** the **.makeText()** and the **.show()** methods one after the other off the Toast object. like this:

```
Toast.makeText(this, alienName, Toast.LENGTH_SHORT).show();
```

After entering the closing bracket, which ends our while loop definition, we'll finally need to **close** (remove the Cursor object from system memory) the alienCur Cursor object, which is currently holding our database data.

This Cursor object can potentially take up a significant amount of system memory, by the way, so it is quite important that when we are done, we use the Cursor class's **.close()** method to clear the Cursor object that we have defined out of the system memory.

This is done using one simple method call off the alienCur object. This is done using Java dot notation, and is shown in the following Java code:

```
alienCur.close();
```

Now we're ready to add Aliens to our Android emulator's Contact database, so that we can test the Permissions, Java code, and XML mark-up which we have just written in the previous sections.

Adding Alien Contacts to the ContactsContract Database

Assuming that you still have Eclipse open, launch the Android emulator, by using the **Window ➤ Android Virtual Device Manager** menu sequence. This work process launches the Nexus S emulator, without having the emulator load and run your Hello World application automatically.

It is also important to note here that if for some reason a **Run As Android Application** work process for any reason does not launch Android's emulator functionality, that this is the way to "**hard launch**" the Android emulator.

When the **Android Virtual Device Manager** dialog appears, select the Nexus S emulator option from the list of emulators we set up earlier in this book, and click on the **Start...** button.

When the **Launch Options** dialog appears, **uncheck** the Launch from snapshot, as well as the Save to snapshot option, and click the **Launch** button.

This then brings up the **Starting Android Emulator** dialog as well as a progress bar that shows the emulator being loaded and launched. Once it launches, you can then close the Android Virtual Device Manager dialog.

What you will see when the Nexus S emulator launches is a Smartphone Start Screen emulator, shown in Figure 19-17 on the left side of the screenshot.

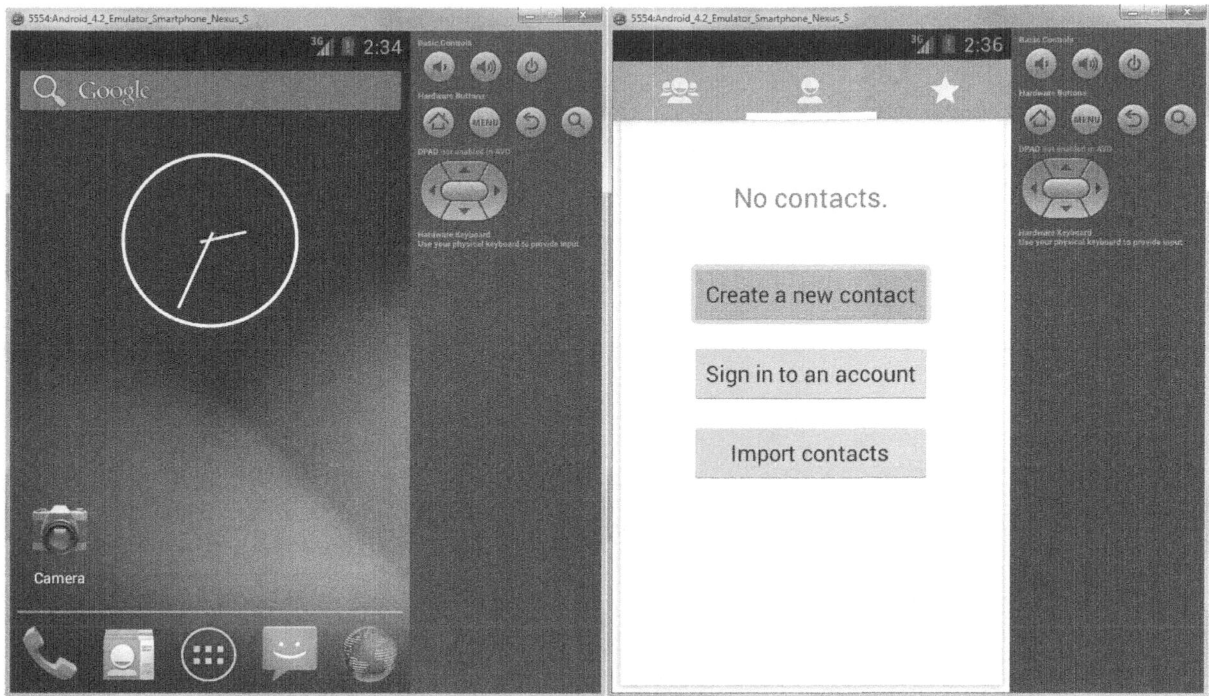

***Figure 19-17.** Using the Contact Database Icon (second from left bottom icon) to create new contact*

The utility for managing your Contacts database is so important that it is right there on the bottom left of your Smartphone Start Screen, indicated by a little talking head inside of a blue contact sheet icon simulation.

Click this icon to launch your emulator's Contact Management Utility, which is shown on the right-hand side of Figure 19-17.

Click the top button to **Create a new contact** in your Smartphone (emulator) Contacts database. This brings up a dialog that informs you that because you are using an emulator, the new contact information that you are about to enter will not be backed up since you are not using a real phone.

In case you want to use the emulator to create real contact database information that can be accessed by your real Android Smartphone account, the dialog then asks you if you want to add an account that would back up the contacts that you enter in the emulator on-line.

Because we are just using this as a testing application for the Contacts database code that we are learning about in this chapter, we are going to select the button option on the left that says "**Keep Local,**" so that the information that we enter is stored on our workstation's hard disk drive, and not "in the cloud" as it were.

This Keep Local dialog is shown in Figure 19-18, and once we select the Keep Local option, we will see the Contact Management user interface.

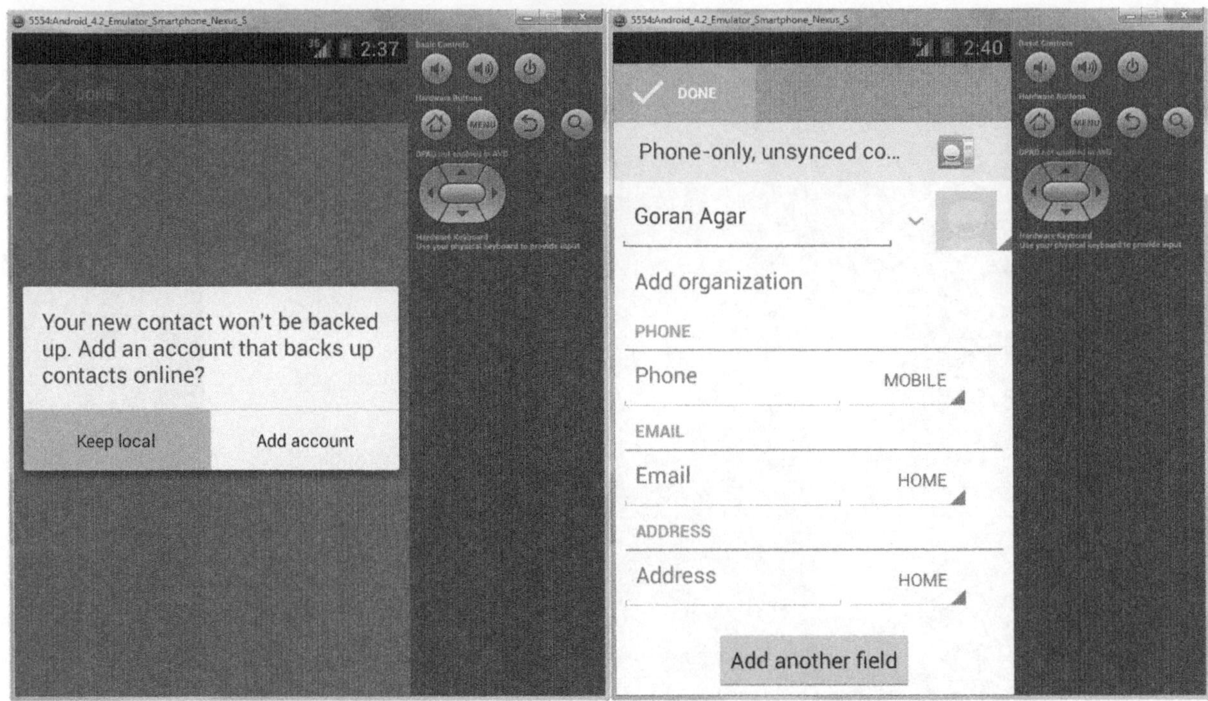

***Figure 19-18.** Keeping our Contacts Database local and adding a new alien named Goran Agar to the database*

Once the Contact Management screen appears, as shown on the right side of Figure 19-18, we will enter our first alien name, Goran Agar, one of the Jem Hadar race, featured on the popular *Star Trek* series.

Once you enter Goran Agar's name on the dark blue line located at the top of the user interface screen, click the light blue **Done** button located right above and to the left of the text entry field, as shown in Figure 19-18.

To see the entry you have just entered in your contacts database, click the left-facing arrow at the top of the screen and you will be brought to the Contacts database listing screen shown in Figure 19-19 on the left.

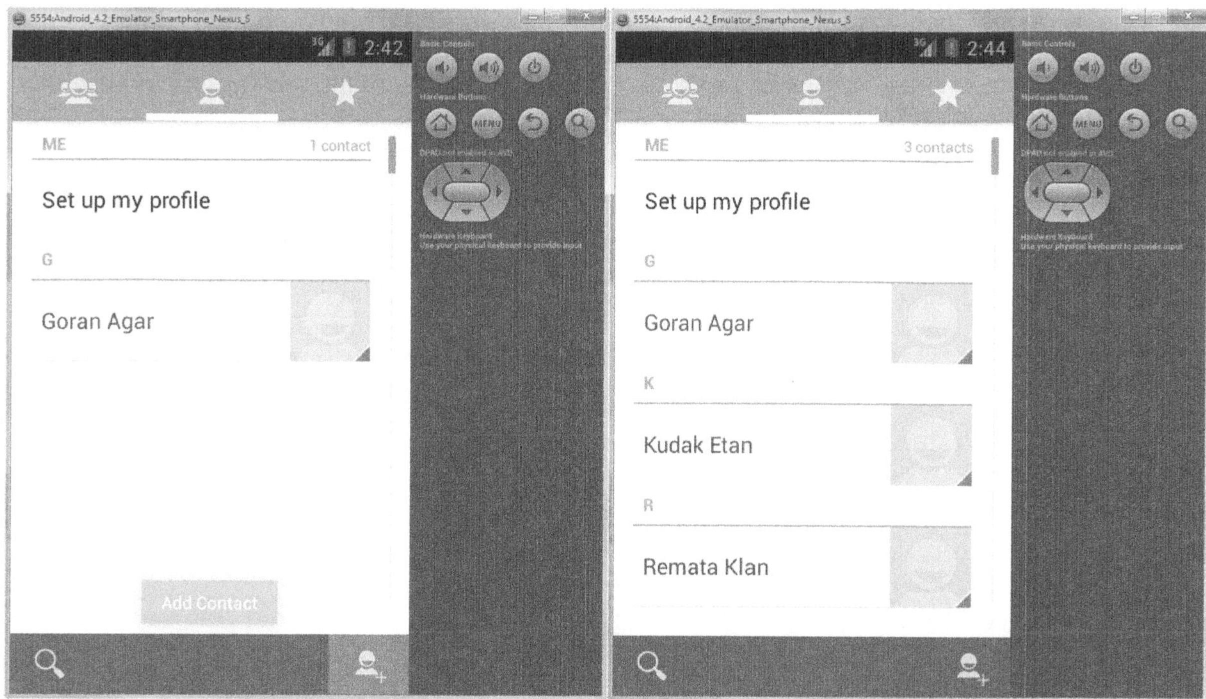

***Figure 19-19.** Viewing added alien contact, and repeating the work process to add Kudak Etan and Remata Klan*

On the bottom right of the Contacts database listing screen, which, at this point in time, only shows our alien friend Goran Agar, if you look closely, you will see a square gray icon of a head with a + symbol next to it. This allows you to add another contact to your Contact database, so click this icon now, and we will add some more aliens to our Galaxy Alliance.

Add two more aliens from the Jem Hadar race, named Remata Klan and Kudak Etan, using the same work process as outlined previously. Once you do this, the Contact Database List Screen should look like it does in the right side of the screenshot shown in Figure 19-19.

Now we have enough aliens in our Alien Contacts database to test our app!

Before we test our AlienContact.java Activity we need to be able to access it from our Home Screen options menu, so let's do that next so that we can test our listAliens() method now that we have the data in the (Alien) Contacts database to do this.

Adding the AlienContact Activity to the Home Screen Menu

The first thing we need to do to add a new options menu entry is to create a <string> constant in our strings.xml file for the menu label.

Following the format for our other menu string constants, let's create a **menu_contact_planet** named <string> tag with the menu label value of **Make Alien Contact**, and place it in the strings.xml file under our other menu string constants, as shown in Figure 19-20. Your XML mark-up for the <string> tag should look like the following:

```
<string name="menu_contact_planet">Make Alien Contact</string>
```

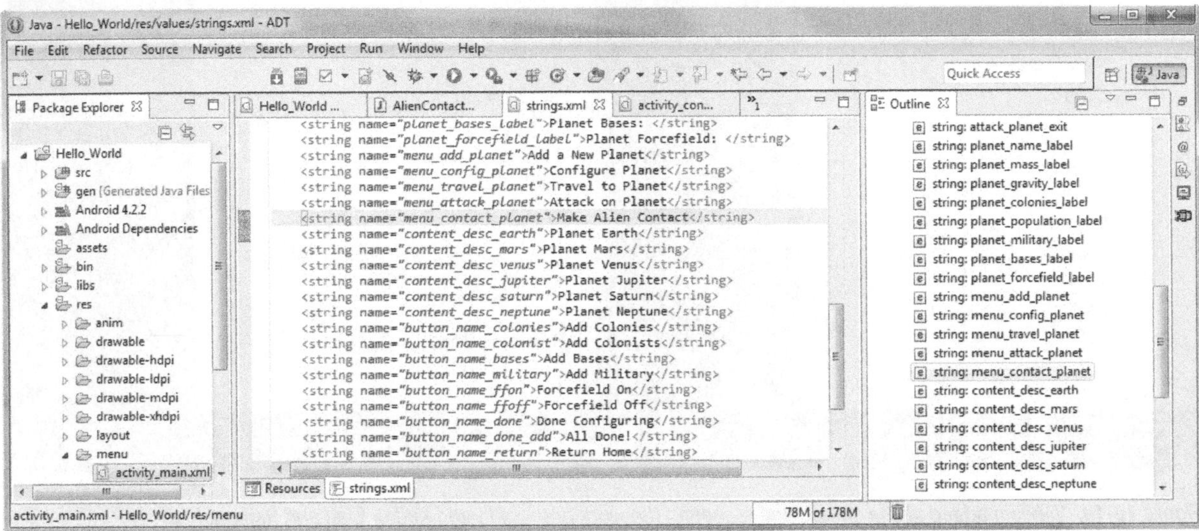

***Figure 19-20.** Adding a fifth menu item label Make Alien Contact named menu_contact_planet to our strings.xml*

Once this is done, we will be ready to change the placeholder fifth menu item entry in our **activity_main.xml** file in our **/res/menu** subfolder with the Make Alien Contact menu option that will call our AlienContact.java Activity subclass. Remember that there are two activity_main.xml files for our application, one in **/layout** for UI, and one in **/menu** for menu design.

Right-click the **activity_main.xml** file, in the **/res/menu** folder, and select the **Open** option (or select the filename in the Package Explorer and then hit **F3**). Edit the last placeholder item in the file to have an android:id setting of **menu_contact** and edit the android:title parameter to reference **@string/menu_contact_planet**, as is shown in Figure 19-21.

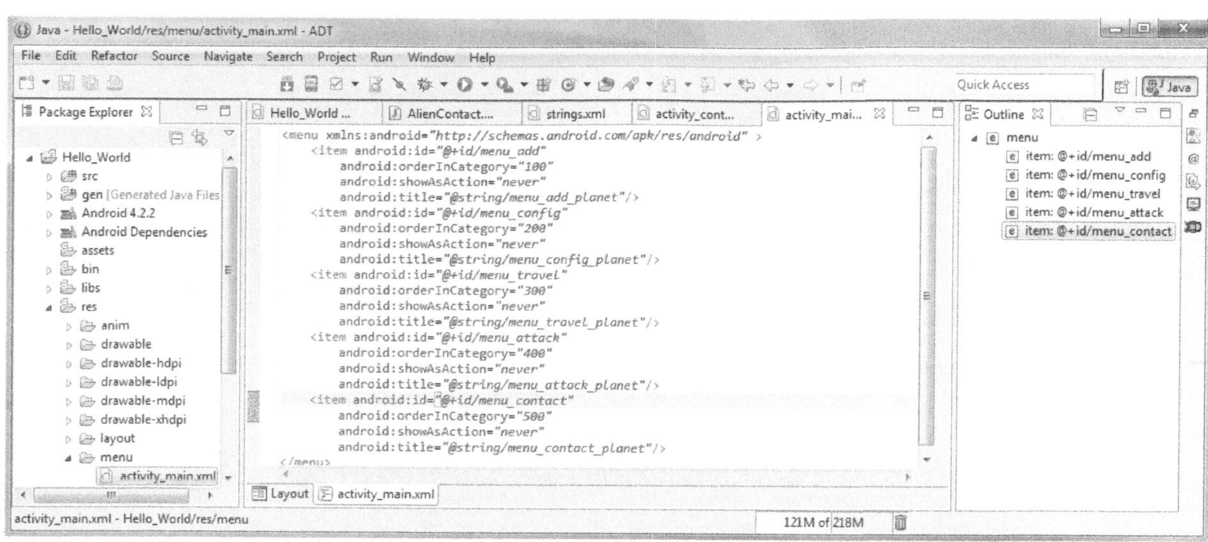

***Figure 19-21.** Changing our fifth menu <item> placeholder tag to menu_contact to access Make Alien Contacts*

Because our **onCreateOptionsMenu()** method already inflates our menu XML file definition, the next thing that we logically need to do is to modify our **onOptionsItemsSelected()** method, and add a **case statement** that handles the **menu_contact** ID and that launches our **AlienContact.java** Activity subclass.

Open your MainActivity.java Activity in the Eclipse central editing pane and close up all the methods except for onOptionsItemSelected() as shown in Figure 19-22. Then, add a **case R.id. menu_contact:** statement that creates an **intent_contact** Intent object, and sets it to call the new **AlienContact** class. Finally, call the **.startActivity()** method, using this Intent object, then use **break;** to exit this section of the case statement.

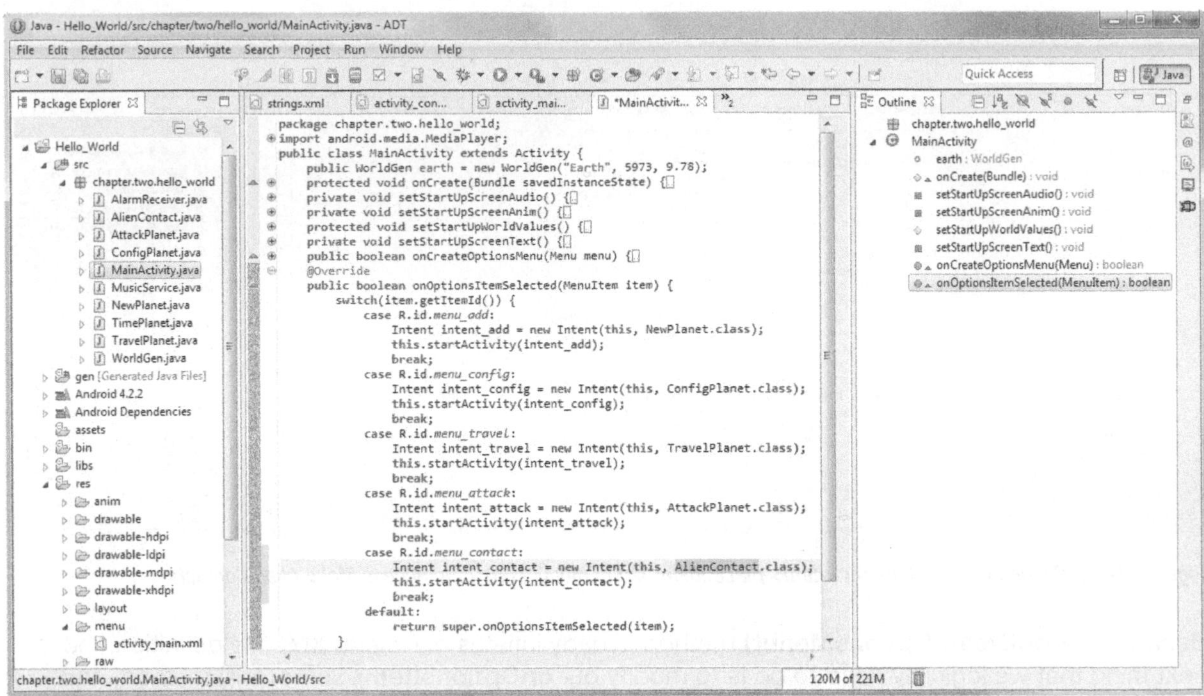

Figure 19-22. Adding a menu_contact entry in the switch() method case statement to open AlienContact Activity

The fifth menu item case statement code should look like the following:

```
case R.id.menu_contact:
    Intent intent_contact = new Intent(this, AlienContact.class);
    this.startActivity(intent_contact);
    break;
```

Now that we have enabled our user (and ourselves) to start the AlienContact.java Activity subclass, we can test our activity_contact.xml user interface design and our Java code that implements it, as well as the ContentResolver that will read our Alien Contacts database entries that we just created in the previous section.

Right-click your Hello_World project folder and then select the **Run As Android Application** menu sequence, or, if you prefer, utilize the **Window ➤ Android Virtual Device Manager** work process we used earlier in the chapter to launch the emulator.

Testing the listAliens() Method in the AlienContact Activity

Once the Nexus S emulator launches, find the Hello_World icon (Saturn) and launch the app. If you used the Run As Android Application menu sequence, this will be done automatically for you.

Once the Hello_World Home Screen appears, click the Menu button on the top right of the emulator, and bring up the options menu that we just created, as shown on the left-hand side of Figure 19-23.

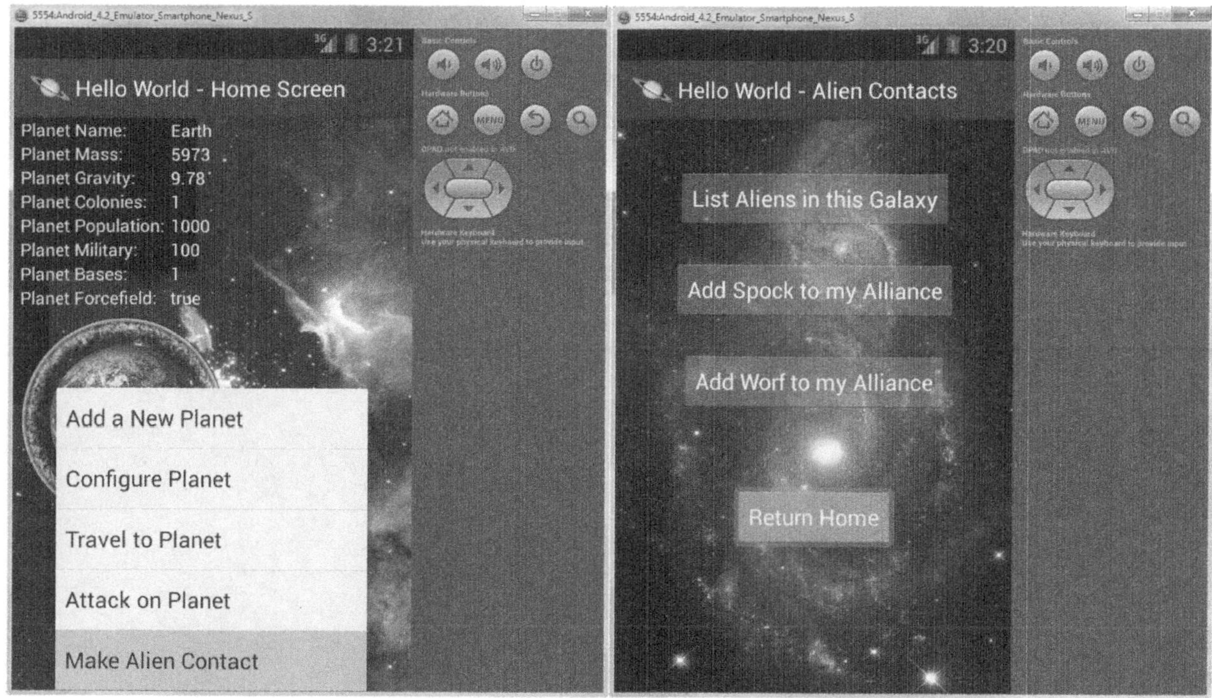

Figure 19-23. Select Make Alien Contact menu item to launch AlienContacts Activity Test Return Home Button

Select the Make Alien Contact menu item at the bottom of the menu and open the Alien Contacts Activity user interface screen shown on the right-hand side of Figure 19-23.

Click the Return Home button as well as the Add Spock and Add Worf buttons and make sure that they call the finish() method and take you back to the Hello_World app Home Screen.

Once you have tested those, click the Menu button in the emulator again, and enter the AlienContact.java Activity subclass, so we can test the **List Aliens in this Galaxy** button and make sure that it is traversing through our Alien Contacts database, using the Cursor object, and listing all our Alien Contacts from the elite Jem Hadar intergalactic race.

When you click the List Aliens in this Galaxy button as shown on the left-hand side of Figure 19-24, you will see the Toast messages appear at the bottom of the user interface screen, listing all three of the Jem Hadar race members in your Alien Contacts database.

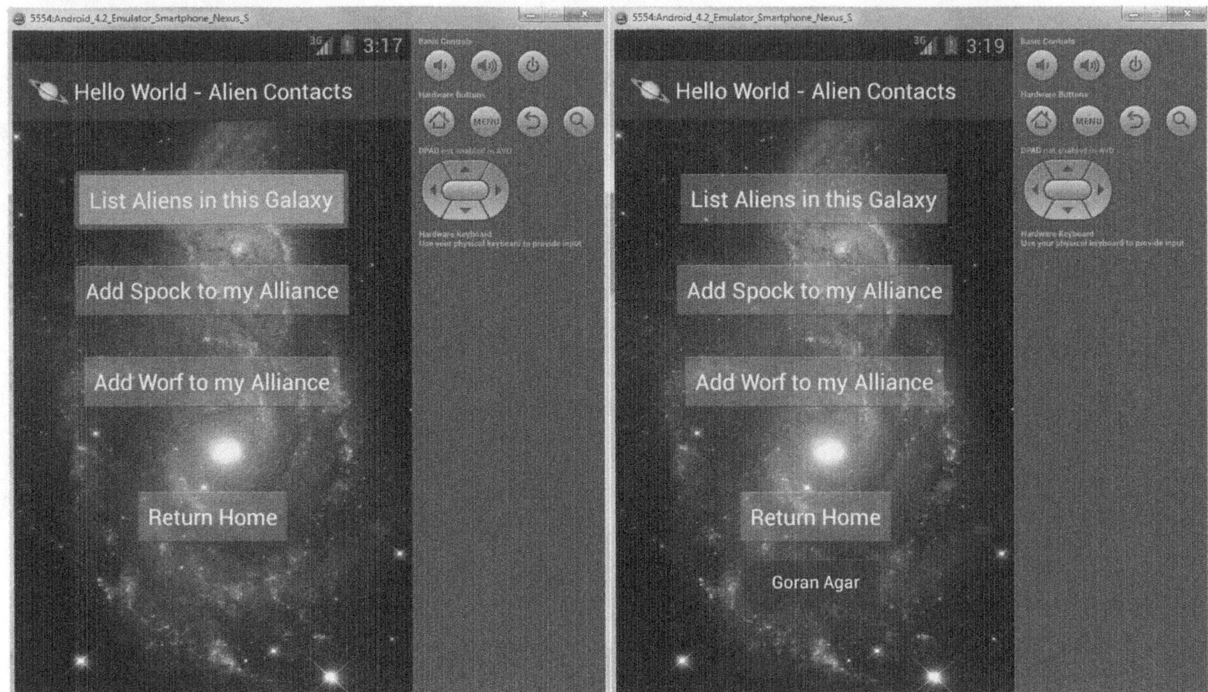

***Figure 19-24.** Testing the ListAliens method using the List Aliens in this Galaxy Button and its Toast messages*

The Toast message for Goran Agar is shown on the bottom right-hand side of the screenshot in Figure 19-24 so our ContentResolver Java code is working perfectly. Next, let's write another Java method called **addToAlliance()**, which shows us how to use the Android **ContentValues** class to enable us to add new Alien Contacts to our Alliance Database, by using our own custom Java code, rather than having to use the Android OSes' Contact Management Utility.

Android ContentValues: Code an addToAlliance() Method

Open up the AlienContact.java editing tab in Eclipse and replace the finish() method calls in the onClick() event handlers for the **spockButton** and **worfButton** code blocks with method calls to the new **addToAlliance()** method that we will be writing. The format for this method call passes a String parameter like this addToAlliance(String Value) so the line of Java code would look like this:

```
addToAlliance("Spock");
```

Once you have added addToAlliance() method calls for Spock and Worf, we need to code the **protected void addToAlliance(String newAlien)** method.

The first thing that we do in our addToAlliance() method is to construct a ContentValues object named **alienContact** using the Java new keyword, using the following single line of Java code:

```
ContentValues alienContact = new ContentValues();
```

After that, we can load the alienContact ContentValues object with the newAlien parameter String data that we passed into the method. We do this by using the **.put()** method, called off of the alienContact ContentValues object, with the first parameter directing where we want the data to be placed, and the second parameter being the data itself to be placed into that field. This is shown in Figure 19-25 near the bottom of the screen.

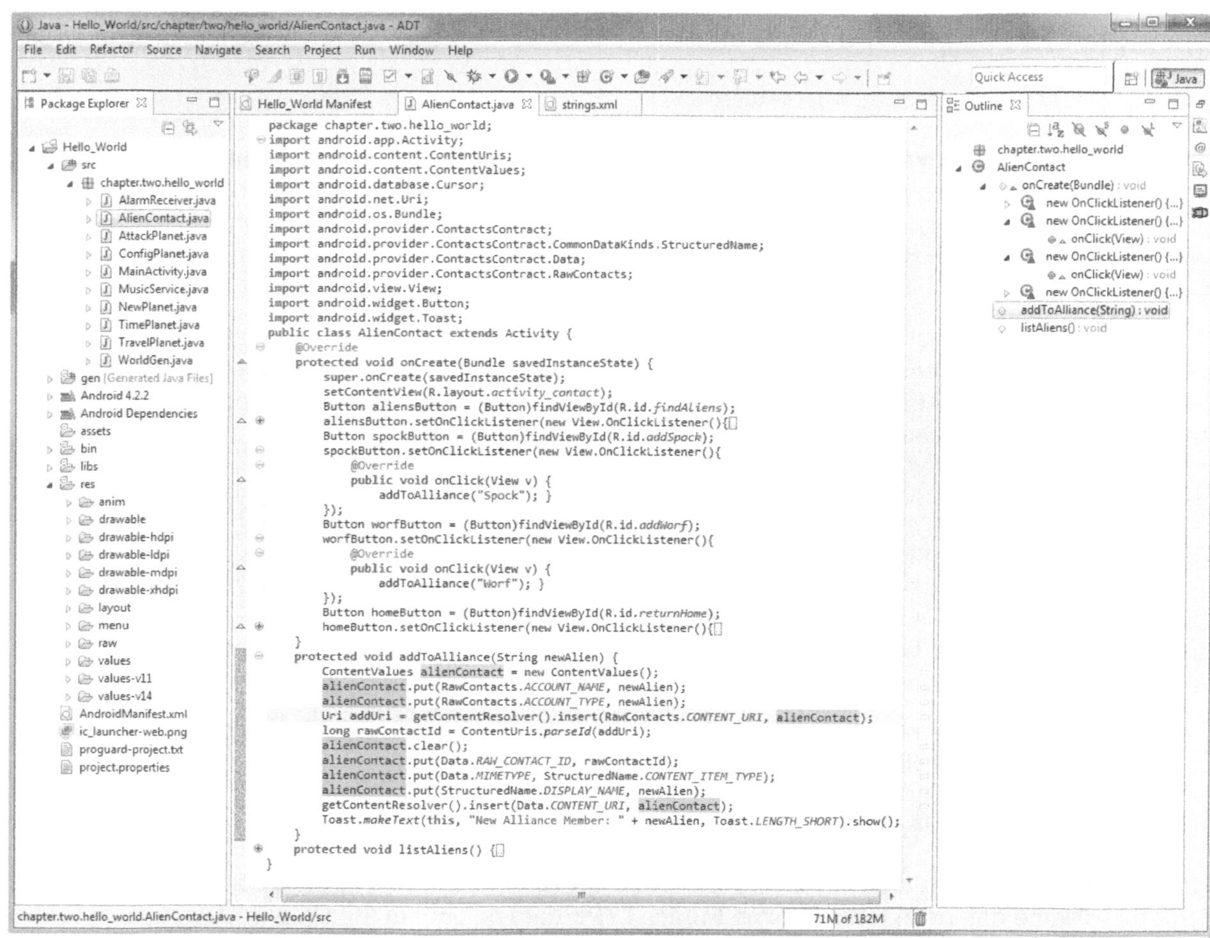

Figure 19-25. *Coding our addToAlliance() method to access the ContentValues class to add Aliens via .put()*

As you can see, this is done for the ACCOUNT_NAME and ACCOUNT_TYPE columns (data fields) in the **RawContacts** database table that we want to specify in the ContentValues object, by using the following two lines of Java code:

```
alienContact.put(RawContacts.ACCOUNT_NAME, newAlien);
alienContact.put(RawContacts.ACCOUNT_TYPE, newAlien);
```

Then we create a **Uri** object named **addUri**, and set that equal to the result of a **getContentResolver.insert()** method call, using the parameters for the database to WRITE to (insert data) and the data to be written. This is the RawContacts database, specified using the

RawContacts.CONTENT_URI constant and the **alienContact** ContentValues object, now loaded with our **newAlien** String data. This is done using the following single line of Java code:

```
Uri addUri = getContentResolver().insert(RawContacts.CONTENT_URI, alienContact);
```

Next we create a **long** variable named **rawContactId**, and set it equal to the result of a **ContentUris.parseId(addUri)** method call, which puts the **addUri** Uri object into long value format compatible with the **.put()** method we are about to call. This is done using the following single line of Java code:

```
long rawContactId = ContentUris.parseId(addUri);
```

Remember that as you type in this new database WRITE operation Java code, any Android class that you call or use, such as ContentValues, ContentUris, or ContentResolver that has not already been imported, that is, an import statement written for it at the top of the class (which, as you have seen, Eclipse will readily do for you) will be highlighted with a wavy red line underneath the offending method call.

Now that we have our database ID in the correct (long) numeric format in our variable **rawContactId**, we can now use the **.clear()** method to **clear** our alienContact ContentValues object, so that we can use it again, to WRITE more data values into the other databases which are interrelated with the Android Contacts database. The line of Java code should look like this:

```
alienContact.clear();
```

This is why database coding in Android is difficult; as I mentioned at the beginning of this chapter, it has to do more with the intricacy of how the database hierarchy is set up than the Java code that is used to access (or to write) the data. You are about to see that here, as we discuss how the rawContactId is used to write the same data you wrote into the RawContacts database table into the related Data and StructuredName database tables.

First we need to put the **rawContactId** value into the **Data.RAW_CONTACT_ID** database table, using the .put() method via this single line of Java code:

```
alienContact.put(Data.RAW_CONTACT_ID, rawContactId);
```

Then we need to put the data value that is in the **CONTENT_ITEM_TYPE** data column of the StructuredName database table into the **MIME_TYPE** data column in the Data database table, using the following line of Java code:

```
alienContact.put(Data.MIME_TYPE, StructuredName.CONTENT_ITEM_TYPE);
```

Then we need to put our **newAlien** String object (alien name) into the **DISPLAY_NAME** data column of the **StructuredName** database table, like this:

```
alienContact.put(StructuredName.DISPLAY_NAME, newAlien);
```

Finally we can insert all this data related to the RawContacts database that we have set up into the **Data** database table using the **CONTENT_URI** and **alienContact** ContentValues object that we have been building over the past several lines of code. We will again accomplish this by using our trusty **getContentResolver().insert()** method call, using the following Java code:

```
getContentResolver.insert(Data.CONTENT_URI, alienContact);
```

Now we are ready to Toast the end-user and tell them what we have just done so that they are aware that the newAlien has been added to the RawContacts (and Data) database table as a New Alliance Member. This is done using the following line of code, which chains two methods together:

```
Toast.makeText(this, "New Alliance Member: " + newAlien, Toast.LENGTH_SHORT).show();
```

Let's test our new **addToAlliance()** Java method via our AlienContact.java Activity inside the Android Nexus S emulator, to see if our new alliance members, Spock and Worf, are being added to the Alien Contacts database.

Launch the Nexus S emulator, and when the Hello_World Home Screen appears, click the Menu button, and select the **Make Alien Contact** menu option.

Once that Activity screen appears, click your **Add Spock to my Alliance** and **Add Worf to my Alliance** buttons, and make sure that the Toast messages appear at the bottom of the user interface screen. Looking great so far!

Now, all that we have left to do is to confirm that the Alien Contact data has indeed been properly added to the Android Contacts databases, as if we had done it using the Contact Management Utilities, which we used earlier.

If we wrote our database code correctly, then our new Alien Contacts data will be in the Android Contact Management Utility when we enter it next, just as if we had added it directly using that utility. If we did not write our database structures correctly, the data will not appear there.

Exit your Hello_World application and return to the Smartphone emulator Home Screen and click the Contact Management icon on the bottom left of the screen as we did earlier in the chapter. When your (alien) contacts list appears, you will see when you scroll down that Spock and Worf are now present and correctly alphabetized in your Contacts database listing!

Note that you can also use your List Aliens Button in your app to test to make sure these two aliens have been added as well if you like.

Summary

In this final chapter, we took a close look at one of the most complex and detailed areas in the Android OS: Data Access, Content Providers, and SQL Database Management Systems. This is a topic that really requires its own separate book, so pat yourself on the back, for a learning job well done.

We first took a look at database terminology and fundamentals, so that we are all on the same page. We learned about SQL and database tables and data rows (records) and data columns (fields) and how data is accessed via an ID or Key or Index.

We then took a look at the open source MySQL database technology, and the memory efficient version of this open source DBMS engine that is a part of the Android OS called SQLite. We learned about the SQLite data types and the caveats of working with SQLite inside of the Android OS.

Next we took an overview of Android Content Providers and Android Content Resolvers, and the different types of places that the Android OS can access stored data from, including preferences, memory, SD card, internal file system, internal SQLite databases, and remote data servers.

We then took a look at how data is accessed inside a database table using a Content URI. We looked at the different sections or parts of the Content URI structure, and put together some sample URIs and finally took a look at the conventions for using a Content URI inside of the Android OS.

Next we took a look at the most prominent Content Provider Java Interfaces which are exposed as part of the Android OS for the Contacts, Calendar and MediaStore functions that are so often used by users. We listed the various sub-tables for those databases and then took a look at deprecated databases that were used before Android 2.1.

Finally it was time to add Content Provider functionality to our own Hello World Android application. We added permissions to our AndroidManifest.xml file using the Visual Permissions Editor in Eclipse and then created an AlienContact.java Activity and all of the string constants, user interface designs, menu design and methods that were needed to implement reading and writing to a built-in Android Contacts database structure.

Finally, we learned about the Android Contact Management Utility so that we could test our database code and created methods that READ our Alien Contact database and WRITE new Aliens into our Alien Contacts database.

Congratulations, you have now finished the extensive introduction to the Android OS and many of its key features, packages, methods, and classes. Now be sure and practice what you have learned here, and build upon it by reviewing all the latest information on the Android Developer website.

Appendix A

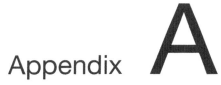

Building an Android IDE for Version 4.12 and Earlier: Acquiring, Installing, and Configuring an Android Development Environment

This appendix matches up closely with Chapter 1 of this book, in fact, it is the Chapter 1 of this book that I wrote when the Android OS was at Version 4.1.2, and there was no ADT Bundle, and thus the Android development environment had to be built from scratch on the developer's side of the equation. With the advent of Android 4.2, Google put everything together on their side and allowed developers simply to download one 400MB "ADT Bundle" that removed dozens of steps from the work process. These steps are contained in this appendix so that you can see what they are (were).

Reading through this appendix will give you some insight as to how the Eclipse IDE and Android SDK are tied together via the ADT Plug-Ins and Google Plug-In for Eclipse 4.2.

For this reason, some of the content in this appendix is the same as or similar to the content found in Chapter 1.

Fortunately for us Android App developers, very powerful 64-bit computers are readily available for a few hundred dollars. If you have a 32-bit computer, that will work just as well for Android App Development, as the Android 4.1 OS is also currently at 32-bit. Android 4.2 also added the option of running a 64-bit development environment across Eclipse and ADT, so users with 64-bit systems can now use 64-bit software for Android development, as of Version 4.2.

Additionally, most the software that we use for app development in this book is free for commercial use, also known as open source, so the cost of starting up your own Android Application Software Development business is quite low these days indeed.

Our Plan of Attack

In this appendix, we make sure that our system has the latest version of the Oracle Java 6 Software Development Kit (Java SDK, also known as the JDK or Java Development Kit) programming environment as well as the Android Software Development Kit (Android SDK). After our JDK is downloaded and installed, we will then download and install an Integrated Development Environment (IDE) called Eclipse.

Eclipse makes developing Android Apps easier by providing a slick Graphical User Interface (GUI), with which we can write, run, test, and debug our Android application code. Eclipse runs "on top of" the Java Runtime Environment (JRE), because Eclipse is written in Java, and thus uses the Java Platform to run its own code that makes up the Eclipse IDE user interface and feature set. This is the primary reason that we downloaded and installed the Java 6 JDK first, so that the Java SDK and JRE are in place on our workstation, so that when we get into installing Eclipse, it can find the Java Runtime Environment (so that Eclipse can launch or run), and so that it can use the Java SDK to build the programming code foundation for our Android Development Environment.

Once we have Eclipse installed and working smoothly on top of Java 6, we will download the Google Android Software Development Kit (SDK), and install that right alongside of the Java 6 SDK and Eclipse Juno 4.2 for Java EE. Once the Android SDK and ADT Plug-Ins are installed and configured properly, they will then modify (enhance) the Eclipse IDE with additional Android-related tools and features, all of which will essentially turn the Eclipse Juno 4.2 for Java EE IDE into a highly customized Android Application IDE.

As part of the Android SDK installation process (the second part), we will install the Android Developer Toolkit (ADT) Plug-Ins, which will live (plug-in) inside of Eclipse, and that will serve to "bridge" the Android SDK and the Java 6 SDK into a single cohesive Android software development environment. As part of this ADT installation process, which you need to be connected to the Internet to perform, your workstation talks with Android Software repositories on Google Servers and retrieves even more Android software APIs to make your Android Development Environment complete.

For a bird's-eye view, if this process were formulated into an equation, it would look something like this:

JDK 6 (Java 6 SDK) + Eclipse 4.2 IDE + Android SDK + ADT Eclipse Plug-Ins = Custom Android IDE

Let's get started with this long and involved process now, so we can get it over with and develop apps!

Foundation of Android Programming: Java 6

The Foundation of Android Application Development, both from a Programming and an Integrated Development Environment (IDE) standpoint, is Java 6. Android Applications are written using the Java programming language (and using XML as well, which we'll get into in more detail in Chapter 2), and Android Apps are developed inside of the Eclipse IDE, which is also written in the Java programming language, and which runs on top of the Java 6 Runtime Environment (JRE). To put it mildly, the exact order in which you set up the software components that make up your Android Development Environment is very important!

So that we have both the Java programming language, which we gain access to via the Java Developer Kit (JDK) , as well as the Java Runtime Environment (JRE), which is part of the JDK, we will go to the Oracle TechNetwork and download the latest JDK6 installation software and install it on our machine. We do this first because Eclipse needs Java to run, that is, Eclipse can be said to run "on top of" the Java Platform and Language. Android also requires Java, as well as Eclipse, for its Android Developer Tools (ADT) Plug-Ins, so we install the Java Platform and Environments first, then Eclipse, and then Android.

Installing the JDK

The first thing we must do is get to the Java SDK Download page. There are two ways to do this; one is generic, one is precise. The generic way, which will always work even if Oracle changes the location of its Java SDK Download page (which it probably won't), is to use Google Search with the keyword phrase "Java SDK Download" that should bring up the Oracle TechNetwork Java Download URL. The second way is to type the URL for the page directly into the browser. Here it is:

```
http://www.oracle.com/technetwork/java/javase/downloads/index.html
```

This points to the Internet (HTTP) and the Oracle website in their TechNetwork area (folder) in the Java area (sub-folder) for the Java SE or "Standard Edition" area (sub-sub-folder) in the Downloads area (sub-sub-sub-folder). There are three primary versions of Java: SE or Standard Edition for individual users, EE or Enterprise Edition for large collections of users, and ME or Micro Edition for mobile flip-phones. Most modern smartphones these days use Android and Java SE rather than Java ME. One of the really cool things about Android is that it uses the full Standard Edition of Java just like a PC does. This is because Android runs "on top of" a full version of the Linux OS Kernel, so an Android consumer electronics device is essentially a computer, for all practical purposes.

After you type in this URL, you arrive at the Java 6 JDK Download page, and you need to find the Java 6 JDK download portion of the page, which looks like the (partial) page section shown in Figure A-1.

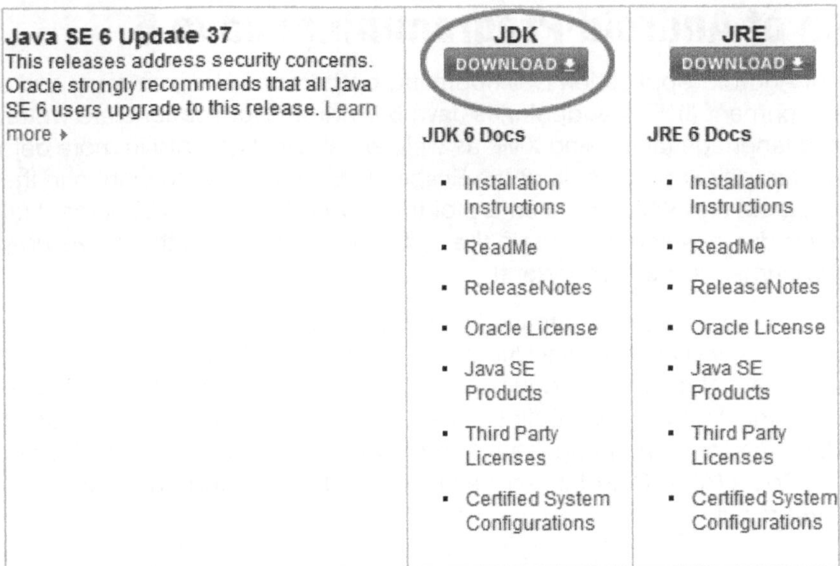

***Figure A-1.** The Java SE 6 JDK download section of the Oracle TechNetwork Java SE webpage*

Click the blue **DOWNLOAD** button under the JDK (remember, the JDK is *both* the JDK and the JRE) shown in Figure A-1 to go to the Java 6 JDK download page where you will accept the software licensing agreement and download the Windows 32-bit version of Java 6. Because Android SDK and ADT are currently 32-bit software, we will use 32-bit versions of Java 6 and Eclipse 4.2 for Java EE, so that everything is 100% compatible.

Remember that 32-bit software runs just fine on 64-bit OSes and workstations, so there will be no problems. Once Android SDK and ADT come out in 64-bit versions, we may eventually be able to put together a 64-bit Android Development Environment (believe me, I've tried to do it). Maybe Android 4.2 will use 64-bit Java 6 and Eclipse, if so, I'll include a chapter on assembling a 64-bit Android IDE, I promise.

Before you can download the x86 Windows 32-bit .exe file, you must click the radio button selector next to the "Accept License Agreement" option at the top of the webpage section, as shown in Figure A-2.

Java SE Development Kit 6 Update 37

You must accept the Oracle Binary Code License Agreement for Java SE to download this software.

Accept License Agreement   Decline License Agreement

Product / File Description	File Size	Download
Linux x86	65.43 MB	jdk-6u37-linux-i586-rpm.bin
Linux x86	68.44 MB	jdk-6u37-linux-i586.bin
Linux x64	65.65 MB	jdk-6u37-linux-x64-rpm.bin
Linux x64	68.71 MB	jdk-6u37-linux-x64.bin
Linux Intel Itanium	53.95 MB	jdk-6u37-linux-ia64-rpm.bin
Linux Intel Itanium	60.67 MB	jdk-6u37-linux-ia64.bin
Solaris x86	68.35 MB	jdk-6u37-solaris-i586.sh
Solaris x86	119.94 MB	jdk-6u37-solaris-i586.tar.Z
Solaris SPARC	73.36 MB	jdk-6u37-solaris-sparc.sh
Solaris SPARC	124.71 MB	jdk-6u37-solaris-sparc.tar.Z
Solaris SPARC 64-bit	12.13 MB	jdk-6u37-solaris-sparcv9.sh
Solaris SPARC 64-bit	15.42 MB	jdk-6u37-solaris-sparcv9.tar.Z
Solaris x64	8.45 MB	jdk-6u37-solaris-x64.sh
Solaris x64	12.18 MB	jdk-6u37-solaris-x64.tar.Z
Windows x86	69.72 MB	jdk-6u37-windows-i586.exe
Windows x64	59.73 MB	jdk-6u37-windows-x64.exe
Windows Intel Itanium	57.89 MB	jdk-6u37-windows-ia64.exe

***Figure A-2.** Accepting the Java 6 SE License Agreement and downloading the Windows x86 32-bit version .exe file*

Once you do this, the download links on the right become bold, and you can click them to download the installation file. Click the **jdk-6u37-windows-i586.exe** link (or whatever that latest update revision happens to be), and then download it to your Downloads folder on your workstation.

Before we install the current Java 6 JDK, we should check our system to make sure that no existing (older) versions of Java are already installed on our workstation. This is done in Windows via the Control Panel, which is accessed via the Windows Start Menu. Launch the Control Panel now, and find the icon labeled "Programs and Features" and launch the Programs and Features dialog shown in Figure A-3.

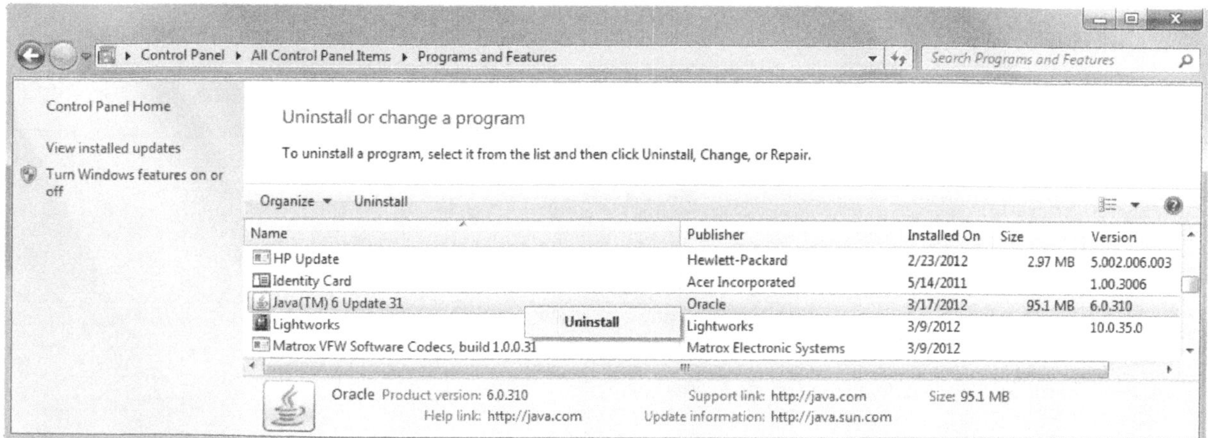

***Figure A-3.** Right-clicking the existing Java installation, and selecting the Uninstall option to remove it from your system*

Notice on my workstation that I already have Java 6 Update 31 installed. Because I want to install the most recent development software possible during this installation process, I am going to Uninstall the previous Java 6 Update 31 installation, as well as any older versions of Eclipse and Android (if they exist, which they didn't on this particular workstation) using the exact same work process. To do this you select the older version of Java and right-click on it and select the **Uninstall** option as shown in Figure A-3. Windows will then proceed to remove the older version(s) of Java (and Eclipse and Android if needed) from your system.

Now go into your Downloads folder (or your desktop, or wherever you put your downloads) and double-click the **jdk-6u37-windows-i586.exe** file to start the Java 6 installation. Accept the default settings for the installation, which should proceed fairly quickly if you have a modern day workstation with a fast hard drive and at least 3GB of memory. Once the Java 6 install is finished, you will be ready to download and install Eclipse Juno 4.2 for Java EE. Let's do that next, so that we have an IDE to use for our Android development.

Installing an Integrated Development Environment: Eclipse

Android's Development Environment is based on a unique and powerful piece of open source software called Eclipse. Eclipse is an IDE, or Integrated Development Environment, which is very similar to a word processor, but instead of publishing documents, it is used for writing, testing, and debugging programming logic. Eclipse supports a number of different programming languages, and the most popular (as you will soon see from the Eclipse download page) of those is Java. Fortunately for us, Java is what Android uses for its development environment, and thus that is what we are going to be downloading and installing.

The first thing we must do is get to the Eclipse IDE webpage, and there are again two ways to do this; one generic, the other precise. The generic way, which will always work, even if Eclipse changes the location of its webpage (which it probably won't), is to use Google Search with the keyword phrase "Eclipse IDE" that brings up the Eclipse website URL. The second way is to type the Eclipse website URL for the webpage directly into the browser. Here it is:

```
http://www.eclipse.org/
```

Once you type in this URL, you arrive at the Eclipse website home page, and you need to find the Eclipse IDE Download banner, which looks like Figure A-4.

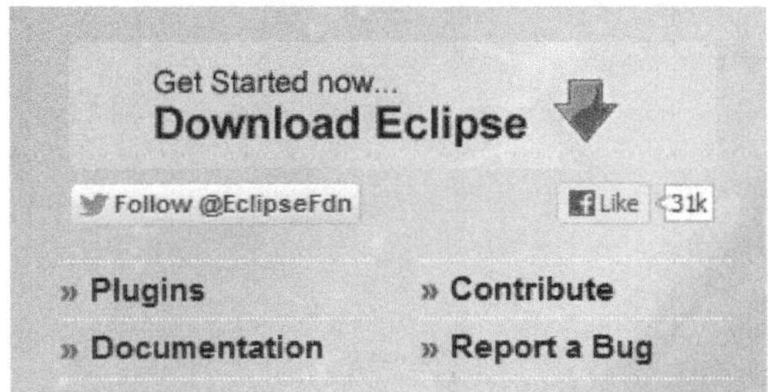

***Figure A-4.** Download Eclipse button found on the Eclipse home page*

Once you click the Download Eclipse button, it takes you to the Downloads page, where you select the first and most popular download, Eclipse for Java EE. Figure A-5 shows what the relevant (top) portion of the Eclipse Downloads page should look like, and shows where to click the 32-bit version download link.

***Figure A-5.** Eclipse Juno 4.2 IDE for Java EE Developers download link for 32-bit Windows version*

After you click the **Eclipse IDE for Java EE Developers** for Windows 32-bit link, you are taken to the download page for that version of the IDE (Eclipse Juno 4.2 Service Release 1 for Java EE 32-bit Windows XP, Vista, 7, or 8 version was the current version at the time this book was written). There you can download the Eclipse Juno JEE software from one of the mirror sites located nearby.

Once the 226MB download has finished, open your Windows Explorer File Navigation and File Management Utility, and find the .zip file in your system's Downloads folder. If you can't find it, put the name of the .zip file (shown in Figure A-6 for this download and install) in the Search box at the upper right, and select your Computer or C:\ drive on the left and the Windows Explorer finds the file for you.

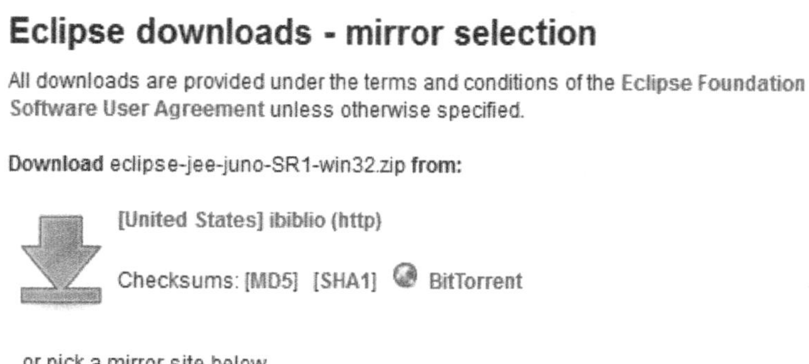

Eclipse downloads - mirror selection
All downloads are provided under the terms and conditions of the Eclipse Foundation Software User Agreement unless otherwise specified.
Download eclipse-jee-juno-SR1-win32.zip from:
[United States] ibiblio (http)
Checksums: [MD5] [SHA1] BitTorrent
...or pick a mirror site below.

***Figure A-6.** Download Eclipse JEE Juno Service Release 1 for Windows 32-bit ZIP file from one of the mirror site selections*

After you find the Eclipse Juno for Java EE installer file, right-click it to get a context-sensitive menu of everything that can be done to or with that file, and choose the **Extract All...** option to extract all the files and folders inside of the .zip archive onto your hard disk drive. This is shown in Figure A-7 circled in red.

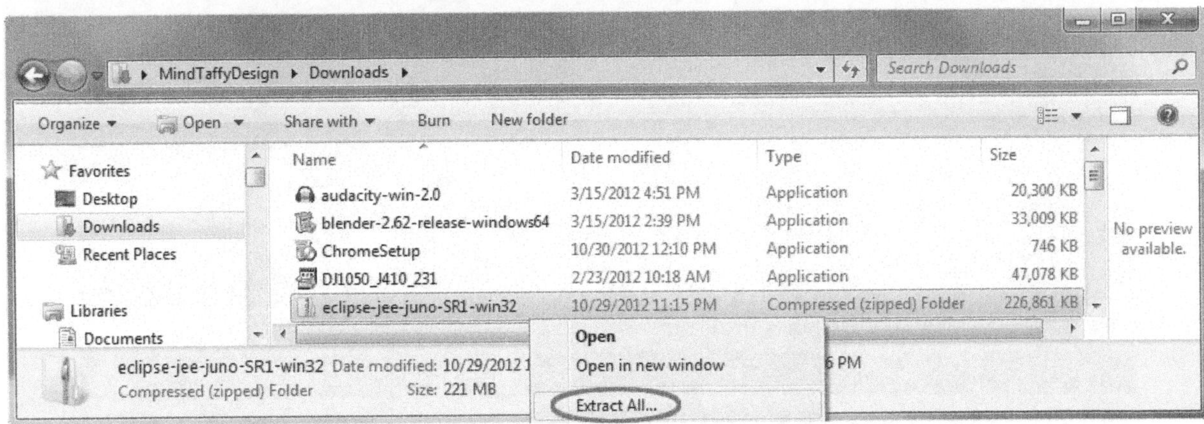

Figure A-7. Extract All files from the Eclipse .zip file by right-clicking the downloaded file in your Downloads folder

Next you see an Extract Compressed (Zipped) Folders dialog asking you to select a destination directory to extract the Eclipse files and folder hierarchy into. As shown in the top dialog of Figure A-8, the archive extraction utility places the current location of the file into your Downloads folder as its destination path, which is not surprising, as it really doesn't know where you want to put it, so it puts itself right where the .zip file is "standing" currently, so to speak.

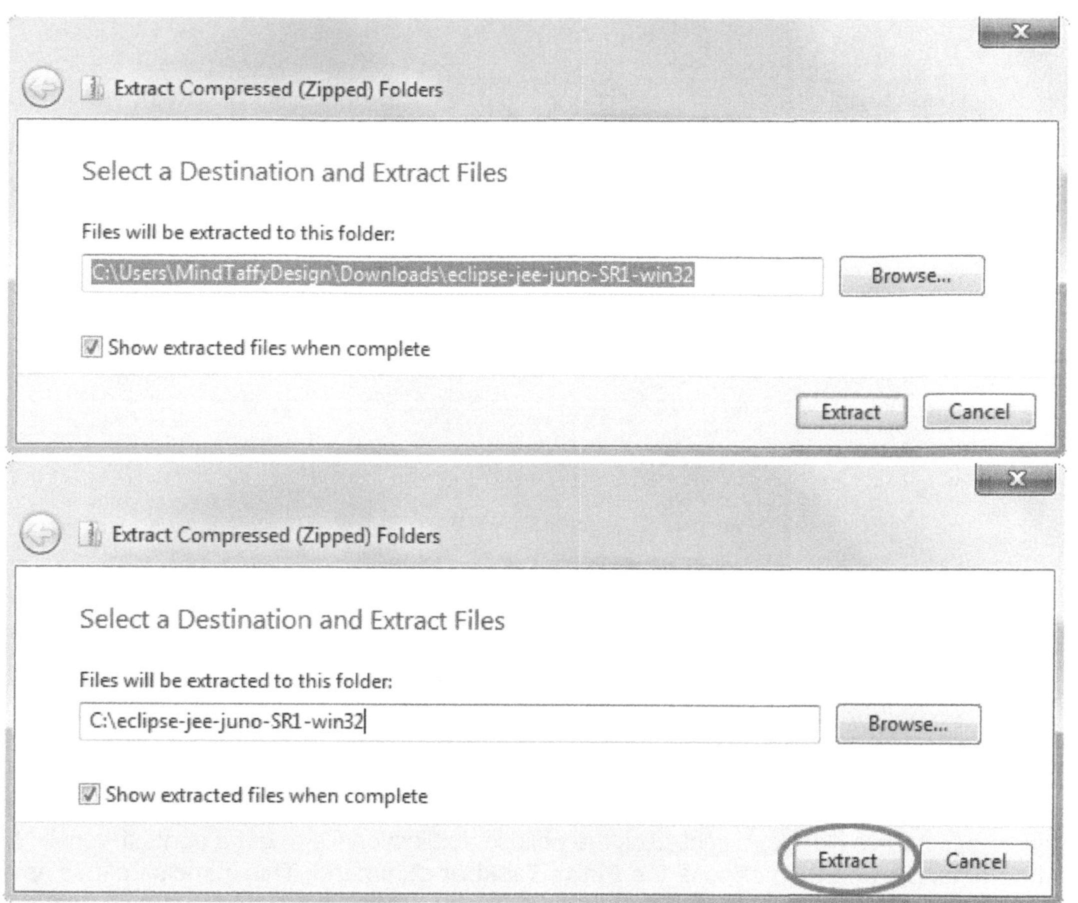

***Figure A-8.** Change Extract Compressed (Zipped)Folders Path from the Downloads directory to a higher profile C:/ (root) location*

Because we don't really want our Eclipse 4.2 for Java EE IDE installed in our Downloads folder (which we use primarily to hold file Downloads), the easiest work process to move it up to the top or "root" of our C:\ primary hard disk drive is to click the cursor right in front of eclipse in the filename, and to then backspace over the Users, (Your Name Here), and Downloads sections of the auto-generated pathname.

In this way, you end up with the C:\ hard drive specifier right in front of the eclipse .zip filename that you just downloaded as your folder name. This installs Eclipse JEE Juno in the root (top) of your C:\ drive, on your primary hard disk partition where you can easily see it and find it anytime you need to. The resulting path is shown in the lower part of the screen shot in Figure A-8.

Once you click Extract, you get a small progress dialog that shows you all the 3,427 items (250 megabytes) that are being rapidly copied to your hard disk drive. After this is complete, open your Windows Explorer file viewing utility, and find the eclipse.exe executable file.

To do this, open the C: drive on the left, and look for the eclipse-jee-juno filename that you downloaded and installed, and under that you will find the eclipse folder and its sub-folders, as shown in Figure A-9.

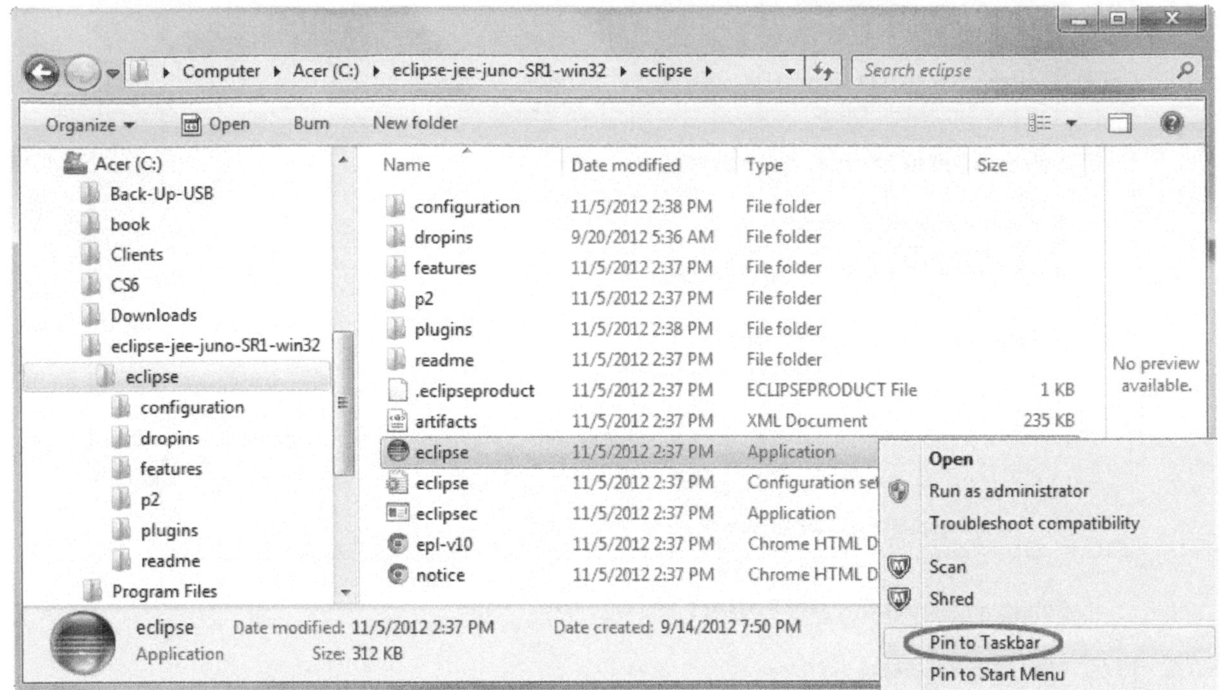

***Figure A-9.** Find eclipse.exe executable file and right-click to access the Pin to Taskbar option to create a launch icon*

Look for a purple sphere next to the word eclipse with a file type of Application and that is your Eclipse IDE software executable file. Next, right-click the Eclipse application file to get a context-sensitive menu of commands, and then choose the **Pin to Taskbar** command. This installs Eclipse as a Quick-Launch icon in your Taskbar Program launch area. This work process is also shown in Figure A-9.

Once you select the Pin to Taskbar command from the right-click menu, the Eclipse Juno purple sphere launch icon appears on your Windows Taskbar, which is usually at the bottom of the screen but which can be docked (via dragging) on the top or the left or right of the screen, as well. Figure A-10 shows the Eclipse for Java EE launch icon on my system along with other open source software (Gimp, Blender 3D, Audacity, Lightworks, OpenOffice, Chrome), some of which we'll be installing later on in the appendix.

***Figure A-10.** Eclipse Juno 4.2 for Java EE Launch Icon is shown on the left side of the Windows Taskbar*

Click once on the Eclipse launch icon and make sure Eclipse fires up; if it does, it means you have Java 6 installed correctly, and that Eclipse has successfully found Java, and is using it to run its integrated Java development environment. Now that we have Eclipse 4.2.1 working for Java development, let's go and get the Google Android SDK, and we'll use it to customize Eclipse to make Eclipse into a custom Android Development Environment as well as a Java SE and Java EE Development Environment.

Android SDK and Android Developer Tools

The Android Software Development Kit, or Android SDK, is essentially all the code and utilities that need to be installed inside of Eclipse so that the Eclipse IDE can not only be used for Java Development but can also be used for the more specialized Android Application Development as well.

Making the Android SDK and Android Developer Tools Plug-in a seamless part of Eclipse Juno 4.2 for Java EE is essentially a six step process:

1. Download the 70MB Android SDK installation file.
2. Run that installation and decompress 110MB of files onto your hard disk drive.
3. Run the Android SDK Manager, and pull even more API files over from a Google Android software repository.
4. Install the Android Developer Tools and the Google Eclipse 4.2 Plug-ins.
5. Check for even more software updates inside of Eclipse, once Android is "plugged in" to Eclipse.
6. Launch Eclipse and you see if you can create a new Android Application Project.

If you can create a new Android Application Project file, then you have succeeded in making Android a seamless, integral part of the Eclipse IDE, essentially making it into an Android IDE. At this point you can finish up by customizing your configuration, checking for the newest file versions and installing an emulator to use throughout the book for testing your applications.

First, get to the Android Developers webpage. There are again two ways to do this; one generic, the other precise. The generic way, which always works, even if Google changes the location of its Android Developer webpage (which it probably won't), is to use Google Search with the keyword phrase "Android Developer Website," which should bring up the `Developer.Android.com` website URL. The second way is to type the URL for the Android Developer webpage directly into the browser. Here it is (I suggest you memorize this one):

```
http://developer.android.com/index.html
```

Once you type in this URL, you arrive at the Android Developers website home page, and you need to find the **Get the SDK** button at the bottom of the page, which looks likes Figure A-11.

About Android | Get the SDK | Open Source | Support | Legal

Figure A-11. Selecting the Get the SDK button to go to the Android SDK Download page on the `Developer.Android.com` *site*

Once you click the **Get the SDK** button you are taken to the **Get the Android SDK** page where you see a large blue button that says: **Download the SDK for Windows** (or Linux or Macintosh, if you are using those OSes). Click this button to download the SDK installer .exe file, as shown in Figure A-12.

Get the Android SDK

The Android SDK provides you the API libraries and developer tools necessary to build, test, and debug apps for Android.

Download the SDK for Windows

Other platforms | System requirements

Figure A-12. Download the SDK for Windows button on the Get the Android SDK page on the `Developer.Android.com` *site*

After you download the file, use the Windows Explorer to locate it in your Downloads folder just like we did for Java and Eclipse and double-click the .exe file to run the installer (or use right-click and Open).

Once you launch the Android SDK Tools Setup installation you will see the Choose Install Location dialog shown in Figure A-13. Accept the default Windows Program Files Folder suggested by the Android SDK Tools Setup utility, which Google wants to see named **Android** with a sub-folder underneath it called **android-sdk**. The full path on a 64-bit workstation, such as the one I am using, will be: **C:\Program Files (x86)\Android\android-sdk** and on a 32-bit OS it would read **C:\Program Files\Android\android-sdk** instead.

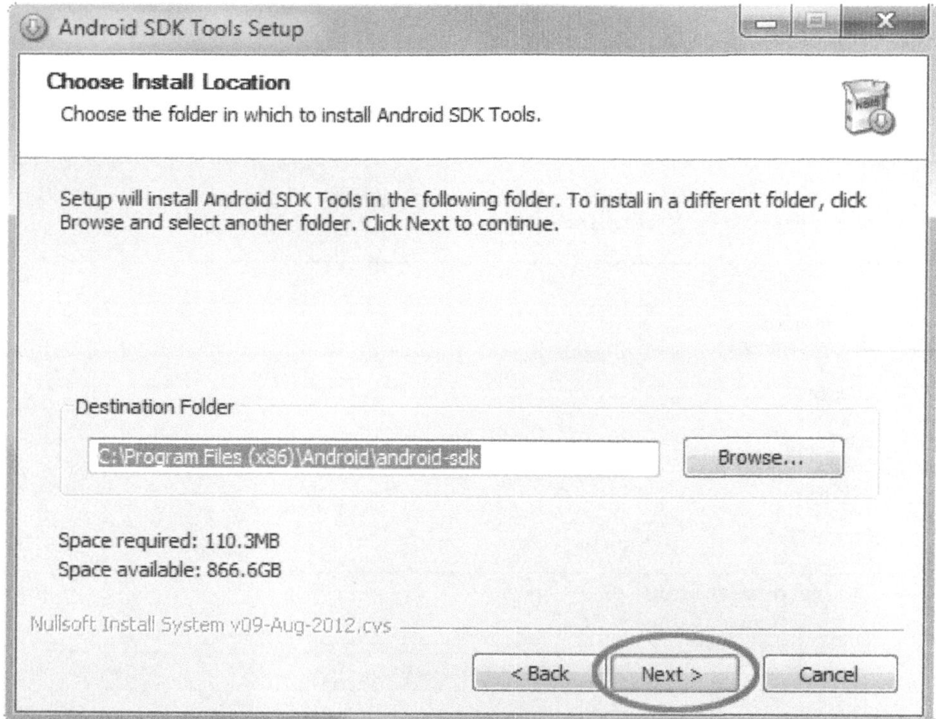

***Figure A-13.** Choose Install Location dialog of the Android SDK Tools Setup process showing default Android folder location and click Next*

This dialog also shows you the space required for the install, which is 110MB, as well as the space available on your hard disk drive (I have a 1TB HDD with 867GB still available). Note that you will need significantly more space than this to install the rest of the Android APIs and Documentation, so make sure you have plenty of gigabytes of free space on your hard disk drive via this space available indicator.

Once you click Next, you will see the Choose Start Menu Folder dialog, which I also recommend that you accept the default folder name Android selects for you, which is **Android SDK Tools**, as shown in Figure A-14. Now you are ready to click the Install button and start the Google Android SDK installation.

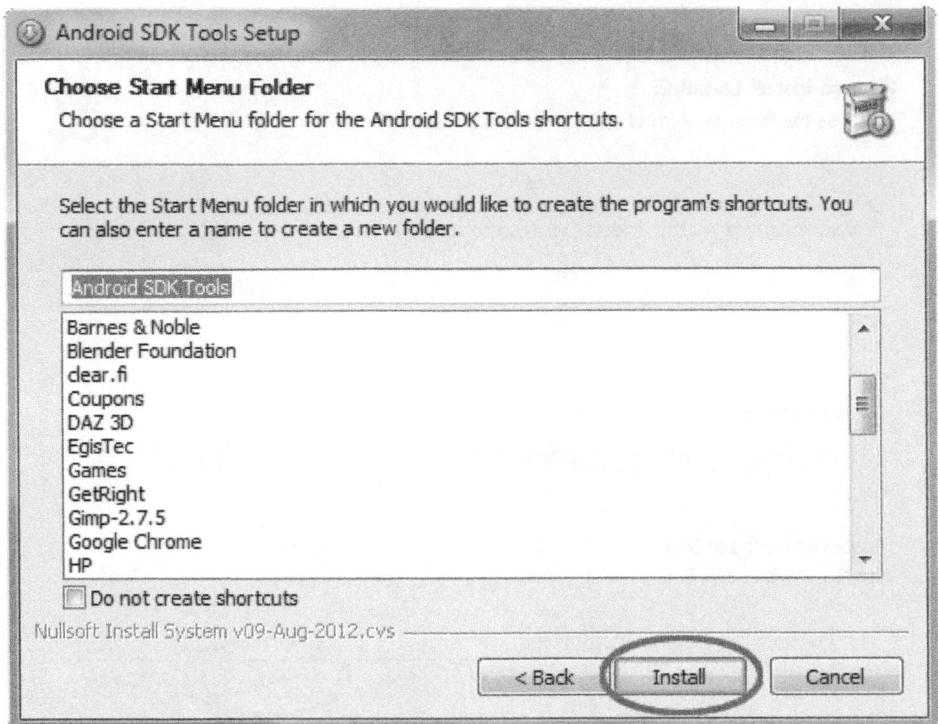

***Figure A-14.** Choose Start Menu Folder dialog in Android SDK Tools Setup process showing default Android SDK Tools folder*

Once the 110MB of Android SDK files finish installing on your system, a dialog called **Completing the Android SDK Tools Setup Wizard** appears, as shown in Figure A-15. Be sure and leave the **Start SDK Manager** checkbox selected, so that once you click the **Finish** button the Android Developer Tools (ADT) Plug-Ins and the Google Eclipse 4.2 Plug-In can be installed.

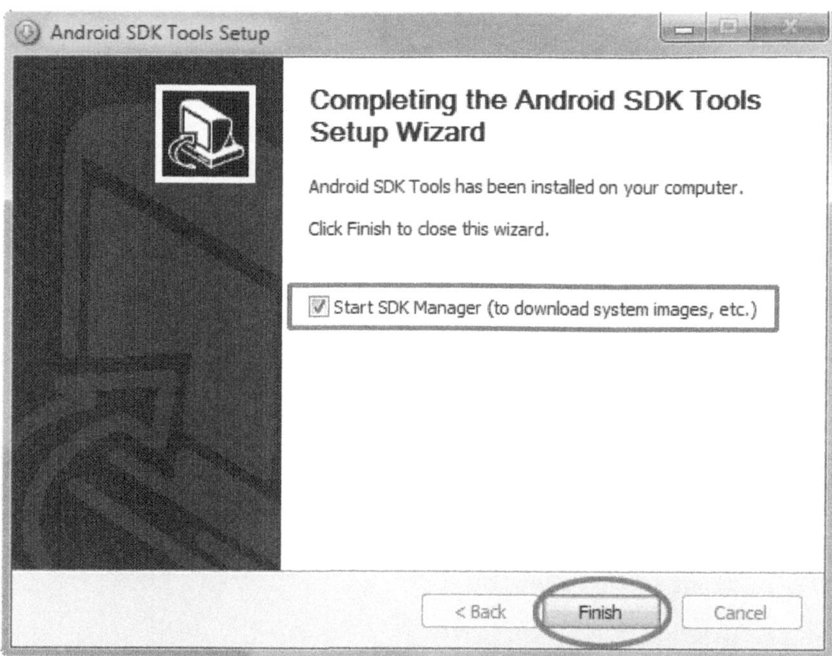

Figure A-15. Start SDK Manager dialog in the Android SDK Tools Setup process (leave checked and click Finish button)

This can be a bit confusing, because you are clicking a Finish button, but you are not even close to being finished yet! Google is finished installing the downloaded "bootstrap" files for the Android SDK, but the SDK Manager ends up doing the real heavy lifting next, by installing significantly more files over the Internet from the Google Android Repository residing on their massive server farms in the Silicon Valley.

In any event, go ahead and click the **Finish** button, and start the Android SDK Manager utility window shown in Figure A-16. Notice that Android SDK Manager pre-selects the current Android 4.1 OS API Level 16 files for automatic installation. The Android Developer website also recommends installing two other packages listed on this screen (I am not sure why they are not also checked as default installs), shown circled (red squared, actually) in Figure A-16.

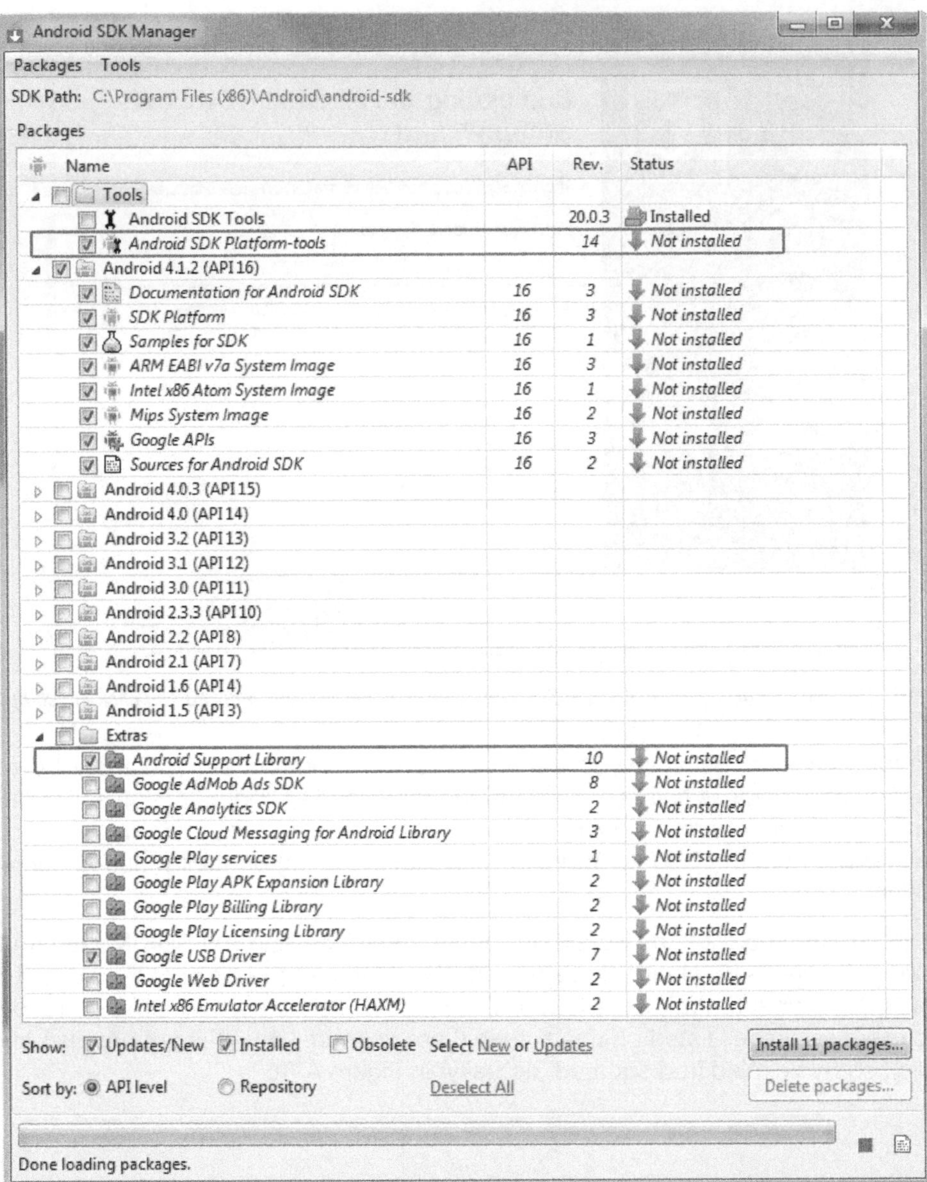

***Figure A-16.** Android SDK Manager auto-select of Android 4.1.2 plus select Android Support Library and SDK Platform-tools*

These options represent the Android SDK Platform Tools and the Android Support Library. So you should also check these options as shown, and once the Install button says "**Install 11 packages**" then click it and install 11 more Android related packages onto your system now. This may take some time, especially if you have a slower Internet connection.

After you click the Install button you get the **Choose Packages to Install** dialog, and you find that there is an easy **Accept All** radio button that you can use to install all of these packages, so that you can develop for all of these Android hardware device technologies (ARM, Intel, Mips, etc.) that support the Android 4.1 API Level 16. Next, select the **Accept All** radio button, and click the **Install** button to proceed as shown in Figure A-17.

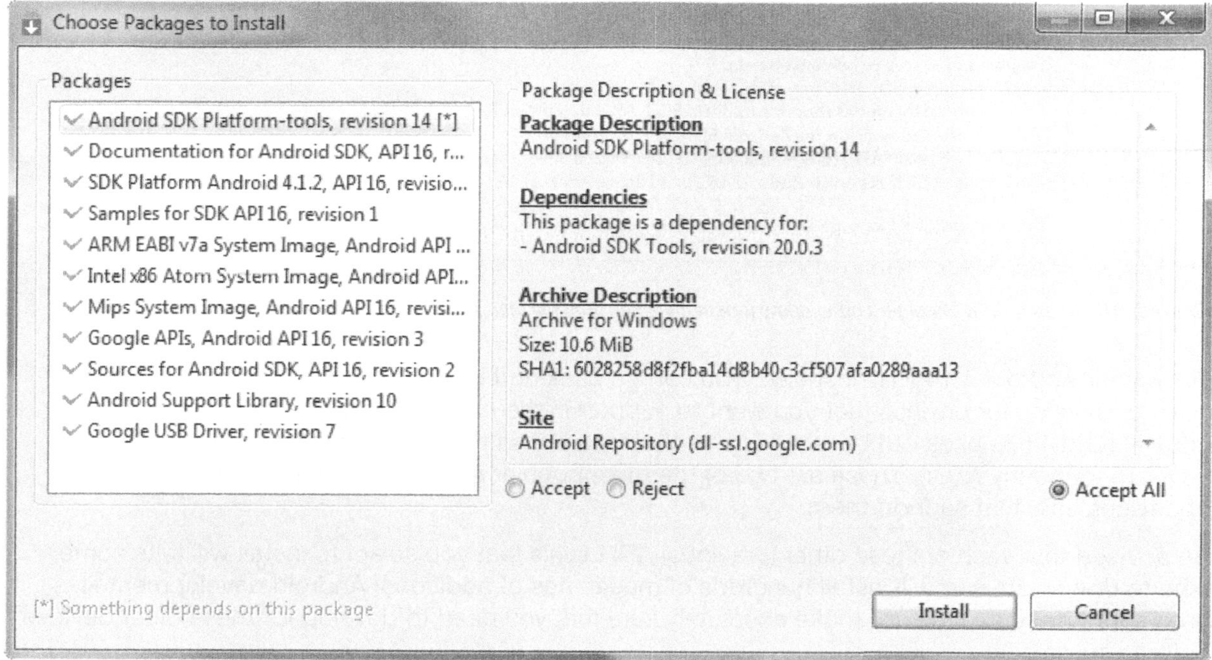

Figure A-17. *Choose Packages to Install dialog (select the Accept All option and then click the Install button)*

Once you click Install you see a Progress Bar at the bottom of the Android SDK Manager similar to what is shown in Figure A-18 that shows you in real-time (if you are interested enough to watch it) which package is being downloaded currently, along with that package's API Level, Revision Number, Percentage Transfer Completed, Data Transfer Rate, and Time Left to Download for that package.

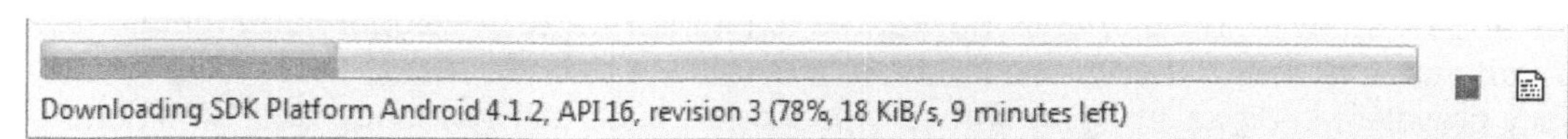

Figure A-18. *Downloading the SDK Platform Android 4.1.2 API Level 16 revision 3 from the Google Android Server Repository*

Note also in Figure A-18 that there is an icon at the far-right corner that opens an Android SDK Manager Log window that actually shows in real-time what is being done on a more detailed level.

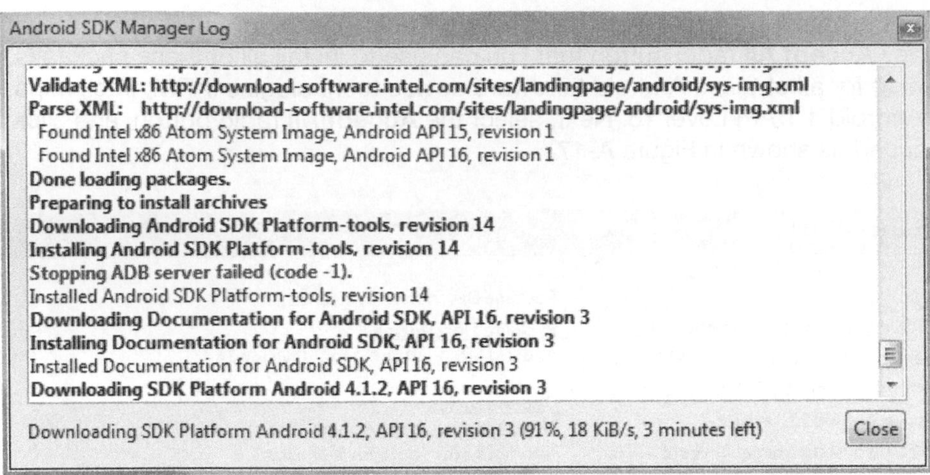

***Figure A-19.** Android SDK Manager Log window (opened via Log Window icon shown at far right side of Figure A-18)*

Once your Android 4.1 API is installed, you can go back and install any other API Levels that you need to develop for devices that you want to support in the Android Market. For instance, the original Kindle Fire uses API Level 10 (currently at 2.3.7) and the new Kindle Fire HD uses API Level 15 (currently 4.0.4). These are two of the more popular API Levels based on the number of devices sold that support them.

Be advised that each of these other (previous) API Levels that you select to install will take some time to download, and will install hundreds of megabytes of additional Android development files onto your hard disk drive, so make absolutely sure that you need to develop for these older devices before you do so.

Eclipse's Android Development Tools Plug-in

The next step in the work process to build a solid Android Development Environment is to show Eclipse where the Android SDK assets are located, and to start to solidify the "bridge" between Eclipse's IDE functionality and Android's Software Development functionality. This is done inside Eclipse via something you may be familiar with called plug-ins, which were invented decades ago by software developers who wanted to let third-party developers add functionality to their software that they did not have the time or resources to code themselves. Plug-ins are especially prevalent in digital imaging software packages, such as Photoshop and GIMP, and allow software development functions to be added to Eclipse, such as being able to turn Eclipse from a Java Development Environment into an Android Development Environment. Let's launch Eclipse via your Taskbar and plug in the Android SDK functionality.

Once Eclipse launches, accept the default workspace location in your Users folder, and then click the Help menu at the top right of the IDE and select the "Install New Software" option near the bottom of the menu. In the **Install Available Software** dialog that appears, click the "Add..."

button on the upper-right to add a new software repository website address to Eclipse; in this case, it will be one of Google's Android repositories. In the **Add Repository** dialog that appears, enter: **Google Plug-In for Eclipse 4.2** in the first data entry field, and in the second data entry field, enter the following exact URL location:

```
http://dl.google.com/eclipse.plugin/4.2
```

Next, click the **OK** button. In case you are wondering, the **dl** before `google.com` stands for download.

Now you will see that Eclipse goes to the Google software repository and fetches the plug-ins for Android Development in Eclipse and populates the center of the Install Available Software dialog with them for you. Select the **Developer Tools** checkbox and the **Google Plug-In for Eclipse** checkbox, and then click on the **Next** button to proceed with their installation. An **Install Details** dialog will soon appear, which will outline in detail the contents of the Android Developer Tools (ADT) plug-in collection, along with the Google Plug-In for Eclipse 4.2, which bridges the new Eclipse 4.2 IDE with the ADT plug-in suite.

Again, click the **Next** button, and a dialog appears that allows you to review and accept the software licensing agreements associated with all the software packages that you are using. Select the **"I accept the terms of the licensing agreements"** radio button option, and click the **Finish** button to proceed to the Installing Software (Progress Bar) dialog that installs the plug-in software that connects the Android SDK to the Java SDK via Eclipse.

Once the installation process is complete, a dialog pops up, asking you to restart Eclipse for the new changes (the Android plug-ins) to be installed into memory. The reason for a restart is because although the software has been installed into Eclipse on your hard disk drive, the software needs to be restarted for these changes to actually be loaded into your system memory, so that they can be used in the Eclipse IDE at runtime.

Enter Eclipse once it restarts, and use the **File ➤ New ➤ Project...** menu sequence to see if you have correctly installed Android Development capability into Eclipse via the ADT plug-ins you just installed.

If you see a folder named **"Android"** in the **New Project** dialog, and it has sub-folders for creating Android Application, Sample and Test Projects, then you have successfully turned Eclipse into a working Android Software Development Environment! Here's the chain of command, so to speak, regarding what talks to (connects with or plugs in to) what, from Java to Android, at this point:

Java ➤ Eclipse ➤ Google Plug-In for Eclipse 4.2 ➤ Android Developer Tools ➤ Android SDK ➤ Android App

So, your Android App uses functions from the Android SDK, which passes them to the Android Developer Tools Plug-In, which implements them in Eclipse, via the Google Plug-in for Eclipse 4.2, and all of it runs on top of both the Java SDK (Java language functions) and JRE (Eclipse runs on top of the Java Runtime Environment in order to run/function). Whew! No wonder it's no walk in the park to set up and configure!

Configuring the Android Development Environment

Finally, let's make sure that our Android Development Environment is configured optimally, before we get into application development in the rest of the book. This is done in Eclipse via the **Window ➤ Preferences** menu sequence, which brings up the Eclipse Preferences dialog. In the left pane of the dialog, you see an Android section with an arrow-head at the left that opens up a sub-section showing all the Android Preference Configuration areas. Select the top primary one (the word "Android") and you will get the main Android Preferences settings area, showing the **SDK Location** at the top along with all the installed Android SDK API Levels underneath that.

You might also encounter the **Thanks for using the Android SDK** dialog, asking you to share your usage statistics for Android in Eclipse with Google, so that Google can make improvements to their ADT plug-in products. I choose to allow this for the good of the developer community, because, as Enterprise First Officer Spock once stated: "The needs of the many outweigh the needs of the one."

Make sure that Eclipse found and set the Android SDK to its proper installed location, and that all the API Levels that you installed are present and accounted for, and then click the **OK** button at the bottom. Just to make absolutely sure that you are leaving no stone unturned, go to the Eclipse **Help** Menu, and select the **Check for Updates** menu item. We are doing this to make sure that you have the very latest revisions of everything that you have installed. Don't be surprised if Eclipse finds updates to the dozens of packages that you have recently installed, it always does find later versions whenever I install a new Android IDE environment onto a new development workstation.

If Eclipse does find any available updates to Eclipse, Android Development Tools, Google Plug-In for Eclipse 4.2, or any of the Android API Level Packages, it will give you an **Available Updates** dialog. If you get this dialog, select the available updates for installation by putting a check in the box next to each update, and then click the **Next** button to proceed.

You will then encounter an **Update Details** dialog, which will give you further detail regarding each software update. Click **Next** in this dialog as well, and then review and accept the software licenses shown in the final **Review Licenses** dialog and click the **Finish** button to begin the Install Process. You should get an **Updating Software** progress bar dialog while the software updates download, and then a **Security Warning** dialog when the software is downloaded and ready to install telling you that you are about to install unsigned content. Click **OK** to install the updates and then click **Yes** when you are asked to restart Eclipse, so that the changes can be loaded into system memory and so that you can now run the newly updated version of Eclipse. Whew! We must be done with this process now, Right?! Almost!

Configuring Your Android Virtual Devices

The last step in the process of getting your Android Development Environment ready for the rest of this book, which we are doing up-front in this appendix so we don't have to worry about it again later, is to set up the Android Virtual Device (AVD. The AVD is an emulator that allows you to test your Android Apps on your workstation using a software device emulator that mimics an Android smartphone or tablet.

This is desirable because the work process of uploading your app onto an actual physical Android device (hardware) is much more tedious than right-clicking your project and selecting Run, which we'll see in the Chapter 2. That's not to say you shouldn't test your app once in a while on a real

Android hardware device, but the AVD allows you to test as you develop with much greater speed and frequency.

Since you've just restarted Eclipse for the final time, go into the **Window** menu, and select the **AVD Manager** option near the bottom. This opens the **Android Virtual Device Manager** dialog, which lists your AVDs, and currently has no AVD set-up, and thus says: **No AVD available** in the central area of the dialog. To add a new AVD to your Eclipse environment click the **New...** button at the top right of the dialog and open up the **Create New Android Virtual Device** dialog.

The first thing to do is name the emulator, so enter **API_16_Emulator** in the **Name** field. Then select the **Target** for the emulator, which is the API Level for the emulator, which is Android 4.1.2 or API Level 16. Select: **Android 4.1 – API Level 16** from the drop-down selection menu. Next set the SD card to be a common 512MB SD card configuration, and check the **Snapshot Enabled** option. Next, set the Default Built-In Skin of **WVGA 800x480** because most smartphones and tablets use at least this resolution.

Finally, you are ready to create your first Android 4.1 emulator, by clicking the **Create AVD** button. If you are developing for some of the other popular API levels, utilize the same work process and add other emulators for Kindle Fire (Android 2.3.7 API Level 10) or Kindle Fire HD (Android 4.0.4 API Level 15), if you need to test your applications for delivery on those hardware platforms.

Index

A

Adaptive Multi-Rate (AMR), 327
Advanced Audio Coding (AAC), 326
Android ADT Bundle, 2
Android application project. *See also* Hello World application
  anatomy
    configure launcher Icon dialog, 43
    drawable folders, 43
    HDPI and LDPI, 43
    key folders and sub-folders, 41
    layout and menu folders, 42
    menu folder, 43
    values folders, 44
  Java coding
    Android classes via import statements, 49–50
    Android 4.2 emulator, 51–52
    Auto Monitor Logcat, 52
    Eclipse central editing pane, 49
    MainActivity class and onCreate() methods, 49
    onCreate() methods, 50
    src and package-name folders, 49
  XML mark-up
    constant values, 47–48
    option menus, 46
    user interface screen layouts, 44–45
Android development environment, 1. *See also* Android Development Tools (ADT)
  3D modeling, rendering, and animation software package, Blender 3D 2.66, 29
  Android Virtual Devices
    emulator, 18
    iTV emulator-GoogleTV, 21, 23–26
    manager menu, 18
    Nexus S Smartphone emulator, 20–21
    Nexus 7 Tablet emulator, 19–20
  digital audio software package, Audacity 2.0.2, 27
  digital imaging software package GIMP 2.8.2, 26–27
  EditShare Lightworks 11, 28–29
  Java 6
    JDK, 3–6
    programming language, 3
  overview, 2
Android Development Tools (ADT), 41
  Android SDK manager tool, 16
    libraries and packages, 16–17
    red X, 18
  configuration
    Android software updates online, 15
    empty Package Explorer, Editing, Console and Outline panes, 15
    Statistics dialog encountered use of, 13–14
  download ADT IDE
    get SDK button, 6–7
    SDK bundle button, 7
    terms and condition agreements, 8
  installation
    adt-bundle zip file, 8–9
    extract files destination folder, 9–10
    URL path, 10–11
  Taksbar
    Android Developer Tools version, 13
    Eclipse 4.2 ADT Bundle Launch Icon, 13
    Eclipse application file, 12
Android graphics design, 165
  color depth, 169
    8-bit indexed color image, 170
    24-bit color/truecolor image, 170
    CMYK color model, 169

Android graphics design (*cont.*)
RGB color model, 169
subtractive color, 169
Drawable class, 166
AnimationDrawable subclass, 167
BitmapDrawable subclass, 166
ColorDrawable subclass, 166
GradientDrawable subclass, 166
InsetDrawable subclass, 167
LayerDrawable subclass, 166
LevelListDrawable subclass, 167
ShapeDrawable subclass, 166
StateListDrawable subclass, 167
TransitionDrawable subclass, 167
image compression, 173–174
image formats, 172
Graphics Information (GIF), 172
Joint Photographic Experts Group (JPEG), 172
Portable Network Graphics (PNG), 172
Web Photo (WEBP), 172
image shaping using pixel, 168
aspect ratio, 169
image resolution, 168
image transparency, 171
alpha channel, 171
blending algorithm, 171
checkerboard pattern, 170–171
image compositing, 171
opacity, 171
PorterDuff algorithm, 171
NewPlanet Activity, 174
screen layout XML editing, 174–175
stars image background addition, 174
TextView tag's textColor parameter adjustment, 176–177
XML tag parameters adjustment, 175–176
pixel, 167–168
TravelPlanet UI, 178
alpha channel inversion, virus selection, 180–182
alpha channel mask creation, 178–180
canvas size tool, mask image re-center, 183–184
GIMP's File Export dialog, 184–186
GIMP XCF native format, 183
Image Resize tool, 186–188
Android IDE, 487
attack plan, 488
configuration of, 506
Eclipse (installation), 492
button download, 492
change of path, 495
executable file, 496
file extraction, 494
Java EE Juno services, 493
Juno 4.2, 493, 496
Eclipse's plug-in, 504
Java 6 programming, 489
jdk-6u37-windows-i586.exe, 491
JDK installation, 489
Oracle TechNetwork Java SE webpage, 490
standard edition, 489
uninstallation, 491
SDK and tools, 497
button for Windows, 498
from Google Android Server Repository, 503
library and platform tools, 502
packages to install, 503
path for installation, 499
SDK manager, 502, 504
setup process, 500–501
virtual device configures, 506
Android Integrated Development Environment (IDE), 2
Android Intents. *See* Inter-application programming
Android Inter-Application Communication. *See* Broadcast receivers
Android vector animation, 239
alpha channel animation, 248
completion of tag, 248
Eclipse view of, 250
Java code for, 250
parameters, 249
startAnimation() method, 250
complex, XML <set>, 257
alpha procedural animation, 263
<alpha> tag, 262
animation (rotate, scale, alpha), 264
execution of, UI elements, 268
frame animation, 258

Java code for, 266
referencing frame animation, 259
repeat parameter, 263
<rotate> tag addition, 260
<scale> tag, 261
scaling (image), 261
startAnimation() method, 265–267
structure, 259
tag configure, 260
motion animation (<translate> parameter), 268
Java code for, 270
options for tag, 269
pulsing LaserCannon, 270
startAnimation() method, 271
tag configure, 269
XML mark-up, 270
procedural and bitmap combine, 251
background (fade), 254
beam effect, 256
frames, special effects, 252, 254
ImageButton, background insert, 254
ImageView tag, 255
Java code for, 256
pong configuration, 253
transporterEffect, 257
XML configure, 252
procedural concepts, 240
rotate, scale and translate (procedure), 240
rotational, attack bomb, 241
cycle duration, 243
interpolation method, 242
Java code for, 244
parameter, Eclipse, 242, 244
repeat count, 243
rotateBomb, 245
rotate tag completion, 242
startAnimation, 245
tween animation, 241
XML naming schema (XMLNS), 242
scalar, attack virus, 245
Eclipse, parameters, 247
Java code for, 247
parameters, 246
ReapeatMode, 246
startAnimation() method, 248
tag completion, 246

Android Virtual Devices (AVDs)
emulator, 18
iTV emulator-GoogleTV
ADV adding Philips GoogleTV USB Stick, 26
AVD creation, 25
AVD Manager Device Definitions tab, 21–23
new device dialog creation, 23
Philips GoogleTV USB stick, 24
manager menu, 18
Nexus S Smartphone emulator, 20–21
Nexus 7 Tablet emulator, 19–20
API. *See* Application Programming Interface (API)
APK (Android PacKage) file, 36
Application Programming Interface (API)
meaning, 55
package
classes and methods, 56
import statements, 56–57
Java import statements, 57
MainActivity.java file, 56
meaning, 56
Aspect ratio, 169
Audio, 321
analog (sound waves and air), 321
compression, digital and formats, 330
Android assets, 339–340
Audacity 2.0 screen, 331
blast digital audio, 341
in Eclipse ADT IDE, 341
FLAC format file, 334
import settings, 330
MediaMetadataRetriever, 333
MPEG-3 format (MP3), 335
MPEG-4 format (AMR), 337, 339
MPEG-4 format(M4A), 336
OGG format file, 335
sample rate, 331
sample resolution, 331
uncompressed PCM, 332
wav format file, 333
digital foundation, 322
frequency, 323
sampling resolution, 322
slicing, 322

Audio (*cont.*)
key attributes, 324
adaptive multi rate (AMR), 327
advanced audio coding (AAC), 326
Audacity 2 setup, 328
bit rates, 325
CD standard, 324
digital streaming, 324
formats, digital codecs, 325
free lossless audio codec (FLAC), 326
HD standard, 324
LADSPA plug in, 329
musical instrument data interface (MIDI), 325
playback, optimization, 327
MediaPlayer class, 342
sound effects creation, 329

B

Background processing, 411
processes (*see* Background processing:threads)
rules and characteristics, 412
threads, 413
caching, 417
foreground process, 415
lifespan of process, 415
onPause() method, 416
onReceive() method, 416
onStop() method, 416
OS spawns, 417
process parameter, 414
startForeground() method, 415
system callbacks, 417
thread-safe, 418
UI threads, 417
XML parameters, 414
threads in Android application, 418
AsyncTask, 418
button tags, 420
class dialog, 426
context reference, 428
Eclipse error dialog, 425
HandlerThread, 418
IBinder() method, 426
Java code, write, 423
lifecycle methods, 419, 427
makeText() method, 428
MusicService class, 419, 422
object intents, 424
<service> components configuring, 422
service subclass, 424
superclass selection, 426
testing MusicService, 430
TimePlanet, reference, 429
UI element, button, 420
Banding, 174
bringToFront() method, 304
Broadcast receivers, 433
conepts and types, 434
implementation, 439
Alarm broadcast, 440
AlarmReceiver BroadcastReceiver UI XML, 442
Android Toast class, 448
Java method, startTimer(), 445
message in Alarm, 448
onReceive() method, 447
parameter configuring, 441
parseInt() method, 445
pendingIntent, 445
<receiver> tag, 443
startTimerButton, 443
startTimer() method, 443
subclass, AlarmReceiver, 446
superclass dialog, 447
testing receiver subclass, 449
UI element label, 440
intents *vs.* activity, 435, 437
NotificationManager class, 437
setPackage(), 436
LocalBroadcastManager, 438
normal, 434
ordered, 434
processing and affects, 438
register, dynamic *vs.* static, 439
security considerations, 436
sendOrderedBroadcast(), 435

C

Codecs, 274
Color depth, 169
Content Providers. *See* Datastores access

D

Dalvik Virtual Machine (DVM), 32
Datastores access
AlienContact class, 464
adding menu, 478
addToAlliance() method, 482, 485
button element, 468
coding addToAlliance() method, 483
coding UI elements, 470
contact creation, 475
ContactsContract DB, 474
getContentResolver().query() method, 472–473
helper options, 472
home screen menu, 477
launch contacts, 481
listAliens() method, 471
naming database, 476
new dialog creation, 467
onCreate() method, 465
onCreateOptionsMenu() method, 479
preparation of, 465
preview in graphical layout editor, 470
RawContacts DB, 485
superclass type, 464
switch() method, 480
test listAliens() method, 480, 482
UI, activity_contact, 466
viewing contacts, 477
write XML mark-up, 469
XML mark-up, 466
deprecated DB structures, 459
MySQL, 453
open source DB engine, 453
OS content providers, 456
CalendarContract DBs, 458
ContactsContract DBs, 458
MediaStore DBs, 457
package and data types, 457
provider, add permissions, 460
Eclipse editor, 460
Eclipse Visual Editor, 463
READ_CONTACTS, 461
types, 461
WRITE_CONTACTS, 462
XML-markup tags, 463
provider addressing, URI, 455
content URI, 455
MediaStore, 456
and resolvers, 454
storage system, 452
SQLite, 453
Digital imaging
color depth, 169
8-bit indexed color image, 170
24-bit color/truecolor image, 170
CMYK color model, 169
RGB color model, 169
subtractive color, 169
image compression, 173–174
image formats, 172
Graphics Information (GIF), 172
Joint Photographic Experts Group (JPEG), 172
Portable Network Graphics (PNG), 172
Web Photo (WEBP), 172
image shaping using pixel, 168
aspect ratio, 169
image resolution, 168
image transparency, 171
alpha channel, 171
blending algorithm, 171
checkerboard pattern, 170–171
image compositing, 171
opacity, 171
PorterDuff algorithm, 171
NewPlanet Activity, 174
screen layout XML editing, 174–175
stars image background addition, 174
TextView tag's textColor parameter adjustment, 176–177
XML tag parameters adjustment, 175–176
pixel, 167–168
TravelPlanet UI, 178
alpha channel inversion, virus selection, 180–182
alpha channel mask creation, 178–180
Canvas Size tool, mask image re-center, 183–184
GIMP's File Export dialog, 184–186
GIMP XCF native format, 183
Image Resize tool, 186–188

Drawable class, graphics design, 166
  direct subclasses, 166
    AnimationDrawable subclass, 167
    BitmapDrawable subclass, 166
    ColorDrawable subclass, 166
    GradientDrawable subclass, 166
    InsetDrawable subclass, 167
    LayerDrawable subclass, 166
    LevelListDrawable subclass, 167
    ShapeDrawable subclass, 166
    StateListDrawable subclass, 167
    TransitionDrawable subclass, 167
  indirect subclasses, 167

E

Events. *See* Intents
Explicit Intents. *See* Intents:explicit intents
eXtra High Density Pixel Imagery (XHDPI), 43

F

Frame(s), 274
Frame animation, XML constructs, 217
  and data optimization, 217
  backgrounds, 222
    AnimationDrawable object, 226
    compositing UI element, 224
    container tag, 224
    execution in Nexus S Emulator, 229
    forcefield animation, 223
    getBackground() method, 228
    <item> tags, 223
    preview, padding, 226
    referencing, 225
    setStartUpScreenAnim() method, 227
  full screen, transitions, 230
    API level support, 232–233
    background image, 236
    Relativelayout container, 232
    set up, 231
    tag elements, 231
    TransitionDrawable, 233–235
  list tag, 218
    add <item> tag, 220
    change of state, 221
    <item> tags, 220
    referencing, attack_virus.xml file, 221
    resource type, drawable, 219
    root element, 219
    state_enabled parameter, 222
Free Lossless Audio Codec (FLAC), 326

G

.3gp, 276
Graphical User Interface (GUI) Design, 191
  custom activity screen, 211
    constants creation, 212
    interface screens, 212
    labels configure, 212–213
    new screen title, 214
    renaming ic_launcher_old, 211
    title labels and icons, 215
  elements compositing, 202
    alpha transparency, 204
    background color, 205
    graphical editor, 204
    home screen preview, 210
    home screen upgrade, 207
    ImageView tag preview, 208–209
    LinearLayout editing, 203
    preview in Nexus S Emulator, 206
    space background, 203
    TextField UI, formatting, 205
  multi-state elements, 192
    attackinvadefocus, 198
    attackinvadepress button, 197
    channel editing mode, 194
    eraser tool, 196
    focused state, 192
    GIMP launch, 193
    gold hoop import, compositing, 195
    hoop layer import, 195
    ImageButton creation, 192
    modal software, 194
    mode conversion, image, 194
    move tool, 196
    normal state, 192
    pressed state, 192
    resolution density, icons, 198
    Soldier's face, 196
  XMl, Android's selector tag, 199
    activity screen layout, 200
    addition of <item> tag, 200
    execution in Nexus S Emulator, 202

new file creation, 199
referencing ImageButton, 200–201
Graphics design. *See* Android graphics design
Graphics Information (GIF) image format, 172

H

Hello World application, 31, 55. *See also* Java programming language
Android application development Lingo
application permissions definition, 36
communications layer, 34
components, 32
data storage layer, 35
DVM, 32
inter-application communications, 35
Linux 2.6 Kernel, 32
presentation layer, 33
processing layer, 33–34
Android application project
ADT, 40
application, project and package, 36
configure launcher icon dialog, 38–39
configure project dialog, 37–38
create activity dialog, 39–40
new blank activity dialog, 40–41
API
meaning, 55
package, 56–57
High Density Pixel Imagery (HDPI), 43

I

Image compositing, 171
Image compression, 173–174
Image data footprint reduction, 173–174
Image formats, 172
Graphics Information (GIF), 172
Joint Photographic Experts Group (JPEG), 172
Portable Network Graphics (PNG), 172
Web Photo (WEBP), 172
Image resolution, 168
Intents, 111
explicit intents, 116
abstract method view, implementation, 122
addition of, intents, 119
AttackPlanet UI event handling, enable, 127
ConfigPlanet UI event handling, enable, 124
constructor, event handler method, 123
event handling (keypads\keyboards), 130
exiting attack mode, 128–129
finish() Intent method, 123
functional activity screens, 119
ImageView object, 121
Java code, ConfigPlanet, 132
layout container, button, 126
MainActivity, 127, 129
menu inflation, 117
OnClickListener() method, 121, 125
onCreateOptionsMenu() method, 117
onFocusChange event, 133
onKeyDown() method, 131
OnKey event handlers, 130
OnLongClick event, 133
onOptionsItemSelected() method, 118
planet intent addition, 118
planet UI event hadling, enable, 120
returnButton, 127
setPlanetColonies() method, 123
TravelPalnet UI event handling, enable, 125
UI definition, 121
unimplemented method, 122
filters, implicit intents, 114–116
high level communication, object, 112
action, 113
component (class) name, 112
constants, 114
data reference, 113
extras, 114
flags, 114
structures, 114
type reference, 113
Interactivity. *See* Intents
Inter-application programming, 383
communications, 35
explicit *vs.* implicit intent, 392
intent messaging, 384
implementation, intent usage, 384–386
structure, intent anatomy, 386–392
intent resolution-implicit, 393
activity, 403
activity, Hello World, 395
Android XML file, 399

Inter-application programming (*cont.*)
atomic clock button, 404
callTimeIntent object, 406
ConfigPlanet.java activity, 405
filter, 394
graphical layout editor, 400
graphic parameters, 401
import statement, 397
<intent-filter>, 394
layout values, 402
LinearLayout XML, 398–399, 405
naming TimePlanet, 396
onCreate() method, 398
returnIntent object, 407
setContentView, 398
string constants, 401
testing TimePlanet, 409
<TextView> UI, 402
TimePlanet, 395, 403, 407
TransitionDrawable UI screen, 408
XML tag, filters, 394
IntWorldGen interface
abstract and static modifiers, 72
interface creation
code statement, 74
implements keyword, 74–75
overridden, 74
WorldGen() constructor method, 73–74
public interface, 72
WorldGen Java class
abstract classes, 73
concrete class, 73
constant, 73
extends, 73
final modifier, 73
public intefrface, 73
template, 73

J, K

Java Development Kit (JDK), 2
download Windows, 4–5
Oracle TechNetwork Java SE webpage, 3–4
uninstall existing Java installation, 5–6
URL, 3
Windows x86 32-bit–or Windows x64 64-bit .exe file, 5
Java programming language
class
child, derived, and extended classes, 59
constructor method, 61
features, 59–60
inheritance, 59
initializing, 61
instance variables, 60
local variables, 60
parent and base class, 59
primitives/primitive data types, 60
string, 60
subclassing, 59
superclass, 59
syntax, 60
variable description, 60
WorldGen objects, 60
IntWorldGen interface
abstract and static modifiers, 72
interface creation, 73–74
public interface, 72
WorldGen Java class, 73
method
access control modifiers, 61
assignment operator, 63
behaviors/functions, 61
CamelCase, 63
constructor, 62
declaration, 61
modifier, 61
parameters, 62
public, private and protected modifiers, 62
return data types, 62
setBaseProtection() method, 64
setColonyImmigration() method, 63
setPlanetColonies() method, 63
turnForceFieldOn() and turnForceFieldOff() methods, 63
WorldGen() method, 62
object
attributes/states, 58
behaviors/functions, 58
code modularity, 59
data encapsulation, 59
instance variables, 58
methods, 58
modules, 59
real-life objects, 57

state, 58
states and behaviors, 58
Java Runtime Environment (JRE), 2
Java 6 Software Development Kit (Java SDK). *See* Java Development Kit (JDK)
Joint Photographic Experts Group (JPEG) image format, 172

L

Layouts and Activities. *See* ViewGroup classes
Linux 2.6 Kernel, 32
Low Density Pixel Imagery (LDPI), 43

M

MediaPlayer, 345
methods, 346
setup and load (digital data), 349
Alien Voiceover Audio, 357
Audacity 2.0, 357
Audio FX button, 360
audio loop play, 355
Background Ambient Audio, 354
ConfigPlanet.java activity, 360
eSpeak application, 356
event handler onCLick() method, 352, 361
getApplicationContext() method, 350
MainActivity looping, 354
MPEG-4 AAC data file, 357–358
onClick() method, 359
setAudioPlayers() method, 349, 351, 353
setLooping() method, 355
special effects coding, 352
start() method, 351, 354–355
value as null, 349
voice synthesis, 356
state engine, 346
bombPlayer, 347
layout of, 346
oncreate() method, 348
preparing state, 347
reset() method, 347
SoundPool class, 348
states of, 347
.mkv, 276
.mp4, 276
MPEG4 H.264, 274
MultiPurpose Internet Mail Extension (MIME), 390
Musical Instrument Data Interface (MIDI), 325

N

NewPlanet Activity, 174
screen layout XML editing, 174–175
stars image background addition, 174
TextView tag's textColor parameter adjustment, 176–177
XML tag parameters adjustment, 175–176
Nexus S emulator
aspect ratio, 305
button UI element, 310
Mars digital video, 305
MediaController Transport, 308
planet surface data, 306
RelativeLayout, 306

O

Object Oriented Programming (OOP). *See* Java programming language

P, Q, R

Pixel, 167–168
Pixels, 274
Portable Network Graphics (PNG) image format, 172
Procedural Animation via XML Constructs. *See* Android vector animation
Pulse Code Modulated (PCM), 327

S

SoundPool, 363
and MIDI, 364
performance data sequencing, 364
sequencers, 364
audio synthesis, 364
compositing, 365
pitch shifting, 365
quadraphonic, 365
and sequencing caveats, 368
stereo, 365
audio synthesis and sequencing caveats, 368
class rules and methods, 366–367

SoundPool (*cont.*)
planet activity, 368
append() method, 379
AudioManager, 373
configure, AudioManager, 372
Eclipse, warning message, 370, 377
HashMap object, 371–372
import, Eclipse helper, 379
load, HashMap class, 371
object setup, 369
parameters, play(), 376
play() method, 376
playSample() method, 375, 380–381
put() method, 373–374, 380
setAudioPlayers() method, 369
SoundPoolFX, 369
SparseArrays, 377
SparseIntArray() method, 376, 378

T

TravelPlanet UI, 178
alpha channel inversion, virus selection, 180–182
alpha channel mask creation, 178–180
Canvas Size tool, mask image re-center, 183–184
GIMP's File Export dialog, 184–186
GIMP XCF native format, 183
Image Resize tool, 186–188
travelVideo.start() method, 314
Troubleshooting
Button tag parameters, 312–313
Java Code, 314
layout_alignParentTop parameter, 312
user experience design, 316
VideoView UI element, 314
XML tags, 314

U

UI Design, 137
AttackPlanet activity, 155
aligning image, 156
chevron < character, 157
compositing image source, 156
image assets, 155
ImageButton tag, 156
Java code, planet UI elements, 161
nested LinearLayout containers, 158
onCick() handlers, 162
preview in Nexus S Emulator, 160
referencing image, 156
text labels to attack icons, 160
XML mark-up, caption, 158
ConfigPlanet activity, 146
Android EditText UI, 148
EditText UI elements, 147
event handlers, 149
getText() method, 151
implemented screen, 152
import EditText, 150
Java code, new UI elements, 149
nested layout containers, 147
setText() method, 151
ImageView UI Widget, 138
aligning, 139
Android Toast class, 145
assets, DPI folder, 138
button add, done, 141
doneAddingButton, 143
Java code, new UI, 144
makeText method, 146
properties panel, 141
referencing, 139
RelativeLayout parameter, 140
screen in Nexus S Emulator, 144
text captioning, 141
TextView tag, 142
interface elements, view and subclasses, 137
TravelPlanet activity, 153
Java code, new UI element, 154
onClick() handler, 154
onTouch() handler, 154
remove UI button tag, 153
VideoView UI elements, 153
Uniform Resource Identifier (URI), 301
Uri class, 302

V

Video, 273
assets, resource's raw folder, 296
DPI resolution, 297
MPEG-4 files, 298
naming resolutions, 298
new file creation, 296

compression, 285
Android settings, 287
codec settings, 291, 293, 295
FPS compression, 288
HDPI resolution, 292
importing files, 286
key frame, 288
MDPI resolution, 290
MP4 video (compressed), 289
Sorenson Squeeze, 285
in Squeeze, Multi-Pass H.264, 290, 292, 294
transcode, 289
digital attributes, 274
bit rate, 275–276
captive data access, 275
data access, 275
high definition (HD), 275
imbedded video, 276
resolution, 275
standard definition (SD), 275
streaming, access data, 275
digital, foundation of, 274
formats (digital), 276
advanced video coding (AVC), 276
codecs in Android, 276
VP8, 277
WebM, 277
Mars Planet creation, 278
animation parameters, 280
animation rendering, 282
anti-aliasing effect, 283
Bryce 7 Proffessional, 278
buttons (set and edit), 282
3D animation options, 281
document resolution, 283
open a file, 280
render engine, 281
render report information, 284
resolution files, 283
terrain generation software, 279
uncompressed frames, 279
playback and resolution, 277
play, VideoView class, 299
Video optimization. *See* Video
VideoView Class, 299, 301
Android MediaController Class
digital video files, 303
TravelPlanet.java Activity, 302
travelVideo VideoView, 304
Uri class, 302
Nexus S emulator
aspect ratio, 305
button UI element, 310
Mars digital video, 305
MediaController Transport, 308
planet surface data, 306
RelativeLayout, 306
Troubleshooting
Button tag parameters, 312–313
Graphical Layout Editor tab, 314
Java Code, 314
layout_alignParentTop parameter, 312
user experience design, 316
VideoView UI element, 313
XML tags, 314
ViewGroup Classes, 77
activity creation, 96
Androidmanifest.xml, 107
attack, LinearLayout, 105
AttackPlanet.java, 107
contentDescription parameter, 99–100
control-spacebar keystroke, 96
FrameLayout container, 104
GLE tag, 98
graphical buttons, 106
ImageButton tags, 105
ImageView tag, 99
ImageView UI elements, 98
layout parameters, 101
LinearLayout container, 102
onCreate() method, 102
package field, 96
RelativeLayout XML mark-up, 101
setContentView() method, 97
string references, 106
subclass, activity definitions, 108
superclass field, 96
toRightof parameter, 100
TravelActivity, 104
UI elements, 103
VideoView UI element, 104
XML file dialog, 98
Android screen layout, 78
layout, Android subclasses, 78
RelativeLayout class, 79, 90

ViewGroup Classes (*cont.*)
- alignStart parameter, 86–87
- coding setStartUpScreenText() method, 89
- data addition, TextView, 85
- definition, menu, 93
- dummy variables, 87
- Eclipse GLE, 86
- Eclipse view, 81
- functioning menu, 95
- getMenuInflater() method, 94
- graphical layout editor (GLE), 86
- inflate() method, 94
- labelling strings, 93
- LinearLayout containers, 82
- MainActivity screen, 79
- marginLeft parameter, 85
- menu inflater, 91
- naming the class, 82
- naming XML definitions, 92
- Nexus S Emulator screen, 84, 91
- orderInCategory, 92
- output screen design, 80
- parameter(s), TextView, 81
- parameter configure, pop-up dialog, 82
- renaming text to data, 86
- setStartUpScreenText() method, 88
- setStartUpWorldValues() method, 88
- setText() method, 89
- start up screen, XML, 80
- string constants, 80
- tag closing of XML, 84
- TextView, subclass, 80–81
- toRightof parameter, 85
- UI elements dataView, Java code, 90
- variables, strings, 83
- various TestView XML tags, 83
- WorldGen method, 88
- write data, Java, 88
- XML menu, 91
- XML tags, 80

user experience (UX), 77
user interface design (UI) design, 77

Views and Widgets. *See* UI design

W, X, Y, Z

.webm, 276

Web Photo (WEBP) image format, 172

WorldGen class, 64. *See* Java programming language
- comments, warnings and errors, 72
- creation
  - Eclipse ADT IDE, 67
  - Java code, 67–68
  - new Java class dialog, 64–65
  - public modifier, 67
  - superclass selection dialog, 65–66
- objects
  - constructor method, 68
  - dot notation, 69
  - earth.setForceFieldOn() method, 71
  - Eclipse object methods, 70
  - Java code, 71
  - MainActivity class, 69
  - new() method, 68
  - onCreate() method, 68
  - setColonyImmigration() method, 71
  - setPlanetColonies() method, 69
  - setPlanetMilitary() method, 71
  - super.onCreate() and setContentView() method, 68

CPSIA information can be obtained at www.ICGtesting.com
Printed in the USA
LVOW021223090613
337669LV00005B/197/P